INCREDIBLE ILLII

BY
BILL NUNES © 2004

Printed in America by Corley Printing of St. Louis, Missouri   ISBN 0-9646934-0-2
bnunesbook@aol.com (618) 288-5185 For autographed copy send $22.95 to 5 Mark Trail, Glen Carbon IL 62034

INCREDIBLE ILLINOIS: AN INFORMAL HISTORY - INTRODUCTION

My thanks to Dan Oberle, Marillyn Watts, Charlie Oliver, Mark Godwin, the Glen Carbon Library, Chris McGinness at Mermet Lake, the Illinois Department of Transportation, the *Chicago Tribune*, the Illinois State Historical Library, the Chicago Historical Society, Illinois Tourism, and the Illinois Historical Society. Special thanks my wife (Lorna), my son-in-law (Roland Jones), and to Bill Jacobus.

A venerable historian once wrote that the history of Illinois is the history of the Midwest. And the history of the Midwest is, to a larger extent than we ever learned in our school textbooks, the history of the nation. Clarence Alvord astutely noted that Illinois "has been shaken by every great force stirring the continent . . . exercising formative influences on its destiny."

The reason I undertook this task was to help correct a bias that seems to exist among most Illinois history books. It is difficult to find a single volume purporting to cover the entire state that does not give short shrift to everything south of Springfield. I have attempted in this work to partially correct those deficiencies and give a balanced treatment without detracting from the northern half of the state.

This is not a scholarly tome, full of big words and tedious footnotes. If you are looking for research or genealogy material, please go to the references cited. This is meant to be a popular highlight history written in a scrapbook style that will appeal to those who normally don't like reading about the past. It's a coffee table book, crammed with fun facts, interesting sidelights and pictures. Nor is it intended to be definitive. It is merely a collection of pictures and material that I have encountered in my research. I did not spend hours haunting dusty archives or sitting at a microfilm reader. I happily abdicate that field to the bookworms. Unlike historians such as Stu Fliegie, I am not a lifelong Illinois history buff and assembling this volume has been a journey of discovery for me.

Not only does *Incredible Illinois* cover historical events, it contains material on science, art, sports, scandals, literature, inventions, legends, lore, cities, counties, gangsters, businesses, mining, manufacturing and entertainers, as well as social, economic and cultural history. I was unable to include an index, but I highlighted each town (except dominant Chicago) that is mentioned.

This book, while hopefully informative, is intended to be sheer fun for general readers. Most residents are unaware of the myriad of amazing facts and stories that abound in the state's history. Outside of New York, Pennsylvania and perhaps Virginia, I can think of no other state with a past that is as rich, significant and intriguing as that of Illinois. It brings to mind the lines from our state song: *"Not without thy wondrous story . . . Can be writ the nation's glory, Illinois! Illinois!"*

It is also my hope to restore a forgotten concept known as "state pride." I remember as a youth hearing a choir sing our state song. My chest swelled, the hair on the nape of my neck stood on edge, and a lump formed in my throat. You can color me dumb - a sentimental sap - but I hope I never lose that soft spot in my heart for my native state and the good ol' U.S. of A.

There is plenty to brag about because Illinois holds a unique history and tradition among the 50 states. It is a leading world center of agriculture, trade, manufacturing and finance. Illinois ranks 7th in overall population among the states and twenty-fourth in area. For decades it was the only state in the union to rank in the top three both agriculturally and industrially. Although coal production has declined since the 1950s, it still has enough reserves to provide the country with an important energy resource for years to come (until replaced by the hydrogen fuel cell). Supported by some of the finest prairie soils in the world, it ranks second only to Iowa in corn production and leads all states in soybean output. Illinois is also second to Iowa in the production of hogs. It ranks third in wheat production. It is roughly 15th in alfalfa-clover-timothy hay production. It can truly be said that Illinois is the "breadbasket of America." Within its 102 counties are huge numbers of jobs in government, manufacturing, trade, finance and agriculture. Illinois is perhaps the most diverse economically of all the states, ranking about 5th or 6th in exports. It has long been a leading air and rail center.

Geographically Illinois is one of the longest states, crossing the traditional North-South cultural divide. Cairo at the southern tip is actually farther south than Richmond, Virginia. Its length is such that fully one month separates the growing season from both ends of the state. Illinois is roughly one-fourth of the way around the globe as the 90th meridian passes through the state. It is bordered by five other states - Missouri, Iowa, Wisconsin, Indiana and Kentucky.

What makes Illinois significant is its climate, central geographic location, and its water resources. Illinois is bordered by the Wabash, Ohio and Mississippi Rivers and bumps Lake Michigan in the northeast. Water from 23 of the 48 states touches its boundaries.

Illinois belongs to neither East, West, South nor North, but is the focal point of all four regions. Historian Richard Jensen called it the perfect microcosm state where roads, rail, waterways and airlines intersect. We are an historic amalgam of races, religions, nationalities, urbanites, farmers and suburbanites. Ironically, this makes the state slightly schizophrenic. A Chicago accent dominates language up north while a southern drawl can easily be heard down south. Northern Illinois was fiercely loyal to the Union while most of "Little Egypt" supported the Confederacy and flirted with secession. The northern tier roots for the Bears, Cubs and Blackhawks while the southern part roots for the St. Louis Cardinals, Rams and Blues. Northerners also tend to forsake the southern region when it comes to hunting, fishing and camping, preferring instead to go to Wisconsin or Minnesota, causing further estrangement. And "downstate" Illinois has long resented the domination of Chicago and its suburbs vis-a-vis political, economic and legislative matters in Springfield.

We are that near perfect microcosm because our history reflects nearly all the basic conflicts and accommodations that have shaped our country's history. Examples: Governor Reynolds and Chief Blackhawk (taming of the frontier vs Native-American rights), Abe Lincoln and Stephen Douglas (slavery as evil vs slavery as benign), Jane Addams vs Know-nothings/nativists (immigration dilemma), Frances Willard (wets vs drys) Pullman and Debs (Robber Baron/Captain of Industry vs worker's rights), Al Capone and Eliot Ness (mobster rule vs law and order), the Democratic National Convention in 1968 (Vietnam "Hawks" vs "Doves") etc.

I am no Baker Brownell, Paul Angle, or John Allen. Most of this book was written in an attempt at self-education. I take full responsibility and apologize for any errors of omission or fact. The writer would appreciate it if those discovering such errors would notify him so that they might be corrected in later editions. Many of these facts were gleaned from sources mentioned in the bibliography and some-times these sources contain errors. Writer Carole Marsh, for example, reports that Ulysses S. Grant was born in Galena when in fact he was born in Ohio. It is certain that I inadvertently repeated some of these errors.

It should also be noted that in an effort to stay within historical time frames, the author has chosen to use words describing certain social and cultural groups that are now considered archaic. Modernized terms such as African-American and Native-American are only used after the 1990 advent of political correctness.

This book is dedicated to those early pioneers who, according to George W. Smith, "planted in this western wilderness the home, the school, the church and the state through their collective struggles, sacrifices, and triumphs." It was they who nurtured and sustained the democratic instutions that make us a great republic and a unique people. We can only imagine what it must have been like for those early immigrants who left oppressive regimes in Europe to come to a land of freedom and opportunity and build a better life. They braved the dangers, hardships, and uncertainty of the frontier and paved the way for the good life that most of us enjoy today. My hat is off to them.

GET YOUR KICKS ON ROUTE 66

A 1995 Illinois Department of Transportation (IDOT) study concluded: "Rarely is the social and cultural impact of transportation engineering on society as evident as it is with the first paved highways created by state governments." U.S. Route 66, although a federal highway, winding its way gloriously for more than 2,000 miles from Lake to shining Sea, may be the single most outstanding example of this legacy in the United States. Over the years Route 66 has acquired an almost spiritual meaning through its billboards, Burma Shave signs, restaurants, motels, service stations, and entertainment spots. Part and parcel of that experience is the natural landscape, geological character, and topography of Illinois that is on display. Today it is possible to travel much (over 300 miles) of the Illinois roads that were once designated Route 66. Some pieces are located under parts of other highways such as I-55. Others are missing, dug up and seeded, or have become frontage roads.

To travel Illinois U.S. Route 66 from Chicago to East St. Louis enables you to capture the spirit of the land and understand why Illinois is called The Prairie State and why agriculture is such a major part of its economy. During most of the trip through the heartland a traveler is presented with a view of various hybrid strains of corn, soybeans, oats, wheat, or other crops. Evidence of large-scale animal husbandry is plentiful. However, a trip from one end of the corridor to the other is also an encounter with a major urban metropolis, county seats, the state capital, and counties filled with urban sprawl, as well as small town America.

It is clear from examining old maps at the Newberry Library in Chicago that there were essentially three different alignments of Illinois U.S. Route 66 that correspond to three distinct eras of construction. This is confirmed by the 1995 IDOT study. Alignment one, for all intents and purposes a temporary route, lasted from 1926-1930. Alignment two takes us from 1930 to 1940. North of Springfield it followed SBI 4 (State Bond Issue 4). South of Springfield, however, the route was shifted eastward away from the towns of **Chatham, Virden, Girard, Nilwood, Carlinville,** and **Gillespie**. It now took us through the towns of **Divernon, Litchfield, Mount Olive and Livingston**. During this construction the road width was increased from sixteen feet to eighteen feet and even wider in places such as Springfield. Alignment three, from 1940 to 1977, was intended to replace much of the old two-lane Route 66 with a divided four-lane highway, foreshadowing the interstates.

By 1900 road building had not improved much since colonial times. There was nothing in America that even remotely resembled Rome's Appian Way, paved magnificently with stones. The first roads used by the Jamestown settlers of Virginia were merely Indian trails that had been cleared and widened. The first big improvement was corduroy roads – so named because they resembled ribbed corduroy cloth – cor du roi, cloth fit for a king. These roads consisted of trees that were felled, stripped of their branches and placed side by side. This took care of the quagmire problem when it rained, but the roads were hard on wheels and axles, and the ride was bone jarring.

The next improvement came with the introduction of plank roads – constructed of smooth wooden boards. These worked fine but were expensive to build and fell victim to decay, rot and termites. To help pay for their cost and upkeep, the turnpike was invented. A turnpike was simply a toll road with a gatekeeper and removable barrier across the road. Once the required fee was paid, the long pole or pike, with a counterbalance on one end, was turned to allow passage, hence "turnpike." These toll roads were universally hated. Officials even had the gall to charge fees for velocipedes (bicycles) when that invention came along. One such tollbooth was on the St. Clair County Turnpike, **the first paved (macadamized) road in the state,** which ran from **East St. Louis** to **Belleville**. It was burned to the ground in 1910. No effort was made to rebuild the structure.

The need for hard roads was not deemed a necessity until large numbers of Americans began buying the "horseless carriage" after World War I. When alternate paths of Route 66 were built during the Depression to take the road through a different set of towns, they were often bricked instead of concreted. A good stretch of the road near **Hamel** was originally bricked before it was later covered with asphalt.

Plank Road

Copyright 1993 by Robert Waldmire. Used with permission. Intinerant artist - does pen and ink drawings of home or business suitable for framing. Has many different scenes on U.S. and Illinois Route 66. Individual Route 66 Postcards are 25 cents each or they can be purchased as a set. They are approximately 4x6 in size. Send Payment to Robert Waldmire, Box 46, Hackberry Arizona. Alternate Address: Box 751, Rochester Illinois, 62563. Arizona phone: (520) 558-1055, Springfield Phone (217) 498-5966.

Greetings from ILLINOIS
near HAMEL
MT. OLIVE
S. of WAGGONER
SPFLD.
SPRINGFIELD
S. of LINCOLN
ATLANTA
CHICAGO
OLD ROUTE 66
ROUTE 66 BEGAN AT THE INTERSECTION OF MICHIGAN AVE. & JACKSON BLVD., IN THE HEART OF DOWNTOWN CHICAGO. THROUGH A "CANYON OF SKYSCRAPERS" THE ROAD HEADED SOUTHWEST, OUT ONTO THE LEVEL PRAIRIE LAND. WHAT ONCE WAS A VAST "SEA" OF TALLGRASS PRAIRIE IS NOW A "CHECKER-BOARD" OF INTENSIVELY-FARMED FIELDS. WATCH FOR REMNANT PRAIRIES ALONG RAILROAD TRACKS PARALLEL-LING OLD 66.
S. of Dwight
CARDINAL
CHICAGO!
SUBURBAN 66 "TOWNS" ARE CICERO, BERWYN, RIVERSIDE, LYONS, McCOOK & COUNTRYSIDE
(PLAINFIELD)
JOLIET
ELWOOD
WILMINGTON
BRAIDWOOD
GARDNER
DWIGHT
ODELL
PONTIAC
CHENOA
LEXINGTON
TOWANDA
NORMAL
BLOOMINGTON
FUNKS GROVE
(FAMOUS MAPLE SIRUP)
McLEAN
ATLANTA
LAWNDALE
LINCOLN
BROADWELL
ELKHART
WILLIAMSVILLE
SHERMAN
Salt Ck.
SANGAMON R.
SPRINGFIELD
GLENARM
DIVERNON
FARMERSVILLE
WAGGONER
LITCHFIELD
MT. OLIVE (SEE MOTHER JONES MEMORIAL)
STAUNTON
HAMEL
EDWARDSVILLE
MITCHELL
GRANITE CITY
MADISON
EAST ST. LOUIS
ST. LOUIS
MISSISSIPPI R.
FLOODPLAIN
66 HALL of FAME at the DIXIE
COZY DRIVE IN & 66 Museum
"OUR LADY of THE HIGHWAY" Shrine, 3 mi. S. of Waggoner.
...LINCOLN HOME & TOMB ARE IN SPFLD.
ABE LINCOLN (1809-1865)
NEARLY ALL OF OLD 66 IS DRIVE-ABLE IN ILLINOIS & BOTH THROUGH & AROUND DOZENS OF TOWNS!
(for a CLOSE-UP VIEW of the CHAIN-OF-ROCKS BRIDGE [CLOSED], TAKE THE CHAIN of ROCKS Road WEST.)
WILD VIOLET
WHITE OAK
RECYCLED PAPER!
R. Waldmire © 1993
31
Lake Michigan

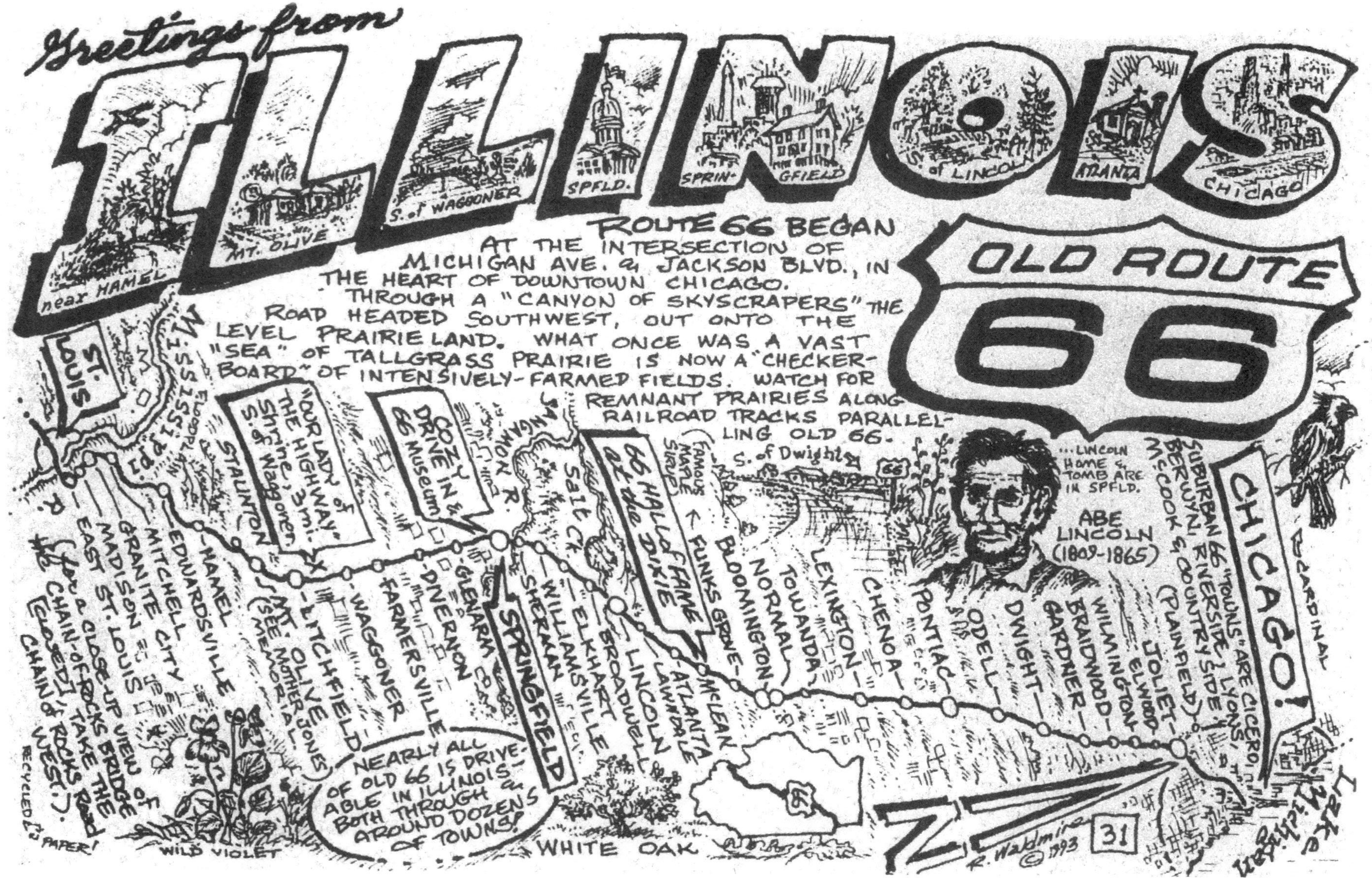

The brick process was used because it was labor intensive and WPA projects like this put more men to work during the Depression.

During the 1920s and '30s Illinois roads were a mish-mash of assorted character. This jumbled variety consisted of graded earth, gravel, oiled gravel, brick, macadam (crushed stone mixed with tar; named for the Scottish inventor), asphalt, asphalt over a concrete base, and Portland cement. The Land of Lincoln was in need of improved roads to enable it to wrest the title "**Crossroads of America**" from those neighboring Hoosiers - roads that would sail past verdant fields of winter wheat in the spring and tawny rows of corn in the fall. Illinois was *the leader* over all of the other states along Route 66 in the paving process. Such roads would sit on top of rich prairie soil that made Illinois the "**Breadbasket of America**;" soil so rich that pioneer farmers boasted, "You can plant nails and harvest crowbars!" These roads could criss-cross the state and connect its pulsating cities with the hinterland and beat the economic drums of trade and commerce.

Before the fabled Route 66 artery existed, there was a dirt road that went from **Chicago** to **East St. Louis**. In 1915 this dirt path was officially dubbed **The Pontiac Trail**. Many called it the Greater Sheridan Road. Dirt roads back then were improved by what came to be known as a split-log drag process. Invented in Missouri, the device used several teams of horses or mules that dragged logs over a dampened roadbed to dramatically improve its utility.

Route 66 started out in 1926 as a patchwork of mixed road surfaces that linked Chicago with St. Louis and St. Louis with Los Angeles. This was the Age of Ballyhoo and showman/entrepreneur C.C. ("Cash and Carry") Pyle drew national attention to the new road in 1928 by organizing an international **Bunion Derby** – a footrace from LA to New York, with the first two thirds to follow Route 66 and go through Chicago. To this day it remains the **single most important event** known to Route 66 in terms of exposure and publicity. A first place prize of $25,000 was offered, drawing 275 contestants. Runners covered a predetermined distance each day. **Red Grange**, the former U of I star and Chicago Bears' football player, was hired to fire the gun each morning to begin the race anew. His celebrity status was used to promote interest in the race at various stops along the way. To help draw crowds, Pyle assembled a circus sideshow that arrived at each leg's destination a day in advance. The show included carnival rides, sideshow attractions (**including a mummified dead outlaw**), games of chance and concession stands. Grange acted as master of ceremonies in some of the featured attractions. When the exhausted runners reached Chicago, a Brit of Italian ancestry by the name of Peter "Iron Man" Gavuzzi clung to a tenuous lead. After a grueling 84 days and a distance of 3,423 miles, with

Early map of Route 66, circa 1927 published by *American Motorist*. Author's collection

numerous contestants dropping out from exhaustion and raw feet, Andy Payne, a young Oklahoman of Native American extraction, claimed the prize at New York's Madison Square Garden. There were only 55 finishers.

Originally labeled Route 60, this proposed road, which would become so revered, was planned by the "**Father of Route 66**," Cyrus Avery, President of the Associated Highways Association of America (what a mouthful). The name change was forced by North Carolina, Virginia, and Kentucky, whose governors whined that a Route 60 should logically start on the East coast - not Chicago - and go through *their* states. At a special meeting in Springfield, Missouri, an Oklahoma engineer named John Page suggested the number 66 be used as a compromise. This intervention by fate, causing a signage change, turned out to be an amazing stroke of luck. It is significant because "Route 60" simply lacks the charisma and magnetic appeal of those incredible double sixes emblazoned on a black and white shield. A Route

60 designation would have been roughly equivalent to Adolph Hitler adopting a yellow flag with an acorn on it instead of the mesmerizing twisted cross, a black swastika within a white circle on a blood red field. Furthermore, can you imagine songwriter Bobby Troupe struggling to pen catchy and rhyming lyrics for Route 60?

The original Route 66 in Illinois followed most of SBI 4 (state bond issue 4, built in 1918 after the war) from **Springfield** to **East St. Louis**. Route 4 traveled along a historic path, a portage trail once traversed by Marquette and **Joliet**. Sixty-six was the **first fully paved road** ("slab all the way") in the state at a cost of $40,000 per mile (6" thick). Some labeled it the "**Great Diagonal Highway**" or the "**Lone Star Route**."

Illinoisans were a practical, pragmatic breed in those jaunty days of "tin lizzies" and hardly gave the new highway thought except for the fact that they could now get from point A to point B much quicker. It was a boon to traveling salesmen and a convenient venue for Chicago bootleggers to keep in touch with their counterparts in Springfield, East

Russel Soulsby's Shell Station in Mt. Olive, Illinois (Dan Oberle Photo)

St. Louis and St. Louis. Leo Brothers, the labor slugger from St. Louis, was convicted of killing reporter Jake Lingle. He traveled Route 66 to make a $10,000 Capone contract hit in Chicago. **Charles Lindbergh** flew along Route 66 and the parallel Chicago & Alton Railroad tracks on his airmail delivery route from St. Louis to the Windy City.

Gasoline back then came as simply regular and ethyl instead of the three octane ratings used today. When Route 66 was completed in Illinois, regular cost about 17 cents a gallon; Ethyl was a penny more. Only Ethyl was leaded because it was introduced in 1923 by Dupont Ethyl Company that made tetraethyl lead. Lead raises the octane rating of gasoline. The higher the compression ratio of a car's engine, the greater the need for a higher octane rating. Both Ethyl and regular gas in the Twenties was clear, like water, as the natural end product of the refining process. Housewives began using leaded gas as a cleaning agent to remove spots on clothes. Since tetraethyl lead was soluble, it penetrated the skin, causing lead poisoning. To discourage this practice, the company added a red dye to the gasoline giving it a pinkish cast. The dye caused a permanent stain on clothing and housewives quickly stopped using ethyl gas as a cleaning agent.

In the 1920s and 1930s gasoline was dispensed mechanically. The attendant pushed a long pump handle back and forth, which brought the gasoline from a storage tank below into a large glass container at the top with markings to show the number of desired gallons. Anything between even gallons was a guesstimate. The nozzle was then placed into the gas tank and the gasoline went into the car by gravity. Quarts of oil (an ugly, thick greenish brown color) at filling stations were stored in glass containers that looked like a pop bottle with a long tapered metal spout for pouring oil into the crankcase. It had the viscosity of sorghum molasses and was not nearly as efficient as modern oil, necessitating frequent "ring jobs."

During World War II drivers were limited to about 3 gallons of gas a week and were encouraged to either use public transportation or carpool. No cars were produced from 1942-45 because auto factories were converted to wartime production. There was a shortage of rubber and car owners were asked to contribute the spare tire in their trunk to the war effort. Punctured inner tubes, instead of being replaced, were fixed with "hot patches." Some patriotic Americans jacked their cars up, removed all of the tires, and left their vehicles on cinder blocks for the duration of the war. And all Americans were expected to strictly obey the nationally imposed speed limit of 35 miles per hour.

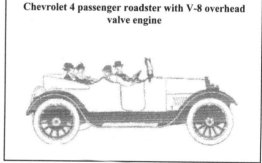

Chevrolet 4 passenger roadster with V-8 overhead valve engine

What kind of autos used Route 66 when it was first completed? Originally called a horseless carriage, the term motorcar was now very much in vogue. Tin Lizzie or "flivver" was the vernacular for cheaper models such as the Chevrolet, Ford and Plymouth. Classic autos of this age of driving by the seat of one's pants included the Packard, Essex, Durant, Nash, Olds, Dodge, Reo, Studebaker, Buick, Auburn, Chrysler, Hudson, Stutz, DuPont, McFarland, Franklin, Peerless, Hupmobile, Cadillac, Dorris, Pierce-Arrow, Willys-Knight, Lincoln, Daniels, Dusenberg, Maxwell, Rolls Royce, Rickenbacker, Stanley Steamer, and Locomobile.

Cars of this happy-go-lucky era, when the journey was almost as important as the destination, generally lacked radios and black box heaters (recycled hot air from the manifold), were optional. Windshield wipers were often found only on the driver's side and were originally operated by hand. Some old models were started with a hand crank. Brakes were mechanical, not hydraulic. Two-seaters with open cockpits were dubbed "roadsters." Some smaller coupes had fold out seats in the rear known as **rumble seats**." The larger square-roofed sedans made for long-distance travel were called "touring cars." Vehicles that took people from hotels to train stations were known as "station wagons." Rear doors were often hinged in the back. If you stepped out of the car and the driver absentmindedly pulled forward with the rear gate open, you could be knocked down and run over, hence the term **"suicide doors."**

Back at the turn of the century there was so much prejudice against motorcars that numerous towns passed ordinances requiring a man holding a red flag to walk ahead of the vehicle. These restrictions often prohibited the use of offensive horns, bells, or whistles. Illinois even passed a 1903 law regulating the top speed of automobiles at fifteen miles per hour. In 1939 the speed limit was *reduced* from 80 to 70 miles per hour.

It can be argued that Route 66 gave birth to a national network of highways, giving rise to the trucking industry. Trucks made it possible for smaller regional stockyards to spring up. This ultimately eliminated the need for huge terminal stockyard facilities, ergo it spelled doom for Chicago's Union Stockyards and the National Stockyards at **East St. Louis**. The trucking industry also put many railroads out of business.

Anne Gregor of Edwardsville next to the Livingston sign she helped correct

Route 66's first eastern terminus (to purists, point of origin) was at Cicero, but it soon was extended to Jackson Boulevard at Michigan Avenue and later to Lakeshore Drive at Chicago's Grant Park. From 1926 to 1930, Route 66 followed Route 4 from **Springfield** to **Staunton**. After that date the road was shifted farther east, and it now ran through **Litchfield, Mount Olive** and **Livingston**.

There was a lot of politics involved back then when determining exactly which route the road would take and what towns would be visited or bypassed. There was so much at stake - just as when the railroads were built back in the 1850s. Towns like **Carbondale, Centralia**, and **Mattoon** that had trunk lines grew and prospered. The American Automobile Association predicted in 1927 that tourist travel along Route 66 towns would amount to an astounding $3.3 billion annually. Places that were bypassed shriveled and died on the economic vine; some became ghost towns or, at the very most, irrelevant. Some towns had big parades to celebrate the opening of a stretch of the road through their boundaries. The new road quickly became a boon to mom and pop stores, motels, filling stations, restaurants, refreshment stands, repair shops, sign painters, and virtually all of the building trades.

I was born on September 1, 1939, and am known as a "Tweener." My generation is neither Depression-era nor Baby Boomer. We were sandwiched between those two groups during the years that Europe and America were at war, almost too young to remember blackouts, scrap metal drives, war bond rallies and rationing. I grew up listening to exciting heroes like Jack Armstrong and Tom Mix and the crazy antics of Fibber McGee and Molly. America still had a large rural population, and Norman Rockwell waxed nostalgic with folksy covers on the "Saturday Evening Post."

I first became vaguely aware of Route 66 when **Nat King Cole**, in his rich velvety voice, sang Bobby Troupe's song about having fun on the open road and getting "your kicks on Route 66." That song tugged at the wanderlust in a great many of us.

There were numerous cousins, aunts, and uncles on my mother's side and many of them lived in St. Louis. Every Fourth of July we had a family get together and picnic at the Chain of Rocks Amusement Park. It was accessed from my house in Washington Park by traveling north on Route 111 and turning west on Route 66 at the Bel-Air Drive-in at **Mitchell**. From there it was a short trek to the Chain of Rocks Bridge - that long trussed structure that had a crick (dogleg) in the middle of it, ostensibly to counter a quirky part of

Nat "King" Cole

the river's current. I remembered wondering why its steel girders looked so different from the camelback trusses of the McArthur Bridge in **East St. Louis**, and why it sat on so many piers when the Eads Bridge, built 50 years earlier, required only two. And like most pubescent teenagers blissfully living in the present, I was barely aware that Route 66 traversed East St. Louis and went across the St. Louis-owned Municipal Bridge. But I did know that in Missouri it headed down a cultural corridor for Illinoisans that included Ted Drewes Frozen Custard on Chippewa, the 66 Park In

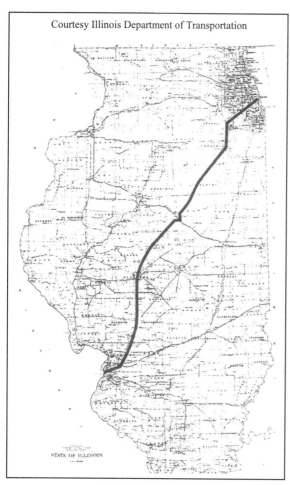

STATE OF ILLINOIS

Theater (Crestwood), and those notorious art deco/glass block Coral Court (no tell) motel units (1953 Bobby Greenlease kidnapping) out on 7775 Watson Rd. in the Marlborough part of south St. Louis County. Furthermore, I had no way of knowing that one day a seemingly ordinary road that went through my hometown would embody a certain magic, a kind of mystical quality that would stir men's blood and capture their imaginations.

Route 66 took on new meaning for me in the early 1960s when Stirling Silliphant began writing screenplays for a four year CBS television series about a couple of nomadic adventurers. It starred freckle-faced Martin Milner as **Tod Stiles**, who usually drove the fawn beige 1960 Corvette, and the brooding, mercurial George Maharis (**Buz Murdoch**). When Maharis (Buz) became ill with hepatitis, actor Glenn Corbett filled in for him. It was one of my favorite programs, and I watched it regularly. And no one has ever written a better road theme than Nelson Riddle's bouncy score for the show's opening credits. Never mind that most of the stories themselves had nothing to do with the highway.

I fell in love, married a pretty Collinsville girl, taught high school at **Collinsville** and **Edwardsville**, and raised a family. I taught social studies but naively came to the conclusion that local and state history were dullsville and focused on the national and international scene. Only since I started writing books back in 1995 did I come to realize that state and local history was the American past firsthand - and it was never boring. I read history – not literature – and didn't know that John Steinbeck had forever embedded the Dust Bowl, Oakies and the highway into our national psyche by terming it "**the Mother Road**" in *The Grapes of Wrath*.

Despite my newfound appreciation of things that are state and local, I am still not a Route 66 "junkie" or a "Rootie." I leave that to the keepers of the highway – the Anne Gregors, Dan Oberles, and Tom Teagues of the world. No book about Illinois would be complete without a cursory look at this national phenomenon, and at groups of people who go gaga over "the most magical road in the world" and haunt the annual Route 66 road tours and festivals. My hat is off to them for helping to preserve this important part of Illinois history.

Route 66 begins exactly where it should begin, in the City of Broad Shoulders by Lake Michigan at Grant Park. Illinois has long been famous for being a champion road builder, butcher to the world, rail giant and transportation hub. But, unfortunately, the quaintness of the highway that is so often associated with small rural towns seems to get lost and swallowed up by Chicago's huge monoliths of concrete, stone, glass and steel. For most of the trip through Illinois, Route 66 parallels Interstate 55, the modern highway with clover leafs that replaced it in the late 1950s and early '60s.

The "**Main Street of America**" loses some of its charm as it is nearly overwhelmed by Chicago's urban tableau. The Masonic Temple, Railway Exchange Building, or the Fine Arts Building have never been favorite groupie landmarks. The venerable road's best Chicago site is probably Lou

Clock/bell tower and unusual octagonal library in Atlanta (Dan Oberle photo)

Mitchell's place at 565 W. Jackson (known for his free Milk Duds in place of after dinner mints). Chicago further irritatingly frustrates purists. While Michigan at Jackson is the Route's point of origin, Jackson is now one way – east. Roadies are forced to begin their trip by heading west on Adams, which is one block north of Jackson. Travelers now

2002 Car lineup at Chicago's Grant Park for Route 66 tour
(Dan Oberle of Edwardsville)

Route 66 going through downtown Edwardsville past Yonaka's Jewelry Store
(Dan Oberle)

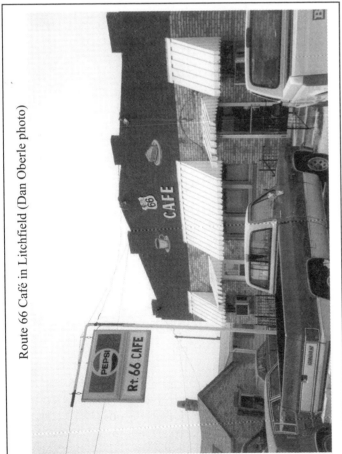

Route 66 Café in Litchfield (Dan Oberle photo)

Route 66 at Williamsville silos and bean field
(Dan Oberle photo)

see the familiar brown and white historical markers on Adams as well as Jackson and Ogden in Chicago.

From Chicago, Route 66 takes a southwest path along Ogden Avenue that was cobbled together and merely followed existing trails that were once used by Indians and buffalo. The next stop is **Cicero** (Henry's Hot Dogs, former location of a giant statue and Bunyon's Drive-in), famous for Bell Telephone's Western Electric complex and Al Capone's Hawthorne Hotel headquarters. Cicero's dark history still exists in the form of tunnels that allowed underworld figures to move unseen from speakeasy to brothel to gang headquarters.

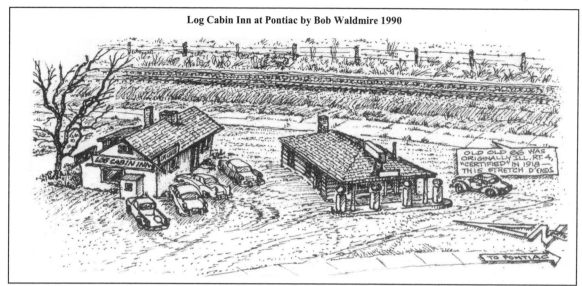
Log Cabin Inn at Pontiac by Bob Waldmire 1990

The next stop is **Berwyn** (Route 66 display at Skylight Restaurant), a residential suburb with a large Bohemian population, where you make a left turn on Harlem Avenue and then right on Joliet Road. This "tips" **Riverside** and goes through **Lyons** (Illinois & Michigan Canal, Hoffman Tower), and **McCook** (DesPlaines River Forest Preserve) and skirts **Hodgkins** and **Countryside** (Route 66 Café and Grill) to **Indian Head Park** (Wolf's Head Inn, Route 66 Root Beer). The road went through **LaGrange** and a later alignment of the road once passed through **Plainfield** and **Shorewood**.

Wilmington Gemini Giant at the Launching Pad Restaurant – photo by Dan Oberle of Edwardsville

The thoroughfare now parallels the DesPlaines River and then heads **for Bolingbrook, Romeoville** (Isle a la Cache Museum 815/886-1437), **Willowbrook,** (Del Rhea's Chicken Basket Restaurant, with a carefully guarded secret recipe, dating back to 1946) and passes through the heart of **Joliet** (Rialto Theater 815/726-6600), bypassing a nearby prison that was termed the "Rock Pile." The Chicago Sanitary and Ship Canal is along the east side of the highway in Will County. South of Joliet, 66 passed a U.S. Army munitions facility – currently a veteran's cemetery and prairie. The road parallels a set of Alton & Chicago Railroad tracks. This will bring back sweet memories to readers who recall flooring the gas pedal and racing side by side with speeding locomotives.

Route 66 now heads past **Elwood** (Illinois Central Gulf Railroad, Jackson Creek, Cedar Creek) for **Wilmington**, a town that is split in two by the Kankakee River. A more recent Wilmington landmark is the jolly green Gemini Giant, a space-helmeted astronaut holding either a rocket or a missile in his hands and who is a mascot for the Launching Pad Restaurant.

Next along the southwest path across the glaciated prairie is **Braidwood** (Korner Keg & Kitchen, Polk-A-Dot Drive-in) in Will County, where Peter Rossi built a grocery store, service station, motor court complex (later called motels) and dance hall. Braidwood is followed by **Godley** (K Mine Park, nearby Mail Pouch Tobacco sign), and **Braceville** (Route 129 bridge, Mazon River). Some of the first great landmarks such as roadhouses, motels, and filling stations appear on this stretch. After **Gardner** (home of Riviera Roadhouse since 1927 and Two Cell Jail) comes **Dwight**, with its correctional center for women, Renfrew Park, Mt. Olivet Cemetery, Feddersen's Pizza Garage, and Mad Max's Dignified Hot Dogs. The Carefree Motel (now gone) and notable Becker Marathon Oil station are also located here.

Odell (Pour Richard's Restaurant), in Livingston County, is enhanced by the historic H. C. Sinclair gas station, (originally a Standard Station), Miller Memorial Park, and a modernistic microwave relay station. Next on the list is **Cayuga** (Wolf Creek Country Club) where there is a restored barnside ad for Lester Dill's Missouri Meramec Caverns, once used as a hideout by Jesse James. (This might have been a bit of hyperbole on Dill's part.)

At **Pontiac**, also in Livingston County (another penitentiary town), the road crosses a set of Wabash Railroad tracks.

Stretch of Memory Lane at Lexington by Dan Oberle

Pontiac - named for the Indian Chief - not the car, is the site of the remodeled Palomar Hotel, Green Parrot Bar, and Old Log Cabin Inn. When a new alignment of the highway placed the inn on its backside, the place was jacked up and moved so it would now face the new route. Pontiac's downtown section boasted the Rodino Square, a brick structure with a tavern, garage and hotel, since demolished. On the outskirts of Pontiac one could find Dreamland Park, another of those Jazz Age dance halls on the banks of Rooks Creek. Route 66 passes an historic district state police building in Livingston County. The road then crosses over Rock Creek before hitting **Chenoa** (Steve's Café, St. Joseph's Church) at the juncture of the Oquawka and Chicago & Alton Railroads.

The next stop is **Lexington** (vintage billboards along Memory Lane during "celebrations," Oasis Cafe), in McLean County, named for the Revolutionary War battle and visited by the old Chicago & Mississippi Railroad in 1857.

McLean County is largely rural except for Normal/Bloomington. Outside of Lexington is another one of those quaint bridges that crosses the Mackinaw River. After Lexington appears the small burg of **Towanda** (Money Creek). From there it's a short drive to **Normal** (Gus Belt's Steak 'n Shake, the nation's first) and the larger adjacent city, **Bloomington**. This town (Beer Nut Factory) celebrates Route 66 with an annual Corvette meet. It's here that the highway crosses over a set of Illinois Central tracks and New York Central & St. Louis tracks.

It's 64 miles from Bloomington to **Springfield**. Sandwiched between are numerous picturesque towns. First on the list is **Shirley** (Sugar Creek) and then **Funks Grove**, named for a stand of ancient of maple trees where the Funk family has been producing maple "sirup" since the turn of the nineteenth century. Perhaps the most notable stop in all of Illinois is the Dixie Truckers Home in **McLean** on S. Main. Built around 1928, it is open 24 hours a day and was rebuilt after a fire in 1965 put it out of business for one day. Mark and Kathy Beeler's place is super famous for its scrump-

delicious food and great pies. Although located in the heart of the Midwest, it was given the southern moniker "Dixie" to denote its friendliness. It is now home to the **Illinois Route 66 Hall of Fame**, maintained by the Illinois Route 66 Association.

Next comes **Atlanta** (Railsplitter State Park, octagonal library and bell tower, and Hawes grain elevator) and then on down to **Lawndale** where the road crosses Kickapoo Creek, made famous in Al Capp's Lil Abner comic strip with its Kickapoo Joy Juice. Like its southern sister city, Atlanta suffered a devastating fire in 1865 that burned most of the town down. Its rebuilt structures were mostly brick. Next on the list is **Lincoln** (Blue Mill tavern), in Logan County, served by the Illinois Central and Chicago & Alton railroads, the only town in America named for Honest Abe while he was still alive. He actually christened the town with juice

Macoupin County Jail at Carlinville – photo by Dan Oberle

from a watermelon. Outside of Lincoln was a hilly, curvy, white-knuckle section of Route 66 that saw numerous deadly car crashes and townsfolk labeled it "Bloody 66" and "Dead Man's Stretch." It was perhaps the most dangerous piece of road in Illinois.

Next it's on to **Broadwell** and **Elkhart**. Broadwell once drew a large crowd of travelers to Ernie Edwards' Pig-Hip Restaurant, famous for its barbeque. Back when it opened in 1937, pork sandwiches could be bought for 15 cents.

Sadly, the Pig Hip pork palace closed in 1991. The town of Elkhart is named for Elkhart Hill, a raised wooded area that jutted up from the rest of the flat Illinois prairie. **Williamsville**, on the northern border of Sangamon County, is followed by **Sherman**, gateway to **Springfield** (Sangamon River), our state capital and home to Abe Lincoln. It's also hometown to the **Cozy Dog** (217/525-1992), sometimes called a corndog or pig in a blanket. The business was started by Ed Waldmire, and he originally called his invention the "crusty cur."

A favorite upscale Springfield restaurant back then was The Black Angus on Sixth Street. A modern Route 66 experience in Springfield is available at Maldaner's Restaurant with some art deco décor and historic Springfield photographs. It's notable for its fine food, "washed coins" given back in change, and second floor "Map Room." Springfield also showcases Bill Shea's Gas Station Museum.

Cozy Dog Restaurant in Springfield – photo by Dan Oberle

From Springfield to St. Louis, the original Route 66 (1926-30) is full of zigs and zags. The Chicago & Alton Railroad was now joined by the Illinois Traction electric streetcar line. You can follow Route 4, the very first alignment of Route 66, past **Jerome** (Lauderbach Giant) on the outskirts of Springfield and then through **Chatham**. Next the famed path goes barely west of **Auburn** (Red Brick Road), through **Thayer**, **Virden** (coal town home to gangster Charlie Birger for about a year), and **Girard** (Otter Creek, Deck's 1884 Drug Store 217/627-2311). The Chicago, Burlington & Quincy slashed through Virden in a diagonal manner. Then comes **Nilwood** (Hurricane Creek) near which is a section of road imprinted with turkey tracks. After the road was poured, and just before the Portland cement hardened, a rafter (or is it gaggle?) of wild turkeys trooped across the road and made their mark for posterity.

Past Nilwood there is **Carlinville**, the seat of Macoupin County, home to a white elephant "Million Dollar" courthouse that is known as the Taj Mahal of the Midwest (in cost overruns – not aesthetically). Carlinville is the original home of the Ariston Café (217/324-2023), a Route 66 landmark run by the Adam family. Ariston comes from the Greek word for "superior." When the highway was reconfigured in 1940 and shifted east, the place was moved to nearby Litchfield. Hubert Humphrey once ate there and so did Tommy Dorsey, who was with his band on his way to play at the **Coliseum**, the famous dance hall/gambling casino in Benld. Al Capone owned a still on the outskirts of town that shipped illegal rotgut back to Chicago.

Gillespie, Benld (Cahokia Creek), **Sawyerville**, and **Staunton** (Ginseng Creek, 66 Terminal, and a roadhouse named DeCamp Junction) were the other stops along the original Route 66. Henry's Old Route 66 Emporium is at Staunton, and it has a collection of auto, truck and motorcycle memorabilia.

On the newer version of Route 66, south of Springfield, are the towns of **Glenarm, Divernon** (Nikorbob Craft Mall), **Thomasville, Farmersville** (Hendricks Café and Gas, Art's Motel) and **Waggoner** (Horse Creek). West of **Raymond**, north of Litchfield in Montgomery County, stands a $400 Italian Carrara marble statue of a praying Virgin Mary on this stretch of Route 66 that road warriors affectionately labeled "**Our Lady of the Highways**." A plaque below the statue reads: "Loving mother of Jesus protect us on the highway." It's been there since 1959, bought by farm kids from St. Raymond's Parish.

Route 66 "junkies" at Henry's Emporium in Staunton – photo by Dan Oberle

At **Litchfield** the road was joined by the Louis-ville & Nashville Railroad. The Litchfield Sky View Drive-in Theater is the oldest continuously operated outdoor theater in Illinois and on all of national Route 66.

Litchfield is popular today for the Gardens Restaurant, Ariston Cafe, and Niehaus Motorcycle Sales, a booming mecca for modern day nomads who prefer to travel on two and three wheels. Sadly, the town's Route 66 Café closed in the spring of 2002.

We are now in the heart of coal mining country and travelers frequently saw coal mine tipples and gob piles, juxtaposed with grain silos and cornfields. **Mount Olive** (Panther Creek) boasted another landmark – Russel Soulsby's Shell Station. Mother Jones is buried here. At one time the fiery union organizer was called the **Most Dangerous Woman in America**. Next comes tiny **Williamson** followed by **Livingston** in northeastern Madison County. The town of **Hamel** (Earnie's Roadhouse) is situated where Route 140 crosses Route 66. Sleepy little Hamel is known by travelers for its St. Paul's Lutheran Church with its blue neon-lit cross, placed there by the Brunworth family whose son was killed at Anzio in World War II.

Hamel also featured the Tourist Haven Restaurant.

Continuing south along Route 157 with a slight curve to the west, the road meanders through **Edwardsville**, the seat of Madison County. It is named for Ninian Edwards, one of the state's early governors who was also a great land speculator. Edwardsville was called home by four other governors as well. In Edwardsville Route 66 sauntered past a Site Gas Station on Hillsboro, the Gothic Revival St. Boniface Church, and made a left on West Street at Hadley House as it curved around the high school, then ducked under a Nickel Plate Railroad overpass. After passing Sunset Hills Cemetery, the road dropped down below the bluffs and traveled along the old floodplain of the Mississippi.

From this point, Route 66 took **three separate paths** to St. Louis. The earliest went down Chain of Rocks Road where it turned left near the Luna Café in **Mitchell**. Next it jogged south along Route 203 (Nameoki Road) and then west along Madison Avenue in **Granite City**. It continued through **Madison** into **Venice** where Madison Ave. becomes Broadwalk. This took you directly to the McKinley Bridge and crossed into north St. Louis. The McKinley Bridge was owned by the city of Venice (named for Venice, Italy, because it flooded so often). The bridge, originally a people traffic and streetcar bridge crossing into north St. Louis, was named for Illinois congressman William B. McKinley, not president William McKinley. McKinley, a **Danville** native, was

Sharp curve on old Route 66 GM&O (?) Railroad underpass near Virden

Old Coliseum Ball Room at Benld – photo by Dan Oberle

responsible for building a large number of streetcar lines in central and Southern Illinois. The bridge has been closed for several years because it has fallen into disrepair but work is progressing and it should be reopened sometime in 2004 or 2005.

Around 1940 a **second route** was created that entered St. Louis through East St. Louis and the Municipal Bridge (later renamed McArthur Bridge). It connected with East St. Louis by splitting off at Hamel, bypassing Edwardsville and Glen Carbon, crossing Route 143 before brushing the edge of **Troy** and Maryville. Linking up with **Collinsville** on Vandalia Street, 66 turned west on the Beltline (U.S. 40) and then went to the base of the bluffs at the current Moto Station. It followed 157 for a spell before heading west on (Collinsville Road) past Evergreen Gardens, Fairmount Park, Cahokia Mounds, **Fairmont City**, and Horseshoe Lake. (Note the slight difference in spelling of Fairmount Park and Fairmont City. Many books erroneously spell them the same). Route 66 went past the Y Café and then sunk beneath a railroad underpass with a set of double tracks used by the Pennsy and B&O and crossed St. Clair Avenue in **East St. Louis** at 9th Street. Then it moved into south St. Louis via the Municipal Bridge at Choteau Avenue. A 1957 alignment went across the Veteran's Bridge.

11

A **third route**, known as a bypass, was established around 1939 across the Chain of Rocks Bridge. As Route 66 dropped below the bluffs from Edwardsville, it followed the old Chain of Rocks Road, which today parallels Interstate 270, then went north of **Granite City** and **Nameoki** (Indian for "smokey"), and passed through Mitchell (Raffaelle's Luna Café). Now the road, graced by the Sun Motel, Chain of Rocks Motel, and Canal Motel, crossed over into north St. Louis at the Chain of Rocks Bridge.

The trussed toll bridge, arguably the most famous on all of Route 66, is named for a stretch of rocks in the river, placed there by ancient glaciers moving down from Canada. They were a hazard to river traffic, and their rapids can still readily be seen. The Chain of Rocks toll bridge (spanning 5,353 feet) was built in 1929 by the Scott brothers. They started construction on the Missouri side *before* they found bedrock on the Illinois side. When they did find bedrock, it necessitated a sharp 47-degree dogleg in the middle of the bridge to reach it. The bend was so severe that two large trucks coming in opposite directions on the 24-foot wide roadway could not pass each other at this point on the two-lane girder bridge.

Unfortunately, highway officials in Illinois and Missouri failed to place the bridge on their maps, jeopardizing the Scott brothers' $2 million dollar investment. The brothers extended the bridge route, and it eventually linked up with Lindbergh Boulevard and this became the bypass around St. Louis. The brothers, discouraged by financial hardship, finally sold the bridge to the city of Madison in 1939 and, as luck would have it, the girdered structure soon became a cash cow.

The old Chain of Rocks Bridge was closed two years after the 4-lane Interstate 270 Bridge opened in 1966. Today the bridge is used as an eagle watch site and a path for cyclists. It is now considered the **World's Longest Pedestrian Bridge**, well over a mile in length.

Because of the dangerous stretch of

Pighip Restaurant on Route 66 at Broadwell © 1990 by Bob Waldmire

river past the chain of rocks, it was deemed necessary to build a canal with a bridge (completed in 1949) to skirt that part of the Mississippi. Up on the bluffs overlooking the bridge was the popular Chain of Rocks Amusement Park that featured an arcade, Ferris wheel, swimming pool, skating rink, dodge-em cars, roller coaster, and picnic area. It closed in the mid-1970s. The two cute little stone castles in the middle of the river near the bridge are pumping stations to send Mississippi water to large settling pools on Riverview Drive in St. Louis for the waterworks department. It is still in operation for this very purpose. Just south of the bridge on the Illinois side is Granite City's Choteau Island. The famed **Lewis and Clark** expedition camped here overnight as they made plans to go up the Missouri River to explore the newly acquired Louisiana Territory. They didn't stay at St. Louis because it was still under control of the Spanish.

All three of these St. Louis access corridors of Route 66 outside Edwardsville traveled along a geographically unique area of Illinois known as the **American Bottom**, carefully researched by **Granite City** native Georgia Engelke. The Bottom stretches from **Alton** to **Chester** and varies from four to twelve miles in width. The flat floodplain was carved out by glacial meltwater and a meandering Mississippi River. The same meltwater also helped form Lake Michigan. Remnants of these earlier channels exist in the form of Grand Marais, Spring Lake, Indian Lake, McDonough Lake, Horseshoe Lake (Madison County) and others. Horseshoe is an oxbow lake that is an abandoned meander of the Mississippi River. The soil on the flood plain is known as gumbo, a sticky, black muck of a soil when it is wet.

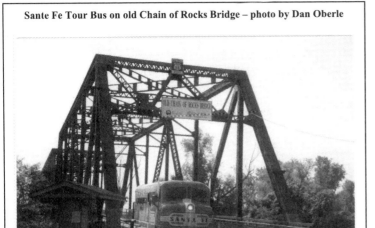

Sante Fe Tour Bus on old Chain of Rocks Bridge – photo by Dan Oberle

Madison and St. Clair counties have long led the nation in the production of a certain crop. That part of Southern Illinois is referred to as the **Horseradish Capital of America**, and the city of **Collinsville** holds an annual Horseradish Festival. First introduced to Illinois by German settlers, it grows robustly in the rich black soil of the American Bottom. Horseradish is used as a condiment on roast beef and is blended with catsup to make cocktail sauce for eating with fish.

It was said that the whole world traveled down Route 66. Not anymore. Route 66 was decertified (decommissioned in official jargon) as a bona fide highway in January of 1977. This meant that the famed conduit would no longer appear on any official highway maps. The new interstates were billed as a triumph over time and space, but in a sense it was a Pyrrhic victory. Travelers would now be forced to drive on dull, mind numbing stretches of boring, homogenized concrete that bypassed practically everything. We sold our souls to the devil in return for the ability to arrive at out destination ten minutes sooner. We gave up a road that was like a gift from God – textured by hills, dips and bumps, girdered bridges, parallel railroad tracks, S curves, classic billboards with catchy slogans, oddball logos, roadhouses, dancehalls, souvenir stands, truck stops, and gaudy neon signs. And for what? It was for nothing more than mind-boggling blandness, bleak as a Dorothea Lange Dust Bowl photo that flim-flamers sold to us as *progress*.

Any other decertified road would have fallen into the dustbin of history and been quickly forgotten. Not so Route 66. Memories of Route 66 soon exerted a powerful grip on our collective imagination. For many of us, that road personified freedom, the wide-open spaces, and postwar prosperity that enabled Americans to buy a car and head to Chicago (if you were from Southern Illinois) or go out West for an annual family vacation. Disparate images of roadway advertising, courthouses, barbed wire, train tracks, and grain silos along the road helped to amplify that perception.

America's love affair with the automobile is as strong as ever. For tourist nirvana while traveling Interstate 55 from East St. Louis to Chicago, pull off at one of those quaint towns along the way to get a true feel for history. Better yet, take a blood oath and don't use I-55 in the first place! Take the road less traveled with those old-fashioned sweeping curves for a slice of Americana and a treasure chest of memories. Sit down with a few old timers on an old porch swing and soak up some local color. Marvel at some of the vintage architecture. Make a trip down memory lane, back to America's glory years of the 1940s and 1950s when commercial buildings had substance and character because they were not cookie cutter images of some franchise in another town. Visit one of the classic family-owned eateries. Talk to a long time resident and discover what it was like back when things were at a slower pace and when we had a greater sense of community. Let them take you back to an era when people took on life's challenges one at a time and had to figure things out with just their common sense. Drive a bit on an old frontage road that was once part and parcel of the original Route 66. Stop, look and listen. You'll discover through its trappings and ambience that Route 66 was much more than just a highway. It's a shibboleth from the past, a touchstone that tells us what we are about.

President Ronald Reagan once said that "If we don't know who we are and where we came from, how will we know where we are going?" If you close your eyes and conjure up a bit of childhood imagination, you might be able to hear some of the sounds from the road's storied past – the whispers of countless ghosts that made the **Colossus of Roads** the most famous and nostalgic in all of our history. Then, with the words of guru Bob Waldmire, you can say: "I still get my kicks on old Route 66!"

Note: Some words, phrases or trademark names mentioned above are property of the trademark holder. We use them for identification purposes only.

Route 66 Association of Illinois
2743 Veterans Parkway, Room 166
Springfield, IL 62704
217/525-7980
teague66@eosinc.com
www.historic66.com, www.enjoyillinois.com

ILLINOIS

Land of Lincoln

FAMOUS ILLINOISANS

My apologies to the dozens of notable people who were omitted from this list. There was simply not room to recognize everyone. Quite a few individuals not mentioned in this section (such as Black Hawk and Joseph Smith) appear elsewhere.

Jane Addams – Founder of Chicago's Hull House (312/413-5353), a halfway house for immigrants; played important role in the founding of the NAACP; unmarried suffragette leader; the outstanding woman of her era; won Nobel Peace Prize in 1931 leader of the Women's International League for Peace and Freedom

Jane Addams

Dankmar Adler – German-born Chicago architect; builder of many museums, churches and public buildings

John Agar – Chicago film star of 1940s and 50s; married to Shirley Temple; *Fort Apache, Sands of Iwo Jima, She Wore a Yellow Ribbon, St. Valentine's Day Massacre* (1967: Dion O'Banion)

Eddie Albert – **Rock Island**-born movie and television actor; undercover spy for U.S. in WW II; TV star of "Green Acres" with Eva Gabor, *The Longest Day, Escape to Witch Mountain, Dreamscape, The Heartbreak Kid, Oklahoma, Roman Holiday*

Ivan Albright – Chicago painter; used dark gloomy themes; masterpiece – *That Which I Should Have Done I Did Not Do*

Nelson Algren – Chicago writer; earned a journalism degree from U of I; lived like a hobo during the Depression; became enamored with Communist party in late 1930s; dressed sloppily and spent much of his life gambling; joltingly realistic portrayal of life; *The Man With The Golden Arm*; *A Walk on the Wild Side*; intensely jealous of Saul Bellow

John Altgeld

Karen Allen – **Carrollton** native; starred in *Raiders of the Lost Ark* with Harrison Ford and *Starman* with Jeff Bridges

Steve Allen - **Hyde Park** comedian, actor, songwriter, and television personality

Robert Allerton – Founder of Chicago's Union Stockyards

John Peter Altgeld – Born in Neider Selders, Germany, (town from which seltzer water gets its name); became Chicago's first foreign-born governor in 1892

Morey Amsterdam – Chicago comedian who starred in "The Dick Van Dyke Show"

John Anderson - **Rockford**-born politician and candidate for president on the Independent ticket; defeated by Ronald Reagan in 1980.

Sherwood Anderson – Contributed to Chicago Renaissance of early 1900's; *Winesburg, Ohio, The Triumph Of The Egg*

Paul Angle – Noted Illinois historian and author of *Bloody Williamson*

Philip Armour – Chicago industrialist; founded Armour Meat Packing Co. and the Armour Institute of Technology

Louis Armstrong – Born in New Orleans around 1900; played his coronet a few years on Mississippi paddleboats; came to Chicago to escape the South's segregation laws; offered a spot in King Oliver's band; his gravely music voice was described as "a piece of sandpaper calling its mate;" invented jazz the way it was played in the 1920s; lost popularity when jazz metamorphosed into swing; described as a "bloated small man with a mouth that looked like piano keys;" songs included: "We Have All The Time in the World" (from *On Her Majesty's Secret Service*), "Mack the Knife," "What a Wonderful World," and "Hello Dolly," making him the oldest performer to reach number 1 with a hit record

Philip Armour

Mary Astor – **Quincy** actress born Lucile Langhanke; silent screen star often teamed with John Barrymore; scandalous affair with playwright George S. Kaufman; married 4 times; won Best Supporting Actress Oscar for *The Great Lie* in 1941; starred in *Maltese Falcon* with Bogart the same year; ended 50-year career in 1964 with *Youngblood Hawke*, playing Hawke's cantankerous mother

Agnes Ayers – 1898-1940 – **Carbondale**-born, **Cobden** reared actress appeared in over 80 movies in the 1920s and 30s - most notably, *The Sheik, The Son of the Sheik, Forbidden Fruit, Racing Hearts;* worked with Valentino and Wallace Reid; talkies killed off her career

Richard Bach – **Oak Park** native who wrote *Jonathan Livingston Seagull* and *Stranger to the Ground*

Josephine Baker – She was just a young girl living in **East St. Louis** when the 1917 race riot broke out. Her family was living in an abandoned railroad car in Boxcar Town on what was known as the Bloody Island area at the time of the riot. She became a dancer and went to Paris where (at the age of 19) she became an immediate sensation at the Follies Bergère. Called "the Black Pearl," she became noted for her eye-popping skimpy outfits, including a celebrated banana skirt she first wore in 1926

John Bardeen – University of Illinois grad; first person in world to win two Nobel Prizes in physics, the first for his work on helping to **invent the transistor** while working for Bell Laboratories, the second for experiments in superconductivity.

Hank Bauer – East St. Louis native; received two Purple Hearts as a WW II marine; Yankee baseball outfielder – holds World Series consecutive game hitting streak – 17 games, owns 8 World Series rings; managed 1966 Orioles to World Series victory over the Dodgers

Frank Baum – Author who lived in Chicago for 20 years and penned *The Wizard of Oz* shortly after the turn of the century

Jennifer Beals – Chicago actress best known for the movie *Flashdance*; also with Sting in *The Bride*, 1985

Rex Bell – Chicago actor who married Clara Bow, the *It* girl; *The Cowboy King, The Man From Arizona, Stormy Trails*

Saul Bellow – *Herzog* and *Humboldt's Gift* author; noted for depiction of Jewish life in contemporary America; Nobel Prize in 1976; three National Book Awards; married 4 times; (not sure why that's important)

Saul Bellow

Jim Belushi – Brother of John Belushi who achieved acting fame in his own right; *The Substitute, The Principal, Mr. Destiny, Little Shop of Horrors*

John Belushi – (1949-1982) Chicago born comedian, raised in **Wheaton**, became famous on TV's "Saturday Night Live;" movies Include: *Continental Divide, Blues Brothers, Neighbors, Animal House;* died 1982 from drug overdose

Jack Benny – (1894-1974) **Waukegan**-born radio and television violin-playing comedian who portrayed himself as a vain miser, perennially 39-years-old – "Now cut that out;" radio show ran from 1932-1955; was good friends with George Burns

Tom Berenger – (1950-) Chicago born actor; *Looking For Mr. Goodbar, The Big Chill, Platoon, In Praise of Older Women*

Edgar Bergen – (1903-1978) Chicago-born ventriloquist famous for his 1930s-1950s act with a dummy, Charlie McCarthy, who is now in the Smithsonian Institute; made a number of films in 1930s; Mortimer Snerd another of his dummies; father of Emmy-winning actress, Candice Bergen

James Belushi

Shelly Berman – Chicago comedian/actor, nightclub performer

Karen Black – (1942-) Born Blanche Zeigler in **Park Ridge**; starred in *Easy Rider, Five Easy Pieces; Cisco Pike; Portnoy's Complaint, Airport 1975; The Great Gatsby, Family Plot, Night Angel*

Harry Blackmun – Nashville, Illinois-born member of the U.S. Supreme Court (appointed by Nixon) who was the swing vote in the 1973 Roe v. Wade decision (4-3), legalizing abortions in the U.S.

Bonnie Blair – Champaign native who became the first woman to win back-to-back speed skating titles by winning the gold in 1988 and again in 1992

Herbert Block – Chicago-born, left-leaning editorial cartoonist with *Chicago Daily News* and *Washington Post* under the name Herblock; severe critic of Joe McCarthy, coining the term McCarthyism; won Pulitzer Prize in 1942, 1954, 1979

Beulah Bondi – (1892-1981) Chicago-born actress, two Oscar nominations; Emmy for "The Waltons"

Tom Bosley – (1927-) Chicago TV actor who starred in "Happy Days," "Charlie's Angels" and "Father Dowling"

Lou Boudreau – Harvey native who was American League MVP in 1948 for Cleveland Indians; stopped Joe Dimaggio's 56-game hitting streak with a bare-handed catch; attended U of I and knew Pick Dehner, both were basketball players

Tom Berenger

Bruce Boxleitner – Elgin-born actor, married to Melissa Gilbert of "Little House on the Prairie" and star of numerous made-for-TV movies shown on Lifetime Channel; starred in the film *Tron*

Walter Boyne – East St. Louisan who is Board Chairman of Wingspan, the aviation cable TV channel; founded Air and Space Magazine; director of the Air and Space Museum at Smithsonian Institute; leading author and authority on air force history

Ray Bradbury - Waukegan native who wrote *The Illustrated Man, The Martian Chronicles* and *Fahrenheit 451*

James Brady – Centralia native who became President Reagan's press secretary. He was shot in the head when mentally disturbed John Hinckley attempted to kill the president in 1981 in Washington D.C. He and his wife became ardent gun-control advocates and urged passage of what came to be known as the Brady Bill.

Neville Brand – (1921-) **Kewanee** actor who played Al Capone on TV's "The Untouchables;" *Stalag 17, The George Raft Story*

Jack Brickhouse – Peoria-born Hall of Fame baseball announcer for the Chicago Cubs; his famous quote: "Anybody can have a bad century;" also broadcast for the White Sox and Bears

Gwendolyn Brooks – Chicago African-American poet laureate of Illinois; received 1950 Pulitzer poetry prize for *Annie Allen;* wrote many children's poems; wrote *A Street in Bronzeville* and *The Bean Eaters*; winner of numerous awards and fellowships; like Richard Wright, much of her writing is sad and bitter

William Jennings Bryan – Salem-born politician and three-time nominee for President of the United States; U.S. Secretary of State (resigned in protest to President Wilson's tough stance on the sinking of the *Lusitania*); prosecutor in the Scopes trial

Ruth Bryan – Jacksonville-born daughter of William J. Bryan; appointed by FDR and became the first woman to become an ambassador to a foreign county (Denmark)

Smiley Burnett – (1911-1967) **Summun**-born actor; Gene Autry's bumbling, lovable sidekick

Daniel Burnham – Designed much of 1893 Columbian Exposition; city planner; developed 1909 plan for Chicago giving it a beautiful lakefront, tall buildings in the business district, an outer ring of parks, and a "miracle mile" of shops and restaurants north of the Loop on Michigan Avenue; his credos: " Let your watchword be 'order' and your beacon 'beauty;' " "Make no little plans. They have no magic to stir men's blood. . ."

Edgar Rice Burroughs – (1875-1950) Chicago science fiction writer (*Princess of Mars*) and creator of Tarzan, the infant English nobleman raised by apes; was the oldest war correspondent in World War II; owned homes in Chicago and Oak Park but lived in La La Land; Tarzana, California, named to honor his creation

Frances Xavier Cabrini – Founded Chicago's Columbus Hospital on Lakeview Street; first American citizen declared a "saint" by Catholic Church; known as the Patron Saint of Immigrants; died in 1917 and canonized in 1946

"Uncle" Joe Cannon - Powerful speaker of U.S. House of Representatives (1903-1911) during Roosevelt-Taft era; first person depicted on cover of Time Magazine; member of House of Representatives variously from 1873-1923 (46 years)

Al Capone – Born in Brooklyn but came to Chicago in 1919; called King of the Gangsters; responsible for St. Valentine's Day Massacre; harassed by Eliot Ness and The Untouchables; convicted of income tax evasion; sent to Alcatraz; offered to find kidnapper of Charles Lindbergh's baby son; died from third-stage syphilis

John Allen Carpenter - Chicago turn-of-the-century composer (1876-1951) who was quite popular in his own time but has since lost celebrity status

Gower Champion - (1923-) **Geneva**, Illinois-born actress; dancer and film director; *The Story of Vernon and Irene Castle*

Raymond Chandler – Chicago-born mystery writer who created the hardboiled detective, Philip Marlowe

Chicago – DePaul University musical group originally known as Chicago Transit Authority; #1 hit in 1976 "If You Leave Me Now"

George Rogers Clark – Hero of the West during Revolutionary War; liberated Illinois from British rule

Hillary Rodham-Clinton – Chicagoan (**Park Ridge**) who became America's most controversial First Lady from 1993-2001; elected New York Senator in 2000; duped by husband Bill Clinton who told her he didn't have an affair with Genifer Flower or Monica L.; polls in 2002 showed that about 67 percent of Americans thought she shouldn't run for President; another poll showed she was most admired female person in the U.S.; author of *It Takes a Village*

Nat "King" Cole – Son of a Chicago minister, became a hit singer in the Fifties era of the crooner; accomplished jazz pianist; formed his Trio in 1937; first African-American to have his own weekly television show; some of his dozens of hits include, "Straighten Up and Fly Right," "Mona Lisa," "Rambling Rose," "Route 66," "Unforgettable," and his own version of Mel Tormé's "The Christmas Song;" died at age 45 in 1965 from lung cancer; daughter Natalie now a star in her own right

Gary Coleman – **Zion**-born actor; on TV comedy, "Different Strokes"

Jimmy Connors – **East St. Louisan** dubbed "Mr. Tennis" in 1975 after winning 3 Grand Slam titles; holds record for most tournament wins with 125; inducted into the tennis Hall of Fame in 1998; taught by mother how to play tennis; holds record for weeks ranked as the number-one player in the world – 273 weeks

Robert Conrad – Chicago actor and star of "Wild, Wild West" and "Baa Baa Black Sheep"

Sam Cooke – Had 1957 #1 hit record, "You Send Me;" killed by motel owner in 1964 whose wife accused him of rape

Louis Cowan – Chicago quizmaster who originated the format for "The Quiz Kids," the "$64,000 Question" and "Stop The Music"

James Cozzens – Born in Chicago but hardly lived there; published his first novel Confusion at age 19; lived in Cuba and Europe; also wrote *The Cock Pit* and *The Sons of Perdition* and *S.S. San Pedro* won the Pulitzer Prize for *Guard of Honor*; died in 1978

Phil Crane – Chicago-born politician; taught history at Bradley University (1963-67); elected to Congress in 1969 to fill a vacancy caused by the resignation of Don Rumsfeld; became a resident of **Mount Prospect**

Michael Crichton – Famous Chicago author (*Coma*, *Rising Sun*) and executive associated with the television program, "ER"

John Cusack

John Cusack – (1967-) **Evanston** actor; *Serendipity, Runaway Jury, High Fidelity, The Thin Red Line, That Championship Season, City Hall, Midnight in the Garden of Good and Evil, Sixteen Candles;* sister Joan Cusack is a prominent actress in her own right

Richard J. Daley – The Kid From the Stockyards; Mayor of Chicago – last of the big political bosses 1955-1976 – elected to 6 terms; loathed by peace Democrats after the '68 convention "police riot;" hated being called "the Last Boss"

Clarence Darrow – Brilliant Chicago defense attorney; defended Eugene Debs, Leopold and Loeb, John Scopes; one of his biggest victories was winning acquittal of radical labor leader Big Bill Heywood, accused of plotting to murder a former Idaho governor who had suppressed a miner's strike; almost went to jail for bribing a jury in Los Angeles; was paid a million dollars to save Leopold and Loeb from the hangman; considered the most influential lawyer of the 20th century

Miles Davis – **Alton/East St. Louis** premier jazz musician; called the Evil Genius of Jazz; quit Juliard in New York because they weren't teaching him anything; had amazing ability to put right artists together to get a desired sound; one of first jazz musicians to experiment with jazz/rock fusion

Bruce Dern

Charles Gates Dawes – America's greatest Vice-president; Chicago banker, lawyer, author, utilities mogul, statesman, soldier, diplomat; Vice-president under Cal Coolidge, Nobel Peace Prize Winner for Dawes Plan to restructure German reparation payments; wrote the song "All in the Game," a hit in 1958 by Tommy Edwards, appointed by Warren Harding as nation's first Director of the Budget; headed Reconstruction Finance Corporation (RFC) under Hoover

Eugene V. Debs – Ran for President on Socialist ticket; head of American Railway Union; jailed for opposing the Great War

John Deere – **Grand Detour** farm equipment inventor and manufacturer; invented new plow to cut through tough prairie sod

Bruce Dern – **Winnetka** actor born 1936; known for playing freaks and psychotics – *All the Pretty Horses, Mulholland Falls, Down Periscope, Middle Age Crazy, Black Sunday, Waterhole # 3, Hang 'em High, The Great Gatsby*

Susan Dey – **Pekin**-born actress starred in "The Partridge Family" and "LA Law"

Will Dilg – Chicagoan and founder of the Isaac Walton League; after son drowned in Mississippi River in 1929, he established the Upper Mississippi River National Wildlife Refuge from Rock Island north, an important site for bald eagles

John Dillinger – Indiana-born bank robber who was shot by the G-Men after attending a gangster movie at the Biograph Theater in Chicago; betrayed by the infamous "Lady in Red," Anna Sage. Chicago true crime writer Jay Nash maintains that the man killed that night was a look-alike so Dillinger could live out the rest of his life in obscurity and spend his ill-gotten loot.

Everett Dirksen

Everett M. Dirksen – **Pekin**-born U.S. Congressman and Senator 1932 –1969, Republican "party whip;" narrated patriotic LP, "Gallant Men;" supported Taft over Ike for President; played critical role in passage of civil rights legislation in 1960's; supported Vietnam War; only 5th member of Senate to have casket at the Capitol rotunda in 1969

Walt Disney – Chicago-born animator, moviemaker; creator of Disneyland and Disneyworld; created Mickey Mouse in 1928

William Dollar – **East St. Louisan** who was the nation's leading American-born ballet performer in 1930s and 1940s; created the ballet for the Ford Motor Company's exhibit at the New York World's Fair in 1939; George Ballanchine choreographed *Transcendence* especially for him; performed 5 different times at the Municipal Opera in St. Louis

Carl Van Doren – **Hope**-born editor, author and publisher; editor of *The Nation* and *Century Magazine*

Walt Disney

John Dos Pasos - (1896-1970) Chicago-born leftist writer; ambulance driver in World War I, wrote *Three Soldiers, The 42nd Parallel, Manhattan Transfer, The Big Money*; jailed for demonstrating in behalf of Sacco and Vanzetti; famous for his impressive *USA* trilogy spanning three decades of American life

Mike Douglas – Appeared as singer with Kay Kyser's Kollege of Musical Knowledge; hosted radio show for WGN; hosted "Mike Douglas Show" on television in 184 cities

Paul Douglas – Economics professor at the University of Chicago; helped draft the first Social Security legislation; fought as a marine in World War II at age 50; elected U.S. senator in 1948; blocked Republican efforts to dismantle New Deal after Ike elected; strong supporter of Vietnam Domino Theory; friend of M.L. King Jr.; called "The Fighting Liberal"

Stephen A. Douglas – The Little Giant (five foot four inches tall); famous for debates with Lincoln; represented the state as representative and senator

Theodore Dreiser – (1871-1945) Newsman, author of *An American Tragedy, Sister Carrie, The Financier,* and *The Titan* (both based on the life of Chicago utilities mogul, Charles T. Yerkes); largely overlooked and unappreciated in his own time; despised Sinclair Lewis who won a Nobel that he thought should have gone to him; only paid $68.50 in royalties from Doubleday for *Sister Carrie*; H.L. Mencken proclaimed him America's greatest writer in 1917; like so many other writers, he dabbled in Communism in 1930s; traveled to Russia where his decadent portrayals of America made him a hero; lived a life beset with personal problems

Katherine Dunham – Chicago dancer who later adopted **East St. Louis** as her home; featured in the film *Stormy Weather, The Bible*; wrote her autobiography, *A Touch of Innocence* in 1959; Communications Building at SIUE was renamed in her honor; fasted for 47 days in 1992 to protest U.S. policy of returning refugees to Haiti

Richard Durbin – **East St. Louisan**; aide to Lieutenant Governor Paul Simon; popular guest on news show *Crossfire*; current Illinois Democratic Senator

Roger Ebert – Film critic of the *Chicago Tribune*; teamed with Gene Siskel to do a weekly PBS show called At The Movies where the pair became the nation's most famous film critics; "two thumbs up" from them meant instant success at the box office; Ebert is only film critic to win Pulitzer Prize

Buddy Ebsen – **Belleville** actor – *Beverly Hillbillies, Davy Crockett, Barnaby Jones, Breakfast at Tiffany's*

Buddy Ebsen

Daniel Ellsberg – Controversial Chicago-born marine/political scientist; worked for Robert McNamara and Rand Corporation think-tank; evolved from a hawk to a dove; his intense war opposition forced his resignation from Rand; Xeroxed copies of classified Pentagon Papers and gave them to Neil Sheehan of *New York Times* in 1971; Supreme Court upheld right of newspapers to publish *Pentagon Papers*, citing 1st Amendment rights; Ellsberg arrested and charged with theft, conspiracy and violation of the Espionage Act, escaped these charges when it was discovered government illegally broke into his psychiatrist's office; also opposed Desert Storm in 1991; wrongly predicted it would cost the lives of 10,000 Americans and 100,000 Iraquis

James Farrell – Author famous for his realistic (meaning poverty, racism and social decay; characters doomed by their environment) trilogy about Chicago Irish life – *Studs Lonigan*; wrote about 52 novels in 50 years; was an ardent Marxist and follower of Leon Trotsky

Edna Ferber – Enshrined in 1990 on the Illinois Authors wall of the State Historical Library; wrote *Giant, Ice Palace, So Big*

Enrico Fermi – Italian physicist; created world's first sustained nuclear reaction at the University of Chicago

George Ferris – **Galesburg**-born inventor of the Ferris Wheel for the Chicago Columbian Exposition of 1893

Eugene Field – (1850-1895) Chicago writer who hated being stereotyped as a writer of child poems "Little Boy Blue" and "Wynken," "Blynken" and "Nod,"as well as the characters "calico cat" and "gingham dog" who eat each other up during a fight in "The Duel;" (his reputation earned him a statue in Lincoln Park)

Marshal Field – (1835-1906) Operated Chicago (world's largest) department store on State Street in the Loop; wealthiest man in Chicago when he died; his slogan: "Give the Lady What She Wants;" created Field Museum of Natural History which cost him $9 million to build

Harvey Firestone – Chicago-born automobile and truck tire manufacturer

Bobby Fisher – Chicago-born, Brooklyn reared, temperamental Boy Robot; responsible for putting chess on the map; youngest grand master ever at age 15; 1972 became chess champion of the world by beating Boris Spassky of the Soviet Union; beat Spassky again in 1992

Bud Fisher – Chicago creator of the comic strip "Mutt (the tall one) and Jeff" (In the strip, they met in an insane asylum.)

Harrison Ford

Betty Ford – Born Elizabeth Bloomer in Chicago; became America's First Lady when husband Gerald Ford became president

Harrison Ford – Park Ridge actor born 1942 – *American Graffiti, Star Wars, Indiana Jones, Regarding Henry, Witness, Patriot Games, The Fugitive, Force 10 From Navarrone, Raiders of the Lost Ark*

Bob Fosse – (1927-1987) Chicago dancer/choreographer; Tony winner for *Pippin, Cabaret, Pajama Game, Dancin,' Damn Yankees, Sweet Charity, Redhead*; 1972 Oscar for directing *Cabaret*; Roy Scheider portrayed him in autobiographical film, *All That Jazz*; had one daughter by Gwen Verdon (Lola in *Damn Yankees*)

John Hope Franklin – Noted African-American historian (*From Slavery to Freedom*) who interestingly views "reparations" for slavery as impractical and counterproductive

Dennis Franz – Chicago born, SIUC educated star of *NYPD Blue;* plays the no-nonsense detective Andy Sipowitz

Walt Frazier – SIUC grad; starred with Bill Bradley on NY Knicks team that won NBA championship

Betty Friedan – Feminist and author; co-founder of NOW – National Organization for Women; wrote *The Feminine Mystique*

Isaac Funk – **Bloomington** cattleman/agriculturalist; founder of Funk Hybrid Seed Company

John Wayne Gacy – **Des Plaines** serial killer convicted of murdering about 32 young men, hiding most of them in the crawl space at his home; called the Killer Clown because he entertained children at parties with tricks and gags while wearing grease paint and dressed up in an outfit; executed by lethal injection

Harry "the Horse" Gallatin – **Wood River**-born NBA Hall of Fame basketball player (New York Knicks 1948-57), Roxana High graduate, head basketball coach of SIU at Carbondale 1958-62; coach of the St. Louis Hawks 1962-65; current Edwardsville resident

Paul Galvin – Founder of Motorola; responsible for making radios that could be placed in automobiles; first made two-way radios used by police and taxicabs; made the Walkie-Talkie for GI's in World War II, early leader in cellular phone industry

Hamlin Garland – Founded Chicago Literary Society; wrote biography of President Grant; wrote *A Son of the Middle Border*

Elbert H. Gary – **Wheaton**-born lawyer and financier; organized U.S. Steel Corp.

Mitzi Gaynor – Chicago actress: *South Pacific, Anything Goes, My Blue Heaven, Bloodhounds of Broadway, Les Girls*

Jason Gedrick – Chicago actor – *Iron Eagle*- portrayed a young fighter jock who was adept only when listening to rock music; *Bad Boys, Backdraft, Born on the Fourth of July*

Sam Giancana – Chicago mobster (and male friend of singer Phyllis McGuire) who was set to testify before a Grand Jury in 1974 but was shot to death in his Oak Park home

Lillian Gish

Lillian Gish – Quintessential silent screen actress; helped sell candy and popcorn at her mother's Majestic Candy Kitchen in East St. Louis; friend of Mary Pickford; started working with D.W. Griffith when he made movies in New York; starred in *Birth of a Nation, Broken Blossoms; Orphans of the Storm, Intolerance,* many others; sister Dorothy also starred in a number of movies

Joseph Glidden – **DeKalb** man who invented barbed wire; it was said to do more for the West than the long rifle or covered wagon

Bob Goalby – **Belleville** native who won the Master's golf tournament in unusual fashion when an opponent forgot to sign his scorecard

George Gobel (1920-1991) – WW II air force pilot; became a regular comedic actor on "Gary Moore Show;" landed his own TV show in 1954; noted for dry humor; appeared as regular on "Hollywood Squares" in 1980s

Arthur Goldberg – (1908-1990) Chicago lawyer named Secretary of Labor and then to U.S. Supreme Court by President Kennedy; wrote majority opinion in *Escobedo v Illinois* that invalidated a conviction made when accused confessed but was denied access to a lawyer; resigned to become ambassador to the United Nations so he could try to convince Lyndon Johnson to quit the war in Vietnam

William Goldman – Chicago author and screenwriter; wrote *Soldier in the Rain, Marathon Man, Heat*; screenplays for *Harper, The Stepford Wives, Butch Cassidy and the Sundance Kid, The Princess Bride, The Great Waldo Pepper*

Benny Goodman – (1909-1986) Chicago-born bandleader ushered America into the Swing Era with famous 1938 concert at Carnegie Hall; King of Swing; was first major bandleader to include both black and white musicians; first musician to play jazz in the Soviet Union (Khrushchev hated it)

Chester Gould – Chicagoan who invented cartoon character Dick Tracy; Eliot Ness was thought to be the prototype for Tracy and Capone was a bad guy in the comic strip, but he was given the title **Big Boy**

Otto Graham – The Waukegan Wonder; at Northwestern, only person to be named All-American in both basketball and football; quarterback for Cleveland Browns; inducted into pro football Hall of Fame in 1965

Virginia Graham – Chicago model and actress; happened to be one of the first people on the scene after the St. Valentine's Day massacre; Virginia Graham radio show; published *My Adventures in Widowhood* after her husband died

Ulysses S. Grant – Born in Ohio; West Point graduate; Galena resident; Civil War general and 18th President of the USA; tried to annex Santo Domingo and make it a black state; died of throat cancer from cigar smoking; considered one of our worst presidents by historians due to many scandals in his administration

Gene Hackman

Harold Gray – **Kankakee**-born cartoonist; creator of **Orphan Annie** and her mentor Daddy Warbucks, dog Sandy, and protector, Punjab; one of those unusually serious strips

Ben Grierson – Music teacher from **Jacksonville** who feared horses; Civil War general who led famous cavalry raid from Tennessee to Louisiana during Grant's siege of Vicksburg, capturing/killing 600 enemy troops, destroying rail lines and capturing horses and mules

Mary and Michael Gross – Chicago-born brother and sister; he – "Family Ties," she – *Feds* and "Satuday Night Live"

Charles Guiteau - A native of **Freeport** and a professional malcontent who assassinated President James Garfield at a train station in 1881.

John Gunther – Chicago writer of *Inside Europe, Inside Africa, Death Be Not Proud*, etc.

Jay Haas - Pro golfer from **Belleville**; graduate of Wake Forest; nephew of Bob Goalby; has been on the pro golf circuit for 27 years; took second place in the March 2003 Players Tournament, earning $572,000; will qualify for the senior tour next year

Gene Hackman – California-born, **Danville**-raised actor attended the University of Illinois; star of films like *The French Connection, The Posideon Adventure, The Package*, etc.

Barbara Hale – **DeKalb** actress – Della Street on *Perry Mason* TV show, *Airport, Seminole, The Far Horizons, Lorna Doone*

George Hale – Chicago-born astronomer; founded Kenwood Observatory in Chicago; convinced Charles Yerkes to build Yerkes Observatory in Williams Bay, Wisconsin; used Carnegie's money to build a big telescope at Mount Wilson in Pasedena; persuaded Rockefeller Foundation to build the 200 inch reflecting telescope at Mount Palomar

Daryl Hannah

Laurens Hammond – **Evanston**-born inventor who patented the electric organ, a machine he did not know how to play

Daryl Hannah – Chicago actress born 1960 – *Splash, Clan of the Cave Bear, Steel Magnolias, Blade Runner, Attack of the 50Ft. Woman; Legal Eagles;* dated John Kennedy Jr.

Lorraine Hansberry – (1930-1965) Chicago born actress/writer; her *Raisin in the Sun* (about her experience growing up in Chicago) is the first play by a black woman (1959) to be produced for Broadway; title came from a Langston Hughes poem

John Marshall Harlan – Chicagoan appointed to U.S. Supreme Court by Eisenhower; spent most of his time trying to prevent liberal Chief Justice Earl Warren from being an activist judge

Harmonicats – Chicago music group consisting of Jerry Murad, Al Fiore and Bob Nes; "Peg O' My Heart" their big hit in 1945.

Barbara Harris – (1936-) **Evanston** actress – *Peggy Sue Got Married, The Seduction of Joe Tynan, Freaky Friday, Family Plot, Nashville*

Jim Hart – **SIU Carbondale** graduate who played quarterback for the St. Louis Cardiac Cardinals holding many of the team's passing records

Paul Harvey – Chicago is the adopted home of this conservative news commentator with the line: "And, now . . . the rest of the story;" heard by 25 million people a day

June Haver – **Rock Island** actress – *Look For the Silver Lining*; married to actor Fred MacMurray

John Hay – Abe Lincoln's secretary and biographer; Secretary of State responsible for Open Door Policy regarding China around 1900; described war with Spain in 1898 as a "splendid little war"

Peter Lind Hayes - **Cairo** actor who starred on TV show "Peter Loves Mary"

Ben Hecht – Chicago newsman who helped make the movie *Scarface,* plus many others such as *The Front Page*; a member of Chicago's Literary Roundtable; moved to Hollywood and became a screenwriter; wrote 10 novels; friend of Burt Lancaster

Hugh Hefner – Publisher of Playboy Magazine; built the Playboy Mansion in Chicago

Ernest Hemingway – **Oak Park** Nobel Prize winning author – *The Sun Also Rises, A Farewell To Arms, The Old Man And The Sea, For Whom the Bell Tolls*; married 4 times; flamboyant, macho headline-maker hunted big game and fished for big fish; considered first author to write dialog the way people spoke; Jake Barnes and Nick Adams were his literary alter egos; committed suicide in Ketchum, Idaho, 1961 (His father also committed suicide with a Civil War pistol.)

Ricky Henderson – Chicago-born all-star baseball player; holds all-time stolen base record

John Hertz - Czech immigrant; started cab company in Chicago; told by University of Chicago that yellow was the most easily recognized color; painted his cabs that bright color to cut down on accidents which cut into profits; Chicago allowed him to install city's first traffic lights at Michigan Avenue and Randolph to cut down on accidents; his Yellow Cab Company was first to install crank operated windshield wipers; invented the taxi meter; bought a company from Walter Jacobs in 1918 and transformed it into a rental car business; fought cab war with Morris Morkin, who started Checker Cab in Chicago and painted his cabs red and lime green because the university study proclaimed them as the next two most easily spotted colors

Whitey Herzog – **New Athens** native managed the St. Louis Cardinals to a World Championship and several National League titles and a World Series championship in 1980s; known as The White Rat

Don Hesse – **Belleville**-born conservative political cartoonist for the *St. Louis Globe-Democrat*

Charlton Heston – Decatur actor – Head of the national N.R.A., *Ben Hur, The Ten Commandments, 55 Days at Peking, Midway, The Warlord, Touch of Evil, The Naked Jungle; recently admitted to suffering from Alzheimer's disease*

Charlton Heston

James Butler "Wild Bill" Hickok – Troy Grove frontiersman, scout, lawman; known for his shooting ability keeping the peace in western cattle towns; holding aces and eights (dead man's hand) when shot in the back by Jack McCall in Deadwood, S.D.

Johann Hoch – The Chicago Bluebeard; known for marrying women for their money, killing them and then collecting on the insurance; his crime spree took place in several cities across the nation, from San Francisco to New York; was caught and hanged in Chicago on February 23, 1906

Malvina Hoffman - Noted anthropologist and sculptor (student of Rodin); commissioned by Field Museum of Natural History in Chicago to create 100 realistic figures of various racial types from all over the world

William Holden - Born Franklin Beedle – **O'Fallon** actor – *The 7th Dawn, World of Susie Wong, Picnic, Stalag 17*

William Holden

Skip Homier – (1929-) Chicago actor – *The Gunfighter, The Ghost and Mr. Chicken, Bullet For a Badman, Comanche Station, Dakota Incident*

Elbert Hubbard – **Bloomington** native who wrote *A Message to Garcia*, about the Cuban revolution and the Spanish American War; perished when the Germans torpedoed the Lusitania

Rock Hudson - Born Roy Sherer in **Winetka** – First film *Magnificent Obsession* in 1954; also *Giant, Pillow Talk, Come September, Spiral Road, Seconds;* popular television series, *McMillan and Wife*; nominated for Academy Award for role of Bick Benedict in *Giant*; disliked James Dean, his co-star in the film; first major Hollywood actor to die from AIDS

Mary Beth Hughes – **Alton** actress – (1919) *Dressed to Kill, Passage West, Young Man With A Horn, El Paso, Rimfire*

Bobby Hull – Chicago Blackhawks star who made the All-Star team 12 of his 14 seasons; scored 1,012 goals in his career and was elected to the Hockey Hall of Fame in 1983

H.L. Hunt – (1889-1974) **Vandalia**-born Texas oil speculator, one of world's richest men; famous for being a recluse; strong supporter of Joe McCarthy; had 12 children by 3 wives

Rock Hudson

Robert Hutchins – President of the University of Chicago; abolished their football program in 1939; chairman of Encyclopedia Britannica from 1943-1974; teamed with Mortimer Adler to produce the 52-volume Great Books of the Western World set

Rex Ingram – (1894-1969) **Cairo** actor – *Hurry Sundown, Elmer Gantry, God's Little Acre, Thief of Baghdad, Sahara*

Samuel Insull – Commonwealth Edison utilities mogul whose holdings were worth $3 billion in 1930; built the $10 million Chicago Civic Opera House in 1929; controlled power generators in 32 states; generously employed blacks; built streetcar systems; built the first grid system that allowed excess power to be sold to other states; broke and indicted by 1932

Burl Ives – (1909) **Hunt/Newton**, Illinois folksinger/actor; wanted to be a coach but dropped out of Eastern Illinois College in 1928; movies: *A Face in the Crowd, Ensign Pulver, Cat on a Hot Tin Roof* (Big Daddy), *The Spiral Road, East of Eden, The Brass Bottle, The Big Country*

Judith Ivey – (1951-) A cheerleader at **Marion** High School - *Designing Women TV, The Long Hot Summer* (with Don Johnson), *Jessica Savitch Story (TV), Washington Square, Brighton Beach Memoirs, The Woman in Red*

Jesse Jackson – Attended University of Illinois; foremost African-American civil rights leader after the death of Martin Luther King Jr., founded Chicago based P.U.S.H. (People United to Serve Humanity); Rainbow Coalition; candidate for U.S. presidency 1988; never elected to any political office; although Chicago is his home base, he encounters strong opposition there; accused by Bill O'Reilly of Fox News of being an extortionist

Mahalia Jackson – Famed New Orleans/Chicago singer; called The Queen of Gospel; disdained singing the blues; joined Pilgrim Baptist Church where Clara Ward and Barrett sisters sang; windows broken when she moved into a white neighborhood in 1956; "Precious Lord" became one of her signature songs; Studs Terkel played her records on his radio show; raised money for M.L. King's civil rights causes; sang "We Shall Overcome" at the 1963 March on Washington; opened beauty parlor and florist shop, becoming a millionaire; married a second time in 1964; divorced in 1972 shortly before her death; 50,000 attended her funeral

Scott-Jacoby – (1956-) Chicago-born actor; played juvenile leads in *Baxter, The Little Girl Who Lives Down the Lane*

John Jakes – Chicago-born formulaic historical novelist; *The Bastard, The Seekers, The Furies, The Titans*

Arte Johnson – (1934-) Chicago actor – TV's *Laugh In and Gong Show, Assault of the Party Nerds, Cannonball Run II, Love at First Bite*

Chic Johnson – Chicago actor, part of Olsen and Johnson comedy team– *Ghost Catchers, Crazy House*

John H. Johnson – Successful African-American; Chicago publisher of *Ebony, Jet, Ebony Jr., EM* magazines; started with Negro *Digest* in 1942; Ebony is upbeat - mostly success stories about African-Americans; 1996 awarded Medal of Freedom

John Johnson

Casey Jones – America's most famous railroad engineer; drove Illinois Central Cannonball Express from Chicago to New Orleans; heroic act saved lives but he was killed in a train wreck; lionized in folk songs

James Jones – **Robinson**-born author of *From Here to Eternity,* made into Academy Award-winning movie that revived Frank Sinatra's career and *Some Came Running* (made into a bad movie with Frank Sinatra and Dean Martin); characters used poor grammar for realism

Quincy Jones – Chicagoan who has garnered more Grammy nominations than anyone in history with over 76, winning more than two dozen times; did music score for *Roots* and *The Color Purple*; in charge of music for Bill Clinton's inauguration

Michael Jordan – Chicago Bulls basketball star considered the greatest player in the history of the sport; led the Chicago Bulls to 6 NBA titles in 1991-93 and 1996-1998

Whitcomb Judson – Chicagoan who invented the zipper that replaced the old hook and eye fasteners

Howard Keel – (1917-) **Gillespie** actor born Harold Leek– *Kiss Me Kate* 1953, *Seven Brides For Seven Brothers, Calamity Jane, Annie Get Your Gun, Show Boat, Carousel, Waco, Across the Wide Missouri, The Big Fisherman,* "Dallas" TV show

Myrna Kennedy – (1908-44) Kankakee-born child actress discovered by Charlie Chaplin

Keokuk – Born near the Illinois River around 1780; became chief by his powers of oratory; usually worked to maintain peaceful relations with the U.S. government; became chief of Sacs and Foxes in 1832; tried to restrain his people from joining Blackhawk in his war on the whites; bitter feeling between Keokuk and Blackhawk resulted in his death by poisoning in 1848

Jackie Joyner-Kersee – **East St. Louis** heptathlon winner at 1988 Seoul Olympics and 1992 at Barcelona, voted World's Greatest Female Athlete in 2,000

Richard Kiley – (1922-) Chicago actor – *Blackboard Jungle, Kismet, Man of LaMancha, Patch Adams, TV's Thornbirds, Endless Love, Looking For Mr. Goodbar, Advise and Consent*

William Wallace Kimball – Chicago businessman; famed piano maker

Jean Kirkpatrick – Conservative no-nonsense head of the U.S. delegation to the United Nations under President Ronald Reagan; attended high school her freshman year at Vandalia and graduated from Mount Vernon High in 1944

Harvey Korman – (1927-) Chicago actor- "Carol Burnette Show" and "Hollywood Squares", *Curse of the Pink Panther, High Anxiety*

James Kraft – Moved to Chicago from Ontario in 1904 and started selling cheese from a horse-drawn wagon; in 1916 he developed a pasteurization process that extended the shelf life of cheese; started selling cheese in 4-ounce tins; introduced Velvetta in 1924; bought Philadelphia Cream Cheese in 1927; added Miracle Whip salad dressing to the line; sponsored the Kraft Music Hall on radio and television; became a rock collector and discovered American Jade

Gene Krupa – Chicagoan who almost became a priest; played with Benny Goodman for several years; formed his own band in 1938; hired jazz vocalist Anita O'Day; frequently voted nation's outstanding drummer

Ann Landers – Jewish advice columnist who started writing in 1955 for Chicago *Sun-Times*; most widely syndicated columnist in the world; her sister, Abigail Van Buren, started writing her California column 9 months later causing a split in their relationship; wrote a column about the breakup of her 36-year-old marriage

Christy Lane – **Peoria**-born (real name Eleanor Johnston) country-western singer who entertained the troops in Vietnam; **songs** include "One Day at a Time, "Footsteps," and "I Believe in Angels"

Frankie Laine – (1913-) Chicago singer born Frank Vecchio – "That's My Desire," "Mule Train," "A Woman in Love," "Jezebel," "Rawhide"

Sherry Lansing – Chicago-born movie producer executive; *The China Syndrome, Kramer vs. Kramer, Black Rain, Fatal Attraction*

Rod LaRocque – (1896-1969) Chicago actor – *Hunchback of Notre Dame, Meet John Doe, The Shadow Strikes, International Crime*

Albert Lasker – Father of Modern Advertising; when told orange trees in California were being cut down because of oversupply, his firm of Lord and Thomas launched ad campaign that started people drinking orange juice; created slogan, "Reach for a Lucky instead of a sweet," considered the most successful slogan in history; convinced Pepsodent to sponsor Amos 'n Andy and Bob Hope; his "Keep that schoolgirl complexion" made a green soap named Palmoilve on top for half a century; delivered $25,000 in hush money to one of Warren Harding's mistresses; in 1942 he dissolved the company and turned his attention to health, science, the arts, and philanthropy

Abe Lincoln

Carol Lawrence – **Melrose Park** actress, dancer; married Robert Goulet

John L. Lewis – Union organizer; head of United Mineworkers Union; founder of the C.I.O.

Gordon Lillie - Born at **Bloomington** in 1866, known as Pawnee Bill in Wild West shows

Abraham Lincoln – **Springfield** lawyer considered by most historians to be our greatest president

Vachel Lindsay – Springfield poet/lecturer – "The Eagle That Is Forgotten," a tribute to Governor John Peter Altgeld who was heavily criticized for pardoning men convicted in the 1886 Haymarket Riot; also: "Abraham Lincoln Walks at Midnight;" "Johnny Appleseed;" committed suicide 1931; known as the wandering Vagabond Poet

John A. Logan – Murphysboro soldier/politician; considered America's greatest political general; fought alongside U.S. Grant at forts Henry, Donnelson and Vicksburg; helped found the G.A.R.; 1884 Republican nominee for U.S. vice-president

Fred MacMurray

Henry Demarest Lloyd – Journalist for *Chicago Tribune*; called the first of the muckraking journalists; wrote *Wealth Against Commonwealth*, 1894

Richard Long – Chicago actor – TV "The Big Valley," "77 Sunset Strip," "Maverick" and "Bourbon Street Beat"

Elijah Lovejoy – Abolitionist editor killed in 1937 at Alton while defending his press; considered America's foremost martyr for freedom of the press

Norman Luboff – Vocal music director born in Chicago; famous for his oft-recorded Norman Luboff Choir

Adolph Luetgert – President of a large Chicago sausage firm who killed his nagging wife for complaining about his sexual appetite for other women; dissolved her body in a chemical bath at his factory but was convicted when police found her ring and pieces of her bone and teeth; received a life sentence in 1898

Archibald MacLeish – Glencoe–born Nobel Prize winner; 1932 for "Conquistador" poem and again in 1952 for collected poems; friend of Hemingway; Harvard professor; Librarian of Congress

John Malkovich

Fred MacMurray – Kankakee actor – *My Three Sons* TV, *The Absent Minded Professor, The Shaggy Dog, Gun For a Coward, The Caine Mutiny, Day of the Bad Man, The Far Horizons, The Apartment, Gun for a Coward, Son of Flubber, Kisses for my President*

Jock Mahoney – Chicago actor – *Tarzan the Magnificent, Tarzan's Three Challenges, Tarzan Goes to India*

Karl Malden – Gary, Ind.-born, Chicago-reared actor; *On The Waterfront, Parrish*; "Streets of San Francisco;" spokesperson for American Express

Dorothy Malone – Chicago actress – *Written on the Wind, The Big Sleep, The Last Sunset, Winter Kills*, TV's "Peyton Place"

James R. Mann – U.S. Representative from the town of **Gilman** on Route 45; sponsored Mann Act that made it illegal to transport women across state lines for immoral purposes

Bobby Joe Mason – Centralia-born, Bradley Univ. graduate who played basketball for the Harlem Globetrotters

Marjorie Main – Acton-reared actress and star of several "Ma and Pa Kettle" films (real name, Mary Krebs)

John Malkovich – Christopher/Benton actor – *In The Line of Fire, Being John Malkovich, Man in the Iron Mask, Con Air, Portrait of a Lady, Mary Reilly, Dangerous Liaisons*

Jasper Maltby – Galena Civil War general who invented the telescopic sight for rifles

David Mamet – Chicago writer; won 1984 Pulitzer Prize for *Glengarry Glen Ross*, based on his own experiences as a high-pressure real estate salesman; also wrote *Sexual Perversity in Chicago;* wrote screenplay for Kevin Kostner's *The Untouchables*

Ann Margret

Ann Margret – Swedish-born New Trier cheerleader; called The Female Elvis; *Viva Las Vegas, Bye-Bye Birdie, Bus Riley's Back in Town*

Virginia Marmaduke – Carbondale-born reporter; dated actor George Raft and coach George Halas, wrote for the *Chicago Sun*; served as hostess for the Illinois Pavilion at the 1965 New York World's Fair

Edgar Lee Masters – Lewiston/Chicago lawyer who also wrote poetry; his *Spoon River Anthology*, a hateful diatribe that rails against small-town America, tells about life in central Illinois through disillusioned spirits of the dead

Bat Masterson – Born in Iroquois County; famed dandy dressing lawman in Kansas and Tombstone, Arizona

Marlee Matlin – Born in **Morton Grove**; first deaf actress to win an Oscar in 1987 (Best Actress for Children of a Lesser God, her very first role)

Bill Mauldin – Chicago *Sun-Times* political cartoonist; did the "Willie and Joe" cartoon (Patton hated them) for Stars and Stripes during World War II.

Mercedes McCambridge – Joliet actress – *Giant, All the King's Men, Cimarron, Angel Baby, A Farewell to Arms*, voice of Satan in *The Exorcist*

Cyrus McCormick – Chicagoan who invented the reaper and founded McCormick Harvester Works

Colonel Robert R. McCormick – Became one of the bosses of the *Chicago Tribune* in 1911; also founded *New York Daily News* and *Washington Herald;* served in World War I and added his rank of colonel to his name; bitterly opposed Wilson's League of Nations; despised Republican Mayor William Thompson; New Deal critic; Anglophobe and leading isolationist of the late 1930s; liked Mayor Richard J. Daley; bought forested lands in Canada which became newsprint farms; made the cover of Time Magazine in 1947 when the *Tribune* celebrated its 100th anniversary; one of the most influential people of his time

Ruth McCormick – Daughter of Marcus Hanna and widow of Chicagoan Medill McCormick; chief political advisor to presidential candidate, Thomas Dewey

Elizabeth McGovern – Evanston actress – *Ragtime, Wings of the Dove, King of the Hill, The Handmaid's Tale, Native Son, Ordinary People*

Donald McHenry – **East St. Louisan**; replaced controversial Andrew Young as head of U.S. delegation to the United Nations

Don McNeil – **Galena**-born performer; his "Breakfast Club" was an early-morning radio variety show broadcast from Chicago aimed at "squares" from church-going Middle America; the national show lasted 35 years

Leo Melamed – Jewish financier; after Nixon said U.S. dollar would no longer be backed by gold, worked with Milton Freidman to open the International Money Market on the Chicago Mercantile Exchange in 1972; investors could now buy monetary futures and Treasury notes the same way they bought grain and pork bellies (bacon); the Father of Financial Futures

Laurie Metcalf – **Carbondale**-born/Edwardsville-reared actress; Jackie on "Roseanne;" *Bulworth, Scream 2, Toy Story, Leaving Las Vegas, Pacific Heights, Internal Affairs, Blink*

Ray Meyer – Legendary coach of the De Paul Blue Demons; had 37 winning seasons in 42 years; 1945 NIT champs; son Joey succeeded him as De Paul coach

Oscar Micheaux – **Metropolis**-born novelist/movie maker; produced 39 films for African-American audiences in 1920s and 30s; has a star on Hollywood Walk of Fame

Ludwig Mies – Built the world's first glass and steel skyscraper in 1951 with an apartment complex in Chicago; the Seagram Building in NYC also illustrates this concept

Donna Mills – Blonde Chicago actress known for her role on television's "Knot's Landing"

Vincentte Minnelli – Chicago-born film director (Oscar for *Gigi*) who married Judy Garland; father of Liza Minnelli

Clayton Moore

Minnesota Fats – **Dowell**, Illinois, resident; born Rudolph Wanderone; considered greatest pool player who ever lived; acquired nickname from the Paul Newman movie, *The Hustler*

Newton Minnow – Chairman of the FCC; made famous by his 1961 comment that television was a "vast wasteland"

Roscoe Misselhorn – From **Sparta** - one of Illinois' most renown sketch artists.

John Mitchell – **Braidwood**-born union organizer who became the head of the United Mine Workers

Dwight Moody – Chicago evangelist, songwriter and publisher

Clayton Moore – Chicagoan who starred as the Lone Ranger on about 220 television shows

Helen Morgan – **Danville** torch singer ("The Man I Love," "Why Was I Born?"), *Showboat, Frankie and Johnnie, Applause, Marie Galante*

Jelly Roll Morton – Infuriated fellow musicians by claiming he invented jazz; concentrated on playing soft music of New Orleans bordellos; loved playing pool and promoting boxing matches; was first person to write jazz music note by note; "Alabama Bound," "Milenburg Joys," "Black Bottom Stomp" and "King Porter Stomp" among his most noted works; career nose dived in 1929, and he died in relative obscurity in 1941; U.S. postage stamp issued to honor him; illogically inducted into Rock and Roll Hall of Fame in 1997

Mr. T – Chicago born-actor (Larence Tero), Rocky boxing opponent (Clubber Lane) and star of TV series, "The A-Team;" celebrated his 37th birthday by cutting down all the trees at his home in Lake Forest

Herman Mudgett – This Chicagoan constructed what came to be known as "Mudgett's Murder Castle" in suburban Englewood. It was 3 stories high and the basement had a crematorium, a dissecting table and a lime pit and a torture table. He lured many of his victims to a large soundproof safe where their screams would not be heard as he murdered them. During the Columbian Exposition he placed ads in newspapers seeking secretarial help. He rented out rooms on the third floor to visitors attending the exposition. Each room had a peephole to enable him to observe the occupants. Mudgett had a medical degree from the University of Michigan and was in the business of supplying skeletons to medical schools. He turned to grave robbing as a source of skeletons, and he refurbished the coffins of the disinterred and sold them to funeral homes. Mudgett owned a pharmacy and earned additional income by performing illegal abortions. Mudgett murdered over 50 people before he was convicted and hanged in Philadelphia in 1896 for the killing of his assistant.

Bill Murray

Martin Mull – Chicago native who starred in "Mary Hartman, Mary Hartman"

Bill Murray – **Wilmette** actor born 1950; Saturday Night Live TV, *Stripes, Groundhog Day, Tootsie, Meatballs, Ghostbusters, Caddyshack, Charlie's Angels, The Royal Tenenbaums*

George Musso – **Collinsville** native; attended Millikin University; only person to play football against two future presidents – Ronald Reagan (Millikin vs Eureka College) and Gerald Ford (College All-Star Game) member of Chicago Bears Monsters of the Midway, Chicago Bears football team; sheriff of Madison County

John Naber – **Evanston** swimmer who won four gold medals and one silver at the Montreal Olympics in 1976

George "Baby-face" Nelson – Chicago gangster who became a member of the Dillinger gang; upset because media referred to it as the Dillinger gang instead of the Nelson gang; cornered in a field near Barrington and riddled with 17 slugs in November of 1934

Eliot Ness – Chicago-born federal agent who led anti-crime group of 10 that became known as "The Untouchables"

Bob Newhart – **Oak Park** comedian – "The Bob Newhart Show;" "Newhart" and "Bob;" Grammy winner for "The Button-down Mind of Bob Newhart"

Mike Nichols - Chicago director; starred with Elaine May at the comedy cabaret, Second City; married May, divorced her and married Diane Sawyer

Arthur Nielson – Chicago-born inventor of famed black box television rating system

Frank Norris – Chicago muckraker who wrote *The Octopus* and *The Pit* (about speculation on the Chicago Board of Trade)

Kim Novak – Chicago actress, *Picnic, Pal Joey, Strangers When We Meet, Legend of Lylah Clare, Moll Flanders, Vertigo, Jeanne Eagles*

Robert Novak – **Joliet**-born political columnist and conservative TV news analyst personality; "Evans and Novak," "Crossfire;" 1952 U of I graduate

Donald O'Connor – **Danville** native – *Singing in the Rain, Francis the Talking Mule, Francis in the Navy, Francis Joins the WACS, That's Dancing, Cry For Happy*

William B. Ogden – Chicago's first mayor; President of the Galena and Chicago Railroad; as president of Union Pacific he drove the golden spike at Ogden, Utah, which completed America's first transcontinental railroad in 1869; according to historian Olivia Mahoney, responsible for forging much of Chicago's railroad dominance

Jesse Owens – Chicago resident who won 4 gold medals at the 1936 Olympics at Berlin; buried at Oak Woods Cemetery in Chicago, along with Harold Washington, 6,000 Confederates who died at Camp Douglas during the Civil War and Big Jim Colosimo; Owens died of lung cancer in 1980 from (you guessed it), smoking cigarettes

Potter Palmer – Merchant Prince of Chicago; said to have "owned" State Street; built plush Palmer House; his wife Bertha had the business acumen to double the value of his holdings after his death

Louella Parsons – **Freeport**-born gossip columnist for Hollywood personalities; worked for newspaper in Dixon; early in career oversaw scripts for Chicago film makers

Mandy Patinkin – Chicago-born actor famous for playing acerbic Dr. Geiger on "Chicago Hope;" starred in *Princess Bride*

Charles Percy – Chicagoan who became wealthy as president of Bell and Howell camera; a Christian Scientist who became a U.S. Senator, lost his taste for the fame of political life after his daughter Valerie was murdered in their suburban Chicago home;

Marlin Perkins – Director of Chicago's Lincoln Park Zoo and host of television's "Zoo Parade" and "Wild Kingdom"

Irna Phillips – Chicagoan who invented the "soap opera" in 1930; helped create "Painted Dreams," "Today's Children," "The Guiding Light" and "As The World Turns." Early soaps focused on the lives of ordinary work-a-day people but most shows today showcase the lives of the well-off and the famous

Charles Post – **Springfield**-born businessman who created the cereals known as Post Grape Nuts and a cereal beverage that tastes like coffee, Postum

John Wesley Powell – Lived in **Carbondale**, taught at Illinois Wesleyan; lost a right arm in the Civil War; led a scientific expedition that explored the Colorado River; it was Powell who named the majestic Grand Canyon which the Paiute Indians called "Mountain Lying Down;" first head of U.S. Geological Survey; honored on postage stamp in 1969

Mel Price – **East St. Louisan** who served in the U.S. Congress for over 40 years; lock and dam at Alton is named in his honor

Richard Pryor – **Peoria** actor/comedian/Grammy winner – *Silver Streak, Harlem Nights, Moving, Critical Condition,, Car Wash, The Toy, Stir, Crazy, Hear No Evil, See No Evil*

Aidan Quinn – Chicago actor; *Practical Magic, Legends of the Fall, Blink, Crusoe, Reckless*

James Earl Ray – **Alton**-born man convicted of killing Dr. Martin Luther King Jr. in April of 1968 at Memphis, Tennessee; Ray fired the shot from a rooming house bathroom when King stepped out on the motel balcony

Robert Reed – **Highland Park** native; father to 6 children on "The Brady Bunch"

Bob Richards – Champion Olympic pole-vaulter born in Champaign; won gold in 1952 and 1956

Levant Richardson – Chicagoan who invented the ball bearing roller skate

Jason Robards – Chicago actor – *All The President's Men, A Thousand Clowns, Beloved, Philadelphia, Legend of the Lone Ranger, Julia, St. Valentine's Day Massacre* (Capone); married to Lauren Bacall

George Lincoln Rockwell – **Bloomington**-born founder of the American Nazi Party; killed by a sniper in 1967

Dan Rostenkowski – Democratic Chairman of House Ways and Means Committee 1980-1994; responsible for 1986 tax cut that paved way for economic boom of 90s; sentenced to 17 months in prison on charges of using stamp money for personal items (stupid is as stupid does)

Mike Royko – Chicago *Tribune* syndicated columnist; wrote *Boss*, about corruption under Mayor Richard Daley; syndicated in more than 500 newspapers all around the country; invented the "Governor Moonbeam" nickname for Jerry Brown of California; "Mayor Bossy" was his moniker for Jane Byrne; won a Pulitzer Prize in 1992; died in 1997

Jack Ruby – Jack Rubenstein was a Chicago entrepreneur who rubbed elbows with the Chicago underworld. He moved to Dallas where he ran a strip joint called the Carousel Club. He shot Kennedy's assassin, Lee Harvey Oswald, in the basement of the Dallas police headquarters while he was being transferred to another facility.

Bob Newhart

Kim Novak

Aidan Quinn

Donald Rumsfeld – Chicago-born U.S. Representative; joined Office of Economic Opportunity under President Nixon; representative to NATO; special presidential Ambassador to the Middle East under Reagan; Secretary of Defense for G.H.W. Bush in 1989; current U.S. Secretary of Defense, known for his sharp wit at press conferences

Damon Runyon – Chicago storywriter who often depicted gangsters as bumbling lovable doakes, best illustrated by his play *Guys and Dolls*

Robert Ryan – **Rugged** Chicago-born movie star nominated for an Academy Award as Best Supporting Actor

Robert Ryan

Pat Sajak – Chicago-born host of "Wheel of Fortune," America's most popular game show on TV

Carl Sandburg – Socialist leaning **Galesburg**/Chicago guitar-playing poet ("Chicago Poems"); 6-volume biographer of Abraham Lincoln; *American Songbags* (collection of folksongs); traveled across America as a hobo; Pulitzer Prize for poem "Cornhuskers;" bitter rival of Robert Frost who called him a sentimental fraud; wrote about common things and common people; widely known for being a cheapskate; honored on U.S. postage stamp; did not become famous until he was 36; author of more than 40 books

Tommy Sands – Chicago singer, "Sing Boy Sing," "Teenage Crush;" had brief film career; married Nancy Sinatra

Abe Saperstein – Chicago sports promoter; called Little Caesar; organized the Harlem Globetrotters in 1927; their first game was at Hinckley, Illinois and the gate receipts bought their meals the next day; their first theme song for warm-ups was "Beer Barrel Polka; in 1948 the Minneapolis Lakers won the NBA title but lost a game to the Globe Trotters

Fred Savage – **Highland Park**-born actor; starred in television series "The Wonder Years"

Phyllis Schlafly – **Alton** resident; right wing social activist and author; arch-enemy of National Organization for Women; credited with the defeat of the ERA Amendment; lost to Mel Price in 1952 for a seat in Congress; Joe McCarthy and Barry Goldwater supporter; produces a newsletter called *The Eagle Forum*; she and her lawyer husband have six children

Fred Savage

Red Schoendienst – Hall of Fame baseball player (2nd base) and manager for St. Louis Cardinals, from **Germantown**

William Scholl – Worked with leather at an early age; apprenticed to a cobbler at age 13, moved to Chicago after turn of the century to work in a shoe store; appalled at the condition of most people's feet; earned a medical degree at Chicago Loyola in 1904 and invented a leather arch support and went into business; added other products to his line such as bunion pads, salves and powders; built a square block factory in 1908 at Wells and Schiller; never married and lived in a single room at the Illinois Athletic Club

Elzie Seegar – **Chester** native who created the popular spinach eating, pugilistic cartoon character with bulging forearms, Popeye

Bishop Fulton Sheen – **El Paso**-born Catholic religious leader, television personality and author

Sidney Sheldon – Chicago born writer of potboiler novels and screenplays; Tony and Oscar winner

Shelton gang – Consisting of Carl, Earl and Bernie, these three brothers engaged in a gang war in Williamson and Franklin counties in the 1920s. They fought a war with the Birger gang for control of a liquor and gambling empire that stretched from Cairo to East St. Louis. The Sheltons won by default when Charlie Birger was hanged in 1928 for killing Mayor Joe Adams, a Shelton ally. The Sheltons were run out of East St. Louis and moved their base of operations to Peoria. Carl was shot to death on his farm at Fairfield in **Wayne County** in 1947. Bernie was killed at a **Peoria** tavern in 1948. Another brother named Roy was killed at his Fairfield farm in 1950.

Sam Shepard

Sam Shepard – Fort Sheridan-born actor – *The Right Stuff* (Chuck Yeager), *Black Hawk Down, Swordfish, Pelican Brief, Thunderheart;* married to earthy (whatever that means) Jessica Lange

William L. Shirer – Chicago-born journalist/author – wrote best-selling *The Rise and Fall of the Third Reich*

Frank Shoddy – **Springfield** native who made woolen goods, primarily blankets, for Union soldiers during the Civil War. He made an inferior product and soon the word "shoddy" became synonymous with poorly made goods.

Paul Simon – Mr. Bow Tie; **Troy** newspaper editor who testified before Kefauver Commission about crime and corruption in St. Clair and Madison counties; teacher at Sangamon State; author; lieutenant governor of Illinois; elected to congress in 1974; elected U.S. Senator; presidential candidate in 1988; current resident of **Makanda** and head of Public Policy Institute in Carbondale

Frank Sinatra – "The Voice" is a Hoboken, New Jerseyite, but will forever be associated with Chicago because of his song "Chicago, That Toddlin' Town," lyrics by immigrant Fred Fisher. He also endeared himself to locals with the prohibition-era film *Robin and the 7 Hoods*, in which he sings the song, "My Kind of Town."

Upton Sinclair – Earned a college degree but early married life and career were in poverty, perhaps helping to form his socialistic bent; his 1906 novel, *The Jungle*, about the Chicago meatpacking industry, was a broadside against capitalism; winner of the 1942 Pulitzer Prize; advocate of free love; dabbled in California politics, running for the governorship; other novels include *Oil, King Coal*; 1934 "Literary Digest" poll ranked him as the 4th most important man in the world, behind FDR, Hitler and Mussolini

Jack Slade – **Carlyle**-born outlaw of the old west, caught and hanged in Montana Territory

Carrie Snodgress - Park Ridge actress – *Diary of a Mad Housewife, Bartleby, Wild Things, Blue Sky, Blueberry Hill, Rabbit Run*

George Snow – Chicagoan who invented the balloon framing method of construction and popularized iron nails instead of wooden pegs

David Soule – Chicago native who starred in 1970's "Starsky and Hutch;" he was the blonde one

Richard Speck – Famous for his "Born to Raise Hell" tattoo; killed 8 student nurses in south Chicago; raised money to buy cigarettes in prison by selling paintings signed R. Speck; was captured when recognized by a hospital doctor after Speck slashed his wrists and tried to commit suicide

Amos Alonzo Stagg – Legendary coach of the University of Chicago who won six Big Ten Conference titles and had five unbeaten seasons; pioneered forward pass; invented the tackling dummy, onside kick, short punt, fake pass, the huddle, the T-formation, numbers on jerseys; first coach to award varsity letters; 5-time member of the Olympic Committee; only man elected to Football Hall of Fame as a player and coach; died in 1965 at age 102

Vincent Starrett - Chicagoan who was an expert on Sherlock Holmes and was one of the founders of the Baker Street Irregulars

McLean Stephenson – Son of a **Normal** physician; played Col. Blake on M*A*S*H*

John Paul Stevens – Chicagoan appointed to the U.S. Supreme Court by Gerald Ford, filling the vacancy left by William O. Douglas; disappointment to conservatives when he leaned to the left; sometimes voted conservative, making him a maverick swing vote

Adlai Stevenson – A man known for his intellect, wit and charm; governor 1948-52; Democratic presidential candidate in 1952 and 1956, ambassador to U.N during Cuban Missile Crisis

Adlai E. Stevenson – **Bloomington**-born politician elected to congress as a Greenbacker, later became Vice-president of the U.S.

Adlai Stevenson

Robert Stroud – **Metropolis** man better known as The Birdman of Alcatraz, played by Burt Lancaster in the movie

Louis Sullivan – (1856-1924) Father of Modern Architecture; his dictum: "Form follows function," meaning banks should look like banks – not cathedrals; formed partnership with Dankmar Adler in 1881; partnership broke up in a bitter 1894 dispute; upset over Daniel Burnham's appointment to design 1893 Columbian Exposition; designed Wainwright Building in St. Louis in 1900; died bitter, drunk and broke

Billy Sunday – Former ballplayer for Pop Anson's Colts; took to the revival circuit and became America's most famous evangelist in the 1920s

Gloria Swanson – Chicago actress – *Sunset Boulevard*, girlfriend of Joe Kennedy, married to Wallace Beery, *Airport 75, Indiscreet, Sadie Thompson*

Gustavus Swift – Chicago meatpacker; developed first refrigerated cars for shipping beef

Carl Switzer – **Paris**, Illinois, actor – Alfalfa in *Our Gang* comedies

Everett Tanner III – Winnetka writer; under the pseudonym Patrick Dennis, created the lovable character of Auntie Mame

Studs Terkle - Chicago oral historian: won Pulitzer Prize in 1984 for *The Good War*, about World War II; also wrote *Working, Hard Times, Giants of Jazz and Division Street USA*

Isiah Thomas – Chicago-born star basketball player for the NBA champion Detroit Pistons

Clyde Tombaugh – **Streator**-born astronomer who discovered the planet Pluto

Gloria Swanson

Roger "the Terrible" Touhy – Downer's Grove altar boy who became a bootlegging king in the Chicago suburbs. He was set up and convicted of a kidnapping committed by Murray "the Camel" Humphreys and other Capone henchmen. After he got out of prison he wrote his memoirs, *The Stolen Years*. Shortly after the book came out, he was gunned down while visiting his sister.

Mel Tormé – Chicago singer-actor known as The Velvet Fog – "The Christmas Song" (chestnuts roasting on an open fire), married actress Candy Tockstein of East St. Louis; fast-draw expert who appeared in several TV westerns, *Walk Like a Dragon, Girls Town, The Fearmakers, Higher and Higher, Pardon my Rhythm,* guest on TVs "Night Court"

Jonathan B. Turner – Illinois College teacher; became nation's leading proponent of Land Grant College idea – federal government grants land to states who then sell it to build agricultural and industrial colleges; Morrill Land Grant Act of 1857 fulfilled his dream

Tina Turner – Singer who lived with Ike Turner in **East St. Louis** from 1958 to the late 1960s, honing their skills in the metro area; movie *What's Love Got to do With It*, based on her autobiography; performed halftime show at 2000 Superbowl; inducted into Rock and Roll Hall of Fame in 1991

Scott Turow – Contemporary Chicago attorney turned novelist; *Presumed Innocent*

Dick Van Dyke – **Danville** native, star of "Dick Van Dyke Show," chimneysweep in film *Mary Poppins*

Jerry Van Dyke – **Danville** native, starred in "My Mother the Car" and "Coach" on television

Robert Wadlow – The **Alton Giant** – world's tallest man; lived a while in **Roxana**, reared in Alton

Clint Walker – **Hartford/Alton** actor – *Cheyenne* TV series, *None But the Brave, Pancho Villa, Yuma, Hardcase, Sam Whiskey, Night of the Grizzly, Fort Dobbs, Yellowstone Kelly*

Irving Wallace – Chicago-born pipe-smoking novelist who wrote *The Prize* and *The Miracle*

Sam Wanamaker – Chicago actor – *Private Benjamin, Raw Deal, Deceptions, Irreconcilable Differences, Death on the Nile*

Aaron Montgomery Ward – Chicagoan called The Father of the Mail Order Business

Arch Ward – A native of **Irwin**, Illinois; Chicago sportswriter who came up with the idea of the Golden Gloves for amateur boxing, the College All-Star Game (defunct in 1976), and baseball's All-Star game, to coincide with the 1933 World's Fair

Harold Washington – First black mayor of Chicago, 1983; served six terms in the Illinois House of Representatives; helped secure state holiday to recognize Martin Luther King Jr.; 1980 elected to U.S. Congress and opposed Reagan cuts in social services; suspended six years from Illinois bar (1970-76); 33 day jail sentence in 1972 for failure to file federal tax return; won a second term for mayor in 1987, but it was cut short by his sudden death; Harold Washington Library in Chicago named in his honor

Muddy Waters – Nickname from playing in mud as a kid; left Mississippi and came to Chicago as part of black migration; brought a new blues sound with him that became known as the Chicago blues; Rolling Stone Magazine and Mick Jagger's band and Bob Dylan's "Like a Rolling Stone," named after Waters' original "Rollin' Stone" composition; recorded for Chess Records; played Carnegie Hall in 1959; played his hit song, "Got My Mojo Working" at 1960 Newport Jazz Festival; died in 1983

James Watson – Child prodigy; entered Univ. of Chicago at age 15; shared 1962 Nobel Prize with Francis Crick for discovery of that tricky, famous spiral molecule known as the double-helix, the structure of DNA

Johnny Weismueller – Stricken with polio at age 9 and started swimming for therapy in Lake Michigan; trained by Coach Bill Bachrach of the Illinois Athletic Club; won three gold medals at the 1924 Olympics and two more in 1928; in ten years of amateur competition was undefeated; star of the 1924 and 1928 Olympics; was given the role in *Tarzan, The Ape Man*, in 1932; said it was perfect for him because he swam a lot and didn't have to say much; made 18 Tarzan films between 1930 and 1947; later starred as Jungle Jim on television.

Raquel Welch – Chicago actress – *The Three Musketeers, Four Musketeers, Fuzz, Last of Sheila, Lady in Cement, Fathom, Kansas City Bomber, Legally Blonde*

George Wendt – Chicago actor who played "Norm" on the television series "Cheers"

Betty White – **Oak Park** Emmy-winning actress on "The Mary Tyler Moore Show" and "The Golden Girls;" animal rights activist

Lee and Lyn Wilde – **East St. Louis** blonde twins who made about 9 Hollywood films, including *Andy Hardy's Blonde Trouble*, with Mickey Rooney, until their careers were ended by the invention of the split-screen process, eliminating the need for twins.

Frances Willard – Founder of the Women's Christian Temperance Union in **Evanston**

Frank Willard – **Anna** native; creator of the popular Moon Mullins comic strip

Daniel H. Williams – African-American Chicago surgeon who was the first to successfully repair a tear in the cardium, the sac around the human heart.

Raquel Welch

Robin Williams – Chicago actor on TVs "Mork and Mindy," movies*: Good Morning, Vietnam, Jumanji, Popeye, Insomnia, Bicentennial Man, One Hour Photo, Good Will Hunting, Jack, Mrs. Doubtfire, Hook, Dead Poet's Society*

Whip Wilson – **Granite City** cowboy movie star of the 1940s and 1950s; did stunt in the movie *The Kentuckian* where Walter Matthau bullwhips Burt Lancaster; *Montana Incident, Night Raiders, Stage to Blue River, Nevada Badmen*

Oprah Winfrey – Came to Chicago from Baltimore in 1984 to host a faltering talk show. WLS (World's Largest Store – Sears) hired her to do "AM Chicago." She quickly became more popular than Phil Donahue. Her TV show went national in 1986; lost gobs of weight, then regained it; decided to marry Stedman Graham in 1992, then changed her mind; sued by the beef industry for saying bad things about red meat on her show (they lost); one of the richest women in America ($550 million in 1997); only one of three women to own a production company (Mary Pickford and Lucille Ball were the others); nominated for Academy Award for her performance in *The Color Purple;* critic of George W. Bush's 2003 "Coalition of the Willing" war on Iraq

Kellen Winslow – **East St. Louisan** who was elected to Pro Football's Hall of Fame in 1995 as a tight end for the San Diego Chargers

Ian Wolfe – **Canton**, Illinois, actor – *Rebel Without a Cause, Reds, Dick Tracy, Frisco Kid, Homebodies, Terminal Man, Pollyanna, Silver Chalice*

Bob Woodward – Reporter for **Washington Post**; teamed with Carl Bernstein to break the Watergate story which brought about the downfall of President Richard Nixon; wrote *The Brethren, All the President's Men, Wired* (life of John Belushi)

Frank Lloyd Wright – (1869-1959) Developed the prairie style of architecture reflecting the horizontal lines of the Illinois landscape; fired by Sullivan in 1893 for accepting private commissions; had 3 wives, several mistresses and 7 children; most famous student of Louis Sullivan; wrote autobiography and several books on architecture; Imperial Hotel in Tokyo, Winslow House, Robie House, Dana House, Falling Water House, Johnson Wax building; first to conceive the idea of carports

Robin Williams

Richard Wright – Grew up in Mississippi where lynchings occurred on a regular basis; migrated to Chicago; joined Communist Party in 1930s; *Black Boy* (his autobiography) and *Native Son* (1940); *Native Son* was first book by black author to be a Book of the Month Club selection; disillusioned, he left America in 1946 to live in Paris

William Wrigley – Chicago founder of Wrigley chewing gum company in 1893 and owner of the Chicago Cubs; president and owner of Catalina Island off the coast of California, which he bought for his wife; first product was called Spearmint

Chic Young – Chicago creator of the popular, long-running Blondie and Dagwood Bumstead comic strip in 1924

Robert Young – Chicago actor; star of TV programs "Father Knows Best" and "Marcus Welby, M.D.;" films: *Secret of the Incas, Half-Breed, That Forsyte Woman, Cairo, Northwest Passage*

Florenz Ziegfield – West Side Chicagoan and showman whose "Follies" launched many a performer's career

ILLINOIS GEOLOGY AND MINERALS

The conventional wisdom holds that the geographical character of Illinois is flat and boring, nothing but corn, soybean and wheat fields – a place to get through as quickly as possible. But this is patent nonsense. Illinois is prairie, bottom land, waterfalls, Silurian reefs, sinkholes, caves, soaring bluffs, dells, wide rivers and rocky gorges. True, there are no granite outcrops in the state, but it exists as a Cambrian underlayment, close to the surface near Rockford and nearly 16,000 feet deep at Chester. Illinois has 14 distinct physiographic divisions: Wisconsin Driftless Region, Rock River Hill Country, Northeastern Moraine, Grand Prairie, Western Forest-Prairie, Upper Mississippi, Illinois River Sand Area, Wabash Border Division, Southern Till Plain, Ozark Division, Shawnee Hills, Middle Mississippi Border, Coastal Plain, and Lower Mississippi River Bottomlands.

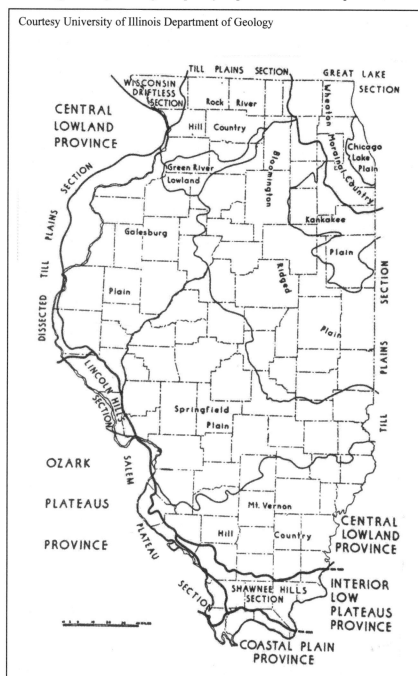

Courtesy University of Illinois Department of Geology

The surface of Illinois, except for the driftless region and southern Ozarks, is an almost unbroken plain sloping very gently from the higher borders of the north and east to the bottom land of the Mississippi on the south and west.

Rudyard Kipling said that geography is destiny, and it can be truly said that Illinois was blessed by Mother Nature with a mild climate, good soil, strategic continental location and magnificent waterways, making it the transportation hub of the nation. In its early geological history, the ocean extended all the way up to northern Illinois. The Ozark Mountains were a mere island in the middle of that sea in the Paleozoic Era. That shallow inland sea (stretching all the way to Chicago) helps explain why shark's teeth and fossils of sea creatures are found in that inverted triangle known as Egypt. This was the site where deposits of limestone, (calcium carbonate) sandstone and shale were formed, making up the bedrock of southern Illinois. The sea receded about sixty million years ago and, much later, was replaced by four great ice ages.

Joe Devera, of the Illinois Geological Survey, has long been searching the area hoping to find evidence of duckbilled dinos—hadrasaurs. A few mastodon bones have been found near **Cypress**.

Some geologists believe the continent almost split in two back in the pre-Cambrian period, millions of years ago along a fault line roughly equal to where the Mississippi River is located. Had that happened, there would have been a great rift valley, much like the one that exists in East Africa. The Mississippi and Illinois river valleys were formed by melting waters from the last great Ice Age. The outwash (sand and gravel deposited at the side or end of a melting glacier) from these meltwaters makes a good reservoir for groundwater. Geographically, Illinois is part of what is known as the Central Lowlands. The lay of the land consists of a slight slope from the northeast to southwest.

Perhaps the most interesting part of Southern Illinois is the area of rich loam known as the American Bottom. The Bottom stretches from **Alton** to **Chester** and varies from two to eight miles in width. The flat floodplain was carved out by glacial meltwater and a meandering Mississippi River. The meltwater also helped form Lake Michigan. Remnants of these earlier channels exist in the form of Grand Marais, Spring Lake, Indian Lake, McDonough Lake, Horseshoe Lake (Madison County) and others. Horseshoe is an oxbow lake that is an abandoned meander of the Mississippi River. The soil on the flood plain is known as gumbo, a sticky, black muck of a soil when it is wet.

According to the Illinois State Geological Survey, there was a huge ancient Mahomet Teays River valley in the vicinity of

Mahomet and **Monticello** that cut deep into Paleozoic bedrock prior to till (deposits) left by the Illinoisan and Wisconsin glaciers.

During the Ice Age, four major glaciers came down from present-day Canada, skimming off vegetation and depositing material in

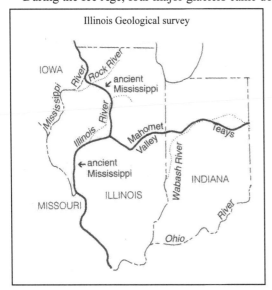

Illinois. Indian legends referred to the Ice Gods that came down from the North. The Labrador Sheet extended farther south in Illinois than in any other state. The fertile soil formed in glacial times is the greatest single source of the wealth of Illinois. About 85 percent of Illinois was covered by glacial ice at least once during the Pleistocene era.

Through plant growth and an accumulation of humus, a chemical and physical process developed our topsoil. Prairie soils, found principally in the east central part of the state, are black and rich in organic matter and lime. They hold water well and sustain crops a long time before wearing out. The topsoil is anywhere from eight inches to thirty-six inches thick, and its underlayment is a poor, recalcitrant soil known as clay pan. Clay pan is a forest soil that has little organic matter. This is why all Illinois farmers worry about the loss of their topsoil through erosion. The earliest, known as the Illinois Glacier (300,000 B.C.), leveled everything except the southern tip of the state and the "driftless" area in the northwest by the state of Wisconsin. This, more than anything else, explains why Illinois has good farmland. The last, known as the Wisconsin Glacier, left most of the state as a glaciated plain. As the water receded and the land began to dry, dust storms picked up silt from the valley and deposited it on top of the surrounding uplands as a yellowish clay known as loess. Only an immature soil is developed on the loess. This loess is quite visible where the bluffs have been cut away for road construction.

The loess sits upon layers of limestone (from shells of sea creatures) and sandstone (river soil). The limestone is exposed at **Alton** and **Dupo**, but is covered with soil and outwash near **Edwardsville, Collinsville and Belleville**.

The treeless prairie developed because repeated fires killed the saplings while the deep-rooted grasses survived the flames. The largest section of this "sea of grass" is to be found just south of Chicago, extending to the middle of the state and is called the Grand Prairie. This tall grass, with large roots extending deep into the soil, could nearly hide a person on horseback. Fortunately, this thick prairie sod protected the rich soil beneath it from erosion.

The northern tier of southern Illinois is physiographically located in the lower part of what is known as the Springfield Plain, which slowly gives way to the **Mount Vernon** Hill Country. This is a gently rolling area with wide valleys and no elevation exceeding 100 feet.

South of **Carbondale** are the Illinois Ozarks (Shawnee Hills, ranging across ten counties). It is an uplifted and folded (tilted) belt, fifteen to forty miles wide and seventy miles long, extending from the Mississippi to the Ohio River. The Missouri and Illinois Ozarks are older than the Rocky Mountains.

This southern part of Illinois escaped glaciation. Much of Little Egypt, defined as the eleven southernmost counties in Illinois, is part of the Shawnee Hills section where some elevations exceed 800 feet. The Big Muddy drains a considerable area of southern Illinois north of **Carbondale** and reaches the Mississippi Valley west of **Murphysboro**.

Pine Hills is slightly north and east of **Wolf Lake** and is part of what is known as the western Illinois Ozarks. The area called the Garden of the Gods (south of Harrisburg) consists mostly of sandstone outcroppings. It is widely believed that the Ohio River flowed north of its present bed along the southern border of the Shawnee Hills section, and an ancient Tennessee River flowed along the state's southern border.

Karst landforms are found in Monroe County around **Columbia and Waterloo**. These sunken or cratered surfaces resulted from small, collapsed limestone caves. Area farmers plow and grow their crops around them.

In Jackson County, near the village of **Grand Tower** on Route 3, there are limestone bluffs along the river known as Devils Backbone. Most think it was so named because a band of Indians killed a group of settlers there in the 1790s. There is also **Walker Hill** and **Fountain Bluff**. A large fault occurred at Walker Hill, south of Bluff Hill, so that the normally horizontal rock layers are tilted at a downward angle. Ancient Indian pictographs can be found on stone walls at Fountain Bluff. Fountain Bluff, an unusual formation that juts from the plain like a loaf on a tabletop, is six square miles in area and has numerous natural springs. Grand Tower Island in the Mississippi River is the **smallest U.S. National Monument**. A major fault, the Rattlesnake Ferry Fault, is present just northeast of Devils Backbone but is mostly concealed by alluvium.

The Indians who lived in Illinois were descendants of Asians who came to North America over the land bridge that existed near the Bering Strait. They first migrated to this area about 10,000 years ago. The Indians of the Archaic Era (8,000 B.C.) were largely hunters and gatherers. This was followed by the Woodland Period (1,000 A.D.), which saw less nomadic activity and a more settled way of life. This was the era of mound building for burial and ceremonial purposes. Urban development obliterated the vast majority of these mounds. The Mississippian Period evolved around 900 A.D., marked by the cultivation of crops, mostly corn. Settlements along Cahokia Creek emerged about 700 A.D. The bow and arrow was introduced around 500 A.D. as evidenced by discoveries of flint arrowheads.

Sandstone, dolomite (magnesium carbonate), shale and limestone underlie much of Illinois deep down in the earth. For millions of years the granite bedrock was covered by sand, clay, and the decaying remains of plants and animals. Gradually this material was pressed to form limestone, sandstone, shale and other minerals. Where the matter was mostly vegetation, coal was formed. Because the earth's crust was in a constant state of flux with sinkings and upheavals, this sagging of the earth, due to tectonic shifts, left some coal deposits 1,000 feet down while other veins were pushed near the surface. The deep part of the sag or basin is near **Fairfield**.

Coal beds remain under nearly two/thirds of the state, enough to last for nearly another century.

Most of the Illinois coal that is presently mined is used by power plants to generate electricity. The Herrin #6 vein of coal at **West Frankfort** is a good fourteen feet thick, making it a major deposit in the state. In recent years, Illinois ranked 4th in coal production, behind Pennsylvania, West Virginia and Kentucky. Coal production was at its height in this state in 1923 when 103,000 men worked 1,136 mines. But coal production fell dramatically in 1950 due to environmental concerns since Illinois coal has high sulfur content.

Another mineral deep in the Illinois earth is oil, and there is some natural gas. Most wells use the water flooding technique where pressurized water is sent down the hole to force the oil to the top.

Illinois was the nation's leading producer of fluorspar (the state mineral), a lavender, quartz-like crystal used in manufacturing antiseptics, insecticides, aluminum, and steel. Fluorspar, not coal, is the "state mineral." There were major deposits of this inorganic substance in **Pope and Hardin Counties.**

No state in the union has a more magnificent system of waterways than has Illinois. The entire length of the Mississippi bordering the state is about 550 miles. The Ohio and Wabash rivers to the east furnish about 300 miles of riverfront while Lake Michigan bathes 60 miles of the state's northeast shore.

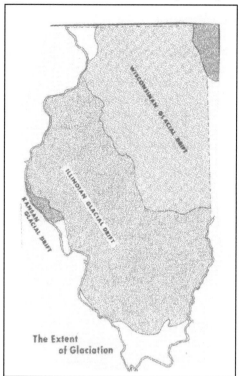

The Extent of Glaciation

YEAR-BY-YEAR ILLUSTRATED HISTORY OF ILLINOIS

200 million B.C. – Cave-in-Rock on the Ohio River begins to form.

12,000 B.C. – Lake Chicago, formed from a melting Wisconsinan glacier, covers all of present-day Chicago. It is the predecessor to Lake Michigan.

8,000 B.C. – The last of the four great glaciers (Wisconsin) retreats from what is now Illinois. When the glaciers retreated they left ridges known as moraines. It was this glacier that produced Lake Michigan. It was the previous Illinoisan glacier that scraped most of the state flat. A group of Native Americans move into present-day Illinois. They are ancestors of tribesmen who first came to North America across an existing land bridge between Alaska and Russia. A process known as Carbon 14 dating places these early Paleo (ancient) Indians at the place known as the Modoc Rock Shelter near Prairie du Rocher in Randolph County.

1,000 B.C. – What archaeologists label as the Woodland Culture begins in Illinois. Whereas earlier tribes subsisted on fruit, nuts, berries and hunting animals, this group forms villages and begins primitive agriculture with corn and squash being the main crops. They also learned how to make pottery and jewelry.

300 B.C. – 500 A.D. – The Hopewellian Indians, in what scientists label the Woodland Culture, comes into prominence. These people are also known as mound builders, their graves often containing several hundred people.

700 – 1500 A.D. - There is the Mississippian Period and an Indian population of six or seven thousand at Cahokia subsists on corn production and hunting. But the destruction of the woodlands denudes the land, causing environmental problems and flooding, forcing them to abandon the site. Mississippian culture declined rapidly after about 1492. It was the Mississippians who built Cahokia Mound around 700 A.D, also known as Monks' Mound, which was apparently used for religious purposes. Situated on old Route 40 to the south and Interstate 70 to the north, near Fairmount City, this huge mound covers 16 acres and contains 22 million cubic feet of soil, making it larger in volume than the Great Pyramid of Egypt! It is about 100 feet tall, 1,000 feet long and 700 feet wide. Incredibly, all of this dirt was carried by hand in buckets and baskets from nearby borrow pits. The great Mound is surrounded by smaller ones that were used as burial sites. Archaeologists later uncovered a circle of wooden posts, believed to be used as an astronomical calendar, that they labeled Woodhenge since it reminded them of Stonehenge, England.

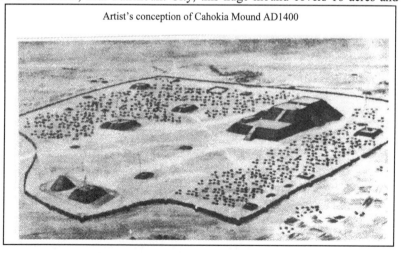

Artist's conception of Cahokia Mound AD1400

1497-98 A.D. - John and Sebastian Cabot explore the Atlantic coast from Newfoundland to Florida, establishing England's first claim to North America. In 1606 King James issued charters to the Plymouth and London companies assigning territory between the 34th and 45 parallels of latitude in what would be called Virginia. These were sea-to-sea charters, and Illinois country existed within these boundaries.

1500 – 1840 A.D. – By 1500 A.D. the Cahokia Mounds site is abandoned. It was first occupied around 700 A.D. After the mysterious decline of the Mississippian culture, the region came to be inhabited by various Algonquin tribes who migrated to Illinois country from back east. The Illinois Indians consisted of the Kaskaskias, Cahokias, Tamaroas, Peorias, Michigameas, Moingwenas and several minor groups. They were haughty of step and referred to themselves as Iliniwek, which meant "superior men," (as if other Indians were mere beasts). It was the early French explorers who shortened the name to Illinois.

These Indians planted corn, tomatoes, squash, tobacco, beans and pumpkins. Tobacco was used mainly for ceremonial purposes and was smoked in a special long pipe called the calumet. After planting season, they hunted rabbits, buffalo, deer, bear and wild fowl. They supplemented this diet by catching fish in rivers and streams. The Illini, consisting of about 12 tribes, worshiped Manitou, the Great Spirit.

War dance performed by Sauk and Fox Indians (author's collection)

Warfare was common and the calumet war dance has been vividly described by early French explorers. Sundry migrations of other tribes into the area brought conflict. Some of the outsiders were the Fox, Kickapoo, Winnebago, Potawatomie, Sauk, Ottawa, Miami and Shawnee. The Potawatomie settled around the shores of Lake Michigan. The Sauk and the Fox roamed the wooded lands of the driftless area. The most feared and hostile of the Illini enemies were the Sioux, from the West and the Iroquois from back East. The Iroquois were the first Indians to acquire firearms. As English settlers pushed the Iroquois out of the Mohawk Valley in New York, they moved east, invading Illinois country around 1655. Around 1667, several of the Illinois tribes, subject to fierce warfare, were forced to leave the area and move westward across the Mississippi River. Such was the state of affairs when the white men first arrived on the scene.

1500 – As a result of Columbus' 4 voyages, Europeans now fully realize that the New World is a barrier to Cathay (China) and the riches of the Far East that they seek. Explorer after explorer will probe the continent, searching for the famed Northwest Passage that will provide quicker access. Around 1521 the Spaniards introduce the first horses and cattle to N. America.

1541 – Hernando DeSoto and his band of Spanish explorers become the first Europeans to see the Mississippi River. *He lands with thirteen pigs in America and discovers the mouth of a great river. He calls it by its Sioux Indian name (Messipi), which loosely means Father of Waters.* Desoto claims the entire area for Spain. DeSoto had been with Pizarro in Peru and was looking for gold and silver. Had that country chosen to follow up with settlements, our southern Illinois heritage could have been Spanish rather than French. On one journey up the Mississippi he reached as far north as Cairo. The Spanish mainly lost interest because Indians in the Mississippi River valley had no gold or silver.

The Cahokia Indians, a sub tribe of the Illini, begin to move into southern Illinois.

1608 – Samuel de Champlain, driven by imperial ambition, lays out the streets and establishes Quebec in Canada, forming the basis for New France. Empire, the fur trade, and Christianizing the Indians becomes the three prime objectives of the French.

1634 – Jean Nicolet is sent by Champlain (from Quebec) to search for a route that would lead him to find the Great Kahn in China. He makes it as far as present-day Green Bay, Wisconsin.

1660 – Estimates place the number of Illinois Indians in the area at 33,000. Twenty years later, their numbers would fall to only about 10,500. Colbert, the finance minister of Louis XIV, develops the idea of mercantilism – that colonies around the world would make the mother country strong and self-sufficient.

1672 – Louis conte de Frontenac is appointed Governor of New France. Lake Michigan is referred to on maps of this era as Lac des Illinois.

1673 – **Louis Jolliet**, a French Canadian adventurer/cartographer, and **Father Pere Marquette** (a Jesuit priest), leave St. Ignace in what is now Michigan's Upper Peninsula to explore and seek new converts. With five woodsmen and several Indian guides, they float down the Mississippi in birch bark canoes and become the first Europeans to see Illinois. This begins the first recorded history of our state. The trip is made in two large canoes with 5 experienced voyageurs to paddle, carry supplies and help with portages

George Catlin depiction of an Iliniwek

(carrying the canoes across shallow water). Young Jolliet was an experienced surveyor and explorer, while Marquette was a Jesuit priest who had mastered 6 Indian languages for the purpose of spreading Christianity. At one point they left the river to explore some land and in the process they encountered an Indian village and learned that the tribe called themselves "Iliniwek" which roughly translated from the Algonquin meant "superior men." They were surprised to discover that the Indians tortured their enemies, tattoos their bodies, captured other tribesmen and practiced slavery, and also ate dog meat. They played a competitive game called lacrosse. They were part of a confederation known as the *Illinois* who were bitter enemies of the hated Iroquois who were thought to be inferior. The French eventually began using the word Illinois to describe this part of the country.

Henry Lewis depiction of Piasa Monster

The Illinois Indians did not bury their dead. They placed the body in the branches of a tree until the flesh rotted away. Then the bones were gathered up and placed in a sepulcher. These Indians, called savages by Whites, made slaves of women and children captured from the enemy. According to a memoir written by Henri Tonti's nephew, captured males were tortured, disemboweled and their hearts eaten raw. Mothers dipped the feet of their young male children into the blood of the deceased's thoracic cavity.

Marquette and Jolliet report seeing "charbon de terre" (coal) at Ottawa and Utica.

They entered the Illinois River from the Mississippi. When they encountered the bluffs on the Illinois River at the future site of Peoria, they marveled at its raw physical beauty and exclaimed, "We have seen nothing like this in all our travels."

When Marquette and Jolliet saw the bluffs near Alton, they referred to the site as the "Ruined Castles" due to the irregular rugged features. They were also the first Europeans to see the petroglyph (rock painting) on the cliff that became known as the **Piasa Monster**. In later years, when the Indians obtained guns from traders, they fired their weapons at the painting of the dragon-like Piasa monster, greatly marring its appearance.

The duo nearly drowned when their birch-bark canoes encountered the turbulence of the confluence of the Missouri River with the Mississippi.

Marquette and Joliet floated past **Tower Rock**, near the future town of Grand Tower. Native Americans were convinced evil spirits inhabited the rock because the dangerous swirls and eddies there claimed so many lives. The **Devil's Backbone**, a half-mile outcrop of rock near Grand Tower, became a famous landmark for steamship pilots. **Grand Tower** at its zenith had a population of about 4,000 and a significant industry flourished with two iron furnaces. Andrew Carnegie once considered expanding the production there to turn it into the Pittsburgh of the West. Instead, that title was adopted by both East St. Louis and, later, Granite City. Devil's Bake Oven is not far from the Devil's Backbone.

Father Marquette

The early explorers had no idea how big the continent was. When the Indians they encountered told stories about mighty rivers that led to distant places, they eagerly explored any significant body of water, hoping it would be the fabled Northwest Passage, a corridor to the fabled lands of the Orient.

Marquette and Jolliet turned back after reaching the point where the Arkansas River flows into the Mississippi. At that point they realized that the Mississippi emptied into the Gulf of Mexico rather than the Pacific Ocean. They made the return trip in 1764 via the Illinois River, portaging to what local Indians called the Checagou River. Father Marquette, weakened by sickness, disease and exposure, died in 1675.

1678 - The Italian Henri de Tonti and several French missionaries place a large wooden cross at the top of Tower Rock in the Mississippi River. They call it Le Cap de Croix, **Rock of the Cross**. Tower Rock is about 62 ft. high and an acre in extent. During the Grant Administration (1870s), the area around it was cleared of rocks that might have proved dangerous to navigation. Tower Rock was left standing because Grant thought it to be a suitable support for a future bridge.

1679 – René de LaSalle and his able companion Henri de Tonti, spurred by reports of the Jolliet/Marquette voyage, travel down the Illinois River searching for a suitable site on which to build a fort. They travel from the headwaters of the Kankakee River down to the Illinois River. LaSalle had earlier secured trading rights from the king of France and had built several forts near Montreal. Now he is sent by Governor Frontenac to extend the French empire. LaSalle and his men build Fort Crevecoeur, which means "refuge of the broken heart," on a bluff overlooking the river on a site near present-day Peoria. It was near a large village of Kaskaskia Indians who were at war with the Iroquois. Tonti displayed bravery and courage when dealing with the local Indians. The Kaskaskians referred to him as "Iron Hand." He had a cast iron replacement hand, having lost the original in an Italian naval battle while in the service of the French. The savages had great respect for Tonti's iron hand, describing it as "great medicine." History has been unkind to Tonti, whose significance was far greater than LaSalle's.

LaSalle left the fort and returned to Fort Frontenac on Lake Ontario in Canada to secure iron for the purpose of building a large ship to transport pelts in the lucrative fur trade. While he was absent, the men at the fort mutinied, wrecked the fort and deserted. The men respected Tonti but hated LaSalle who was vain, ambitious, and arrogant.

Robert de La Salle

Robert de LaSalle and Henri Tonti, encouraged by reports from Joliet and Marquette, decide to explore the Illinois River and go all the way to the mouth of the Mississippi River, looking for that fabled route to the Far East to "La Chine." They claimed the entire region for King Louis XIV of France and call it Louisiana. They returned to Illinois and constructed Fort St. Louis on a bluff that later came to be known as Starved Rock. Several thousand Illini were persuaded to settle near the fort since LaSalle and Tonti (his lieutenant) promised them protection from the Iroquois.

1680 – LaSalle, Tonti, and Father Hennepin build Fort Crevecoeur on the east side of the Illinois River, three miles below Peoria. It was later overrun by the Iroquois who attacked and killed large numbers of the Iliniwek.

1685 – Louis XIV, through the influence of Madam de Maintenon, revokes the Edict of Nantes which had previously granted religious freedom to French Protestants. Large numbers of them will migrate to America to escape religious persecution. Many then simplified or anglicized their names. For example, Waudleaux became Wadlow.

1687 - LaSalle was a poor leader of men. He was removed as commander of Fort St. Louis and he returned to France in 1683 to plead his case before the crown. He gained support for an expedition to build a settlement near present-day New Orleans. But his group missed the mouth of the Mississippi river and landed farther west in what is now Texas. **He was murdered** in 1687 by discouraged and mutinous members of his party. Tonti ventured forth a year later in an effort to find his friend's body, but was unsuccessful. In 1690, Tonti was granted all the rights and privileges from the French crown that had previously been given to LaSalle. Despite his death, LaSalle had laid in Illinois the foundation of a French colony.

1692 – French forces are unable to protect the Illinois tribes from attack by the Iroquois. After holding a pow wow with the local chiefs, Tonti agrees to build a new fort in a safer area. Fort Pimitoui, sometimes called Fort St. Louis, is built near Lake Peoria, at Starved Rock, not far from the old Fort Crevecoeur site. Lake Peoria is a misnomer, simply being a wide part of the Illinois River.

1696-1700 - The Mission of the Guardian Angel is built on the future site of Chicago.

1699 – An explorer by the name **St. Cosme** travels down the Mississippi and confirms the Marquette/Jolliet sighting of the **Piasa monster** on the cliffs near the future sight of Alton.

The French Seminary For Foreign Missions, led by Bishop de St. Vallier of Quebec, sends three priests to the site of Cahokia to minister to the Indians. The Cahokia settlement is not on the Mississippi River but on the east side of Cahokia Creek that emptied into it. Before Cahokia, most Frenchmen engaged in the fur trade and did not extensively farm.

The French build a chapel and a house at Cahokia, making it the **oldest settlement in Illinois**. The Church of the Holy Family is the **oldest west of the Appalachians**. The Cahokia courthouse (Saucier house) is built. Now roughly 300 years old, it is the oldest existing structure in the state of Illinois. Settlers from France, (*habitants*) arrived and raised crops and cared for livestock. It grew into a sizable trading post due to *coureurs de bois* (runners of the woods), French trappers. In its early history, this community exercised jurisdictional control over a vast area that included the present site of Chicago.

French farms were different from those of British colonialists. Because of the importance of accessibility to the river, they used the long-lot system, measured in arpents. A typical farm might be a quarter of a mile long and only 40 feet wide. These ribbon farms also allowed tillers from adjacent farms to plow side-by-side, affording more protection from Indians. Most of the Frenchmen married squaws from the different tribes.

Somehow, French residents in Illinois also escaped the feudal system used elsewhere in New France where land was granted to *seignors*, who, in turn, leased holdings to other settlers. The French in Illinois had their land fee simple, owning it outright. French cabins

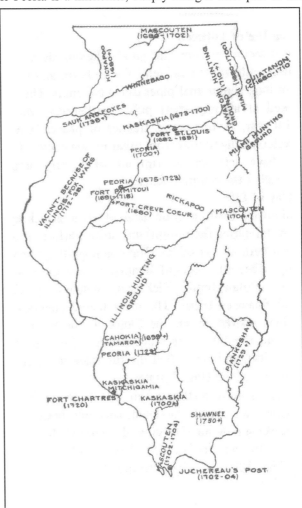

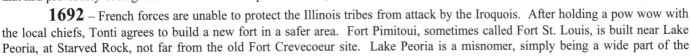

were also constructed differently. Instead of placing logs horizontally, the French used the post en terre system, placing the logs vertically, sometimes in the ground, or on a wooden footing.

1700 – A French trader known as LeSeuer discovers lead near the Galena River (he called it the River of Mines) in what is now known as Jo Daviess County.

1701 – Louisiana Governor Antoine Cadillac establishes a French settlement at Detroit. The War of the Spanish Succession (1701-13 rages on the continent.

1702 – Henri Tonti dies of yellow fever in Mobile. Shortly after Fort Pimitoui was built, the French government cancelled his fur monopoly. He left Illinois and went south, establishing a fort at Biloxi, Mississippi. For a few years he served as an advisor to the government in what came to be called Lower Louisiana. Tonti and LaSalle failed in their dream, but their string of forts from Canada to the Gulf of Mexico laid the foundation for New France and paved the way for future European settlement in Illinois Country.

1703 – The French village of Kaskaskia is established, making it the second oldest community in Illinois. It is on a peninsula between the Mississippi and Kaskaskia rivers. The local Indian tribes depart and establish a new village about 5 miles farther north. Settlers construct a church made of logs near the bank of the Kaskaskia River that same year. The roof is made of thatched straw. A second church, made of stone, was built in 1740 at the expense of the French government. Yet a third church was built in 1775. It was made of vertical palisade posts, but it deteriorated quickly and was torn down in 1838. A new brick church was then constructed. It was torn down three years after the 1881 flood, and the materials were used to build a new church farther west and south at the site of New Kaskaskia.

Henri de Tonti – empire builder and LaSalle's assistant

Kaskaskia ruled as the social and commercial center of Upper Louisiana for more than a century. The site was so prosperous that the gay social life earns it the title, the "Versailles of the West."

The pirogue or dugout canoe from the trunk of a cottonwood tree or a sycamore became a common method of river travel for the French settlers.

1717-1720 - A Scotsman named John Law arrives in Paris and soon becomes a French minister of finance. He establishes a land speculation scheme to promote trade and colonization of Illinois Country. It became known as the **"Mississippi Bubble."** In addition to enriching himself, his scheme proposed to pay off French government debts through empire building. The term "millionaire" was invented to describe him. It was a grand plan to colonize southern Illinois with settlers and exploit its natural resources (gold and silver). The Galena area was included as part of his scheme. For decades the French held to the mistaken belief that the Illinois country contained a vast mineral wealth of gold and silver. Silver Creek in St. Clair County was so named because small amounts of the precious metal were found in it. Law envisaged that factories would be established to weave cloth from buffalo wool and that farmers would till the land by hitching buffalos to plows.

He convinced the Duke of Orleans, regent for Louis XV, to issue France's first paper money (billets d' état), backed by a vast trading and colonizing enterprise, to pump new life into France's economy. He painted an exciting picture of Illinois and its great opportunities, but Law knew little about the area he was promoting. Although his scheme, through the issuance of millions of pamphlets, did result in more settlers moving into the area (mainly at Prairie du Rocher (pronounced Roash-er), most investors in company shares lost their shirts. This episode became known as the Mississippi Bubble. Law returned to London and died in poverty.

Illinois country became part of the French Colony of Upper Louisiana in 1717. Furs, lumber and farm produce were the staples of the trade sent down to New Orleans. Despite their economic success, French settlements in Illinois numbered only around 3,000 at the time of the outbreak of the French and Indian War in 1756.

1718 – Bienville, the governor of Louisiana, founds the city of New Orleans and it quickly becomes an important shipping point. The English, French and Spanish were now contending for supremacy in North America.

1720 - **Philippe Renault** brings craftsmen, engineers and 500 Negroes to build and operate silver and lead mines in southern Illinois. Negroes were also taken to Galena where mining was found to be more profitable. When the mining in southern Illinois proved unprofitable, the slaves were sold to settlers, thus establishing the institution of slavery in Illinois. The enterprise went broke in 1740 and they surrendered their concession to the king.

The French government decided to strengthen its hold on Illinois. Pierre du Boisbriant built **Fort Chartres**, the first French fort in southern Illinois, located 15 miles north of Kaskaskia. It was named for the Duke de Chartres. In 1753, it was refurbished by Jean Babtiste Saucier and **Richard McCarty**. McCarty was an Irishman who became commander. The wooden walls were replaced with stone over a three-year period at an astounding cost of one million dollars. The sum nearly bankrupted the French government. This largest French fort in North America, covering 4 acres, protected settlers from the nearby Piankeshaws and other tribes, augmented by the fierce Iliniwek further north. After the French and Indian War, Richard McCarty built a grist mill on the present site of East St. Louis and named his small settlement St. Ursule in honor of his Canadian wife. But McCarty sold the mill and began operating a ferry service to St. Louis. He later abandoned everything and joined up with George Rogers Clark to fight the British in the Revolution.

1723 - **Prairie du Rocher** (prairie by the bluff) becomes the third most important French settlement in Illinois, founded by Pierre Boisbriant along Prairie du Rocher creek. He was the commandant at Fort Chartres. Plots of land were assigned to settlers in the "long lot" arpent French traditional system and they ran from the bluffs to the river. (French arpent is equal to 0.85 acre) By 1766 the town had twenty-two dwellings.

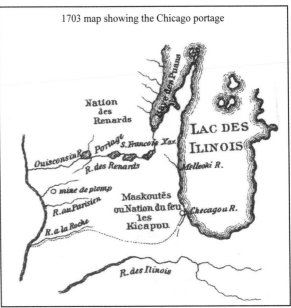

1703 map showing the Chicago portage

French settlers were noted for their adherence to the law and raucous parties and celebrations. It became the custom on New Year's Eve to blend voices with violins and sing the traditional song, "La Gui-Annee."

It was the French who developed a variety of uses for that otherwise useless weed known as the dandelion. The leaves could be used in a salad, the roots were ground up and used as a coffee substitute, and wine was processed from the flower.

Antoine Blais and Abraham Lee were prominent businessmen at du Rocher by the 1860s.

The oldest house in Prairie du Rocher was the old Creole House, built in the mid-1700s, now owned by the Brickey family. The descendants of the original French settlers were referred to as Creoles.

1727 – A group of people known as the Amish migrate to America. They are followers of Jacom Ammon and revolt from the Swiss Brethren of Switzerland who had separated from the Catholic Church. For years they led simple lives and rejected automobiles and the use of electricity. They also interpreted the Bible literally.

1729 – A Frenchman named M. deLery discovers a large limestone cave on the Ohio River and names it Caverne le Roc; Cave in Rock.

1732 – The village of Cahokia reports 182 slaves (106 Negro and 76 Indian) living among the residents.

1735 – The French take control of the salt springs from the Indians at Equality on the Saline River in Gallatin County.

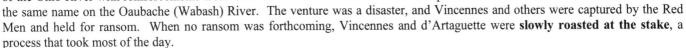

1736 - Pierre d'Artaguette, commander of Fort Chartres (in present-day Randolph County), is given orders to lead a military expedition against rampaging Chickasaw Indians. The expedition started in February, and they were joined at the mouth of the Ohio River with reinforcements from **Chevalier Vincennes** from his French post of the same name on the Oaubache (Wabash) River. The venture was a disaster, and Vincennes and others were captured by the Red Men and held for ransom. When no ransom was forthcoming, Vincennes and d'Artaguette were **slowly roasted at the stake**, a process that took most of the day.

1741 – King Louis XV presents the parish at Kaskaskia with a 600-pound cast metal bell. The bell, which is still preserved and on display, bears the inscription (in French): "For the church of the Illinois, with the compliments of the King from beyond the sea." The bell was made by Normand in the seaport town of LaRochelle in France. In time new bells were procured from St. Louis and the old one placed in storage. It took many months to bring the bell up the river from New Orleans on a raft. The bell was recovered from an old building in 1918 and transferred to New Kaskaskia, west of the Mississippi. In 1948 the state of Illinois erected a new brick structure to house the historic bell, known as the "Liberty Bell of the West." When George Rogers Clark took control of the territory from the British during the American Revolution, French citizens rang it loudly to proclaim their new freedom from the hated British.

1744 - A French explorer by the name of Francois Charlevois discovers Cave-In-Rock on the Ohio River. Back in 1721 he reported that the future site of Cairo would be a strategic site for a city and fortification. King George's War (1744-48) breaks out on the European continent. Illinois wine, from locally grown grapes, is so good that the French government forbids its import for fear of having their own industry ruined.

1748 - The Ohio Company, a group of Virginia land speculators, receives a charter for establishing settlements along the upper Ohio River. The French and Indian War hindered its development.

1750 – Prairie du Pont, French for "prairie across the bridge," which later was shortened to Dupo, is settled by people from Kaskaskia.

1752 – Hoping to block British expansion into the Ohio River Valley, the French build an impressive Fort at the strategic juncture of the Allegheny and Monongahela rivers, the site of modern Pittsburgh. It is named Fort DuQuesne. A year later, Fort Chartres is rebuilt and called the "Louisbourg of the West."

1754 - Southern Illinois is responsible for firing the first shots of the French and Indian War (1756-1763). The French had made claims to this area in 1749 by depositing lead plates at various points along the Ohio River. The next year, Christopher Gist, an agent for the Ohio Land Company from Virginia was sent to the area to pave the way for English settlements. George Washington, a surveyor, went along with Gist on one of these dangerous missions.

In 1754, George Washington, in charge of a militia unit sent by Virginia governor Dinwiddie, made a bold and daring attack on a French group of explorers in Pennsylvania near the strategic fort of **DuQuesne** at the juncture of the Allegheny and Monongahela Rivers (the beginning of the Ohio River). In retaliation, a group **from Fort Chartres**, led by Neyon de Villiers, made plans to avenge the attack. His "100 Picked Men" and their Indian allies headed for Pennsylvania. They were joined by other forces at Fort Duquesne, located on the modern site of **Pittsburgh**. Washington and his men met with near disaster and built a makeshift palisade (vertical logs), **Fort Necessity** at Great Meadow, Pennsylvania. His outnumbered force surrendered, but he and his men were later released.

Chief Pontiac

1757 - Fort Ascension (Massac), opposite the mouth of the Tennessee River, is established by French Canadians. Its elevation afforded a view of the Ohio River for twenty miles down and ten miles up the river. Some think it was named for the site of a massacre but most historians believe it was named for a local Indian chief. A band of Cherokee Indians, who were allies of the British, burned the French fort in 1765. It lay in ruins during the remainder of the British occupation era.

1754-1763 – The British and American colonists fight the French and their allies in the French and Indian War. This is a global struggle between France and England and in Europe the conflict is known as the Seven Years War, lasting from 1756-1763. The turning point in the war was the battle for Quebec on the Plains of Abraham in 1759 where General Wolfe defeated Montcalm.

During the war, Fort Chartres is used as a supply center and a holding prison for captured British troops. But as a whole, Illinois is confined to a marginal role because it is too far from the main conflict back east.

1763 - France, defeated in the French and Indian War by the colonists and Britain, gives up (by the Treaty of Paris) all of her territory east of the Mississippi River (except New Orleans), including Illinois Territory, to the British. This closes a 90-year period of French rule and immigration. The French, never here in large numbers, leave little in the way of heritage except in place names such as Dupo or Vermilion. Everything west of the Mississippi River is ceded to the Spanish, a reward for belatedly entering the war on the side of the British. At no point did the French in Illinois number much more than 3,000. Perhaps their biggest mistake was in not allowing religious dissenters, such as the Huguenots, to migrate to New France.

The Ottawa Chief Pontiac leads an Indian rebellion against encroaching English settlers like Daniel Boone, pushing settlements west of the Appalachians. **He forms a confederation of Ottowas**, Potawatomis, Delawares, Seneca, Ojibwas and Shawnee. Their main targets are a string of British frontier forts such as Detroit, Fort Ouiatanon on the Wabash, and Fort Michilimackinac on the straits of Mackinac. Detroit escaped destruction, but nine of the other forts fell before the onslaught. French authorities at Fort Chartres told Pontiac they would not assist him in his struggle against their old enemy. General Jeffrey Amherst helped the British regain the initiative and the Indian conspiracy was defeated in 1764.

The first roads for American settlers moving into Illinois country are buffalo trails.

The British government issues the Proclamation of 1763, declaring everything west of the Appalachians off limits for further settlement, putting Illinois country back into the territory of the savages.

1764 - **St. Louis**, planned before the end of the French and Indian War, is founded as a fur trading post (especially beaver fur) by Auguste Choteau and Pierre LaClede. It was named in honor of the reigning king, Louis 15th, whose patron saint was Louis 9th, (better known as Saint Louis) who was killed while on his way to participate in one of the crusades. LaClede came up to Fort Chartres from New Orleans with the intention of planting a colony of fur traders. He learned that Illinois country had been lost to the British. He supposed, mistakenly, that France still held territory west of the Mississippi so he selected a high spot on the river a few miles north of Cahokia. The important fur trade, which had centered at Cahokia, now shifts to St. Louis.

Many of the French residents in Illinois leave their homes and move to St. Louis, St. Genevieve, or New Orleans rather than live under British control. It takes a while for Spanish authorities to arrive and assume political and military control of St. Louis, located in what is now called Spanish Louisiana.

The St. Louis Trace is an old Indian trail that runs from Louisville to Cahokia.

Chief Pontiac and his Ottawa tribe settle in Illinois on the Kankakee River at the point where it joins the Des Plaines to form the Illinois. They are regarded as aliens by the Illinois tribes.

1765 - British efforts to take control of Illinois Country are initially thwarted by Pontiac's Rebellion, but the Indian eventually agrees to make peace. The British, under Captain Thomas Stirling, set out from Fort Pitt (the new name for Duquesne), sail down the Ohio River, and take control of Fort Chartres from the French commander. The red cross of St. George replaces the gold lilies of France and it is renamed Fort Cavendish. This is the last French flag to fly in Illinois territory. French commander Louis Bellerive wept when the French flag was replaced with that of the British. Witnesses say that even the stolid Indians there shed tears. The French settlers burned Fort Kaskaskia in 1766 to prevent British occupancy. As colonists back east became more unruly due to passage of the Stamp Act, British forces in Illinois were sent to quell the uprising. By the time of the outbreak of the Revolution, there were no British troops in Illinois.

Richard McCarty builds a grist mill and a trading post on Cahokia Creek, just west of where National Stock Yards were later located. In 1770 he sold the mill and began operating a ferry service to St. Louis. This is the first settlement of any kind on land that would become East St. Louis. The mill and post were later washed away by a flood.

1769 - A notable murder in Cahokia is that of the powerful Ottawa **Chief Pontiac,** in Maplewood (Cahokia), by the Illini chief, Kinneboo, a member of the Peoria tribe. One report says he was killed while in a state of drunken debauchery after a masquerade party in Cahokia. His confederacy had been responsible for the deaths of hundreds, perhaps thousands, of settlers in the region. Pontiac's war started after the French and Indian War and for several years delayed further settlement of Illinois country.

The sudden demise of Chief Pontiac

He was killed after attending a social event, wearing a uniform given to him by his friend, General Montcalm, before the Battle of Quebec in 1759. A white British trader named James Wilkinson is said to have hired another Indian, with the promise of a barrel of whiskey, to dispatch the great chieftain. The whereabouts of his remains are unknown because there is no grave marker. He was taken by a St. Louis friend, Saint Ange de Bellerive, and buried somewhere near a fort in St. Louis close to present-day south **Broadway**.

1770 - When Chief Pontiac was murdered by a Peoria Indian at Maplewood, on the outskirts of Cahokia, the vengeful Chippewa, Potawatomi, Miami and Kickapoo sought revenge for the incident. Pontiac's body was boiled and the flesh reverently removed from his bones. With his skull and crossbones nailed to their standard, they set out to avenge their murdered chief. Illinois Indians tried to escape their enemies by seeking refuge on the flat-topped surface of a place the Indians called The Rock, on the Illinois River. According to legend, they were encircled and starved into submission, giving the place a new name, Starved Rock. They were almost totally annihilated.

According to the story, an Illini wedding ceremony was interrupted by the final attack. When the young maiden saw her betrothed's skull split open by a tomahawk, she committed suicide by flinging herself from the rock into the river below, giving Illinois another one of those famous haunted places. Another legend holds that there is buried gold somewhere near Starved Rock, left there by Henri Tonti. Happy hunting!

1772 - The Father of Waters overflows its banks all the way to the bluffs, causing numerous families to abandon their settlements on the American Bottom flood plain. The encroaching river has been inching closer and closer to Fort Chartres and it now reaches its walls, causing the British to abandon it. It was never again used for military purposes.

Cahokia Courthouse-oldest west of the Appalachian Mountains

1773 – Jean Baptiste du Sable arrives in present-day **Peoria** but leaves about 6 years later to become the founder of Chicago.

1774 - In another move that angers colonists, the British pass the Quebec Act, placing Illinois and the rest of the Northwest Territory under the control of Canadian officials and making it part of Canada. They are outraged because in their view, this is land they fought and died for in the French and Indian War. The onset of the Revolution prevented its full implementation.

1775 – The first skirmishes of the Revolution take place at Lexington and Concord, outside of the Boston area. Benedict Arnold leads a failed expedition to capture Canada. This forces the British to station large garrisons to protect Montreal and Quebec.

1776 – The Americans, angered over British efforts to control them through legislation and taxation (without representation), declare their independence. The revolution is largely a frontier movement. Most loyalists who remained sympathetic to the crown resided in the tidewater area along the eastern seaboard. From the hill country of the Appalachians to the Mississippi River, one found strong support for independence.

1777 – **Thomas Brady**, a Pennsylvanian who is now a resident of Cahokia, leads a party of 16 volunteers to capture the British post at St. Joseph. On his return he was taken prisoner on the Calumet River by a pursuing force, but escaped and returned to **Cahokia**. Later he was made sheriff of St. Clair County. He was commonly called "Mr. Tom."

Jean Baptiste DuSable of Chicago

1778 - The American Revolution is now three years old. **George Rogers Clark**, a Virginian by birth, was living in Kentucky and was a major in the militia at the outbreak of war. Clark, a surveyor before the war, had never read a military strategy textbook. Clark, in charge of defending Kentucky settlements, sent spies to Illinois country. They returned with information that the British were rewarding the Indians for attacking Kentucky settlers. That also gave him astonishing news: the overconfident British had stores of military supplies in Cahokia and Kaskaskia, but hadn't bothered to garrison troops in those villages. Under orders from Governor Patrick Henry of Virginia, he is assigned the daunting task of wresting control of the western frontier from the British. Virginia laid claim to Illinois Territory on the basis of an original sea-to-sea charter, granted to the Jamestown settlers in 1607. Clark and his brave men set out from Corn Island, in the Ohio River near Louisville, and floated down the river to **Fort Massac**. He raised the American flag, and this was the only day he ever spent at the fort.

They marched overland from there, led by a man named **John Duff,** to Kaskaskia. For the most part, they followed the Le Grand Trace, an old French military road. With a meager force of 178 men, they took the Fort Gage by surprise, capturing commander Rocheblave as he slept in his bed. They captured Kaskaskia without firing a shot by making noise and disturbance in the streets to make inhabitants think they had been invaded by a large army. Clark explained to locals that they would be afforded freedoms and privileges of Americans if they sided with him against the British. Clark quickly wins over Father Gibault by promising religious freedom. During the festivities, the **Liberty Bell of the West** was rung. The French Kaskaskians called the Virginians "Long Knives." Clark next captured **Cahokia, St. Philippe, and Prairie du Rocher** without a struggle. At Cahokia, Francois Trottier, the commandant, prepared for a spirited defense, but when he saw his friends and relatives from Kaskaskia among the invaders, he surrendered the town and joined the American cause.

Clark held a powwow and smoked the peace pipe with the leaders of local Indian tribes. They called him **Long Knife**. His skillful diplomacy won them over. Clark then sent emissaries to Vincennes and told the authorities that he and his men, allied with the French and Indians in southern Illinois, were now in control and that they should throw in their lot with him. Clark pulled a surprise bluff that worked. He told the British and the Indians he was the vanguard of a larger nearby force awaiting his orders. They promptly surrendered.

In the **Year of the Great Snow**, thousands of buffalo die by starvation, trapped before they could head to the southern part of the state.

France, thanks to the diplomacy of Ben Franklin, declares herself to be an ally of the United States.

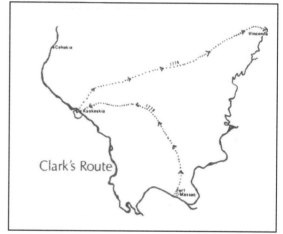
Clark's Route

1779 - Henry Hamilton, the British governor at Detroit, sends a huge force and recaptures Vincennes. The fickle French simply take new loyalty oaths. He is known as Hamilton the **"hair buyer"** for he begins the practice of offering bounties for the scalps of his enemies. Clark deems the fall of Vincennes intolerable. From there, the British could launch attacks on Kentucky and southern Illinois.

As a result of Clark's exploits, the Illinois region will become a county of Virginia.

Realizing that the British had designs on their holdings at New Orleans and St. Louis, Spain belatedly enters the Revolutionary War on the American side.

The **first Americans** arrive to make permanent homes in Illinois at **Bellefontaine** in the Kaskaskia district.

Spain declares herself to be an ally of France, and thus an ally of the United States. Spain hopes to recover Florida and Gibraltar, lost to the British in 1763 and 1703, respectively. **Casmir Pulaski** is killed at the battle of Savanna.

George Rogers Clark and his men crossing the Wabash

1780 - George Rogers Clark, along with Richard McCarty and a force of 170 men at Kaskaskia, with blessings from Father Gibault, begin the "Impossible March" of about

200 miles to recapture Fort Sackville at Vincennes, on the Illinois/Indiana border along the Wabash River. Father Gibault, who ministered to the flock at Vincennes, went there in advance of Clark to help secure their allegiance. Clark shrewdly determined that Hamilton would never expect an attack in the dead of winter. Richard McCarty was with Clark's expedition and commanded a group of men from Cahokia. The twenty-two day midwinter trek through swampy marshland of the Little Wabash River is exhausting, and they were near starving, having run out of provisions. They cross the Wabash by building crude rafts. Clark sent secret messengers to tell the French villagers he had arrived, warning them not to join the British. Clark's reputation was so great, they not only failed to join the British, they didn't even tell them Clark and his men had arrived.

Hamilton was loathe to surrender the fort, but Clark tricked him into thinking he was being attacked by a superior force. Clark and his men captured a raiding party coming back to the fort with American scalps. Clark had them dispatched with tomahawks in full view of Hamilton and his men who were inside the fort. Fearful for their lives, they surrendered on February 25th. Fearful of Clark's power, the remaining hostile Indian tribes were won over to the American side. Hamilton was sent to a prison in Williamsburg, Virginia.

McCarty convinces Clark to spare the life of Chief Pontiac's son because Pontiac had once spared McCarty's life during his rebellion.

Clark next wanted to attack Detroit, but he lacked sufficient numbers of men and resources. He was forced to spend most of the remaining years of the war maintaining a defensive posture, holding on to what he had captured. In 1781 he joined Baron von Steuben in the defense of Virginia against British attacks, led by the traitorous Benedict Arnold. Clark spent the remaining years of his life unappreciated, in ill health and near poverty, near Louisville, dying in 1818.

In 1778 the state of Virginia embraced Virginia and West Virginia of to-day, plus the present state (then county) of Kentucky.

Clark acquires the nickname, the **George Washington of the West**. A junior high school in E. St. Louis will be named in Clark's honor, and a bridge in Alton will be named for a brother. It was his younger brother, **William Clark**, who led the Lewis and Clark expedition in 1804. Clark's military leadership and diplomacy skills were exceptional. He is one of the true heroes of the Revolution. The suffering he and his men endured in their Vincennes campaign was remarkable and should stir the patriotic blood of all Illinoisans.

There is a statue of George Rogers Clark in the rotunda of a memorial to Clark on the site of old Fort Sackville at Vincennes. Seven murals there depict his heroic exploits. There is another statue of Clark at Fort Massac, near Metropolis.

Clark retired and lived out the rest of his life in near poverty in a house near the Ohio River.

In 1778 Illinois took a definite place on the map as an enormous county.

Theodore Roosevelt wrote in *The Winning of the West* that Clark's only reward for his heroism was the sword given him by the Virginia legislature. After the war he fell upon hard times and died in near poverty. Clark is remembered as the **Father of the Northwest Territory**.

When the war was over, Clark's men carried back good reports of the country they had seen, which caused many emigrants to come seeking new homes. After the war, new settlers (largely Scotch-Irish and English) poured into Illinois Country from North Carolina, Kentucky, Tennessee and Virginia. From these migrants the great majority of "Egyptians" have descended, and their cultural traditions, Southern in character, prevail generally in this region.

From around 1779 to 1780 settlements in the American Bottom were under the civil authority of John Todd, an able administrator appointed by Patrick Henry. But John Todd was killed in an Indian battle in Kentucky in 1781. John Dodge is appointed Indian agent for Illinois and with the help of local commanders at Kaskaskia and Bellefontaine, impose tyrannical restrictions on French locals. Dismayed, a large number of them leave and settle in St. Louis.

In 1784 Illinois became a part of the Northwest Territory.

John Dodge and his notorious band looted, stole and raped for nearly 6 years because there was no organized authority to stop them due to the Revolution.

1781 – Shadrach Bond senior, one of George Rogers Clark's soldiers, arrives in Illinois, becomes a member of the territorial legislature, a judge of the court of common pleas of St. Clair County, and uncle of Shadrach Bond, first governor of the state of Illinois.

Richard McCarty decides to return to Montreal to be with his French-Canadian wife and children. On the trip home he is captured by Indians and killed and scalped by a group of Weas (a branch of the Miami Indians) near the Wabash and Ohio Rivers.

William Herschel uses his telescope to **discover the planet Uranus**. His Uranus telescope is now on display at the Adler Planetarium in Chicago.

1782 - New Design, south of Bellefontaine, is established. It soon will become the largest English settlement in southern Illinois. A Baptist minister, David Badgley, led a group of settlers overland from Fort Massac, to bolster the town's number by another 154. His church there is the first Protestant church in Illinois, and he is the first Protestant minister.

1783 – The British sign the Treaty of Paris, formally ending the war with its American colonies. Because of George Rogers Clark's victories, Illinois and the land from the Appalachians to the Mississippi River were detached from Canada and became part of America. The impact of British rule in Illinois from 1763-1783 is minimal, mostly due to the short duration and the great distance separating the territory from the main British settlements.

The American negotiators in Paris were ready to give up claims to Illinois County in exchange for fishing rights off the coast of Newfoundland near the Grand Banks. But the British Prime Minister, Lord Shelburne, offered it to Ben Franklin in hopes of drawing the Americans toward Britain and away from France and Spain. (We should have named a county after this man.)

There is a 3-year delay in the ratification of the Articles of Confederation, the new plan of American government, due to quarrels over claims to western lands. Virginia breaks the deadlock by agreeing to vacate claim to this land and creating public domain, a priceless resource for the new government. Virginia's claims were the strongest of any states, based on their sea-to-sea royal charter and the exploits of their own George Rogers Clark in the Revolution. French inhabitants of Illinois country would be guaranteed title to their land, freedom to worship as Catholics, and the right to keep their Negro slaves.

After the Revolution, thirty-five Indian tribes meet and decide to resist the expansion of white settlers into the Northwest Territory, created officially in 1787. It includes Illinois, Ohio, Indiana, Michigan, Wisconsin and part of Minnesota.

When the war is over, soldiers, visitors and settlers send letters to people back East, praising the virtues of Illinois country.

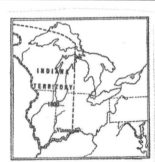

In 1800 Illinois was a part of Indiana Territory. Vincennes was the capital.

1784 – Oxford-educated **John Rice Jones** migrates to America and begins practicing law in Philadelphia. He heard about the western frontier and decided to explore the excitement. In 1786 he reached the falls of the Ohio River at Louisville where he joined the army of **George Rogers Clark** and his army of 1,000 to suppress the hostile Wabash Indians. For his service, he received a grant of 100 acres near Vincennes. He located at Kaskaskia in 1790 and **became the first man to practice law in Illinois**. He acquired more land and became an extensive owner of property in Indiana and Illinois. His law practice prospered and in 1808 he paid taxes on 16,400 acres in Monroe County alone. In 1801 General Harrison commissioned him as Attorney General for the Indiana Territory. His son, Rice Jones, began practicing law in Kaskaskia in 1806. John Rice Jones later made his home in Kaskaskia, the capital of Illinois Territory. Jones supported the move to set aside for 10 years the 6th article of the Northwest Ordinance of 1787 forbidding slavery in the Northwest Territory. Although not a slave owner himself, many prominent leaders in Illinois at the time were slaveholders.

Other proslavists were Pierre Menard, Ninian Edwards, Nathaniel Pope, Sidney Breese and Shadrach Bond.

In 1809 Illinois was at last a separate division with a local government of its own. Kaskaskia was the seat of the simple form of government.

The question now arose as to whether Indiana Territory should be split with the other half becoming Illinois Territory. Rice Jones in Randolph County and John Messinger of St. Clair County were zealous divisionists. William Henry Harrison was anti divisionist. Congressional enactment created Illinois Territory in 1809. Jones later became involved in Missouri politics and helped draft that state's first constitution at St. Louis in 1820.

His son, **Rice Jones** became involved in a bitter political dispute with **Shadrach Bond**, who later became the first governor of the state. Bond **challenged Jones to a duel** and Jones accepted the challenge to mortal combat under *code duello*. The principals and their attendants and surgeons met on an island in the Mississippi River between Kaskaskia and St. Genevieve. In those days pistols had hair triggers requiring only slight pressure to discharge. The parties had taken their respective positions and were awaiting the word "fire," when Jones inadvertently touched the trigger and that caused the weapon to explode, the shot entering the ground close to where Jones stood. Jones explained to the satisfaction of Bond that the shot was accidental. But Bond's second, a Doctor James Dunlap, said that was Jones' actual fire and that Bond should return the fire in retaliation. But Bond scorned the suggestion. Since the differences between the two men were political and not personal, Bond called off the duel. But James Dunlap had a personal hatred for Jones and on December 7, 1808, shot and killed Jones on a street in Kaskaskia. Dunlap jumped on his horse and rode to his house where he told his wife, in the presence of John Menard, that he had "shot that rascal Jones." However, Dunlap's friends claimed the killing was in self-defense. He was ac-

Illinois a state in 1818.

quitted in a jury trial, but two of the men on the jury were his friends. (from **Bill Lane** of St. Louis, a descendent of John R. Jones)

Jean Baptiste du Sable, a French mulatto from Santo Domingo, builds a cabin and trading post on the north bank of the "Checagou" River, thus becoming the founder of Chicago. Chicago is an Anglicization of the Indian word Checagou, which translates to "stinking onion," for the common plant found in the swampy marshes. Several years earlier, he had married a Potawatomi Indian maiden named Catherine. They traveled all the way to Cahokia so they could have a Catholic wedding. The marriage produced 2 children, Jean Baptiste and Susanne. He became very prosperous but for unknown reasons sold out and moved to St. Charles, Missouri. **John Kinzie**, another prosperous trader, later acquired the du Sable property at the land office in Palestine and enlarged and improved it. Kinzie Street in Chicago is named for him for it was he who strove to make Chicago a thriving and prosperous city. Kinzie was also the first Chicagoan to kill another man, a guy named Jack Lalime, in self-defense.

Virginia gives up its western lands and cedes the Illinois region to the U.S. government.

The renegade John Dodge and his brigands seize control of the ruins of old Fort Kaskaskia. He and his men will loot and pillage for two years before order is restored.

1785 - The Land Ordinance of 1785 mandates that Illinois and the Northwest Territory be surveyed by the township grid system. It replaces the old "metes and bounds" system used by early colonials. Based on cardinal directions, each township has thirty-six sections (one square mile each), and section sixteen is reserved for the support of public schools. It provides for the survey and sale of public lands at a dollar an acre. Minimum size purchase is a full section of land or 640 acres. The east-west lines are called township lines or parallels (parallel to the equator) and the north-south lines are called range lines or meridians. The revenue from section 16 in every township was set aside for the support of public education.

The checkerboard patterned range system causes roads to hug section lines and cross each other perpendicular at right angles. This new system allowed for orderly land sales helping Illinois to avoid the debilitating land feuds that plagued Kentucky. When viewed from the air, the grid pattern is clearly visible in roads and property lines.

The **greatest Mississippi River flood ever** (according to the Indians) takes place. It floods the American Bottom all the way to the bluffs. Settlers were in awe and they dubbed it "I'annee des grands eaux" or Year of the Great Waters.

Thomas Jefferson draws a map of the Northwest Territory calling for rectangular embryo states with illogical names and boundaries. He suggests Greek and Indian names such as Assenisipia, Polypotamia, Sylvania, Michigania, Chersonesus and Metropolitamia.

1786 - The **largest massacre** of whites by Indians in Southern Illinois occurs on this date. A large group of emigrants floated down the Ohio, preparing to settle in **Kaskaskia**. The passengers disembarked at the rapids near **Grand Tower**, so the crew could cordel (portage) past the rocks. Indians who were hidden nearby, attacked the party and killed everyone except for a teenage boy named John Moredock who hid in the bushes. Moredock lost 6 brothers, two sisters and his mother. Moredock walked to the village of Kaskaskia where he told his grisly story. Moredock spent the rest of his life taking revenge on the Indians, earning the title **Indian Slayer**. Moredock spent the rest of his life in Monroe County near **Valmeyer**.

Future president James Monroe visits the Northwest Territory and mistakenly describes it as "miserably poor" and a "hopeless desert" area that was not much of an asset to the United States.

1787 – The U.S. government under the Articles of Confederation passes the Northwest Ordinance, sometimes called the **Magna Charta of the West**, which prohibited but did not prevent slavery in the Northwest Territory. The Territory encompassed land north of the Ohio River and East of the Mississippi, which included Illinois. This apparent contradiction was never fully resolved, and agitation over slavery remains a bone of contention during Illinois' territorial era. Arthur St. Clair, new governor of the territory, added to the confusion by reassuring the French slaveholders. St. Clair was probably wrong in his interpretation that Article 6 merely prohibited the introduction of new slaves to the area. St. Clair should have sought an opinion from the U.S. Attorney General.

The Ordinance provided a process whereby new states could be created and admitted to the confederation on an equal basis with the other states. Ultimately, Indiana, Illinois, Michigan, Wisconsin and Minnesota were carved out of this region.

The ordinance was comforting to settlers wanting to move west. Now they could do so without fear of losing their citizenship.

1788 – U.S. Congress passes legislation granting 100 acres of land in St. Clair County to males serving in the Illinois militia and 400 acres if they were head of a family.

John Dubuque, the first settler in Iowa, obtains permission from the Fox Indians to mine lead ore on both sides of the Mississippi. Lead was thought by many to be a useless metal until demand for it increased as a material for bullets. The town of Galena gets its name from the deposits of lead sulfide (galena) near the Fever River. The river received its name from a smallpox epidemic there. By 1840, twenty-eight percent of the nation's lead supply came from the Jo Daviess County "driftless" region.

Other deposits of lead would be found in southeastern Illinois in Hardin County where silver and fluorspar was also mined.

1790 – A West Indies Negro named **Moreau is hanged at Cahokia** for practicing witchcraft and casting spells on people. Another (Emmanuel) is shot for the same offense. Some of these Caribbean slaves poisoned their masters and practiced secret rituals. A Salem Massachusetts-type witch hunt ensued and several slaves were put on trial for practicing witchcraft.

For about the next twelve years, the settler/Indian wars continue unabated, resulting in the loss of life of about ten percent of the population.

Governor Arthur St. Clair arrives in Kaskaskia and proceeds north to visit Cahokia. St. Clair County, named for Scottish-born Northwest Territory governor St. Clair, is organized, making it the first in the state. It is the **largest county in the world**, extending

Land Ordinance of 1785

THIRD PRINCIPAL MERIDIAN

FOURTH MERIDIAN

BASE LINE

BASE LINE

Township

6	5	4	3	2	1
7	8	9	10	11	12
18	17	16	15	14	13
19	20	21	22	23	24
30	29	28	27	26	25
31	32	33	34	35	36

6 MILES

6 MILES

Section

HALF SECTION 320 ACRES

160 ACRES

80 ACRES

40

1 MILE

1 MILE

to parts of the Canadian border.

A milling law is passed giving millers 1/5th of the wheat they process; rye, corn and oats = ¼ and malt = 1/6th.

There is a scoundrel by the name of Duff who engages in counterfeiting in the area at Cave-In-Rock. All we have from past records is his last name, and his Christian name remains unknown. It is quite possible that this fellow named Duff is the same man named John Duff who was known to assist George Rogers Clark as a trail guide at Fort Massac when Clark and his fellow Virginians were on their way to capture Kaskaskia.

Duff lived in a hamlet named Caseyville, Kentucky, which was just across the river from Battery Rock. It was rumored that this man named Duff was involved in all sorts of illegal activities but the only thing we know for sure is that he engaged in the manufacture of spurious specie coinage. From time to time Duff shifted his base of operations to Cave-In-Rock and other times to Island Ripple, about 13 miles from the mouth of the Saline River. Duff would secure lead from the mines on the Saline River and separate the silver content from the lead. He joined forces with a whitesmith named Schammel who made counterfeit molds from real coins and fire clay. He also made gold coins in a similar manner and in each instance would lessen the amount of precious metal in each fake coin. There were other men named Blakely, Hall and Hazel who helped him spend the counterfeit coins.

Duff had a loyal slave named Pompey who assisted him in his ventures.

Arthur St. Clair

There was a military fort located some miles below Cave-In-Rock. An expedition managed to capture Duff and his men while he was securing white metal in Illinois for shady purposes. On the way back to the fort, Pompey helped the men overwhelm the soldiers, and they managed to escape. The fort's commander hired a Canadian and a group of Indians to go up the river to Duff's Fort and kill him, which they did in 1799.

There are all sorts of legends about Duff's great wealth and buried treasure in the areas around Cave-In-Rock, similar to stories about Captain Kidd's treasure being hidden away somewhere on Long Island in New York. Somewhere out there in southern Illinois in Pope or Gallatin County might be fabulous wealth underground or in some hidden and undiscovered cave. The region is rife with stories about those who have tried to find it but as far as we know, none of Duff's treasure has ever been found. Good hunting!

1792 - Captain Robert Gray discovers the Columbia River and gives the U.S. claim to that territory. In 1807 John Jacob Astor will later organize the American Fur Company in the Pacific Northwest. He later will invest in a huge tract of land in East St. Louis in an area that becomes known as Denverside.

1793 – **Nathaniel Hull** of Massachusetts commands a party of 8 which defeats a force of Indians twice that size at the battle of Big Spring in what is now **Monroe County**. Joseph Ogle and James Lemen were two of the men with him. Lemon went on to become a leading Baptist minister.

Peter Zip is killed and scalped on the road from New Design to Kaskaskia.

1794 – **Michael Huff** is killed by Indians on the road between Prairie du Rocher and Kaskaskia.

Mad Anthony Wayne, hero of Stony Point in the Revolutionary War, defeats the Miami Indians at Fallen Timbers (named due to a tornado), Indiana. This avenges earlier defeats of Americans by the Indians. General Josiah Harmar lost to them in 1790 (near the Maumee River) and the aged St. Clair suffered a big defeat in 1791. A year later (1795), the treaty of Greenville (Ohio) was signed. Chief Little Turtle ceded 25,000 squared miles of Midwest land to the U.S. government. This included present-day Peoria and 6 square miles of land consisting of bogs and sloughs at the mouth of the Chicago River, where a great city would be built. The name for the place came from the Ojibwa word – checagou. When Father Jacques Marquette preached to the Indians at the site back in the 17th century, he reported one Pierre "The Mole" Moreau was selling firewater to them.

1795 – **Randolph County** is organized making it the second oldest in the state. The British sign the John Jay treaty and agree to abandon the Northwest Posts, which they had held on to illegally after the Treaty of Paris, 1783.

1796 - The Public Lands Act raises the price of public lands for sale from a dollar to two dollars an acre. A year's credit is allowed as long as half the purchase price is made originally.

The U.S. and Spain sign accords that are significant for Illinois country, the Pinckney treaty, giving Americans access to unimpeded navigation on the Mississippi River and the right of deposit of goods at the port of New Orleans. It must be remembered that Spain owned most of the land on the west side of the Mississippi River by the Treaty of Paris that ended the French and Indian War.

America and Britain sign the John Jay Treaty, whereby Britain promises to abandon forts in the Northwest Territory.

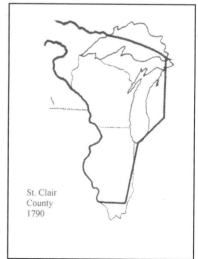
St. Clair County 1790

Predators become so troublesome to cattle and sheep that bounty laws are passed. Two dollars was offered for bodies or pelts of wolves and one dollar for foxes. In one town a wolf was **skinned alive** and set free to run back to its compatriots with a burning torch tied to its tail, hoping this might frighten the rest of them away.

Governor St. Clair finishes his legal code for Illinois Territory, helping to make up for his numerous deficiencies as an administrator.

The first Baptist church in Illinois is built at **New Design**.

Major James Lusk builds a cabin in Kentucky directly across from where Lusk Creek empties into the Ohio River near Golconda. He began to operate a ferry and later moved to the Illinois side to show his opposition to Kentucky's slavery. He created primitive roads that led to his ferry site just north of **Golconda**. Illinois Route 146 currently follows the path of one of his roads. Lusk Creek and **Lusk Creek Canyon** derive their respective names from him.

1797 – Captain James Piggott, a Pennsylvanian who fought at Brandywine Creek and Germantown, lays the foundations for East St. Louis by building two cabins and a bridge over Cahokia Creek. He begins operating a ferry service to St. Louis. He also builds an all-weather road from the ferry to connect it with Cahokia.

1798 – Steven Pensoneau, along with two brothers and two cousins, migrates from Canada to Cahokia. He will play an important role in early Cahokia, East St. Louis and Belleville as a businessman and entrepreneur. Brother Louis ran a ferry service to St. Louis from Cahokia.

1799 – The first meeting of the Territorial Legislature meets in Cincinnati. Shadrach Bond represented St. Clair County and John Edgar, Randolph County.

Nicholas Jarrot builds a two-story home in Cahokia. It is thought to be the first brick structure in Illinois. It is located on the east side of Route 3 at the juncture of Route 157.

1800 – The minimum amount of public land purchase is reduced from 640 acres to 320 acres.

Jonathin Boone, brother to pathfinder Daniel Boone, builds a mill on the future site of New Haven in southern Illinois.

Cave-in-Rock

There is a place in southern Illinois known as **Cave-In-Rock**. Located in what would become Hardin County, about twenty miles below **Shawneetown** on the Ohio River, the natural limestone formation became a notorious den for riverboat highwaymen around the turn of the century. The opening of the cave is in a limestone bluff overlooking the Ohio River (near the juncture of the Saline River), not many miles from where the river joins the Mississippi at **Cairo**. The cave was formed in some remote geological age and was possibly the drainage for one of the many sinkholes in the area. Almost directly in front of the cave is the lower end of Cave-In-Rock Island, which becomes submerged during high water. A stone carving of a sitting man, unearthed in 1918, suggests that prehistoric natives may have used the cave for religious rituals. **Henry Schoolcraft**, an early historian, visited the cave in 1818.

The elliptical opening at the mouth of the cave is about 55 feet wide. The cavern extends to the rear about 160 feet at a uniform width of about 40 feet. The floor and ceiling are smooth and contain no stalagmites or stalactites. There is a gradual incline from the front of the cave to the back.

As flatboats made their way down the river, the pirates had a confederate hail a passing boat, yelling out to occupants that they were stranded. When the boat came ashore for rescue, the crew was attacked and the boat was robbed of its supplies and provisions. Sometimes the crew and boat would be released but often the people were killed and their bodies, weighted down with rocks, were thrown into the river.

One group of cutthroats turned the cave into a pleasant-looking inn and by this deception ensnared weary travelers. Another ingenious band of robbers used the treacherous serpentine river channel at that point to good advantage. They stationed a confederate about ten miles above the cave near **Battery Rock**. He would pose as an experienced pilot and offer to steer the boat safely past the sandbars for a sum of one dollar. He would then proceed to run the boat aground so it could be attacked by his partners. The fact that the West (as this part of the country was known) was so sparsely settled at this time made these outlaw attacks on the citizenry possible.

Probably the most brutal persons to occupy the cave were the **Harp(e) brothers**. They seemed to have had a lust for blood. They were a couple of backwoodsmen native to North Carolina, their fathers having been immigrants from Scotland. According to historian Doris Lane, they passed for brothers, but were cousins. They fought against the Americans on the side of Banastre Tarlton, the British commander at the battle of King's Mountain in North Carolina during the Revolution. They spent much of the war as members of a Tory outlaw gang that pillaged the N.C. countryside.

The oldest, Micajah "Big" Harpe, a big-boned man with huge limbs, curly hair, and a weather-beaten face, claimed two women as his wives, Betsy and Susan. Susan Wood had been kidnapped from her family by Harpe during the forays. His brother/cousin, the red-haired Wiley "Little" Harpe was married to a woman named Sally Rice. They left a trail of murder, arson and thievery in the frontier areas of Tennessee and Kentucky. Big Harpe was known for splitting opponent's skulls open with a big tomahawk that he carried in his belt.

The whole clan was once arrested for killing a man named Thomas Langford. While they were in the Danville, Kentucky, jail, all three of their only children were born. But the two brothers eventually escaped from the jail, leaving their wives and babies behind. The court and townsfolk took pity on the abandoned women and released them, thinking they would seek a fresh start in life. But instead they made their way to Cave-In-Rock where they rejoined their murderous husbands. The Harpes killed three men as soon as they crossed into Illinois. The trio was sitting around a campfire at Potts Station near the mouth of the Saline River. There were other outlaws at the cave while the Harpes were there, but most of the men left and went elsewhere, fearing that too many of them would bring in the authorities.

One day a flatboat came down the river and stopped about a mile north of the cave to make some repairs. Two passengers, a young man and his sweetheart, decided to go for a walk to the top of the bluff where they sat down to take in the view. The Harpe brothers rushed from the woods and pushed them off the cliff above the cave. The man and woman fell forty feet but miraculously landed on a sandy beach below, and neither was seriously hurt.

Pioneers on flatboats used rivers as highways

There was another time when a boat was captured and passengers were taken prisoner and robbed. They stripped one of their captives naked and tied him to a horse. The Harpes then led the horse to the top of the cliff and placed a blindfold on the animal. They frightened the horse with yells and gunshot, and the horse raced blindly over the cliff and fell 100 feet to the rocky shore below. Both the man and the horse were crushed. The Harpes often **gutted their victims** and placed rocks in their stomach cavities to weight them down when they tossed them in the Ohio River.

The Harpe family left Cave-In-Rock and continued their killing spree in Kentucky and Tennessee. The Harpes even killed several children who came upon them by chance, seemingly for the sport of it. There was one instance where Big Harpe grabbed his own young infant from the arms of his wife and **bashed its brains out against a tree**. In all, the Harpe cousins committed infanticide on their own flesh and blood on four occasions.

Finally, after the Harpes had been responsible for the brutal murders of more than twenty people, a vigilante group took out after them. In a desperate shoot-out, Big Harpe was mortally wounded but managed to lead his pursuers on a short chase until they finally caught up with him. After giving him a chance to make his peace with God, which he ignored, they shot him again and killed him. Then one of the men named Steigal **cut off his head as a trophy**. The decapitated body was left to be devoured by animals.

Little Harpe managed to escape and continued his criminal ways in other states. The women, seemingly glad to be free of their polecat husbands, and the recipients of much sympathy, were not charged.

The severed head of Big Harpe was placed in the fork of a tree near a public road in rural Kentucky as a grisly reminder to all monstrous outlaws. Today, it is known as **Harpe's Head Road**.

Old map: Cave-In-Rock, Goshen Road and the Natchez Trace

There was one wily fellow by the name of **Samuel Mason** who came up with an imaginative scheme. He made Cave-In-Rock his headquarters around 1797 and stayed there for nearly a year. Both Mason and the cave already had nefarious reputations, so he schemed to avert suspicion. He changed his name to Wilson, and he converted the cave into an inn of hospitality. He and his family brought in tables and chairs, and he erected a large sign outside that read: "Wilson's Liquor Vault and House for Entertainment." Thus for a spell, the place was known as **Cave Inn Rock**. But Wilson had nothing but skullduggery, robbery and booty on his mind. After about a year, fearful that authorities would organize an expedition against him, he transferred his activities to **Wolf Island**, near the juncture of the Ohio and Mississippi rivers. After a while, Mason gave that up and continued to make a disreputable living by robbing travelers on the Natchez Trace.

There was a large reward on his head, and that ultimately was the cause of his demise. One night in 1804, by a campfire, he was counting his loot when one of his associates buried a tomahawk in his brain. The head was then taken to the governor of Mississippi by two men, **James May** and **John Setton** who tried to collect the reward. Someone recognized Setton and claimed that he was really "Little" Harpe. Setton denied that he was Little Harpe, but a mole on his neck and certain body scars, left

44

authorities in Greenville, Mississippi, convinced it was Little Harpe. Both men were tried and found guilty of various charges. They were taken to a field where a log was placed horizontally so that it rested in the forks of two different trees. Two nooses were tied to the pole. The men were led from the jail and made to climb ladders to reach their hangman's rope. Then the ladders were kicked out from under them. After their execution, their **heads were placed on poles**, on opposite sides of the road, along the **Natchez Trace** as a warning to other outlaws.

The three wives survived. Maria Davidson, also called Betsey Roberts, remarried and raised a family in Illinois. The other two went back to Tennessee and eventually remarried.

Historian John Allen wrote that Cave-In-Rock was the setting for a large number of 19th century novels, the first of which was *Mike Fink, A Legend of the Ohio* by **Emerson Bennett**. It was published in 1848 and was quite successful. There is wild and woolly action aplenty in this Middle West melodrama. The chicanery centers around a band of outlaws who make a predatory attack from Cave-In-Rock on Mike Fink's flatboat, crew, and passengers. The cave figures prominently in the plot.

Fink, although an actual person, became one of those fabled characters of lore cut from the same cloth as Paul Bunyan. This likable rogue was described as being part-man, part-alligator, part-horse, and part-snappin' turtle. The exploits and deeds of Fink, John Henry and Pecos Bill have filled volumes. He looked danger straight in the eye and spit in its face. Mike Fink came to be a legendary hero of the flatboat era. The "**King of the Keelboats**" once jumped across the Mississippi, but sensing he would fall just short of the shore, turned back in midair and landed at his starting point. It is considered the greatest jump on record.

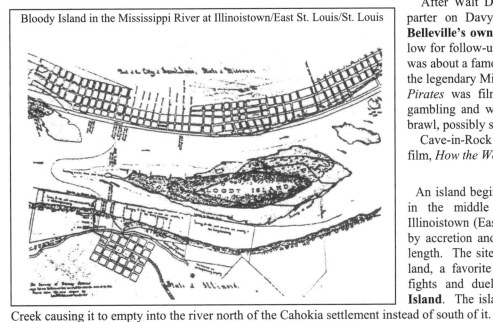

Bloody Island in the Mississippi River at Illinoistown/East St. Louis/St. Louis

After Walt Disney did his highly successful three-parter on Davy Crockett (starring Fess Parker and **Belleville's own Buddy Ebsen**), he searched high and low for follow-up material. The next Crockett segment was about a famous keelboat race between Crockett and the legendary Mike Fink. *Davey Crockett and the River Pirates* was filmed at Cave-in-Rock. Fink saw his gambling and womanizing days come to an end in a brawl, possibly shot by another man he offended.

Cave-in-Rock was also featured in the Cinerama film, *How the West Was Won*.

An island begins to shoulder its way above the water in the middle of the Mississippi River between Illinoistown (East St. Louis) and St. Louis. It expands by accretion and ultimately grows to nearly a mile in length. The site ultimately became sort of a no-man's land, a favorite place for bare knuckle brawls, cock fights and duels, earning it the nickname, **Bloody Island**. The island made the river intrude on Cahokia Creek causing it to empty into the river north of the Cahokia settlement instead of south of it.

The island received its baptism of blood in 1817 in a duel between two lawyers, **Charles Lucas** and **Thomas Hart Benton**, the future U.S. Senator from **Missouri**. The two had exchanged heated words while on opposite sides in a trial. Lucas was only wounded in the exchange of fire but was killed when the duel was refought and the distance was closed from 30 to 10 feet. The duel created a national sensation and gave rise to the image of St. Louis as a wild and violent place in the "Kentuckyan" image. There were five duels fought on the island. In the late 1830s **Robert E. Lee** (of future Civil War fame) and the U.S. Army Corps of Engineers built a series of dikes that caused the island to become permanently attached to the Illinois shore. Lee was promoted to Captain in 1838, in part, due to his efficient work on this project.

Sketch of duel at Bloody Island

Congress divides the Northwest Territory into Ohio and Indiana Territories. Illinois is now part of Indiana Territory, of which William Henry Harrison played a significant part in its creation.

The Indians, with little or no resistance build up of their immune system, are decimates by European diseases such as measles, smallpox and tuberculosis.

1802 - The Shawnees, occupying land between the Wabash and Big Muddy Rivers, engage in a great battle with the Kaskaskia tribe in a quarrel over hunting grounds and saltworks. This is sometimes called the **Salt War**. The Kaskaskia's lands were between the Big Muddy and Mississippi Rivers. The battle took place about three miles below the present town of Old West Frankfort, and the fierce Shawnees nearly destroyed the Kaskaskias (led by the aged chief John DuQuoin).

Twelve delegates are chosen in a general election to attend a conference at Vincennes, Indiana to discuss the problem of slavery. Among the delegates are Pierre Menard, Shadrach Bond and William Biggs. Most were strongly pro-slavery except for William Biggs and another representative of Clark County. Governor William Henry Harrison presided over the convention. They sent a petition to the federal government asking for a ten-year suspension of the provision prohibiting slavery but the request was denied.

Elexander Denis is killed by the Potawatomie Indians returning to Cahokia from Chicago, near the present town of **Edwardsville**.

1803 – Settlers of Illinois country petition congress to allow slavery in this part of the country. The U.S. government rejects these petitions so the territorial government enacts statutes to evade the provisions of the Northwest Ordinance that prohibits slavery. Under the new statutes, settlers are allowed to have indentured servants for virtually unlimited periods of time. Negroes brought in under these new terms were virtual slaves. They could be beaten and punished by their owners and jailed for escape attempts.

A detachment of soldiers, led by Captain John Whistler, leaves the fort at Detroit to build a new fort at the Chicago Portage near the old du Sable trading post on the Chicago River. Whistler brings along his wife and 15 children. It is named Fort Dearborn, to honor Henry Dearborn, Revolutionary War hero and Secretary of War. Whistler is considered the founder of modern Chicago. Except for a brick powder magazine, the fort was constructed from logs. One of the citizens living outside the fort was Antoine Ouilmette, best known for his name being used for the village of Wilmette, site of a land grant to his Indian wife and children.

Whistler was transferred to Detroit in 1810, a move that probably saved his family since Dearborn was destroyed by Indians 2 years later. By surviving, his grandson, James McNeil Whistler, later became an artist, famed for his portrait in gray and black, better known as "**Whistler's Mother.**"

Seven Indian tribes enter into a treaty with the United States whereby our government promises to deliver 150 bushels of salt a year (from the Saline Salt Springs) to the council chiefs. In return, they relinquish claim to some 14,800,000 acres in southern Illinois, virtually abandoning the area. William Henry Harrison is so eager to secure land for settlement, he frequently doesn't bother to check whether the signatories have the authorities to sign such treaties. In the treaty of Vincennes, signed by Anthony Wayne and William H. Harrison, it was stated that the Kaskaskias constituted "the remains of and rightfully represent all the tribes of the Illinois Indians," including the Michigamia, Cahokia and Tamaroi.

Charles IV of Spain discovers that maintaining land west of the Mississippi is expensive. He transfers ownership to Napoleon of France by treaty. Napoleon, deciding that he needs money to finance his European wars, sells the Louisiana Territory to the United States, nearly doubling the size of the fledgling country.

This moves Illinois closer to the center of the United States. Its lands are used as staging areas and jumping off points for settlers and explorers.

Depiction of Native-Americans in a 1925 textbook

The savages of Illinois were wild men indeed, for they knew nothing of the mineral wealth and almost nothing of the farm value of the Illinois lands. One could hardly call the inhabitants men; yet these savages loved to call themselves Iliniwek or superior men. Their influence on Illinois history amounts to little, for they gave up their lands to the white men with hardly a protest and left practically nothing besides a few barbarous relics and some Indian names. The Indians taught the white man to smoke and

---

1804-06 - There is a historical marker on Route 67 in Madison County. It is the site where Lewis and Clark set out in May of 1804 with 43 unmarried men from Camp Dubois at Wood River, across from the mouth of the Missouri River, to begin their twenty-eight month exploration of Thomas Jefferson's Louisiana Purchase. This was the most significant exploring expedition ever sent out by the U.S. government. One of the men on the expedition, on the return trip, stayed out west and discovered Old Faithful at present Yellowstone Park. A 1948 tornado in Wood River took down most of the old trees that were in the area.

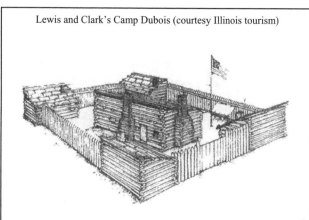
Lewis and Clark's Camp Dubois (courtesy Illinois tourism)

Illinois would play a significant role in the trans-Mississippi expedition. In preparation for the journey, the expedition of about 22 men floated down the Ohio River from Louisville in a keelboat and landed in Illinois Territory in present-day Gallatin County. They continued south to Fort Massac on November 11, 1803. Here, several more men were recruited for the expedition. They left Massac and arrived at present-day Cairo on November 14. Clark then sketched a map of the confluence of the Ohio and Mississippi. Lewis and Clark's boats landed at Fort Kaskaskia on November 26 and they recruited 12 more men. Lewis rode on horseback to Cahokia while Clark brought the party in boats. They stopped briefly for provisions at Bellefontaine. Clark's group landed at the mouth of Cahokia Creek on December 7. The party then traveled further up the river to establish a camp for the winter at River Dubois (Wood River). For 5 months the group trained and prepared for the quest ahead of them.

A new Lewis and Clark Visitor/Interpretive Center was recently built on Route 3 at **Hartford**, Illinois. The exact site of Camp Dubois was probably farther north but the exact location on Wood River (not to be confused with the town of Wood River) is not known due to changes in the river channel from floods. A life-size replica of the fort is being built for the 200th anniversary celebration in 2004.

A federal land office is established at Kaskaskia. The first sale would not be recorded until 1814. Settlers already there become known as squatters.

1804 – The Sauk and Fox Indians sign a treaty at St. Louis, giving up territory west of the Illinois and Fox Rivers. Black Hawk, a prominent leader, refuses to sign the treaty.

Etienne Pensoneau begins operating a ferry from Cahokia to Missouri at a point a couple of miles below St. Louis. A year later he acquired land near the Piggott ferry in Illinoistown and built that city's first brick structure, a two-story tavern at present Main and Market streets.

John Kinzie, the first white settler, arrives in Chicago.

At St. Louis, territorial governor William Henry Harrison plies 5 Sauk and Fox chiefs with whiskey and persuades them to sell 50 million acres between the Illinois and Mississippi Rivers in exchange for yearly payment of $1,000 a year in cloth, shoes, guns and trinkets.

Ninian Edwards – Governor of Illinois Territory 1809-1818, Governor of Illinois 1826-1830

1805 - The American Bottom is hit by high winds that devastate numerous cabins and is later referred to by settlers as the 1805 hurricane because it drew water out of the Mississippi River.

Former Vice-president Aaron Burr visits commander James Wilkinson at Fort Massac near Metropolis and plots a military expedition. Mad Anthony Wayne and Zebulon Pike (his son discovered Pike's Peak) had rebuilt the fort during Washington's administration after it was destroyed by Cherokee Indians. Some say Burr was plotting to separate the western territory from the rest of America and set himself up as king. Others speculate that he was planning an operation to conquer Mexico. He was seized and accused of treason but the courts held that while he might have been plotting something, he had not actually committed the act. Edward Everett Hale's *The Man Without a Country* is loosely based on this incident.

Galena, stricken with lead fever, leads the nation in the mining of that mineral.

Zebulon Pike receives orders to find the true source of the Mississippi. He makes preparations for the trip on the American Bottom and leaves his family at Fort Charles, across the river from Alton. His expedition is a failure but in a subsequent expedition he discovers the peak named for him. He reported more than 5,000 Indians living near present-day Rock Island.

1806 - Thomas Jefferson authorizes the construction of the Cumberland Road from the Potomac to the Ohio River. The idea was that of Albert Gallatin, his Secretary of the Treasury, and it was to be financed from the sale of public lands.

A horse race is held on the frozen Mississippi between St. Louis and Illinoistown/East St. Louis. People haul wagon loads of grain and lumber across the ice to avoid paying the charges of Piggott's ferry.

Trappist monks discover coal in the Illinoistown area when they observe a bolt of lightning ignite the earth near the bluffs.

1807 – By this date, most of the land in Illinois has been ceded to the government by some 17 different treaties between 16 different tribes with the Indians. In most cases, Indians gave up their land for a few thousand dollars plus promises of food, salt and tobacco.

One pioneer settler at Fort Piggott, south of Cahokia, wrote: "The tomahawk and scalping knife were our continual dread. To use the words of the Prophet Jeremiah. We got our bread by the peril of our lives, because of the sword of the wilderness." Thus it was with the greatest difficulty we procured the necessaries of life, laboring with one hand, while in the other we held a weapon of defence; our food and raiment being of the coarsest kind, and scanty withal. No coffee nor whisky, without which numbers, cannot live in these days of plenty." "Our currency consisted of deer-skins, three pounds being equal to one dollar in silver; and they were a lawful tender. Our amusements were the contemplation of better days. We had no minister of the Gospel; our manner of worship was to assemble on the Sabbath, read the Scriptures, and sing a few psalms or spiritual songs. We had no schools."

Jesse Walker, (the Daniel Boone of Methodism) a pioneer Methodist circuit rider, holds the first camp meeting in the state near Edwardsville.

1808 - The last known buffalo in Illinois is killed. The animals were so large a special weapon, the "**buffalo gun,**" was invented to kill them. It was a much larger weapon than the traditional rifle, and it had a sizable kick.

1809 - Illinois, having more than reached the required 8,000 population figure, is separated from Indiana and becomes Illinois Territory, with the capital at Kaskaskia. The move was championed by Jesse Thomas, Speaker of the Territorial House of Representatives. Various factions in Indiana opposed the move because it probably meant that Vincennes would now be on the border of Indiana and the capitol would move to a more central location, such as Indianapolis. Ninian Edwards, a Kentucky slave holder, is the first governor of the territory. Nathaniel Pope, the territorial secretary, was his cousin. Edwards was given 1,000 acres and settled on a large farm near Kaskaskia.

In part, the separation occurred due to Illinois settlers favoring slavery while those in Indiana opposed it. In later years, because of their similarities, the two are referred to as sister states.

The territory's first laws were to be selected from the laws of other states. Since most of the representatives came from places like Kentucky, Tennessee, Virginia, Georgia and the Carolinas, our first laws were distinctly southern in character.

Since southerners were riverine people, they settled along the rivers, avoiding the prairies that were often feared as great barren expanses of the dreadful unknown.

PIONEER ILLINOIS PENALTIES

Burglary - 39 lashes on bare back
Larceny - 31 stripes
Hog-stealing - 25-39 lashes
Bigamy 100-300 stripes
Disobedient children - 10 lashes
Hunting on the Sabbath - the pillory
Profanely cursing - Branding
Treason - Hanging
Murder - Hanging
Arson - Hanging
Rape - Hanging
Horse-stealing (2nd time) - Hanging

A full colony of Trappist monks, originally expelled from France because of the Revolution, **establish a monastery on the Great Cahokia Mound**. The mound was owned by Nicholas Jarrot, a prominent citizen of Cahokia, and he allowed them to use it free of charge. The original mound was 100 ft. tall, featured three terraces, and had a base that was larger than the Great Pyramid of Egypt. At first, geologists thought that the mounds were natural formations. It probably took more than two centuries to construct as workers and slaves carried baskets of earth from borrow pits to build the mound. For reasons unknown the site was abandoned by 1500 A.D. When the French settlers asked the Cahokians about it, they had no knowledge of their predecessors. Archaeologists consider it one of the most important sites in North America.

In the late 1800s a man named T. Amos Hill had a house on top of the mound.

Indiana Territory is divided into Indiana and Illinois Territories.

1810 - The first commercial production of Illinois coal is in Jackson County where William Boone dug a mine into an exposed outcrop (a drift or slope mine) along the banks of the Big Muddy River near present-day Highway 127, long known as the Black Diamond Highway. It appears Boone loaded the coal on a barge and sold the cargo in New Orleans. A to have been the first commercial mine in the state. A settlement, known as **Scotch Town**, grew up near the mine and was named for Scotch miners who came over to lend their expertise. Boone lived in **Brownsville**.

Indians knew about coal due to occasional outcroppings, but there is no evidence that they ever used it as a fuel.

Robert Fulton of New York, inventor of the steamboat, builds another one called the *New Orleans*. It is the first steamboat in western waters, and it makes a trip from Cairo to St. Louis. A brilliant comet streaked across the sky as the boat docked and blew its shrill whistle. Hundreds of people on both sides of the shore came down to the river **to see if the comet had fallen into the Mississippi River.**

According to the census, only 12,181 whites live in Illinois Territory.

The thick timber and numerous river bottoms in Illinois make it an excellent place for raising hogs. They eat practically anything and can grub for acorns. They are impervious to snake bites and usually consume the offending reptile. The hogs were usually butchered after the first hard freeze, to retard spoilage. "Fried down" and smoked meat remained edible for many months.

A group of surveyors is sent by the Madison administration to lay out and plat the town of Shawneetown. **This makes it the only town besides Washington D.C. to be laid out by the federal government.** Shawneetown is described as having more business activity than any other town west of Pittsburgh.

About 60 percent of the state is covered by tall prairie grasses. Prairie is a French word that means covered by grass. Much of this land was probably covered by timber but fires from lightning and fires started by Indians destroyed much of it. Unable to regenerate, it was replaced by tall prairie grass.

Pioneers begin arriving in southern Illinois in large numbers, mostly southerners of English or Scotch-Irish

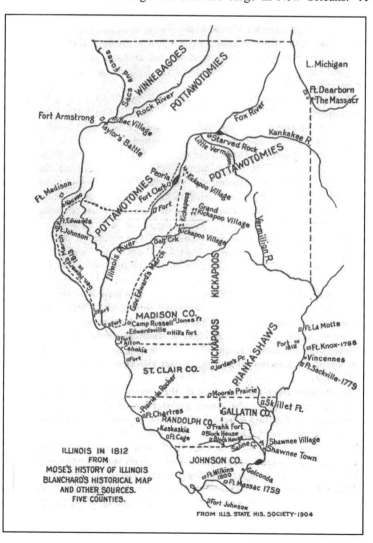

ILLINOIS IN 1812
FROM
MOSE'S HISTORY OF ILLINOIS
BLANCHARD'S HISTORICAL MAP
AND OTHER SOURCES.
FIVE COUNTIES.
FROM ILLS. STATE. HIS. SOCIETY-1904

descent. They fled from states like Kentucky and North Carolina where the rich gained control of the best parcels of land and gained influence in the legislature, threatening to turn those less fortunate into "white niggers." A majority are poor, yeoman farmers who led a simple life of subsistence farming. A saying develops: "The frontier is easy for men and horses, hard on women and oxen."

Corn was the most popular crop for it could be fed to domesticated critters, milled by hand and turned into johnnycakes distilled into whiskey.

Famed New Orleans naturalist James Audubon visits Shawneetown and the Cache Basin Swamp in southern Illinois.

1811 - The Shawnee Chief **Tecumseh** and his brother, known as The Prophet, criss-cross southern Illinois in an effort to unite tribes against the encroaching Americans. He bans the use of American goods and "firewater." He also forbade the sale of any more land to the Americans. He sided with the British in the War of 1812, and his forces were defeated at the battle of Tippecanoe Creek in Indiana, near the Illinois border. Tecumseh is later slain at the battle of Thames at Canada. In Illinois, the followers of Main Poc, a powerful Potawatomie, made life difficult for isolated settlers and weary travelers. At Alton, one man was killed and another wounded.

The first steamboat to come down the Ohio River to Cairo is the *Comet*.

A massive earthquake, due to slippage at the New Madrid Fault, destroys Fort Massac. It had been rebuilt after the Revolutionary War, so ordered by George Washington. It was quickly rebuilt after the earthquake as a fortification during the War of 1812. A replica of the 1794 fort, with vertical timbers, has been reconstructed near present-day Metropolis and features tours and a historic museum. A statue of George Rogers Clark overlooks the Ohio River. **Quincy** has also erected a statue honoring Clark.

The earthquake would have probably been about an 8.4 on the present Richter scale. It collapsed some bluffs along the river, caused the Mississippi to temporarily flow backwards, formed Reelfoot Lake on the Kentucky-Tennessee border, changed the course of the river and formed new islands in it. Because the area was so sparsely settled, there were few deaths. It rang church bells in Philadelphia and people as far away as Quebec felt the tremors. The entire state only had a population of about 5,000 at this time. This "prime event," the "great shakes" as old timers called it was said to have shaken the ground in long waves that would rock and roll. Due to the basket-like construction of pioneer homes back then, where no iron or nails were used, there was only damage. One eyewitness said that the stock was very much disturbed and frightened; horses nickering, cattle lowing, hogs squealing, chickens squawking. The domestic animals all came running to the house for protection.

There were numerous aftershocks that lasted from November until March of 1812.

The federal government begins constructing the National Road (Route 40). It will run from Baltimore to St. Louis. It stops when it reaches Vandalia. The stoppage is due to a lack of funds and a dispute over whether it should end at Alton or Illinoistown. Route 40 eventually is extended through East St. Louis.

1812 –During the War of 1812 against the British and Indians, Territorial Governor Ninian Edwards assembled about 350 Illinois frontiersmen at **Fort Russell**, a wooden stockade just north of present-day Edwardsville. They were organized as mounted cavalry, and they were supplanted by 3 companies of United States Rangers commanded by Colonel Russell. They moved north along the Illinois as far as Lake Peoria and destroyed tribes that had allied themselves with the British, suffering only 1 casualty. Future governors John Reynolds and Thomas Carlin participated in the campaign.

Other Illinois forts included Fort Armstrong at Rock Island and Fort Crawford at Prairie du Chein and Fort Clark at Peoria.

There are no battles with the British fought in Illinois during the War of 1812 but British influence coupled with bribes cause the natives to wreak havoc on settlers in the area. About 22 forts are built in settlements along the Mississippi from Alton to Kaskaskia. Settlers are murdered at **Covington, Carlyle and Albion**.

Territorial Governor Ninian Edwards meets with tribal leaders at Cahokia in a vain effort to dissuade them from the warpath.

The Northwest Indians, led by the Shawnee chief Tecumseh, declared war on white settlers in a last desperate attempt to save their homeland. In April a farm on the outskirts of Fort Dearborn was attacked, causing all the settlers to enter the stockade for protection. News came in July that war against Great Britain had been declared. The Fort's commander, Captain Heald, was ordered to evacuate the fort and proceed to Fort Wayne, Indiana. The evacuation took place in August, consisting of 55 soldiers, 30 friendly Miami warriors, 12 volunteer militia, 9 women and 18 children. They had gone barely more than a mile when the attack came. All the militia were killed and 2 women and 12 children fell victim to the onslaught. Captain Heald surrendered on the promise survivors would be spared. About 6 of the captives were tortured and killed. All told, about 60 whites and 15 Indians were killed. Many of those who remained were taken back to Indian villages. Captain Heald and his wife managed to escape, and many of those remaining were eventually rescued. But the fort was destroyed and would not be rebuilt until July of 1816.

1813 – The territorial legislature passes an important preemption law. For years settlers were coming to the area to settle on lands, but could not

Sweet's Tavern at Kaskaskia-visited in 1824 by Lafayette

buy them because no land office had been established for that purpose. Those who had settled on the land and had made improvements were now given the first option to buy the land when it came up for sale. This new law changed everything. Squatters were allowed to pay 1/20th of the purchase price of a quarter section of land (160 acres.) Squatter anxiety dissolved, leading to a land rush.

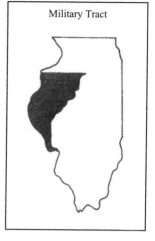

Military Tract

Suffrage in Illinois at this time is limited to white males who were 21 years of age and were freeholders (owned land).

Illinois and Missouri are placed under the control of General Benjamin Howard of St. Louis, much to the disgust of Ninian Edwards. Under his orders, Fort Clark is built at **Peoria** and it forms the basis for the beginning of that city.

Conrad Will (Will County) begins an extensive salt works operation along the Big Muddy south of **Murphysboro**. The town of **Brownsville**, once the 3rd largest town in Illinois but now extinct, developed near the site.

1814 – Several members of the **Abel Moore** and **Reason Reagan** families are killed near the Alton/**Wood River** settlement. Only one of the attacking party was killed as the others managed to escape the clutches of a company of rangers led by **Captain Samuel Whiteside**. The dead Indian had the bloody scalp of Mrs. Reagan dangling from his belt.

The first newspaper in Illinois is Matthew Duncan's *Herald*, printed at Kaskaskia.

The Goshen Road is extended from Shawneetown to Edwardsville. It reaches Alton in 1839.

Illinoisans suffer two War of 1812 defeats in the north. The first occurs at Rock Island and another takes place at Prairie du Chein.

The federal government sets aside nearly three million acres of land in central/western Illinois, between the Illinois and Mississippi Rivers (and north of Alton) as land bounties to veterans who served in the War of 1812. The government was rich in land and poor in currency, so it followed a precedent established after the Revolutionary War. This becomes known as the Military Tract.

The territorial legislature enacts a law offering a bounty of $50.00 for the body of any Indian killed attacking an Illinois village.

1815 – The Treaty of Ghent, negotiated by Henry Clay and John Quincy Adams, ends the War of 1812. The treaty essentially provides for a return to the status quo before the war broke out in 1812. For a second time, Americans had invaded Canada in an effort to wrest control of that territory, but this attack, like the one during the Revolution, ended in failure.

In the aftermath of the War of 1812, the Americans build Fort Armstrong at Rock Island and Fort Edwards at Warsaw.

The first book printed in Illinois Country is a compilation of territorial laws by Nathaniel Pope.

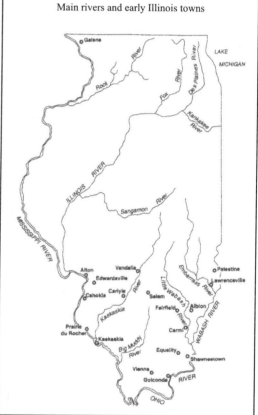

Main rivers and early Illinois towns

1816 – The U.S. Congress, at the behest of the Illinois Territory, appropriates $8,000 for the purpose of cutting out a road from Shawneetown to Kaskaskia. After Kaskaskia declined, when the capital was moved to Vandalia, the road went to St. Louis by way of **Benton** and **DuQuoin**.

Thanks to John Marshall, a prominent merchant and trader, **Shawneetown** had the **first bank in the state of Illinois**. He chartered the bank in 1816, with permission of the territorial legislature. It could not charge more than six percent interest, and it had the authority to issue its own currency. Shawneetown soon was referred to as the financial capital of the state. When developers from **Chicago** traveled 300 miles south and sought a $2,000 loan, the **bank officials refused because it thought Chicago was too far north and too far from navigable rivers to ever amount to anything**.

Around 1800, people from the Ohio River Valley, who wanted to go to St. Louis, floated down the river by flatboat and landed at Shawneetown. They went overland from there to St. Louis because it was difficult for flatboats to go upstream. Shawneetown's location near the Ohio, Wabash, and Mississippi Rivers led to rapid population growth and to its becoming an important commercial center. But the bank closed in 1823 due to stiff competition from the bank at St. Louis.

Monroe County is formed from parts of Randolph and St. Clair Counties.

John Jacob Astor, fur-trading baron, sends a representative to Chicago, Jean Baptiste Beaubien, to open a branch trading post for his American Fur Company.

Territorial governor Ninian Edwards hoodwinks the Indians into believing that a canal connecting the Illinois River to Lake Michigan, and they turn over a hundred-mile strip of land for a trifle.

Fort Armstrong is established at the south end of **Rock Island**. Fort Edwards is built at **Warsaw** for protection from the Potawatomi Indians.

1817 – The minimum amount of public land that can be purchased is reduced to 80 acres.

Albion is founded by a couple of affluent Englishmen, **Morris Birkbeck and George Flower**. The two were unhappy with political and economic life in England. It was Flower who helped convince Robert Owen to establish his utopian religious town of New Harmony, on the Wabash River in Indiana. Near the Wabash River on Illinois' east border, **Albion** was away from slavery in the south, away from brutal cold in the north, and away from the troubles of the Napoleonic Wars in Europe. Together, they purchased more than 26,000 acres and advertised extensively to attract working-class Brits. By 1818 they had 200 settlers, mostly from Surrey, Liverpool and Bristol. They secured food and supplies from settlers in "Harmonie," Indiana. Birbeck's *Notes on a Journey* and *Letters From Illinois* were widely read and attracted many visitors and settlers. The town's chief claim to fame was the creation of the first public library in the state.

Settlers in Albion brought with them the Georgian style of architecture, popular in England at the time, reflected in their 1842-built library.

Albion, **Bishop Hill** and **Nauvoo** are examples of *colony* settlements within the state. In all, there were about 40 such settlements of varying makeup and size. Colony settlements were established by groups of people who had one thing in common. Albion was an English settlement. Nauvoo was a Mormon town. Bishop Hill was Swedish. Hecker was a German settlement. **Princeton, Galesburg and Wethersfield (now part of Kewanee)** were all established by church groups who were unhappy with their congregational life on the east coast.

The first log cabin in Sangamon County (Springfield) is built.

The first steamboat to come up the Mississippi as far north as St. Louis/Illinoistown arrives.

Nathaniel Pope added 14 northern counties

1818 – The Territorial Legislature charters the Bank of Cairo, a land bank created for the purpose of developing 1800 acres at the peninsula where the Ohio meets the Mississippi.

The oldest English-speaking Catholic parish in Illinois is established at the O'Hare settlement near present-day **Ruma**.

East St. Louisans get their first taste of corrupting public officials in 1818. They bribed a public official who was taking the census so he would pad his numbers. Some families were counted twice to insure that the figure of 40,000 would be reached, the number needed to insure the status of statehood. It took a lot of padding of the census figures along with some creative accounting to push the figure to 40,258 (even visitors to the state were counted). As certain officials looked the other way, Illinois sneaked into the Union illegally with a mere 34,620 residents, **making it the smallest state ever admitted**.

President Monroe, who signed the act of statehood, had earlier visited Illinois country, thought the area to be "miserably poor" and would never attain a sufficient number of settlers to ever be admitted to the confederacy.

Newspaperman **Daniel Pope Cook** (Cook County) and **Nathaniel Pope** (Pope County) were behind the push for statehood, and with good foresight, Pope pushed the boundary of Illinois forty miles north of the boundary set by the Northwest Ordinance, so that the new state would border on Lake Michigan and include the valuable lead mines at **Galena**.

Nathaniel Pope was Daniel Pope Cook's uncle. Ninian Edwards was Cook's future father-in-law. Pope was the territory's delegate to Congress in Washington D.C. His lobbying efforts resulted in the creation of an enabling act in the House of Representatives outlining the necessary steps and procedures. In April Congress was preparing to vote on the bill when delegate Pope submitted an amendment that changed the course of Illinois history. His proposal pushed the northern boundary of the state roughly 41 miles farther north. This gave the new state a shoreline on Lake Michigan, and his foresight meant that 14 counties plus the city of Chicago would be in Illinois instead of the future state of Wisconsin. Without that extra territory, Illinois would rank about sixteenth in population.

Cook, who lived in **Kaskaskia**, wrote editorials in the *Illinois Intelligencer* campaigning for statehood. Territorial Governor Ninian Edwards appointed Cook the clerk of the territorial legislature. At the close of its 1817 session, Pope proposed a census be taken to see if Illinois had the 40,000 minimum population required. Judge Pope predicted that by the adoption of such a line Illinois might become at some future time "the keystone to the perpetuity of the Union." The inclusion of this northern land to the

Territory added to Illinois by statehood

state of Illinois helped Illinois identify with northern states instead of the South. The counties in this northern district gave Lincoln the presidency, and Grant (Galena) to Illinois. The first capital of Illinois (the 21st state) was located at **Kaskaskia**. **Shadrack Bond** became the first Governor (annual salary of $1,000) and Pierre Menard the Lieutenant Governor.

Morris Birbeck

Illinois' first meat packing plant is built near the mouth of **Wood River**.

John McLean of **Shawneetown** became the state's first congressman, defeating Cook by 14 votes. (McLean's brother, William McLean, founded the town of **McLeansboro**.)

But a year later the seat of government is moved to **Vandalia** and Kaskaskia declines rapidly in importance.

Thirty-three delegates met in August at Kaskaskia to construct a frame of government. The Illinois constitution borrows heavily from the one in Indiana. The governor is given extensive appointive powers. While most executive officers were required to be U.S. citizens for 30 years, this proviso was omitted for the office of lieutenant governor so that recently naturalized Pierre Menard could fill the post. The practice of having indentured servants was sanctioned by the new Constitution. The new state constitution did not free any existing slaves in Illinois, despite the fact that the Northwest Ordinance of 1787 prohibited slavery. Arthur St. Clair interpreted the clause forbidding slavery to apply only to new slaves, not existing ones. However, no new slaves were allowed to be brought in, and no further indentured servants were to be imported.

Gazetteer author John Mason Peck

President Monroe signed the congressional resolution creating the 21st state on December 3, 1818.

The only grounds for divorce at this time are bigamy, adultery and impotence.

Ninian Edwards gives up farming and moves from Kaskaskia to **Edwardsville** and becomes a land speculator.

Morris Birbeck of **Albion** writes *Letters From Illinois*, printed in Philadelphia and London. Birbeck and George Flower found an English colony in Edwards County on Boltenhouse Prairie. The two men had a falling out when the younger Flower married Eliza Andrews, a woman Birbeck had intended to marry. Flower was responsible for the founding of Albion while Birbeck settled a few miles away at a place he called Wanborough. New families came down the Ohio and landed at Shawneetown, then walked the 45 miles north to Albion. Birbeck drowned in 1825 while trying to cross a flooded river with his horse. Flower and his wife lived on and the pair subsequently **died on the same day** in their daughter's house. It was thought that farming on prairie soils was difficult due to the thick grass cover but it was Birbeck who argued and persuaded otherwise. Until Birbeck, nearly all Illinois settlements were along timbered watercourses.

John Mason Peck, a Baptist missionary, compiles a gazetteer and attracts many immigrants to Illinois by writing about it in glowing terms. Peck also wrote *A Guide For Emigrants* in 1831.

In the Treaty of Edwardsville, negotiated by Ninian Edwards and August Choteau with 5 tribes, the 1803 treaty is confirmed and over 7 million acres of additional land is ceded in consideration for annual monetary payments and 640 acres in Missouri.

Lincoln's mother, Nancy Hanks, dies from "**milk sickness**" while the family is living in Indiana. The family will move to Illinois, in part, to escape the disease. The family had moved to Indiana from Kentucky to get away from slavery and due to difficulties with land titles in Indiana. Lincoln bemoaned the lack of educational opportunities in Indiana and when he left that state his only education was learning readin', writin', and cipherin' (math).

Edward Coles frees his slaves: drawn in 1886 by an unknown artist

1819 – The Depression of 1819 (lasting to nearly 1825) causes bank failures and ruins land speculators such as **Rufus Easton**, the founder of **Alton**. Local politicos **Ninian Edwards** and **Nathaniel Pope** take advantage of Easton's hardship and try to gain title to Easton's former land holdings. The matter dragged on for years until a settlement was finally reached. Easton then moved to St. Louis and had a daughter named Mary who married a certain George Sibley. **The couple was responsible for the founding of Lindenwood College in St. Charles.**

Virginian Edward Coles migrates to Illinois and on reaching the border of the state unexpectedly frees his slaves. He gave each family 160 acres of land. Thomas Jefferson, his neighbor and friend back in Virginia, tried to talk him out of manumission. Coles was elected the state's 2nd governor in 1822, and his pro-slave political enemies, at the Edwardsville courthouse, successfully charged him with illegally freeing his slaves. Coles had unwittingly violated a new law, passed just before his arrival in the state. Coles had made out the necessary certificates of manumission, but failed to post $1,000 bond for each slave freed, as required by law. The bond was thought to be necessary to ensure that the public would not have to support the newly freed slave.

Illinois enacts its first Black Code, based on laws in Virginia and Kentucky. It is forbidden for someone to bring slaves into the state for the purpose of emancipating them.

Illinois' two senators persuade the U.S. Congress to make a land grant closer to the geographic center of the state for the purpose of a new capital. This, they argued would increase the sale of public lands and bring money into the federal treasury. The site selected was called Vandalia, located on the west bank of the Kaskaskia River. It was a wilderness area and virtually uninhabited. Our first statehouse was a modest two-story frame building, built at a cost of $500. When the Second General Assembly met in December of 1820, lodging was so scarce, many of the men had to sleep in the capitol building.

Vandalia receives a boost in population when Ferdinand Ernst, a wealthy German liberal, brings in 30 families from Hanover to escape political repression.

In **Belleville**, two men get into a quarrel. It seems that **Timothy Bennett's** horse repeatedly got into Alfonso Stuart's cornfield and ate his crops. Each made serious threats against the other. Two of their friends, Nathan Fikes and Jacob Short, thought the affair to be silly and proposed that the matter be settled with a sham duel, using rifles with powder but no bullets. The duel was fought on a vacant lot according to code duello with Fikes and Short acting as seconds. Bennett loaded his rifle with ammunition, fired first, and killed his opponent. Bennett was the **first man in St. Clair County to be hanged**. It was done on September 3, 1821, in front of a large crowd.

The Kickapoo tribes of the Illinois Indians sign a treaty at **Edwardsville** and cede large sections of their land in central and southern Illinois, including land in Clark County. Ninian Edwards, Benjamin Stephenson and Auguste Chouteau were present at the ceremony. Nearly a million new acres are gained.

Section of wooden pipe from U.S. Saltworks at Equality

The Gallatin County salines near **Equality**, using over 1,000 slaves, produces nearly 300,000 bushels of salt. The Great Half Moon salt lick is one of the largest in the U.S. and covers about 13 acres. The making of salt at Equality ceased about 1870 because it could be produced cheaper elsewhere. The brine was collected in large metal kettles that were brought in from Pittsburgh. The kettles held about 60 gallons of water. A fire was kept constantly burning under the kettles. The fuel was wood from nearby trees. The water was brought from the salt wells to the kettles by wooden pipes made from twelve-inch diameter trees that had the centers bored out. Iron bands were fitted over the jointed sections of the logs. Around 1840 coal came to be used as fuel instead of wood and new furnaces were built.

During the early years of working the salines, the bones of a woolly mammoth were discovered.

A large and important salt lick at **Danville** is converted into commercial production of salt.

Edwardsville has the state's first library, but lack of support causes its dissolution in six years.

Jacksonville has a total population of nineteen souls.

1820 – The cost of public land is reduced to $1.25 an acre. Thus an entire farm can be purchased for as little as $100 dollars. Illinois has a preemption law that gives squatters the first opportunity to buy the land that they were on before it was surveyed and offered for sale at the land office.

The state capital is moved to **Vandalia**, a more centralized location and away from the flooding Mississippi River. There was no existing town on the site but it was on the Kaskaskia River, with a good spring, and surrounded by woods and good farmland.

The state's population at this time is 55,211.

The First Bank of Illinois is chartered to deal with the problem of a shortage of capital, but it does poorly. The parent bank was at **Vandalia** with branches at **Edwardsville**, **Brownsville** (Jackson County),

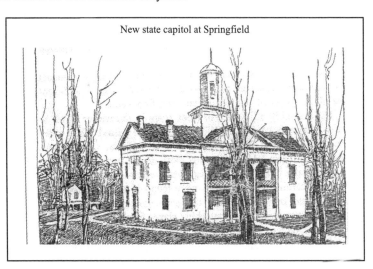
New state capitol at Springfield

Shawneetown and **Alton**. The printing presses were set in motion and "wildcat" bank notes or paper currency was printed. Gold or silver money was referred to as specie. The bank notes slowly fell in value to the point where they were worth only 25 cents on the dollar.

Illinois at this time has only 22 counties (eventually 102).

The first steamboat to travel up the Illinois River makes it as far north as **Peoria**.

A 33 foot-wide road is cut connecting Shawneetown with **Edwardsville, Alton, and Carlyle**, with a branch to Kaskaskia. It is called the Goshen Road.

The national census shows that there are only 917 Negroes in the state of Illinois, mostly household servants that are leftovers from the early French regime. Plantation slavery, so well rooted in the Deep South, simply does not exist in Illinois.

The census shows marriage to be uncommonly common as only one single female trying to make it on her own is recorded in the Illinois head count. Men on the frontier tended to marry earlier than men in towns and settled areas. Most women gave birth every other year and had an average of ten children, with many young ones dying before reaching the age of 7. Children who reached that age could expect to live to about age 50. There was no need for nursing homes on the Illinois frontier since only two percent of the population was over 60 years of age. But part of this was due to Illinois being settled by younger couples who did not reach old age until about 1860.

Henry Clay of Kentucky helps forge the Missouri Compromise in the U.S. Congress. According to its terms, Missouri is admitted to the union as a slave state, Maine as a free state, and slavery is prohibited north of the 36 degree-30 minute line of latitude in the territory that was part of the Louisiana Purchase.

Land sales in Illinois dwindle for ten years after the U.S. government reduces the price from two dollars an acre to a dollar and a quarter and acre, but now requires cash instead of credit. Too many farmers had defaulted on their loans but remained on the land. The minimum purchase was 160 acres.

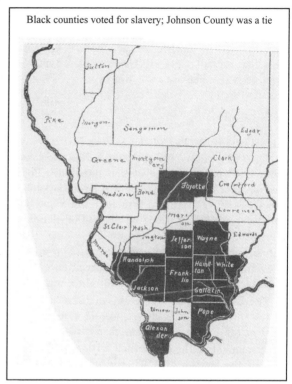

Black counties voted for slavery; Johnson County was a tie

1822 – The Illinois constitution prohibits Shadrach Bond from succeeding himself. Incredibly, Edward Coles, who had been in the state a mere 3 years, wins the governorship, defeating 3 rivals. Two candidates were anti-slave and two were pro. Coles had settled in Illinois as owner of 6,000 acres, purchased on a previous trip in 1818. Coles, a former secretary to James Madison, secured a commission from Madison to become registrar of the recently established land office in Edwardsville. For the next two years after his election, the issue of whether the fledgling state would be slave or free, was hotly debated in taverns, inns, churches and in the legislature.

Shadrach Bond: first delegate to Congress from the Illinois Territory and the state's first governor

Coles strenuously argued that the Black Code should be abolished and all slavery in Illinois should be abolished. When the general assembly voted on whether to submit the question of slavery to a convention, the issue passed in the senate but fell a vote short in the House. A fellow named Nicholas Hansen of Pike County, who had switched from yes to no, was dealt with swiftly. The next day the House conducted an inquiry into his election and decided that his rival had actually won. John Shaw was summoned to **Vandalia**, and his positive vote made the difference. Poor Hansen was also stripped of his position as a canal commissioner. It was expected that had the call for a convention been successful, it would have led to Illinois becoming a slave state and perhaps part of the Confederacy. Slavery was not totally abolished in the state until 1848.

The state has only 4 weekly newspapers at this point in time: The *Vandalia Intelligencer*, the *Edwardsville Spectator*, the *Kaskaskia Republican*, and the *Illinois Gazette* of Shawneetown. The two southern newspapers supported the convention, and the two northern ones opposed.

EDWARDSVILLE SPECTATOR 1820

FOR SALE, AN INDENTURED NEGRO MAN: Said Negro is about 23 years of age, and has 13 years to serve; is well acquainted with farming; a pretty good rough shoemaker, and has attended a distillery and possesses good moral character. For further information apply to the printer.

Morris Birbeck of **Albion** on the "English Prairie," the Englishman who had arrived in the state only 3 years before Coles, wrote a series of "Jonathan Freeman" letters that pointed out the evils of slavery, and that it would cast a dark shadow over the state. At the time the number of free and slave states in the union were equal. It is reasonable to believe that Birbeck's eloquence helped turn the tide. James Simeone, in *Democracy and Slavery in Frontier Illinois*, asserts that as a whole, Baptists and Calvinists in "The Bottomland Republic" favored the convention, while most Methodists and Scots-Irish Presbyterians opposed it. Yankee townsmen were usually against slavery, while southern yeoman farmers were sympathetic to it. In the 1824 general election, the anti-slave forces won by a margin of 57 to 43 percent and the

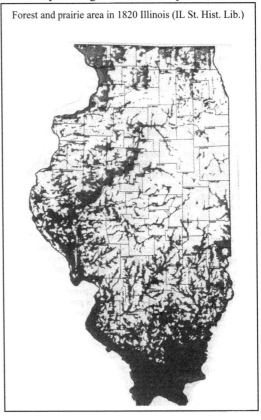

Forest and prairie area in 1820 Illinois (IL St. Hist. Lib.)

special assemblage was never held. This was the last time that slavery would be an issue in Illinois but it would be another 20 years before the state courts abolished slavery completely in the state. Many historians feel that it was Coles, Cook and Birbeck who saved Illinois from becoming a slave state.

Due to the Greek war for independence against the Turks, the Greek Revival style of architecture becomes popular, reflect in the construction of county courthouses. The old state capitol building in **Springfield**, designed by Rague, has a pedimented Greek portico.

The first steamboat reaches **Galena**.

Daniel Cook champions the cause in Congress of building a canal that would join the Illinois River to Lake Michigan.

1823 - There is a Bloody Island duel at Illinoistown/St. Louis between U.S. District Attorney Joshua Barton and Thomas Rector. Barton, who had accused General Rector of corruption in office, is killed in an exchange of gunfire.

It is estimated that income from the salt works in Gallatin County provides 1/7th of the state revenues. Salt was a necessity for preserving food and for tanning hides.

The settlement of **Galena** begins when a man named Moses Meeker obtains a lease from the federal government to begin mining operations there. (Even though Illinois has achieved statehood, much of its land is still owned by the federal government.) Picturesquely located on a high bluff on the Galena River, with access to the Mississippi River, the city grew by leaps and bounds due to prosperity brought on by the lead mines. With more than 10,000 men flocking to town to mine and smelt the lead, it quickly replaced Shawneetown as the most important city in the state. Galena's chief problem was that it was smack dab in the middle of Indian country, and there was constant danger from raiding parties. And being so far north, getting enough supplies there in winter was difficult. The first steamboat to arrive in Galena was the *Virginia*. **Galena has the distinction of being the nation's first mining boomtown.**

Major Stephen Long arrives in Chicago on a government survey project and agrees that a canal through the portage site is feasible. Long would later explore the plains west of the Mississippi and erroneously label them the **Great American Desert**. Henry R. Schoolcraft, who wrote a glowing report about Chicago, enthusiastically agreed with the assessment.

Lewis C. Beck publishes a gazetteer of Illinois and Missouri and describes Illinois as a "dreary uninhabited waste."

The town of **Salem** is founded as the halfway station on the stagecoach route between Vincennes and St. Louis.

St. Louis begins using coal mined from the bluffs along the American Bottom.

Native-American with salt from U.S. Salines at Equality

1824 - Governor Edward Coles is convicted (at the courthouse in Edwardsville) of illegally freeing his slaves by his political enemies.

Illinois is divided into 3 political districts and in the race for the U.S. Presidency, J.Q. Adams wins in one district and Andrew Jackson wins in two. Of the four candidates running for president, none gained a majority of the electoral votes so the election was thrown to the U.S. House of Representatives. John Pope Cook, Illinois' only member of the House of Representatives, disregarded the will of his constituents and cast his vote for J.Q. Adams, a move that would later haunt him.

1825 - Don Adams of **Edwardsville** sets up a press and begins the **first commercial production of castor oil in southern Illinois**. His press produced 500 gallons of oil that sold for $2.50 a gallon. By 1830 he had two presses producing 10,000 gallons annually. **Sparta** and **Chester** were two other towns that became heavily involved in castor oil production. The oil was used for medicinal purposes and as a lubricant. After the petroleum refining process was discovered, castor crops and castor oil production fell off dramatically in Illinois.

Reverend John Mason Peck, a Baptist minister from the American Bible Institute back east, builds Rock Springs Academy/Seminary between **Belleville** and **Greenville near Shiloh**. Its first roster included about 25 students. In 1832 he moved the school to Upper Alton. A fundraising effort back east netted the handsome sum of $10,000 from a Boston physician, **Benjamin Shurtleff**. This act of philanthropy prompted the trustees to change the name to Shurtleff College. In 1957 the facilities were purchased by Southern Illinois University that also held classes in the old East St. Louis High on Tenth and Ohio in **East St. Louis**. SIU would build a new campus in **Edwardsville**, and the old **Alton** facility became the site of its dental school.

Thomas Ford 1800-1850

One of the classroom buildings at SIU in Edwardsville is named the Peck Building in his honor.

The Erie Canal is completed, running from Buffalo on Lake Erie to Troy on the Hudson River. The *Seneca Chief* makes the first run from Buffalo to New York harbor. A barrel of Lake Erie water is ceremoniously poured into the harbor to commemorate the event. This links the entire Great Lakes region and the Midwest with the Atlantic seaboard and European trade. Goods shipped to the Midwest would now come through Chicago rather than New Orleans and St. Louis. More than anything else, the growth and success of Chicago as one of America's greatest cities is now insured. It will also bring Illinois settlers from New England and New York (Yankees) and help ensure that the state remains loyal to the Union in the Civil War. Interestingly, the new settlers brought with them a spirit of vigor and energy and a hard work ethic that they saw lacking in the earlier settlers who were now their neighbors. They generally regarded these "ragtags" from Kentucky, Tennessee, Virginia and North Carolina as inferiors, barely one step up from the savage Indians. The Yankee settlers were generally more prosperous, better educated and more eager to establish schools and newspapers than their predecessors.

The southerners resented this and began telling tall tales about inept Yankee city slickers who had book learnin' but little common sense. Anyone cheated in a business deal was said to have been "yankeed."

A good illustration of this culture clash can be found in a 1919 book by Christina Tillson, *A Woman's Story of Pioneer Illinois*. In it, she relates how she and her husband move from Connecticut to **Hillsboro**, and discover significant differences with their neighbors.

Future governor Thomas Ford is practicing law at this time in **Waterloo** and at **Edwardsville** with his half-brother, George Forquer, of Edwardsville. Ford's *History of Illinois* was published shortly after his death in 1850.

1826 – The Illinois Supreme Court reverses the decision of the circuit court and relieves Edward Coles of the penalties and fines for freeing his slaves.

1827 – A new state-maintained prison facility with twenty-five cells is authorized by the legislature to be built at **Alton**. Illinois' first prison was on a plot of ten acres and was financed from land sales belonging to the salines near **Equality**. By 1857 it had 286 cells. A second prison was built in 1858 at Joliet. The Alton prison was abandoned in 1860 after the conditions there were heavily criticized by reformer **Dorothea Dix**. During the Civil War Confederate prisoners were sent to the old prison facility at Alton with disastrous results. When a smallpox epidemic broke out the town's population became alarmed at the death rate, so officials moved the captives to a place in the Mississippi River that became named Smallpox Island. Well over one thousand men died in confinement.

A law is enacted imposing a fine of $500 or six months in jail for anyone found harboring a runaway slave.

Settlers up north participate in the Winnebago War near **Galena** and Fort Snelling. Several prominent Indians were arrested. Some were executed, others were released. Black Hawk was among those released. After its conclusion, Chief Red Bird signs several treaties yielding four and a half million acres in return for land in Iowa and annual payments of salt, tobacco and free blacksmithing services. Pierre Menard was one of the chief negotiators of these treaties. Black Hawk would have nothing to do with these agreements.

Gurdon S. Hubbard earns the nickname, the **Paul Revere of Illinois**. Hubbard frantically rode from Fort Dearborn to **Danville** in less than 24 hours in a desperate attempt to secure volunteers to defend the fort from an impending Indian attack. Fortunately, the Winnebago Indians never attacked. Hubbard was responsible for hacking out the eastern trace that went from Chicago to Vincennes. Hubbard's Trace eventually became Illinois Route 1.

A group of soldiers from Fort Dearborn cut a channel through the sandbar blocking direct entrance to the Chicago River.

1829 - Southern Illinois in particular, and Illinois as a whole, became a magnet for emigrants looking for economic opportunity. It seemed as if all roads and rivers from back East led to this state. They

Indian land cessions in Illinois

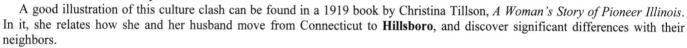

came from New York and New England, traveling along the Mohawk River Valley and the Erie Canal through the Great Lakes. From the middle states like Pennsylvania, Maryland, and Virginia, they floated down the Ohio River to southern Illinois. Through Ohio and Indiana they could travel along the National Road. From southern states they went through the famous Cumberland Gap, then followed Daniel Boone's Wilderness Road through Kentucky and into southern Illinois.

Early pioneer song: Way down upon the Wabash/ Such land was never known;/ If Adam had passed over it,/ The soil he'd surely own;/ He'd think it was the garden/ He'd played in when a boy/ And straight pronounce it Eden,/ In the state of El-a-noy.

Typical early pioneer log cabin (Illinois State Historical Library)

The powerful Wiggins Ferry monopoly at Illinoistown/**East St. Louis** convinces the legislature to pass a bill for the construction of the Great Western Mail Route, which is an extension of the National Road from Vandalia to East St. Louis.

The state's first institution of higher learning, Illinois College at **Jacksonville**, is established.

The first steamboat reaches **Peoria**.

Gurdon Hubbard establishes Chicago as a meat packing area by driving 400 hogs there to be butchered. Four years later he builds a warehouse and a packing plant.

1830 - The racial enclave of **Brooklyn** is founded by eleven families, ex-slaves from Missouri, which was a slave state. The community became a haven for maroons - runaway slaves. The town was platted and named in 1837 by white abolitionists. After the Black Valley was destroyed in the 1917 race riot in East St. Louis, a new vice district sprang up in Brooklyn that included taverns, brothels, gambling parlors and dance halls.

The state legislature outlaws the use of the pillory and whipping post.

The town of **Old Madison**, near Gillham Landing on Choteau Island in the Mississippi, is established near the Chain of Rocks. In its early years it is a flourishing village visited often by steamboats.

In the romantic (but dangerous) days of steam boating, there are more than seventy-two boiler explosions on the Mississippi, killing more than 600 people in the decade of the 1830s.

Abe Lincoln's family moves from Indiana to Illinois. Abe was twenty-one at the time, lived in **New Salem**, and found a job splitting rails and later operated flatboats on the Sangamon River. Lincoln lived in Kentucky 7 years and Indiana 14 years.

A legendary and romantic figure from **Hardin County** was **Dr. Anna Bigsby (Bixby)**. She studied medicine in Philadelphia but came to practice in southern Illinois. Her fame spread quickly when she solved the riddle of milksick that caused mysterious deaths every fall. **Abe Lincoln's** mother, Nancy Hanks, died in 1818 from the disease when he was only ten years old. Superstition attributed the sickness to witches but Bigsby proved it was caused by the white snake root plant, also known as nightshade. Farmers eliminated the problem by destroying the plant wherever it was found.

Farther north, the city of **Chicago** is finally platted by James Thompson, a surveyor for the state canal commission. He also gave names to streets in the northern loop area.

Chief Black Hawk

Illinois now has 56 counties. There are 6 land offices in the state: **Palestine, Quincy, Edwardsville, Vandalia, Shawneetown, Kaskaskia**. A few years later, there will also be land offices in **Dixon, Galena**, and Chicago.

Settlers coming into Illinois from back east often traveled in wagons dubbed "**prairie schooners.**" These ponderous, wide-bodied vehicles had canvas tops and were likened to schooners with white sails. The Conestoga wagon was another name used to describe these 4-wheeled behemoths. The drivers often smoked cigars, and these were labeled "**stogies,**" which became a slang expression for a cigar.

John Dixon obtains a contract to carry the mail on the new **Peoria-Galena** route. Where the trail crosses the Rock River he established a ferry service. He then moved his family to the river crossing and founded a town that bears his name.

James Hall establishes in **Vandalia** the *Illinois Monthly Magazine*, the first literary periodical west of the Ohio River.

The state is saved from bankruptcy by Samuel Wiggins, a Cincinnati capitalist who owns the powerful and rich Wiggins Ferry monopoly at Illinoistown/East St. Louis. In debt due to the folly of going into the banking business back in 1821 and issuing bank notes, Wiggins agrees to loan the state $100,000 in return for payments of money from taxes on land with a favorable interest rate on his money.

William McKendree, the first American-born bishop of the Methodist church, donates 480 acres of land to help establish Lebanon Seminary, later called McKendree College.

Illinois Monthly Magazine is published in **Vandalia**. It is the first literary periodical west of the Ohio River.

1831 - Settlements from all over southern Illinois send volunteers to fight in the war against Chief Black Hawk, leader of the Sauk and Fox tribes in northern Illinois. Keokuk, chief of the Sauk Indians, saw the folly of fighting the whites and peacefully moved his people across the Mississippi into Iowa. Black Hawk, a malcontent war chief who had served with Tecumseh, opposed Keokuk and chose war. Ford's *History of Illinois* says Black Hawk was known for his courage and integrity. Abe Lincoln was a captain of Illinois volunteers in the war, but he did not participate in any battles with the Indians. Lincoln's grandfather had been killed by Indians back in 1786. Zachary Taylor and Winfield Scott also fought in the war. It was during this war that he met Vital Jarrot of **Cahokia**, the two Whigs becoming fast friends. Governor John Reynolds of **Belleville** took charge of the militia and made Jarrot his personal adjunct. The 15-week campaign saw the capture of Black Hawk, thus ending the Indian threat in Illinois once and for all.

The problem developed back in 1829 when the federal government, in response to settler demands for farmland, decided to relocate Sauk and Fox Indians from their lands in northwestern Illinois across the Mississippi into Iowa. The war was precipitated

The Battle of Bad Axe

by the destruction of Indian burial grounds to make way for settler corn planting. Most of them obeyed but some, in an effort to retain the land of their forefathers, went on the warpath. Their homes were destroyed and crops were burned. The elderly chief of the Sauk, Black Hawk, tried to negotiate, pointing out that white actions were in violation of signed treaties. But most whites remained insensitive to the wants and needs of the Native Americans. Black Hawk was forced to sign a new treaty. But life in a foreign land proved difficult for the Indians. Game was not plentiful and the land was hard to till. Desperate, Black Hawk and his people violated an 1804 treaty and crossed the river and came back into Illinois to raise crops. When news of the Indians' return reached the whites, they sent out the army and militia. **Besides Abe Lincoln, General Winfield Scott and Colonel Zachary Taylor par-ticipated in the Black Hawk campaign.** Lincoln did not see any military action in the war. Five future governors, including Thomas Ford, also serve in the war. Lincoln was with a group of volunteers that assembled at **Beardstown** where the company he was assigned to elected him captain. The Beardstown volunteers left and traveled to Fort Armstrong at **Rock Island**.

In one of the first skirmishes of the war, a surprise counterattack by the outnumbered Black Hawk scattered the enemy whites and sent the state into near panic. White plight worsened when an attack on settlers resulted in the death of 16, with two young girls being taken captive. At **Kellogg's Grove**, the Indians slaughtered 47 from houses that were built outside the fort. The whites regrouped and put together an overwhelming force of 4,000-armed men. The overmatched Indians were chased into Wisconsin. Sheriff James D. Henry of Sangamon County, brigadier general of volunteers, became the hero of the war for his success at Wisconsin Heights. Black Hawk held off the whites at a battle near present-day Madison. Black Hawk then headed west, hoping to escape across the Mississippi. Both sides, however, reached the river at the same time. Black Hawk tried to surrender but angry whites were out for blood. Black Hawk suffered his final defeat at the battle of **Bad Axe** in what would more appropriately be called a tit for tat slaughter of men, women and children. Sioux Indians, sworn enemies of the Sauk, were employed by the army and waited on the west bank of the river to kill those who made it across. The Indians suffered 600 casualties and the whites 72. The defeat of Black Hawk is significant because it ended the Indian threat in Illinois. He was captured and imprisoned. Later released, Black Hawk died on an Iowa reservation in 1838.

Judge Sydney Breese

The unfortunate war was both needless and avoidable. At war's end, all Indians were expelled from the state, whether they had participated in the war or not. The war marked the passing of the Indian from Illinois country, 150 years after Marquette first met them on one of his voyages.

A 48-foot-tall, 100 ton statue of Black Hawk would later be placed along the Rock River near the Mississippi to honor Chief Black Hawk. It is made of reinforced poured concrete; executed by Lorado Taft, critics feel that the figure is much too peaceful-looking in its countenance.

The winter of the "deep snow" (1830-31) **gives rise to the label of "Egypt" for the lower third of Illinois**. There were crop failures in the north so caravans were organized to go south to purchase grain for food and seed. When others asked where they were going, the voyagers, thinking about the story in the book of Genesis when there was a famine in the land of Canaan, replied: "We're a-goin' to Egypt, just like the story of Joseph and his brothers. In many parts of the state, the snow was six foot deep with drifts that were much deeper.

The 1831 volume of *Breese's Reports* by Sidney Breese, a collection of law reports, was the **first book ever** printed in Illinois.

Abe Lincoln and two other men are paid by Denton Offut to take a boatload of stock down the Sangamon, Illinois, and Mississippi rivers to New Orleans. Lincoln saw slaves on the auction block while he was there.

1832 – **Alton's** first newspaper, *The Spectator*, is founded. A few years later, the Alton *Telegraph* was started.

A man from Grafton, Massachusetts, by the name of James Mason constructs several log cabins at a place where the Illinois River empties into the Mississippi. He lived in **Edwardsville** and was in the real estate business and married into a prominent St. Louis family. His St. Louis friends were concerned that the city of **Alton** was growing so rapidly that it threatened to replace St.

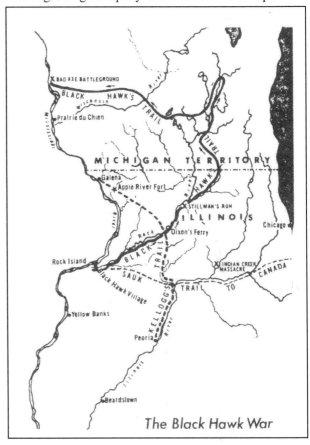

The Black Hawk War

Louis as the premier city in the Riverbend area. Mason and his friends purchased land north of Alton and attempted to have commerce bypass the city by establishing roads, rail lines and ferries at the site. Mason died in 1834, and his widow named the new town **Grafton** after her husband's birthplace. The city enjoyed brief prosperity. Grafton's prosperity waned with the demise of steamboats and the railroads. It was not until the Great River Road was extended in the 1960s did Grafton enjoy a revival.

The first stage of **Alton's** penitentiary with 24 cells is completed.

Ben Godfrey builds a home near **Alton**. Godfrey will be the founder of Monticello College, the first school for girls in the Midwest. Godfrey rejected Edward Clarke's thesis that the physical strain and demanding study in college would permanently damage women's health. The house becomes the property of the William Walters family in 1895. Walters will become a successful farmer and naturalist, collecting Indian artifacts all his life. His large and unique collection will later be housed in the old Godfrey House. Waters' property was at one time the site of an emergency landing field for United States Mail planes, and was laid out as such by Colonel **Charles Lindbergh**. The field had a beacon with a revolving light. Lindbergh and another man built the tower in 3 days. The first night mail flight from St. Louis to Chicago, with 24 total beacons on the route, was flown 0n January 13, 1927. A few years later, R. G. Carpenter of **Alton** built a monoplane that was successfully test flown at Waters Field.

Poet William Cullen Bryant visits the Illinois frontier and is unimpressed. "In looking for a place to feed our horses I asked for corn at the cabin of an old settler named Wilson. Here I saw a fat dusky woman barefoot with 6 children as dirty as pigs and as shaggy as bears. She was delousing one of them and cracking the unfortunate insects between her thumbnails."

Bryant visits the Indian Mounds of southern Illinois and writes about them in his poem, **"The Prairies."**

There is an epidemic of **Asian cholera** in southern Illinois. The disease was first apparent after there was an outbreak among Winfield Scott's troops, brought here to fight the **Black Hawk War**. The disease soon spread to the general population. Little was known about the disease, and it was thought to be caused by **miasma** - inhaling vapors of rotting vegetation. Death came quickly, often within five or six hours. Former governor Ninian Edwards is stricken in Belleville.

It was particularly bad in cities. In 1833 **St. Louis had 3,262 deaths** in a period of six months. If you visit old cemeteries in places like **Pomona** and **Walker Hill**, you'll find that there was another bad outbreak in 1847. In 1847 the *Cairo Delta* reported that

there were deaths on nearly every steamboat on the Mississippi. There was a place just below **Chester** that became a convenient burial spot, and the boat bodies were disposed of quickly.

A druggist in **Jonesboro** sold a remedy called Egyptian Anodyne, its formula supposedly taken from hieroglyphics on the walls of Egyptian tombs. The disease was treated with a variety of ineffectual home remedies that included powdered castor seeds, camphor, snake root tea, grapevine smoked and inhaled into the lungs, and odd combinations of alcoholic spirits sprinkled with mustard seed.

Near a point where the **Big Kincaid Creek** joins the Big Muddy River, the last of the Indians in southern Illinois left for Kansas. William Boon(e), a cousin to Daniel, once lived in the area.

The Illinois Indians sign a treaty and cede all their lands east of the Mississippi except a tract reserved for Ellen

Emigration to the West by Robert Sears

Ducoigne (DuQuoin), the daughter of their late chief.

The Whig Party forms in Illinois, largely in opposition to the policies of President Andrew Jackson of Tennessee, a Democrat. Their symbol is the raccoon. The Whig party, nationally led by Henry Clay and supported by Abe Lincoln, favored spending federal money on internal improvements – roads, canals, and later, railroads. They also advocated high tariffs and a national banking system. In Illinois as well as nationally, the Whig party was a minority party. The Whigs inherited ideas from the old Federalist party of Washington, Adams and Alexander Hamilton – a modern, commercial and industrial nation. The Whig party evolved into the Republican Party. Democrats traced their roots back to Thomas Jefferson and James Madison. They wanted an agrarian nation supported by independent yeoman farmers and distrusted big banks, favored low tariffs, and disliked spending huge sums of money on internal improvements.

Chief Shabbona

Elizabeth Armstrong leads the successful defense of a fort on the Apple River during the Black Hawk War while most of the men are away. The nearby town that later sprouted was named in her honor.

The Great Northern Stage Route, running from **Galena**, through **Quincy**, **Alton**, **Illinoistown**, **Cahokia**, **Waterloo**, and ending in **Chester**, is completed. It was called the Great Road From the North and later the Great River Road.

Fort George Rogers Clark at **Peoria** was rebuilt as preparations were being made for the war with Chief Blackhawk.

The Seminary at **Alton** is founded by the Rev. John Mason Peck. Ben **Godfrey** founds Monticello College for girls.

Hostile Potawatomie Indians massacre 15 men, women and children of the Indian Creek Settlement in north central Illinois. Chief Shabbona had warned the settlers of an impending attack and urged them to flee.

Fort Dearborn on the Chicago River

1833 – Chief Sauganash (Sau-Ko-Noek) is swindled out of Chicago swampland for some whiskey, tobacco and a few trinkets. By 1853 the land sold by the Indians for pennies an acre would be worth $3 million. Seventy-six other chiefs made their mark on the treaty and one signed his name. The first annuity payment was made by piling a heap of goods near the modern corner of Canal and Randolph Streets. The Indians then grabbed what they could carry in their arms in haphazard fashion. The final payment was made in 1835. As many as 6,000 Indians gathered in Chicago to witness the treaty. The Ottawa, Ojibwa, Chippewa and Potawatomie sold 5 million acres of land in northern Illinois and moved west across the Mississippi River. They sold the land to the white invaders for about 2 cents an acre. At this session, many of the braves dressed in war paint and armed themselves with clubs and tomahawks. Before leaving the area forever, they did a mock war dance and marched through the streets and rushed up to every cabin door and brandished their weapons in a threatening manner.

Sauganash saw to it that cooler heads prevailed and that there was no massacre. He was born in Detroit in 1812, the son of an Irish colonel and a Potawatomie maiden. Chicagoans called him Archibald "Billy" Caldwell. He had attended a Jesuit school and knew English. When land speculators moved in they developed a motto: buy the acre, sell by the foot. Billy Caldwell, the half-breed son of a British army officer was the person mainly responsible for convincing the Indians to sign. During the Fort Dearborn Massacre, it was Billy who saved the lives of the Kinzie family. For his role in the treaty, Billy was given two sections of land and an annual $600 annuity by the government. After the ceremony about 30 half-naked braves celebrated by dancing their way from Fort Dearborn to South Water Street.

Startled Illinoisans witness a **Leonids meteor shower** on November 12 and refer to it as "the night the stars fell." A firestorm of shooting stars, silent but overwhelming, filled the sky. This was a spectacular event – a tempest of falling stars over the earth. One account says: "the sky was scored in every direction with shining tracks and

Leonids meteor shower

illuminated with fireballs. The frequency of meteors was estimated to be about half that of flakes of snow in an average snowstorm. Their numbers . . . during the 9 hours that they fell were estimated to be 240,000."

In 1878 historian R.M. Devens listed the event as one of the 100 **most memorable events in U.S. history**. For the religious, morbid, and superstitious, many believed it to be the arrival of Judgment Day. Impromptu prayer meetings were held in many places. These meteor showers are called Leonids for their place of origin is the constellation Leo. They occur around mid November of each year but some years are more spectacular than others. The shower is caused by the Earth being peppered with pebbles about the size of marbles that are vaporized in the Earth's upper atmosphere.

According to one account, an Illinois woman at Chicago said that she washed her hands and face with the stars, as though they had been snowflakes. She carried her baby out to see the sight and saw the stars fall on the baby's face and wiped them off.

Father Loisel constructs the parish house, a private dwelling made of brick in **Cahokia**. Loisel Village in East St. Louis will later be named for him.

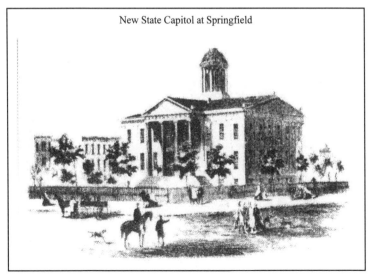
Mary Todd – 1846 daguerreotype

Chicago is incorporated as a village. It has about 150 wooden structures along the Chicago River. Many land speculators foresaw that Chicago had possibilities of developing into a great city, and land prices were booming and population was surging.

The U.S. Congress acts on the recommendations of young army engineer **Robert E. Lee** and appropriates $25,000 to cut a canal through the sand bar blocking the entrance to the Chicago River.

New Yorker **Stephen A. Douglas** arrives in Illinois and begins teaching in subscription schools at **Whitworth and Winchester**. He begins reading law from borrowed books and is later elected to the legislature from **Jacksonville**. In 1843 he was elected to the U.S. Congress at the age of thirty. He used the income from teaching to study law and in 1834 was admitted to the bar and quit teaching.

Ann Rutledge, the first love of Lincoln's life, would die in a few years from a fever at age 22. Lincoln lived in New Salem at the Rutledge tavern and fell in love with the innkeeper's daughter. Sudden death is still a common occurrence on the Illinois frontier where folk remedies, snake oil concoctions, bleedings by barbers and harsh purgatives take their toll. Doctors are mistrusted and are referred to as "sawbones" due to their inclination for amputating infected limbs. Lincoln might have had a much happier life had he married Ann rather than Mary Todd. This love affair is one of the most notable in American history, and much of it came from Lincoln's law partner, William Herndon. Many historians believe Herndon loathed Mary Todd and invented the Rutledge romance to humiliate her. Incidentally, Lincoln was 9 years older than Mary Todd.

Edgar Lee Masters wrote a lovely epitaph for Ann in his *Anthology*. Masters had a great capacity for intellectualizing the theme of the past and its meaning. A scornful realist, he wrote a slanted biography of Lincoln in 1931, full of ill-founded insinuations and marred by his own personal beliefs and hatred for Christianity and the Republican Party. Masters died penniless in 1950.

The Chicago to Vincennes Road is routed along the old trail established by Gurdon Hubbard back in the 1820s, later approximated by state Route 1.

Abe Lincoln is appointed postmaster of **New Salem** by President Andrew Jackson.

1834 – A statewide referendum is held on the question of where the state's capital should be located. The three leading contenders were **Alton, Vandalia** and **Springfield**. Abraham Lincoln is elected to the state legislature and with a group known as the Long Nine lobbied hard for Springfield. The vote was inconclusive, with each town receiving about 1/3 of the vote. In 1837 the state legislators took another vote and chose Springfield, since the state's population was slowly shifting northward. The Long Nine managed to "buy" votes for the **Springfield** site by promising internal improvements for those areas that supported their position on

the new capital. An impressive Greek revival domed structure with rotunda, columns and porticos was built of local sandstone for the new capitol.

The government cuts a channel through a sandbar at the mouth of the Chicago River, allowing great lake ships to enter its mouth.

John Hart Crenshaw builds a three-story structure with colonnaded porches on Hickory Hill near Equality in Gallatin County. The house overlooks the Saline river valley. It has been a landmark for over a century and is called **"The Old Slave House."** The third floor has many small windowless rooms where slaves were kept. There were metal rings attached to the floor in some rooms to prevent the slaves from escaping. Crenshaw employed a good deal of slave labor and Negro indentured servants at his extensive salt works on the **Saline River** (hence the name Saline). He probably engaged in the practice of kidnapping free Negroes because there are court records in

New State Capitol at Springfield

Shawneetown showing him charged with this offense. Crenshaw owned 30,000 acres of land plus three of the nine furnaces that reduced the salt water to crystals. Abe Lincoln stayed one night at the house but did not know slaves were on the third floor.

The first Norwegian settlement in Illinois establishes itself in **LaSalle County** on the Fox River. Led by Cleng Peerson, it is only the 2nd Norwegian settlement in the nation. Scandinavians tended to bypass the towns and settle on farms.

Stephen Douglas becomes the unofficial leader of the Democratic Party in Illinois and holds that title until his death shortly after the outbreak of the Civil War.

Quincy adopts an ordinance making it illegal to abandon the carcass of a dead animal in town.

The **Shawneetown** bank reopens and for a while enjoys a brisk business. But the main political and economic interests of the state were shifting north. After the panic and depression of 1837, the bank was forced to close.

Dr. John Emerson, an army physician, is stationed at a fort in **Rock Island**, Illinois. He brings a slave with him by the name of Dred Scott. Scott will later sue for his freedom on the basis that he lived in a free state. In 1857 the U.S. Supreme Court ruled against him in the famous **Dred Scott Case**.

Vandalia's Madonna of the Trail – tribute to pioneer women
(photo by Steve Schlager)

1835 – Ann Rutledge, Abraham Lincoln's (mythical?) first love, suddenly dies in the summer of this year. It took him nearly two years to get over this blond-haired, blue-eyed beauty of New Salem. Lincoln was a melancholy man for much of the rest of his life. Two years later he passed the bar exam and left New Salem, his home for six years.

Alton Seminary becomes Shurtleff College.

1836 – Long John Wentworth arrives in Chicago and publishes its first newspaper, the *Chicago Democrat*.

St. Louis enhances its reputation for violence in the **Francis McIntosh** affair. McIntosh, a mulatto steward on a steamboat, was arrested after a skirmish down on the levee. He was charged with interfering with the duties of law enforcement officials. McIntosh broke free as they were taking him to jail. He killed **George Hammond** by cutting his throat, and he seriously wounded the other officer, **William Mull**.

Historian James N. Primm says McIntosh was captured and sent to jail where an angry crowd of about 2,000 people gathered. They rushed the jail and overpowered the sheriff and took the prisoner out to hang him. When someone in the crowd suggested that hanging was too good for him, they took him to a tree at 10th and Market and bound him to it. A fire was lit, and he was slowly roasted alive. Someone in the crowd asked if he "felt any pain," and he replied with an anguished *yes*. He expired after about eighteen minutes of torture. None of the newspaper accounts of the incident ever identified any specific persons as the ringleaders, and no one was prosecuted for the crime.

The winter of 1836-37 is very severe and much of the state is hit by an ice storm or blizzard. One man, near frozen to death, managed to make it to an inn and called for help. When those inside rushed to his rescue, they found him **frozen to his saddle**. He was carried inside, saddle and all, and thawed in front of a roaring fire. The **Great Freeze** reportedly froze chickens and hogs in their tracks. Another man supposedly saved his life by killing his horse and climbing into his belly. According to a history of Logan County by L. Stringer, the mercury dropped in a matter of minutes from 40 degrees above to 30 degrees below zero.

Elijah Lovejoy

Additional branches of the Second Bank of Illinois (chartered in 1835) open in **Belleville, Quincy, Danville and Mt. Carmel**. There were already branches in **Alton, Springfield, Chicago, Vandalia, Galena** and **Springfield**.

Following a failed rebellion in Poland in 1831, Congress grants exiles the privilege of settling on land either in Michigan or Illinois.

The **Alton *Telegraph*** was highly critical of lack of government's initiative in stopping the mob in the McIntosh affair. **Elijah Lovejoy**, editor of a religious weekly, incurred the wrath of St. Louisans by keeping the issue alive week after week in his inflammatory abolitionist newspaper, the *Observer*. Judge **Luke Lawless** (actual name, no kidding) held a grand jury probe that, to no one's surprise, indicted no one.

Lovejoy now stepped up his attacks and lambasted judge Lawless and the jury. He inferred that Judge Lawless's faulty logic was attributable to his Irish birth and Catholic upbringing. After Lovejoy's editorial attacks, his office was twice broken into and damaged. He opted to move to a "safer" location in **Alton**, 20 miles north of St. Louis and located in a "free" state. Lovejoy became a member of the College Avenue Presbyterian Church. Owen Lovejoy, his brother, also became a leading abolitionist.

Whig legislator Abe Lincoln and Democrat Stephen Douglas vote in support of a Springfield bill that authorizes funds for the construction of the Illinois & Michigan Canal. Lincoln built wooden ship models and patented a never used invention that purportedly had air chambers to enable vessels to navigate shallow canal waters. Governor Joel Matteson embezzled Illinois and Michigan Canal script that cost the state an enormous sum of nearly $400,000.

Alexander Jenkins, of Jackson County, resigns as lieutenant governor to become president of the Illinois Central Railroad. In 1847 he was a delegate to the state constitutional convention.

Here is another story about Mother Nature wreaking havoc with what is known as the **Sudden Freeze**. The icy storm hit the state, killing dozens of people caught out in the open. One man was driving a herd of 1,000 hogs toward St. Louis. Nearly 500 of the animals were killed as they piled on top of each other, seeking warmth. The result was a macabre frozen pyramid of dead animals as the ones on top froze and those on the bottom suffocated.

The National Road (Route 40), begun in 1811 at Cumberland, Maryland, reaches the outskirts of **Vandalia**.

George Washington Gale, a New York Presbyterian minister, convinces about 50 families in his congregation to purchase land in Illinois for settlement. Each family received an 80-acre parcel of land and the town was named **Galesburg**. Mr. Gale founded Knox (John Knox) College the next year. Other similar planned communities include: **Bloomington, Ottawa, Kewanee**, **Mt. Hope**, **Metamora** and **Princeton**.

Abe Lincoln is re-elected to the state legislature.

NOVELS ABOUT PIONEER LIFE

The Graysons by Edward Eggleson – life in early **Illinois**

Beyond the Bedroom Wall by Larry Woiwode – about a **German family near Pekin**

Land of Strangers – By Lillian Budd – **Swedish immigrants in Chicago**

The Murphy Stories by Mark Costello – **early Decatur**

The Valley of the Shadows by Francis Grierson – **frontier life around 1800**

Children of the Market Place by Edgar Lee Masters – **English immigrants in Illinois Country**

John Russell claims to have seen a cave in the cliff near Alton that was filled with human skulls and old bones, giving credence to the story of the Piasa (Illini for "Bird That Devours Man") monster.

1837 - November 7. An angry mob in **Alton** attacks and kills **Elijah Lovejoy**, a newspaper editor who hated slavery but thought abolitionism was inexpedient. He died in a warehouse defending his press. The 35-year-old Lovejoy had been married just two years to the 23-year-old Celia Ann French. She died several years later, prematurely old, never getting over the shock of her husband's murder.

Lovejoy was born in Albion, Maine, in 1802, and failing to find employment on the east coast, walked to **Hillsboro** in 1927. Finding no suitable work there, he went to St. Louis and started a private high school. He went back east and became a minister after studying at Princeton Seminary School. He came back to **St. Louis** as editor of *The Observer*, a Presbyterian newspaper. He was outspoken against tobacco, alcohol, Catholicism and working on the Lord's Day. As he grew more critical and outspoken about slavery, threats of violence from pro-slave sentiment in that town was so strong he moved to Alton in 1836. At the time, **Alton was the largest city in the entire state** and was considered progressive and cosmopolitan. Many of its citizens had migrated there from the South. Alton also enjoyed favoritism from state legislators who wanted to see Alton grow and prosper at the expense of its Missouri rival, St. Louis.

Lovejoy further angered people when he criticized bankers and unscrupulous real estate speculators and said the Depression of 1837 might be "God's way of punishing the people of Alton." His first press was destroyed and thrown into the river in 1836. A second press and a third were destroyed, so he ordered yet another. He was shot and killed as a mob tried to set fire to the warehouse near the riverfront that housed his fourth and newest machine.

As the angry mob first began to gather, Alton's mayor, **John Krum**, tried unsuccessfully to try and stop the violence. There were about twenty other defenders inside the building with Lovejoy. A bell from Alton's First Presbyterian Church began to ring out a warning, hoping to enlist aid for the defenders. The crowd started throwing stones, and nearly every window in the place was broken by hurled paving stones. The defenders tossed earthenware pots down from the second story on the attackers. Ladders were then brought and burning torches were readied to be tossed on the roof of the building. Lovejoy was shot five times while trying to push away one of the ladders.

Alton mob attacks Elijah Lovejoy

Lovejoy is considered the nation's number one martyr regarding freedom of the press. No one was ever convicted of his murder. Numerous prominent townspeople, who had been supporters of Lovejoy, moved away.

The economic and population boom that had marked the three previous years was reversed. This incident reflected how divided the country was becoming. Martin Van Buren, president at the time, was against slavery. He was Andrew Jackson's hand picked successor, yet Old Hickory was an ardent slave owner. Alton was a microcosm of the national battleground with the Whig *Telegraph* versus the Democratic Alton *Spectator*.

The *Alton Telegraph* currently has part of one of Lovejoy's presses (reclaimed from the river in 1915) in their newspaper office. In the 1960s, the SIU library at Edwardsville was named in his honor. His monument in Alton cost $30,000 with most of it being furnished by the state.

The reputation of St. Louis is damaged when newspaper reports indicate that St. Louisans were part of the mob that killed Lovejoy. Lovejoy was an important martyr in both the anti-slavery movement and the struggle for freedom of the press.

A syndicate headed by Vital Jarrot and John Reynolds builds the **first railroad in the state at Illinoistown**. Reynolds had been defeated in a bid for congress and having nothing else to do, conceived the idea for the railroad. The Illinois & St. Louis carried coal from the bluffs across a bridge at Grand Marais (great swamp), to the Wiggins Ferry on the riverfront. The first rails were made of wood and the cars were pulled by horses and mules. As demand for coal slowly increased, by 1867 the Short Line was the **richest dollar-per-mile railroad in America**.

The town of **Brooklyn** is platted as a "paper town" by five white men who gain control of the government of this Negro community. It will not be incorporated until 1874, and it is named Lovejoy, for Elijah Lovejoy. By 1910 the community had become wholly Negro.

John Deere, a blacksmith of **Grand Detour,** invents the self-cleaning steel plow. He later moved to **Moline** where he had better access to steel. Earlier plows, made back east, were of iron. The Illinois soils stuck to the moldboard of these plows, necessitating frequent cleaning with wooden paddles. Deere's new steel plow was self-scouring.

The state legislature votes to move the capital from **Vandalia** to **Springfield** as a result of the lobbying (trading favors for votes) efforts of the "Long Nine." Abe Lincoln was a member of the junta, so called because all nine members, from Sangamon County, were over six ft. tall. According to legend (meaning it's probably a fairytale), Lincoln jumped out of the statehouse window in order to break a quorum that was ready to vote to keep the capital at Vandalia another 20 years. The Long Nine also supported the passage of an internal improvements bill, allocating ten million for that purpose through the sale of bonds.

Sauganash Hotel in Chicago (Philo Carpenter's drug-store was next door)

Chicago's first city census lists 4,170 people.

The state debt, brought on by the Panic of 1837, stands at $15 million.

Chicago's first permanent theater is established in the Sauganash Hotel.

President Andrew Jackson signs a bill to distribute surplus money in the federal treasury to the states. Illinois receives about $640,000 and the General Assembly, led by Abe Lincoln and Stephen Douglas, votes huge appropriations for internal improvements that ruins the state's credit for years.

John S. Wright comes to Chicago and becomes involved in real estate. He eventually founds a newspaper in 1841 called *The Prairie Farmer* specifically aimed at farm life and farm problems. The newspaper still functions today.

Abe Lincoln makes a proposal of marriage to Mary Owens, but she turns him down for his lack of financial substance. Lincoln met Mary, a Kentuckian, while she was visiting her sister in **New Salem**. The ill-fated romance had lasted a little more than two years. They also didn't see eye to eye on politics. Fortunately, Lincoln was only mildly in love with her.

Reverend John Mason Peck takes a grand tour of Illinois for the purpose of writing a gazetteer.

Restored iron furnace near Rosiclare

1838 – Monticello Female Seminary in **Godfrey** opens under the leadership of Theron Baldwin from Yale University. It soon gained a nationwide reputation for academic excellence. Today the school is the site of Lewis & Clark Junior College.

The production of iron begins in southern Illinois with the establishment of Chalon Gaurd and Company which sold out to Illinois Furnace Company. It was located at **Hog Thief Creek** about four miles north of **Rosiclare** in Hardin County. Iron ore deposits known as limonite came from nearby Shawnee hills. About 1,800 bushels of charcoal were required daily. The furnace, about fifty-three feet high, had an eight ft. diameter inner core lined with firebrick. At full capacity, the furnace could produce as much as nine tons of pig iron a day. It became an important source of iron used by the naval yards at **Mound City** during the Civil War. Most of the equipment was removed in 1883, but the state of Illinois has restored the furnace. Farther up Hog Thief Creek was another producer called Martha Furnace, built in 1848 and used for nine years.

There is a plaque near the Saline River that marks the road to Nigger Spring. At this spring brine would slowly ooze to the surface, giving off an unpleasant, pungent odor of salt and sulfur. This liquid was placed in heated iron kettles that hastened the evaporation process. Salt making,

Illinois' oldest industry, was so important that the Illinois Constitution of 1818 exempted the works near **Shawneetown** from the antislavery clause, and a man named Crenshaw was allowed to lease slaves from Kentucky. The surrounding forest was cut to provide fuel for the process that made 500 bushels of "white gold" (salt) daily. The site declined as other sources of salt were found, and it was abandoned in 1875.

Abe Lincoln once visited the place and spent a night in the Crenshaw home.

1839 - In March the last of a group of Indians passed through southern Illinois over a route that would become known as the **Trail of Tears**. This was made notorious by Helen Hunt Jackson in her famous book, *A Century of Dishonor*. The trail was over 800 miles long and was necessitated by the Indian Removal Act under President Andrew Jackson. About 14,000 Indians, mostly Cherokee from Georgia, were rounded up from their homes by 7,000 troops under General Winfield Scott. A marker on Route 146 near Route 3 says 3,000 of them died.

The group had traveled about half the long journey from Tennessee to their destination when they reached **Golconda** on December 15, 1838. They passed through **Allen Springs, Wartrace, Vienna**, **Mt. Pleasant**, and **Jonesboro**, and planned on crossing into Missouri at Cape Girardeau. But the river was choked with ice floes, so they had to make camp in freezing weather. Most lacked proper clothing and many suffered from pneumonia and tuberculosis. Many died and were buried in the vicinity of Jonesboro. The proud and valiant Cherokee were allies of Andrew Jackson, helping him to defeat the Creek Indians in the War of 1812. The Cherokee were among the most advanced Indians, having an alphabet devised by the leader Sequoya, and a government with elected representatives. At the zenith of their power, they held sway over Tennessee and Kentucky, and portions of Virginia and the Carolinas. But their lands in Georgia were taken from them, and they were sent to a reservation in Tennessee, and then resettled in Indian Territory (present-day Oklahoma).

Citizens of **Illinoistown** secure an injunction to halt dike work by St. Louisans on Bloody Island.

Jacksonville is chosen by the legislature as the site for the Illinois School for the Deaf. It later was given money to establish schools for the blind plus an insane asylum.

Andrus Plouch Manufactory where John Deere invented the steel plow

Legend says that a young man named John Chapman plants a grove of trees along the Goshen Road between Saline and Hamilton counties. He will be known in history as **Johnny Appleseed**.

The states first passenger rail line opens in Morgan County and connects **Meredosia**, on the Illinois River, with **Morgan City**, a distance of 12 miles. Early rails were made of wood and topped with strips of iron. The Chicago and Galena Railroad was the first to adopt the all-metal T-shaped iron rail in 1851.

The Mormons flee persecution in Missouri and arrive at **Quincy** with about 5,000 people. After the passing of winter, the Mormon group moves 70 miles north and establish a new town in the wilderness. Their theocratic state violated the American tradition of separation of church and state.

Between 1839 and 1876 **Williamson County** has approximately 50 murders committed there. Only 6 are successfully prosecuted.

1840 – Coal is discovered in the **Godfrey** area in a place along Mill Creek. The coal is mined and transported to the docks at Alton for shipment elsewhere.

The Golden Age of Steamboats on the Mississippi begins. It will last about 20 years.

Union Brewery is founded in **Alton** by a German immigrant named **Phillip Yakel**. It later becomes **Bluff City Brewery** when it was purchased by **William Nelzhammer** in 1886. During Prohibition it made root beer. The place closed down in 1950.

A magazine called "**The Prairie Farmer**" names Randolph County the "Castor Oil Center of the Nation."

The state grows to 476,183 people.

As more and more Yankees migrate to northern Illinois, a kind of class warfare begins to develop. Northerners picture themselves as hard working, industrious, cultured, inventive and educated. Numerous references to southerners in the state, from sermons, books and newspaper articles, deride them as ignorant, slothful, drunkards. Southerners struck back with stereotypes of northerners as greedy, swindling and untrustworthy and utterly lacking in hospitality.

There are still about 3,000 slaves in the state, most of them at the Saline Salt Works near **Equality**.

"Crazy" Hugh Newell **builds the state's first aeroplane at Newton**, 6 miles west of **Danville**. The Ornithopter was a "wing-flapper," the motion caused by turning a crank. It was launched from the top of a large haystack but crashed on its maiden voyage.

The national Liberty Party is organized in Illinois and advocates the abolition of slavery. Illinois, thanks to strong Democratic Party organization, supports Martin Van Buren for re-election, but he loses to the Whig candidate, William Henry Harrison. In general, Whigs support federal money for internal improvements, a protective tariff, and a national bank - all opposed by Democrats.

The National Road reaches **Vandalia**.

1841 – An examination of records showed that about 1100 steamboats landed at Alton's harbor. Alton sought to become the equal of St. Louis but was hampered in this effort by the size of its harbor and a large sandbar located near the wharf.

The state of Illinois grants a charter to the Alton & Sangamon Railroad, linking Alton with Springfield. Benjamin Godfrey and Simeon Ryder were the moving force behind this project. Toward the end of the Civil War plans were made to construct the Alton & St. Louis Railroad. There was also an effort at this time to build a bridge across the Mississippi at **Alton**, but the lack of any significant town on the other side hampered efforts to raise funds for the project.

In the case of Kinney v. Cook, the Illinois Supreme Count decides that in lawsuits involving the status of a black living in the state, the presumption will be in favor of liberty and the onus falls on the owner to prove a status of servitude.

The "diamond plow," a John Deere invention, is introduced. It is the first plow to turn the soil completely over, and it starts a revolution in agriculture.

Sarah Marshall of **Shawneetown** writes *Early Engagements*, making her the first novelist of Illinois.

There is a criminal group in the **Oregon**, Illinois, area. Known as "**Banditti of the Prairie**," they terrorize the area for nearly a decade in DeKalb and Ogle counties. They are led by John Driscoll, a man named Taylor and Driscoll's four sons. John Campbell, captain of the Regulators (vigilante group), is assassinated by these prairie bandits. A band of Regulators catches up with them around 1841 and kill Driscoll and a son named William. Each is shot by about 55 men. Over 100 regulators were tried by a jury for committing this act but were acquitted. A third Driscoll son (Pierce) was spared because he was only thirteen.

1842 - **Abraham Lincoln fights a serio-comic duel** with large cavalry broadswords on Sunflower Island in the Mississippi near **Alton**. (Some accounts place the location at Tow Head Island near Missouri.) James Shields, the Democratic State Auditor, was offended by a lampooning **Tremont** newspaper article written by Mary Todd, Lincoln's betrothed. The cause for the attack was Shield's order that state taxes could not be paid with state bank notes, which had fallen dramatically in value. It was common back then when discussing politics to write letters from some imaginary backwoods place and to sign a fictitious name. One article Lincoln wrote was from "Lost Township" and signed "Aunt Rebecca." The Rebecca letters also ridiculed Shields' pomp and vanity in social circumstances. Lincoln accepted responsibility for both letters, thought the challenge was absurd, and responded by choosing sabers as weapons. Shields would have been at a great disadvantage for he was short with stubby arms. A plank ten feet long was placed on the ground as a dividing line between the two men. Thanks to urging from a mutual friend, Dr. R.W. English, Lincoln apologized, and the duel was called off at the last second.

Shields pulled a trick on the crowd of observers on the Illinois side by placing a log covered with a coat stained with blood (red paint) in the returning boat of his party while he stayed behind. Onlookers were horrified, thinking he had been mortally wounded. Shields made

Lincoln lops off a willow limb with his saber (courtesy James Meyers)

the trip on a second crossing, and everyone laughed at the outrageous prank. This affair proved to be a political embarrassment the rest of Lincoln's life. Shields went on to become a highly decorated hero in the Mexican War.

In November, Abe Lincoln and Mary Todd of Kentucky, after a broken engagement called off by Lincoln, are wed in the Springfield home of Ninian Wirt Edwards, the son of territorial governor Ninian Edwards. Abe and Mary had met while she was staying with her sister, who was married to Wirt Edwards. Mary Todd's family (her father owned slaves) opposed the marriage, believing they were at opposite ends of the social spectrum, and that she was marrying *below* her station in life.

Slave mother Susan Richardson escapes from Randolph County with her three children. They are aided by William Hayes of Columbus (**Sparta**) and various elements of the Illinois Underground Railroad. Andrew Borders, her master and a large landowner, sues Hayes in 1844 for recovery. In a case decided by the Supreme Court in Springfield, Borders reclaims the children, but not Susan Richardson.

A visitor to Illinois notes in a letter that the buffalo, beaver, and elk were virtually extinct.

Fourteen northern counties send representatives to a protest meeting at **Oregon City** (now Oregon) and try to **secede from Illinois** and join with the newly forming state of Wisconsin. Lower taxes were probably the main factor behind this failed effort.

Some of the state's earliest shaft mines (as opposed to surface coal in drift mines) are sunk near **Belleville**.

Charles Dickens, the English writer, visits his brother in St. Louis. He also plans to inspect some land investments he has made near **Cairo**. Dickens and his companions crossed the Mississippi on a Wiggins Ferry boat. He describes in his *American Notes* Black Hollow (**Illinoistown**) as a quagmire of "muck and mire;" **Belleville** as a small collection of wooden houses huddled together in brush and swamp;" Cairo as a "detestable morass . . . a breeding place of fever, ague and death." He also visited **Lebanon**, staying at the Mermaid House, and traveled a bit farther east to see the famed Illinois prairie. He was unimpressed, calling it "lonely and wild, but oppressive in its barren monotony." Dickens relied too much on his memory, and it failed him in his description of Looking Glass Prairie. He says that he was looking at the setting sun, but looking east from Lebanon, the setting sun would have been behind him to the west.

Dickens lost money in his Cairo City and Canal Company investment because of the annual spring flooding. Perhaps

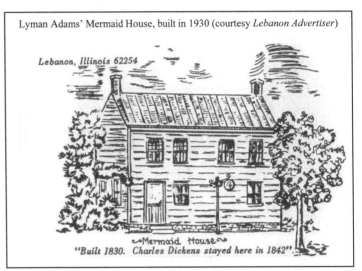

Lyman Adams' Mermaid House, built in 1930 (courtesy *Lebanon Advertiser*)

Lebanon, Illinois 62254

~Mermaid House~
"Built 1830. Charles Dickens stayed here in 1842".

this accounted for his caustic, unfair, inaccurate and stinging criticism of southern Illinois. Citizens rejoiced when they learned that his *American Notes* was not a big seller.

Stephen A. Douglas tries for the U.S. Senate but narrowly loses out to Sydney Breese in a vote by the legislature.

1843 – **Owen Lovejoy**, Congregationalist minister and younger brother of slain Alton abolitionist newspaperman Elijah Lovejoy, is arrested for aiding in the escape of two women from slavery. His two-story frame home was well known as a shelter for runaway slaves. He later was elected to Congress and strongly supported Abraham Lincoln when he issued the Emancipation Proclamation.

A vigilante group in **Gallatin County** attains prominence. They become known as **Regulators**, and they were formed to "regulate" the Negroes and to intimidate abolitionists who showed sympathy toward them. They threatened, intimidated, and whipped disobedient Negroes and captured freed slaves and placed them back in bondage. A group known as the Vigilantes was eventually organized to oppose them. The leader of the Regulators was 'Leather' Moore—so named because he was a stealer of leather goods.

Chicago with its large Catholic population becomes the See, Catholic headquarters for the entire state.

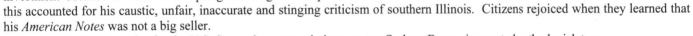
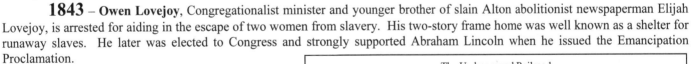

The Underground Railroad

LIBERTY LINE.

Rev. George Gale established Knox Manual Labor College and the town of **Galesburg**.

The state legislature decides to quit the banking business and passes laws giving the state bank and its branches four years to wind up their business and liquidate.

1844 - One of the worst floods ever hits the region extending from **Alton to Kaskaskia**. The American Bottom is completely flooded, allowing steamboats to travel inland about 7 miles to the bluffs. Much of **East St. Louis** is simply washed downstream. The water stood eight feet deep in the streets of **Kaskaskia** and 12 feet in Illinoistown. Steamers were able to travel from the river all the way to the bluffs to pick up those who are stranded.

The flood proved to be a blessing in disguise for the town of **Grafton**. Although the flood severely damaged the downtown business district, a larger harbor was created which in turn ushered in an era of robust steamboat activity.

In the early 1820s a devout man named **Joseph Smith** prayed to God and asked him what church he should attend. Smith claims he was visited by an angel named Moroni who led him to a cave near the family farm at Palmyra, New York. Smith was given a record of God's dealing with former inhabitants of the North American continent. He put on a pair of "magical" spectacles that enabled him to translate the strange writings on golden plates into English. This became the basis for the Book of Mormon and the beginning of a new Christian religion. The Mormons believed that native Americans were one of the lost tribes of Israel. They also believed that Jesus Christ had come to America after his crucifixion and Resurrection, and ministered to the natives. Smith founded the Mormon Church in 1830 at Fayette, New York. Believers were urged to avoid the use of tobacco, alcohol and coffee. Their most controversial belief was the practice of polygamy – having more than one wife. The movement spread westward, first to Kirtland, Ohio, and then Independence, Missouri. In each instance they met pressure and opposition from their neighbors, causing

them to move on. The Mormons left the Independence area in 1833 and moved to an unsettled area in Clay County, which they reorganized into Mormon County. For political, economic, and religious reasons, they once again came into conflict with their Gentile neighbors. In 1838 the Missouri governor signed an "Extermination Order," saying that the hated Mormons needed to be driven from the state. The Mormons fled the settlement and left for **Quincy**, Illinois, where they found sympathy from local citizens.

Joseph Smith

Joseph Smith (The Prophet), who had been imprisoned in Liberty, Missouri, escaped and joined his flock at Quincy. The Mormon leaders purchased land in nearby Commerce and renamed it **Nauvoo** – Hebrew for "beautiful place of rest." Previously the land was occupied by Fox and Sac Indians. The new town was located on a unique bend in the Mississippi River across from Iowa. The old Ripley's *Believe It Or Not* claimed it had the **only Main Street in the world with a river at both ends**. About 5,000 believers flocked to the site in 1839. It is believed that the practice of polygamy began around 1841. Non-Mormons were referred to as gentiles. The Mormons were adept at missionary work and converts migrated to the new city from Canada and Europe. Special arrangement with state legislature allowed Mormons to have their own courts, militia and university. It was virtually an autonomous entity within the state. By 1846 Nauvoo, with about 15,000 people, was the **largest city in the state**.

The Mormons established a militia and its "legion" was the largest military force in the state and **second in size only to the U.S. army**. Mormons were also feared for their political activism. They voted as a large bloc and had significant influence in the state. This gave them control over the balance of power between Whigs and Democrats. One prominent writer accused the Mormons of plotting to take over about 5 Midwestern states so they could

establish a religious oligarchy. This was seen by opponents as a threat to democracy. Other rumors spread like wildfire. One said that women from local communities were being kidnapped, forced to live in sin and serve in **polygamous Mormon harems**. Local communities, such as **Carthage** and **Warsaw**, feared Mormon manifest destiny and took to mob violence and lynchings against the "saints." Smith was seen as a fugitive from justice back in Missouri, one who set himself above the law. Perhaps the straw that broke the camel's back was when Smith and his army destroyed an opposition printing press, *The Expositor*, which opposed polygamy. Joseph Smith and his brother Hyrum were arrested for treason and taken to the jail in Carthage, the seat of Hancock County.

The Hancock County Jail at Carthage

In 1844 an angry mob, led by members of a disbanded militia, stormed the Carthage Jail where Governor Thomas Ford had Joseph Smith and his brother (Hyrum) confined for their protection. **Carthage** was the county seat of Hancock County. **Both men were killed**. Joseph Smith wounded four men with a brace of pistols before he succumbed. The assailants were probably part of a posse from Warsaw that made pre-arrangements with the jailers to load their guns without balls so none of the intruders would be killed. After a faux show of resistance, they allowed themselves to be subdued.

Persecution and mob violence by "gentiles" dropped off after the murders but soon became resurgent. A two-year period of violence following the murders is referred to as the Mormon War. Governor Thomas Ford finally sent a commission, headed by Stephen Douglas, to persuade the Mormons to leave Illinois. Under the leadership of Brigham Young, the Mormons left Nauvoo and settled in Salt Lake City, Utah. In 1848 their temple back in Nauvoo was burned to the ground by an arsonist. A group of French Icarians, led by Etienne (Steven) Cabet, bought the abandoned Mormon property and tried to establish a socialist/communal society. They rebuilt the temple that had been burned, but it was destroyed by a tornado. The community fell into disorder and eventually failed.

Governor Thomas Ford

In 1846 **Brigham Young**, the new leader, led 5,000 of the Mormons from Nauvoo in a westward trek that would end with the establishment of Salt Lake City, Utah. Joseph Smith's first wife stayed behind because she did not care for polygamy. She later married a non-Mormon.

When Brigham Young died, one enterprising political cartoonist drew a picture of "Bigamy" Young's wives in mourning. Six of them were depicted crowded together in a large bed, wiping their tears with handkerchiefs.

Nauvoo had been unique. It was a carefully planned city, with farms located on the perimeter. Many of the houses were constructed of brick. Their Nauvoo House was the largest hotel in the entire area. The Temple, built of bluff limestone, was situated on the highest point in the city. The National Park Service has designated Nauvoo as a National Historic Site. A huge restoration effort was started in 1962, led by **James Kimball**, resulting in the town becoming a huge tourist attraction.

1845 – A city in Will County named Juliet, founded by Juliet Campbell's father, changes its name to Joliet, to honor the explorer. (Note: Jolliet spelled his name with two l's.)

Cyrus McCormick arrives in Chicago and builds a factory to produce his mechanical reaper that will make him a millionaire. It has been said that his reaper played a major factor in the North winning the Civil War. Nearly half a million men were released from farm work to fight in the infantry while the efficient machine took up the slack. In 1858 he introduced the idea of installment buying, offering his machines for $30.00 down and the balance of $90.00 due 6 months later.

Lyman Trumbull

Peoria is incorporated as a city with a population that is strongly German. It becomes known for producing beer and whiskey. There would eventually be a large influx of Lebanese in that town, most of them migrating from the town of Itooli. By the 1920s Peoria had the nickname "**Earthworm City**" because it was the headquarters for the Caterpillar Company.

An important step in education is taken when the Secretary of State is given responsibility for schools. Teacher requirements at the time included a demonstration of ability in reading, math, geography, grammar, and history. By the Civil War, most communities had ungraded primary public schools. Male teachers were paid about $45 a month and females earned $30. Males were paid more because it was believed they maintained better discipline.

The **Irish Potato Famine** begins, causing thousands of residents from the Emerald Isle to come to the U.S. Many of them found work in southern Illinois building the railroads. Being Catholic, they faced harsh discrimination in urban areas where businesses often posted signs, "No Irish Need Apply."

The Illinois Supreme Court eliminates all remnants of slavery in the state in the case of Jarrot v. Jarrot. In 1845 one of Vital Jarrot's slaves sued for his freedom. **Lyman Trumbull** represented the slave in the case against his master. Trumbull successfully argued that the slave should be free because slavery had been forbidden in Illinois by the Northwest Ordinance of 1787. This case ended slavery in Illinois. Trumbull, the senator from Illinois after the Civil War (he lived in Alton from 1855-73), was the author of the **13th Amendment** to the U.S. Constitution, outlawing slavery. Henceforth, the descendants of the old French slaves were no longer valid property of anyone in Illinois.

Vital Jarrot, who briefly served as mayor of Illinoistown/**East St. Louis**, was ruined by the Panic of 1873. Destitute, he traveled to South Dakota, lured there by General Custer's tales of gold. He found no gold, fell ill of fever, and died at the age of seventy-one.

Thanks to its lead mines, **Galena** becomes the busiest port on the Mississippi north of St. Louis and commercially the richest town in the state.

Elizabeth Reed is convicted of **poisoning her husband** (arsenic-flavored sassafras) so she could marry another. She tried to escape the **Palestine** jail by burning it down so she is

Old Beliefs Make Mormons Unpopular

The Mormons became a persecuted sect, in part, because of their unorthodox beliefs in "Christian" America. According to a 1900 textbook: 1. They taught that all wealth in the world belonged to them. 2. They taught that they were God's chosen people. 3. They were clannish and forbade followers to have anything to do with people of other faiths. 4. They believed that Adam was the primary God. 5. They taught that Mohammed, Christ, Joseph Smith and Brigham Young were lesser gods. 6. They maintained the largest army in the state. 7. They held the belief that the dead could be baptized. 8. They believed that Indians were the lost tribe of Israel. 9. They believed in men having more than one wife – polygamy.

moved to the county jail in Lawrenceville where she is hanged. A crowd of 20,000 gathers to watch the first and **only execution of a female** in Illinois.

The lead mines around **Galena** produce about 83 percent of the total U.S. output at this time. These surface mines will begin to be exhausted in the 1850s, leading to a rapid decline in production.

1846 - War between the **Regulators and the Flatheads** (lawbreakers) becomes so intense in Massac, Pope, and Hardin counties, it becomes a national story in the press. Many of the rogues lived in canebrakes along the river bottom and preyed with impunity on their victims. They engaged in counterfeiting, rustling, thievery and murder. The Flatheads were defeated in a battle near **Brookport** and several of their leaders were lynched.

Galena: Wells Western area circa 1851 (Illinois State Historical Library)

The St. Andrew Society is formed in Chicago as a benevolent society to help take care of newly arriving Scottish immigrants. It is the oldest philanthropic society in the state.

The Liberty Party, established for the purpose of ending slavery, holds the balance of power in 13 northern Illinois counties.

Dorthea Dix, Massachusetts feminist reformer, arrives in **Jacksonville** and begins a tour of Illinois jails, almshouses. Due to her urging, the legislature appropriates money for a mental institution at centrally located Jacksonville. The first patient arrives in 1851. In 1869 the state ordered additional asylums to be built at **Anna** and **Elgin**.

George Donner assembles a group at the square in **Springfield** to head for California. Attempting to find a new route through the Sierras, they were trapped by snow. Of the ninety in the **Donner party**, forty-two died with some of the survivors resorting to **cannibalism**.

Reverend Peter Cartwright

Abe Lincoln is the only Whig elected to congress from Illinois, defeating clergyman Peter Cartwright. A famous Lincoln story says that Lincoln attended one of Cartwright's sermons during the campaign. At the end of the sermon, Cartwright called on those who planned to go to heaven to stand. Lincoln remained seated. Thinking he would place Lincoln in an awkward position, Cartwright asked all of those expecting to go to hell to stand. Lincoln didn't budge. Whereupon Cartwright thundered, "I am surprised to see Abe Lincoln sitting back there unmoved by these appeals. If Mr. Lincoln does not plan to go to heaven and has no plans to escape hell, perhaps he will tell us where he does plan to go." Lincoln slowly stood up and announced in a loud firm voice, "I am going to Congress."

Lincoln was hurt by a whispering campaign that accused him of being a Deist because he attended no organized church and had nearly fought a duel. Little is known about Lincoln's religious views because he never discussed them with his friends or his wife. With the advent of the Mexican War he introduced the Spot Resolution, insisting that he be shown the exact spot where American blood was shed on American soil in the disputed southern boundary of Texas. His anti-war stand was unpopular, and he lost his bid for re-election. Senator Stephen Douglas, also elected in 1846, supported the popular war.

Northerners and Whigs generally opposed the Mexican War and saw it as a plot by Democrats and President Polk to add new states to the South from conquered territory. This would upset the balance between "free" and "slave" states and give southerners the political advantage in Congress.

Belleville was the recruiting center for Illinois regiments during the war, and **Alton** was the staging area.

Illinois troops distinguish themselves during the war at Buena Vista (defeating Santa Anna) and Cerro Gordo. Colonel John Hardin of **Jacksonville**, in command of the 1st Regiment, was killed at Buena Vista. One Illinois commander, rallying his troops at a battle famously roared: **"Come on, you Illinois bloodhounds."**

Pioneer Festivities and Celebrations

German settlers in Belleville celebrated Fastnacht (fast night) on the Tuesday before Ash Wednesday. Women prepared cookies, pastries, popcorn balls and baked apples. Children put on masks and costumes to depict historical characters. The children went from farm to farm collecting treats in flour sacks.

The birth of Jesus was celebrated with a Christmas tree that was decorated with homemade wooden ornaments, garlands of dried berries and popcorn surrounding the tree. Wooden stars, each inscribed with a different name of a family member, and sized according to age, were hung on the tree. An angel or a star, usually a family heirloom, passed down to successive generations, graced the top of the tree. Painted pinecones were placed around the bottom of the tree.

After a Christmas dinner consisting of Wiener-schnitzel, sauerkraut, potato pancakes and German chocolate cake, the family gathered around the hearth to sing "Stille Nacht" and other carols.

Santa Anna is credited with introducing chewing gum (chicle from the sapodilla evergreen) to the United States.

Northern counties of Illinois, at the urging of Wisconsin officials and feeling neglected by the rest of the state, vote overwhelmingly **to join Wisconsin territory** and become a part of that state. These were 9 of the 14 counties added to the state at the insistence of Nathaniel Pope in 1818. Governor Carlin ignores the petition, and nothing comes from the **attempt at secession**.

1847 – Social reformer **Dorothea Dix** makes an inspection tour of the state prison facility located at Broadway and Williams Streets on the **Alton** riverfront. She condemned the conditions there as filthy and pest ridden.

The Sons of Temperance are organized in Illinois. Following the lead of Maine temperance laws, they work with evangelical churches to secure dry laws in **Quincy, Rockford and Springfield**.

Zadoc Casey

Former Lieutenant Governor Zadoc Casey addresses a convention of delegates in Springfield who plan to revise the state constitution of 1818. Casey attacked the power of the General Assembly and said that the state's ills for the past ten years could be traced to the curse of "too much legislation." The twelfth General Assembly, ending in 1841, passed an astounding 273 laws. The new constitution of 1848 would give more power to the governor and limit the ability of the legislature to borrow money and incur debt. The new constitution severely limited the amount of time the assembly met. This new constitution, drawn up by 76 farmers and 44 lawyers, lasted a mere 22 years.

The Chicago *Tribune*, a Whig paper, prints 400 copies of its first edition, 4 pages long, which sold for a penny each.

St. Louisans and Illinoistown/East St. Louisans **fight a mini-war over Bloody Island**. An 1844 flood washed away much of the work on the dikes performed by **Robert E. Lee** and the Corps of Engineers. St. Louisans now had to use their own men and money to finish the project. East St. Louisans took umbrage at this invasion of their territory and sent a force that **drove the St. Louisans back** across the river. They then built fortifications and brought in cannons to ward off any further incursions. Cooler heads prevailed, and the dispute was mediated by the Illinois legislature. St. Louisans were allowed to finish the work but in return had to build a raised dike road (Broadway) that ran the breadth of the island.

Ben L. Wiley, a resident of **Makanda**, near Carbondale in Jackson County, signed on with Company B to fight in the **Mexican War**. As the group made its way southwest to join the fighting, they had a brief encounter with the famed frontiersman, **Kit Carson**. His group got as far as Las Vegas, New Mexico, when they received notification that the war was over. He was discharged at **Alton**. Wiley, along with Owen Lovejoy, went on to become one of the founding members of the **Republican Party** in Illinois and was a lieutenant colonel in the cavalry during the Civil War.

The legislature authorizes the formation of plank road companies and a road-paving craze sweeps the state. The venture proved to be expensive and unsatisfactory. The boards warped and companies did not set aside enough reserves for repairing the roads.

James Semple, a U.S. Senator who lived near **Alton** at Semple Town, takes an old steam locomotive (from the abandoned Northern Cross Railroad) and has it refitted with broad flat wheels to make it suitable for travel over roads. Semple's land schooner made its maiden run from Alton to **Edwardsville**, traveling along the plank road. Near **Carlinville**, on his way to Springfield, the smoke-belching vehicle fell into a hole and broke an axle. It was abandoned on the side of the road, and the rusting hulk became known as **Semple's Folly**.

Semple was instrumental in founding the towns of **Elsah, Tamaroa, and Highland**. At Elsah, he offered lots to settlers who would build with stone, ensuring durability.

East St. Louis becomes the western terminus of the national telegraph lines.

Three thousand delegates from all over the country converge on Chicago for its first convention. Called the River and Harbor Convention, its purpose was to persuade President James Polk to spend federal money to develop the rivers and harbors of the northwest.

Congressman Stephen A. Douglas moves to Chicago and becomes involved in railroad development schemes.

The St. Clair County Turnpike (now State Street) is paved by a new process invented by Scotsman John McAdam. Also called Rock Road

Illinois and Michigan Canal script money (author's collection)

due to the crushed stone from Alton quarries, it is the **first macadamized (paved) road in the state of Illinois**.

Blasting operations on the bluffs near **Alton** destroy the original painting of the Piasa Monster. The rocks are crushed to make ballast for railroad tracks.

1848 - Free-soilers (anti-slavery) hold their convention in **Ottawa**.

Forty persons in **Collinsville** die from an outbreak of cholera. By 1850 the casualties from Madison County were over 600 people, many of them young infants.

Cyrus McCormick's Reaper

Cyrus McCormick sells 800 of his new machines in his first year of operation in Chicago.

The Chicago Board of Trade opens and engages in the farm commodities market. By 1995 a seat on the Exchange cost $710,000.

Chicago receives its first telegram by wire, only four years after Samuel Morse sent his historic message, "What hath God wrought?" The first line was strung from Baltimore to Washington D.C. In the western part of the state, the telegraph ends at Illinoistown. Dispatches are carried to St. Louis by ferry. Efforts to string the wires across the river fail, and ultimately the wires are laid on the riverbed encased in gutta percha tile conduit.

Public mistrust of the medical profession leads to passage of a state law that makes grave robbing (for anatomical research) illegal, subject to a fine of up to $500.

The Chicago & Galena Union, led by entrepreneur **William Ogden**, the city's first mayor, becomes the city's first railroad. It was Ogden who convinced Chicagoans to build bridges over the Chicago River.

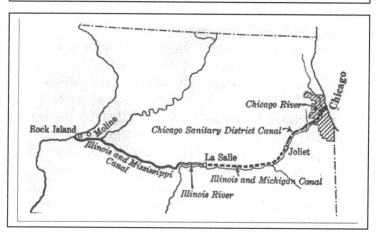

The Illinois/Michigan Canal, dug mainly by Irish contract laborers, opens for business, bringing yet another population boom to Illinois. Back in 1673 Louis Jolliet had proposed such a canal. Albert Gallatin in 1801, President Madison in 1814, and Nathaniel Pope in 1818, all talked about the need for such a canal. Its purpose was to connect the Chicago River and Lake Michigan with the Illinois River. Progress was slow and work was halted by the Panic of 1837. The completion of the canal connected New York with an all-water route to New Orleans. Its biggest problem was that during the summer, low water in the canal and in the Illinois River held back traffic.

Back in 1816 a treaty was signed with the Indians, extinguishing their title to the land along the proposed canal route. Congress first authorized the building of the canal by granting the state of Illinois alternate sections of land, one square mile each, along the proposed route. The state could then sell this land to settlers and use the money for construction purposes. The U.S. Congress financed the canal by authorizing the sale of alternate sections of land, one square mile each along the proposed route. The towns of **Ottawa** and Chicago were platted for this purpose and lots were offered for sale. Many of the lots in Chicago sold for only a few dollars – disappointing to say the least. Another hindrance was lack of support from southern Illinoisans, thinking the canal would

not benefit them. The General Assembly had passed an Internal Improvements Enabling Act back in 1837, authorizing the start of construction. But work was slow and was further impeded by the depression of 1837. Work was halted completely in 1842. Channels were cut by the use of black blasting powder. Then workers removed the loose dirt by hand with shovels. And with the advent of railroads, there were those who doubted the usefulness of such a canal. Subsequent events proved them to be right. Ten million had been authorized for canal and railroad construction, but now the state was short on funds. Governor Thomas Ford decided to secure a loan of $1,600,000 from British investors. This was a bold move since in any given year, the average tax revenue the state received was only about $100,000. Construction resumed in 1846, and the canal was opened on April 23, 1848, twelve years after the initial groundbreaking. The 60 foot wide canal is about 96 miles long, running from **Bridgeport**, west of Chicago, to **LaSalle-Peru** in north central Illinois, connecting the Des Plaines River with the Illinois River.

Lock on the I&M Canal at Marseilles

Unfortunately, the canal fell into disuse after the Civil War because of the advent of railroads. And when larger ships were built, the canal was not deep enough to accommodate them. But the canal made it easier for farmers to market their produce to eastern markets. And many of the contract laborers from Ireland decided to stay when their work was completed, settling in Chicago and numerous communities in southern Illinois, especially **Alton** and Illinoistown (E. St. Louis). They bought land with scrip money they received as wages. It was called the canal that opened Chicago to the world. Despite being eclipsed by the railroads, the canal stood second only to the Erie Canal in national importance.

Stephen A. Douglas' wife inherits 150 slaves as a result of her father's death in Mississippi. Douglas decides to take a neutral stance on the controversial issue of slavery. He becomes a proponent of "**Popular Sovereignty**," let the people of a territory decide whether it is to be slave-owning or free.

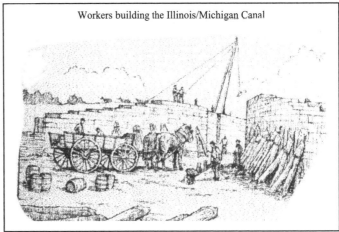
Workers building the Illinois/Michigan Canal

The first liberty pole in Williamson County is raised by the Whigs.

The 2nd Illinois Constitution is adopted. It bans slavery but also forbids free Negroes from coming to the state. It granted suffrage to white male residents age 21 and have resided within the state for one year. Another improvement is the requirement for the secret ballot. Before, voter names and choices were recorded in a book. The House of Representatives was limited to 100 members. Suffrage is granted only to free white males 21 years of age or older.

New Yorkers replace Kentuckians as the dominant immigrant group in Illinois.

Chicago gets its first railroad depot at Kinzie Street from the Galena & Chicago Union Railroad.

1849 – Illinois experiences another outbreak of cholera, killing people by the thousands.

A significant number of young men leave the state and head for the gold rush in California.

Chicago is inundated by a flood as the Des Plaines River spills across Mud Lake, wrecking more than 100 ships.

The federal government gives 60 million acres of land, much of it in Illinois, to Mexican War veterans.

The city of **Belleville** becomes known for its liquor consumption. It has 40 establishments with licenses to sell liquor and perhaps an equal number in service but avoiding the quarterly license fee.

The practice of kidnapping free Negroes and selling them in the South is a regular practice in Illinoistown and Shawneetown.

Protestant Portuguese exiles from the island of Maderia, fleeing Catholic persecution, are invited to settle in Springfield and **Jacksonville** at the behest of various Protestant groups hearing of their plight. It is believed that this is the origin of the Nunes family in Illinois. The settlement in Jacksonville is called Portuguese Hill.

The Wiggins Ferry Company at **Illinoistown** buys Bloody Island from the federal government for $1.25 an acre.

The legislature passes a law that makes it easy to incorporate plank road companies. The state goes on a plank **road-building craze**. These were sometimes called "farmers' roads" and "poor man's roads." These toll roads were built at a cost of about $15,000 per mile. After heavy rains, some farmers reported driving on the plank roads, and the ooze beneath would squirt up between the cracks and plaster drivers and horses alike.

Miners abandon **Galena** in droves and head for the California gold rush.

Stephen A. Douglas

1850 - **William H. Bissell**, of Monroe County, is elected Illinois congressman after serving in the Mexican War. **Jefferson Davis**, a Democrat from Mississippi and future President of the Confederacy, took offense at a speech made by Bissell (a Whig) in the House of Representatives and challenged him to a duel. Bissell accepted the challenge and proposed that muskets be used at six paces. Friends on both sides persuaded the men to forego the contest.

The federal government, which still owned a significant portion of Illinois land, passes a law granting the state all the swampland still unsold. This amounts to about a million and a half acres.

John Evans and a group of Methodist brethren establish Northwestern University on the shore of Lake Michigan. Evanston, site of the University, is named for him.

Alan Pinkerton establishes a detective agency in **Chicago**. During the Civil War he heads a spy group for the North. Pinkerton was a Scotsman who migrated to the Scots-Irish community of **Dundee**. He later came to Chicago and was a successful businessman before becoming a deputy sheriff in Kane County. His detectives were hired to protect railroads, infiltrate unions, arrest pickpockets at circuses, and various other activities. Alan Pinkerton was Lincoln's personal bodyguard. James McParland, a Pinkerton man, infiltrated the infamous **Molly Maguires**, a secret, violent group of miners in the Pennsylvania coalfields. The famous scout **Tom Horn** worked as a Pinkerton man to go after train robbers. Detective writer **Dashielle Hammett** worked for the

Pinkerton Agency three years, giving him invaluable background and insight for his stories. Pinkerton's motto: "The Eye That Never Sleeps." (The dominant immigrant groups in the state at this time are German, Irish, English, Canadian, Scottish and French.)

Illinois has a grand total of 110 miles of railroads. The federal government's decision to invest heavily in railroad and canal building in Illinois results in a thirty-year population boom.

Eric Janson, the leader of the Swedish colony at **Bishop Hill**, is murdered by John Root, who was married to Janson's cousin. Janson was shot at **Cambridge** while defending the Colony against lawsuits in Henry County. Root was found guilty of manslaughter and sentenced to serve 2 years at the **Alton** Prison. After serving one year, he was pardoned by Governor Matteson.

Stephen Douglas sponsors a bill in Congress that provides funding for a railroad to be built in Illinois that will connect Mobile, Alabama, and Dubuque, Iowa, with Chicago. This is the basis for the Illinois Central Railroad. The law contained provisions for generous land grants to the builders, making it the **first land-grant railroad in our nation's history**.

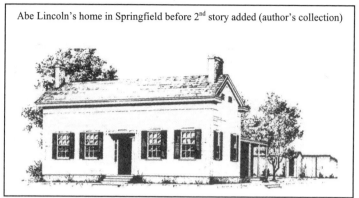
Abe Lincoln's home in Springfield before 2nd story added (author's collection)

1851 – The state passes the "free banking law," so called because it was not necessary to secure a charter from the state to go into the banking business. The only requirement was the posting of security deposits with the auditor of public accounts. The banks that sprouted were called wildcat banks (so-called because one of their early banknotes depicted a wildcat), a term widely used to describe any irresponsible act. In later years when workers were unionized, unauthorized strikes were called wildcat strikes. Because so many different kinds of bills went into circulation, counterfeiting became a big problem.

The Illinois legislature votes for a series of regulations, known as the **Black Laws**, proscribing the behavior of Negroes. They were not allowed to serve on juries nor in the militia. Neither could they hold public office nor testify in court against a white man. Free Negroes were not allowed to come to the state for the purpose of settling here. Any white person found guilty of bringing a Negro into the state was subject to fine.

Work begins on the Illinois Central Railroad. The federal government gave the company a huge land grant that was made in alternate sections, six miles deep - thus retaining half of the land for the D.C. government. The company received the even numbered sections while the government retained the odd ones. (There are 640 acres of land in a section.) This can be pictured if one thinks of red and black squares on a checkerboard. **Stephen Douglas** played an important part in convincing the government to make these land grants to help develop the country and is considered the **Father of the Illinois Central**. The IC was responsible for founding many towns in the central part of the state. Until the coming of the railroad, most of Illinois' population was along riverbanks.

The Illinois Central received more than two and one-half million acres of land. These grants were actually given to the states, and the states, in turn, passed them on to the railroad companies. In return, the Illinois central agreed to pay seven percent of its gross revenues each year into the state treasury. The company's directors included Governor John Reynolds, Pierre Menard and Illinois Supreme Court Judge Sidney Breese (**Breese, Illinois**). The Illinois Central went from **Galena** to **Cairo**, with an additional diagonal line from **Chicago**. As many as 100,000 men worked on construction from 1851-56. When it was completed, it was the **longest railroad line in the world**.

New towns sprang up practically overnight. In 1850 there was no such town as **Centralia**, **Mattoon** (named for railroad contractor, Bill Mattoon), **Kankakee** or **Du-Quoin**. As the railroads spread across the state, towns like these sprang up overnight along rail lines providing fuel, water, storage and various other support facilities. **Pana** sprang up at the juncture of the Illinois Central and the Terre Haute (translated high land) & Alton Railroad. **Paxton, Gilman, Rantoul, and Seidel** are all places where stations were located and named for a railroad official or construction engineer. By 1856, most of these towns were linked economically with Chicago, sending it raw materials and foodstuffs and buying goods in return it had processed. Land prices jumped and an economic boom hit the state. Since Chicago was linked to eastern markets, now, more than ever before, when war comes, the state is linked to the Union cause.

When railroads begin to switch from burning wood to consuming coal, a totally new mining industry is born.

Land grants to the IC Railroad

There was a downside to the railroads. Some towns that were bypassed became extinct. Stagecoach and plank road business dwindled, and steamboat traffic was undermined. Also, enthusiasm for the building of the Illinois & Michigan Canal waned.

Judge Sydney Breese, another **Father of the Illinois Central**, knew that if the railroad was to survive, it would need to have towns develop along its path. Officials advertised heavily and sent agents to Europe to recruit settlers. When railroad officials platted and gave names to these towns, they chose names that would appeal to certain nationalities. If you remember the Tyrone Power film, *Captain From Castille*, **Sandoval** was a lieutenant to Hernan Cortez, the conquistador. **Odin** is the chief Norse god. It was hoped that the town of **Beaucoup** would draw French settlers and **Kinmundy**, named for a stockholder, would attract Scotsmen.

The railroads allowed farmers in southern Illinois to take advantage of the rich promise of Illinois soil. The railroad also gave them access to Illinois inventions, such as Deere's steel plow, Joe Glidden's barbed wire, and McCormick's reaper. And for cattlemen, the railroads eliminated the need for the long drives "on the hoof" to the markets.

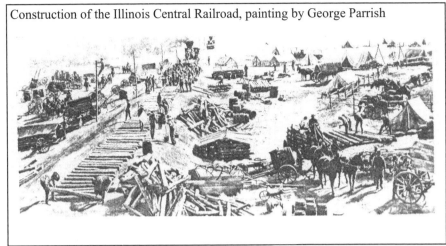
Construction of the Illinois Central Railroad, painting by George Parrish

Perhaps the most important effect of the railroads was the political effect. Before the railroads, Illinois was tied psychologically to the South by means of the Mississippi River and its tributaries. The railroads tied the state economically with the north and the east, making its ties with the Union that much stronger. And the superior rail network in the North brought the saying that "victory rode the rails."

Father Charles Chiniquy, a priest who quarreled with his superiors, begins writing articles about the attraction of Illinois around Kankakee County. This leads to a French-Canadian migration around towns such as **Bourbonnais, Kankakee, St. Anne, Momence**, and **Manteno**.

West Jacksonville organizes the state's first public high school.

1852 - A man named **Edward Judson** leads an election-day riot in **St. Louis** in the month of April. The riot produced much property damage, many injuries and one death. Judson took issue with drinking and gambling. He was also opposed to foreign immigration and helped found the American Party that was later called the Know-Nothings. The state militia had to be called in to put down the disturbance. He was arrested and jailed but posted bond and then fled to **Carlyle**, Illinois, where he edited *The Prairie Flower,* a political newspaper that failed. A few years later he moved west, met **William F. Cody**, and induced him to star in a Chicago play that he produced. Judson began writing stories about the West under the pen name, **Ned Buntline**. He gave Cody **the nickname Buffalo Bill** and soon became the father of the **Dime Novel**.

He had the Colt Company make a special order of guns that he called the Buntline Special. The .45 revolver had a long twelve inch barrel, and it became the favorite weapon of lawman **Wyatt Earp**.

Rock Road, a macadamized turnpike from Belleville to East St. Louis on the river, is completed. Tolls are charged to help pay for its construction. It was authorized by the Illinois Legislature and is the first paved road in the state.

James Semple, a politician, inventor, and land speculator buys land in the area known as Jersey Landing. It was long known as a site where cutters felled trees to provide fuel for steamboats. He plats the land and names it Ailsah for a town in Scotland where his ancestors lived. In later years, the postmaster of the town simplified the name to **Elsah**.

In the 1870s railroad mogul **Jay Gould** was frustrated in his attempts to gain control of the

Illinois Central's Engine Number One with cowcatcher and diamond smokestack

Eads Bridge at St. Louis for his railroad empire. Gould formulated plans to build a railroad line from **Springfield** to **Grafton** with a bridge over the Mississippi River at Elsah. But getting past the bluffs proved to be daunting. At first a tunnel was considered, then a trestle. The railroad line was quickly abandoned when Gould gained control of the Eads Bridge and the downtown tunnel at St. Louis.

The boiler of the steamer *Prairie State* explodes, killing many at **Pekin**.

1853 - **Walt Whitman** writes a poem about the river that the French called La Belle Riviere. It was titled "Sailing Down the River at Mid-Night," and it describes his first trip on the Mississippi River.

The state adopts oppressive "Black Laws." The bill was created by John Logan and said that any Negro who entered the state could legally be sold into servitude.

The Chicago, Alton & St. Louis is the first rail line from Chicago to reach the Mississippi.

A "slave catcher" arrives at a house in **Alton** with legal papers and demands that the owners surrender a light-skinned girl. They were reluctant to do so, but the new fugitive slave law that came out of the Compromise of 1850 gave federal agents authority to assist those seeking those who had absconded. Word got around town and enough collections were taken to purchase the mulatto's freedom. This became a national story, and it helped mitigate the dark image of Alton engendered by those who remembered the murder of Elijah Lovejoy. Resistance to the new fugitive slave law brought about what came to be known as the Underground Railroad. Slave catchers would be hot on the trail of a fugitive slave, and then all of a sudden the trail went cold. It was as if they had vanished into thin air, or perhaps escaped on a mythical underground railroad. According to tradition, that is how the phrase came into existence.

The Illinois Supreme Court upholds an ordinance in the city of **Jacksonville** banning the sale of alcoholic beverages, declaring liquor to be a public nuisance.

Chicago's first City Hall is constructed, also housing the Cook County Courthouse. A dome would be added in 1858 to provide an uninterrupted view of the entire city.

With the rapid construction of railroads all over the state, stagecoach lines fall off drastically in popularity.

1854 - The Illinois Central Gulf Railroad is founded in **Centralia**. Engine 2500 is currently on display at Fairview Park.

The Illinoistown/Cairo Short Line opens for business, connecting the two cities. More riverboats land in **Cairo** this year (3,798) than at St. Louis (3,006).

Illinois now has 100 counties, leaving only two more to be created.

The Illinois Supreme Court rules in favor of permitting local legislation by supporting a **Jacksonville** ordinance in favor of declaring the sale of liquor to be a public nuisance. In general, Catholics and Democrats were against temperance laws while Protestants and Whigs favored them.

Stephen A. Douglas, the "Little Giant," a foot shorter than Abe Lincoln, introduces the Kansas-Nebraska Act in Congress. The act is controversial because it calls for people in Kansas to vote slavery up or down, a concept known as popular sovereignty, thus repealing the Missouri Compromise of 1820, which limited slavery below the 36 degree – 30-minute line. Kansas will become a bloody battleground as anti-slave forces clash with pro-slavery groups for control of the territory. Kansas and Missouri are bitter sports rivals today, dating back to this event. Pro slavery border ruffians from Missouri crossed over into Kansas to influence elections being held there.

General George McClellan, chief engineer on the Illinois Central in the 1850s and Civil War general

This controversy brings Abe Lincoln out of retirement. Discouraged by repeated political failures, he had, in recent years, eschewed politics in favor of his law practice. Lincoln gave his first speech denouncing slavery at Peoria as rebuttal made there by Stephen Douglas earlier in the day. It is considered by most to be his first great speech.

1855 – Ninian Edwards, the son of former governor Ninian Edwards, is named the first state superintendent of schools. He helps craft a law that creates the basis for our modern system of public education. The length of the school year back then was about six months. An important provision required teachers to pass an examination before being allowed to teach. School districts were given the power to levy taxes for the purpose of public education. These funds would be supplemented with money from the state. The number of students in public schools increased dramatically after passage of this law. Male teachers generally received higher pay than females because it was widely believed that they could maintain better discipline. Students sat on wooden benches rather than at desks.

Charles Barry's magnificent and resolute Abe Lincoln

Abe Lincoln and other Illinois legislators become snowbound in a blizzard while on a train in route from Chicago to **Springfield**. The seats in one of the cars had to be burned for warmth before they were rescued.

Chicago elects Dr. Levi Boone as mayor, an anti-Catholic, anti-foreigner Know-Nothing. He secured passage of a law that raised tavern licenses from about $50 a year to $300. He also vigorously enforced a Sunday saloon-closing blue law. About ¼ of Chicago's population at this time were beer-loving Germans, who largely lived on the north side. They staged a demonstration that left one dead, several injured and dozens arrested. This incident is known as the **Lager Beer Riot**.

Chicago now has 2,933 miles of railroad track with 10 trunk lines and 11 branch lines.

The first coal mined by digging a deep shaft occurs at **DuQuoin**.

According to a survey, 405 of the states' 1,233 churches are of the Methodist persuasion. Baptists had 282 churches. Catholics had 59 parishes.

Friedens Church, near **Caseyville,** becomes a link in the Underground Railroad.

Local women in **Earlville** are the first in the state to organize a local suffragette organization.

The **first bridge to span the Mississippi River** is built by Lucius Boomer of the American Bridge Co. A railroad bridge for the Rock Island Railroad, it connects **Rock Island** and Davenport, Iowa, April 21. Shortly after the completion of the railroad bridge, a pier is rammed by the steamboat *Effie Afton*. Abe Lincoln represented the railroad in a lawsuit that followed. William Ogden's Galena & Chicago Union followed, crossing the river into Iowa at Fulton.

1856 – The **Chicago & Alton Railroad** is completed. The line was chartered by the state in 1841 and was originally known as the Alton & Sangamon. The rail line reached Springfield in 1852. **Benjamin Godfrey** (Godfrey, Illinois) is one of the moving forces behind this railroad construction. The Chicago & Alton line eventually merged with the Illinois Central.

The Illinois Republican party is organized in **Bloomington** by anti-Kansas-Nebraska Act Democrats, Free Soilers and Whigs. Joseph Medill, editor of the *Tribune*, was the guiding force behind the organization of the party in Chicago.

The 4th annual Illinois Fair is held in the city of **Alton**. The fair included horse racing, steamboat races, a circus and assorted carnival rides. State Street, which had been a plank road, was mcadamized for the event with a mixture of tar and crushed rock. People from all over the state, plus residents of St. Louis, made it one of the few fairs of that era that did not lose money.

The Bit Act is passed making land at the **Shawneetown** land office available for twelve and one half cents an acre. These were bargain prices, and there was a mad scramble to get to Shawneetown. One scored section, or bit, from old Spanish Pieces of Eight, the coin of the realm in colonial days, was worth twelve and a half cents.

John C. Fremont, The Pathfinder, becomes the first person to run for the U.S. presidency on the Republican ticket. His slogan was "Free soil, free speech, free men – Fremont." Only two men from **Johnson County** voted for him as it was considered a disgrace to vote for a "Black Republican" (abolitionist). In the 1858 election that pitted Abe Lincoln v Stephen Douglas, a Methodist minister at **Vienna** voted for Lincoln. When his congregation learned of this, they refused to pay him. He was forced to perform manual labor for the remainder of his term.

Lincoln and Douglas speak in **Olney** on the same day (Sept. 20) but at separate rallies in the presidential campaign (Buchanan vs Fremont). Lincoln and Senator Lyman Trumbull challenged the Democrats to a debate, but, confident of victory, they refused.

Hull House is constructed in Chicago by Charles Hull in southwest Chicago. In 1890 Jane Addams leased the place on Halstead Street, and its first use was a kind of day care center. Addams, a social reformer, later used it as a settlement house to help the poor and feed the hungry. Addams would later win the **Nobel Peace Prize** in recognition for her work in the peace movement.

Captain George B. McClellan, of future Civil War fame, resigns from his $1,300 a year position in the military to become Chief Engineer for the Illinois Central for $3,000 a year.

A group of temperance women in **Farmington** take matters into their own hands and launch the **Whiskey War** by marching into saloons and smashing barrels of Demon Rum.

The Chicago, Burlington & Quincy Railroad bridges the Mississippi River.

1857 - **Illinoistown** is connected to the East by the Ohio & Mississippi Railroad, which will later become the Baltimore & Ohio. Ground had been broken near Main and Brady back in 1852 when John O'Fallon dug the first ceremonial shovel of dirt. Jan 7, 1852 is referred to as the "Birthday of East St. Louis."

The nation as a whole suffers from another one of those economic downturns, peculiar to capitalism.

A huge fire rages along Lake and South Water streets in Chicago, killing 21 and causing $3 million in damages.

Illinois elects its first non-Democratic governor, Republican William Bissell.

Rev. Gideon Blackburn, a Presbyterian, raises money for the establishment of Blackburn College at **Carlinville**.

In order to build the Illinois-Michigan Canal, trustees had issued scrip money until bonds to finance the project had been sold. When these bonds were finally redeemed, they were sent to the state house and stored in boxes. Just before Governor Joel Matteson (a Democrat) went out of office, he presented $250,000 worth of this script for payment. A subsequent inquiry found that this was script that had already been redeemed and his property was seized and sold to recover the losses. The governor lived out the rest of his days in disgrace.

Captain Eber Ward starts the steel industry in Illinois with a rolling mill in Chicago.

The legislature passes acts creating the teaching school at **Normal** and the establishment of a second penitentiary at **Joliet**.

1858 – The **Three Mile House** is built north of **Edwardsville** by a St. Louis barber named Frederick Gaertner. Two years later the three-level brick tavern/inn opened its doors to passengers on the St. Louis-Springfield Road. Many people say that the structure was a way station on the Underground Railroad. It was said that there were tunnels and secret passages beneath the property. After railroads became more popular and stage traffic was discontinued, the owner closed the place and went back to his native Pennsylvania. The place sat empty for 25 years until bought by **Orrie Dunlap**, a road builder and contractor. He was in the process of paving the future Route 159, and he bought the place and renovated it for his headquarters. Dunlap also built the storm sewer system in **East St. Louis** and developed what is now known as **Dunlap Lake** in west **Edwardsville**. Later owners used the house as a bootlegging headquarters during Prohibition and a bordello during the Depression.

Joseph Gillespie was a Whig political friend of Abe Lincoln. When Lincoln came to town and gave a speech on Nov. 11, 1858, he went to a reception at Gillespie's brother's house at 606 N. Main Street in Edwardsville.

The average wage for female teachers in southern Illinois is about $155 a year. Male teachers made about twice that amount.

Abraham Lincoln and Stephen Douglas contest a U.S. Senate seat by engaging in a series of 7 debates that are a precursor to the great Civil War (**Ottawa, Freeport, Charleston, Jonesboro, Galesburg, Quincy, Alton**). In his nomination acceptance, Lincoln gives his famous "House Divided" speech. "A house divided against itself cannot stand," he said. In these debates, Abe Lincoln, a man with southern roots, argues for the abolition of slavery. Douglas, a man with New England roots, argues sympathy for slave owners because he fears interracial marriage and the destruction of white society. Although Lincoln did not believe in total racial equality, he was against slavery. Lincoln probably would have won the election if it had depended on a popular vote, but the matter back then was still decided by the state legislature. The direct election of senators would not come until the Wilson administration.

The first debate is held in **Ottawa**, lasts 3 hours, and is heard by 10,000 people. The second debate is at **Freeport** where Douglas coins his **Freeport Doctrine**, popular sovereignty currency that would cost him the presidency in 1860. The debate at **Jonesboro**, Douglas country, was the least attended. At **Charleston**, before 12,000 people, Douglas falsely accused Lincoln of favoring miscegenation – intermarriage between whites and Negroes. **Galesburg** drew the largest crowd – 20,000 people. A monument at **Quincy** by Laredo Taft honors the two men in the 6th debate. The last of the seven debates is held in **Alton**. Lincoln reportedly visited with friends in Edwardsville and stayed at the **Wabash Hotel** on 1101 N. Main, in **Edwardsville**. Abe Lincoln then traveled to Alton and stayed at the Franklin House Hotel located at 208 State Street. Senator Lyman Trumbull dined with Mr. and Mrs. Lincoln at the hotel.

It was at **Clinton** where Douglas falsely accused Lincoln of supporting political equality for Negroes. Lincoln's famous rebuttal? "You can fool all of the people some of the time, and some of the people all of the time, but you can't fool all of the people all of the time."

Map of the 7 Lincoln/Douglas debates

- Freeport
  August 27
- Ottawa
  August 21
- Galesburg
  October 7
- Quincy
  October 13
- Charleston
  September 18
- Alton
  October 15
- Jonesboro
  September 15

THE DOUGLAS-LINCOLN DEBATES OF 1858

At **Jonesboro**, Douglas made his way from **Cairo**, and Lincoln came by train from **Springfield**. They departed their respective trains at **Anna** and proceeded to the public square at Jonesboro in Union County. It was obvious to all who attended the Jonesboro debate that the crowd supported Douglas. This debate was poorly attended (only about 100 people) compared to the six others.

Douglas proposed **Popular Sovereignty** - let the people in a territory decide whether or not they wanted slavery. But Lincoln saw bondage as an evil and sought legislation to prevent the extension of slavery into western territories. The **Mason-Dixon Line** at this time ran along the Ohio River and then looped around southern Illinois to the northern border of Missouri. People from Egypt were emotionally in border country. Many of them felt like southerners trapped in a free state. Lincoln received meager support in this region of Illinois.

Douglas won the U.S. Senate seat, but his stand on popular sovereignty made him an unacceptable candidate to southern Democrats in the upcoming presidential race of 1860. Lincoln, meanwhile, became famous overnight as a result of the debates.

The U.S. Supreme Court renders its controversial Dred Scott decision. The case started in the old courthouse in **St. Louis**, which is now a historic landmark. Dred Scott, living in Missouri, a slave state, sued his master for his freedom. His case was based on the fact that he and his owner, a Dr. Emerson, had lived for a while in **Rock Island**, Illinois, where slavery was forbidden by the Northwest Ordinance. The court, dominated by southerners, held that slaves were property, and that Scott did not have legal standing on which to bring a lawsuit.

The *Olney Times* becomes the first U.S. paper with this type of headline: "For President in 1860, Abe Lincoln."

Philip Gundlach of **Belleville** invents an improved seed drill for planting crops.

Dr. C.V. Dyer, head of the Chicago, Burlington, & Quincy, arranges for slaves to ride in his boxcars, earning him the title, "Conductor" of the Underground Railroad in Illinois.

Chicago gets its first horse-pulled trolley cars, operating on State Street.

The Illinois Coal Company Railroad, carrying both coal and passengers, extends from **Caseyville** to **Brooklyn**.

Young men from Illinois sign up to be riders on the Pony Express. The pay is $25 a week, if they live long enough to collect it. Riders make the dangerous 2,000-mile trip through Indian country from St. Joe, Missouri, to Sacramento, California, in 10 days. The service only lasts 18 months, and ends when the transcontinental telegraph is completed in 1861.

The Illinois State Fair is held in **Centralia**. A man named Samuel Wilson had a featured attraction - rides in a hydrogen filled balloon. Two children, Martha and David Harvey, were in the basket of the balloon when it was suddenly pulled loose from its moorings by a gust of wind. The balloon traveled all night and passed over the town of **Mount Vernon** where large crowds watched helplessly. The **runaway balloon** finally came down and landed in a tree on a farm that belonged

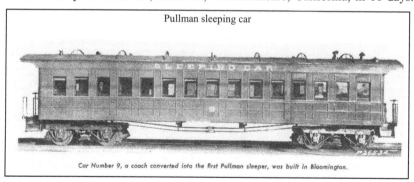

Pullman sleeping car

Car Number 9, a coach converted into the first Pullman sleeper, was built in Bloomington.

to Ignatius Atchison. The two children, unharmed, were aloft for more than 13 hours. (See picture on page 86.)

Popular songs of this era are "One-Eyed Riley" and "Buffalo Gals" (won't you come out tonight . . .).

1859 - A shipyard called **Marine Way** is completed at **Mound City** by a company from Cincinnati, which also planned to build a company town. It was to be called Emporium City. It was situated ten miles above Cairo where romantic steamboats were built and kept in good working order. The Marine Way repair facility consisted of a series of inclines where the boats were hoisted up by huge chains attached to a steam winch.

During the Civil War, the government took over operations and built the gunboats "Carondelet," "Mound City," and "Cincinnati." These ships gave valuable support to General Grant in his campaigns in the West. An old bronze bell from Mississippi was used at the shipyard and was struck at half hour intervals to mark the time of day. It came from a plantation where it had been used to rouse the slaves in the morning and strike a curfew at night. For a while the bell was in a schoolhouse to summon students to task. Today the refurbished bell is located on a stone foundation in **Pulaski County Memorial Park.**

Chicago Wigwam, courtesy H.W. Fay of DeKalb

The Seventh Annual United States Agricultural Society Exhibition is held in Chicago. It opened on September 13th and drew more than 5,000 visitors.

The last county in the state of Illinois is created (Ford), giving it 102. The state's first art exhibit is held in Chicago.

1860 – Lincoln gives his Cooper Union speech at New York in February, which introduces him to eastern Republicans. His best line: "Let us have faith that right makes might, and in that faith, let us, to the end, dare to do our duty as we understand it."

Illinois Republicans hold a party meeting in May at **Decatur** and agree to back the nomination of Abraham Lincoln. The fledgling Republican Party holds its presidential nominating convention in Chicago's "Wigwam." It is so named because it was hastily constructed specifically for the convention. The two leading contenders to carry the party banner were Abraham Lincoln, a former Whig, and New York Senator William Seward. Lincoln supporters packed the 10,000-seat arena and Lincoln won the nomination on the third ballot. Seward, the favorite going into the convention, would become Lincoln's Secretary of State and was mainly responsible for the U.S. purchase of Alaska from Russia in 1867.

The Democratic Party is split as the northern faction nominates Douglas, but the southern wing of the party walked out and held their own convention and tabbed John C. Breckinridge of Kentucky.

In the critical 1860 election, both of the major candidates for the presidency are from Illinois. Lincoln is a Republican and Douglas is a Democrat. It was an unusual election by today's standards in that there were no debates, nor did Lincoln or Douglas give any statements to the press or make speeches. Although Lincoln had promised to merely limit slavery, not end it, he was depicted as an abolitionist by southern firebrands. Eleven southern states seceded from the Union after his election.

Threats against Lincoln's life were made, and detective Allan Pinkerton of Chicago escorted Lincoln on his trip to Washington D.C., which he entered through the back door from Baltimore.

The ensuing Civil War will stimulate Illinois industry. Small shops almost overnight will turn into bustling factories churning out wartime goods. The Civil War hurts Illinois farmers at first when they are cut off from southern markets, but they make economic gain by being called on to feed the northern army. Crop failures in Europe at this time also increase demand for foodstuffs. Cotton will become a big crop in Little Egypt.

Southern counties in the state, which briefly toyed with secession, will ultimately send more volunteers to fight the South than was originally expected of them.

To the credit of Stephen Douglas, when war comes, he supports the Union and rallies Chicago's Irish to volunteer and fight for the cause.

A cyclone blows away the Kingdom Chapel in **Metropolis**, but in a strange twist of fate, the Bible is left on the pulpit. The Grinnel School of Massac County changes its name to Hurricane.

Illinois now ranks second among all states in total railroad mileage.

The *Lady Elgin*, a side-wheeling excursion boat carrying about 400 people, is rammed in a fog by the schooner *Augusta*. Incredibly, the extent of damage was not readily perceived, and the captain of the schooner was told to proceed to his destination instead of commencing rescue operations. Efforts were made to plug the hole with mattresses, but water continued to gush in. Two hundred head of cattle in the hold were driven overboard to lighten the ship. The ship sunk in Lake Michigan near **Winnetka**. Only about 100 survivors safely reached shore. A Chicagoan wrote a song "Lost on the Lady Elgin" that was sung in saloons all through the 1860s.

On November 8 the steamer *Globe* explodes at Hales Dock (Clark and Wells streets), killing twenty-five in Chicago. (See picture on page 80.)

Mayor Wentworth arranges for Albert Edward, England's Prince of Wales, to visit Chicago. But Edward insists on no pomp or ceremony and visits incognito as Baron Renfrew. Chicagoans surprised him with a parade attended by 50,000

Railsplitter Abe divides the Union with a joke

people. He later became King Edward VII. In the evening, the prince left on a train for **Dwight**, where he planned to do some royal hunting.

Chicago now has 300,000 people with more of them being foreign-born than native-born.

Illinois leads the nation in producing corn, wheat, and oats.

U.S. Grant and his wife arrive in **Galena**, and he begins to work in his father's leather store. Before that, they lived on the outskirts of St. Louis in a log cabin, and he eked out a living by hauling cordwood into town. He called his place "Hardscrabble." Grant loved animals and hated working for his father cutting hides from flesh to be used for tanning. Up to this point in his life, he was pretty much a failure. The notion that Grant would become president in 8 years would have been incomprehensible to him.

Illinois, with a population of 1,711,172 residents, is the fourth largest state in the union.

1861 - The city of **East St. Louis** is created by merging Illinoistown, St. Clair, Illinois City and by annexing Bloody Island (the river landing owned by Wiggins Ferry) and Washington. Bribery reared its ugly head when a referendum was held to determine whether the name Illinoistown or East St. Louis would be used for the newly incorporated city. Railroad officials were already using the name East St. Louis on signs, stationery, and buildings. They paid railroad workers a dollar to vote for the name East St. Louis.

With the outbreak of the Civil War, Bloody Island became a gathering place for lawless characters. East St. Louisans became outraged when **St. Louis courts** made it a Botany Bay - a dumping ground for miscreants and do-badders. When the lawbreakers repeated their offenses and were apprehended, city officials placed them on a skiff in the Mississippi and shipped them to some unsuspecting town downstream.

The first national coal miners' union meets in **West Belleville**.

Chicago has a thriving area north of the

Nov. 8, 1860, explosion kills 25 on Chicago steamer *Globe*

Chicago River known as the Sands. It is a shantytown full of prostitutes, gambling dens, pickpockets and thieves. Mayor "Long" John Wentworth (six feet ten inches tall) arranged to have a dogfight on the city's outskirts to lure the adult males away from the shanties. He then took a large police force and marched into the area and gave everyone an ultimatum, ordering them to vacate the premises. A half an hour later, **he torched the place**.

The impetuous newcomer from New Hampshire later became unhappy with his police force and fired the lot of them. Chicago went for 24 hours with protection before a new force could be organized. Wentworth was later elected to congress for 6 terms as a Democrat.

When Confederate forces fired on Fort Sumter, South Carolina, on April 12, Lincoln issued a call for northern governors to furnish 75,000 volunteers for 90 days of service to put down the insurrection. Lincoln held that secession was illegal and was determined to preserve the Union. Lincoln's call for volunteers resulted in large numbers of men going to **Springfield** to enlist. Illinois would eventually supply six regiments. Many of the groups organized along ethnic lines. Chicago provided an Irish brigade, and there were two German and two Scotch brigades.

Governor Richard Yates called the General Assembly into an emergency session. Three and a half million dollars were appropriated for the war effort. This was money that the government did not have so banks in various cities, mostly Chicago and **Springfield**, came to the rescue with no interest loans.

It became obvious to strategists that the **Cairo area**, where the Ohio River joined the Mississippi, was an important locale. Union forces from Chicago were sent south, barely arriving before the Confederates. One small group left the train at **Carbondale** to guard the nearby Illinois Central Railroad bridge across the **Big Muddy River**. Fortifications were established and cannons were set in place to control traffic on the river. The massive earthen fortifications at Cairo were named **Fort Defiance**. Cairo was at the southern tip of the state and pointed like a dagger at the heart of the Confederacy. It was from this crucial salient that the drive to control the Mississippi River and split the Confederacy in two was launched.

Vital Jarrot uses his considerable influence to keep citizens in the American Bottom region loyal to the Union. During the war, the Ninth Illinois is also known as the American Bottom Unit.

Governor Richard Yates 1861-65

Illinois units participated in several skirmishes in Missouri that helped keep that state in the Union.

General U.S. Grant was appointed commander of troops in **Cairo** by John C. Fremont. Grant had resigned his commission in 1854 because he thought there were limited chances for promotion in peacetime. He met and married a St. Louis woman named Julia Dent. Grant tried his hand at farming in St. Louis on land given to him by his father-in-law but did not prosper. After failing in a St. Louis business venture, he took his family to **Galena** where he worked as a clerk in his father's leather store. His record at West Point in 1843 was less than impressive, but he had served capably in the Mexican War.

After war broke out, Grant became a drillmaster at Camp Yates in Springfield and miraculously transformed the 21st Illinois Infantry into a group of model soldiers. Grant arrived from **Springfield** and took control of Fort Defiance, staying at the St. Charles Hotel, later known as the Halliday House. When the war broke out Grant volunteered his services and was appointed quartermaster general for Illinois regiments. His personal friendship with Galena Congressman Elihue Washburne brought him a quick promotion to brigadier general. (Galena would furnish the Union with a total of 9 generals.)

It was in **Cairo** that Grant first attracted attention as an aggressive and capable leader. Cairo's Ohio Street, along the river, was once one of the busiest ports in the world and frequented on numerous occasions by Mark Twain in his riverboat days. Today the buildings along the street are in ruin, and the place is nearly deserted.

Perhaps as many as 1/3 of the people in southern Illinois were sympathetic to the Confederate cause. Some organized and called themselves the **Knights of the Golden Circle,** but unionists disdained them as snakes in the grass - "Copperheads." They secretly met and plotted in the hidden canyons of Giant City Park near **Makanda**. Giant City received its name from huge blocks of sandstone that resembled the walls of a large medieval fortress. The Knights stimulated resistance to the draft, circulated treasonable publications in the Union ranks, and carried on espionage for the South. The subversive nightriders, who were never caught, presumably set up their printing presses in the deep recesses of these canyons.

Two romantic novels about this aspect of the Civil War in southern Illinois are: *Vinnie and the Flag Tree* by Mabel T. Rauch, and *The Flag on the Hilltop* by Mary T. Earle.

Southern sentiment was especially strong in **Hamilton, Franklin**, and **Williamson** counties. Many from there celebrated the news of Lincoln's assassination by a southerner. There was one group of men who had to be arrested and imprisoned for their opposition to the Union cause. The story is told in an 1880 book by John Marshall, *An American Bastille*.

In the middle of the year, in Williamson County, Captain Thorndike Brooks recruited a company of soldiers to serve in the Confederate Army. There was strong opposition to the draft in Southern Illinois, and no large-scale draft ever took place there. For a time, there was talk of southern Illinois seceding from the rest of the state if the war was prosecuted too vigorously.

In November the gunboat *Mound City*, carrying iron armature, slipped into the Ohio River from the Mound City shipyards. Ft. Massac, abandoned since the War of 1812, was reactivated. It is where the 131st regiment of the Illinois Cavalry, containing 815 men from nearby counties, train to fight for the Union.

The Civil War battle nearest to **Metropolis** was at Paducah, with many women and children fleeing to the Illinois shore. Union gunboats secured the victory.

On June 3rd Stephen Douglas dies from typhoid fever. In his last speech on May 1st, at the Wigwam in Chicago, he exhorted his followers to remain loyal to the Union.

A steamboat named ***City of Alton*** is used to transfer weaponry from the St. Louis arsenal (hence the origin of Arsenal Street) and transport them to safety in Illinois. It was feared the ordinance might be stolen by southern sympathizers whose numbers in St. Louis were extraordinary. Captain **James Stokes** was in charge of the assignment. Muskets, carbines, pistols, cartridges and cannon were removed and ultimately shipped to **Springfield**.

Frank B. Moore organizes a company of men that are known as the **Madison County Rangers**. This group bravely fought with Missouri guerrilla bands and successfully captured prisoners, weapons, and supplies. Two of Frank's brothers had been killed in the **Wood River** massacre by Indians.

A measles epidemic causes Union forces to abandon Fort Massac. This is the last time it will be occupied for military purposes.

The *Chicago Tribune* becomes the first 7-day-a-week newspaper in the state to meet the demand for news during the Civil War.

A mass meeting held in **Marion** results in passage of a resolution to **divide the state into two halves** with the southern portion attaching itself to the Confederacy. There is a serious effort by copperheads in Williamson County in southern Illinois to have that county secede from the rest of the state. Proponents planned to call the new Confederate county by the name of Egypt.

The 5th county courthouse, with Doric columns, is constructed in **Belleville** at the cost of $100,000.

Colonel Elmer Ellsworth of **Springfield** is killed while taking down a Confederate flag outside a building at Alexandria, Virginia. He becomes the first Illinoisan killed in the war.

Fort Defiance at Cairo: from *Frank Leslie's Illustrated*

1862 - The largest military cemetery in Illinois is authorized by Congress. **Mound City Cemetery** is located about six miles north of **Cairo** at the confluence of Highways 51 and 37. The cemetery contains the areas' dead from the Mexican War and Civil War. There are also a small number of Confederate graves. Bronze markers throughout the cemetery contain stanzas from Major Theodore O'Hara's famous poem, **"The Bivouac of the Dead."**

In early February, Grant captures Fort Henry. John Pope captured the strategic Island Number 10 on the Mississippi with the help of 7 "alligator" ironclads built by James B. Eads at Carondolet, Missouri. In March, Grant's forces took Fort Donnelson and won the battle of Pea Ridge in Arkansas. Some Illinois **soldiers were scalped** by Cherokee and Choctaw Indians who fought with the Confederates. In the Union's costly victory at Shiloh, Illinois suffered about one third of the total casualties. Ironically, of all the Illinois generals, it was General Pope, not John McClernand or Grant, who was held in highest esteem from the military brass in the aftermath of Shiloh.

McClernand put forth a proposal to President Lincoln that he should be placed in charge of a campaign against Vicksburg which would enable the North to control the entire Mississippi Valley. From there, the armies could move east, destroying Confederate railroads as they went. Illinois regiments cheerfully went into battle singing "The Battle Cry of Freedom."

Abe Lincoln appoints his good friend, Judge David Davis of **Pekin**, as associate justice of the U.S. Supreme Court. The 300-pound man was a judge on the Eighth Circuit, where Lincoln argued cases. It was Davis who had helped secure the nomination of Lincoln to head the Republican ticket in 1860. Davis went from room to room, lobbying hard for his good friend.

In a "bye" or off-year election, Democrats gain control of the Illinois legislature and do everything they can to harass Governor Yates and Abraham Lincoln. They become known as "peace at any price" Democrats. Democrats are also the majority in a convention designed to draw up a new state constitution, but it is so partisan that voters reject it overwhelmingly.

There is a large influx of settlers from the South. Due to the war, thousands of anti-slavery southerners and political refugees pour into the southern Illinois to find a new home.

A group called the **Knights of the Golden Circle** is officially organized in Egypt. Originally they were a gang of filibustering brigands who sought to invade Mexico and Americanize that country. The Knights more or less became the forerunner of the KKK. It was rumored that both Williamson and Union Counties harbored a large number of Federal deserters.

Southern Illinois contributed more than its quota of men to Mr. Lincoln's Army. Interestingly, the 73rd Illinois was composed mainly of Baptist ministers.

Illinoisan John Pope, hero of New Madrid and Corinth, is elevated to top command in the East but suffers defeat at the Second Battle of Bull Run.

One of several river gunboats built for the Union by James B. Eads

In September, after the Battle of Antietam, Lincoln, under pressure from radicals within his party (Horace Greeley and Lyman Trumbull), issues the Emancipation Proclamation, freeing (at least on paper) the slaves in states that were in rebellion. He did not free all of the slaves for fear it would anger slaveholding states such as Kentucky, Missouri, Maryland, and Delaware that had rejected secession.

Lincoln's proclamation bitterly divided the state and was highly controversial since many Democrats had remained loyal only because they had been told the war was being fought to preserve the Union. Many Illinois soldiers had joined the ranks to protect the Union – not to free the slaves.

During the war, Lincoln met with Negro leaders (the first president to do so) and **suggested that they establish a colony in Central America (Panama).** Lincoln believed that whites in this country would never accept Negroes as their equals. The leaders turned down his suggestion.

Actor John Wilkes Booth stars in the play "Richard III" at the McVicker Theater in Chicago.

The government builds an arsenal at **Rock Island** at the site of Fort Browning, and it is used to house 1,200 Confederate prisoners. It serves the nation through future wars and conflicts and currently features the John Browning Museum and a time capsule. A major addition was completed in 1893.

1863 - After Lincoln issues the Emancipation Proclamation, numerous volunteers are so upset that they desert the army. The woods of Union County soon became filled with men who were hiding from the authorities. Professional informers were paid a $30 bounty for every man captured by the provost marshal.

FIVE DOLLARS FINE FOR DRIVING MORE THAN 12 HORSES, MULES OR CATTLE AT ANY ONE TIME OR FOR LEADING ANY BEAST FASTER THAN A WALK ACROSS THIS BRIDGE – Old sign at the Red Covered bridge near Princeton, one of 5 remaining covered bridges in the state.

The Democrats had been a powerful force in Illinois politics ever since the election of Andrew Jackson in 1828. An obstruction-ist faction within their ranks begins to cause trouble. Democrats in Springfield prepared a list of 15 grievances against Abe Lincoln and Governor Yates. They hindered the Illinois' war effort by blocking important legislation. Governor Yates grew so disgusted with the legislature that in the spring of this year he prorogues (dissolves) the Assembly and orders it not to meet until January of 1865.

In June, 40,000 dissatisfied citizens, led by Democratic members of the legislature, hold a convention and pass a resolution calling for a national convention to "restore the Union." One of the members of this anti-war rally is William Quantrill.

On August 19 a former schoolteacher in **Mendota**, Illinois, by the name of **William Quantrill** leads a raid on Lawrence, Kansas. Quantrill threw in his lot with the Confederacy when the war broke out, and he organized a force of "raiders" consisting of 450 men. He and his marauders killed 150 men and boys in the Kansas town that was noted for its abolitionism. They shot the townspeople as if they were hunting rabbits. This massacre of civilians **has no equal in any American war**.

William Quantrill

Frank and Jesse James were sympathetic to the South and rode with Quantrill. When the war was over and the brothers became robbers and outlaws, they frequently stayed at the home of Ignatius Burch, on **Kaskaskia Island**, when the heat was on. According to a son named Charlie Burch, the James brothers rode in after dark and had a secret knock on the door as a signal to make their presence known.

A treasonous guerrilla band is organized and terrorizes folk in Montgomery, Bond, Fayette, and Christian counties. Led by a murderous cutthroat named Josiah Woods, he frequently used the alias Klingman, so the band became known as the Klingman Gang. The group sympathized with the Confederate cause and terrorized residents in the area. A posse of nearly 800 men finally chased the brigands out of Illinois. Klingman was later hanged in Missouri for having committed murder. Remnants of the gang were still around as late as 1895. According to the *Alton Telegraph*, there was a man near **Oconee** who was killed because of his Union sentiments.

Camp Douglas, a Confederate POW camp, is established in Chicago at 33rd St. on the lakefront.

McClernand proposes a plan in January to capture Fort Hindman on the Arkansas River, which ends up being a successful campaign. The victory gave a much-needed boost to the soldier's morale.

In July U.S. Grant and General John Logan capture the strategic town of Vicksburg on the Mississippi River, giving the North full control of that important commercial waterway. Texas and Arkansas are now cut off from the rest of the Confederacy.

McClernand, the Hero of Donnelson and Shiloh, lost his command after Vicksburg. To his credit, he continued to espouse the Union cause in Illinois. In early 1864, Lincoln overruled his officers and restored his Springfield friend to command of the XIII Corps.

In November Illinois regiments play an important role in capturing Missionary Ridge in the capture of Chattanooga, paving the way for Sherman's "march to the sea."

Copperhead cartoon 1863

The state's policy of allowing only whites to serve in the Civil War is changed by the government at **Springfield**. This allows the 29th U.S. Colored Infantry to be organized. Officially, 1,811 Negroes from Illinois served in the war, but many believe the actual number to be higher.

Chicago begins an era of mayorships with terms lasting only two years.

The Chicago *Tribune* strongly supports the North in the war while the Chicago *Times*, edited by Copperhead Wilbur F. Storey, is sympathetic to the South. General Ambrose Burnside (whose muttonchops gave us the term "sideburns") is so angry, he issues orders from his headquarters in Cincinnati to suppress the newspaper. A mob of 20,000 gathered in Chicago's streets and threatened to destroy the *Times*. Lincoln sent a message to Burnside, urging him to reconsider, and the order was revoked. Several years after the war was over, Story audaciously accused Lydia Thompson, the star of a Chicago stage play of lascivious conduct. Shortly after, Thompson attacked Story near his home and **administered an embarrassing horse whipping**.

Abraham Lincoln gives his Gettysburg Address in November to dedicate the battlefield cemetery. Edward Everett, a famed orator, was actually the featured speaker and Lincoln was invited as an afterthought. Everett's speech was two hours, Lincoln's lasted two minutes. ". . . And that the government of the people, by the people, for the people shall not perish from the earth."

In **Jacksonville**, at Strawn's Hall, George Bailey brings a circus to town and P.T. Barnum displays Charles Stratton, better known as Tom Thumb, to enthusiastic crowds who temporarily forget about the Civil War. Tom Thumb was a mere two feet, one inch tall, and was from a Connecticut family where other members were normal size. Barnum named Stratton Tom Thumb after the dwarf at King Arthur's court. Tom Thumb died prematurely in 1883.

The Mississippi River freezes over at **East St. Louis** during the winter.

George Pullman builds the "Pioneer," the first sleeping car built from the ground up that was not a converted day coach.

1864 - Seven Confederate prisoners are killed when an escape attempt is made by prisoners of war at the **Alton** prison. Five of the prisoners were wounded. At its peak, the facility held more than 2,000 men from all parts of the South. About 1300 men would later die from smallpox. The epidemic lasted from the winter of 1863 to the spring of 1864. There is a three-story brick structure on State Street in Alton called the Mansion House that had been used since 1834 as a hotel. It was converted into a hospital by an Ursuline order of nuns from St. Louis. Because numerous Confederate prisoners died there, the place is said to be haunted by ghosts who still walk the halls. The building currently houses a number of private apartments.

The national draft now affects Illinois but its impact is slight due to the state's large number of volunteers. Only 55 men paid the state a $300 commutation fee to avoid service. About 3,583 men were drafted.

Illinois' contribution to the Civil War is significant. Illinois residents ranked 5th out of 22 states paying the Civil War tax to support the preservation of the Union.

The 29th U.S. Colored Infantry from Illinois is sent to Washington D.C. Whites do not trust them to fight on the front line of battle, so they are given the task of protecting Grant's supply lines as he makes his march towards Richmond to capture the Confederate capital and end the war. Confederates attacked them in a determined bid to sever this vital link. The colored troops fought well and repulsed the attack, allowing Grant to proceed with his effort.

In the northeast part of **Hamilton County**, near **Skillet Fork**, a tributary of the Little Wabash River, stood Fort Shipley. The makeshift fort was occupied by a band of renegades from a tri-state area. They called themselves **Knights of the Golden Circle**. Many were draft dodgers, opposed to the 1863 Union conscription law. This motley group of 80 to 100 men caused the government enough worry that an order was sent to **Springfield** to send a company of men against the fort. A group of about 30 heavily armed men moved against the fort, headed by Captain John R. Moss. When the group arrived they found that its occupants had fled for parts unknown. The military band proceeded to lay waste to the fort, completely destroying it in the "bloodless" battle of Fort Shipley. The apparent leader of the group, Thomas Shipley, went on to become a respected lawyer in the community of **Dahlgren**.

Sympathy for the Southern Cause was strong in **Little Egypt**, and there is documentation of numerous roving bands of "Copperheads" throughout the Illinois Ozarks.

General John Logan

In March, a band of "Copperheads" attack a group of Union soldiers from the 54th Infantry on furlough in Charleston. The soldiers harassed a group of men dressed in homespun (Butternuts) by questioning them about their sympathy and then taking them before a Justice of the Peace and forcing them to swear loyalty to the Union. Several days later, the men who had been harassed came back to town, and this time they were armed with guns and Arkansas toothpicks (Bowie knives). Words were exchanged and shots were fired. Nine were killed and 12 were wounded. About 35 members of the Mattoon Rifle Company were rushed by locomotive to Charleston. The principal perpetrators of the melee escaped and were never arrested. The **Charleston Riot** is probably the most famous Civil War incident in Illinois.

A similar, but less bloody, encounter between the two factions took place at **Paris**, the seat of Edgar County. Six soldiers mixed it up with 14 Copperheads. The fight was over an arsenal of weapons collected by the Butternuts in an effort to defend the local Democratic and pro-South newspaper, the *Paris Times*. Two soldiers were wounded and one Copperhead was killed.

Danville was the scene of two such war incidents between members of the Union League and Sons of Jefferson Davis.

In the summer, another group of "Copperheads" hatch a plot to attack Camp Douglas in Chicago and free all the prisoners. Confederate prisoners were held in the north rather than border states to make such liberation plans less likely. The U.S. Secret Service learned about the plan and foils it by arresting the leaders.

Abe Lincoln, the "Railsplitter From Illinois," wins a second term of office by defeating Democratic candidate, General George McClellan. McClellan won the nomination at the Democratic convention held at the Wigwam in Chicago. In an effort to appease the border states, Hannibal Hamlin of Maine is dropped from the ticket and replaced by Andrew Johnson of Tennessee. Johnson was the only southern Senator to remain loyal to the Union when the Civil War began. Lincoln's re-election was in doubt until General Sherman captured Atlanta, Georgia. General Logan was one of the heroes in the battle of Atlanta. Illinois soldiers voted overwhelmingly for Lincoln.

Confederate prisoners at Camp Douglas plot the **Chicago Conspiracy.** It is a bold plan hatched by Captain Thomas Hines, a Confederate spy. Once freed, the prisoners would conspire with other Copperheads to stuff the ballot boxes at the Republican presidential nominating convention, and replace Lincoln with a peace candidate who would end the war. On the eve of the election, Union counterspies foiled the plot and arrested most of the ringleaders. About 6,000 Rebels died in the camp during the war from sickness and disease.

Military punishment at Camp Douglas - "Riding the Rail"

Chicagoan Henry Clay Work writes the popular Civil War song, "Marching Through Georgia." Chicagoan George Root wrote the wildly popular, "The Battle Cry of Freedom." Root and Florenz Ziegfield would later establish the Chicago Musical College. Ziegfield received his first taste of theater when he attended a performance of William F. Cody's Wild West Show. He responded to an audience challenge from **Buffalo Bill** and promptly hit the bull's eye on a target. Buffalo Bill's show was produced by **Ned Buntline**, who once published a newspaper in **Carlyle**, author of numerous dime novels.

Zeigfield introduced the world to many stars, including Fanny Brice, W.C. Fields, Will Rogers, Eddie Cantor and Billie Burke (whom he married).

Jennie Hodgers, an Illinois woman, **dressed like a man** and enlisted to fight in the Civil War. This was done in other states as well, but she **holds the record** for remaining undetected the longest. Her gender was not discovered until she was in a 1911 car wreck and was sent to a veteran's hospital for treatment. During the war she used the name Albert Cashier.

Jenny Hodgers/Albert Cashier

Abe Lincoln declares the last Thursday in November to be set aside as a national day of thanksgiving.

The Chicago & North Western Railway carries the first railway post office (from Chicago to **Fulton**) in the United States. Assistant Postmaster George B. Armstrong of Chicago devises a way to have a crew of clerks sort and re-sack the mail as the train sped along the tracks.

1865 – The only state to send a proportionately higher number of men into battle than Illinois was Kansas. The state also excelled in the area of leadership by furnishing the war with 177 generals.

Illinois becomes the first state to ratify the 13th Amendment, abolishing slavery.

Altonite Lyman Trumbull is the author of the act that creates the Freedman's Bureau. This agency, administered by General O.O. Howard, sought to look out for the welfare of newly freed slaves under the aegis of the 13th Amendment, of which Trumbull was also the author. Senator Trumbull was a close friend of Abraham Lincoln. His home in the Middletown section of Alton is a national historic landmark.

Paris-born *Octave Chanute*, an engineer, designed and supervised the construction of Chicago's Union Stock Yards – the largest in the world.

The steamship *Sultana*, heavily overloaded with 250 hogsheads (large barrels) of sugar and 2,200 passengers, bursts into flames when its faulty boiler explodes. The ship was only licensed to carry 376 passengers. The *Sultana*, going from New Orleans and on its way to St. Louis, had passed Memphis and was headed for **Cairo** when disaster struck. At least **1,900 people perished**. It is the **largest marine disaster in the annals of our history**. Many of the men who died had just been released from Confederate prisons at the end of the war. Illinois lost more men in the Civil War to disease (19,934) than from action in battle (8,908).

Chicago, only two feet higher than the Chicago River, completes a ten-year project, started in 1855, that lifts the city out of the mud. Streets and sidewalks were raised an average of ten feet. Young engineer George Pullman, who later became a railroad inventor, supervised the raising of the Tremont Hotel. Twelve hundred workers with jackscrews lifted the five-story building six feet higher without significant damage. Some houses in Chicago have their entrances into the second story because of this project.

Mary Ann Bickerdyke

About twenty-five years later, **East St. Louis** undertook a similar project because, like Chicago, it too had been built on a sandbar. When cattle were driven down Collinsville Avenue on the way to the stockyards, cowboys joked that they lost part of their herd in the mud. Some houses and businesses in both cities today have entrances into the second story because the street and sidewalk were raised ten feet.

The Illinois General Assembly repeals its infamous Black Code and becomes the first state to ratify the Thirteenth Amendment to the U.S. Constitution, which abolished slavery in the U.S.

On April 9th, at Appomattox Court House in Virginia, General Robert E. Lee surrenders to U.S. Grant. The Civil War finally ends. Ely Parker, a full-blooded Seneca Indian from **Galena**, was Grant's military secretary. It was Ely who drew up the document outlining the terms of surrender. General Grant is forever remembered for the courtesy and generosity he showed to Lee and his troops.

"Mother" Bickerdyke of Galesburg and **Mary Jane Safford of Cairo** gain fame as angels of the battlefield, nursing wounded men on the front lines of the war back to health. In her time, Bickerdyke was nearly as famous as Grant or Sherman. Chicago women organized a Sanitary Commission that did relief work similar to the Red Cross. Bickerdyke, the **Cyclone In Calico**, traveled with Grant throughout the entire western campaign of the Civil War. She saved many lives by improving sanitary conditions in hospitals. There is a memorial statue of Bickerdyke on the courthouse lawn in **Galesburg**.

James Wilson, a native of **Shawneetown**, leads the military unit responsible for capturing Robert E. Lee.

Abraham Lincoln is assassinated on April 14 by John Wilkes Booth while watching the play "Our American Cousin" at Ford's Theater in Washington D.C. The assassination was part of a larger plot that was supposed to kill U.S. Grant, Andrew Johnson and William Seward. William Seward was attacked and stabbed, but he recovered from his wounds. Booth was hunted down and killed. The other conspirators were arrested and hanged. Mary Surrat, a woman who ran a boarding house and mother to one of the conspirators, was executed with the others.

Samuel Mudd, a doctor who treated Booth's broken leg, was also imprisoned. Tradition holds that this is the origin of the expression, "If you do that, your name is mud." John's brother Edwin, the most noteworthy American Shakespearian actor of his day, found his career to be ruined because of his last name.

On May 1 Lincoln's body was brought to the Cook County Courthouse where 125,000 mourners paid tribute to the fallen leader. From there, the body was taken to **Springfield** for burial.

A bill is introduced to move the state capital to **Peoria** but is tabled. **Springfield** citizens hastily pony-up money needed to construct a new building in their city.

James H. Wilson of Shawneetown helped capture Jefferson Davis

Chicago's Union Stock Yards open and are considered the largest and most modern in the world.

The nation's first steel rails are produced in Chicago.

Illinois casualties from the Civil War include 34,834 dead including 1,700 who died in Confederate prisons. One out of every 7.3 soldiers who served died in battle. There were 19,934 men who died from disease, more than were killed in actual combat.

Chicago surpasses Cincinnati in population and now looks to catch rival St. Louis, whom it hates and detests. Chicagoans are thoroughly Yankee while they consider St. Louis southern. St. Louis newspapers disdainfully refer to Chicago as that "Babylon on the Mud."

1866 – President Andrew Johnson visits **Chicago, Springfield and Alton** in a vain effort to explain his reconstruction policies after the Civil War. He is accompanied by General Grant and **General George A. Custer.**

Johnson County is hit by a cyclone, devastating the town of **West Vienna.** It killed about 5 people and injured 18-20.

Dr. Benjamin F. Stephenson of **Decatur**, who had served as a surgeon in the 14th Illinois Infantry, works with John Logan and Governor Oglesby to **organize the G.A.R.** (Grand Army of the Republic), a fraternal organization for Union veterans.

Parker Earle, of Cobden, perfects a method of shipping strawberries, first in wooden casks filled with ice, later in a special boxcar car that had space along its inner sides to hold ice and sawdust. The ice came from a nearby pond owned by J.B. Broadway. This is claimed to be **America's first refrigerated railroad car**. Earle's innovation leads to the development of truck farming and an orchard industry in southern Illinois that persists to this day. Earle became famous for his tomatoes and made that town the **tomato growing capital of the United States**.

Two sisters, Tennessee Claflin and Victoria Woodhull, arrive in Chicago, claiming to be clairvoyants. They hold séances at 365 Wabash Avenue. It was not known that they had fled from **Ottawa**, Illinois, under indictment for murder. They later advocated free love but left the city in 1870 for New York where they became stockbrokers.

The town of **Galena** donates a $16,000 house to its favorite son, Ulysses S. Grant.

The first observance of Memorial Day occurs in **Carbondale** on April 29 at the Woodlawn Cemetery. General John Logan was one of the organizers of this event. Two years later Logan issued a memo to all G.A.R. posts, requesting them to observe this event annually. It eventually becomes a **national holiday.**

The nation's first recorded sextuplets are born in Chicago to Mr. and Mrs. Bushnell.

1867 - The state of Illinois makes plans to build a new statehouse. A $3,000 prize is offered to the architect whose plans are adopted. The architect who won the prize later claimed that he spent $2,700 in bribes to win the competition.

The Illinois Industrial University, a land-grant school, is founded at **Urbana**, under the auspices of the Morrill Act of 1862. It became the University of Illinois in 1885.

An investigation finds that there have been at least 133 boats that sank in the dangerous waters between St. Louis and Cairo, a stretch river men called the "**Graveyard.**"

Illinois becomes the first state to legislate the 8-hour working day.

The national Pi Beta Pi Sorority is founded in Holt House at **Monmouth College**.

The Crib, a large octagonal of about 50 feet in diameter, is built on the shore of Lake Michigan and then towed two miles out and sunk. An iron tube about ten feet in diameter was fitted to the crib, and it was joined to the city waterworks by an underground brick tunnel roughly 6 feet in diameter. The Crib supplied Chicago's water needs, and Mayor J.B. Rice called it an engineering marvel.

William L. Jenny establishes an architectural firm in Chicago, and it is responsible for training Louis Sullivan and Daniel Burnham in what came to be known as the "Chicago School."

1868 - The beginning of what came to be known as the **Bloody Vendetta** in Williamson County occurs in an argument over a 4th of July card game near **Carbondale** that ended in a fight between the **Bulliner** and **Henderson** families. Historian John Allen wrote that the **Sisney** family was drawn into the intrigue due to a lawsuit over a crop of oats. It was said that jealousy over a woman was the third cause of the vendetta. Four large families were ultimately involved in the ongoing dispute - the Bulliners and the **Crains** vs the Sisneys and Hendersons. Whenever members of these families had chance

U.S. Grant from Galena: President 1869-1877

encounters with their sworn enemies, words were exchanged, fists flew, and hot lead began to fly. In this feud, which had political overtones, Democratic families were aligned against Republican families.

When **Milo Erwin** later wrote about the feud in a 1914 book, *The Bloody Vendetta*, he was forced to flee Illinois and live out his remaining years under an assumed name because of the animosity that arose.

A general melee at **Carterville** in December of 1872 served to solidify the opposing factions. And with each subsequent encounter, the bitterness was intensified. Over an eight-year period, the feud resulted in a never-ending series of brawls, assaults, ambushes and murders. **George Bulliner**, traveling to **Carbondale**, was ambushed and killed near the Jackson County line on December 12, 1873. His murder was never solved. Four months later, **David Bulliner**, a son of the slain man, was set upon by assassins on his way home from church and was also killed.

This feud, reminiscent of the Hatfield-McCoy imbroglio, got so bad that a bill to appropriate $10,000 for the purpose of ending the brouhaha was actually introduced in the Illinois General Assembly. The hanging of **Marshall Crain** for the murder of **William Spence**, and two other men being sent to the pen for killing **George Sisney** ended the long-standing feud.

The *Thunderbolt Express* of the Illinois Central Railroad Company becomes the **first train in America to use refrigerated cars** to preserve fresh fruit. Strawberries, peaches, apples and Keiffer pears were the principle crops sent north from **Centralia** to Chicago.

Chicago's famed Lincoln Park Zoo is started when NY Central Park donates a pair of swans. Its featured attraction would ultimately be Bushman, a huge **600-pound gorilla** purchased from an animal trader in 1930. Bushman grew ill in 1950 and 120,000 people flocked to see him, thinking he was dying. He recovered but succumbed in 1951. His impressive stuffed remains are on display at the Field Museum.

Andrew Carnegie's Keystone Bridge Work constructs a 7-span, wrought iron railroad bridge over the Mississippi River, between Illinois and Dubuque, Iowa. It is for an Illinois Central lease line, and it is built at a cost of slightly more than a million dollars.

Children in runaway balloon (see story p. 77)
Frank Leslie's Illustrated

The Republicans hold their national convention at Chicago's Crosby Opera House and nominate U.S. Grant for president. As it turned out, Grant was a failure at the job, appointing political cronies to positions, providing weak leadership, and tolerating an administration that was rife with corruption.

The first blast furnace for processing iron ore is built in Chicago by the Chicago Iron Company. The molten iron extracted from the ore was poured into molds that reminded workers of rows of suckling piglets, so the resulting ingots were called "pig iron." Interestingly, Illinois will become one of the leading steel producers in the nation (ranked 4th in 1880) despite not having deposits of iron ore.

In 1871 the **Joliet** Iron and Steel Company produces a second blast furnace. A large steel making complex would develop after the turn of the century in the metro-east downstate area of **East St. Louis, Alton**, and **Granite City**.

The first meeting of the Patrons of Husbandry, a farmers' organization founded in 1867 by O.H. Kelley, an employee of the Department of Agriculture, is held in the Chicago office of the *Prairie Farmer*. The organization **evolves into the "Grange"** which, in turn, later becomes the NFO. The word grange is a French term for a barn.

The official state seal is adopted. It depicts an eagle standing on a rock with the dates 1818 (statehood) and 1868. One talon is holding a red white and blue shield with stars and stripes on it. The eagle has a ribbon in its mouth with the state motto: State Sovereignty, National Union.

Bushman the gorilla

1869 - Grand Tower Mining Company operates a brick furnace on the site of what is known as the Devil's Backbone near **Grand Tower**.

A normal school for teacher training is established at **Carbondale**. It will evolve into Southern Illinois University. In the 1950s it was one of the fastest growing colleges in America. It was called the Suitcase College because many of its students went home to other communities on weekends. Today, Carbondale graduates more African-American students than almost any other large university in the state.

Frederick Weyerhauser and C.A. Denkman begin lumber operations at **Rock Island**. Weyerhauser eventually moves to the state of Washington as the nation expands, and today is a giant in the lumber industry.

Chicago inventor Ives McGaffrey is issued a patent for the vacuum cleaner.

The National Prohibition Party is formed in Chicago.

The steamer *Stonewall* catches fire near **Cairo** and burns, killing 200.

Chicago replaces St. Louis as the headquarters of the U.S. Army's Division of the Missouri, because of Chicago's superior connection to the Great Plains area by railroad and telegraph. The war against the plains Indians for the next ten years would be directed from Chicago by Philip Sheridan. While the destruction of the Indians and their culture and way of life is tragic, it must be remembered that the U.S. government was only doing what was demanded of it by whites who wanted Indian land for homesteading.

Stern wheeler and side wheeler steamboats in Illinois waters

1870 – A convention in 1869 draws up a new constitution for the state of Illinois that goes into effect a year later. This is the third constitution for the state. The 1848 constitution was seen as outdated and too restrictive. The legislature was given the power to regulate railroad and warehouse rates. The consideration of "private bills," affecting just one person (as in a name change) was now forbidden. Prior to this, there were almost as many private bills as there were for the public good. Cumulative voting to better enable minority representation was an interesting feature. Also, the General Assembly was forbidden to propose no more than one amending article per session. The new document gave the General Assembly the power to regulate railroads and grain elevators. This led to the historic case of **Munn v. Illinois** where the U.S. Supreme Court affirmed the right to regulate railroads for the public good. Salaries of public officials could not be altered during the incumbent's term of office. The Supreme Court was increased in size from 3 to 7 members. A 2/3 requirement was needed to pass a bill over a governor's veto instead of a simple majority. No suffrage was granted to women or Indians. This constitution cured most of the ills of the 1848 constitution and lasted one hundred years. This revised constitution served as a prototype for the new western states that were coming into the union. This same year, Gail Borden developed a process for making condensed milk in **Elgin**.

The most **famous steamboat race** in the annals of history takes place. The *Robert E. Lee* and the *Natchez* tried to set a new record in an upstream trip from New Orleans to St. Louis. The old record was a little more than three days and twenty-three hours. It was originally conceived as part of a 4th of July celebration in St. Louis. There were so many people who bet on the outcome of the race that estimates ran as high as a total of a billion dollars in wagers. The *Natchez* was favored because for years its captain had held the record.

A pistol shot started the race, and the *Robert E. Lee* pulled ahead of the *Natchez* before the crowd lost sight of the boats. Engine troubles and fog kept the *Natchez* in second place the entire race. When the two boats reached southern Illinois, crowds were lining the levees, and telegraphers were on hand to send reports to the newspapers. The *Robert E. Lee* stopped at **Cairo** to prematurely celebrate an obvious victory and then disaster; it got stuck in the mud. The captain pulled it free just as the *Natchez* came into view. People from all over the region were in St. Louis eagerly awaiting the victor. The *Robert E. Lee* arrived in St. Louis in record time, trimming the old mark by about one hour. The race was immortalized in song and a Currier and Ives print.

D.L. Moody (author's collection)

The fabulous era of steamboats brought to prominence such towns as **East St. Louis, Chester, Grand Tower, Elizabethtown, Cairo, Mound City, Metropolis, Golconda, Moline, Rock Island, Quincy, and Savanna.** Most river towns, especially East St. Louis and Cairo, become notorious for being lawless, wicked and immoral (reputations richly deserved).

A disputed election in **East St. Louis** results in two different city governments and two opposing police forces. The two law enforcement groups battle it out in the streets, leaving **two dead** and several wounded. The skirmish ends with the **arrest of fifteen officers** who are fined $500 each, a tremendous sum in those days.

A group of German Sisters establish the Precious Blood convent at **Ruma**.

D.L. Moody, a Massachusetts transplant, establishes a ministry in Chicago and becomes America's first crusading evangelist, a forerunner of men like Billy Graham, Oral Roberts and Pat Robertson. In 1873 he travels to England and wins enough converts and financial support that he returns to Chicago and builds a church at Chicago Avenue and LaSalle Street. In 1896 he founds the Moody Bible Institute which today remains as one of the largest of its kind in the world. It was said that Moody "**reduced the population of hell** by over a million souls."

The town of **Raleigh** in Saline County leads the state in tobacco production.

Illinois now ranks first among the states in corn and wheat production.

German Chancellor Otto Von Bismarck says: "I wish I could go to America, if only to see that Chicago. Chicago's nickname, The Garden City, becomes increasingly popular.

Both piers of the Eads Bridge, being built at East St. Louis, now project above the water line in the Mississippi River.

The University of Illinois accepts women for the first time.

John Logan, the "Black Eagle," defeats Richard Oglesby to become U.S. Senator.

William Deering invents the "binder" which was eventually replaced by the combine.

A coal shaft is sunk at **St. Johns**, north of **DuQuoin**. Saltwater is discovered instead, and large amounts of the commodity are shipped to market until falling prices cause the operation to shut down in 1906.

1871 – One dry October night,
When everyone was in bed;
Mrs. O'Leary's cow
Kicked over a lantern in the shed,
And said . . . "There'll be a hot time in the old town tonight."

Currier & Ives print of Chicago fire with flames in wrong direction – auth. col.

On October 9th Chicago is devastated by a fire that ravages about 80 blocks. Hundreds of people from Illinois, Wisconsin, and Indiana board trains and visit Chicago to see the damage wrought by Mr. and Mrs. Patrick O'Leary's famous pyromaniac cow (at 137 DeKoven St.). It had been a summer of drought and Chicago, a city of 300,000 people, had wood block streets, plank sidewalks, and mostly wooden buildings - a veritable tinderbox. From the southwest side of Chicago, the fires burned their way north and east, taking out the central business district, ending at Fullerton Avenue. The charred area covered 3.3 square miles, killed about 250 people, destroyed 17,500 buildings, and damage estimates were well over $100 million. **Ironically, Mrs. O'Leary lost her shed, but her house survived intact**. The ravaging flames ran out of fuel after 27 hours and began to die out when fickle Mother Nature decided to send a steady cooling rain to soak the charred remains. Millionaire Potter Palmer, in Europe at the time of the fire, lost 95 buildings to the flames. Nearly 100,000 were left homeless. The only two structures in the main path of the fire to survive were the masoned water tower (looking like an Islamic totem pole) and its sand castle-like pumping station across the street.

President Grant sent a personal check to the city for $1,000.

Civil War General Philip ("**The only good Indian is a dead one**") Sheridan was brought in to establish martial law. Looters were shot on sight. The Union Stockyards and most grain elevators, rail facilities, rolling mills and the dockage on Lake Michigan escaped harm. "The Chicago packers at the yards reportedly used every bit of a hog except his squeal, boasted Gustavus Swift. In 1915 it was amended to … and were planning on selling that to Henry Ford for his auto horns.

After the fire, a group of merchants gathered on State Street and looked at the smoldering ruins of their business establishments. They conferred and then voted on whether to rebuild or move to a more promising area. The only one who stayed was Marshall Field. (A wise choice because Chicago grew to 503,000 by 1880.)

The upside of the fire is that old wooden buildings were now replaced by those of marble, concrete, and steel. Another positive is that it led to the nation's first concerted effort at city planning with strict new building codes.

Towns from all over the country sent trainloads of food, clothing and medical supplies. In another act of generosity, Queen Victoria of England sent books from her personal collection, thus the start of Chicago's public library. It was supplemented by donations of 8,000 other books by Brits from all walks of life.

Prior to the fire, there was strong sentiment in political circles to move the capital from **Springfield** to Chicago. The fire was so devastating that it ended, once and for all, such talk. Peoria was another site that lobbied to be the site of relocation.

Many new homes after the fire took on the architectural look of the Gothic/Victorian style with turrets and mansard roofs. The old McCormick mansion was a fine example.

Author Mel Waskin in the book *Mrs. O'Leary's Comet,* theorizes that the Chicago fire was started by fragments of Biels's Comet that fell to earth that fateful day. According to a number of witnesses, there was a thunderous roar moments before the fire began. A monument has been erected on the site of the O'Leary barn. Named the Pillar of Fire, it is a bronze piece nearly three stories tall, shaped like flames reaching toward the sky.

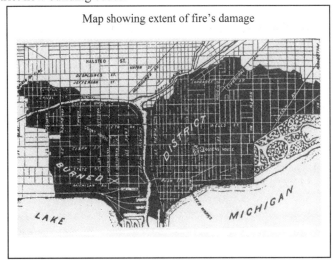

Map showing extent of fire's damage

Myra Bradwell passes the Illinois bar exam but is refused admission by the Illinois Supreme Court solely on the basis of her sex. She persisted and in 1892 became the first female member of the bar association. She also championed the cause of Alta Hulett for admission to the bar. Myra was the founder and publisher of Chicago's *Legal News*.

The **Pontiac Reformatory** for boys under age 16 opens. When state prisons become overcrowded, the age limit is raised to 21 in 1891.

The Baltimore & Ohio Railroad, much to its chagrin, finds it necessary to convert its wide-gauge tracks to the narrower standard gauge used by most railroads. Not wanting to interrupt service between St. Louis and Cincinnati, an army of 1,000 gandy dancing tracklayers are hired to do the conversion overnight.

"Buffalo Bill" Cody

1872 – An act of the General Assembly of Illinois, March 7, is the first free public library law enacted by any state in the union.

The city of **Evanston** passes a local ordinance forbidding the sale of ice cream sodas on Sunday. The reason? It was thought that the "fizz" produced intoxication. William C. Garwood, a drug store owner, began the practice of placing flavored syrup on top of ice cream (which was legal), **thus inventing the ice cream sundae**. The odd spelling of sundae was merely a reflection of the town's Sunday blue laws at the time.

Aaron Montgomery Ward establishes the first of the great mail order houses. He begins a joint venture with his brother-in-law, George R. Thorne, with a capital investment of $2,400. Operations began in a small store with 168 sq. feet of space at Clark and Kinzie Streets in Chicago. The first "catalogue" was a sheet of paper listing items for sale, their price and ordering instructions. Ward had lived and worked with farmers much of his life and was familiar with their special needs. He catered to their interests by designating Ward's as a Grange supply house. Group orders were encouraged to reduce shipping costs and a policy of cash on delivery kept the company solvent. Growth was further insured when the government developed the system of rural free delivery. Catalogues were classified as learning materials, placing them in a cheaper category.

Ned Buntline - wrote about the exploits of Buffalo Bill, "Wild Bill" Hickok, and Wyatt Earp

The Illinois Department of Agriculture is established in **Springfield**.

Reform Republicans, led by Lyman Trumbull, try to wrest control of the party from the Grant faction, but Grant's popularity as a war hero insures another disastrous four years in office. The liberal Republicans nominate a weak candidate, Horace Greeley, and Grant easily defeats both Greeley and the Democrats. Grant's tenure is called the **Era of Good Stealings**.

Buffalo Bill Cody arrives in Chicago to start a theatrical career that evolves into a very popular Wild West Show.

Peter Cartwright, that brawny, sharp-tongued, heavy-fisted fighter for righteousness and Methodism, dies.

1873 – A steamboat named the *Mississippi Queen* departs from Memphis in April. About 12 hours after her departure, the boat disappeared without a trace. A year later the *Iron Mountain*, a very large steamboat with 57 passengers, also vanished. It's possible that both boats were attacked and plundered by river pirates. The boats were either completely dismantled and hidden or burned to destroy evidence.

Hapgood Plow is established in **Alton**. Charles Hapgood, John Lane and George Laughton were the firm's partners. Their improved farm implements sold well both nationally and internationally.

John Hayner purchases a bankrupt glass factory. He also establishes Alton Box Manufacturing that employed over 80 men to make cigar boxes, barrels and crates. He later sells out to Edward Levi and William Smith who become the founders of the Illinois Glass Works in Alton. The works were at Belle Street near Tenth. A few years later, Smith invented the **world's first glass ashtray**. By 1892 the plant employed about 2200 people, and it became the **largest glass producer in the world**. But like the Obear-Nester glass plant in East St. Louis, Illinois Glass fell victim to plastic bottles and aluminum cans. Both factories are now abandoned.

Aaron Montgomery Ward

The huge 665 acre National Stockyards in **East St. Louis** are completed, setting the stage for the city's tremendous growth. Mayor Bowman pocketed $115,000 on the sale.

A huge circus comes to **Metropolis** and other southern Illinois towns, featuring exotic animals, acrobats and the famous petrified man known as the **Cardiff Giant** (later proved a hoax).

There is a national recession and many Illinois towns are forced to open their city hall to provide shelter to families who have no other place to stay.

Spring Grove farmer Fred Hatch, seeking a way to prevent grain spoilage from rain and dampness, **invents the silo**.

1874 – A number of Confederate bodies on Smallpox Island near Alton in the Mississippi River are washed away due to a dike that caused part of the island to wash away downstream.

When Mrs. O'Leary's cow kicked over a lantern and started the Chicago fire in 1871, this led to the bankruptcy of several large insurance companies. The volatile mixture of heat and dust at storage granaries made going without insurance a risky business. David Sparks, owner of several flourmills in **Alton**, decided to start his own insurance company due to the high cost of insurance. This leads to the creation of Miller's Mutual Insurance Company that continues to do a multi-million dollar business in Alton.

Farmers in southern Illinois support the Greenback Party. They wanted the government to print paper dollars, called "greenbacks," so that money would become less scarce and make it easier to pay off their mortgages to banks.

The Workingmen's Party of Illinois is launched, asking for compulsory education, the 8-hour day and the abolition of child labor and prison labor, except on public works. Behind their lofty goals is the notion of a Communist state.

Adlai E. Stevenson of **Bloomington** is sent to congress as a Greenbacker. He is the great-grandfather of the Adlai Stevenson who later became governor. The movement died out by 1884.

Adlai E. Stevenson

Fourteen men are killed while completing construction of the **Eads Bridge** at East St. Louis/St. Louis (1868-74). Most of them died from what they called "caisson disease" (the bends) from going below the water to work on the piers. They took to wearing copper bracelets to ward off the mysterious disease. Before the war, Eads made a fortune salvaging wrecked steamboats from the bottom of the Mississippi.

President Grant officially opened the bridge. It is named one of the Seven Wonders of the Modern World and James B. Eads, the builder, will be hailed as one of the **five greatest engineers of all time**. Built at a cost of $9 million, it is the first pedestrian bridge to cross the Mississippi. A saying soon developed. The Mississippi: discovered by Desoto, explored by Marquette, spanned by Eads. The project took over five years to complete.

Eads, a self-taught engineer, had earlier devised diving bells to descend to the bottom of the Mississippi River to salvage items from boat wrecks. During the Civil War, he built ironclads for the Union. Many ridiculed the bridge upon its completion, saying it would not support any great weight and was destined to fall into the river. The first test of the bridge came with a man who walked across while leading an elephant. The bridge passed its final test with flying colors – 14 locomotives on the arched spans at once. The bridge has two levels, the bottom tier for trains and the upper deck for pedestrians and carriages.

Joseph Glidden of **DeKalb** invents a new kind of fencing material called barbed wire, becomes a millionaire, and later donates the land for the construction of Northern Illinois University. Glidden formed a partnership with Isaac Elwood and the product was sold from Elwood's store in DeKalb. Interestingly, the pair had a bitter competitor named Jacob Haish, who sold his own brand of barbed wire in DeKalb.

Southern Illinois State Normal University is founded. It became the largest teacher-training institute in the state and is home to the Irvin Pheitman exhibition of Indian relics.

1875 – A.G. Spaulding of **Rockford** moves from the Boston Red Sox to the Chicago White Stockings. Spaulding later established a prominent sporting goods company.

For the next twenty-five years the small towns in Illinois enter into what is known as a Golden Era. The towns of this period were beautiful, peaceful, and self-sustaining. With the coming of the automobile at the turn of the century, everything changed. Small manufacturing shops, common in nearly every small town, were eventually put out of business by large concerns that tended to locate in large urban centers.

Northern Illinois Normal School at DeKalb (author's collection)

Mark Twain writes *Life on the Mississippi* in which he describes the Illinois shore of the Mississippi. He mentions a railway and the penitentiary at **Chester** and describes **Grand Tower** as "one of the most picturesque features" of the scenery of that region.

The old courthouse in **Marion**, built in 1858, burns to the ground. All the houses on the same block are also burned. Up to this point, this is the only fire in Marion of any consequence.

Logan Belt, a notorious desperado, born in **Hardin County**, kills Elisha T. Oldham at a dance. As a youth he was almost constantly in trouble, and Belt once nearly killed another youth by attacking him with an ax. At **Shawneetown**, in 1879, he receives a 15-year penitentiary sentence. Governor Oglesby pardoned him six years later and thought he was a changed man. (He was now a Baptist preacher.) Belt was married to Mary Frailey of **Cave-In-Rock**, but he divorced her and abandoned his large family and married his cousin. Less than a year later he was indicted for the murder of Luke Hambrink. Belt was acquitted in Gallatin County, but a year later (in 1887) he was murdered by an unknown assassin.

Mary Todd Lincoln is sent to the Fox Hill Home in **Batavia** after a judge finds her to be insane with grief over the death of her son Tad in 1871. Another son named Eddie had died at an early age back in 1850. Willie, the third son, died in 1862. The only Lincoln child to live to maturity was Robert, born 9 months after their marriage (1843-1926).

Freeman Graham of **Rockford** builds the first sour mash distillery in Illinois.

1876 - Finding the original state capitol building in Springfield too small to meet the expanding needs of government, a new and larger statehouse is constructed. This is the state's present capitol building.

Wild Bill Hickok, famed frontier sheriff from **Troy Grove** in LaSalle County, is shot in the back and killed by Jack McCall. Hickok was playing cards at the time and was holding aces and eights, now known as the "**dead man's hand**" in poker. When **Hickok's gun was examined there were seventy-two notches on it**, none of which were for Indians.

The Ohio River freezes over at **Metropolis**. Ice blocks floating down the river destroy many boats. This will not happen again until 1917-18.

William Hulbert and Albert Spaulding found the National Baseball League in Chicago.

Ben Boyd, a counterfeiter, concocts a **plot to steal Lincoln's body**. He was in prison at the time, and his gang planned to snatch Lincoln's body, bury it, and tell Ben Boyd where it was to use as blackmail for his release. The Secret Service learned of the plot and waited until the gang actually tried to steal the body. One of the officers accidentally discharged his gun and in a terrible mix up, the officers began shooting at each other. In the confusion, the perpetrators escaped but were later apprehended. They were given the maximum sentence allowed – one year for grave robbing.

Out west, General George A. Custer, who graduated last in his class at West Point, leads the 7th Cavalry to doom at the battle (massacre?) of Little Bighorn in Montana. "Yellowhair" was among the last to die and was scalped.

According to historian Milo Erwin, about 50 murders occur in **Williamson County** between 1839 and 1876.

1877 - It was the Civil War that helped make America an industrial nation, and this in turn created a demand for more labor. The large factories that arose and the changes they wrought raised new questions about the relationship of management and labor. Management felt that it had the right to decide wages, hours, and working conditions, and by and large labor accepted this philosophy. But the Depression of 1873 changed all of that. When economic conditions worsened, management cut production, lowered wages, and made layoffs. When prosperity returned after a few years, some managers refused to restore wages to their previous levels. This set the stage for future labor battles in Illinois that would gain national recognition.

Wild Bill Hickok

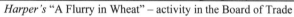
Harper's "A Flurry in Wheat" – activity in the Board of Trade

Aaron Montgomery Ward begins a 13-year battle, using his own funds, to clear an area at the edge of town next to the lake, east of Michigan Avenue. An 1837 city ordinance forbade the erection of any structures on that property in perpetuity, but it had not been enforced for years. After great expense and numerous court struggles, railroad tracks were removed and buildings torn down, creating what is now known as **Grant Park**. It was with great reluctance that Ward later allowed the Art Institute to remain and the Field Museum of Natural History to be built there.

Some of the new immigrant laborers were German, and workers' unions were fairly common where they came from. Unions were now organized in the mining and railroad industries. The year 1877 became known as the year of the strikes, and a succession of riots resulted in a mob attacking the Chicago Burlington & Quincy roundhouse at **Galesburg** and battling police. Strikers also shut down mines and railroads at **East St. Louis, Peoria, Urbana, and Decatur**. Governor Shelby Cullom was forced to ask President Rutherford B. Hayes to send six companies of militia to Illinois before the violence was quelled.

In Chicago, mobs urged on by speeches from the Workingmen's Party attacked factories and burned railroad cars. In one melee, 7 rioters were killed and 25 were seriously injured. Sixteen policemen were hurt.

Rioters marched with red flags (the blood of humanity) and black flags (symbolizing starvation), sang the *Marseillaise* in English or German, and called the new Chicago Board of Trade Building the "Temple of Usury."

J.B. Thomas becomes the first Negro to be elected to the state legislature.

1878 – **Frances Willard of Evanston** becomes president of the Women's Christian Temperance Union –WCTU. She traveled all over the country speaking out against the evils of Demon Rum. During the 1890s the office of the WCTU was an 11-story temple on Chicago's LaSalle and Monroe streets. Her efforts would lay the foundation for the passage of the 18th Amendment that went into effect in January of 1920. She died from the flu in 1898, and in 1905 Illinois honored her with the first likeness of a woman to be placed in Statuary Hall in Washington, D.C. Willard never married or bore children but was a leading advocate of domesticity and motherhood, while calling for women to be given a greater role in public life.

Frances Willard

Work on a new prison at **Chester** is completed. The facilities at **Joliet** had become inadequate, and the state legislature authorized the construction of the new complex.

People from all over southern Illinois flock to St. Louis to see the first annual Veiled Prophet celebration. A huge parade is held, and colorful floats from the New Orleans Mardi Gras participate.

T.C. Moy becomes the first Chinese immigrant to settle in Chicago. She likes it so well she writes to her friends in San Francisco to come join her. Chicago's Chinatown will become the largest in the Midwest.

George Crofutt of Chicago begins publishing a travel guide for people visiting the West. His Great Trans-Continental Railroad Guide contained a detailed description of over 500 towns along with handy travel and "how to" tips. Rand McNally bought him out in 1890.

Police call box

1879 – Western Military Academy is founded in **Alton** by **Edward Lyman**, a transplant from St. Louis University. Like many others of its kind, the academy fell victim to the anti-military stance of the Vietnam era protestors. Declining enrollment forced the Academy to close its doors in 1971. Thanks to the new social milieu created by the anti-establishment groups of the Vietnam War era, Christian schools became *more* popular as public schools grew dangerous and secular. Today the facilities of Western Military Academy are being used by the Mississippi Valley Christian School.

1880 - The town of **Rockwood** is a thriving river port in Randolph County. But the course of the Mississippi river begins to shift, and eventually the town is about a mile from the river. In its early history, it had the name Liberty because it was a stopover point for slaves escaping from Missouri. One of the way stations in the Underground Railroad was a local farmhouse on the road to **Sparta**.

The state's population stands at 3,077,871.

After the Chicago fire turned his first hotel to ashes, Potter Palmer built a new hotel on a filled in frog pond on Lake Shore Drive, giving birth to Chicago's Gold Coast, named for the collective wealth of the people who live there.

James and Joseph Tucker, two IC Railroad officials, develop the idea of shipping bananas up from New Orleans in refrigerated cars to cities in Illinois. For the first time in history, most citizens of the state taste the tropical fruit that would become so popular in the form of a banana split ice cream sundae.

Chicago becomes the **first city in the world** to install police telephone booths to assist the force in its duties.

The Dial (1880-1928) becomes a noteworthy Chicago literary magazine.

Adrian "Pop" Anson's White Stockings team wins its first of five pennants in a row.

Peoria is the **largest corn-consuming center in the world** due to its large number of breweries, distilleries and factories producing corn syrup, starch, and grits.

Dwight-born Dr. Leslie Keeley treats several patients for alcoholism, sent to him by Joseph Medill of the *Chicago Tribune* on a bet. He wins the bet by turning them into gentlemen, and from this he develops the "Keeley Cure," a famous method of treatment for addicts.

The Chicago White Stockings revolutionize the game of baseball and extend the career of pitchers by coming up with the idea of a **pitching rotation.**

Potter Palmer's mansion

A certain Mr. Paquette tells the **DuQuoin** newspaper that while he was fishing in Stumpy Pond, his boat was nearly overturned by a sea-serpent-like creature.

A resort is built at **Creal Springs** in southeast Williamson County. It all started when a malaria-stricken family camped near some springs that had mineral water on the farm of Ed Creal. After drinking and bathing in the water, they claimed to have been cured. The Ozark Hotel and a large bathhouse were constructed, and eventually the town of **Creal Springs** developed around the resort. A city park now occupies the spot of the old resort.

The state's largest mineral springs resort was located in Pike County, a few miles northeast of **Perry**. The site is currently owned by J.L. Wade of **Griggsville**, known for making metal birdhouses for purple martins.

1881 - The Mississippi overflows its banks in April and cuts a new channel through the Kaskaskia River (also known as the Okaw) and around the small town of Kaskaskia. The place suddenly becomes an island, and it is the **only part of Illinois that is now west of the river**. With each successive year, more and more of the original site washed away until nothing was left. The swollen flow of the Mississippi River current fed into the Kaskaskia River that was not capable of carrying such a volume. Since the eastern bank of the Kaskaskia River was composed of limestone rock, the additional riverbed needed was gouged out by washing away the western bank of the Kaskaskia, placing the town in the state of Missouri.

When **Kaskaskia** was first settled, the Mississippi River lay nearly two miles away. But the intervening land was slowly eroded, and prior to the 1881 flood the river was a mere 400 feet away.

With Kaskaskia now on the other side of the Mississippi River, the state of Missouri tried to claim it. There was a huge legal battle that the Supreme Court eventually settled in favor of Illinois. It ruled that Kaskaskia had historically been part of Illinois and that a whimsical act of nature should not change its attachment to that state.

This is the peak year for tonnage on the Illinois-Michigan Canal.

The infamous **Libby Prison**, a notorious fortress holding Civil War Union soldiers at Richmond, Virginia, is brought to Chicago and reconstructed stone by stone. Its walls later became part of the Coliseum, home to numerous political conventions.

Southern Illinois Normal University at Carbondale (author's collection)

1882 - August 8 has long been celebrated as **Emancipation Day** in Southern Illinois. Lincoln signed the Emancipation Proclamation in January, so the August date is perplexing. Most likely, with a majority of Negroes in Egypt being farmers, it was chosen because this was a slack time between planting and harvesting, allowing time for celebrating.

The first recorded observation of this "holiday" was recorded in 1882 at **Elizabethtown** in Hardin County. **Metropolis, Brookport and Carbondale** followed suit. But the biggest annual celebration of this day was held at **Paducah**, Kentucky, where perhaps as many as 10,000 people came on trains from southern Illinois and western Kentucky to attend the festivities. When the KKK rose to national prominence in the 1920s, they derisively called it "Nigger Day."

Traffic on the Illinois & Michigan Canal reaches a peak and then begins a steady decline until it falls into disuse because of railroads. Also, the Sanitary Ship Canal, wider and deeper, opened in 1900.

Oscar Wilde visits Chicago and confounds its citizens with zany and offbeat remarks. His best advice was that Americans should end their fascination with European culture and start developing one of their own, especially in art.

George "Cap" Streeter accidentally grounds his ship on a shoal at the edge of Chicago's shoreline, just west of the present day John Hancock Building. Stranded for good, Streeter convinces local builders to dump fill material at the site, creating the small burg that becomes known as Streeterville. Because the land had been reclaimed from the lake, Streeter claimed that the city of Chicago had no jurisdiction. He set himself up as the ruler. City officials and judges were vexed for decades by the legal technicalities this presented. Finally, old man Streeter was evicted for violating an old blue law prohibiting the sale of liquor on the Sabbath.

It must be remembered that in 1820 the Chicago shoreline, where the Chicago River empties into Lake Michigan, was farther west of its present site. Back then the shore was just short of present-day Michigan Avenue.

Illinois University at Normal (author's collection)

1883 – Land is cheap in Johnson County, selling for only $10 or $15 an acre. In central Illinois the land sells for about $25.00 an acre.

The state legislature enacts the first law for compulsory education for children under the age of 14. Reading, writing, arithmetic, physical training, and proper care of teeth were required subjects. In 1897 the effect of alcohol and narcotics became required.

Governor John Hamilton is forced to send state militiamen to **Collinsville** to disperse striking miners there. The troops were fired upon by the miners, and in an exchange of gunfire, one striker was killed. Twenty-six miners were arrested in the fracas. A year later Governor Oglesby was forced to send the troops to **East St. Louis** to quell striking railway switchmen.

Franklin County becomes the leading coal producer in the state. Underground drownings in Illinois coal mines for this year total sixty-nine dead.

General Philip Sheridan marries a Chicago girl and organizes the Washington Park Jockey Club in Chicago.

Robert Ridgeway of **Olney** organizes the American Ornithologists' Union. He helped create the "official checklist" which all birdwatchers use. The **Mount Carmel**-born Ridgeway also reportedly brought the white albino squirrels to Olney in 1902.

The Romanesque style of architecture is revived, especially in Chicago. Henry Richardson was the originator of this movement featuring low rounded arches.

Three brothers with a sausage shop in Chicago start a company called **Oscar Mayer**. It's hard to believe that from such humble beginnings would come the incredible, the fantastic, the stunning . . . *Wienermobile.*

Jenney's Home Ins. Bldg. – world's first skyscraper

1884 – William L. Jenney designs Home Insurance Co., **the first skyscraper in the world**. It was torn down in 1931. A cast iron frame was used and walls were simply "hung" on the frame. This is still the basis of modern skyscrapers, although steel has replaced iron. Some earlier structures, like the Monadnock Building, had to be raised on stones that were six feet thick.

Thirty-two children, twenty-six nuns, and four novices are killed in a tragic fire at the Immaculate Conception Convent/School, across from St. Peter's Church, in **Belleville**.

Opium dens become popular in Chicago. Opium was legal at the time and was used by many for medicinal purposes and as a painkiller. The substance was usually smoked in a two-foot long bamboo pipe in a dimly lit den, known as a hop joint. Most of the dens were located in Chinatown, often in the back room of a laundry. In 1894 the city passed an ordinance against the practice, shutting down most of the places within a year. Somehow an urban legend grew about how to determine whether a Chinaman was telling the truth or not. According to tradition, a **Chinese lie detector** involved cutting the head off a live chicken and then dipping the yellow man's fingers in the warm blood.

Senator John Logan, one of the most popular politicians in the state, tries to secure the Republican nomination for president but loses out to James G. Blaine in a convention held at the Chicago Exposition Building. Logan accepts the second spot on the ticket but for the first time since 1856, Democrats win the presidency with Grover Cleveland.

The Whiskey Trust is organized by Joseph Greenhut of **Peoria**, forcing smaller concerns out of business. Six of the 12 largest plants in the trust were in **Peoria**. The monopoly was not dissolved until the trust-busting era of Taft and Teddy Roosevelt.

A skating rink called the Casino opens in Chicago. It is one of the largest facilities of this type ever built with room for 1,000 skaters at one time and 3,000 spectators.

Illinois-born lawman, Bat Masterson

1885 - Four-time mayor of East St. Louis, **John Bowman,** is assassinated near his home at 10th and College. At the time he was involved in a contentious lawsuit against the powerful Wiggins Ferry monopoly. His killer is never found, and East St. Louis will become infamous for its unsolved murder cases. **Thomas Furlong**, a railroad detective working out of **St. Louis** for railroad magnate Jay Gould, finds two witnesses who claim that Bowman's killers were a couple of policemen, but the witnesses mysteriously disappear, and the murder is never solved. In a memo to his boss, Furlong calls East St. Louis the "toughest of the tough towns— **tougher than Dodge City**, Kansas," which had to be tamed by Wyatt Earp.

George Pidgeon of Cairo publishes a book - *Diluvium or the End of the World* - in which he predicts that the canal-building activities of mankind would bring about climatic changes that would **destroy life on Earth**. Climatic changes, he said, would cause the polar caps to melt. Such a large shift of water mass, he claimed, would cause the earth to wobble on its axis and result in great trauma. He predicted the end would come sometime between 1889-1892.

In later years, a St. Louis scientist named Iben Browning claimed that he knew the exact day in 1990 when the **New Madrid Fault** was going to destroy much of the area with a quake of strong magnitude on the Richter scale. Southern Illinois towns foolishly spent thousands of dollars preparing for an event that never happened. In Madison County, most schools were either dismissed for the day, or officials had school busses waiting to take kids home at the first sign of a tremor.

The Illinois Central now has branch lines all the way to Sioux City, Iowa, in the West and to New Orleans in the South. The lower extension ran in a straight line from **Cairo**, through Kentucky, Tennessee, and Mississippi, down to the port of New Orleans on the Gulf of Mexico. Its slogan was "**The Main Line of America**."

A structure that would become known as the Fine Arts Building is completed in Michigan Avenue. Frank Lloyd Wright had an office there, and it was once an assembly plant and showroom for the Studebaker Carriage Company. The Indiana-based company was the only buggy maker to successfully make the transition to manufacturing cars.

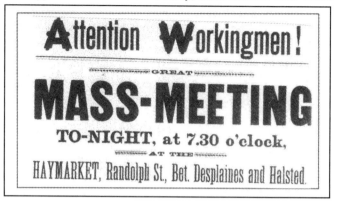

1886 – Octave Chanute teams with Joseph Card and establishes Chicago Tie Treatment Company. To validate the life span of the creosote treated ties, dated spikes were used. It was determined that the treatment increased the life span from about 6 years to over 20.

Richard Warren Sears, a train station agent, begins selling watches through other station agents. When he accumulates enough capital, he moves to Minneapolis and establishes the R.W. Sears Watch Company. After a year he moved to Chicago and hired another watchmaker, Alvah C. Roebuck, who would become his lifelong partner. They added jewelry to their inventory and began selling by mail order, requiring a 50-cent deposit. In 1891 Sears sold out to his partner but changed his mind a week later and ended his retirement at age 27. In 1893 the name was changed to **Sears, Roebuck and Company**. The mail order business expanded through aggressive advertising, selling guns, shoes, organs, sewing machines and even automobiles and houses. The partners started producing a catalog, enabling residents of rural America to have access to items heretofore available only to city dwellers.

Richard W. Sears (author's collection)

Holabird and Roche begin construction of Chicago's Tacoma Building.

Deputy sheriffs **kill six rioting workers** on the Cahokia Creek Bridge (East St. Louis) during a contentious railroad strike. The rioters on the bridge were pelting trains below with brickbats and large stones. The sensational story, complete with lithographs, appeared in *Frank Leslie's Illustrated* magazine.

Organized labor kept pressing for an eight-hour day and better wages and conditions. A group of anarchists began spreading their radical doctrine among immigrant workers in Chicago. August Spies, editor of the *Arbeiter Zeitung*, wrote editorials urging workers to take up arms. There was a strike at the McCormick Reaper Works near **Chicago**. Management brought in Pinkerton strikebreakers, and **two workers were killed** in a skirmish outside the factory. The next day a meeting was called by anarchists to protest the killings. A police battalion came to the square and ordered the crowd to disperse. Someone from the crowd threw a homemade bomb, wounding sixty-seven and killing seven policemen. Seven of the anarchist leaders were tried, found guilty, and four were executed. The men were convicted largely on circumstantial evidence and by radical statements made in favor of anarchy others testified they heard them make. Albert Parsons once called dynamite "democratic" because it made everybody equal. One of the convicted, Louis Lingg, committed suicide by **exploding a dynamite cartridge between his teeth**.

Even before the bombing, Chicago was a hotbed of anarchist activity with six radical newspapers being printed on a weekly basis. About forty percent of Chicago's population was foreign born.

Combined river and rail shipments give **Cairo** the **highest per-capita commercial valuation in the United States**.

The state's first producing oil well is drilled. Thirty–four of the state's 102 counties will eventually produce oil.

Haymarket Square riot executions

1887 – August Spies, Albert Parsons, Adolph Fisher and George Engle are hanged for their roles in the Haymarket Riot of the previous year.

Fort Sheridan is established along Lake Michigan after Chicagoans lure the federal government there with 600 acres of free land in return for the security of having federal troops close at hand to protect private property.

In **Murphysboro,** a group is formed known as the "Jackson County Anti-Horse and Mule-Thief Association." It soon spreads its activities to curbing the theft of chickens and other livestock. Their authority extended to a five-mile area around the town.

A group of St. Louis industrialists, spurred on by the high cost of bringing coal into St. Louis because of the Eads Bridge/Wiggins Ferry monopoly, form the **Madison** Land Syndicate to promote the construction of the Merchants Bridge (1890). The new bridge had the unintended effect of diverting St. Louis capital to the embryo Tri-Cities in Illinois. The American Car Foundry built a plant on the site of Madison in 1891. Two rows of small houses near the foundry were incorporated as the village of Madison by the Land Syndicate.

By 1939 Madison's population was 7,661. Nearby **Venice,** smallest of the Tri-Cities in 1939 at 5,362, dates back to 1804 when a ferry was established there. It was named for the Italian city due to the frequent flooding of its streets. A switchyard, built in 1891 near the Merchants Bridge, promoted a considerable growth in population.

The other town designated as one of the tri-cities is **Granite City**.

George Hancock, a reporter for the Chicago Board of Trade, hating to give up baseball during the course of winter, **invents the game of softball**, which was played indoors with a larger, softer ball.

An excursion train belonging to the Toledo, Peoria & Western Railroad falls from a burning culvert and 85 passengers are killed (some reports place the figure at 81). Earlier in the day a road gang had purposely started a fire to clear the area around the tracks of dry prairie grass. They left without noticing that the fire had not gone completely out. Strong winds rekindled the blaze which burned the wooden supports of the bridge.

A round trip ticket to see Niagra Falls had cost a mere $7.50 – quite a bargain. Eleven coaches crashed to the ground, killing scores and injuring about 140 people. The Niagra Falls Special had started its journey in **LaHarpe** in Hancock County and had passed through **Peoria** earlier that morning. This was to be one of the worst train wrecks in Illinois history.

Entrepreneur Potter Palmer

1888 - **Carl Shelton** is born to Ben Shelton (born 1861) and Agnes Gaither Shelton, a Wayne County girl. Ben's father came to **Wayne County** from Kentucky. His parents farmed 120 acres near **Merriam,** a hamlet five miles east of **Fairfield**. All nine of Ben's children were born here, with five boys and two girls reaching adulthood. Brother Earl was born in 1890, and Bernie was born in 1899. Carl would become the leader of a notorious southern Illinois gang.

A tornado strikes **Mt. Vernon** and the casualties are so numerous that **Clara Barton,** founder of the Red Cross, converts a building on 14th and Main into a hospital.

East St. Louis pulls itself out of the mud by raising street levels an average of twelve feet. The staggering cost of the project is nearly a million dollars. The engineer in charge of the project makes a miscalculation and raises the streets nearly a foot higher than intended, costing the city an extra $100,000. The despondent man, his reputation tarnished, committed suicide. Several years later, rising floodwaters threatened to once again inundate the city. The only thing that prevented it was the extra foot "mistake" by the engineer.

1889 – A woman, whose last name was Chris, claims to have seen a ghostly funeral procession going silently from the old Fort Chartres to a cemetery in **Prairie du Rocher**. Those who believe in the supernatural say that the woman saw a replay of a funeral that dates back to when the French occupied the fort. According to the tale, a local man got into a violent argument with one of the officers of the garrison and was killed. The commander at Kaskaskia advised that the whole sordid affair be kept as quiet as possible and suggested that the local man be buried in the middle of the night at the Prairie du Rocher cemetery.

Jane Addams, born in 1860 in **Cedarville,** co-founds Hull House at 335 Halstead for Chicago immigrants. She will be awarded the Nobel Peace Prize in 1931.

Dr. Patrick Cronin is murdered in Chicago by the Clan-Na-Gael, a secret group working for Irish independence from England. Five men were caught and given prison sentences. Cronin was involved with the clan but was thought to be a British spy.

The Whitechapel Club is formed in a Chicago saloon by morbid news reporters. This drinking/social club was named for London's **Jack The Ripper,** who gave newsmen plenty to write about. Consisting of about 90 members, the group had a fascination with death and festooned the walls of its club with hangman's nooses, guns and skulls. In one odd event, the members drank toasts to a Chicago man who committed suicide to prove he had no fear of death. The club took his body to some sand dunes on Lake Michigan and cremated it while drinking and reading poetry. After about 6 raucous years of existence, the club went bankrupt when one of its members embezzled its funds.

Louis Sullivan

Dankmar Adler and Louis Sullivan are engaged as architects and design the new Chicago Opera House. This afforded the *nouveau riche* an opportunity to show off their finery and indulge in pleasures they could now afford. A huge debate occurred when the question of appropriate female attire arose. A new fashion coming in vogue was the low-necked dress known as the décolleté gown. Mrs. Marshall Field expressed a preference for the high neck dress, similar to those worn by actress Sarah Bernhardt. Mrs. Reginald De Koven, wife of the composer who wrote, "O Promise Me," pooh-poohed rumors that wearing such revealing dresses was unhealthy and would lead to catching a cold.

An act by the General Assembly creates the Illinois Historical Library at **Springfield**. It has the nation's second largest collection of Lincolniana, behind the Library of Congress.

The legislature passes what becomes known as the Edwards Law, making public school attendance compulsory until the age of 12.

1890 – **East St. Louis** is hit by a record snowfall, receiving over 20 inches of snow on March 30-31.

Illinois achieves the ranking of 3rd in the nation in industrial production and 8th in agricultural output.

Chicago is now the number two ranking city in population in the nation, earning it the title SECOND CITY, a title it holds for 94 years, being eventually eclipsed by L.A. (thanks largely to illegal immigration). From 1860 to 1870 Chicago tripled its population to 300,000; no other city in world history grew with such astonishing speed. The census shows it to be the third largest state population wise, ranking only behind New York and Pennsylvania.

At this point in history it must be remembered that most funerals of immigrant families took place in the home, and the body was on display for two days in the parlor. The

Crowd attacking police Patrol Wagon near McCormick's Reaper Works 1886

undertaker was responsible for preparing the body for display and furnishing a 6-horse carriage to transport the silk-lined pine casket to the cemetery. Inside the house, it was tradition to cover all mirrors and stop all clocks. In the 1920s, all radios were turned off. Before the funeral, the casket was placed in a slanted upright position and members of the family and friends stood around the casket for a picture to be taken. The trip to the cemetery, led by a small band, was a long affair often lasting most of the day.

A Chicago Literary Renaissance begins and lasts into the 1920s. H.L. Mencken of the *Baltimore Sun* called Chicago the **literary capital of the United States**. The group included Hamlin Garland, Frank Norris, Theodore Dreiser, and included cartoonists, novelists, poets, essayists and a prominent literary magazine called the "Dial."

The Farmers Mutual Benefit Association elects 50 members to the Illinois legislature, enough to give them the balance of power.

Leslie Keeley, a graduate of Rush Medical School, establishes Keeley Institute for the treatment of alcoholism in **Dwight**. Keeley held the odd belief that alcoholism was a disease rather than a moral weakness.

Archaeologists make their first attempt to excavate the great Indian mound at **Collinsville**. A fourteen-foot square pit is dug slightly south of the center, unearthing Indian bones, skeletons, pottery shards, arrowheads and primitive tools. It is believed that when originally built, the mound was a mere 200 yards from the river that had receded by about half a mile.

About 28 counties, mostly in southern Illinois, have grown smaller as a result of residents leaving rural areas and moving to the large cities.

1891 – An earthquake with an estimated magnitude of 5.8 on the Richter Scale hits **Cairo**, Illinois.

Two Catholic parishes in East St. Louis purchase 135 acres at 10101 West Main to establish Mt. Carmel Cemetery in **Belleville**. St. Mary's, one of the parish churches, was torn down in the 1960s due to construction of the Poplar Street Bridge across the Mississippi.

The Chicago firm of Root and Burnham draw plans for the 16-story Monadnock Building. The owner insisted on a building with little scrollwork and few projections, designed to keep pigeons off. It still stands in the Chicago Loop. This same year, the firm of Burnham and Root design the Women's Temple. Burnham's famous dictum: "Make no small plans."

Architect Daniel Burnham

Theodore Thomas establishes the Chicago Symphony Orchestra.

The Socialist Party is organized in Chicago.

Ignaz Schwinn begins manufacturing bicycles in Chicago at 1718 N. Kildare Dr. By 1918 his factory was producing 25 percent of all bicycles in the United States. In 1911 he began manufacturing Excelsior motorcycles on a ten-acre site at Cortland and Lawndale.

Several oat milling companies join together in an effort to produce packaged goods. The result is the **Quaker Oat Company** of Chicago.

Women in Illinois are granted suffrage in school elections.

There is fierce competition between Chicago and New York in the bidding for the site of an exposition to commemorate the 400th anniversary of Columbus' voyage to America. Charles Dana of the **New York Sun** criticized Chicago boosterism efforts and claimed that they were a bunch of windbags and that "its people could not hold a world's fair, even if they won it." This is the origin of Chicago being called the **Windy City**. It has nothing to do with the wind speed in Chicago which is only slightly above average at best. Dana, by the way, was the inventor of the **Gibson Girl**, the idealized version of the All-American-Girl of the 1890s.

Illustrator Charles Gibson immortalized the Gibson Girl look with his pen and ink drawings. The idealized Gibson Girl had hair piled on top of her head and a tiny waist that defied belief. The popularity of this icon declined after World War I.

"Beauty on a bike" 1889

The Australian Ballot Act is passed by the legislature. Henceforth, the government, not political parties, will be responsible for the printing of ballots used in elections.

William Wrigley comes to Chicago as a baking powder salesman. As an added incentive, he gave away a pack of chewing gum with each box of powder sold. He will soon discover there is more money to be made from Central and South American chicle than baking powder.

1892 – Franklin Olin starts a company named the Equitable Powder Manufacturing Co. This evolved into the Olin Corporation whose plant is still on the original site on Powder Road in **East Alton**. The company originally made black powder that was used for blasting in area coalmines. **Western Cartridge Company** was started in 1898. Since ammunition was housed in metal cartridges, a brass mill was added to the complex in 1916. During the Great War the company profited by selling ammunition to the Allies. In 1931 the company bought out the Winchester Arms Co. of Connecticut. This led to the development of the famed M-1 army carbine that helped win World War II. Currently, the company makes the "sandwich" metal that is used for most coins at the U.S. mint.

The 22-story Masonic Temple in Chicago, built by the firm of Burnham and Root, becomes the world's tallest building.

What will become known as the **Pope County Stone** becomes involved in its first of several ownership disputes. The use of a "**madstone**" back then was quite common as a home remedy for bites from insects, snakes, and rabid animals. This rectangular shaped stone, about an inch in length, was thought to have come to this country from Italy. The owner claimed that it had been used about a hundred times and was effective in every instance, save one. The stone, said to have magical healing powers, was placed directly over the site of the wound. When Louis Pasteur discovered a real cure for rabies, madstones quickly fell out of favor.

Chicago cable car (author's collection)

Chicago's elevated transit system, the "El," opens. Originally pulled by steam locomotives, the system was changed over to electric by means of a 3rd rail. It eventually loops around the entire downtown district. Many mistakenly believe this is the origin of The Loop, but this moniker goes back to the 1880s when cable car tracks looped around the downtown district. The El became famous for its use in a chase scene in the Steve McQueen movie, *Bullitt*.

Washington Square Park in Chicago is nicknamed "Bughouse Square." It becomes a popular discussion site where people meet to rehash issues of the day or give soapbox speeches on topics such as crime, woman's suffrage, the economy, or Marxism.

Newsman Finley Peter Dunne creates a cartoon character named **Mr. Dooley**, modeled after an Irish saloonkeeper he knew. His character made witty and caustic observations about life and politics in the 1890s. Dooley's foil was based on real-life John McKenna, an alderman of the 6th Ward. McKenna's alter ego was named Mr. Hennessey. The characters spoke about everyday events as well as national issues. One piece on Admiral Dewey's victory at Manila Bay in the Spanish-American War launched the characters into national prominence.

Julius Rosenwald of Sears

The new Chicago University, built with donations from men like John D. Rockefeller and Marshall Field, opens its doors for business. The original had gone bankrupt in 1886.

The Klondike gold rush will draw many young Illinoisans to Alaska but the *Tribune* publishes an editorial stating that economic opportunity in Chicago is still the best gold rush.

Chicago streets at this time are mostly paved with cobblestones or cedar blocks. The first automobile appears on Chicago's streets, an electric vehicle. Some Illinois towns despise the new horseless carriage and pass ordinances requiring a man with a **red flag to precede the car as it moves down the road**.

Democrat John Peter Altgeld becomes the first foreign-born and the first Cook County man elected governor of the state. He was supported by a farmer-labor-Democrat coalition. Altgeld appoints Florence Kelly, an associate of Jane Addams at Hull House, to be a factory inspector. Altgeld is also responsible for initiating the parole system in the state prisons as a reward for good behavior.

Grover Cleveland wins a second term as president and his vice-president is Adlai E. Stevenson of Illinois. Stevenson was added to the ticket to bring in votes for the Democrats in the Midwest.

The Lone Star Saloon, located in a Chicago vice area known as Whiskey Row, is run by a rascal named **Mickey Finn**. He becomes famous for a drink called a Mickey Finn Special. It was laced with a white powder Finn had obtained from a Caribbean voodoo doctor. The knockout concoction rendered its victims unconscious, whereby Finn would pick their pockets and then dump them into the alley. His name becomes a part of our national lexicon.

Eleven people die when the steamer *Frankie Folsom* capsizes at **Pekin**.

Woodrow Wilson, a professor at Princeton, turns down an offer to become president of the University of Illinois for $6,000. He rejects it because he has little sympathy for co-education, and the offer does not include housing.

The federal government begins to build the 75-mile long Hennepin Canal (later renamed the Illinois and Mississippi Canal) from **Bureau** on the Illinois River to **Milan** where the Rock River meets the Mississippi. This **Hennepin Canal** links up with the Illinois and Michigan Canal in the west at **LaSalle**. As a commercial success, the $7 million dollar canal was a failure. The idea for such a canal was conceived in 1834 at the town of Hennepin. The canal would be closed to traffic in 1951.

A fire destroys the hotel and mineral springs resort at **Okawville** in Washington County. A new hotel is built and the business, started shortly after the Civil War, is still thriving.

The Free Methodists establish **Greenville College** in Greenville in Bond County.

1893 - Chicago hosts a world's fair – the Columbian Exposition, celebrating the 400th anniversary of Columbus' discovery of America. President Cleveland officiated at the opening ceremonies. Admission was fifty cents. The famed Polish pianist Padereweski performed at one of the concerts, insisting that his instrument be a Steinway. Her Royal Highness, the Infanta Eulalia of Spain and her husband attended the fair with much fanfare. Potter Palmer's wife held a reception in her honor. John Philip Sousa's band provided the entertainment. Another visitor was Archduke Francis Ferdinand, heir to the throne of Austria-Hungary. His assassination in 1914 would be the spark that lit the fire for World War I.

Little Egypt (author's collection)

The prominent Frederick Law Olmstead was hired as landscaper. He had secured his fame by planning New York's Central Park. Since buildings would be torn down after the exposition, White City was cheaply clad with a mixture of plaster, cement and jute fibers. The only building constructed of sturdy materials was the Palace of Fine Arts, which in 1933 became the Museum of Science and Industry. Unfortunately, there is also a financial panic and national recession in 1893.

Daniel Burnham, engineer in charge of construction, managed to create from scrub marshland an impressive modern white complex with refreshing green spaces containing serene pools and fountains. The entire exhibition site was simply magnificent. Thousands of residents from Illinois flock to Jackson Park on Chicago's lakefront for the festivities. Three replicas of Columbus' sailing ships, the Niña, Pinta and the Santa Maria, graced the harbor. Buffalo Bill Cody and Annie Oakley were featured performers and Clarence Darrow, Samuel Gompers, and Frederick Douglass gave symposiums. Frederick Jackson Turner read his paper on "The Significance of the Frontier on American History."

Another popular draw was an Egyptian dancer (Fahreda Mahzar) known as **"Little Egypt,"** who gyrated the hoochie coochie to the soulful sounds of a flute. She died in Chicago 43 years later.

Illinoisan **George Ferris** introduced his impressive "wheel" at the fair. It was 250 feet high, and each of its thirty-six compartments held forty people. One compartment held a band that played tunes as the wheel revolved. Called by some a "monstrous bridge on an axle," Ferris wanted something for the fair that would rival the Eiffel Tower of the Paris Exposition of 1889. Another sideshow attraction was the European strongman Sandow, brought to the event and managed by showman Florenz Zeigfield Jr.

A German immigrant named F.W. Rueckheim served fairgoers a new treat that consisted of popcorn coated with molasses and placed a small prize inside each package. One person, tasting it for the first time, exclaimed, **"That's a Cracker Jack,"** thus giving the new confection a name.

There were 17 major buildings and numerous smaller ones from 46 foreign countries and most of the states. The Manufacturers and Liberal Arts Building was the **largest in the world** at the time. These buildings will cause architects throughout the country to turn away from old Victorian and Romanesque styles and revert to a "white classical" style with traces of Saracenic (Moslem) influence. Louis Sullivan was not happy with the buildings of the fair and condemned their influence. (Probably sour grapes because he was left out.) Exhibits that were left after the fair ended formed the nucleus of two museums – the Museum of Natural History (later endowed by Marshal Field), and the Museum of Science and Industry. The **incandescent light** was one of the new marvels on display at the fair. The fair also featured the famed Midway with carnival games.

Thomas Edison's kinetoscope (movie projector) drew large crowds at the exposition. The wooden cabinet showed a 50-foot long movie to one person at a time. Chicagoans George Spoor and William Selig soon developed projectors that cast images on a screen.

Impoverished Negroes were drawn to exhibits when a "Colored Day" was held, promising 2,000 free watermelons.

Octave Chanute organized an International Aeronautics Congress as part of the Columbian Exposition – America's first aviation meeting.

A Viking longship sailed into Chicago harbor, and its Norwegian crew was given a 21-gun salute. Magnus Andersen, a merchant seaman, sailed the ship from Norway to prove to the world that Vikings could have reached the new world before Columbus. The *Viking* was a replica of a ship called *Gokstad*, built circa 900 A.D. The ship crossed the North Atlantic in 28 days, and thousands of visitors to the World Fair flocked to see it.

Meatpacker Gustavus Swift

Buffalo Bill was not invited to participate at the fair because his show was merely considered entertainment. Miffed, he rented 14 acres across from the main entrance to the fair and sold thousands of tickets to his Wild West Show, featuring Chief Rain-in-the-Face (who claimed to have killed Custer) and "Little Sure Shot," **Annie Oakley**.

The fair ended on a sour note when Chicago's 5-time mayor, Carter Harrison, was assassinated. Harrison was shot and killed by a visitor to his home. W.S. Chalmers, president of Allis-Chalmers Steel, who lived across the street, heard the shots and rushed over to the house to give aid. The assassin, a deluded man named Patrick Prendergast, escaped but later walked into the Des Plaines police station and announced that he had killed the mayor. Prendergast was tried, convicted and hanged for the murder.

Litchfield's Planet Mill burns. It was capable of producing 2,000 barrels of flour daily.

John Peter Altgeld (the Eagle Forgotten), a German-born governor, commits political suicide and pardons 3 anarchists who were convicted in Chicago's Haymarket Square Riot. Altgeld was the first Democrat elected governor since the Civil War.

"The Democratic party (in Chicago) is built upon bribery, intimidation, bulldozing of every kind, knifing, shooting and the whole swimming in whiskey." – William T. Stead

The Bá'hà'í faith is introduced to Chicago by a missionary who attends the Columbian Exposition. The eastern faith is an offshoot of Islam, founded by Mírzá Ali-Muhammad, who proclaimed to be a new messiah. He was branded a traitor by traditional Muslims and died in a Palestinian jail in 1892. His son carried on his teachings and writings. The religion teaches equality among the sexes and stresses peace and education. In 1906 the group bought a site in Wilmette, near Lake Michigan. In 1953 its converts built a strikingly beautiful temple that has become a Chicago landmark. Its pylons contain symbols of all the world's great religions and include the Crescent, the Christian Cross and the Swastika, the ancient symbol of good luck used by Hindu and American Indians. (708-256-4400)

Hundreds of people from all over the state join Jacob S. Coxey of Massilon, Ohio, in his march of the unemployed, known as **Coxey's Army**, on Washington, D.C. to protest hardships brought on by the Depression of 1893.

Peoria ranks number one in the country in the amount of revenue paid to the U.S. Treasury. This is due mainly to the 14 distilleries located in or near the city.

Chicagoans Swift, Armour and Nelson Morris build packing plants in East St. Louis. In size, its stockyards will be second only to Chicago **and will surpass Chicago** in the horse, mule, and hog markets.

A marble likeness of General James Shields is sent to Statuary Hall in Washington D.C., but due to lack of space, is placed in the Hall of Columns. Shields was a brigadier general in the Mexican and Civil Wars, and a senator and governor of Oregon Territory.

Illinoisan Charles Cretors receives a patent for his invention of the **popcorn machine**.

Paul Beich establishes a candy business in **Bloomington** on East Front Street. His company will grow to become one of the best-known candy companies in America.

Future evangelist **Billy Sunday**, an outfielder for Chicago, sets the record for stolen bases in baseball with 83 thefts. Ty Cobb will break the record in 1915.

Meatpacker Nelson Morris

1894 – The architectural firm of Adler and Sullivan completes the 13-story Chicago Stock Exchange building at LaSalle and Washington, razed in the 1970s.

One of the most bitter labor disputes in history takes place at the Pullman Sleeping Car Factory near Chicago. The workers lived in a company town, but it was not a model of progressiveness. Some said it smacked of feudalism. It lacked home ownership and local self-government. When the Depression of 1893 hit, the coldhearted Pullman cut wages by 25 percent but did not lower rents.

Federal troops guard a train during the Pullman strike (author's collection)

The frustrated workers finally went on strike and were joined by the American Railway Union, led by Eugene Debs. Debs and his officers sought to meet with Pullman to negotiate an end to the strike. But an obstinate Pullman refused to budge. Mail cars were attached to the trains and an injunction was issued to prevent the strike from interfering with the delivery of mail. Debs was imprisoned for violating the injunction. Embittered, he became a radical and **founded the American Socialist Party**.

Within a few days rail workers all over the state were on strike, and rail traffic ground to a halt. Railroad managers asked President Grover Cleveland to send federal troops, and he did so to keep mail delivery alive. When Debs violated an injunction he was sent to jail for six months, despite being defended by Lyman Trumbull and Clarence Darrow. The strike was broken.

Residents of **Shakerag** (the town's saloon hoisted a rag to indicate a new arrival of whiskey) move their town on rollers and rename it Johnston City for B.F. Johnston, president of the new Chicago & Eastern Illinois Railroad in their area.

A decision is made to hold all future state fairs in the city of **Springfield**.

The University of Chicago baseball team plays a game wearing maroon socks, giving rise to the nickname, Maroons.

1895 – Hampered by the need for better local transportation for securing raw materials and distributing finished products, Levi and Smith combine with sundry area investors to form the Illinois Terminal Railroad.

Chicago's rise in immigrant population causes it to be the second largest city in America. "Chicago is the second American city, the fifth German city, the third Swedish, the second Polish. . . ." – G.W. Steevens

Chicago's meatpacking barons are among the city's richest and most eccentric. Gustavus Swift thought it extremely bad taste to live ostentatiously and for years resided in a modest home near his plant at the stockyards. When he did move to a nicer brick home, he only adorned the windows with curtains after his wife threatened to leave him.

Few, if any, of the sons of Chicago's *nouveau riche* were able to successfully follow in their father's footsteps - probably because they had been given softening cultural advantages and were pampered their entire lives, making them unfit for the rigors and challenges of the business world.

Nelson Morris is reputed to be the finest judge of cattle in the entire world. He was said to be able to immediately be able to tell what part of the country the steer had come from when he consumed a steak.

Philip Armour devoted all of his time to his business and had no other outside interests except attending church on Sunday.

Rudyard Kipling visited Chicago, the city that he called "the most American of cities," but was critical of its crass materialism in one of his poems:

"I know thy cunning and thy greed/ Thy hard high lust and willful deed/ And all th' glory loves to tell/Of specious gifts material"

George Huff becomes football and baseball coach at the University of Illinois and helps make athletics an integral part of university life. He helps form an athletic conference that includes Northwestern, the University of Chicago, Wisconsin, Purdue, Michigan and Minnesota, leading to the formation of the Big Ten.

Early Duryea automobile

The first mineshaft at **Herrin** is sunk; the town incorporates in 1898.

The *Chicago Times-Herald* sponsors the first American auto race, a contest billed as the "Race of the Century." It was won by Frank Duryea and his brother, bicycle shop owners from **Peoria**. The race course is from Jackson Park to Evanston and back, a total of about 40 miles over which they averaged about 5 miles an hour.

Streetcars make their first appearance in Chicago on Clark Street.

1896 – Chicagoan Octave Chanute successfully flies a bi-wing glider at Miller Beach on the nearby Indiana Dunes by the Calumet River on Lake Michigan. His aeronautical research helps usher America into the Age of Flight. Many of his books and a model of his 1896 glider are on display at the John Crerar Library at the University of Chicago (773-702-8717).

A devastating **tornado** strikes the southern part of St. Louis, barely missing the main downtown district, **killing about 114 people**. It crosses the Mississippi, after destroying many boats in the harbor, and wreaks havoc in East St. Louis, killing 115. It is the single worst catastrophe ever to befall either city. Damages in **East St. Louis** were estimated at $4 million and in St. Louis at $11 million.

Three days earlier, a cyclone capsized the ferryboat *Katherine* at **Cairo**, killing eleven of sixteen people aboard, including Wood Rittenhouse, father of Maud Rittenhouse. He was manager of Three States Ferry Service. Maud Rittenhouse of **Cairo** kept a fascinating diary that was published in 1939 (*Maud*) that tells about living in southern Illinois during the post-Civil War era.

A mild earthquake strikes southern Illinois causing the waters of many springs to be muddy for several days.

The entire state is swept by a craze for velocipedes. Riding a bicycle becomes a popular form of both entertainment and exercise. Cycling guides dominate most the best-seller booklists.

The Democratic national convention is held in Chicago and William Jennings Bryan is given the nod. Altgeld wanted the nomination but his foreign birth prevented that. Bryan mesmerized delegates with his "Cross of Gold" speech, advocating a bimetal monetary standard (silver and gold) for the nation at a ratio of 16-1. Bryan was defeated by Republican William McKinley.

1897 – George Pullman, the millionaire of Pullman railroad sleeping car fame, dies three years after the bitter Pullman strike of 1894. It was feared that angry workers who had been fired from their jobs might try to steal the body. The solution was to pour several tons of concrete and reinforced steel on top of the casket. Robert Todd Lincoln, the president's son, became the new president of the company. Lincoln, a lawyer, had the misfortune of being close at hand for the assassination of three presidents, his father, James Garfield and William McKinley.

The first suburbs begin to appear in the state just outside the boundaries of large cities in an effort to escape what are perceived to be "disliked" elements.

A statewide strike of coal miners begins at **Mount Olive**, led by a colorful orator by the name of "General" Alexander Brady. Brady wore a Prince Albert coat and top hat. The cemetery at Mount Olive, where miners are buried, will become a shrine of unionism and a scene of annual memorial services.

Adolph Leutgert, a Chicago sausage maker, is charged with the murder of his wife. After she disappeared, the police searched the premises and found some of his wife's teeth and body parts in a large cooking vat. They also found her wedding ring with her initials and last name inscribed on it. **Wiener and sausage sales were markedly down** after the story broke.

F.Y. Hedley (Scottish), editor of the ***Bunker Hill Gazette***, fatally shoots the mayor of Bunker Hill, J.R. Richards. The two men had a long-standing feud stemming from an alleged relationship between Hedley and Richards' wife, Ella Brown. The affair between Hedley and Brown began when Hedley, the organist at the local Congregationalist Church, was assigned the task of instructing Richards' wife to be the alternate organist. At the time, Richards was about 65, his wife 35, and Hedley was age 53.

Since Richards had started the fracas by striking Hedley with his cane, a county jury in **Carlinville** saw fit to acquit the accused assailant of manslaughter. Hedley left Bunker Hill about a year later and was subsequently divorced by his wife who charged him with adultery. He later married Ella Brown.

Liliuokalani, former Queen of Hawaii, visits the city of Chicago.

1898 – Negroes are hired by coalmine operators in **Virden** to replace striking workers and crush the strike. A similar thing happens in **Pana**.

During the Spanish-American War, 385 men die from battle wounds. But an astounding 4,795 die from sickness and disease. General Nelson Miles (the man who captured Geronimo) blames a large number of these deaths on **"embalmed beef," from unsanitary packinghouses in Chicago** and **East St. Louis**.

The only Illinoisans to see action were members of the First Regiment from Chicago in the battlefield around Santiago. General Wesley Merritt, a native of **Salem**, led the occupational forces at Manila in the Philippines.

J. Mason Reeves of **Tampico** is aboard the *U.S.S. Oregon* when it leaves San Francisco on a 3,000-mile voyage around Cape Horn to Cuba. By the time the battleship reached its destination, hostilities were drawing to a close in the Spanish-American War. This incident dramatized the need for a canal to be built at the Isthmus of Panama.

On October 12 a number of men are killed in a gun battle between armed guards and union men over a strike

Mother Mary Jones Memorial at Mount Olive (courtesy Neal Strebel)

dispute at a coal mine in **Virden**. Some of the dead were buried in **Mt. Olive** at Miners Cemetery. In that same cemetery, next to the miners, is the grave of **Mary Jones**, who became a great spokesperson for the cause of labor. She traveled all over the country for the cause of the working class, often leading mop parades of protesting women supporting their husbands. Clarence Darrow described her as a fearless woman who often wore a black bonnet. Her husband and 3 children were killed in an 1861 yellow fever epidemic. When she died in 1930 at the age of one hundred, 50,000 miners attended the dedication of her memorial. To many business executives, Mary "Mother" Jones was the **most dangerous woman in America**.

The levee on the Ohio River breaks, and twenty-five people are drowned in a disastrous flood at **Shawneetown**.

The Eads Bridge at East St. Louis becomes the **first in the nation to be depicted on a U.S. postage stamp**.

Chicago bakeries are forced to reduce the price of a loaf of bread to a nickel after housewives boycott the new six-cent price.

Two male cats, known as the **Lions of Tsavo**, go on a rampage in British East Africa and kill about 130 railway workers. John Patterson, a civil engineer on the construction project, killed the pair. These stuffed mammals, unusual in that they were maneless,

Eads Bridge 1898 Trans-Mississippi issue

were purchased by the Field Museum in Chicago and placed on display. This story was used as the plot for the first 3-D movie ever made (starring Robert Stack), *Bwana Devil*. A later, more accurate, remake was titled *The Ghost And the Darkness*.

1899 -There is a strike at the **St. Louis & Big Muddy Coal Mine** in **Carterville**, the top producing mine in Illinois. The strike is about wages and working conditions. The mine superintendent continues to operate the mine with a reduced force, then brings in a trainload of Negro miners. The group of Negro miners, brought in with their families from **Pena** is attacked by an angry mob. **One woman is killed, and twenty men are wounded**. Two companies of state militia are called in to restore order, and things quiet down temporarily. Two months later, after the militia have been sent back home, another mob attacks the mine and **kills five Negro workers**. The accused were brought to trial in **Vienna** (my parents called it VI-anna, but locals say VI-enna), but were acquitted.

The Mississippi River **freezes so hard** people on both sides of the river can walk across at East St. Louis. Vendors set up refreshment booths to add to the festivity.

Martin Kingman, who formerly built Prospect Heights Summer Hotel, builds Kingman Plow factory near Peoria. The Robert Avery Co. has a large corn planter manufacturing business in **Peoria** at this time. They also built steam tractors.

Aaron Montgomery Ward builds Chicago's tallest building, a warehouse and corporate offices at Michigan and Madison.

1900 - The Farmer's Union, one of the first farm and anti-monopoly organizations in America, was born at the Grange Hall near **Murphysboro**. Railroads were the chief enemy of the farmer in those days. They were accused of favoring big producers and charging exorbitant shipping rates for farm produce.

The first car travels over the new **Collinsville, Caseyville and East St. Louis** electric railway.

The Chicago Sanitary and Ship Canal is completed. A canal was built connecting the Chicago River to the lower, and nearly parallel, Des Plaines River. The two rivers were linked at **Lockport**. The canal reverses the flow of the Chicago River and solves the polluted drinking water problem of the city. Back in 1885, a six-inch rain had flooded the river, contaminating the city's supply of drinking water. The canal was dug deep enough to accommodate ocean-going vessels, and only the Suez Canal was a larger artificial waterway.

Casey Jones postage stamp issued in 1950

HONORING RAILROAD ENGINEERS OF AMERICA
3 CENTS 3
UNITED STATES POSTAGE

Because of the interconnecting waterway, the Chicago River is known as the **river that runs backward** and has been featured in Ripley's "Believe It Or Not." The Illinois River was soon nicknamed the "Crap Ditch" by some because it flushed all of Chicago's waste into the Mississippi and down to the Gulf of Mexico. St. Louisans are incensed that Chicagoans have the audacity to flush their wastes down the Illinois River where it empties into the Mississippi only 14 miles from the city.

The top coal producing communities in Egypt are **Staunton, Mt. Olive, Virden**, **Hillsboro, Collinsville, Belleville, Mascoutah, DuQuoin**, and **Coffeen**. St. Clair County is second in the state, and Madison County is sixth.

Famed engineer **Casey Jones** of **Centralia** dies in a train wreck at Vaughn, Mississippi. His *Cannonball Express*, engine 382, struck an IC freight train that was sticking out on the main track from a siding. He was found in the cab with his hand on the brake control and slowed the train down enough so that no passengers were killed. He will become the first person to be enshrined in the Railroad Hall of Fame. In an era where train wrecks were all too common, this was the only one where the only fatality was the engineer.

Ada Everleigh

The Everleigh Club, a posh brothel at 2131 South Dearborn in Chicago, run by two sisters whose father was a Kentucky lawyer, announce that henceforth they will be open 24 hours a day. This splendid establishment boasted over 50 rooms. **It was a formal policy that Illinois legislators were admitted free.** Marshall Field's son, age 37, died from a fatal gunshot wound, and many believe it happened at the Club but was taken elsewhere. The girls paid protection money, and the conduit to the politicians was **Big Jim Colosimo**. They went too far when they printed up an illustrated brochure that described its fancy parlors and many attractions. A reform mayor closed the club in 1911, and the sisters left Chicago and eventually retired in New York.

The population of Illinois has grown to 4,821,550.

Chicago's First Ward gains the reputation of being the most wealthy, corrupt and sinful in all of Chicago. It encompasses the central business district to the lake. Its colorful areas include **Bed Bug Row, Hell's Half Acre, Hair-Trigger Block, the Badlands**, and **Gambler's Alley**. Its two "odd couple" physical opposite aldermen are Mike "Hinky Dink" Kenna and John "Bathhouse" Coughlin who became known as the "Lords of the Levee." Coughlin acquired the nickname "Bathhouse" because he once worked as a massager at the bathhouse of the Palmer Hotel. It was Kenna who once boasted, "**Chicago ain't no sissy town.**"

Chicago issues 95 permits for electric cars, 55 for gasoline vehicles and 44 for steam operated cars. No offensive horns or whistles are allowed on these "horseless carriages."

Novelist Henry B. Fuller writes: "Chicago is the only great city in the world to which all its citizens have come for the avowed purpose of making money."

A **Litchfield** resident, Perry Commodore Oller, is the oldest living pioneer Indian fighter/scout alive. He was born in 1820. In one famous encounter he was captured by Indians who made preparations to burn him at the stake. He was able to slip a hand loose, jerk a knife from a nearby Indian's belt, thrust it into his body, pick up the pistols dropped by his foe, kill most of those remaining, and escape.

Lincoln's body is moved to a reconstructed Lincoln Memorial. His casket is opened by officials just to make sure that the body belongs to Abraham Lincoln.

The American League is formed for professional baseball, and it has a Chicago team, the White Sox.

Joliet Junior College begins as an extension of Joliet High School and gains the distinction of being the **oldest community college in the nation.**

Chicagoan Carrie Bond publishes a book of songs, one of which is "**I Love You Truly**," still popular at weddings.

Charles Walgreen, born in **Galesburg**, called the "Father of the Modern Drugstore," borrows $2,000 from his father to open his first store in Chicago. It was Walgreen who later introduced the innovation of the lunch counter and the soda fountain.

It becomes fashionable for men and women in cities to carry "calling cards." These were engraved cards about the size of today's business cards with the owner's name and address printed on them. Women's cards were larger than men's and had the day of the week that visitors were welcome to call. Special trays or baskets were placed on tables so the visitor could place his or her card there after the visit, which customarily only lasted about 15 minutes.

Spirit of Peoria on the Illinois River (Illinois Department of Tourism)

1902 – Future mayor Richard Daley is born of Irish Catholic parents on Chicago's south side. An only child, he attended Mass regularly throughout his life.

Patrick Doyle is hanged in **Edwardsville** on January 16 for the murder of a hobo in **Mitchell**, Illinois.

The Coal Belt Line becomes the first electric interurban streetcar line south of East St. Louis. It connects **Marion and Harrisburg with Carterville**.

The Pittsburg(h) Reduction Company opens a plant on 225 acres at 3300 Missouri Avenue in East St. Louis. It will become **the largest processor of bauxite** (for making aluminum) in the world. Because of its many and varied metal and manufacturing plants, East St. Louis is called the "Pittsburgh of the West," a title also claimed by **Granite City** because of its steel mills. By this date, all the Captains of Industry have held investments in East St. Louis including John Jacob Astor, Andrew Carnegie, Philip Armour, Gustavus Swift, Nelson Morris, Andrew Mellon and J.P. Morgan. A saying soon developed: "**If you can't find a job in East St. Louis, you won't find work anywhere.**"

A.F. Callahan of Chicago patents the first envelope with an address window.

1903 – Another major flood hits the southern area (June 8) from **Alton** to **Kaskaskia**. Railroad traffic in East St. Louis came to a standstill. When the floodwaters receded, it was discovered that a new mouth to the Missouri River had been formed several miles downstream from the original.

One Negro, inexplicably caught in the act of destroying the levee by removing sandbags, was shot and killed. East St. Louis was flooded when the Illinois Central Railroad embankment gave way. Residents were awakened by the cries of several men who ran through the streets warning that the flood was coming. Women fainted from fright, and there was disorder everywhere. The whole town became panic stricken. Over 20 lives were lost in **East St. Louis, Venice, Brooklyn, Madison** and **Granite City**. Seven hundred people were rescued from their housetops. Dozens of animals drowned at the National Stockyards, on the northwest side of East St. Louis.

Residents of small houses on 3rd Street abandoned their flooded homes never to return. When the waters receded, the buildings, only a block from City Hall, will formed the core of a new red light district known as **the Valley**.

Granite City's mayor, John Edwards, went to the pump station to restart the engine at the levee. It exploded when he lit a match, and he died eight days later from severe burns. A Madison-St. Clair County levee district was later formed to deal with flood control, and it will become the source of much patronage and much corruption.

A special citizen's committee appointed by Mayor W.J. King secures funds from Andrew Carnegie to construct a library at State and Union streets in **Litchfield** at a cost of over $16,000. It opens in 1905.

A group of circus showmen kidnap six-year old John Layton of **East St. Louis**, place berry stain on his skin and **cage him with monkeys** to turn him into a **"wild boy"** as a sideshow attraction. The boy escaped and notified the police who arrested Sylvester Baker, a Negro, as the man who had caged him. Baker was transported to the county jail in Belleville to prevent a lynch party from forming.

William Hobbe of **Brooklyn**, known as the **Southern Illinois Giant**, died in **Belleville**. Hobbe, age 33, attained the incredible height of seven feet five inches and weighed approximately 234 pounds. Both of his parents were taller than the average person at that time.

David Wyatt, a Negro teacher from **Brooklyn**, Illinois, shoots **Charles Hertel**, County Superintendent of Schools. Wyatt was angered by Hertel's refusal to renew his teaching certificate. Wyatt is dragged from his jail cell by an enraged mob and **lynched at the Public Square in Belleville**.

Thanks to the efforts of the Daughters of the American Revolution, Fort Massac, near **Metropolis**, becomes the **first state park of Illinois**.

The city directory lists **East St. Louis** as the **Queen City of Egypt**.

On December 30, during a holiday matinee of *Bluebeard Jr.*, starring Eddie Foy, a disastrous fire breaks out in the five week old, fireproof **Iroquois Theater** in Chicago's "loop." The 7 story high building held 1,900 people. There were **570 men, women, and children killed within fifteen minutes. The fire started during the second act when either a carbon-arc light or a gas light touched the fabric of a drape. When stagehands lowered the fireproof asbestos drape, it caught on a bank of lights. There were 27 exits but some of them had been locked to prevent gate crashing. Some youngsters were trampled underfoot and suffocated during the mad rush to the exits. The disastrous fire killed more than twice as many people as the Great Chicago Fire 32 years earlier.** Mayor Carter Harrison II canceled the city's New Year's celebration. Most of the cast members took an elevator to the ground level and escaped through a rear exit door.

Two years later, a disastrous fire struck on Broadway in **Johnston City**.

Illinois passes a law regulating the top speed of automobiles at fifteen miles per hour.

The St. Louis Valley Railroad (Iron Mountain) is completed. It runs from **East St. Louis to Thebes**. This railroad on the American Bottom evolved into the Missouri Pacific.

Louis Sullivan designs Chicago's Holy Trinity Orthodox Church at 1121 North Levitt. The Tsar of Russia contributed money for its construction. There were no pews installed for the congregation stood during the entire service. It is now a Chicago landmark.

Frank Norris writes *The Pit*, a protest novel about the Chicago Board of Trade and the wheat market.

1904 – Lincoln R. Steffans, a muckraker, pens *Shame of the Cities*. In it he lambasts Chicago and St. Louis for being cities that were known for being "wide open" and where corruption, bribery and protection were the order of the day.

Hot dogs, ice cream cones and iced tea are introduced to the public at the St. Louis World's Fair. George Ferris' wheel, that was introduced at the Columbian Exposition, was transported to the fair in 175 freight cars and reassembled. When the fair ended, the wheel was dynamited, and the scrap sold for $1,800. **Foot-long hot dogs** were first introduced in the 1930s at Chicago's Riverview Amusement Park.

There was an **East St. Louis Day** and an Illinois Day at the fair. The Cahokia Courthouse, the oldest west of the Appalachians, was moved to the fair and displayed. The Illinois Pavilion features statues of Lincoln and Douglas. When the fair is over, the Lincoln/Douglas statues are placed on the lawn in front of the new Rock High School in East St. Louis.

The national Amalgamated Meatcutters and Butcher Workers Union of North America calls for a huge strike in Chicago's Union Stock Yards and at National City in **East St. Louis**. The strike is broken when scab workers, many of them Negro, are brought in by the company owners. As a result, the power of the union is nearly destroyed. From 1904-16 wages will remain constant in this industry, despite the fact that inflation rises by over 25 percent.

Illinois becomes the first state to adopt the 8-hour workday and 40 hour week for children.

Encouraged by the formation of coal miner unions, teachers in **Harrisburg** form the Saline County Teachers Association, thought to be the **first teacher's union in America**. A schedule of salaries was drawn up for different districts, based on assessed valuation and tax rates.

Coal is discovered in Franklin County, and Peabody No. 19 becomes the first mine.

Riverview Amusement Park, billed as the **"world's largest,"** opens in northwest Chicago on the north Branch of the Chicago River.

A long circulation war between Colonel Robert McCormick's *Tribune* and William Randolph Hearst's *Examiner* begins in Chicago. Moe Annenberg is in charge of Hearst's circulation

Marshall Field and Company: circa 1899 (author's collection)

department, and he employs slugger Frank McErlane to do his dirty business. Before it ends in 1913, rival newspapers, costing a penny each, are burned, delivery trucks are overturned and destroyed, and **27 news dealers are killed**. Annenberg, a German Jew, rejected all religion and saw it as a trap to keep poor people docile. This is similar to the view of Karl Marx who once said, "Religion is the opiate of the people."

Teddy Roosevelt is nominated for president at the Republican convention held in Chicago.

William Scholl, a Chicago shoemaker, decides to expand his business by making products for the feet to help ease the pain of bunions and fallen arches, corns etc. Today there is a museum of podiatry called Feet First at the Scholl College of Podiatric Medicine. One of the more interesting exhibits is a **fluoroscope** that shoe salesmen used back in the 1950s to X-ray customer's feet to insure a proper shoe fit.

Walter Boyle Jr. of Chicago is fined for breaking the state speed limit of 15 mph in an automobile.

Hall of Fame pitcher Ed Walsh begins his career with the White Sox. He is generally given credit for **inventing the "spitter."**

1905 - **Fifty-four men are killed** in an explosion at the **Zeigler Coal Mine** in **Franklin County**. The Leiter brothers believed the mine was blown up on purpose by strike sympathizers. A coroner's jury implied that gunpowder had been involved in the explosion, and that it was not an explosion of gases. Later investigations attributed the disaster to marsh gas and poor ventilation. The mine was owned by **Joseph** and **Levi Leiter** who first bought the acreage in 1902. There was a strike at the mine in 1904 when Joe Leiter reduced tonnage wage rates. Non-union workmen were brought in, violence broke out, and the state militia was called in.

The mine facility was modern and up-to-date, and it led the state in productivity. A company town of **Zeigler** was built, and it was a model community. The houses were weatherized, calcimined and plastered. There was a park in the center of town, and streets radiated out like the spokes on a wheel. There was also a brick schoolhouse and a modern, well-equipped hospital.

Instead of paying the men the going rate of 50 cents a ton, the Leiters paid them only 38 cents and insisted on an open shop. This meant that no worker would be forced to join a union against his wishes.

Mining inspectors closed the shaft, but on January 10, 1909, another explosion **killed a clean-up crew of twenty-six men**. Mine officials decided to ignore a closing order and sent a crew down to make preparations for reopening the mine. On February 9 another explosion killed three men. Later that month, the mine closed forever.

The Southern Illinois and Missouri Bridge Company builds a two-lane railroad bridge across the Mississippi at **Thebes**.

The town of **Dupo**, south of Cahokia, is laid out by Charles Mousette (Mousette Lane).

Dredge boat building levees on Illinois River

The first **Tongs** (Chinese Mafia) are organized in Chicago. The Hip Sing begins as a social club and an organization for helping arriving immigrants. But they also ran gambling parlors and houses of prostitution.

The Pike County community of **Detroit** begins manufacturing a car called La Petite, a two-seater with a one-cycle engine.

A statue of Francis Willard, founder of the WCTU, is placed in Statuary Hall, Washington D.C. It is the **first statue of a woman to be placed in the hall.**

Rotary International is founded in Chicago. In 1955, the U.S. government issued an 8-cent stamp commemorating the organization.

The Chicago Cubs' president signs a larceny complaint against a fan who catches a foul ball and keeps it.

The IWW, a radical labor organization, is founded in Chicago by Eugene Debs and "Big Bill" Haywood.

1906 – An electric interurban trolley line begins service from **Alton** to St. Louis and continues operations up to 1953. The depot was located near the riverfront. The first interurban between **Bloomington** and **Decatur** is completed with runs between the two cities made every hour. The line was later extended to **Champaign**. One line was run from Bloomington to **Lincoln** and another went to **Peoria**. This line took in towns of **Danvers, Lilly, Mackinaw, Morton, Agles, Zook, and Woodruff**.

Upton Sinclair publishes *The Jungle*, a scathing indictment of unsanitary conditions in the Chicago meat packing industry. Sinclair, a socialist, is biased and one-sided in his exposé of Porkopolis. A particularly nauseating part of the book was his description of the putrid waters of the branch of the Chicago River that ran through the yards called **"Bubbly Creek."** Sinclair thought his novel would inspire workers to organize. Instead it caused an outraged public to demand reform, leading to the Pure Food and Drug Act. "I aimed at the public's heart, and by accident I hit it in the stomach," Sinclair observed. At one time, the stockyards employed nearly 30,000 workers.

In reality, packinghouse wages were relatively high. Business giants such as Armour, Swift and Morris were not nearly so cruel or callous as depicted by Sinclair in his novel. They often yielded to the concerns of the Illinois Humane Society and responded to public pressure for better meat inspection measures.

Frank Lloyd Wright designs the famous **Robie House** in Chicago's Hyde Park with its cantilevered roof.

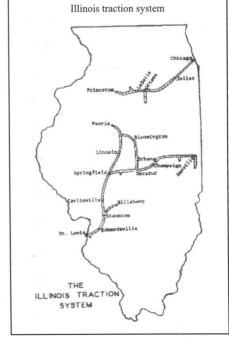
Illinois traction system

THE ILLINOIS TRACTION SYSTEM

Charles Comisky's White Sox take on the Chicago Cubs in the World Series. The mighty Cubs were heavily favored over the "Hitless Wonders," a team that didn't have a single .300 hitter. The Sox won in 6 games.

A Chicago company produces the **state's first candy bar**, the Tango. By 1956, one out of every four candy bars produced in the nation comes from Chicago.

Oil production begins in the state with the introduction of wells in Clark, Crawford and Lawrence counties. Two years later, Illinois **ranks 3rd in oil production** among all states.

Glide automobiles, made in **Peoria** by J.B. Bartholomew, are a popular motorcar. When President Roosevelt visited the city he rode in a Glide and called Grand View Drive the "**world's most beautiful drive.**" This was immortalized by Peoria's radio station that adopted the call letters WMBD. Charles Duryea was another early automaker in Peoria.

John Hertz, the auto leasing genius, made cars in Illinois for his leasing firm up until 1928.

The John Deere Company of **Moline** produced a 4-cylinder, 5-passenger car in the early days of the automobile.

Newsman William Randolph Hearst takes historical interest in the connection of Abraham Lincoln with the village of New Salem. He purchases the site and then donates it to the state. The legislature appropriated sufficient funds to enable part of the place on the Sangamon River to be reconstructed and filled with furnishings and artifacts authentic to the early Lincoln era. **New Salem** declined after its founding when it was discovered that the river wasn't suitable for navigation. It ultimately became a ghost town.

Commercial freshwater fishing on the Illinois River is surpassed only by the Columbia River.

Mrs. W.P. Halliday presents the city of **Cairo** with a nude statue in memory of her husband, Captain W.P. Halliday. The plaque on the statue base reads: "A vision of men laboring on the shore of a flood hewing and dragging wood to save the people from death and destruction." Noted sculptor Lorado Taft said the Hewer statue (by George Barnard) was one of the two finest nudes produced in America.

William Patrick Rend constructs a coal mining operation in **Franklin County** near the Big Muddy River. He used Clydesdale horses instead of mules at the mine. Rend Mine No. 1 employed about 300 miners. Rend was a bit more benevolent than most mine owners and painted the houses in his company town in cheerful colors. He sold the mine and left for Chicago in 1920, and the mine was renamed Old Ben No. 17. The Army Corps of Engineers dammed the Big Muddy in 1972 and created Rend Lake covering almost 1900 acres.

1907 - President Theodore Roosevelt makes a visit to **Cairo** on October 3. He delivers a rousing speech that contradicts the sour remarks about Cairo, made in 1842 by writer Charles Dickens. He stated: "Here was the breeding place not of disease, but of heroes, the best people that ever trod the face of the earth." The country that Dickens so bitterly assailed is now one of the most fertile and productive agricultural territories in all the world, and the dwellers here represent a higher average of comfort and intelligence than the people of any tract of like extent on this continent." President Taft visited Cairo in 1909.

The **Chicago Cubs win the World Series and repeat again in 1908**. They haven't won since. Meanwhile, their arch rivals, the St. Louis Cardinals will be world champs 9 times in the same span, more than any other national league team. Yet in head-to-head competition, the Cubs have the edge on the Cardinals.

Essanay Studios is formed, making Chicago the **Movie Capital of the World** for a ten-year span. The company had **Gloria Swanson**, **Charlie Chaplin** and Bronco Billy Anderson under contract. Actually, Essanay was founded by Billy Anderson and George Spoor, the operator of a **Waukegan** opera house. Another Chicago studio was the Selig Polyscope Company. Louella Parsons, a cub reporter from downstate Illinois, supervised script writing for Essanay. **Frank Baum**, of Wizard of Oz fame, was employed by Selig. Essanay's first release starred a cross-eyed actor named **Ben Turpin** who earned his keep by also sweeping the floors. When Selig went on

Essany Studios of Chicago (author's collection)

location to Oklahoma to film a story about cowboys and Indians, they sought technical advice from U.S. Marshall **Tom Mix**. Mix, a veteran of the Spanish-American War, went on to star in more than 200 Selig westerns between 1910 and 1917. Chicago's central location and its reputation as a theater town fueled its early success. But the emergence of Hollywood undermined Chicago's position, and talent began heading for the fair weather of southern California.

Chicagoan Francis Boggs, frustrated by Chicago weather while filming *The Count of Monte Cristo*, makes a decision. He will leave that town and take his production company with him to the sunny climes of southern California. Hollywood was founded by Horace Wilcox in 1886. **His wife named the town after a friend's summer house in Illinois.**

An editorial in the Chicago *Tribune* condemns the city's one hundred and sixteen 5-cent movie houses called Nickelodeons. They are said to be "without a redeeming feature to warrant their existence," and were thought to contribute to juvenile delinquency.

(Some people said the same thing about comic books in the 1950s.)

Chicago institutes a four-year mayoral term of office.

Albert Michelson, head of physics dept. at the University of Chicago, is the first American awarded Nobel Prize in science for his work on measuring the speed of light.

The **largest steam engine in the world** is #601, owned by the Chicago and Alton Railroad Company.

Illinois schoolchildren vote to adopt the native violet as the state flower.

The 22-story LaSalle, the **world's tallest hotel**, is built at Madison and LaSalle in Chicago for 6 million dollars.

Fred Busse becomes the mayor of Chicago. A year later he secretly marries. Soon all of Chicago is buzzing with the gossip that Mrs. Busse is a mulatto. Apparently the mayor didn't learn of his wife's racial mixture until just before their marriage.

1908 - The state's **first race riot** takes place in **Springfield**. The wife of a streetcar conductor claimed that a Negro had broken into her house and assaulted her. An angry mob formed a lynch party, but the police had spirited the man away to safety in **Bloomington**. The frustrated mob vented its wrath on the colored in an effort to drive all of them from the community. It took 5,000 militiamen to quell the two-day riot. When it was over, **two Negroes were lynched, four whites were killed, 70 persons were injured**. This riot led to the formation of the national NAACP in 1909.

Standard Oil of Indiana builds a plant in Wood River, hires about 400 employees and begins refining crude oil. The towns of **Wood River, Hartford and Roxana** come into existence due to the local refineries. International Shoe Company also locates in Hartford and secures its hides for leather from the National Stock Yards in East St. Louis.

Chicagoan Clifton Wooldridge writes an autobiography titled: *Twenty Years a Detective in the Wickedest City in the World*. He describes a raucous town filled with gangsters, grifters, grafters, gunmen, pickpockets, murderers, thieves, gamblers, prostitutes, con men and rowdies of all hue and stripe.

The University of Chicago wins the national intercollegiate basketball title by defeating the University of Pennsylvania, 16-15.

1909 - A mob in **Cairo** lynches William James, a colored man. He was accused of assaulting and then murdering Anna Pelly, a young white woman. The mob first tried to hang him from the steel arches spanning Commercial Avenue at 8th Street. Finding it slow and difficult, they shot him instead and took his body to the scene of the crime where they burned it. They then proceeded to the courthouse and dragged Henry Salzner from his cell. He was a white man who had been charged with murdering his wife. They took him to a telephone pole and hanged him and then riddled his body with bullets. Cairo's sagging reputation for being a hard town was fully restored.

Thirty-one-year-old New Yorker Johnny "The Fox" Torrio arrives in Chicago to work for Uncle Jim Colosimo, supervising his brothels and arranging for the deaths of his boss' enemies.

Holt Mfg. Company of **Peoria** has 65 employees and makes track-type tractors. It will grow into Peoria Caterpillar Company and make Peoria the "**Earthmoving Capital of the World**." Komatsu is currently its chief competitor.

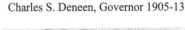

Charles S. Deneen, Governor 1905-13

It was the army corps of engineers, many of which were former caterpillar employees, who built the famed Burma Road during World War II. The Peoria Cats were charter members of the Industrial Basketball League.

The Lincoln penny is issued by the U.S. Mint. It is the **first coin ever to bear the image of a President**. The coin was controversial because some thought it smacked of monarchy where kings and tyrants placed their likeness on coins. Others protested the fact that the designer promoted himself by placing his initials VDB on the obverse side of the coin. Southerners, of course, also did not like the coin.

The state's worst coalmine disaster occurs at Cherry Mine 12 in **Bureau County**. It started when a load of hay, used to feed animals that pulled the coal cars, caught fire from a kerosene torch. The small fire was momentarily ignored by two workers who had more pressing chores. When they returned to douse the fire, it had grown to menacing proportions, igniting timbers and chunks of scattered coal. The fire was sucked through the ventilation system, and 259 miners lost their lives. This disaster is also one of the worst in the U.S. and resulted in the passage of a state Workmen's Compensation Act.

Lorado Taft sculpts "Eternal Silence," an ethereal hooded figure for Graceland Cemetery in Chicago. It is rather spooky looking, and locals have dubbed it "the Statue of Death." It is rumored to be unphotographable (poppycock, of course).

1910 – **Samuel P. Wilson** writes an exposé about Chicago's thriving vice trade and its Cess-Pools of Infamy. **William Stead** wrote a similar tome, *If Christ Came to Chicago*. Incredibly, he included a map to show locations of many of the town's brothels. Most thought the map was included to insure that it would become a best seller. Critics called it a **SIN DIRECTORY**.

It is estimated at this time that the number of brothels in Chicago numbered around 1,000 with an annual gross of about 60 million dollars.

Edwardsville's Griffin House, at 705 St. Louis Street, is built by Walter Griffin. He was an associate of Frank Lloyd Wright and designed the place using Wright's distinctive horizontal Prairie Style.

Thomas Scott Baldwin becomes the **first person to fly under the Eads Bridge** in his *Red Devil*. Baldwin was a pioneer aviator from **Quincy**. Baldwin had earlier been a daredevil high wire circus performer and later performed parachute stunts from hydrogen balloons at local fairs. Baldwin built the *California Arrow*, the nation's first powered dirigible (1904), propelled by a Curtiss engine. Twenty-six years after his death in 1923, the airport at Quincy was named in his honor.

The University of Illinois establishes the practice of holding a Homecoming celebration for its alumni. It becomes the **first university in the nation to do so**. The university's *Daily Illini* is also the **nation's oldest**.

A total of over $4,000 in fines is levied against **East St. Louis prostitutes** working in The Valley on 3rd Street near City Hall. A *Journal* reporter can only find records where just $3 of that amount found its way into the city treasury. This was mute testimony to the fact that these offerings constituted graft that went to police and various public officials. One of the most notorious dens of iniquity was the **Monkey Cage** on South Main Street in East St. Louis. **Charlie Birger** once told his wife that it was one of his favorite hangouts.

Senator William McKinley (no relation to the president), a member of the Illinois General Assembly, heads a consortium that builds the **McKinley Bridge** in **Madison/Venice**. The group built an electrified railway system over much of that part of southern Illinois. He was a friend of the Neidringhaus brothers of **Granite City** and headed the state transportation committee. His original

McKinley Bridge, Granite City, Ill

plan was to gain access to St. Louis over the **Merchant's Bridge** (for rail traffic only) or the Eads Bridge. But neither of those two entities were interested in sharing their monopoly, so he was forced to build his own bridge.

Under the McKinley Bridge, which connects Granite/Madison/Venice with St. Louis, is Kerr Island. It becomes attached to the Illinois shore and is taken over as a dwelling place by more than 1,000 Negro squatters. Their huts are built from scraps of tin and wood, and a variety of materials salvaged from river and alley.

This is the peak year of popularity for public bathhouses in Chicago. When first introduced in the 1890s, large numbers of neighborhood folk complained, marched and protested, fearing that they were going to be forced to take baths. The typical charge for a luxurious bath was 5 cents. For Jewish women, the bathhouses became popular as a place to perform the mikvah, a ceremonial cleansing after completion of the menstrual cycle.

Chicago is scandalized by a theater performance of the Richard Strauss play, *Salome*. The play was based on a poem by Oscar Wilde, who had earlier visited Chicago and offended its citizens by loathingly describing the town's water tower as a "castellated monstrosity with pepper boxes stuck all over it." In the offending scene, the severed head of John the Baptist is brought to the dancer on a platter, around which the bejeweled dancer writhes and passionately kisses. Soprano Mary Garden, the prima donna of the Chicago Opera, performed the Dance of the Seven Veils. One critic described it as lacking in artistry and said she wallowed around **like a cat on a bed of catnip**. There was so much public uproar that the Chicago Opera Company cancelled the final sold-out performance. Garden was born in Aberdeen, Scotland, but grew up in Chicago and was trained in Paris. In a later performance, a mentally disturbed man walked on stage and tried to shoot her but was disarmed by a police officer. In 1921 she was named directress of the Chicago Opera Company. She resigned after a year that saw the company lose money and had several death threats against her. She went back to being a performer and retired in the late 1930s, returning to live the rest of her life in Scotland.

The man most responsible for the creation of the Chicago Opera Company was Harold McCormick and his wife, the former Edith Rockefeller. McCormick was the son of the reaper king, Cyrus McCormick. They lived in a turreted gray stone mansion at 1000 Lake Shore Drive and dominated Chicago's social scene. She served her guests with golden dinnerware, once given by Napoleon to his sister Pauline, consisting of 1,000 pieces. She was snobbish and wrote out her instructions to her chauffeur so she wouldn't have to talk to him. Mrs. McCormick separated from her husband for 8 years in 1913 and left for Switzerland to study psychology with Dr. Carl Jung. Harold became enamored with Ganna Walska, a European singer of limited ability. He tried in vain to secure a divorce from his wife and when finally successful, was crushed to discover she had married Alexander Cochran, reputed to be the

world's richest bachelor. They soon divorced enabling the 51-year-old McCormick to marry Walska. **He had a gland transplant from a younger man to sustain his youth**. Floyd Gibbons, the famous reporter for the *Tribune* covered the wedding. They divorced in 1931, and it cost McCormick 6 million dollars.

A paraphrased version of Longfellow's poem became popular in drawing rooms:

Under the spreading chestnut tree,/The village smithy stands;/the smith a gloomy man is he/McCormick has his glands.

McCormick later developed a big interest in flying and sponsored the first international aeronautical show in Chicago.

A coal miner's massacre takes place at **Virden**.

Harold McCormick and Ganna Walska

Julius Rosenwald, half owner of Sears-Roebuck, becomes the company's president. His philanthropy becomes legendary as he gave away 63 million dollars while he was alive. It was Rosenwald who remodeled the Fine Arts Building from the Columbian Exposition and converted it into the Museum of Science and Industry. Another significant building on the lakefront, the Adler Planetarium, was a gift from Rosenwald's brother-in-law, Max Adler. Adler was also an executive at Sears. (Rosenwald pic on p 99)

U.S. Speaker of the House Joe Cannon, a **Danville** native, is stripped of his dictatorial power in a move led by George Norris of Nebraska and other progressives. Cannon was the **first person pictured on the cover of Time Magazine**.

After a visit to England where he learned first-hand about Baden Powell's Boy Scouts, **William Boyce of Ottawa founds the Boy Scouts of America** in Chicago.

The National Road Race is held in **Elgin** and is won by Ralph Mulford who averages about 62 m.p.h. Eddie Rickenbacker is a participant in this race.

Jones Park in **East St. Louis** opens, consisting of 330 acres near the Lansdowne section of town. The Jones family, who owned the land dating back to Civil War times, donated the property to the city with the stipulation that the name never be changed.

A capacity crowd fills the Chicago Coliseum to hear explorer Robert Peary describe his trip to the North Pole.

Illinois is **second only to Michigan as an auto producing** state. Michigan has 49 auto factories and Illinois has 39.

1911 – LaClede Steel is founded in **Madison**. The company expanded a few years later by buying an economically troubled steel mill in **Alton**.

Peabody Mine #7 is sunk near **Kincaid** and continues operation until May of 1952. Peabody Mine #8 is sunk near Tovey and continues operation until July of 1954. The town of **Tovey** was founded by miners.

Reform Mayor Carter Harrison II closes down the notorious Everleigh Club, a famous brothel in the First Ward.

Illinois passes the **nation's first pension law** for mothers with dependent children.

Ronald Reagan is born in **Tampico**. He is the only Illinois-born president. While working as a lifeguard in his youth, he was credited with saving 77 lives.

Chicago evangelist H. Van Meter denounces mixed dancing and proposes that boys should dance with boys and girls with girls.

1912 - A four-sided monument in **Edwards-ville's** City Park is built to commemorate the Madison County Centennial. There are figures on each of its sides that pay tribute to early pioneers representing: Plenty, Virtue, Justice and Wisdom.

The Anti Saloon League starts a national campaign to secure a prohibition amendment to the U.S. Constitution.

Carl Sandburg and his wife move to Chicago from Milwaukee where he becomes a columnist and movie reviewer for the *Daily News*.

Rockford native **Julia Lathrop**, friend of Jane Addams, is appointed by President Taft to be the first head of the U.S. Children's Bureau, a position held until 1921. Lathrop also helped establish the world's first court for juveniles.

Harriet Monroe, who made her literary debut with "Columbian Ode" in 1893 at the Chicago fair, founds a magazine called "Poetry." For the next two decades she published nearly every American poet of note including Carl Sandburg, Robert Frost, Amy Lowell, T.S. Eliot and Ezra Pound.

Maude Van Dusen, a Nebraskan, commits suicide by leaping from the McCormick Building on South Michigan in Chicago. She leaves a note behind explaining that she had been forced into prostitution. This leads to the adoption of the Mann Act, making it illegal to transport women across state lines for immoral purposes.

Lansdowne Park opens in **East St. Louis**. It has a large lagoon, carnival rides and a covered/open air dance hall. To commemorate the gala opening, a recreation of the Civil War battle between the Monitor and the Merrimac is staged. In later years when the city held Labor Day parades, the CIO group ended their parade at the park and then spent the rest of the afternoon with a picnic. The rival AFL, which looked down on the CIO because they were unskilled workers and admitted blacks, held their picnic at nearby Jones Park.

The progressive wing of the Republican Party meets in Chicago at the Coliseum and nominates Teddy Roosevelt for president on the Bull Moose ticket. The conservative wing re-nominates Taft, causing a split that enables Woodrow Wilson and the Democrats to win the election.

Centennial Monument in Edwardsville (Neal Strebel of Collinsville)

Julia Lathrop (author's collection)

Harriet Monroe

Cpl. Frank Scott becomes the first enlisted man to be killed in an aviation accident on American soil. Scott was riding in a two-man airplane that crashed near College Park, Maryland. In 1917 the War Department announced it would establish an aviation field on 640 acres in **Shiloh Valley**, naming it Scott Field, in honor of Cpl. Scott. (Picture on 113)

The nation's dance masters meet in Chicago to protest "ragtime" music, claiming it is anathema to dancing. Ragtime had earlier been denounced as immoral.

1913 - Mrs. John A. Logan publishes *Reminisces of a Soldier's Wife.*

There is another disastrous flood at **Joppa**, **Metropolis** and **Shawneetown**. A local ballad of unknown origin described a similar earlier flood:

> All at once the bells were ringing, With a wild and awful ring,
> As the fearful flood broke over one and all, Oh! that faithful levee broke
> Pale the lips of those who spoke, While that roaring, crashing, awful flood came in. . . .

The 16th Amendment goes into effect, levying a national tax on incomes. The tax was a flat 1 % of one's income. Tax freedom day back then was January 4. Today it doesn't occur until May. Illinois contributes a significant amount to the national treasury because it **ranks 3rd nationally in the number of millionaires**. Only New York and Pennsylvania have more. Gutsy Illinois was the first state with a large urban population to ratify the amendment.

Illinois becomes the first state east of the Mississippi to allow women to vote in local and state elections. Known as the "Illinois Law," it quickly became a model for other states. Illinois women cast their first ballots in the spring of 1914 in local elections. Suffragette **Carrie Catt** refers to the vote in Illinois as the turning point that would enable females to cast their first ballot in the 1920 presidential race. The national press referred to the victory in Illinois as "amazing." Machine politicians in places like **Rockford, Peoria, East St. Louis** and Chicago opposed female suffrage, fearing honest, intelligent and independent female voters would not be as easy to manipulate as their male counterparts.

The town of **Kincaid** is founded by F.S. Peabody. Under the supervision of the Kincaid Land Association, a subsidiary of Peabody Coal, workers built an infrastructure that consisted of 5 businesses and over 80 homes. It was incorporated as a village in 1913.

A sand-bottomed swimming lagoon at Jones Park in **East St. Louis** is created. Fed by an artesian well, it is the **largest inland beach in America**.

Charles Pajeau of **Evanston**, a stone mason by trade, gets an idea from watching children play with empty spools of thread. He markets a toy with wooden pieces that children can tinker with and invents an American classic – **Tinker Toys**. A few years later in 1916, J.L. Wright, the son of Frank Lloyd Wright, started manufacturing a children's toy called **Lincoln Logs**.

Thomas Dunham of **Aurora** establishes a company called Equipto that becomes famous for making steel shelving used in stores.

1914 –The citizens of Chicago pass a referendum to create nearly 100 square miles of Cook County Forest Preserves, a belt of parks and trees nearly encircling the city. They reject a proposal for building a subway.

The Panama Canal opens with metal floodgates that are produced in **East St. Louis** and locks with bricks made in **Murphysboro**.

Owner negligence in meeting mine safety standards causes a mine explosion at **Royalton** that kills 52 miners.

Chicagoan Ralph Chaplin, a member of the radical IWW (Wobblies) labor group, writes the popular song, "Solidarity Forever."

Calumet Sag Channel is dug through a slough to create a barge route between the Illinois Waterway and Calumet harbor.

1915 - **Earl Shelton** enters Pontiac Reformatory at age 25 on October 29. He and another man named **Thomas Draper** had been arrested back in March for robbing Cloyd Wilson. About this same time, **Carl Shelton** is arrested for stealing a car in St. Louis, and he receives a year in the St. Louis Workhouse. Earl serves 18 months in prison and is released for good behavior.

The **Mascoutah** business district is inundated in the August Hog River flood.

When the steamship **Eastland** overturns in the Chicago River on July 24th, **812 people drown**. The boat was loaded with more than 2,000 employees of Western Electric ready for a holiday cruise and picnic. When about 900 people on the top deck rushed to one side, attracted by a passing tugboat and to wave goodbye to friends, the boat tipped over and capsized. The boat was docked near the Clark Street Bridge at Wacker Drive. It was one of the largest peacetime naval disasters in U.S. history. It was ironic that most of the people died in relatively shallow water, not far from the water's edge. All of the crew members survived. Most of the employees were of Polish and Bohemian (Czech) descent. A court of inquiry placed responsibility for the disaster on an engineer who failed to fill the ballast tanks. Some blamed the tragedy on new restrictions, imposed after the sinking of the Titanic, which required huge number of lifeboats, making the ship unstable and top heavy.

The Eastland Disaster (author's collection)

A makeshift morgue was set up in the Armory Building on Washington Avenue. Today this is the location of Oprah Winfrey's television studio. **Oprah claims she has felt the presence of the spirits** of the victims on several occasions.

One of the lucky ones was future Bears coach, George Halas. He had attended a college football game and arrived at the dock too late to get on board.

Lillian Gish, a former resident of **East St. Louis**, stars in the film, *Birth of a Nation*, by D.W. Griffith. Based on the novel, "The Clansman," it showed "coloreds" as virtual brutes from the jungle who preyed upon whites. The film was largely responsible for the rebirth of the KKK. By the early 1920s, they had at least three million members. In Chicago, city ordinance banned the showing of the movie on the grounds that it preached racial hatred. The film's producers tried to show it again in 1924 and the police arrested the theater owner. When movie officials threatened to sue the city for damages, the film was allowed to be shown, breaking all attendance records. When a 1939 version with added sound was shown, Negro groups protested the showing and the matter once again went to court. A judge ruled that the movie could be shown, but only in one theater at a time. A music score was added and the film was re-released in 1970 and shown at the Wilmette Theater without any major problems.

Chicago utilities mogul Charles Yerkes

The white state flag of Illinois is adopted. It features an eagle with a ribbon banner in its mouth. The banner contains the state motto. The name "Illinois" was added at the bottom in 1970 when chief petty officer Bruce McDaniel complained that no one in his mess hall could identify the Illinois flag.

Republican **Big Bill Thompson** wins his first term as Chicago's mayor.

Oscar de Priest becomes the first Negro elected as an alderman on Chicago's City Council.

Chicago Radio Laboratory is established by two local ham operators, R.G. Mathews and Karl Hassel. Eugene McDonald joined the group in 1921, and they formed the new **Zenith Radio Corp**. Zenith gave our country the first portable radio (1924), the first push-button radio (1927), the first black and white TV and the first color TVs for sale. Zenith also developed national FM radio as approved by the FCC. Zenith was the last independent maker of color television sets in America before succumbing to the Asian market.

1916 - **Alfonso Magarian**, three-year-old son of an **East St. Louis** Armenian baker, is found murdered. The child's father had complained to the police that a house of prostitution was being operated next door to where he lived. One of the prostitutes confessed that she assisted with the abduction, but before the trial of arrested gang members took place, her mangled body was discovered on a set of railroad tracks.

Carl Sandburg's 1916 poem about his adopted city: Hog Butcher for the world,/ Tool maker, stacker of wheat,/ Player with railroads and the Nation's Freight Handler;/ Stormy, husky, brawling,' City of the Broad Shoulders.

James Thomas of **Makanda** publishes *Poems of Egypt and Other Poems*.

The dog population becomes a problem in **Wood River**. Police officers are instructed to shoot any dogs running loose. Officer **John Phipps** dies after being bitten by a rabid dog that he was trying to kill.

Financiers Ogden Armour and William Wrigley Jr. head a syndicate that purchases a baseball team called the Cubs from the Taft family of Cincinnati. Wrigley, the chewing gum magnate, had no interest in the game but thought such a team should be locally owned.

The Kathleen Mine opens near **Dowell** and the town's population climbs to nearly 1,000. When it closes around 1959, the town will be left without an economic base.

The Chicago school board fires 68 teachers and principals for belonging to the Chicago Teachers Federation (union).

Over 3,000 women brave a downpour and march on the Republican national convention in Chicago, demanding full suffrage. The Republicans nominate Charles Evans Hughes to challenge Woodrow Wilson for his second term.

Big business moguls are stunned to learn that the Sears Company now offers a profit sharing plan for its employees.

1917 – The United States declares war on the Central Powers after the sinking of the Luisitania and resumption of unrestricted U-boat warfare. Industries in southern Illinois, especially those in Alton, Granite City and East St. Louis, give credence to the slogan "Production Will Win the War." Western Cartridge in **East Alton** ships ammo to the Allies, and its reputation for quality allows it to be the only U.S. munitions maker to keep its own primer specifications. Fort Sheridan in Chicago became a training camp for officers. Sailors (50,000) trained at an expanded Chicago's Great Lakes Naval Station, built in 1904. Illinois had two aviation bases, Scott Field near **Belleville** and Chanute Field at **Rantoul**.

(left) Cpl. Frank Scott (Scott Field)

Chicago, **Peoria** and **East St. Louis** led the way in war output. East St. Louis was noted for its packing houses, aluminum production, chemical plants, fertilizer plants, foundries, machine shops, zinc production, feed plants, paint mills, roofing products and railroad repair shops.

"Food Will Win the War" was a slogan used by the Creel Committee, and Illinoisans took it seriously. Numerous farmers were given deferments to enable them to stay home and grow crops. City folk planted "victory gardens" in their back yards. More than 850,000 citizens in the state signed pledge cards to conserve food and eat less.

Utilities mogul Samuel Insull, appointed to head the "Defense Council," used his own money to provide a six-story building for his staff. He trained a group of speakers known as "Four-minute Men" to give patriotic speeches before the start of movies and plays. Illinoisans bought $1.3 million worth of War Bonds. In cooperation with the Federal Food Administration, Illinoisans pledge "meatless Mondays" and "wheatless Wednesdays."

Jane Addams, considered a near-saint before the war, opposed it and fell under heavy criticism. As head of the Women's Peace Party, she opposed the war on moral and humanitarian considerations.

The winter of 1917-18 is remembered as the **Winter of Deep Snow**. It snowed in **Johnson County**, off and on, for nearly 4 weeks and covered the ground for almost 2 months.

After congress declared war on the Central Powers, the War Department quickly opened ground schools at 8 colleges and established 27 flying fields to train pilots. Congress appropriated $640 million, and the War Department built Chanute Field, (honoring the early aviation pioneer) as one of the sites. Its topography was level, close to the Illinois Central Railroad, and could depend on nearby **Rantoul** for water and electricity. It was built at a cost of $1 million and was completed by July 4. During the first 6-months there were 50 crashes. Chanute Field trained 525 pilots for WWI combat duty.

There is a two-day race riot, July 2-3, at **East St. Louis**. **Forty-eight people are killed – 39 Negroes and 9 whites**. This is the largest riot ever in America in the number of African-American lives lost. Factory managers in the city had invited some 10,000 Negro workers to move from the South to take care of labor shortages and to use as pawns in labor-management disputes. A grand jury blamed the riot on racism, inept politicians, and agitators from both races. Governor Lowden sent the state militia, but the young men did little to stop the riot.

Lowden, a two-term congressman married to George Pullman's daughter (Florence), was unique among Illinois governors in that he announced shortly before his inauguration that he would only serve one term and then step down. Lowden was a serious contender for the Republican presidential nomination in 1920, but the "darkhorse" candidate, Warren G. Harding, was chosen by the Old Guard in a smoke-filled room.

Captured German soldiers from the Great War (WW I) are housed in **Waterloo**. After the war, some of them decide to stay and settle there.

The Illinois unit with the most brilliant military record is the 149th Field Artillery of the **Rainbow Division**. It helped smother General Ludendorff's last offensive and was outstanding in the Marne, Chateau-Thierry, Saint Mihiel, Meuse-Argonne campaigns. Camp Grant at **Rockford** is the training ground of the 86th Black Hawk Division. The Naval Training Station at Great Lakes produced 71,440 men. Fort Sheridan graduated 7,000 officers. Twenty squadrons of aviators trained at Chanute Field near **Rantoul** and Scott Field near **Belleville**. Illinois was one of only 3 states to furnish a complete National Guard unit for the war, the Prairie Division. Illinois Medal of Honor winners were Harold Goettler, John J. Kelly, Weedon Osborne, Thomas Pope (all of Chicago) and Fred E. Smith of **Rockford**.

The Chicago White Sox are the world champions of baseball.

Illinois reaches its peak year in coal production with 810 mines producing 86 million tons of coal.

An automobile called the Commonwealth is produced at **Joliet** from 1917-1922. It ultimately becomes the Checker taxi. **Decatur** produces an auto called the Comet from 1917-22.

A posse of 300 men fan out in the Sangamon River area of **Decatur** to look for a huge cat that has been terrorizing people in the area.

The horse and mule market at the stockyards in **East St. Louis** becomes the **largest in the world** in terms of volume of animals bought and sold.

A huge tornado rips through **Mattoon**, killing 53 people. Another 38 were killed at **Charleston**. The twister stayed on the ground for 293 miles, the longest tornado path ever recorded. The 1925 twister that hit southern Illinois killed more people but covered only 219 miles.

Early oil rig at Salem, Illinois

Thomas Gulliet, a **Decatur** resident, is mauled while picking flowers near the Sangamon River. A huge posse was formed to scour the countryside, but the **lion is never found**.

The Office of Mines and Minerals is created as a state authority to protect the health and safety of miners. At this time, Illinois ranks third in the nation in coal production with 810 mines.

Chicago Cub pitcher Jim Vaughn pitches a no-hitter against Cincinnati, but is matched by opponent Fred Toney, who also tosses a no-hit gem. Vaughn loses the game in the 10th when Jim Thorpe, of Olympic fame, singles home a run for Cincinnati.

1918 – **Roxana Petroleum** begins refining crude oil at the Shell Oil refinery.

The influenza epidemic strikes southern Illinois killing thousands. **More people lost their lives to this Spanish Flu epidemic than on the battlefields of Europe**. Schools were closed, and large public gatherings were forbidden.

Robert Wadlow is born in **Alton** on February 22, weighing a healthy (and normal) 8 pounds, two ounces. His family lives in **Roxana** during his grade school years and later moves to Alton. By the time he attended grade school he was over 5 feet tall. Peters Shoe Company of St. Louis made his specially fitted shoes for free in return for various promotional appearances. By the time he reaches manhood, he will become the **tallest person who ever lived**. (picture on 134)

A new state constitution for Illinois is drawn up by the legislature at the urging of Governor Frank Lowden, but it is rejected by voters at the polls.

During World War I, on April 5, the city of **Collinsville** receives a black eye when a German sympathizer and a socialist named **Robert Prager** is plucked from his jail cell, dragged through the streets, and lynched by an angry group of drunken miners. Wesley Beaver, a local agitator who also participated in the East St. Louis riot of 1917, was one of the mob leaders. It was the third time in a week mobs had tried to punish him for his statements. A rumor was also circulated that he was a spy. Prager, 32, had applied for a union card to work in the mines but was turned down when officials learned about pro-German statements that he had been making. Prager lived in an apartment at 208-A Vandalia Street. He was hanged from a tree limb at the intersection of Collinsville and Caseyville roads by an angry mob of nearly 400 miners. When the mob went to the jail, **Mayor Siegel** told them he had been spirited away to some unknown place. But 28 year-old **Joe Riegel**, an ex-soldier, was allowed to search the jail, and he was the one who delivered Prager to the mob. Before Prager was hanged, he was allowed to say a prayer and write a note to his parents. The body was left in the tree from 11 p.m. that night until eight in the morning when a man from **Vincent Herr Funeral Home** cut him down.

Governor Frank Lowden sent an investigator to look into the incident. The Collinsville Justice of the Peace refused to issue arrest warrants on the five mob leaders. Eleven men were later brought to trial, but a local jury refused to convict them. Prager's funeral in **St. Louis** was attended by over 500 people, and he was buried in St. Mathew's Cemetery. Beaver, the agitator, was so haunted by the incident that two years later he committed suicide.

Chicago is hit by 42 inches of snow in the month of January.

Howard Knotts of **Springfield** becomes an air "Ace" during the war.

The excursion steamer *Columbia* sinks after hitting a submerged stump on the Illinois River near **Pekin**; 87 lives are lost.

George Cassens settles in **Hamel** and purchases all 4 corners at the intersection of Route 66 and 140. He then proceeded to build a gas station, auto showroom, an office building and Tourist Haven Restaurant on those corners. He and his brother Louis started a Chrysler/Plymouth dealership in **Edwardsville**. Along with their sons Albert and Arnold, they also began a lucrative auto transport business.

1919 – Southern Illinois black film pioneer **Oscar Micheaux**, who worked outside the Hollywood system for 30 years, directs and produces his first silent film, *The Homesteader*.

Likker-lovin' Illinois is one of only 12 states without statewide prohibition. Downstate, dominated by native-stock Americans that were largely Baptist, Methodist or Presbyterian, generally supported prohibition and looked upon Chicago, **Peoria** and East St. Louis as wide open cities where Catholics and recent immigrants drank in saloons and provided the bought

Filmmaker Oscar Micheaux

votes that kept corrupt political machines going in the state's two largest cities. Historian Harry Englemann has referred to Chicago as a "a city upon a still."

The legislature met and ratified the 18th amendment with the dry law going into effect a year later on January 14. About six months later, Illinois, Wisconsin and Michigan tied in the race to become the first states to ratify the 19th Amendment, women's suffrage.

Another race riot breaks out, this time in **Chicago**. On Sunday, July 27, a young Negro crossed the dividing line swimming area on Lake Michigan. A crowd of whites started throwing rocks, and the boy drowned. The riot was on, but this time the Negroes fought back. Six thousand militiamen were needed to quell the **five-day riot**. They were assisted by a drenching downpour of rain that fell on the city. **Fifteen whites were killed and 178 injured while twenty-three Negroes were killed**, and 342 were injured. The large number of white deaths happened because many of the Negro men in the riot area still had their service revolvers left over from the war. Over a **thousand homes were burned**.

One of the gangs that participated in the violence was the Hamburgs, and one of its members was a youth named Richard J. Daley. After he became mayor and was asked if he had participated in the riot, Daley always responded with a "no comment."

Chicago is the site of **America's first commercial aviation disaster**. The Goodyear blimp Wingfoot Express catches fire and crashes through the roof of a bank in the Loop, killing 13 people.

Shoeless Joe Jackson of the Chicago White Sox hits the last home run of the old "dead ball" era in baseball. Benjamin Shibe invented a lively cork-centered baseball that replaced the old one with a solid center. Jackson received his nickname when he batted shoeless (due to blisters) and hit a home run in an exhibition game. Jackson also batted .408 as a rookie, but lost the hitting title to Ty Cobb who hit .420.

Eight Chicago White Sox players are banned from baseball by Judge "Kennesaw Mountain" Landis, the commissioner. Infielder Eddie Collins was not implicated. These men were accused of taking money from gamblers in exchange for "throwing" the series to the Cincinnati Reds. **Shoeless Joe Jackson** (Ray Liota portrayed him in *Field of Dreams*) was one of the players banned. He claimed innocence, noting that he had 12 hits in the 8 game series (best of 9) and batted .375. Many blamed tightwad owner Chuck

Comisky for the debaucle. Pitcher Ed Cicotte won 29 games that year and was in line for a big bonus if he reached 30. Comisky ordered the manager not to start him the last two weeks of the season.

Johnny Torrio sends for Brooklynite and former Five Points Gang member Al Capone to come to Chicago. Capone's first duties were bodyguard, bartender and brothel capper.

Chicago's blustery and unpredictable Big Bill Thompson wins re-election as mayor.

The Chicago Crime Commission is organized. In April of 1923 they publish a list of 28 crime figures that become known as Public Enemies. Capone topped the list, followed by bodyguard Tony "Mops" Volpe and Ralph Capone.

A legislative act authorized the passage of a bond issue for the construction of a canal with a depth of eight feet between **Lockport** and **Utica**, to provide water transportation between the two towns.

The Communist Party of America is organized by the left wing of the Socialist Party in Chicago. They had split over the question of whether to support the Revolution in Russia and the overthrow of the Czar.

George Halas is the MVP for the Fighting Illini at the Rose Bowl.

"Shoeless" Joe Jackson (author's collection)

1920 – **Big Jim Colosimo**, a restauranteer and vice lord of the Chicago district known as The Levee, is gunned down by Frankie Yale in the lobby of his own establishment. His death enables Torrio and Capone to enlarge their holdings in vice and racketeering. Yale probably murdered Colosimo so he could expand his own empire. Colosimo fell in love with a young singer named Dale Winter and had recently divorced his wife and married Miss Winter. When he fell head over heels in love, this was a sign to the rest of the underworld that he had gone soft. The murder was never officially solved. It was Johnny Torrio who now presided over the operation of countless brothels, speakeasies and gin joints. Colosimo was Torrio's uncle, and it was he who first persuaded Torrio to leave New York and come to Chicago. Although a Catholic, Colosimo's funeral was conducted by a Protestant clergyman because the local archbishop forbade any diocese priest from performing rites on a gangster.

Some say the cause of his death was his lovely new wife, a former Methodist church choir singer. She was hired as a featured singer at Colosimo's club. He immediately fell for her and she for him even though she was half his age. He catered to Dale's every whim and fancy. Everyone in the underworld said that Colosimo had "gone soft." To the sharks of gangland Chicago, that was like blood in the water. There were fifty-three pallbearers and honorary pallbearers at his funeral. Nine aldermen, 3 judges and a couple of Congressmen attended the ceremony. His grieving widow soon discovered that technically their marriage had no legal basis because they were married before the mandatory yearlong waiting period after Jim's divorce from his first wife. The family, however, decided that the happiness she had given to her husband was worth about $6,000.

The Cook County Jail forces 200 inmates to watch the hanging of a desperado so they will learn how to behave themselves.

The **Volstead Act**, designed to enforce the national Prohibition laws, goes into effect on January 17th. **The first violation of the law** occurred about an hour later in Chicago by men who raided a railroad car and hijacked a load of whiskey that had been marked for medicinal use only.

Johnny Torrio, in a masterful diplomatic move, meets with various local gangs and proposes a plan whereby territories are marked out and a monopoly is established for supplying illegal beer and hard liquor to area saloons, bawdy houses, restaurants and cabarets. Any outsider that tried to move in would be dealt with collectively. Torrio would supply all the beer for $50 a barrel. Peace and prosperity would last among thugdom until 1923 when Spike O'Donnell got out of Joliet Prison and began hijacking Torrio's beer trucks, starting the so-called **Beer War**.

In a smoke-filled room at Chicago's Blackstone Hotel, (suite 804-805) Republican party bigwigs made a deal that made Warren G. Harding of Ohio their "dark horse" candidate for president.

Johnny Torrio

Few, if any, states could lay claim to playing a more significant role than Illinois in the passage of the so-called Progressive amendments for the income tax, the direct election of senators, women's suffrage, and Prohibition.

East St. Louis, the fastest growing city in America for the last thirty years, doubling its size every decade, reaches a population of over 70,000 people. It is now the 86th largest city in America, and the **third largest city in Illinois**. The total population for Illinois is 6,485,280. Downtown merchants organize the Jaycees, making it the **second oldest Jaycee group in the nation**.

Prohibition has a significant impact on all of Illinois. "Black Leg" mobsters saw opportunities for enormous profits and opened illegal "speakeasies." The Shelton brothers were dominant in **East St. Louis** and brought in illegal slot machines and prostitutes to their establishments. One of the Shelton Gang, **Jardown "Blackie" Armes**, was a good automobile mechanic and put his talents to work modifying cars to outrun prohibition agents. This was done by others all over the South with the same goals in mind. From these efforts at modifying car engines came **stock car racing** as we know it today. Armes was also adept at rigging cars with hidden containers for smuggling liquor.

Prohibition was largely responsible for the growth and development of organized crime and the Mafia empire as it now exists. Prohibition corrupted police and city officials in all major cities because it gave them a chance to supplement their meager salaries with bribes and kickbacks in return for looking the other way.

September 15. **S. Glenn Young**, a neophyte Prohibition Agent, along with two **Granite City** police officers, make a raid on a home in nearby **Madison**. They found a small still, mash, whiskey and arrested the occupant. They then went to the house next door where a relative of the arrested man lived and found a 25-gallon container of liquor. The occupant, **Luka Vukovic**, pulled a gun and tried to shoot Young, but the weapon misfired. Young, in self-defense, shot and killed the man.

Decatur starch manufacturer, A.E. Staley sells his football team to **George Halas**, a former U of I standout under coach Robert Zuppke. Halas met with 10 other owners in Canton, Ohio (this is why the Hall of Fame is there), and formed a professional league called the American Professional Football Association. Halas' team won the title that year with a 9-1-1 record, playing their games at Cubs Field (later Wrigley Field). The next year, Halas changed the name from the Staleys to the Bears (to create a connection with the Cubs) and the APFA became the NFL. Halas would win ten NFL championships.

Al Capone (UPI)

On a Sunday, March 20, a tornado strikes **Elgin, Melrose Park**, **Maywood**, **Evanston** and **Wilmette** on the northwest side of Chicago killing 103 people. Around 1 p.m. the bright sunny skies grew dark, releasing rain and hail the size of robin eggs. The roof of the First Congregational Church in Elgin collapsed injuring scores and killing three. The Red Cross provided temporary shelters, and the militia was summoned to maintain law and order, with orders to shoot looters. Relief trains from all over the state arrived, bringing food, clothes and medical supplies. Damage was estimated at $10 million.

Chicago has its own version of New York's Tin Pan Alley with dozens of music publishers and lyricists flourishing in the city, centering in the Randolph Building and the Garrick Theater Building. Tin Pan was a slang expression for the music pounded out on cheap, tinny upright pianos. Stephen Foster is considered to be the first person to make a living at writing songs. He penned *My Old Kentucky Home* and *I Dream of Jeannie*. The success of popular songs began with the rise of vaudeville in the 1890s.

Chicago produced the hit, Rudolph the Red-nosed Reindeer. It was written in 1939 by Robert May, a Montgomery Ward copywriter, who wrote it to accompany a Christmas story for the store's holiday promotion.

East St. Louis ranks third in population and third in the state in industrial output behind Chicago and **Peoria**. The biggest concerns in the Metro-East at this time are Hunter, Armour, Obear-Nester, Shell Oil, American Zinc, Alcoa, Granite City Steel, Alton Boxboard, American Steel, Monsanto, Standard Oil of Indiana, American Smelting and Refining and Laclede Steel.

The steel making complex along the Calumet River in Chicago becomes known as the **Ruhr of North America**. It became the nation's largest steel producing area.

The **Mascoutah** Brewery changes its name to Mascoutah Products Company and to comply with prohibition begins manufacturing a beverage called Old English Ginger Beer and Masco near beer (3.2 percent). The company is fined in late 1920 for making 4 percent beer, and in 1924 federal authorities closed the plant. After it was later found to still be making beer, new owners from **Joliet** were given jail sentences, and the plant was dismantled.

A ship called the *Sprague* is the **largest boat operating on the Mississippi River**. It is owned by the Aluminum Ore Company of East St. Louis and is used for hauling Arkansas bauxite to their plant site.

Jim Thorpe, Olympic champion and **great grandson of Chief Blackhawk**, becomes president of the National Football League. Thorpe was voted the greatest athlete of the first half of the Twentieth Century.

Only about 50 percent of eligible Illinois voters bother to go to the polls. This number has steadily been declining since 1896 when it had peaked at 79 percent.

Montgomery Ward, with 1,050 workers, is the largest Chicago employer of colored women. Because it did mail-order business, customers had no direct contact with them and never had to know they were served by black clerical workers.

Ronald Reagan's parents leave **Tampico** and move to **Dixon** when he is 9 years old.

1921 – Illinois governor **Len Small** is indicted and accused of embezzling a half million dollars when he was state treasurer. He wins acquittal, but many believe he was successful in bribing some of the jurors.

After the death of his father, Al Capone builds a two-story brick home at 7244 South Prairie Avenue in anticipation of his mother coming to live with him, along with his wife and his son.

Construction begins on Wacker Drive in Chicago, making use of concrete double decking to carry traffic.

Edith Rockefeller divorces Harold McCormick and gives him $3 million for title to their homes on Lakeshore Drive and in **Lake Forest**.

A woman in **Danville** goes on a 48-day fast to convince her husband to give up drinking, smoking, and join her church.

Adam "Mule Pole" Fritz, owner of a popular saloon in the heart of the city, complete with a spacious, ornate gambling parlor in the rear, is the most notorious gangster in **East St. Louis**. He eventually becomes a partner with the Shelton gang—Carl, Bernie and Big Earl.

June 6. **S. Glenn Young** is tried in a federal court in **Springfield** for killing Luka Vukovic of **Madison**. He had entered the man's home without a warrant, and the dead man's widow claimed that her husband was unarmed and that Young had planted the gun on his body. Young was exonerated, but it was a bittersweet victory because his wife divorced him (she claimed physical abuse), and he lost his $150 a month job as a Treasury Agent. He remarried later that year to a woman named Maude. One of the reasons given for his firing was an unauthorized interview he gave to the **East St. Louis** *Journal,* which gave the department "improper publicity."

People read with shocked delight about the first-ever Miss America Beauty Pageant, describing a host of beautiful young women wearing revealing one-piece bathing suits.

Female telephone operators in **Danville** are forbidden to chew gum and must reply to callers in pleasant singsong tones and phrases.

The state's first radio station, WDZ of **Decatur**, begins operation in **Tuscola**.

1922 – **Big Bill Thompson**, corrupt and "wet" mayor of Chicago, makes the charge that villainous England, under the leadership of King George V, is planning to invade the United States. This absurdity is pure politics designed to win over the Irish vote in upcoming elections. Thompson, a snaggle-toothed hulk who was a former athlete, was first elected mayor of Chicago on the Republican ticket in 1915. He soon fell in league with pimps, gamblers, thugs and assorted racketeers. He actually had little interest in politics and only **decided to run for mayor to win a bet**.

The nation, already in the grip of a nationwide coal strike, is shocked by the **Herrin Massacre** which takes place on June 22. The infamous incident occurred during a bitter coal miners' strike against the **Southern Illinois Coal Company**. The company tried to break the union by firing its unionized workers. Next, the management imported armed guards and replacement scab workers from Chicago to work the Lester strip mine. There were mine strikes all over the nation at this time, ordered by **John L. Lewis** and the United Mine Workers of America. The millionaire owner of the mine sought to profit by continuing to mine coal that would be sold at a premium price due to shortages.

Gunshots were exchanged as striking workers attacked the mine, and in the ensuing mayhem, **three union miners were killed**. Enraged, the belligerent miners surrounded the facility, cut power and telephone lines, and lay siege to the place.

Terrified, everyone in the besieged strip mine surrendered on the promise that they would leave Williamson County. As they filed out, the angry mob began striking the scabs, shouting ugly epithets. Then they dragged off C.K. McDowell, the mine superintendent, and shot him twice, killing him. A man in an automobile drove up and told the mob not to kill the captives on the highway where it might be seen by women and children. The men were herded into a woodland and told to run as fast as they could back to Chicago. But most of them were shot and killed trying to flee. One small group was held captive in the Herrin schoolhouse until the mob of about 200 people worked itself into a frenzy and dragged the men to a cemetery about a mile away. The group of six men, pleading for their lives, while yoked together by a large rope, were beaten and shot. Those who managed to survive, with bodies broken and bleeding, had their **throats cut** by a man with a pocketknife. When it was over, authorities found a total of **nineteen strikebreaker bodies**. Two separate trials were held for the remorseless murderers, but acquittal was the verdict in each case.

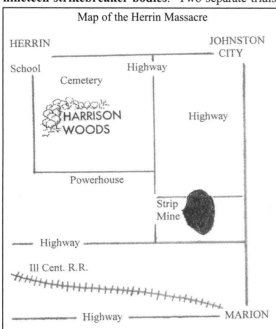

Map of the Herrin Massacre

S. Glen Young was one of the guards at the mine before he became a prohibition agent. Young is credited with bringing the first machinegun into Williamson County. Young will become the leader of the KKK forces in the county.

An article in the June 24, 1922, St. Louis *Globe-Democrat* described the massacre as . . . "the most brutal and horrifying crime that has ever stained the garments of organized labor." After the massacre, Williamson County gained a national reputation as **"Little Hell."**

William Allen White, the Kansas newspaper editor, saw the emergence of a new doctrine in the conflict. Labor was beginning to believe that skill had the same status as property. The right of a worker to apply his skill in a place where it would produce value was beginning to be seen as a human right. The right of a laborer to work for profit was gaining equal status with the right of owners to make a profit.

Winnifred Mason Huck of Chicago becomes the first woman elected to congress from Illinois.

Robert Zupke, **University of Illinois** football coach, **introduces the huddle** as a means of communication during the game. Under his leadership, Illinois won or tied for the Big Ten title 7 times in the next fifteen years, including the **national championship in 1927**.

Louis Armstrong, encouraged by coronetist Joe "King" Oliver, follows in the footsteps of "Jelly Roll" Morton and comes to Chicago. Armstrong and others would make Chicago a hotbed of the new distinctly American artform called *jazz*. Other notable performers in Chicago include Eddie Condon, Hoagy Carmichael, Ben Pollock, Benny and Harry Goodman.

The Illinois State police are organized. Its purpose is to enforce the provisions of the Illinois motor vehicle law. Troopers are expected to purchase their own firearms.

The Sag channel, a 24-mile long extension of the Chicago Sanitary and Ship Canal to connect with the Calumet River (south of Chicago), is completed. Like the Chicago River, the Calumet River no longer drains into Lake Michigan.

Early picture of the Illinois Highway Patrol (courtesy Illinois Highway Patrol)

After nearly three years of work, a new state constitution is submitted to voters. Downstate voters accept the new document but ratification fails when Chicago area voters overwhelmingly reject efforts to "modernize" the 1870 constitution.

After the Great War, Ed Stinson, a navy test pilot, moves to Chicago and begins the manufacture of Stinson airplanes. It was Stinson who discovered that lack of air speed caused tailspins and saved thousands of lives by teaching pilots how to come out of a spin.

The American Fiber Company of East St. Louis is the **world's largest maker of burlap-type bags**. Instead of making them from jute, they are made from yucca plant fibers from plants grown on their plantation in Arizona.

The Lincoln Memorial in Washington D.C. is dedicated. Henry Bacon, an architect from **Watseka**, is the man who designed it.

Al Capone makes newspaper headlines for the first time in Chicago when he accidentally rams a taxi and then pulls a gun on the driver. The story got his name wrong and referred to him as Alfred Caponi.

Pilots at Canute Field in **Rantoul** are ordered to wear parachutes for the first time.

Lottie Holman O'Neill becomes the first woman elected to the General Assembly, a position she holds for 38 years.

1923 – The Ku Klux Klan stages a huge rally on the outskirts of East St. Louis at the prehistoric site on **Collinsville Road** known as Monks Mound, sometimes called Cahokia Mound. Some estimates placed their crowd of supporters as high as 10,000. But the Klan was largely unsuccessful in East St. Louis because the city had large contingencies of Irish, Catholics and Negroes, the groups it hated the most.

There are few Negroes in Johnson County until this year when many migrate from the South to assist in the new industry of raising cotton.

It is estimated that Chicago has 20,000 speakeasies.

Jack Dempsey, the colorful heavyweight champ since 1919, frequents the Chicago nightclub scene. Most politicians have his autographed picture on their desks. Dempsey fights Louis Firpo, the Wild Bull of the Argentine pampas. The fight only lasted 2 rounds, with Dempsey winning by a knockout. There were twelve knockdowns in about 4 minutes, making it the most ferocious action ever in a fight of such limited duration. The 6'3" and 220-pound Firpo knocked Dempsey down several times, once through the ropes and out of the ring. Ashcan artist George Bellows immortalized the incident on canvas.

The power of the Ku Klux Klan was broken in **Franklin County** in what came to be known as the battle of Mattox Farm. Jack Mattox was a prominent farmer who owned land at a place called Crawford Prairie. The local Klan, in their usual manner, was planning to pay him a midnight visit to give him a serious warning. But among the Klan group was a fellow Mason and friend of Jack Mattox. He warned Mattox of the impending visit, and he promptly organized a posse of about 40 men. They lay in ambush along the roadside and waited for the nightriders. There was an exchange of gunfire, and several Klansmen were injured and one killed in the ensuing melee. One of those wounded was convinced through trickery that his wounds were fatal. To salve his conscience, he gave authorities a long list of members. The governor of Illinois authorized a special group of 100 men to round up and arrest the Klansmen. The power of the KKK was broken forever in Franklin County.

The KKK arrives in **Marion** and holds a rally some 2,000 strong with a cross burning ceremony. Dismayed over the inability of law officials to enforce prohibition, the Klan hires S. Glen Young, a former Prohibition Agent to clean up the area. The war between the wets and drys was on.

> ## THE KU KLUX KLAN
>
> The KKK invites all able-bodied, law abiding, Christian men of the Protestant persuasion to come join us in our fight to purify our nation from those who seek to drag it down through lawlessness, Romanism and the mixing of inferior blood.
>
> Defenders of true Americanism are invited to come to our meeting this Thursday, April 23, at 9:00 p.m. in the large field south of Mine #3 at Carterville. New members will be initiated.

Charlie Birger purchases 40 acres of land in Williamson County and makes plans to build Shady Rest, a clubhouse for his gang. Bootlegger Charlie Birger was one of the people caught in a Young-led raid at **Benton,** and he vows to get even.

Johnny Torrio, after an assassination attempt that severely wounded him, quits the business and hands everything over to Al Capone. Torrio leaves the country and visits Naples, Italy.

Reform-minded Democrat Michael Dever becomes Chicago's new mayor, replacing "Big Bill" Thompson. It was Dever's pressure on Capone that forced him to leave Chicago and move his base of operations to the Hawthorne Inn at Cicero.

A big earthquake in Tokyo destroys most of its buildings. Left standing is Frank Lloyd Wright's Tokyo Hotel that he designed to be quake resistant.

The state buys historic Monk's Mound from the Ramey family that owned it and lived in a brick house on the site.

Red Grange (author's collection)

Robert Millikan becomes **first Illinois-born native to win the Nobel Prize**. It is awarded for his oil-drop experiment by which he determined the amount of electrical charge in a single electron.

About 500 members of the Ku Klux Klan are sworn in as Prohibition Agents to combat illegal drinking in southern Illinois. Politics makes strange bedfellows as Baptist churches, also strong supporters of Prohibition, find themselves in an unholy alliance.

Robert Abbott, founder of the *Chicago Daily Defender*, begins the practice of including a column for Negro children in his newspaper. A few years later he created a character named Bud Billiken (a Billiken is a guardian angel for children) and held a Bud Billiken Festival the first Saturday in August. It was marked by a parade, special singers and performers, and a picnic after the parade with soda, candy, ice cream and competitive games and races. This festival is still going strong.

1924 - Harold Red Grange, from **Wheaton**, leads the University of Illinois to a stunning victory over Michigan. Grange scored four times in the first quarter, and in the second half, ran for yet another and passed for a 6th touchdown. Michigan at the time was ranked number one in the country and had a 22 game winning streak. Illinois won the game 39 to 14. Grange ran for 402 yards and passed for 64 more. His first four touchdowns were on runs of 95, 67, 56, and 44 yards, a feat that will probably never be matched. In 1925 Illinois played Penn, the Ivy League school. The mighty Penn team was undefeated and had crushed powerful teams like Yale and Chicago. Easterners said Grange's exploits were exaggerated and due to luck. Illinois won 24 to 2 with Grange running wild for 363 yards and three touchdowns. Grange would go on to play pro ball for the Chicago Bears. Grange quit the Illini team after Thanksgiving and was signed by George Halas for $100,000. This led to a new rule that pro sports could not sign college athletes until after their class graduated.

The state of Illinois passes a law that prohibits males from appearing in public wearing masks. One of the two negative votes against the bill was cast by Representative Bandy of **Williamson County**.

S. Glenn Young seizes control of governmental machinery in **Herrin** and, acting as self-appointed judge, finds Sheriff George Galligan guilty of murdering Klansman Caesar Cagle in a shootout and orders him thrown in jail. In all, some 40 men were arrested for some connection with Kagle's killing, but Galligan and the others were later released.

Young is attacked by the Shelton gang while traveling with his wife from **Marion** to East St. Louis. His car is raked with gunfire near **Okawville**. He is wounded, and his wife is blinded by buckshot.

In August there is a big shootout between Klan and anti-Klan forces at a garage in **Herrin**, and 6 people are killed. The sheriff's anti-Klan forces take refuge in a hospital, and there is another shootout at that site.

Chicago's Soldier Field, seating capacity 45,000, opens in the fall to host athletic events. Its name at the time is Municipal Grant Park Stadium.

Architect Louis Sullivan dies broke and unappreciated. He started out as a member of William LeBaron Jenny's office staff. His talent and contributions would not be appreciated until long after his death. He studied in Paris and then joined the Chicago firm of Dankmar Adler.

Al Capone's men use violence and intimidation at the polls in Cicero in an effort to oust reform Mayor Dever who has been cracking down on their operations. An hours-long afternoon pitched battle ensues. Brother Frank Capone is killed in a shootout with police. Al Capone escapes under cover of night. Florist/gangster Dion O'Banion orders $20,000 worth of flowers in anticipation of a brisk funeral business due to the carnage. Fortunately for Capone, his slate of public officials won the election.

Charles Lindbergh, working for Robertson Aircraft of St. Louis, flies airmail on the St. Louis to Chicago run by following railroad tracks. Stops along the way include **Springfield** and **Peoria**.

An explosion in a food plant at **Pekin** kills 42 people.

Leopold and Loeb, the two youths who killed young Bobby Franks just for the thrill of it, and defended by Clarence Darrow, plead guilty to murder and are sentenced to life plus 99 years in jail. Chicago has six newspapers at this time reporting about the Crime of the Century.

Community players begin what comes to be an annual event in **Bloomington**, the American Passion Play depicting the life of Christ at the Scottish Rite Temple (309/829-3903).

Capone kills Joe Howard by pumping 6 bullets in him. Capone's friend, Jake Guzik, complained that Howard had slapped him around. Capone confronted the man, and when he mouthed off, filled him full of lead. Capone escaped prosecution when no one at the scene of the crime identified Capone as the shooter.

Congress passes a law extending the full rights of citizenship to native-Americans for the first time.

William Wrigley, the chewing gum magnate, builds the terra cotta Wrigley Building. It quickly becomes a Chicago landmark.

The divorce rate in Illinois stands at one in every seven marriages. (This is considered a scandalous statistic.)

Cicero, a town of about 70,000, the 5th largest city in the state at the time, is west of Chicago, but it is still in Cook County. Capone's new headquarters became the Hawthorne Inn at 4833 Twenty-second Street.

The small town of **Ina**, south of **Mount Vernon**, is rocked by a religious scandal. Lawrence Hight, a married Methodist minister, falls in love with a young member of his flock, Elsie Sweeten, a married woman with 3 children. After a torrid affair that included clandestine trysts following Wednesday night prayer meetings, the love-struck couple decided to murder their spouses. Wilford Sweeten, a coal miner, was the first victim. Ptomaine (food) poisoning was common back then, and many assumed that was the cause of death. But when Anna Hight died an agonizing death 6 weeks later, ugly rumors forced the county coroner to order autopsies. Sweeten's body was exhumed, and an analysis of the stomach found traces of poison. Arsenic was also found in Mrs. Hight's body. The reverend was sentenced to life imprisonment at Menard, and Elsie was given 35 years at Joliet. Two years later the Illinois Supreme Court ruled that Elsie should have been tried separately. A second trial, despite much damaging evidence, ended with an acquittal.

Dion O'Banion, Capone's Irish rival, is killed in the famous "handshake murder." Three men came into his flower shop in Chicago and when O'Banion (who always carried 3 guns) offered a handshake, one of the men held him fast, the other helped immobilze him, and the third shot him dead. Hymie Weiss now assumed leadership of the O'Banion Gang. O'Banion had been responsible for about 25 killings.

1925 – Illinois adopts an official state song, "Illinois," written by Charles H. Chamberlain and sung to the tune, "Baby Mine." "By thy rivers gently flowing, Illinois, Illinois . . ." The song pays tribute to Lincoln, Grant and General John Logan. No state in the union produced 3 men as important as these to the Civil War effort. "Not without thy wondrous story, Illinois, Illinois, Can be writ the nation's glory, Illinois, Illinois . . . ." This great song makes the hair on the back of your neck stiffen.

Victor Motors of 28th and Locust in St. Louis, a truck manufacturing firm since 1923, completes the renovation of an old factory at 24th and McCasland in **East St. Louis**. The facility was first used by St. Louis Bed Company in 1905 and then was used by St. Louis Cotton Oil Company before Victor revamped the 360,000 sq. ft. building for about $500,000. In April of 1926 the company started producing buses holding 28-35 passengers. The company apparently went out of business around 1929. The building was later occupied by Nelson Concrete Culvert Company.

It is estimated that warfare against the KKK by the forces of Sheriff Galligan, allied with the Birger and Shelton gangs, is responsible for 52 deaths in Williamson County. Allied with S. Glenn Young and the Klan were large numbers of Protestant ministers.

In a shootout at the European Hotel in Herrin, there is a gunplay between Birger's men and S. Glen Young and his supporters. Four people are killed in the fracas, including S. Glenn Young. The power of the KKK wanes after his funeral. It is completely broken after another shootout (1926) in front of the Masonic Temple in Herrin where 7 men were killed.

Chicago's most successful criminal defense lawyer, Clarence Darrow, defends John Scopes in the famous Monkey Trial about evolution in Dayton, Tennessee. This sensationalized trial was heavily covered by the press. It turned out to be a battle between old-fashioned fundamentalists who believed in a literal interpretation of the Bible, and modernists who believed the Old Testament to be a collection of fairy tales. William Jennings Bryan of **Salem** prosecuted the case and died a week after the trial was over.

Clarence Darrow

March 18. A series of tornadoes ravage southern Illinois and the Midwest, killing more than **891** people in the **worst series of storms** to ever hit this part of the country. Twenty-six towns were hit over a five state area **injuring 2,832 people**. Whatever might have been missed by the tornadoes was finished off by fires in numerous places. Missouri, Illinois, Indiana, Kentucky and Tennessee were the devastated states. The heaviest loss of life and greatest destruction was reported in **Murphysboro**.

This part of Illinois becomes known as Tornado Alley. Seven other states have tornadoes more frequently than Illinois, but our state **ranks first in tornado-caused deaths**.

East St. Louis *Journal*: The swirling death wind which late Wednesday swept over southern Illinois has caused property damage in excess of ten million dollars. The death and injured figures were based on bodies recovered from the stricken area, and upon the number

SALESMAN SUCKED THROUGH ROOF

East St. Louis *Journal*, March 20

A traveling salesman in Carbondale, B.B. McPherson of St. Louis, told the amazing story of being sucked head first through a roof.

He was inside a frame store when the tornado struck. It pulled him head first through the roof and then set him down outside in front of the building.

He said his trousers were torn entirely off him leaving nothing but the belt. Physicians in St. Louis said that he suffered from two scalp wounds, a possible fractured skull, a fractured shoulder and an injured ankle.

of persons still unaccounted for in the storm-ridden territory. The original figures were revised upward daily. The rural communities still have to report their loss of life, and this is expected to swell the totals.

Twenty-three towns in three states were swept by the storm, many of the places being virtually flattened.

1925 TORNADO CASUALTY FIGURES		
Town	Dead	Injured
Annapolis	2	25
Benton	7	0
Biehle	10	18
Bloomfield	7	24
Bush	10	60
Caldwell	2	16
C.Girard.	12	41
Carbondale	25	61
Carmi	2	11
DeSoto	150	400
Gallatin,Ten.	80	10
Gorham	40	70
Griffin Ind.	100	100
Logan	10	60
Louisville,Ky	5	5
McLeansboro	10	25
Murphysboro	400	700
Owensville,Ind	6	30
Parrish	25	25
Princeton,Ind	100	200
Poseyville,Ind	5	30
Royalton, Ind	3	25
Thompsonville	9	32
Vergennes	38	30
W. Frankfort	250	400

The city council of **East St. Louis**, led by **Mayor M.M. Stephens**, voted to send $1,000, and the state legislature was expected to vote $500,000 in relief funds. The St. Clair County Board voted to send an additional $1,000. **William R. Brown**, potentate of the Ainad Temple in East St. Louis, organized a group of his fellow men for relief work. A relief train, filled with doctors, nurses and supplies, immediately left from Chicago. Others were sent from St. Louis and East St. Louis.

Governor Len Small dispatched the state militia from **Quincy** to affected areas. Men were also sent from **Jefferson Barracks** in Missouri to help clear the wreckage and establish order. There was some reported looting initially, but after more guardsmen arrived the practice of thievery came to an end.

Murphysboro was the hardest hit with nearly half the town being flattened. Nearly a third of **West Frankfort** was gone. The fires that subsequently broke out were so bad that dynamite had to be used to create firebreaks.

More women than men were killed in Illinois because many men were down in the coalmines when the tornado struck.

The largest industrial site damaged was the Southern Railroad shops at Princeton, Indiana, which employed 450 people.

The Red Cross, of course, was on the scene in every town and immediately set up soup kitchens and tents.

Nearly half of those killed in **Desoto** were children as the winds struck a large school complex shortly before 3:00 p.m.

In Indiana, scores more were burned to death as they became trapped in the debris, and fires swept through the ruins with indescribable scenes of horror. The deathly odor of burning flesh was smelled for miles around as volunteer fire fighters struggled to check the flames. The fires were started mostly by overturned stoves whose burning embers set fire to the rubble.

Spectators described the tornado as a sausage-shaped greenish cloud that roared in with the sound of a locomotive from the west. They said it was humid and that hail began to fall just before the cyclone struck.

Automobiles did not escape the destruction as they were often piled together in small heaps. Some of them were tossed completely through the sides of buildings.

East St. Louis Commissioner **John Connors** came back from a visit to the devastated district and said there was a pressing need for serums, especially the anti-toxin for tetanus. He also said there was a shortage of undertakers.

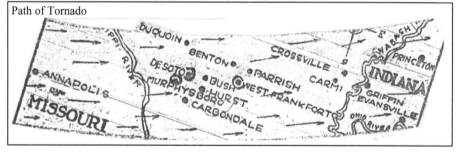

Path of Tornado

Around midnight, the skies around **Benton**, **Harrisburg** and **DuQuoin** were reddish-orange with flame from the fires that were still destroying Murphysboro.

Forty-six of the injured were taken to hospitals in East St. Louis. Seven of the most severely injured died on the train while in route to St. Mary's and Deaconess (Christian Welfare).

For several days after the tornado, all roads and highways were clogged with sightseers wanting to get a glimpse of the carnage. Most were turned away for fear they would hamper relief efforts. Tented cities sprang up for the homeless. A crew of about forty men set about digging graves in Murphysboro.

Author Dean Koontz would later write about the tornado in *From The Corner of his Eye*.

April: The Sheltons have a falling out with the Newmans. Bess Newman orders the brothers out of the Arlington Hotel in East St. Louis. A few days later, one of the Shelton's men, **Charlie Gordon**, provoked Art Newman into a street fight, and Newman shot and killed Gordon. Newman was acquitted on self-defense, but he decided that it was time to get outta Dodge. Art sold the hotel, and the couple left for Memphis. After the heat was off, they decided to return to the area to **hook up with Charlie Birger**, making him a much more formidable foe for the Sheltons.

Harry Houdini, the renown escape artist, comes to Chicago. While not engaged in the business of death-defying escapes, Houdini took it upon himself to debunk those who claimed to be fortunetellers and spiritualists. One such person sued Houdini, saying that his crusade was making it impossible for him to communicate with the spirits, thus costing him money. Houdini

Charlie Birger

won his case in court when he proved the man to be a fraud by challenging him to reveal the nickname Houdini's father had given him. The irony of all this is that before his death in 1926, Houdini promised to try and communicate with his wife from beyond the grave, prompting annual séances on every Halloween, the anniversary of his death.

A city ordinance makes it illegal to kill a white squirrel (rats with bushy tails) or take one out of the city of **Olney**.

George Halas, owner of the Chicago Bruins, helps establish the American Basketball Association pro league. The Depression wipes out the league, and in 1937 the NBA is formed. In 1947 the Chicago Gears signed George Mikan and won the championship. Maurice White took his Gears into a new league that he formed. It collapsed and Mikan was signed by the Minneapolis Lakers (now the L.A. Lakers).

The Chicago Cardinals win the NFL championship.

Harold Red Grange becomes football's first $100,000 a year player when he signs with the Chicago Bears. His contract is unusual in that it also calls for a percentage of the gate take. He quits the team a year later and forms his own league when they turn down his request to become 1/3 owner.

The editor of the student newspaper *Daily Illini* calls the popular shimmy dance "that insult to our whole moral code."

Al Capone applies for life insurance but is rejected by 3 different companies.

Bugs Moran and Hymie Weiss gun down Johnny Torrio as he and his wife return from a shopping trip. He was shot several times in front of his home and was thought to be mortally wounded, but he miraculously recovered.

Elgin wins its second straight prep basketball championship.

1926 – The Chicago Tribune Tower opens on July 6.

Chicago evangelist Billy Sunday lambasts the automobile for the decline in church attendance and the loosening of morals. "We've put the red light district on wheels," he warned.

Thousands of Chicagoans turn out to see the body of actor Rudolph Valentino who had recently died from a perforated ulcer in New York. He was on the way to his burial place in Hollywood. Police officers, fearing a repeat of a riot in New York, cordon off the area, and only a few catch even a glimpse of his casket. The swarthy Italian-born Valentino rose to fame by starring in the *Four Horsemen of the Apocalypse* and *The Sheik*.

The federal government and the states work in conjunction to create **Route 66**. It begins in Chicago at the intersection of Jackson Boulevard and Lake Shore Drive. It coursed 2,400 miles in length and ended in California near Los Angeles. Approximately 1/8 of the highway was in Illinois. It was fully paved by 1936.

Samuel Insull, the Chicago utilities giant, proposes that the city build a subway system. Aldermen turned him down. His company was now operating in 11 states and furnishing electricity to 385 cities. Insull ran utilities and electric streetcar systems in the northern half of the state, while **Champaign** politician William B. McKinley ran things in the southern half. McKinley's Illinois Traction System became the largest in the Midwest. The McKinley Bridge over the Mississippi at Madison/Granite City was built by him.

Insull spent his mornings at his People's Gas Light & Coke Company and his afternoon at Chicago Commonwealth Edison. His wife, the former Gladys Wallis of stage fame, tried to resurrect her stage career 25 years after the birth of her son, but with little success. Insull kept a preferred list of 1600 Chicagoans whom he sold stock to at below market price.

When Harold McCormick was no longer willing to support the Chicago Opera Company, Insull stepped in and agreed to underwrite it for a 5-year period. He built a new structure that would have an opera house combined with office space. The idea was that the office rents

---

Rank of Illinois cities in 1925 according to annual manufacturing value of products

1. Chicago, $3 ½ billion 2. Joliet $82 million 3. East St. Louis $77 million 4. Rockford $74 million 5 Cicero $57 million 6. Peoria $57 million 7. Moline $44 million 8. Granite City $43 million 9. Chicago Heights $41 million 10. Decatur $38 million 11. Alton $31 million 12. Aurora $30 million 13 Pekin $25.2 million 14. Elgin $ 25 million 15. Waukegan $24 million 16. Quincy $23 million 17. Springfield $22.7 million 18. Rock Island $22 million 19. Freeport $18 million 20. Kewanee $16 million 21. Danville $15 million 22. Maywood $14.4 million 23. Belleville 14 million

Writer Edgar Lee Masters

CHICAGO GANGSTERS OF THE 20s and 30s

Johnny Torrio - The Father of Modern Gangsterdom

Dion O'Banion - Capone rival - shot in his flower shop

Hynie Weiss - O'Banion successor, gunned down on streets of Chicago

Al Capone - Voted "Man of the Year" by Time Magazine

Machine Gun McGurn - Ex-boxer turned Capone gunman

Jake "Greasy Thumb" Guzik - Capone's treasurer

Bugs Moran - Capone rival whose men were gunned down in St. Valentine's Day Massacre

Anselmi, Guinta and Scalisi - Beaten to death at a banquet with a ballbat by Capone because they were traitors

Eliot Ness - Capone nemesis, leader of Untouchables

John Dillinger - Gunned down in Chicago by Melvin Purvis and FBI

Anna Sage - The Lady in Red - woman who fingered John Dillinger for the FBI at Chicago's Biograph Theater

Murray "the Camel" Humphreys - Man who quietly headed the Capone organization during much of the 1930s

would pay for the support of the opera. A month before the grand opening, the stock market crashed. Insull was 70 years old at the time. In July of 1932, his fortunes declining, his Board of Directors forced him to resign. The crash of Insull stock caused one bank failure and brought losses to thousands of investors. Insull's brother (Martin) was guilty of using more than $500,000 of company money to cover the margin on his personal brokerage account. After various lawsuits were filed, both brothers fled, Samuel to Europe and Martin to Canada. Samuel Insull was finally apprehended, but he was acquitted by the jury in a controversial trial.

Frank Smith wins the U.S. Senate race against William McKinley. But the U.S. Senate refuses to accept him on the grounds that his Insull-backed campaign had spent too much money on the campaign and "bought" the seat. The same thing happened to Senator William Lorimer who was expelled on similar grounds ten years earlier.

It is claimed that 900 different items bear the label, "**Made in Peoria.**"

According to the legend, Mary and John Kent of Smallville (Illinois) adopt a child they find along the roadside. While in the process of growing up, Clark discovers that he is incredibly strong and has X-ray vision - powers he hides until he grows up and takes a job as a mild-mannered reporter at the *Daily Planet* in Metropolis.

William Stout, a native of **Quincy**, establishes the nation's first airline service, offering flights from Detroit to Grand Rapids, Michigan.

The first Eucharistic Congress opens in Chicago and is attended by over a million people.

The **East St Louis Flyers** and the **Belleville Maroons** begin a football rivalry that lasts until 1974 by playing an annual Thanksgiving Day (morning) football game that, more often than not, determined the conference championship. Some of the crowds were as large as 11,000 people.

According to August Maue in his *History of Illinois*, geography experts predict that by the year 1950, Chicago will have a population of 10 million.

Chicago upstart **Rand McNally** publishes his first atlas.

Coffee baron Frederick McLaughlin buys a Portland hockey team and moves it to Chicago where they become known as the Blackhawks. They play their games at the Coliseum, a former Civil War prison. McLaughlin was married to movie star Irene Castle.

There is a falling out between Charlie Birger and the Sheltons when it becomes apparent that Charlie Birger is skimming profits from the slot machine business they were supposed to share equally.

The Sheltons hire a barnstorming pilot to fly over Shady Rest, Birger's hangout, while one of them tosses homemade bombs out of a two-seat JN-4 Jenny. Blackie Armes was the bombardier, but his nitro/dynamite bombs missed the target, killing only one of Birger's pets. In a later story that appeared in Ripley's Believe It Or Not, this incident was considered the **first aerial bombing attack carried out on American soil.**

Emil Fricker becomes the last man publicly hanged in **Madison County**. Fricker, a dairy farmer in **Highland**, was convicted of murdering the husband of a milkmaid on his farm with whom he had fallen hopelessly in love. He was also suspected of killing her first husband.

Assistant State's Attorney William McSwiggin is gunned down by a passing motorcade on the streets of Chicago. It was probably the Capone mob that did it, but 4 grand jury investigations failed to lead to a conviction.

1927 – Jack Dempsey, who lost his title to Gene Tunney, gets a rematch. The fight is at Soldier Field in Chicago. It was rumored that Capone had big bets on Dempsey, and had sent him a note that warned him not to lose. Capone even met with the referee, Davey Miller, and told him he had bet $50,000 on Dempsey and that he wanted him to give Dempsey a fair shot. Shortly before the fight, Miller was replaced as referee. Dempsey knocked Tunney down in the 7th round and would have won the fight had he gone to a neutral corner. Referee Dave (Long Count) Barry had to push Dempsey in the right direction before starting his count.

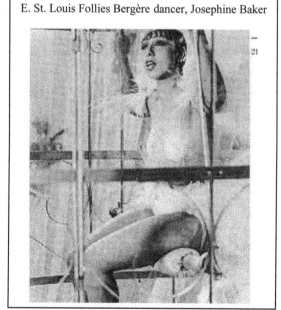

E. St. Louis Follies Bergère dancer, Josephine Baker

Tunney barely got off the canvas before the count of ten, having been given 5 extra seconds. Tunney went on to win by decision in the controversial fight.

Interestingly, it was the same Davey Miller shot by Dion O'Banion four years earlier outside the LaSalle Theater.

Giant City State Park, south of **Carbondale** in the Illinois Ozarks, is created and so named for its orderly 35-foot high blocks of sandstone. Its large stone lodge was built by the Civilian Conservation Corps (CCC) during the Depression. During the Civil War the site was a hideout for treasonous Knights of the Golden Circle, Confederate sympathizers

Chicago opens a new municipal airport that becomes known as Midway. It has a single runway and occupies a quarter of a square mile.

Entertainer Joe E. Lewis becomes known as "**the man the mob couldn't kill.**" Lewis was a comedian at the Green Mill in Chicago but wanted to sign a new contract with another club. He ignored threats on his life and planned to continue his career at the New Rendezvous. He was beaten and horribly slashed by several of Machine Gun McGurn's men. It took him nearly ten years to recover. He doggedly resumed his career as soon as he was able. His story was told in the Frank Sinatra vehicle, *The Joker is Wild*.

Jim and Marian Jordan of **Peoria**, playing **Fibber McGee and Molly** on radio, help **make Chicago the radio capital of America**.

William McAndrew, Chicago Superintendent of Schools, is suspended and placed on trial by the School Board. He is accused of being unpatriotic and pro-British in his views. McAndrew is a victim of former Mayor Big Bill Thompson's bid for reelection based on a zany crusade against the British in an "America First" platform. Famed lawyer Clarence Darrow proclaimed, "Why it's the craziest thing I ever heard of." The school district's head librarian suggested that all of the pro-British books be placed in a cage and only "mature" historians be allowed to read them. A former congressman combed the system's books for 6 months and declared that England was conquering America, "not by shot but by a rain of propaganda." After months of hearings and 6,000 pages of testimony, the Board voted to remove McAndrew from his position. Thompson won election for his third term as mayor but was defeated in 1931 by Anton Cermak.

Chicago mayor "Big Bill" Thompson (a.c.)

George and Ben Probst, proprietors of the **New Athens Brewery**, are fined $1,000 each and sentenced to 90 days in the Franklin County jail for violation of the Volstead prohibition act.

Illinois becomes the last state to adopt a motor fuel tax to pay for road improvement. This was due partially to farmers not wanting fuel used in tractors to be taxed. A tax of two cents a gallon is imposed to build and maintain roads in Illinois.

Litchfield resident **Ray "the Cracker" Schalk** becomes the manager of the Chicago White Sox. He established records by catching 1,719 baseball games in 17 years. He also played in the 1917 and 1919 World Series.

Miles Davis and his parents move to **East St. Louis** a year after he is born in **Alton**. His father is a dentist.

Famed Jazz musician Duke Ellington records a peppy tune on the RCA label called "East St. Louis Toodle Oo." The tune is a vague reference about having a good time in the notorious Valley district of the town. The song became nationally famous because it heralded his popular radio show throughout the 1930s.

When a tornado approaches a school in **White Hall**, teacher Annie Keller urges the children to take refuge under their desks and she faces the tornado's rage at the room's doorway. She is killed, but all of the children survived. A monument to her was later sculpted by the renowned Lorado Taft.

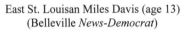
East St. Louisan Miles Davis (age 13)
(Belleville *News-Democrat*)

Lois Delaner of **Joliet**, a high school student and only 16 years old, is chosen Miss America.

The ship *Favorite* capsizes off North Avenue in the Chicago River, killing 27.

The Buckingham Fountain is built at Grant Park and Lake Shore Drive in Chicago. The fountain spouts water almost 150 feet into the air and at night has a dazzling light display. It is modeled after a fountain at Louis XIV's palace at Versailles and named for its donor, Katherine Buckingham, a patron of the arts.

The new airport in **Springfield** will be named for Charles Lindbergh who helped plan its construction before his famous transoceanic flight.

"Roosting Joe" Powers remains atop the flagpole at Chicago's Morrison Hotel for 16 days, two hours, and 45 minutes. Flagpole sitting is a fad that sweeps the nation at this point in time.

The Avalon, the greatest of John Eberson's "atmospheric" movie palaces opens in Chicago.

Shady Rest, Charlie Birger's hangout is dynamited and burned to the ground. At first it was thought to be the work of his enemies – the Shelton gang. But it was later thought to have been done by Birger himself, ostensibly to kill Elmo Thomasson, a young man Birger had hired to kill Joe Adams, Mayor of West City and a hated ally of the Sheltons. Birger was also responsible for the murder of Lory "Slim" Price, a state trooper whom Birger suspected of duplicity. Harry Thomasson, who had been a partner with his brother when they killed Joe Adams, confessed to the crime and admitted he had been paid by Birger to commit the murder.

Birger and several other members of his gang are convicted of murder and are sentenced to be executed. The state has recently replaced hanging with electrocution, but Birger gets a date with the hangman because his crime was committed before the new law was passed.

Carl Sandburg composes the song "El-a-noy:" Then move your family westward,/ Bring all your girls and boys/ And cross at Shawnee ferry'/ To the state of El-a-noy/

1928 – Charlie Birger becomes the last man in the state of Illinois to be legally hanged. He is executed at the Benton Jail for the murder of Joe Adams of **West City**. Birger was seen by many as a modern-day Robin Hood (overlooking the fact that he was a cold-blooded killer) and was perhaps the most colorful gangster in Illinois history after Capone and Dillinger. While in jail awaiting execution, Birger was visited by evangelist **Billy Sunday**. Birger was also allowed to have conjugal visits from his wife. Birger's favorite drink was said to be an **Egyptian cocktail** – corn liquor mixed with port wine.

The 9-piered Chain of Rocks Bridge is built, spanning the Mississippi River in North St. Louis at Route 66. It is a steel structure of the cantilever type and is one-and-a tenth mile in length. The name is derived from Rocks Shoal.

The Lewis and Clark bridges open in **Alton**, giving access to St. Charles County and north St. Louis.

7-Up is invented and marketed in St. Louis by C.L. Grigg. It took him 2 years and 11 different formulas before he perfected the lemon-flavored drink. The red spot on the drink come from the inventor who had red eyes because he was albino.

Coalmine operators begin installing new loading machines and conveyors in Illinois mines to modernize and make operations more efficient. This results in large layoffs of miners who have never known any other kind of work. With the Depression about to begin, this will lead to economic hardship and labor strife.

The Manny Company of **Rockford** is absorbed by the J.I. Case Implement Company.

Two whites, Charles Correll and Freeman Gosden, launch a Chicago radio career with a blackface vaudeville act they had been performing. Within a year **Amos 'n' Andy** was a hit on NBC radio.

Freeman Gosden of Amos 'n' Andy

1929 – Congress passes the Jones Law, providing for heavy fines and up to 5 years in jail for bootlegging and other violations against the Prohibition Amendment.

At roughly 10:30 a.m. on the morning of February 14, four men in a car, two of them wearing police uniforms, pull up in front of a garage on Clark Street. A sign on the building read SMC Cartage Company. and it was a favorite hangout for the Bugs Moran gang. Their Cadillac touring car even had a Klaxon gong on the running board. Thinking it was just a police raid, the seven men inside meekly lined up against the wall and were cut down in a hail of bullets. One of the men killed was Reinhardt Schwimmer, an optometrist who hung around with the gang for the sport of it. One of the victims, Frank Gusenberg, lived 3 hours with 14 bullets in him. When asked who shot him, he maintained the underworld's code of silence and said, "nobody." It is believed that the shooters were Tony Accardo, Machine Gun McGurn, Fred Burke and John Scalisi.

Al Capone was purposely in Florida at his estate so that he would have an alibi. He was informed every step of the way by McGurn who made frequent phone calls. Moran, one of the main targets, escaped the slaughter when he arrived a few minutes late for a meeting, saw the "police car" pull up, and walked away in the other direction.

As a result of public outrage over the St. Valentine's Day Massacre in Chicago on February 14, the **nation's first major crime laboratory** is established at Northwestern University. The lab was affiliated with the Northwestern University School of Law in the hopes that this would prevent political interference.

Calhoun is the only county in the state without rail service.

Al Capone attends a big gangster meeting in Atlantic City, New Jersey. Sensing that other mob bosses are unhappy with the notoriety he is bringing to organized crime, he fears for his life. He gets himself arrested on a concealed weapons charge in Pennsylvania on the way home from the meeting. Thinking the judge will give him a month or two in jail where he will be safe, he is astounded when a stiff yearlong sentence is pronounced.

Eliot Ness, a Norwegian-American graduate of the University of Chicago, becomes the head of a special task force to make raids on Capone's breweries and to gather information that will help the U.S. government make a case against Al Capone for tax fraud. The word soon gets out that Ness and his men can't be bribed, and they are labeled **The Untouchables** by the press.

Bloody aftermath of the St. Valentine's Day Massacre

Jake Lingle, the "**World's Richest Reporter**" is shot and killed in a pedestrian subway under Michigan Avenue. Lingle was killed shortly after Al Capone was released from prison in Pennsylvania, getting time off for good behavior. Thousands of people showed up at his funeral. At first he was thought to be a martyr for freedom of the press. But it soon came to light that this $65 a week *Tribune* reporter led a fancy and expensive lifestyle. He was on the take as a middleman between the Chicago police and the underworld. Lingle was killed one day prior to a meeting he was supposed to have with Colonel McCormick and some Treasury agents. Leo Brothers, a St. Louis hit man, was later convicted of the killing.

Chicago real estate entrepreneur Oscar DePriest becomes the **first black man from a northern state elected to congress**. Unfortunately, he voted against Roosevelt's New Deal and lost his seat four years later.

The wild and woolly decade comes to a crushing end on Thursday, October 24, when the stock market crashes in New York with a one-day loss of $32 billion. By the end of the year, the losses amounted to a staggering $40 million. Overproduction by farmers led to falling commodity prices, and business over expansion during the booming decade also added to the economic woes. Stock prices had soared to unrealistic dizzying heights, fueled by feverish investor speculation that bought on margin (10 percent down) and gambled everything on even higher prices. The state of Illinois, like the rest of the nation, would now suffer through a decade-long depression. Illinois coal mines closed one after another due to lack of industrial demand.

Because most people could no longer afford to ride trains, the Illinois Central was forced to lay off nearly half of its 60,000 work force.

Numerous banks were financially unsound because they too had speculated and made risky loans at the prospect of high profits. When large numbers of people started withdrawing their savings to cover living expenses, shortfalls occurred which led to runs on banks and financial panic. Numerous banks were forced to close causing many people to lose their life savings.

Construction is nearly complete on the two-block long Merchandise Mart in Chicago, which remains for decades as the **largest commercial building in the world**. Completed in 1930, it has 95 acres of total floor space. Originally intended to serve wholesaling business needs, in 1991 it opened several floors to retail shoppers.

Cartoonist Elzie Segar introduces a new character into his ten-year-old "Thimble Theater" comic strip. He is **Popeye**, a spinach-eating sailor with bulging muscles in all the wrong places (forearm instead of biceps). The Popeye characters are based on real people known by Segar in **Chester**. Olive Oyl was modeled after a shopkeeper named Dora Paskal. The Wimpy character with the hamburger fetish was based on Bill Schuchert, owner of the Chester Opera House. Popeye was the alter ego of Frank "Rocky" Fiegel, a riverboat operator.

Ernie Nevers of the Chicago Cardinals **scores 40 points** in a football game against the Bears.

Chicago loses a national lawsuit, filed in 1908 by surrounding states. It was finally decided by the U.S. Supreme Court. The decision held that Chicago had legally been authorized by the secretary of war to divert 4,167 cubic feet of water per second from Lake Michigan, but for years had unlawfully increased that amount to 8,500. Chicago had argued that the levels of the great lakes were rising, not falling, and that the latter volume of water was necessary to maintain navigability of the Illinois River.

Chicagoan Ruth Hanna McCormick serves a two-year term as a Republican representative in Congress.

Al Capone commits the most vicious act of his infamous career. Suspecting several of his men to be traitors, he staged a large banquet at a roadhouse near Hammond, Indiana. Joe Guinta, Albert Anselmi, and John Scalise were among the dozens of mobsters invited. Late in the evening, he accused the trio of disloyalty, bound them to their chairs and beat them to a bloody pulp with a baseball bat.

Illinois claims more miles of paved roads than any other state in the nation. Every county had at least one paved road.

1930 - **Connie Ritter**, a fugitive from justice for the murder of Joe Adams and Lory and Ethel Price, is apprehended and sentenced to life imprisonment. Ritter, a Charlie Birger thug, was the one who shot **Ethel Price**. He had been captured in Gulfport, Mississippi, eight months earlier. **Ernest Blue** was an important member of the Birger clan who escaped prosecution, but authorities believed various reports that he was already dead.

Chief of Police **James P. Leahy** issued an order for certain crooks to **stay out of East St. Louis** for six

King Features Trademark

Depression era, Capone-run soup kitchen for the unemployed

months. The order was issued on the Shelton brothers, Earl, Carl and Bernie, who sold illegal liquor, ran gambling and prostitution resorts, and were linked to several murders in Southern Illinois. **Bernie Shelton**, youngest member of the bootlegging brothers known as the Shelton gang, was sentenced to six months in jail in August of 1930 for violating the order. He was nabbed by a squad of detectives in East St. Louis and charged with vagrancy and carrying a concealed weapon. Superintendent of the Workhouse, Adolph Briesacher, said Shelton would be made to work on the rock pile six days a week just like the other prisoners. A newspaper account reported that "no other gang plied its illicit trade and served so little time in the penitentiaries as the Shelton boys."

The last known bear is shot and killed in the state of Illinois.

127

The Madison Kennel Club, a dog racing facility on **Collinsville Road** (Route 40), closes after two years of shady activities. Two miles west of Fairmont Park, it was only a quarter of a mile long and was one of the first facilities of its type to be lighted for night racing. One evening the state police raided it, their objective being the mechanical rabbit, but management was tipped off and secured an injunction. State troopers were turned away as the band struck up *Hail! Hail! The Gang's All Here*, and illegal betting continued.

The heavily populated Black Belt of Chicago spawns a neighborhood that becomes known as **Bronzeville**. It becomes a center of literary and cultural achievement. Prominent African-Americans who lived there include: Katherine Dunham, Richard Wright, Gwendolyn Brooks and sociologist Horace Cayton. The ornate Regal Theater in that neighborhood was played by all the great black entertainers in the 1930s, 40s and 50s.

Route 66 is reconfigured through **Litchfield** to give it a more direct alignment to **Springfield**.

The lowest temperature ever recorded in the state occurs at **Mount Carroll** at –35 degrees Fahrenheit.

Baseball slugger Babe Ruth makes a deal with a candy company to start selling a candy bar with his name on it. Unfortunately, the courts hold that this is an infringement on the **candy bar** invented over a decade earlier by Otto Schneering, founder of Curtiss Candy Company in Chicago. His first product was called Kandy Kate and was very popular. A re-name contest was held and the winner was "Baby Ruth," named for President Cleveland's oldest daughter who died at age 12.

The **pinball machine** is invented in Chicago by the In and Outdoor Games Company.

The Hostess snack food known as **Twinkies** is invented by James Dewar, manager of Continental Baking Company in **Schiller Park**. Dewar ate two Twinkies every day and lived into his eighties.

Chicagoan Eliot Ness (auth. col.)

The new saltwater Shedd Aquarium in Chicago is supplied with its ocean water by 160 boxcars from Key West, Florida.

Edwin Perkins, a Nebraskan, builds a plant in Chicago to produce Flavor Smack, which later became known as **Kool-Aid**. The company was acquired by General Foods in 1953.

Hack Wilson of the Chicago Cubs drives in 190 runs, a record that may never be broken.

Al Capone makes the cover of Time Magazine when he is chosen as the weekly's Man of the Year.

Dominic Tarro of **Benld**, one of the owners of a roadhouse called the Coliseum, is called to Springfield to testify before a grand jury. The state's attorney wants to question him about $50,000 worth of sugar he allegedly sold to a Capone still on the outskirts of Benld. Dominic never made it to testify. His body was found in the Sangamon River a few months later.

1931 – Southern Illinoisan **Oscar Micheaux** makes his first sound movie, *The Exile*.

Ralph "Wide Open" Smith flees the city of **East St. Louis** and heads for parts unknown. He is a familiar bootleg speakeasy owner of an establishment on Broadway. He was told by tipsters to get lost after he saw gunmen "rub out" three men in his establishment. He died of natural causes in Florida in 1947.

March: Carl Shelton is arrested by the Feds and charged with violating the Prohibition Law and the Dyer Act (interstate transportation of a stolen vehicle). Carl hijacked a $21,000 shipment of shoes, thinking the truck was loaded with alcohol. He was fined $500 and sentenced to six months in jail. While in jail, he helped rescue a jailer who had been slugged by a man in an escape attempt. He locked up the felon and fetched a doctor for the jailer.

June 12: Al Capone and 68 others are indicted and charged with 5,000 violations of the prohibition laws.

June 16: Capone pleads guilty to violating the liquor laws and income tax evasion for the years 1924-1929, thinking a bargain had been struck, and he would get off with a fine and light jail sentence.

July 24. **Earl Shelton** and two other men (who couldn't swim) are rescued from a sinking boat off the Georgia coast by Prohibition agents. The boat was rum running and had run aground in shallow water. Thinking the water was deep, Earl didn't try to escape. Earl claimed the liquor wasn't his, and that he had simply rowed out there to buy some. When the boat began to sink, the crew took his boat and rowed to safety, leaving him to drown. He was charged with violating Prohibition and tariff laws.

Writer Sherwood Anderson

July 30, 1931: Judge Wilkerson tells Capone he won't be bound by any deals. Capone changes plea to *not guilty*.

October 24, 1931: Capone is found guilty and sentenced to 11 years in prison and a $50,000 fine. Capone is stunned. He was expecting a sentence of two years.

The state begins the practice of sending money to schools based on their enrollment and attendance.

Decatur defeats **Galesburg** for the state championship in high school basketball. Decatur will repeat in 1936, 1945 and 1962.

Chicago's Home Insurance Building, the world's first skyscraper, is torn down to make way for a more modern bank building. Only now does architect William L. Jenney receive his due for this achievement.

General Robert Wood, President of Sears, founds **Allstate Auto Insurance Company**, a cash generator for years until fires, hurricanes, earthquakes, riots and floods causes Sears to finally sell it off.

1932 – Chicagoan Thomas Dorsey, his life saddened by personal tragedy, writes "Take My Hand, Precious Lord," and starts a new phenomenon called **Gospel Music**. His wife and baby daughter died in childbirth. Dorsey, a Negro, also wrote "Peace in the Valley" and started the first gospel publishing company. It was Dorsey who trained the first generation of gospel singers such as **James Cleveland, Mahalia Jackson and Clara Ward**.

Howard Hughes produces the movie *Scarface* starring Paul Muni. It is the first film about Al Capone, and it is a big hit. Chicagoan Ben Hecht wrote the screenplay.

Phillips Petroleum opens a plant in **Monsanto,** Illinois, between East St. Louis and **Cahokia**. The dispute between organized labor and the Phillips Company goes back to February of 1931 when the oil firm began constructing its first of ten huge oil storage tanks south on Route 3. Non-union men, many of them from Chicago, were hired to work on the project. In March, several non-union workers were attacked and beaten while on their way to work. Phillips said that they could save thousands by having non-union men spray paint the storage tanks. Union workers would take longer to do the job by hand with brushes.

Daniel H. Williams, Chicago heart surgeon

Imported gunmen are blamed by East St. Louis Chief of Police **James Leahy** for the killing of **Alden (Ollie) Moore**, 37, of 1628 Cleveland Avenue, president of the Central Trades and Labor Union. Moore was shot at the Central Trades building, 504 St. Louis Ave. Moore was also business agent for the Boilermakers Union # 362. The killing was an outgrowth of a three-day labor war in a dispute with the Phillips Petroleum Co. Eight men were beaten severely during the outbreaks, the attacks having been made by union sympathizers.

Belief that local gangland may have been responsible for Moore's murder leads Chief Leahy to order the arrest of **Carl Shelton** on the hunch that he is the key to solving the crime. Carl had an alibi and said he was talking to a deputy sheriff at the time of the shooting. Blackie Armes was arrested on suspicion and was found to have a machine gun and a sawed off shotgun. He said he was going squirrel hunting. Ray Walker was also picked up but was later released.

The shooting happened so quickly, witnesses were unable to identify the number of men in the car when the shots were fired. Forty-five minutes before his death, Moore told two deputy sheriffs that Carl Shelton offered him a $30,000 bribe to stay out of labor disputes. He promptly turned down the offer. The Sheltons threatened him by saying, "We know where you live." Moore was armed at the time of his death, due to the numerous threats that had been made against him.

Sheriff Jerome Munie said **Carl Shelton** told him he was employed by the Phillips Co. "to work a compromise and get this thing settled between labor and Phillips." Moore's murder is never solved.

Henry Horner, an honest reform politician, is elected governor of Illinois. He contacts Sheriff **Jerome Munie** of St. Clair County and gives him broad authority to deal with crime and corruption. Munie was given two radio-equipped police cars and a couple of investigators. Munie, a storekeeper, hated the Sheltons because he was honest, and they made fun of him. They claimed his election in 1930 was a freakish accident. They said he was a sissy and couldn't be very tough because he always had a smile on his face. Munie set up the Southern Illinois Crime Commission - six men with badges whose job was to harass the Sheltons and force them to leave the area. A lot of people didn't like the way the group operated, but many said that it was the only way to deal with the Sheltons.

Illinois writer Vachel Lindsay

It is estimated that the number of murders in Chicago during the Capone era is 350.

In response to the unhappiness of coal miners represented by the corrupt United Mine Workers union, workers in **Christian County** organize their own union, The Progressive Miners of America, formed at **Gillespie**. They immediately call for a strike against Peabody Coal. The rebellion, in part, was a demand for job security since miners were being laid off in increasing numbers due to mechanization. The straw that broke the camel's back was a new contract that was going to cut worker's pay a dollar an hour (ostensibly due to the Depression). The original contract was voted down. John L. Lewis negotiated a new contract with more fringe benefits, but still containing a reduction in pay. The ballots were sent to **Springfield**, but someone broke into the office and stole them. Lewis declared a "state of emergency" and declared the new contract to be valid. Striking miners resorted to violence to close down the mines, even blowing up railroad bridges. A majority of the workers at all the mines in **Pana** voted to go "progressive."

In August, a large caravan of **Taylorville** and **Pana** miners went to **Mulkeytown** near the Franklin County border to picket mines in southern Illinois. The sheriff of **Williamson County** was alerted and met the invasion with armed deputies. In what came to be known as the **Mulkeytown Riot**, the striking miners were beaten and shot, their cars and trucks overturned, and chased all the way back to central Illinois. When striking miners were arrested, there were too many to keep in the jails so they housed them in the **Christian County** courthouse. The angry miners tore the place up, tossing chairs out the windows, causing nearly $500,000 worth of damage. Thirty-six miners were given prison sentences for interference with interstate commerce and the mails.

The Chicago Cubs lose to the New York Yankees in the World Series four games to none. The biggest controversy was whether or not Babe Ruth called his home run shot in game 3. A home movie shows him pointing to something (some say the pitcher, some say the center field bleachers) and on the next pitch he hit one of the longest home runs ever at Wrigley Field. Did he predict the homer? That question has been debated by fans ever since.

There is a holdup at a delicatessen in the stockyards district of Chicago, during which Officer William Lundy is killed. Joe Majczek and Ted Marcinkiewicz were arrested and convicted of the crime, each receiving 99-year sentences. The pair were convicted largely on the testimony of Vera Walsh, the owner of the store at 4312 South Ashland. "Those two . . . were right in my face," she testified. Majczek's mother believed her son to be innocent and cleaned offices for 12 years until she had saved enough money to offer a $5,000 reward for the real killers. Her newspaper ad caught the eye of *Times'* reporters Jack McPhail and James McGuire. They discovered startling inconsistencies in Vera Walsh's testimony. They also uncovered the fact that her delicatessen was a front for a speakeasy, and that she was nearly arrested on bootlegging charges. They concluded that the men were victims of a "crime crackdown," ordered by Mayor Anton Cermak, on the eve of Chicago's World's Fair. The new evidence was presented to Governor Dwight Green who granted Majczek a pardon and an award of $24,000. The courts released the other man 5 years later. **The incident became the basis for a Hollywood movie,** *Northside 777*.

Franklin D. Roosevelt breaks with tradition and flies to Chicago Stadium, site of the Democratic national convention, to accept his party's nomination for president of the United States.

John McCutcheon of the *Chicago Tribune* wins the Pulitzer Prize for newspaper political cartoons.

Lake Park at Grand Marais is turned into a municipal park in **East St. Louis**. With over 1,300 acres, it is the **third largest municipal park in the nation**. It currently is the site of Frank Holten State Park, named for a city official who served in the state legislature for 40 years, thought to be a record.

The General Assembly appropriates $20 million for emergency relief funds for the calendar year. The funds are gone after six months. Governor Emmerson asks state employees to give up one day's pay a month to help out, and they willingly oblige. Emmerson, like president Hoover, had trouble with the concept of giving people dole money without requiring work in return, fearing it would destroy the work ethic.

Ronald Reagan graduates from **Eureka College** where he played football and joined the drama club.

A little known singer named **Gene Autry** records "The Death of Mother Jones," paying tribute to the nationally famous union organizer.

Bronco Nagurski helps lead the Chicago Bears to an NFL title. He is on the team when they repeat in 1933 and 1943.

A Moweaqua mine disaster kills 54 men. An unprecedented drop in barometric pressure allowed methne gas to leak into the mine. The 8:00 a.m. explosion was ignited by open flame carbide lights.

George Halas

1933 – Banks all over the state are shut down by President Roosevelt's declaration of a "Bank Holiday." This stopped the run on banks and when the closure ended, only banks deemed to be sound were allowed to reopen, boosting public confidence. Governor Emmerson chose not to run for another term and was replaced by Democratic Governor Horner who died in office from the day-after-day strain of dealing with depression problems.

Alton businessman **August Luer**, age 77, is kidnapped. He is the founder of Alton Banking and Trust and the Mineral Springs Hotel. He also was the owner of Luer Meat Packing. Luer was taken from his home by two men and a woman. On July 10th. after 6 days of captivity, he was released without explanation. The *Alton-Telegraph* published its first "Extra" edition to announce his safe return. About 7 people were involved in the plot, and all were eventually caught, convicted, and sentenced to prison. Luer was held captive in a dark cellar and was given food and medicine by his kidnappers. An elaborate communications scheme with the police was concocted, but no ransom money was ever collected.

The Army Corps of Engineers begins to dredge Smallpox Island in preparation for a new lock and dam at **Alton**. Large numbers of human skulls are found, presumably belonging to Confederate soldiers who died there from the smallpox epidemic during the Civil War.

George Halas of the **Chicago Bears** realizes that professional football is dull and that college games outdraw the pros by an average of 45,000 fans to 5,000 fans per game. He urges the rules committee to legalize the forward pass, as long as it is thrown behind the line of scrimmage. The pass was already being used in college. His Bears win the first NFL championship game against the New York Giants.

Ozark Airlines, originally called Parks Air Lines, is started as a class project by students of Parks Air College in **Cahokia**. During World War II, Oliver Parks used his college to train pilots for the Army Air Corps.

Denny Cochran of **East St. Louis** High begins his 3-year career where he earned 6 varsity letters in football and basketball.

Carl Totsch of Central Catholic in East St. Louis begins his career as a great running back. He starred in the backfield with Bob Shea and Johnny Nunn. All 3 later starred at St. Louis University. Totsch declined a pro baseball contract with the Detroit Tigers in 1935. He went on to become president of Midwest Rubber.

There is a lengthy gun battle between Progressive Miners and the mine guards at Peabody Mine #7 at **Kincaid**. Two people are killed, 12 wounded and 30 arrested. Similar battles took place at **Taylorville** with the state militia being called out to protect property. Illinois governor Henry Horner met with leaders of the UMW and the PMA. They signed an agreement not to picket in **Christian County** and acquiese in occupation by the National Guard to maintain order. In October, Governor Horner ordered the closing of Mine #43 at **Harrisburg** to avoid bloodshed.

Chicago hosts a centennial celebration, **A Century of Progress**. This fair, smaller and less ambitious than the Columbian Exposition, was held at Northerly Island near Grant Park. This later became the location of Meigs Field. Twelve large buildings housed exhibits that focused on modern science, industry, and transportation. The **Adler Planetarium** and the **Shedd Aquarium** were especially built for this gala event. The fair was sponsored by Chicago businessmen, not financially strapped City Hall. Kate Buckingham, a big sponsor of the Chicago Art Institute and donor of the famed Buckingham Fountain on the lakefront (312/742-PLAY), was disappointed in the modernism that dominated the art show at the fair. So were most of the critics. Only one painting at the show was sold.

The fair was a boon to the city's economy during hard times, so it was held over for a second year. Total attendance was nearly 40 million visitors – quite impressive. The leading "cultural" attraction at the "Streets of Paris" section was 28-year-old **Sally Rand** with her daring "fan dance." Sally had gained notoriety earlier by appearing as **Lady Godiva** at an art ball. She went on to appear as the star attraction in numerous other fairs, her naked body mostly hidden by strategic use of two large ostrich feathers, in the United States and Europe. When Mayor Edward Kelly visited the fair and saw the nudity, Rand was forced to don a transparent gauze costume. The oft-arrested Rand was earning a salary of $3,000 a week at the height of the Depression. Her name Rand was taken from a Rand-McNally atlas.

Texas Guinan, famous for her brassy "Hello, suckers" welcome, was running a nightclub at the fair called the Pirate Ship. Protesting that officials were trying to take all the fun out of the fair, she packed up and left. Unfortunately, she was one of those who fell victim to an attack of amoebic dysentery that marred the first summer of the fair.

President Roosevelt lauded the fair and praised the organizers for emphasizing achievement and progress, bringing hope to millions of Americans. Ironically, both Chicago fairs were successfully held in the midst of economic downturns. The U.S. Post Office issues one cent and three-cent stamps, commemorating the "Century of Progress" Chicago World's Fair.

One unnoticed visitor to the Fair on July 11, 1934 was notorious bank robber **John Dillinger** who attended with his girlfriend Mary Longnaker.

John Barleycorn is back. The 21st Amendment is passed repealing the Volstead Act and Prohibition. In a little more than a year the city of **East St. Louis** has over 200 taverns.

Leo Quick, president of the Central Trades and Labor group and agent for the boilermakers, became involved in an argument with **Frank McCarthy**, president of the Ironworkers, in a jurisdictional dispute. Leo shot and seriously wounded him outside the Labor Temple. His dispute was with the Ironworkers over which union should be responsible for building a smokestack at Central Brewery on Broadway.

Mayor Anton Cermak of Chicago is accidentally **shot and killed** in Miami, Florida, by a man named Joe Zangara. He was riding in a car next to president-elect Franklin Roosevelt, for whom the assassin's shots were intended. Zangara, an Italian who hated politicians, was executed 3 weeks later. As Cermak was being taken to the hospital, he whispered to FDR: "I'M GLAD IT WAS ME INSTEAD OF YOU." Some writers assert that Cermak was the intended target all along, the victim of a Chicago mob hit. Roosevelt won the nomination in Chicago, and Cermak had supported Al Smith over FDR. Cermak had gone to Miami to mend his political fences. Cermak started his life of work in the coalmines of southern Illinois.

In October the U.S. government sets aside 801,944 acres and calls it Shawnee National Forest, managed by the U.S. Forest Service. It consists of two units, one

Chicago Century of Progress Fair, 1933 (U.S. Army photo)

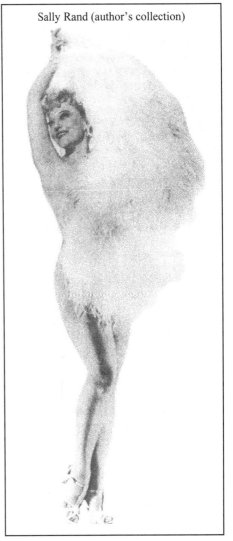

Sally Rand (author's collection)

bounded by the Mississippi River and the other bounded by the Ohio. There is a break in the middle that runs on a straight line from **Marion** to **Vienna** and to the southern border of the state. It is the only national forest in the state.

Chicago's Comiskey Park hosts the **first All-Star game** between the National and American leagues. It was the idea of Chicago mayor Ed Kelly, who wanted something exciting as an adjunct to the World's Fair. Babe Ruth was the star, hitting the first home run, as the American League won 4-2.

The Everleigh Club is torn down. Built in 1900 in the middle of Chicago's red light district on South Dearborn, this famous brothel contained 50 rooms, many of them soundproofed.

Governor Horner is responsible for the state's first-ever sales tax at 3 percent. The state Supreme Court ruled it unconstitutional because it exempted farm products and gasoline. A new bill was passed with a two percent tax levy with no exemptions. As the depression deepened in 1935, the tax went up to three percent.

The **East St. Louis** Bridge Company is the **largest dry shipyard in the nation**, manufacturing ship hulls. Walworth Valve in East St. Louis is the **world's largest manufacturer of industrial valves**, making the huge units used for the hydroelectric plant at Hoover Dam.

The Illinois Deep Waterway Project, linking the Great Lakes with the Gulf of Mexico, is finally completed. It has been called the single most important factor in the economic development of Illinois.

The state buys the Sinnissippi farm, developed by ex-governor Frank Lowden who was married to the daughter of railroad giant, George Pullman. Located in the **Rock River Valley**, it contains 1,196 acres and was owned by Lowden's grandson. Sinnissippi is an Indian word that means Rocky River. Lowden planted over 500,000 seedlings when he owned the land that now becomes a state forest. Other state forests are: Trail of Tears at **Jonesboro**, Sand Ridge at **Forest City**, Big River at **Oquawka** and Hidden Springs at **Strasburg** in Shelby County.

The **Ma Barker gang** robs a Federal Reserve mail truck in Chicago.

Flyer Tito Falconi sets a record (of some kind) by flying a plane upside down all the way from St. Louis to **Joliet**.

Dr. Francis Townsend, a native of **Fairbury** in Livingston County, becomes an advocate of the government collecting extra taxes from citizens so that they could retire at age 60 and receive a pension. In 1935 Franklin Roosevelt signed the Social Security Act into a law that embodied many of the ideas of Dr. Townsend.

Charles Holzmeier is arrested in Chicago and admits to being the leader of the Ping Pong gang that committed more than 200 robberies in **Belleville, Mascoutah, Columbia, Waterloo, Signal Hill, Collinsville, Edwardsville** and **Hamel**. Ping Pong is an area in east-central East St. Louis between Pittsburg Lake (Grand Marais) and the Day Line Railroad tracks. It eventually incorporated as Midway when the city of East St. Louis refused to extend fire protection that far out.

Ruth Bryan Owens, eldest daughter of William Jennings Bryan and a **Jacksonville** native, becomes the nation's **first female ambassador** when she is appointed minister to Denmark.

Many school districts in Illinois adopt the policy of not hiring married women. It was thought that such a policy would make it easier for single women and husbands to find employment during the Depression.

1934 - **Carl Shelton** and his attorney file a lawsuit against the city of East St. Louis and officer Bob Sweeney. Sweeney hated the Sheltons, and when he found out that Carl was in the hospital, he dragged him out of his bed and arrested him on some minor charge. The lawsuit was later dropped.

Al Capone is transferred from the federal penitentiary in Atlanta to Alcatraz. Alcatraz had opened a year earlier, and it soon gained a reputation for being the toughest prison in America. It was America's version of Devil's Island.

On August 22, Joe Medwick, Leo Durocher, Terry Moore and other members of the Cardinal Gas House Gang come to **Belleville** and battle the local Griesedieck Stags at the new **Belleville Athletic Field**. It was a rare off day for the Cards who were in the middle of a pennant race. The stadium was at South Illinois and Cleveland Avenues. The grandstand seated 1,500. Incredibly, the Stags christened the new stadium by pummeling the St. Louis Negro All-Stars 18-2. The year before, the Negro team compiled an amazing 58-6 record. The spunky Stags outhit the Cards 16-11 but lost in 11 innings.

The first **Steak and Shake** restaurant opens in **Normal**, Illinois.

Chicago Democrats Edward Kelly and Patrick Nash

Future mayor Richard Daley earns his law degree at DePaul University. He never uses it, deciding instead to go into politics.

The Chicago Blackhawks, who began their first season in 1926, win Lord Stanley's cup for the first time. They would win again in 1938 and 1961.

Ted Fleming and Harley Potter launch a business venture in **Peoria**, printing whiskey labels for Hiram Walker. The business grows and evolves into the **largest U.S. printer of promotional stamps**, including Easter Seals, Christmas Seals, and promotional stickers for Publisher's Clearing House.

The Illinois State Historical Society begins the practice of installing markers along roads and highways to describe persons and events important to the history of the state. Each marker is co-sponsored by at least one local organization.

Despite Capone being in the slammer, Chicago maintains its reputation for lawlessness with 35 gangland-style killings. For the rest of the decade and until 1947, the Kelly-Nash Democratic political machine rules Chicago. The City Council named Edward Kelly Mayor after Anton Cermak was shot. Patrick Nash, a wealthy contractor, was chairman of the Cook County Democratic Central Committee.

John Dillinger (author's collection)

Notorious bank robber **John Dillinger** is gunned down July 22 by Melvin Purvis and FBI agents in an alley near the Biograph Theater in Chicago. Dillinger had been laying low in Chicago, posing as Jimmie Lawrence, clerk for the Chicago Board of Trade. He was staying at a rooming house run by Anna Sage, a Romanian immigrant. She became the Lady in Red, fingering Dillinger that night when she went to a Clark Gable movie (*Manhattan Melodrama*) with Dillinger and his girl friend, Polly Hamilton. Sage was about to be deported and gave Dillinger up in an attempt to stay in America. The government gave her a reward and then deported her anyway. Interestingly, Anna Sage wore an orange skirt that night but to reporters and bystanders, it looked red in the marquee lights.

Fifteen thousand Chicagoans came to view Dillinger's body in the morgue. Back in May, Dillinger had plastic surgery performed on him in an effort to alter his appearance. Dr. Wilhelm Loeser performed the surgery in a Chicago building at 2509 North Caldwell.

The Chicago, Burlington & Quincy Railroad's Pioneer Zephyr, America's first diesel passenger train, makes its first run. It makes a 1,015-mile run from Denver to Chicago (for the Exposition) breaking all records with an average speed of over 90 miles per hour.

1935 - Gladys McEvilly, born in **Wartburg**, is Queen of the Pageant of Progress in East St. Louis.

Irv Nicholson of East St. Louis High begins his outstanding career starring in football (halfback) and track (220 relay team).

When a PMA (Progressive Miners' Association) commissary is blown up, it marks the 55th such bombing in that town since the start of mine troubles back in 1932. Much of the violence was blamed on the UMW, the old union that set out to destroy the new one. Progressives would bomb buildings and bridges, and the UMW would bomb homes. In the end, the PMA was finally disbanded with most of the miners drifting back to the UMW.

Anna Sage – the Lady in Red

Most of the scabs the companies brought in during the many depression strikes were from Kentucky, Pennsylvania and West Virginia. Some of the scabs came from southern Illinois and were derisively labeled "swampies." In light of the 1922 Herrin Massacre, where striking miners killed guards and scabs, it is ironic that the "swampies" from southern Illinois now give the same justification for replacing striking miners. They largely claimed that they didn't mean to take away anyone's job, they were simply unemployed and trying to survive.

St. Louisan **Lou Thesz**, considered the greatest professional wrestler who ever lived, has his first professional wrestling match at the East St. Louis Social Center at 9th and Summit. He earns the grand sum of $3.

The Ames Street Guide lists **East St. Louis** as **the largest maker of roofing materials in the world**.

East St. Louisan Bill Walker, a member of the 1934 World Champion Cardinals' Gas House Gang, is the starting pitcher for the National League in the All-Star game.

Jay Berwanger of the University of Chicago (Big Ten) wins the first Heisman Trophy in college football.

The first Roller Derby event is held in Chicago.

Famed evangelist Billy Sunday dies in Chicago. Sunday had been an exceptional baseball player, being signed by the Chicago White Stockings in 1883. After playing professional ball for 7 years, he quit and turned to preaching and evangelizing. Over a twenty-year period he was the most famous evangelist in America, speaking to over 100 million people. He used many baseball metaphors and railed against lipstick and rouge, against alcohol, against modernism, against motion pictures.

Chicago's American Can Company introduces the nation to beer in steel cans. Despite lining the inside to prevent the metal from affecting beer taste, those traditional dark brown bottles remain popular all the way up to about 1960.

Clarke Ansley of **Swedona** publishes a general one volume Columbia Encyclopedia.

The IHSAA (IHSA) adopts a new rule that eliminates a jump ball at the center of the court after every basket or successful free throw. This rule allowed high school teams with a tall center to dominate games.

1936 – A character named Eugene the Jeep appears in a **Popeye the Sailor** comic strip written by E.C. Segar of **Chester**, Illinois. H.L. Mencken maintained that the name for the army vehicle named the *jeep* comes from this source. Others say it comes from **general-purpose vehicle**.

The town of **Elkville**, population 1,133, suffers extensive damage when a fire of undetermined origin sweeps through its business district.

The motion picture *Earthworm City* (**Peoria**), starring Joe E. Brown as an optimistic tractor salesman, premiers.

Edward Ravenscrift of Abbott Labs in Chicago secures a patent for **the first screw-cap for bottles**.

Richard Leob is slashed to death in a prison shower by an inmate who complained that he was making homosexual advances.

Chicago's Hart, Shaffner & Marx introduce zippers to men's pants, replacing traditional buttons.

Robert Wadlow, the world's tallest man, travels to Dallas, Texas, which is holding a Centennial Celebration. On the fair's Illinois Day, Wadlow meets Illinois Governor Henry Hoerner. At a rival centennial celebration in Fort Worth, Wadlow met Vice-president John Nance Garner and dancer **Sally Rand**. He then visited the State Fair in **Springfield** and made $1,800 appearing on stage in one of the shows.

1937 – Robert Wadlow, the **Alton Giant**, joins the Ringling Brothers/Barnum & Bailey Circus out on the east coast. Dr. Frederick Fadner of Shurtleff College writes the Wadlow biography, *The Gentleman Giant* in 1941. Wadlow died from blood poisoning in 1940 from a blister on his ankle made by a metal brace. He was 8 feet, 11.1 inches tall and is listed in Guinness records as the tallest person who ever lived. Wadlow had been a Mason and a Boy Scout.

Robert Wadlow as a teenager (courtesy Mad. Cnty. Hist. Soc.)

The first crosses at Bald Knob at **Alto Pass** are constructed by members of the Civilian Conservation Corps, which had a camp near there. Wayman Presley and Rev. William Lively were responsible for the erection of a giant 111-foot tall cross on that spot in later years.

The **Goldenrod Showboat**, once anchored at **Cairo** and New Orleans, becomes a permanent part of the St. Louis riverfront at the foot of Locust Street. It was said that **Red Skelton** learned the buck and wing dance on the Goldenrod. It is currently anchored on the Missouri River at St. Charles.

January 24. Southern Illinois suffers one of the worst floods in its history. The rampaging Ohio River and its tributaries cause over $75 million worth of damage. **Shawneetown**, with a population that had dwindled to 2,000 people, suffered $500,000 in damages from floodwaters that reached 57 feet. Thirty straight hours of rain in the upper Ohio valley and six inches of snow in southern Illinois proved to be disastrous. Both Shawneetown and **Cairo** had sixty-foot levees along the river, but the one at Shawneetown did not hold. Nearby towns of **Golconda, Rosiclare**, and **Elizabethtown** became isolated islands in the middle of the swollen floodwaters.

Cairo is the lowest point in the state, and most of the town was evacuated because the river was predicted to crest above sixty feet. It reached 59.62 feet but the levee miraculously held. The wall was originally a series of 10 ft. square concrete boxes filled with tamped earth. The base width was 16 ft., narrowing to 10 ft. at the top, allowing sufficient room to add to the height if necessary. The city also constructed an earthen levee system that rings the city.

Cairo was the only town in the area that did not fall victim to the raging waters. Even Paducah, only thirty-five miles away, had waters that reached the second stories of buildings. Since no flood has ever breached its walls, Cairo is known as "The City That Never Floods."

By late February, **Shawneetown** still had ten feet of water in its streets. After the flood, authorities reluctantly decided to relocate the town on higher ground, creating an "Old Shawneetown" and a "New Shawneetown." This was done with help from the state, the RFC, and the WPA.

During a bitter CIO strike at Republic Steel, on Chicago's south side, police clash with demonstrators and picketers. Rocks were thrown and shots were fired. When it was over, 10 people were dead and thirty were wounded. Although no one was prosecuted, an investigation led by Senator Robert LaFollette of Wisconsin blamed the police for using excessive force. This event is remembered as the **Memorial Day Massacre**.

Pure Oil Company drills 75 new oil wells near **Salem**. Petroleum, a greenish-black substance created from the remains of plants and animals, was formed millions of years ago during the Pleistocene Period.

Carl Hansberry, a Negro real estate broker, buys a home for his family in the Hyde Park section of Chicago. The family is harassed and hauled into a court on the charge of violating a deed restriction forbidding the sale of the property to a Negro. The Hansberry family loses in the Illinois Supreme Court but wins in the 1941 decision of the U.S. Supreme Court in the case of Hansberry v. Lee. This incident is dramatized in daughter Lorraine Hansbery's 1959 book, "**A Raisin in the Sun**."

Joe Louis takes the heavyweight title away from James Braddock in a fight at Chicago.

P.K. Wrigley orders all advertising signs in the outfield at Wrigley Field to be taken down and ivy planted instead. He refuses to install lights for night games because he didn't want neighborhood residents disturbed by crowd noise.

One hundred and twenty-five thousand fans pay a dollar each to see a Chicago prep league championship played at Soldier Field. The big draw for the crowd is to see prep star running back Bill DeCorrevont do his thing. He did not disappoint, scoring three touchdowns and passing for another leading his Austin team to victory. Against an earlier team, he touched the ball ten times and scored 9 touchdowns. **No college or pro player has ever drawn a crowd as big** as 125,000.

Martin Johnson, a native of **Rockford**, is killed in a plane crash in Los Angeles. He was the only member of Jack London's crews on Jack London's *Snark* to complete the round-the-world cruise.

1938 – Ludwig Mies van der Rohe leaves Nazi Germany and migrates to Chicago. He quickly becomes a dominant figure in American architecture. His celebrated phrase "Less is more," led to the construction of buildings that were remarkably similar from top to bottom. Some of his renown works include the Tugendhat House in Czechoslovakia, the Barcelona Pavilion, The Illinois Institute of Technology, the Seagram Building in New York, and the New National Gallery in Berlin. He also designed the metal and leather seat that became known as the Barcelona chair. His Farnsworth house near **Plano** is his most famous dwelling.

Robert Sherwood's play, *Abe Lincoln in Illinois*, starring Raymond Massey, opens on Broadway and wins a Pulitzer Prize.

Charles M. Neely publishes "The Death of Charlie Burger" (Birger) in *Tales and Songs of Southern Illinois*.

A tornado rips through East St. Louis and destroys the roof of George Rogers Clark Junior High. It levels fifty homes near West Main and **kills eight people in Belleville**.

Leo W. Quick, belligerent labor leader and minor politician, is shot to death in the back yard of his home. The .38 revolver used in the shooting was found by a youth in Madison, and it was a gun that had been purchased by Quick himself. Police Commissioner **A. P. Lauman** speculated that Quick was shot by two men he had hired to kill another man with whom he had a labor dispute. The trio apparently had a falling out, and the two men shot Leo seven times and robbed him of a diamond tie pin and a roll of bills worth about $500.

Quick had been involved in bitter disputes with individuals and labor organizations the last few years. He had recently been defeated in January for re-election as the head of Central Trades and Labor union. Quick was killed in the same methodical manner in which his predecessor, Alden "Ollie" Moore was killed in 1932. Quick's career was marked by controversy and violence. He came from the old school of labor leaders who sought to achieve goals through violence and confrontation, instead of negotiations at the bargaining table. Quick was selected by his union as the man to succeed Ollie Moore as its business agent. He was responsible for ending labor's dispute with Phillips Petroleum by securing their agreement to use union labor. His murder is never solved.

After several robberies and stick-ups in other states, Orelle and Clarence Easton, a couple of bored Illinois farm boys, commit several robberies in other states. They later kill a state trooper in South Bend, Indiana. There is a shootout with authorities on a farm near the **Will-Kankakee County** line near **Wilmington**. Clarence was killed by a hail of bullets and Orelle surrendered. He was wounded in his right shoulder, both ears and lip. The young killer was executed less than a year later.

John L. Lewis establishes the CIO, Congress of Industrial Organizations, for unskilled workers.

A radio program on the Mercury Theater is interrupted with the announcement that Professor Farrell of Mt. Jennings observatory in Chicago has discovered life on Mars, leading to the great Orson Wells hoax that New Jersey was being invaded by Martians with death-ray guns. Incredibly, this science fiction "War of the Worlds" radio program caused a panic on the East Coast. Obviously, **there is no Mt. Jennings Observatory in pancake-flat Chicago**.

Mies Van Der Rohe

1939 - **Dora Shelton**, mother of the Shelton boys, files a lawsuit in the county courthouse and sues her sons for "maintenance." Earl Shelton was working at Scott Field at the time.

The girlhood diary of Maud Rittenhouse, a **Cairo** belle of the 1880s, is published. Her family lived on the corner of 7th and Walnut. She loved the theater and was an accomplished amateur actress, gaining small roles in productions at the Cairo Opera House. She later married and moved away to Brooklyn, NY. The next year, Anne West published *It Happened in Cairo*, a book that filled in some of the blanks from the diary.

The University of Chicago, believing sports to be extraneous, drops varsity football from its program.

Carl Sandburg

Chicago gangster Al Capone is transferred from Alcatraz, suffering from degeneration of the central nervous system due to advanced syphilis, to finish his remaining ten months in a Los Angeles correctional facility.

Poet Carl Sandburg (Swedish), who earlier in his life favored socialism, gives serious consideration to running for president against Franklin D. Roosevelt in 1940, who plans to break with tradition and run for an unprecedented 3rd term.

Keystone Fence of **Peoria** celebrates its 50th anniversary. It is the **largest independent steel and wire fence mill in the world**.

The lanes on Route 66 are widened from 8 or 9 feet to eleven feet. In addition, the speed limit was reduced to 70 miles per hour. A few years later, a 12 foot standard was adopted, one that is currently used on modern highways.

Sid Luckman becomes quarterback for the Chicago Bears and holds that position until 1950, a Bears' record. He wins championships in 1940, '41, '43 and '46.

Robert Wood of Sears, along with Colonel McCormick of the *Tribune* and Colonel Charles Lindbergh, form the anti-war America First Committee. They oppose Roosevelt's measures to help the Allies, fearing that actions such as Lend-Lease will drag us into another European war. Many Americans disliked the America First Committee because it was perceived as being anti-semitic. The organization ceased to exist after Pearl Harbor.

Edward O'Hare, father of Butch O'Hare, is gunned down on Ogden Avenue in Chicago. O'Hare was successful at building tracks for dog racing, going into partnership with Al Capone. O'Hare is killed shortly after Al Capone is released from prison. His death was thought to be payback for being a snitch for the government at Capone's tax trial.

The lanes on Route 66 are widened to 11 feet. A year later, this is increased to 12 feet, the standard still used today.

1940 – Starting in 1940 and continuing up to 1960, approximately 350,000 poor whites from Appalachia migrate to Chicago, looking for employment and a better life.

Illinois population stands at 7,897,241.

Dwight Green, the prosecutor who helped send Al Capone to jail, is elected governor. He reduces taxes for the only time in the century, dropping the sales tax to two percent. However, for the first time ever, the state enacts a cigarette tax. The state treasury surplus reached a hundred million dollars helping Green win re-election in 1944.

The U.S. Post Office issues a 5-cent stamp at **Evanston**, paying tribute to Frances Willard, founder of the WCTU.

The **Granite City Warriors**, led by Andy Phillip, Andy Hagopian, George Gages, Babe Champion, John Markarian and Gus Lignoul, defeat the **Herrin Tigers** in the last IHSA game played at the old Huff Gymnasium at the University of Illinois.

Ronald Reagan, a Democrat, marries actress Jane Wyman. He also stars in the movie *Knute Rockne* and portrays football halfback George Gipp.

1941 – Coach Wirt Downing of **East St. Louis** High produces 4 state wrestling champs – still a state record. One was Herb Littlefield who went on to become president of Southern Illinois National Bank in Fairview Heights. Downing's football coaching record would be 144 wins, 18 losses and 7 ties, winning 12 Southwest Conference championships.

The Chicago Bears, the Monsters of the Midway, defeat Sammy Baugh and the Washington Redskins in the NFL title game 73-0. They will repeat as champions in 1943, 1946 and 1963.

Marshall Field III begins publication of the *Chicago Sun*, mainly to counter the isolationist and Republican tone of the rival *Tribune*.

Illinois ranks third in the nation in agricultural output and industrial production, a claim no other state can match.

When the U.S enters World War II after Pearl Harbor, the Great Lakes Training Center, the largest in the nation, trains 1/3 of our enlisted personnel for the navy.

Scott Field near **Belleville** becomes known as the "Radio University of the Army Air Corps." A special training school for military police is established at **Mount Vernon**. Illinois sends a little less than a million men and women into the armed services during the war.

Robert G. LeTourneau buys the Avery Co. in **Peoria** and begins manufacturing earthmoving equipment.

Donald Nelson, head of Sears and Roebuck, is appointed by Roosevelt to head the nation's War Production Board. Colonel Frank Knox, publisher of the Chicago *Daily News*, becomes Secretary of the Navy.

The town of **Seneca** produces "The Trojan Horse," LST (landing ship tanks) boats that are floated down the Illinois and Mississippi rivers to New Orleans for use by the navy.

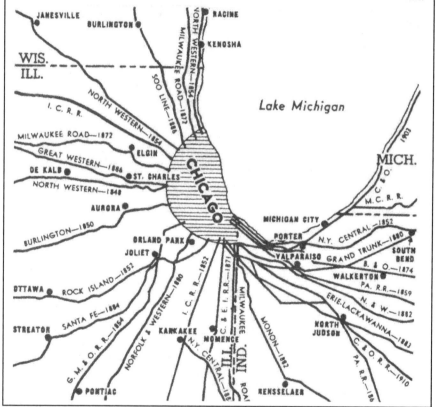

Illinois led the nation in production of ammunition (especially Western cartridge in East Alton) and artillery ordinance during the war. Auto plants were converted to producing airplanes and airplane engines. **Kenney**, a small DeWitt County village of 483, won national recognition as the **first community in which every house was participating in the war effort**.

The war restores prosperity to farmers. Their income nearly triples and the value of their land doubles.

In a game against the Maple Leafs, the Blackhawk's coach pulls the goalie in the closing minute and replaces him with a forward in a desperate effort at scoring a tying goal. This precedent has now become standard practice at the end of close games.

1942 – When the General Assembly meets in January, under the leadership of Governor Dwight Green, they begin to deal with mobilization for the war effort. Curiously, one member proposes that Santa Anna's wooden leg be sent back to Mexico in an effort to secure that country's goodwill and cooperation. Camp Robert Smalls, named for a former slave and hero of the Civil War, is established in Chicago.

Roughly 361 draft boards were set up to handle manpower problems. Illinois furnished nearly a million men and women for the war effort, with more than 24,000 of them losing their lives.

Women were not used in combat but they held positions as nurses, secretaries, administrators, photographers and many other positions and served as WACs (Women's Army Corps), WAFS (Women's Auxiliary Ferrying Squadron, and WAVES (Women Accepted for Volunteer Emergency Service).

Fort Sheridan served as a training center and later in the war as a camp for prisoners of war. Scott Field near Belleville became the top communications training center in the nation. Great Lakes Training Center, 1,000 miles from the closest ocean, trained 1/3 of the navy.

Ben Reitman, Chicago's "Clap Doctor" dies. He was a reformer who worked among Chicago's poor, treating and giving aid to drunks, prostitutes, hoboes and drifters. Doc took on evangelist **Billy Sunday** and called him an enemy of the needy.

The world's first controlled atomic reaction occurs on December 2 in a squash (handball) court under the west grandstands of the Alonzo Stagg Stadium of the University of Chicago. A latticework of graphite bricks, containing uranium slugs, were arranged in a spherical shape, thus constructing a 28-foot high nuclear "pile" or reactor, held together by a crude wooden frame. In case something went wrong, two young scientists stood on top of the pile, ready to pour a cadmium solution on it. **Enrico Fermi**, who had fled Mussolini's Fascist Italy some years before, directed the experiment whereby control rods were withdrawn to produce a sustained reaction. This was the first step in producing an atomic bomb – the dawn of the Nuclear Age. Arthur Compton, dean of the school's physical science department, sent a coded message to President James B. Conant of Harvard: "The Italian navigator has landed in the New World." Fermi then moved on to Los Alamos, New Mexico to work on the Manhattan Project to create the first atomic bomb.

"Nuclear Energy" by Henry Moore (courtesy Univ. of Chicago)

War Bond drives were very successful in Illinois with all 8 of them being oversubscribed. Marshal Field III bought $10 million worth of bonds to support the war effort. Civilians helped in other ways by planting victory gardens, cooperating with the OPA rationing program and collecting scrap metal. Women saved bacon grease and lard and took it to the local butcher who gave it to the government for making explosives. People in **Peoria** saved enough aluminum pots and pans to create an "Aluminum Mountain."

Three German-American couples in Chicago are sentenced to jail terms after being convicted of treason.

An explosion at a munitions ordinance plant at **Elwood** kills 49 people.

Chicagoan James C. Petrillo, head of the American Federation of Musicians, scores a victory by forcing record companies to pay a royalty to musicians for every record they sell.

William Heirens, a 17 year-old University of Chicago student, is captured while trying to burglarize a home. It turns out that he is the subject of a massive Chicago manhunt. He had previously murdered and callously dismembered a six-year-old girl. He denied having committed the murder but confessed when forced to undergo an injection of sodium pentathol, better known as "truth serum." As of 1999, he had been incarcerated over 50 years and was the state's longest-serving prisoner.

1943 - A **Nameoki** Transit bus is hit by a train at 2700 Nameoki Road in Granite City. Nine are killed and thirteen people are seriously hurt in the city's worst traffic disaster.

There is a severe flood along the Illinois River when it crests at a 99-year peak.

Patrick Henry McMahon of **Wyanet** is on the PT 109 when it is cut in two by a Japanese destroyer in the Soloman Islands. His life is saved when **skipper John F. Kennedy**, swimming with him on his back and the strap of his life jacket clinched between his teeth, swims to safety. McMahon's name is mentioned in the hit song by Jimmy Dean, "PT 109."

Illinois has 26 Medal of Honor winners in World War II.

P.K. Wrigley, owner of the Chicago Cubs, founds the nation's first women's professional softball league. He wanted them to look like women, so he insisted that they wear skirts. Makeup and shoulder-length hair were also standard fare. Illinois had four teams: **Springfield** Sallies, **Peoria** Redwings, **Rockford** Peaches, Chicago Colleens. The league finally folded in 1954. Their story is told in the 1992 Geena Davis/Tom Hanks movie, *A League of Their Own*.

The 551 mile long oil pipeline from Texas to **Norris City** is completed.

A new subway system for passenger travel opens in Chicago.

1944 - At White Castle Tavern, near **Herrin**, **Blackie Armes** is shot and fatally wounded by **Thomas Propes**, the owner. Propes, figuring that Armes was dead, turned his back and was fatally shot in the back of the head by a dying Armes.

The Jefferson Barracks Bridge is completed, connecting **Columbia, Dupo and East Corondelet** (Route 3) with south St. Louis County.

Two days before the Normandy invasion on June 6th, the United States Navy **captured its only U-Boat of World War II**. Chicagoan D.V. Gallery led the capturing force of U–505 and had it towed to a base in the Caribbean. When the war was over he worked to get the sub donated to the Museum of Science and Industry in Chicago. The subs were called U-boats because the German word "unterseebooten" described an underwater boat.

Bill Mauldin goes to work full-time as a cartoonist for *Stars and Stripes* military magazine. His portrayal of characters Willie and Joe are loved by dogfaces slugging it out with the enemy in the mud. General Patton hated the one panel cartoon and thought the feature fostered an anti-authoritarian attitude. Tom Ewell would star in a 1951 movie about Willie and Joe, *Up Front*.

Due to high winds, tornado, or poor engineering (take your pick), a 640-foot section of the Mississippi River Bridge at Chester falls into the water.

Three-time Chicago mayor Big Bill Thompson dies in Chicago at age 75. His mayoral salary was about $22,000 a year, but when Treasury Agents search his home they find strong boxes stuffed with money, banknotes and gold certificates. The hoard amounts to $1,750,000.

1945 – The original grandstand of the state fairgrounds at **DuQuoin** is destroyed by fire. A new 10,000-seat grandstand is built at a cost of one million dollars.

Enrico Fermi, nuclear physicist

Charlie Menees becomes the southern Illinois' first jazz disc jockey, working at WTMV in the Broadview Hotel in East St. Louis.

Two Chicago restauranteers, Ike Sewall and Rick Riccardo, open Pizzeria Uno for business and feature deep pan pizza. Up until then, pizza served in Chicago's Little Italy was thin crusted and thought of as an appetizer. Thus was born **Chicago-style pizza**.

Frank "the Enforcer" Nitti commits suicide rather than face a jail sentence for labor racketeering. Tony "Big Tuna Accardo steps in as one of the syndicate's big bosses.

Five Chicago gunmen go to **Peoria** to try and collect a reward offered by the Syndicate on each of the Sheltons. The amount was reportedly $10,000 each. They were members of the **Bookie Gang** that had the audacity to make raids on Syndicate handbook operations. The gang made an appointment with the Sheltons to discuss selling a truckload of whiskey stolen in Chicago. Two of the gang were waiting in ambush, but Carl got suspicious at the last minute and brought a carload of men with him. Discouraged, the gunmen went back to Chicago.

George Mikan of De Paul University is the NCAA scoring leader with 454 points. He will repeat in 1946 and go on to star as a center for the Minneapolis Lakers pro team.

The Chicago Cubs make it to the World Series but lose to Detroit. Both clubs were said to be mediocre, and it was predicted that neither team would win. This marks the last time that the hapless (but lovable) Cubbies will make it to the Fall Classic – a major league record.

1946 - Orville Hodge of **Granite City** wins his first term as a Republican representative in the General Assembly, representing Madison and Bond Counties in the 47th district.

Clyde Choate of Anna receives the Congressional Medal of Honor for his actions in a tank battalion near Bruyeres, France during World War II. He was later elected to the Illinois General Assembly and became the assistant minority leader in 1969.

The entire City Council (including the mayor) of **East St. Louis** is indicted for malfeasance of office for failure to take action against illegal gambling. The indictments will later be dismissed by a circuit court judge for being too vague.

One of the worst fires in Chicago's history breaks out at the LaSalle Hotel. The blaze started in the 22-story complex shortly after midnight on June 5. The fire began in an elevator shaft on the ground floor. There was a disastrous 20-minute delay in sounding the fire alarm as employees vainly fought the blaze with bottles of seltzer water. The Hotel survived and remained open until 1976 when it was closed and demolished. Sixty-one men, women and children perished, most dying from asphyxiation or smoke inhalation.

Meigs Field for small aircraft is established in Chicago at the lakefront, on the site of the former world's fair. It is named for Merrill C. Meigs, a publisher who was a foremost aviation booster.

Joe Tinker SS, John Evers 2B and Frank Chance 1B, members of the great Chicago Cubs double play combination, are elected to baseball's Hall of Fame.

Preston Tucker acquires the old Dodge plant and begins making cars in Chicago. He is charged with fraud and securities violations. He ultimately wins vindication but the controversy wipes out his capital and only a handful of the innovative Tucker sedans were sold. His car had a number of innovations that were ahead of their time. The car had a center "swivel" headlight that moved left or right, depending on the direction of the car. **Only 51 Tucker cars** were produced. They had a flat six engine that gave it a top speed of 120 mph. The aircraft-inspired doors made it easier to enter and depart. Rear fender vents cooled the helicopter-inspired engine located in the trunk.

Between the two wars a new crop from Manchuria arrives on the Illinois scene – soybeans. With seeds that contain oil and valuable protein that was useful both as a food and industrial use, **Decatur** quickly becomes the soybean capital of the world.

More changes are made in historic Route 66. Four lane bypasses are constructed around towns such as **Joliet** and small towns are completely bypassed. However, there are still some intersections where Route 66 crosses other major highways.

Rock Island-born Joe "Iron Man" McGinty is elected to baseball's Hall of Fame. Five times in his illustrious career he pitched two complete doubleheaders.

There is a train wreck at **Naperville** when one train rear-ends another, killing forty-five.

The nation's first drive-in banking service is started by a Chicago firm.

1947 - **Carl Shelton**, nearly sixty years old, decides to quit the rackets and farm his 900 acres on Merriam Road near Fairfield. He still operated a small gambling place called the Farmers Club above a restaurant on the courthouse square. But Carl became involved in a quarrel with the Harris and Vaughn families who owned farms nearby in the Pond Creek Bottoms. Charlie Harris fell behind on his tax payments, and Carl bought the delinquent tax certificates, causing hard feelings. In June there was a quarrel over some cattle. Local gossip said that Carl got into the protection racket on soybeans - trying to force the Pond Creek families to pay him a nickel a bushel royalty on their crops.

On October 23rd Carl was driving his Jeep to pick up a load of soybeans. Following behind him in trucks were **Ray Walker**, a bodyguard, and **'Little Earl,'** the 28 year-old son of Carl's other brother, Dalta. There was a black car on a side road as Carl's Jeep neared a bridge over a creek. Someone fired some shots from the underbrush and Carl was hit. He fired back with a pistol, but the men got in the car and drove off. Carl died at the age of fifty-nine from his wounds. The "brains" of the Shelton Gang was dead. Little Earl accused **Blackie Harris** of firing the shots, but Ray Walker said the man was dressed in a suit and thought he was Frank Wortman, a man from East St. Louis. Blackie Harris, who had also retired and was living on a nearby farm, was charged with the crime, but the grand jury failed to indict.

The third worst mine disaster in the state hits **Centralia** Coal Company's No. 5 mine on March 25th. A device used in blasting the coal misfired and caused the explosion. After several days of rescue efforts, the **death toll was fixed at 111**.

A few months later there was another mine disaster at **West Frankfort,** and twenty-seven miners died in another mine explosion.

Paul Simon, the son of a Lutheran minister, borrows $3,600 to buy the *Tribune*, a newspaper in **Troy**. The young Simon became a crusading editor and ran many stories about alleged vice and corruption in St. Clair and Madison Counties. His article and editorials caught the attention of Governor Adlai Stevenson, who sent in the state troopers to raid the dens of iniquity. When the Kefauver Committee came to town in 1951, Simon was called as a "star witness" and achieved national fame by the age of twenty-two.

The steamer *Golden Eagle*, the last St. Louis river packet, sinks on May 18 in the Mississippi River at **Grand Tower Island**. All passengers are rescued.

H. Allen Smith, a former resident of **McLeansboro**, writes *Lo, the Former Egyptian*. It is a collection of reflective musings on life in southern Illinois.

Republican state Senator **Paul Broyles** chairs a committee that investigates subversive communist activity in the state of Illinois. Clyde Choate of **Jonesboro** and **John Thomas** of **Belleville** were also on the commission. The committee recommended an investigation of the University of Chicago to determine the extent of communist infiltration among the faculty and student body. The group secured passage of a bill that would have required teachers and public employees to take a loyalty oath but the proposed legislation was vetoed by Governor Stevenson.

A cluster of **Thunderbird sightings** occur in Illinois. A retired army colonel named Walter Siegmund claimed to have seen a gigantic bird flying over **Alton**. Several days later, a farmer in **Caldonia** named **Robert Price** spotted a "monster bird." On April 10th Mr. and Mrs. Clyde Smith of **Overland** claimed to have spotted a bird the size of a small airplane. Several different residents reported sightings of huge birds in the St. Louis area. The last sighting took place in early May by an Alton resident named Arthur Davidson. Some researchers believe these birds might have been modern-day relatives of the prehistoric pterodactyls that somehow managed to survive.

The *Daily Times* merges with the *Chicago Sun* to become the *Chicago Sun-Times*.

January 19: Al Capone dies at his Palm Island villa in Key Biscayne, Florida, at age 48. Ironically, he passed away just one week after the death of Andrew Volstead, the author of the Prohibition law. He is buried in a simple ceremony at Olivet Cemetery in Chicago. Later, in a secretive fashion, Capone's body was exhumed and moved to Mt. Carmel Cemetery where many of Capone's enemies slept *sub specie aeternitatis*.

Illinois defeats UCLA in the Rose Bowl, 45-14. Illinois wins again in 1952 (40-7 v Stanford) and 1964 (17-7 v Washington).

The Chicago Cardinals win the NFL championship with a record of 10-3. This will be only the second championship ever won by that franchise. They relocated to St. Louis in the 1960s and are now in Phoenix.

Billy Reay scores a goal in a Blackhawk-Canadian hockey game and raises his stick to allow the press and fans to more easily identify the goal scorer. This eventually becomes standard practice.

1948 – Chuck Gottfried of **East St. Louis** becomes the Big Ten wrestling champ in his division.

Connie Ritter, one of Charlie Birger's lieutenants, dies in Menard Prison at Chester.

Bernie Shelton, the youngest brother, is shot and killed at the Parkway Tavern in **Peoria** at the age of fifty. He died at St. Francis Hospital and was buried at Parkview Cemetery, not far from his tavern.

Coca Cola Co. DuQuoin, sponsor of annual State Fair (Neal Strebel card)

One of the most famous historical photographs of all time is taken. It is a picture of President Harry Truman holding up a copy of the *Chicago Tribune* with the embarrassing headline: DEWEY DEFEATS TRUMAN. The mistake was made because the newspaper was under a deadline and nearly all of the polls had predicted a Dewey win. A last minute check with the paper's Washington D.C. correspondent validated that assumption. Truman, of course, with his famous "whistle-stop campaign," snatched victory from the jaws of defeat in one of the greatest upsets in history.

Democrat Adlai Stevenson, grandson of Grover Cleveland's vice-president, defeats Dwight Green's bid for a third consecutive bid as governor. The Green administration was racked with political scandals. Democrat Paul Douglas, a former economics professor at

139

the University of Chicago is elected U.S. senator. The Stevenson-Douglas landslide helped Harry Truman carry Illinois and pull off the greatest upset in presidential campaign history by defeating Thomas E. Dewey.

Senator Paul Douglas

Stevenson is tough on organized crime and sends out the state police to break up crime rings in **East St. Louis, Peoria, Joliet, Springfield**, **Decatur** and **Rock Island**.

A railroad fair and exhibition, commemorating 100 years of railroading, opens in Chicago.

Mrs. Ralph E. Smafield (I'm not being sexist – that's how women signed their names back then) of **Rockford** becomes the first woman to win the national Pillsbury Bake-Off Contest with her recipe for Water Rising-Twists.

Walter Siegmund claims to have sighted an "enormous bird" about the size of a small plane, giving rise to speculation about a new Piasa creature lurking in the **Alton** area.

The Chicago Bears have a sterling trio of quarterbacks in Sid Luckman, Johnny Lujack, and Bobby Layne.

Bill Veeck of the Chicago White Sox signs 41-year-old rookie Satchel Paige to a contract. Paige made the All-Star team in 1953 at age 47.

Henry Hathaway's *Northside 777* is filmed in Chicago – where it happened. It is about a Chicago reporter's (James Stewart) attempt to locate a witness who can prove the innocence of a Polish-American (Richard Conte), sentenced to prison for his complicity in a murder. The movie is superlatively shot in and around various Chicago locales.

Diamond Mineral Springs, a health spa in **Grantfork** (Madison County) closes. Today there is a large popular restaurant located on the site.

1949 – (Jan. 29) Susan Perry, East St. Louis film actress who began her career in a St. Louis war plant (Emerson Electric) minstrel show, weds **Mel Tormé**, the crooner known to bobby-soxers as the "Velvet Fog," on February 12. Nat 'King' Cole, Peggy Lee, and Dorothy Kilgallen were at their wedding at the Ambassador Hotel in Chicago, where Mel's family lives. Plans call for a honeymoon in Europe before Tormé fills a London engagement in May.

The actress, born Florence Tockstein in Vienna, Mo., is the daughter of Mrs. Teresa Tockstein, 1655 North Thirty-ninth, East St. Louis. Tormé will open a stage engagement at the St. Louis Theater next Thursday with Jimmy Dorsey's orchestra.

Miss Perry, the eldest of 6 children, attended St. Joseph's parochial school and St. Teresa Academy in East St. Louis. During the war she was employed as a parts inspector.

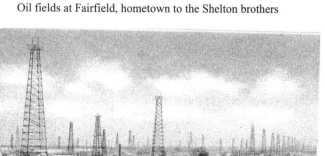

Oil fields at Fairfield, hometown to the Shelton brothers

The actress at one time was employed as a model at Famous-Barr Company, where she was known as Candy Toxton. She left a modeling career in St. Louis and went to Chicago where she steadily dated bandleader Tommy Dorsey for more than a year. Then she left Chicago for New York where her modeling career further blossomed. While in New York, she dated Frank Sinatra who had a radio show. An agent for the Feldman Agency convinced her to go to Hollywood. She won a contract and the studio changed her name three times. She has been known previously as Linda Howard and Brooke Chase. While in Hollywood she met Tormé. After several years of marriage, she divorced Tormé and married his friend, Hal March, host of TVs *$64,000 Question*. Candy previously dated Frank Sinatra, Buddy Rich, Tommy Dorsey and Peter Lawford. Candy starred as Humphrey Bogart's wife in the film that introduced John Derek to the world, *Knock On Any Door*. Candy currently lives in Rancho Mirage, near Palm Springs, California.

Governor Adlai Stevenson and Attorney General Ivan Elliott join forces and order the state police to make a raid on the gambling house known as the Hyde Park Club, located near the McKinley Bridge in Madison County. For a quarter of a century it was patronized by well-heeled patrons from St. Louis who were given souvenir silver dollars by uniformed doormen.

Stevenson, who was divorced by his wife because she hated political life, was the state's first divorced governor.

A tragic fire at St. Anthony's Hospital in **Effingham** kills 77 people.

The Illinois legislature passes a new prison law. It is now a felony for a prisoner to break out of jail or prison. Before, if an inmate broke out of prison and didn't hurt anyone or commit another crime, no additional time was tacked on to his sentence.

Northwestern defeats California 20-14 in the Rose Bowl.

Mercedes McCambridge of **Joliet** wins Best Supporting Actress Oscar for her performance in a film about demagogue governor Huey Long of Louisiana, *All The King's Men*.

Phillies baseball player Eddie Waitkus is shot in a Chicago hotel room by an obsessed female fan who is then committed to a mental institution. This incident was used in the book *The Natural*, by Bernard Malamud, which was made into a Robert Redford movie.

Orchard Place Airport in Chicago is renamed for Butch O'Hare, Medal of Honor winner and hero of the battle of Midway. Chicago Municipal becomes Chicago Midway, and Northerly Island becomes Merril Meigs Field.

G.S. Suppiger and Brooks Foods build a 70-foot tall water tower shaped like a catsup bottle, sitting on a 100-foot tall base - the **tallest in the world**, located on Route 159 in south **Collinsville**; it was restored in 1995 at a cost of $75,000

The **Mount Vernon Rams** win the state championship in basketball. They will repeat in 1950 and again in 1954.

"Three-Finger" (yes, he was missing a finger) Mordecai Brown, star pitcher for the Chicago Cubs, is elected to baseball's Hall of Fame. His record was 229-131, with an ERA of 2.06. The Cubs secured him in a trade from the St. Louis Cardinals. The Cardinals later got revenge when they traded pitcher Ernie Broglio to the Cubs in 1964 for future Hall-of-Famer, Lou Brock.

Talk television is invented when NBC produces a show on the 19th floor of the Merchandise Mart called "Dave Garroway at Large."

1950 - Life Magazine publishes the June 19th article, "Gunfire Lays Low One More Shelton." Roy Shelton, the eldest, is shot while riding on a tractor on Carl's farm. The bullet entered his back and severed his spinal cord. It was a gruesome death for the sixty-five year-old brother when the trailing disk ran over his body after he fell to the ground. After attempts on the lives of Big Earl, Little Earl and Dalta, the three disappeared from the **Fairfield** area.

Illinois reaches its zenith ranking fourth nationally in agricultural output, third in manufacturing, and fourth in population.

Poet Gwendolyn Brooks

The center of U.S. population moves from Indiana to Illinois. It is now in a **Dundee** cornfield about nine miles north of **Olney**.

Johnny Wyrostek, the Polish kid from **East St. Louis/Fairmont City**, is selected to the All-Star team from the Cincinnati Reds. Wyrostek is the idol of a Cincinnati kid named Pete Rose.

Illinois' population expands to 8,712,176.

Gwendolyn Brooks becomes the first black woman to receive the Pulitzer Prize in poetry.

East St. Louis businessman Frank Buster Wortman is dubbed "the Crown Prince" by the local news media. He ran a string of gambling houses – the Prevue, the Corona, the Red Rooster, the Harlem Club, and others.

Ozark Airlines becomes the biggest air operator in Illinois and starts off with a Chicago-Champaign-Decatur-Springfield route.

East St. Louisan Bill Lawrence is the featured singer on the Arthur Godfrey television show, a spot he loses to Julius LaRosa when he is drafted for the Korean War.

A Chicago Transit Authority streetcar hits a gasoline truck and 33 people are killed.

The town of **Dixon** holds an annual Petunia Festival for 4 days during the 4th of July weekend. After Dutch elm disease killed off many trees, the Dixon Men's Garden Club planted petunias along the barren roads leading to town.

Max Hill wins the race for St. Clair County sheriff over Republican Ed Lehman 34,543 to 34,162. Lehman, whose brother Albert ran Lehman Sheet Metal at 4100 State in East St. Louis, asks the decision to be overturned because of voter fraud in Centreville Township. County Judge Quinten Spivey overturns the outcome and declares Lehman to be the winner.

According to a census taker, the Louis and Bertha Vander Pluym family, recently relocated from **Breese** with 11 children, is the largest in **Belleville**.

Bob Shaw of the Chicago Cardinals catches 5 touchdowns in a game against the Baltimore Colts.

Luke Appling ends a 20-year career with the White Sox. The future Hall-of-Famer owns most of the club's hitting records. Incredibly, old "aches and pains" hit a home run at RFK Stadium, at age 75, in a 1982 old timer's game.

East St. Louis, the birthplace of several national unions, becomes the most unionized town in America.

Dixon, Illinois, the town with the Petunia Festival

1951 – Orville Hodge, a state representative from **Granite City**, meets a woman named Bonita Lillie and began seeing her on a regular basis. He told her that he and his wife had been separated for years, and that Mrs. Hodge lived in Florida.

Dr. Thaddeus Szewczyk, overseeing ophthalmological care at Christian Welfare Hospital in **East St. Louis discovers a cure for incubator blindness** in premature babies. He figured out that the oxygen being administered to the incubator was causing the blindness. Musician Stevie Wonder, born in 1950, was a victim of the disease. Dr Szeweczyk published his findings in the American Journal of Ophthalmology in December of 1951. In 2002 the doctor was honored when Congressman Jerry Costello of **East St. Louis/Belleville** entered a tribute in the Congressional Record.

DQ Joe, the Indian mascot of **DuQuoin High School** is originated by **R. P. Hibbs**, principal of the high school. The school mascot was designed with the assistance of **Virginia Green** and **Jerry Givens**. The mascot soon came to be used by all athletic teams and was placed on the baseball team uniforms. Joe the Indian was soon painted on the basketball floor jump circle in the gymnasium. He also graced the tile floor of the gym lobby. The *Magnavox*, the school newspaper, carries the logo with every issue. Joe, dressed in the school colors of red and black, is a cartoon caricature of Chief DuQuoin. When the student chosen to represent

141

Chief **DuQuoin** graduates, a new mascot is chosen from the freshman class to promote school spirit. **Mike Coffel** served as the first mascot. **Jamie Swallows** also served in that capacity. Collinsville High has a similar tradition for their Chief Kahok.

The Argonne National Laboratory, located 25 miles southwest of Chicago near **Lamont**, builds the **world's first breeder reactor** to produce electricity. The lab, under the auspices of the University of Chicago, was established after World War II by the Atomic Energy Commission to explore peaceful uses of atomic energy. The Laboratory covers more than 350 acres and is staffed by about 852 scientists.

DuQuoin High School Indian mascot/logo

Carl Baldwin, East Side reporter for the *Post-Dispatch*, writes more than 100 stories about corruption in the metro area construction industry. This leads to FBI, congressional, and grand jury investigations, resulting in the indictments of sixty men.

There was an explosion and fire at the New Orient Mine No. 2 at **West Frankfort, killing 119 men**. It was the second worst mine disaster in the state's history. Some electrical equipment touched off a pocket of explosive methane gas. The fire was fed by coal dust and other pockets of gas. Only one man survived the blast and fire. As a direct result of this disaster, the federal Coal Mine Safety Act was passed the next year.

Sam "Jet" Jethroe, of **East St. Louis**, wins the National League Rookie of the Year title with the Boston Braves. He is still the oldest player to win that award in either league. He batted .273 and led the league in stolen bases.

Jimmy Durante, Tony Martin, Frank Sinatra, Bob Hope, Dean Martin and many others give a performance in Chicago known as the Night of Stars. Murray "the Camel Humphreys" came up with the idea of a benefit performance to send the pook kids of Chicago to summer camp.

Senator Estes Kefauver of Tennessee holds national televised hearings on organized crime in St. Louis and subpoenas various officials from Madison and St. Clair Counties to testify. They are heavily criticized for their failure to take action against betting through Western Union wire services and handbook/policy numbers betting. Paul Simon, editor of the *Troy Tribune,* testifies as a friendly witness to the veracity of wide-open gambling in the bi-county. Otto Kerner claimed that Chicago was a clean city, but after conducting hearings in that town the committee said: "If we had gone no farther than Chicago and East St. Louis for evidence of a direct link between organized crime and politics, we could have written a complete report in miniature."

Ralph Capone & Tony Arresso

Alcoholic Dorothy Anderson is found in a Chicago alley on a cold winter night. **Her blood, legs, and eyeballs were frozen solid**, but she was thawed and regained consciousness within 24 hours. Her legs had to be amputated, but she lived until 1971.

Manager Bill Veeck (a Chicagoan) of the St. Louis Browns, stuns the baseball world by inserting a Chicago midget (Eddie Gaedel) into his lineup. Predictably, the three feet, seven inches tall Gaedel drew a walk.

A Chicagoan named Paul Harvey is arrested for breaching security by scaling a fence at Argonne National Laboratory in Lamont. He insists he did it to expose lax security. Paul Harvey would later become famous for his daily Chicago radio news-commentary show of ABC and for books containing his "the rest of the story" famous surprise endings.

In 1957 this plant produced the **nation's first nuclear-powered generator**.

A.J. Liebling, a connoisseur of street life and a writer for *The New Yorker,* composes a piece that accuses Chicagoans of trying (and failing) to emulate New Yorkers. It was titled "The Second City." Realizing that complaining or bellyaching about the article would accomplish little, Chicagoans adopted Second City as one of the unofficial nicknamed for Chicago.

Geneva begins the practice of holding an annual Swedish Festival around the third weekend in June. A parade with bands and floats is held. Local merchants hold sidewalk sales and music includes guest performers, folk dancing, barbershop quartets, Sweet Adelines, and drum and bugle corps contests.

Chuck Connors, a former *cager* for the Boston Celtics, plays 66 games for the Cubs at first base before heading to the West Coast to star in the television series, "The Rifleman." Basketball players once played on a *caged* court to protect them from unruly crowds.

A grand jury in Chicago convenes for the purpose of investigating Ralph Capone's tax problems with the IRS. One of the people called to testify is **"Two-Gun" Hart**, the most famous and violent Prohibition agent west of the Mississippi. It turns out that Hart is actually a brother to Al and Ralph Capone – the so-called Lost Brother.

1952 – **Orville Hodge** wins the race for state auditor. He had wanted to run for governor but was persuaded by party officials to run for auditor instead. He had previously served 3 terms in the General Assembly. It was believed by many that Hodge had been staked for campaign funds by Frank Wortman and others on the promise that he would help legalize gambling after the election. It was no secret that Hodge had a lot more money to spend than any other candidate in 1952. Phil Brown, state police superintendent, said Hodge went to him and asked if he could ease up on the gambling spots in and around East St. Louis.

At the Republican National Convention, held in the International Ampitheater in Chicago, delegates choose Dwight D. Eisenhower, a man who has never held political office, over the venerable party leader, Senator Robert A. Taft of Ohio. The Democrats met in Chicago and nominated Stevenson who preferred to be governor.

Adlai Stevenson, the man from **Libertyville**, campaigns for the presidency against Eisenhower in East St. Louis on October 10. He curried the black vote by greeting **Henry Fuller**, who was born in slavery. **Ben Day** of the East St. Louis Democratic Committee and Mayor Alvin Fields helped plan Stevenson's visit to the city. Eisenhower wins 98 of the 102 counties in Illinois.

A bill passes the Illinois legislature that requires the "Broyles oath." It is named for the congressman from Mt. Vernon who sponsored it. It is a product of the McCarthy era. All state employees and teachers are required to sign a paper, swearing that they are not members of the Communist party.

Encyclopedia Britannica publishes Great Books of the Western World. Britannica started out as a Scottish company, but was later bought out by Sears and became Chicago based. Britannica bought the Compton Company in 1961 and in 1983 moved its headquarters to the Britannica Center on Michigan Ave. at Marshall. It has more than 250 offices worldwide.

Republican William G. Stratton wins the first of his two terms as governor.

The U.S. Post Office issues a 3-cent stamp in Chicago honoring establishment of the AAA, American Automobile Association.

Chicago Blackhawks player Bill Mosienko accomplishes the incredible feat of scoring **3 goals in 21 seconds**.

Leo Stefafanos, Greek owner of a confectionery at 61st and Pulaski in Chicago, creates the first **Dove Bars**.

The Chicago Bears draft Eddie Macon, and he becomes the first black to play for them.

Ronald Reagan marries actress Nancy Davis after they star together in *Hellcats of the Navy*. Reagan, who became the nation's first divorced president, separated from Jane Wyman because she thought his obsession with politics was ruining their marriage.

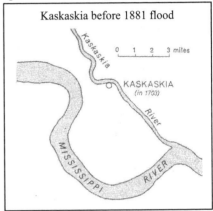
Kaskaskia before 1881 flood

Tiny Hebron, led by Paul and Phil Judson, completes the most famous Cinderella season in state history. They defeat powerful **Rock Island** in the semi-finals and talented **Quincy (led by All-stater Bruce Brothers)** in overtime in the championship game, ending a fabulous 35-1 season.

The Fighting Illini make it to the Final Four in basketball.

Chuck Berry fills in for another act and performs at the Cosmos Club in East St. Louis, helping to usher in the era of rock and roll.

1953 –Central and southern Illinois investors put up money for the new Cahokia Downs racetrack on Route 15 on the outskirts of East St. Louis.

Art Newman, former Birger gang member, is released from prison and goes to California to raise flowers. By 1979 he was living in Arizona.

Ruby Berkley Goodwin publishes *It's Good to be Black*, a coming-of-age memoir about the **DuQuoin** area.

Chicagoan **Hugh Hefner**, a 1949 graduate of the University of Illinois and a copywriter for Esquire Magazine, gambles that American males are ready for a magazine that features sexy naked women. Starting with a mere $600 investment, he decides to publish a magazine called *Stag Party*, after the term used to describe "adult" films. At the last minute he changes the name to *Playboy,* and it features a nude pinup of Marilyn Monroe. He prints 72,000 copies of "Playboy" magazine. It cost Hefner $200 for the rights to use the photo. He raised $10,000 worth of capital by selling stock to his friends. Not sure how well the magazine will do, he leaves the word December off the first issue. He soon divorced his (high school sweetheart) wife, Mildred Williams. Circulation hit an all-time high in 1972 with 7.2 million copies sold. Hefner's "Playboy philosophy" soon came under heavy fire from feminists and religious groups. He built a 48-room mansion (expanded to 69-rooms) at 1340 North State Parkway on Chicago's Gold Coast. Many of the playmates lived in dormitories at the mansion. In 1982 his daughter Christie became President of Playboy Enterprises, and she rescued it from the doldrums of the 1970s. In 1989 he married Kimberly Conrad. They separated in 1998.

Chicago surpasses Pittsburgh as the nation's leading steel maker.

Forty million catalogs are mailed out by Chicago companies that include Sears, Montgomery Ward, Spiegel and Aldens.

The Chicago Mercantile Exchange is the **largest market in the world** for butter, eggs, potatoes and other farm produce. Chicago's Board of Trade is the **world's largest grain market**.

The **Litchfield** bowling team wins the Elks Club national tournament in Chicago. Their five-man team consisted of Carl Diehl, Mason Bouillon, Ralph Walls, Gene Phillips and Harvey Lehnen.

William Holden of **O'Fallon** wins Best Actor award in the World War II German prison camp film, *Stalag 17*.

Illinois Medal of Honor winners in the Korean War include William F. Dean of **Carlyle**, John Kilmer of **Highland Park**, Chicagoan Ed Krzyoswki, James Poynter of **Bloomington**, Richard Wilson of **Marion** and Chicagoan William Windrich.

The Chicago plant of the Haber Corporation catches fire, killing 35 people.

Rocky Marciano defeats Jersey Joe Walcott in a heavyweight championship boxing match in Chicago.

Bears' quarterback George Blanda leads the league in completions with 169, but also throws 24 interceptions.

1954 - Massac County Memorial Hospital, named for the war dead, is built on six acres of ground donated by Charles Adkins Sr.

William Holden of O'Fallon

East St. Louis detective Robert Sweeney, the "**Law in East St. Louis**" who killed as many men in the line of duty as Frank and Jesse James, quits the police force when ordered by superiors to "lay off" hoodlums who were "home town boys." Sweeney was a member of the department for over 30 years. Sweeny killed 12 men in the line of duty, as many as Frank and Jesse James combined. He was noted for having run Ben "Bugsy" Siegel and Ma Barker's nephew out of town on separate occasions.

Willie Dixon, bass player, songwriter, and arranger, joins with guitarist **Muddy Waters**, and they begin making records for the blue and silver label of Chess Records, on 2120 South Michigan Avenue. Their bold, playful and ribald music ushers blues music into a new era.

Chicago's Union Stockyards slaughters its billionth animal.

Mayor Richard Daley

The **Mount Vernon** Rams win their 4th state basketball title by beating Chicago DuSable, 76-70.

The temperature reaches 117 F. in East St. Louis on July 14, **the state record**.

Olin Industries merges with Mathieson Chemical. Franklin Olin started the Equitable Powder Company in **East Alton** back in 1892. He formed Western Cartridge Company in 1898 as an outlet for excess production of black powder used in the coal industry.

1955 – Richard Daley, Cook County clerk since 1950, becomes mayor of Chicago for his first of 6 terms. Despite controversy and corruption in government, Daley wins numerous re-election campaigns on the slogan "Chicago: The City That Works." He became America's most powerful big city "boss" and was proud of the many public works projects completed during his reign. Daley lived his entire life in the Irish neighborhood of **Bridgeport**.

Construction begins on Frank Wortman's "moat" home in southeast **Collinsville**. The East St. Louis businessman probably got the idea from an old associate, Irving "Waxey Gordon" Wexler, who surrounded his New Jersey headquarters with a moat. Fred "Bo" Beuckman, of Beuckman Ford in Collinsville, bought the 126-acre estate around 1971, shortly after Wortman's death in 1968.

Only 13,000 men are working in 198 southern Illinois coalmines, down from the 103,000 peak in 1923.

Muddy Waters

Arlington resident **Ray Kroc**, a malted-milk mixing machine salesman, encounters a thriving hamburger business in San Bernadino, run by Mac and Dick McDonald. He talks them into the idea of selling him a franchise. He will later buy them out for $2.7 million. His first McDonalds, with its 15-cent hamburgers, 10-cent fries, and golden arches was built in **Des Plaines**. Ironically, **McDonalds** did not become teen hangouts because Kroc wouldn't install jukeboxes or pay phones. Kroc bought out the McDonald brothers in 1971 and became owner of the San Diego Padres baseball team. The first logo of McDonalds was a fellow named "Speedee" (for fast food), but Kroc replaced him with the golden arches. McDonalds franchises exist all over the world and have sold over 100 billion hamburgers – and that's no bull. The term "hamburger" comes from the Hamburg steamship company that served beef patties to immigrants coming to America on its ocean going vessels.

Kroc's original restaurant was torn down with a new replica built in its place, becoming the McDonalds Museum.

A downtrodden blues singer from St. Louis walks into the Chicago office of Chess records and persuades them to record his song "Ida Red." Released under the new title *Maybelline*, it becomes the company's first hit record and makes **Chuck Berry** a star. The company was the creation of Leonard and Phil Chess, two Polish-born Jews who had previously run nightclubs in Chicago that featured Billy Eckstine and Ella Fitzgerald. Chess Records was also the home of Muddy Waters, a Mississippi transplant who was a deliveryman by day and played the nightclub circuit at night. A financially strapped Sam Phillips of Sun Records once offered to sell his label to the Chess brothers. But they had just signed **Bo Diddley** to a contract and couldn't see buying up a contract of some hillbilly singer from Tupelo, Mississippi, named **Elvis Presley**.

Tony Accardo of the Chicago Syndicate moves aside making way for the rise of Sam Giancana. Future boss, Joey "Doves" Aiuppa, continues to move up in the ranks.

The U.S. issues an 8-cent **Rotary International** stamp honoring its Chicago beginnings in 1905.

Illinois **leads the nation in the production of corn and soybeans**. Cook County leads all other counties in the nation in industrial production. The state leads all others in meatpacking, agricultural machinery, electrical machinery, and packaging products.

Midway Airport is designated as a port of entry by the U.S. government. It is the **first inland airport so designated**. O'Hare airport begins its first commercial operations.

Rockford West wins two consecutive IHSA basketball championships by defeating Elgin (61-59) and Edwardsville (67-65) in 1956.

The General Assembly adopts "Land of Lincoln" as the state slogan and begins adding the words *Land of Lincoln* to all license plates.

Frank Tully of **Joliet** discovers the "Tully Monster," a soft-bodied marine creature that lived 280 million years ago and has only been found in Illinois.

1956 – Incumbent **Orville Hodge of Granite City** runs against Democrat Michael Howlett for state auditor in November.

George Theim, a reporter for the *Chicago Daily News*, acting on a tip begins to investigate Hodge's extravagant lifestyle in May. He examined the auditor's payroll list and discovered friends and relatives on the list in an apparent effort to broaden his political base. He also discovered Hodge had a plush suite of rooms at the St. Nicholas Hotel in **Springfield**. Hodge was a joiner and a member of the **Belleville Country Club** and the **Sunset Country Club** in **Edwardsville**. He had formerly run an insurance agency at 1915 Madison in Granite. He also owned a hotel in Florida, Cadillac cars, two airplanes, a summer home on the lake, a new hardware and appliance store, motorboats, and farms stocked with expensive Aberdeen-Angus cows. A trip to Granite City made it obvious that his real estate business hadn't paid for these extravagances.

When asked on the stand about stolen funds and forged checks, Hodge tried to lay the blame on his confederates. And he denied using tax money to pay personal hotel, food, and liquor bills.

Hodge was often seen with **Paul Powell**, a Democrat from **Vienna** and Speaker of the House, and former governor (back in 1940) **John Stelle of McLeansboro** at Cahokia Downs in East St. Louis where Stelle was a significant stockholder. Powell visited Hodge a few times when he was sent to Menard Prison at Chester.

The final audit of Hodge's three and a half years as state auditor listed over a million dollars worth of embezzled state warrants and misappropriation of another half-million of bank funds.

Hodge was sentenced to 12-15 years at Menard in Chester. The state was able to recover about half of the total amount stolen.

The town of **Summerfield**, just east of **Lebanon**, is hit by a tornado on February 25th, killing three people.

Robert "Polecat" McMillan (of **Centralia**) becomes the third person enshrined in the Railroad Hall of Fame.

Women now constitute 1/3 of the workforce in the state.

Only about 17,000 men are employed as coal miners, but they produce twice the amount of coal dug by twice as many workers in 1898.

Franklin, **Williamson** and **Macoupin** counties lead the state in coal production.

Ernie Banks

More than 8,400 have lost their lives in Illinois coal mining and twice that number have been injured in accidents. Today, coal mining is the third most dangerous occupation in the U.S.

Seventy-seven Hungarians resettle in **Peoria** after the Russians crush a revolt in Hungary.

East St. Louisan Miles Davis releases an album called *Birth of the Cool* and is voted the top jazz artist in the nation.

Chicagoan Dorothy Malone wins Best Supporting Actress for her performance in the film, *Written on the Wind*.

White Sox shortstop Luis Aparicio wins Rookie-of-the-Year honors.

1957 - A wolf hunt is held in **Goreville** to rid the area of this pesky predator.

Barbara Zobrist, age ten, of **Highland**, wins the national roller skating tournament in Oakland, California.

The Greyhound bus terminal in Chicago is the **largest in the nation**. And Chicago is the rail hub of the nation with 30 interstate trunk lines. East St. Louis ranks second with 27 major trunk lines.

The University of Illinois at **Urbana** is now the largest school in the nation outside of those in New York City.

Gangster Bernie Shelton

The Methodists lay claim to being the largest Protestant denomination in the state.

Construction of the 41-story Prudential Building is completed. This started a building boom that saw construction of the Sears Tower, John Hancock Center, Lake Point Tower and the Amoco Building.

SIU at **Carbondale**, led by Delyte Morris, expands and takes over the old Shurtleff College in **Alton** and begins offering classes. In 1958 it purchases the old East St. Louis High School at Tenth and Ohio and offers classes there. A permanent extension campus opened at **Edwardsville** in 1965.

East St. Louis sets the state record for rainfall as 16 and ½ inches fall within 24 hours on June 14. The average yearly rainfall amount in the state is 38 inches with this figure being higher in the south and lower in the north.

Wheaton College wins the NCAA Division II national basketball championship; it is the only Illinois college to do this.

A tornado rips through Murphysboro killing 9 people.

Cardinal Stritch of Chicago bans rock and roll from all Catholic high school functions.

There is a power outage in the southern Illinois town of **Tamaroa**. Several people claim it was caused by a UFO hovering near the place. (UFO's, first seen by an Air Force pilot in 1947, are, of course, a Modern Myth.)

1958 – Author **Taylor Pensoneau** graduates from **Belleville West** High School. Pensoneau's father ran The Toggery, a clothing store for men on Main Street. Pensoneau ran track in high school and competed against **Jim Brady of Centralia High** in the mile event in track. Brady will go on to become President Reagan's press secretary. He was seriously injured when John Hinckley tried to assassinate Reagan in 1981. The Brady Bill gun control measure is named for him.

Mayor Richard Daley proclaims Chicago to be "The Convention Center of America." By 2003, the city had hosted 14 Republican presidential nominating conventions and 11 Democratic assemblages since its first in 1860.

Harvey Dungey, a member of the old Birger gang, is shot and killed by a night watchman while trying to rob the Midway Tavern near **Desoto**.

East St. Louisan **"Bullet" Bob Turley**, pitcher for the N.Y. Yankees, wins the Cy Young Award.

East St. Louis builds a new high school at 4901 State Street. SIU moves into the old building.

Three nuns and 93 students perish in a fire at Our Lady of Angels School in Chicago. The fire started in a wastebasket filled with paper, set by a fifth grader. In the aftermath, Chicago passes an ordinance requiring the installation of sprinkler systems in all schools and linked fire alarm systems directly to the fire department.

For the first time in a decade, operating revenues of the Illinois Central are down. The trucking industry is beginning to make significant progress in replacing the railroads as carriers of the nation's freight.

Bill Veeck buys the Chicago White Sox.

Under pressure from the NAACP, Riverside Amusement Park in Chicago discontinues an attraction called The African Dip. Young black males would taunt patrons into throwing baseballs at a target. If a bullseye was scored, the "victim" was dumped into a pool of water.

The U.S. Post Office issues a 3-cent International Geophysical Year stamp at Chicago.

The U.S. Post Office raises first-class mail rates and issues a 4-cent Lincoln-Douglas commemorative debate stamp.

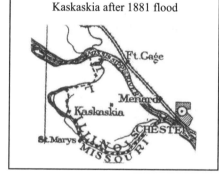
Kaskaskia after 1881 flood

Baker Brownell writes *The Other Illinois*, and describes the southern third of the state (between the 37th and 39th parallels, from **Vandalia** to **Cairo**) as an area suffering from economic depression (poor as Job's turkey). He identifies **Cairo** (pronounced Kerro) as having one foot in the Mississippi River and the other in the Ohio. He staunchly maintains that it is the most beautiful part of the state, and that it has more varieties of trees than the whole of Europe.

Kankakee loses the Little League baseball championship to a team from Monterray, Mexico.

Sugar Ray Robinson defeats middleweight champion Carmen Basilio in a title fight at Chicago Stadium.

Ernie "Let's Play Two" Banks of the Cubs wins the National League MVP award. He becomes the first player to win it back-to-back when he repeats in 1959. Baseball's goodwill ambassador, he was later heavily criticized for not taking a strong stance to support the Civil Rights movement.

Bobby Hull, (the Golden Jet) of the Blackhawks, scores 47 points in his rookie season, but is edged for Rookie-of-the-Year honors by Frank Mahovlich. Hockey was a sport dominated by Canadians and ignored by Americans until Hull came along.

Edwards County, in east central Illinois, is proclaimed the **Chowder Capital of America.**

Marshall High becomes the first prep Chicago team in modern times to win the state championship.

The number of Drive-in movie theaters reach their peak in the state of Illinois.

Frank Lloyd Wright

1959 – **Ray Page** coaches the **Springfield Senators** to the state basketball championship. In 1962 he will win a stunning political victory by being elected state superintendent of public instruction.

Chicagoan Frank Lloyd Wright dies in his sleep. He will be feted as the **greatest American architect of all time**.

The opening of the St. Lawrence Seaway connects the city of Chicago to the Atlantic Ocean making the Great Lakes our nation's "fourth seacoast." Chicago, now a seaport, holds a Trade Fair at Navy Pier, and it's visited by Queen Elizabeth II and Prince Philip in their royal yacht *Britannia*.

The General Electric Company builds a nuclear power plant for Commonwealth Edison near **Morris**, Illinois, called the Dresden plant. It was the largest commercial reactor in existence, capable of 700,000 watts of power daily.

The Chicago White Sox win the national League pennant but lose the World Series (4-2) against Sandy Khoufax, Don Drysdale and the Dodgers. When the pennant was clinched, Fire Commissioner Robert Quinn ordered the sounding of the city's air raid sirens for 5 minutes setting off a panic. The nation was in the midst of the Cold War, and Nikita Khrushchev had recently delivered his famous "We will bury you" speech.

A cabaret/theater club called **Second City** opens in Chicago. Some of the featured performers are Paul Sand, Joan Rivers, Barbara Harris, Mike Nichols, Elaine May, Chevy Chase, Alan Arkin and Shelly Berman. When Saturday Night Live started in the mid 1970s, the cast included such Second City veterans as John Belushi, Gilda Radner, Dan Akroyd and Bill Murray. Several years later a syndicated Second City TV series came along and featured Harold Ramis, Andrea Martin and John Candy.

Mobster Roger (the Terrible") Touhy is shot and killed four days before Christmas, shortly after being released from prison. According to tallies by the press, he becomes the **1,000th mobster to be killed** since the advent of prohibition. Murray "the Camel" Humphreys had set him up on a kidnapping charge against Jake "the Barber" Factor. Roger wrote a book while in prison that came out about the same time as his release from prison (after 25 years behind bars) in late 1958. It was called *The Stolen Years* and most figure that Roger was killed because he said too much about his enemies in the book.

The Illinois Central begins to fight the union practice of featherbedding. In order to save jobs, union contracts stipulated that a fireman would sit next to the engineer. In the old days, the fireman shoveled coal and tended the boiler. Modern diesels no longer required the services of such a worker. The railroad association maintained that featherbedding cost railroads an unnecessary expense of over a billion dollars a year.

Ernie Banks, Chicago infielder, becomes known as "Mr. Cub."

Evanston-born Charlton Heston wins the Oscar for Best Actor in *Ben Hur*: A Tale of the Christ.

The first boat to pass through the St. Lawrence Seaway arrives in Chicago.

The Little Grassy Fish Hatchery, southeast of **Carbondale**, is established by the state for the purpose of stocking lakes. Largemouth bass, bluegill, redear sunfish, channel cat and striped bass are among the fish raised here ((618/529-4100). The place is enlarged and remodeled in 1979.

1960 – Television history is made when a debate between Democratic Senator John F. Kennedy and Republican Vice-president Richard M. Nixon is held in Chicago and broadcast nationally. The event is a disaster for Nixon. His gray suit blended in with the background. By contrast, the camera loved Kennedy's dark blue attire. Nixon used pancake makeup to hide his 5 o'clock shadow. The hot lights caused it to become streaked halfway through the debate. Finally, Nixon and his staff guessed that the first of 3 debates (domestic politics) would attract the fewest viewers, and interest would build for the last, about foreign policy – his greatest strength. Just the opposite happened. Ironically, most radio listeners thought Nixon had won the debate while TV viewers gave the nod to Kennedy. Nixon went into the debate with a lead in the polls over his rival. John F. Kennedy narrowly defeats Richard Nixon in Illinois and narrowly in the electoral vote. Many Republicans believed to their dying day this was due to vote stealing by Richard Daley's political machine in Chicago. Nixon bitterly complained of voter fraud in Chicago but belatedly declined to challenge the vote count.

During the campaign, actor Ronald Reagan, a Democrat, gives 200 speeches for "Democrats supporting Nixon."

Route 66 is immortalized by a television show of the same name, starring Martin Milner and George Maharis, two buddies driving along the famed road in a Corvette convertible, with stories taking place at various stops along the way. Singer Nat King Cole had earlier brought fame to the roadway by singing a song with the lyrics: "Get your kicks on Route 66."

A marker is placed in Fred Kleiboeker's soybean field near **Shattue**, in Clinton County (not far from **Centralia**), marking the new geographic center of U.S. population.

Though in a slight condition of decline, **East St. Louis** is still the state's 5th leading industrial producer. It is named by Look Magazine as an **All-America City,** one of 11 such cities in the nation.

East St. Louisan **Hank Bauer** retires as right fielder for the N.Y. Yankees. He has eight world champion-ship rings and the World Series record for hitting in seventeen consecutive games.

Southeastern Illinois College is founded. The 148-acre campus of this two-year school is located five miles east of **Harrisburg** on Route 13. The first classes were held in a wing of Harrisburg Township High in 1961. It serves Gallatin, Hardin, Pope, Saline and parts of four other counties. Enrollment has gone from 314 to 4,700 students. Most of the current buildings were completed in 1976. The Forensic Falcons won the national speech championship in 1986. (618-252-6376)

Fleetwood Restaurant on Route 66 in Springfield (courtesy Neal Strebel)

Illinois' population expands to 10,081,158.

Industrial firms in Illinois, concerned by heating costs, aging facilities and high union wages and strict work rules, begin an exodus to the Sun Belt in the South. This is a national trend that will leave large numbers of unemployed workers and idle factories known across the Midwest as the Rust Belt.

The Metro-East towns in Madison and St. Clair Counties are among the top 40 industrial regions in America. This includes East St. Louis, **Wood River, Alton, Roxana, Belleville, Edwardsville, Collinsville** and a host of smaller towns.

The Cantigny War Memorial opens on the estate of the late Robert Rutherford McCormick at **Wheaton**. It has two dioramas, one of the Battle of Cantigny and the other of the D-Day landing at Normandy.

147

Otto Kerner, a Democrat, wins the first of his two terms as governor of Illinois, defeating William G. Stratton in a bid for a third term. He is married to the daughter of assassinated mayor of Chicago, Anton Cermak.

The Dresden nuclear power plant at Morris, built by Commonwealth Edison, becomes the first private nuclear plant in the U.S. Seven more reactors were subsequently built in northern Illinois, and more were planned until concerns about safety and waste disposal and pressure from environmental groups caused those plans to be abandoned. Nevertheless, the existing reactors were enough to place Illinois **second among all states** in the total amount of electricity produced by nuclear power. With a growing demand for the nation to become energy self-sufficient and less dependent on Arab oil, there is increased public sentiment to build more nuclear plants.

Mayor Richard J. Daley appoints professor Orlando Wilson to clean up a corrupt police force after 8 Chicago policemen are arrested for burglarizing the North Side and using a patrol wagon to haul away the loot. Policemen can now be fired for accepting "free" donuts from appreciative businesses.

Cub pitcher Don Cardwell throws a **no-hitter** in his first start for the Cubs, a feat that had never before been accomplished.

Fisherman John Nathan discovers an unusual amphibian caught in his nets anchored at a spot called **Rattlesnake Ferry** on the Big Muddy River. Entangled in the net was a monster **160-pound alligator turtle**. A man named Jesse Grammer owned a furniture store in **Grand Tower** and bought the creature at a price of $25 to attract customers. Big Bill, as the turtle was called, later became a feature attraction at the Illinois State Fair in **Springfield**.

Chicago begins a new tradition by placing green dye in the Chicago River to celebrate St. Patrick's Day.

1961 – **Andy Phillip**, a guard on the Granite City basketball team that won the state championship (24-22) against Herrin in 1940, is inducted into the **NBA Hall of Fame**. It is believed this was the first team from southern Illinois to win the championship. In 1989 he was named one of the 100 greatest players of all time. **John Markarian**, **Andy Hagopian** and **George Gages**, three other members of the 1940 team, still live in **Granite City**. He was a member of the legendary U of Illinois 1941-43 whiz Kids. In 1957 he was a member of the Boston Celtic team that won the NBA championship against the St. Louis Hawks. In 2002, efforts were being made to raise money for a 7 foot bronze plaque to commemorate the event.

Chicago's O'Hare Airport surpasses Midway and becomes the *busiest in the world*, ultimately handling over 70 million passengers a year, creating nearly 300,000 jobs and generating over $13 billion a year in revenues for the city.

The Chicago Blackhawks, led by Stan Mikita and Bobby Hull, defeat the Detroit Redwings, led by Gordie Howe, **to win the Stanley Cup**.

Bozo The Clown and his Circus debut on WGN TV in Chicago. The red-haired, hyperkinetic, flop-shoed clown was played by Bob Bell. Bozo was portrayed by many other characters in numerous other cities (weatherman Willard Scott in Washington D.C), but out of 182 markets, Chicago had the highest ratings. **Dave** *"Garroway at Large"* and **"Kukla, Fran and Ollie"** were other early TV shows that originated from Chicago.

Dave Garroway graduated near the bottom of his announcing class

The shift from coal power to diesel fuel by the Illinois Central is now complete. Not only is diesel fuel more efficient and cleaner than coal, the company saves over a million dollars a year by not having to use water for steam power. The diesel engines are not cheap. In 1954, new units from General Motors cost $256,500 each.

Billy Williams of the Chicago Cubs is named Rookie of the Year.

The **Collinsville** Kahoks crush Thornton for the IHSA basketball title by the incredible score of 84-50. Collinsville wins again in 1965 by defeating **Quincy**, 55-52.

McDonald's Hamburger University is founded in **Oak Brook**.

Chanute Air Base at **Rantoul** begins training airmen for Minuteman ICBM maintenance. The Minuteman Missile was launch ready with nuclear warheads and stored in underground silos. These can now be seen on museum tours.

1962 - Charles Boewe publishes *Prairie Albion: An English Settlement in Pioneer Illinois*.

Mermet Lake in Massac County is dug by the Illinois Dept. of Conservation. Water covers 452 acres of the 2,580 acres that were formerly an old cypress tree swamp. Bass, catfish and panfish abound. This area boasts the state record for its numbers of the willow oak tree.

Illinois passes the Open Cut Mining Reclamation Act requiring waste or gob piles to be flattened. A subsequent revision in 1973 and 1977 required the land to be made level or gently rolling.

Ten miners are killed near **Herrin** in an accident at the Blue Blaze Mine.

Chicagoan **Gene Chandler** has a #1 hit with "The Duke of Earl."

During the Cuban Missile Crisis in October, former governor Adlai Stevenson, now Ambassador to the U.N., makes a dramatic accusation that the Russians were providing Cuba with offensive missiles that would threaten the U.S.

Ronald Reagan officially switches allegiance from the Democratic to the Republican Party.

Nationally syndicated columnist Drew Pearson lists the **Springfield Godfather**, Frank Zito, as one of Illinois' "worst hoodlums."

Edith Sampson becomes the first black woman elected judge when she wins a Chicago municipal judgeship.

1963 – John F. Kennedy, 35th president of the United States, is assassinated by Lee Harvey Oswald in Dallas, Texas on November 22. His weapon was a World War II vintage Carcano Manlicher bolt-action rifle. The bullet that killed Kennedy was manufactured by the Winchester-Western plant, located next to the Olin brass mill in **East Alton**.

Joseph Valachi, a Neopolitan, testifies before the Senate Permanent Subcommittee on Investigation about the Mafia and organized crime in America.

Lake of Egypt, a 2,300 acre man made lake, is constructed to provide water to cool the steam generating plant at the Southern Illinois Power Co-operative dam. It is near **Goreville** east of the point where Interstate 24 intersects Interstate 57.

The Alcoa Aluminum plant at **East St. Louis** closes, leaving behind 20 million tons of spent ore waste bauxite tailings known as "red mud" for making bricks and 15 million tons of gypsum, used in the production of cement.

The Illinois General Assembly creates the Nature Preserves Commission. The state acquires places like Vole Bog, Lusk Creek Canyon, Goose Lake Prairie, Wildcat Bluff, and Beall Woods as nature preserves. John Schwegman and George Fell played important roles in this conservation movement.

St. Louisan **James Franciscus** stars as "Mr. Novak," a television series about an English teacher in the Chicago public school system.

George Halas' smash-mouth Chicago Bears defeat Y.A. Tittle and the New York Giants by a score of 14-10. A temperature of 9 degrees in a game played on December 29th also froze the vaunted NY offense. Chicago fans feared the Bears might never win another championship under Halas who was notoriously stingy and not very innovative on offense. Linebacker Larry Morris was the game's MVP.

The **Metropolis High** basketball team goes to the state finals in Champaign-Urbana. Here they lose their only game of the season, but Trojan forward **John Turner** scored the first IHSA basket ever at the new Assembly Hall.

Wayman Presley's 111-foot tall cross on Bald Knob at **Alto Pass** is finished.

Due to declining revenues, IC diversifies and now is known as Illinois Central Industries.

Goalie Glenn Hall of the Chicago Blackhawks wins the Vezina Trophy as pro hockey's best goalkeeper.

An Islamic Student Union is formed at the University of Illinois. It evolves into a national leadership role, establishing an Islamic Awareness Week on the campuses of many of the nation's universities.

Illinoisan Johnny Gilmer hits #1 on the pop charts with "Sugar Shack."

Loyola of Chicago wins the NCAA Division I basketball title. They are the only Illinois team to accomplish this feat.

The U.S. Post Office issues a 5-cent stamp at Chicago commemorating the Emancipation Proclamation.

George Harrison comes to **Benton** to visit his sister, Louise Harrison Caldwell, for a month. The Beatles were already popular in England but were just getting ready to begin a tour known as the British Invasion. The radio station in **West Frankfort** becomes the **first in the nation to play a Beatles song**.

The state creates the Lincoln Heritage Trail, marking the route the family traveled from their original home in Kentucky, through Indiana, to Macon County.

Huff Gymnasium at the University of Illinois is retired in favor of a new and larger Assembly Hall. Illinois is 8-1-1 in football.

All of the famed Burma Shave road signs in Illinois are taken down along the highways.

1964 - Richard Dorson publishes *Buying the Wind*, a book about folklore from seven different regions of the U.S. He selects southern Illinois as the area that best represents folklore of the upper Mississippi Valley.

The *U.S.S. Cairo*, a Union gunboat that was sunk during the Vicksburg campaign in the Civil War, is raised from the Mississippi and placed on display in Vicksburg.

Illinois outproduces Iowa in corn with 891,664,000 bushels. The two states compete yearly for the national championship with Iowa winning most of the time. **Decatur** calls

The new Assembly Hall, Univ. of Illinois at Champaign/Urbana (courtesy of U of I

itself the soybean capital of America and Illinois annually leads the nation in soybean output.

The new campus of Southern Illinois University at **Edwardsville** opens for business. The student newspaper is called **The Alestle**, a composite of its three sites - Alton, East St. Louis and Edwardsville. The Meridian Room in the University Center is so named because it sits squarely on the 90th meridian of longitude, exactly 1/4 of the way around the globe.

Cicero police chief Erwin Konovsky admits to having made only one vice arrest in **Cicero** from 1963-64. Cicero acquires the nickname "The Walled City of the Syndicate," known for its lax law enforcement.

The **Pekin** "Chinks" (now Dragons) defeat the **Cobden** "Appleknockers" 50-45 for the IHSA title. They repeat as champs in 1967, defeating the **Carbondale** Terriers 75-59.

U.S. Congress passes the Civil Rights Act, a law made possible by the compromise talent of Illinois Senator Everett Dirksen. His talents are essential a year later in securing passage of the Voting Rights Act of 1965.

Linebacker Dick Butkus leads the University of Illinois to a 17-7 Rose Bowl victory over Washington University.

Ronald Reagan gives a speech supporting Barry Goldwater's bid for the presidency against Lyndon Johnson. It impresses California conservatives who urge him to run for governor. He will serve in that capacity for two terms, a total of 8 years.

Brian Piccolo makes the Bears' team as a free agent after leading the nation in rushing at Wake Forest his senior year.

Ken Hubbs, Chicago Cub Rookie-of-the-Year and Gold Glover, is killed in a plane crash.

The U.S. Supreme Court rules in the case of **Escobedo v. Illinois** that Danny Escobedo, convicted of killing his brother-in-law, had been denied the right to legal counsel before making a confession to police.

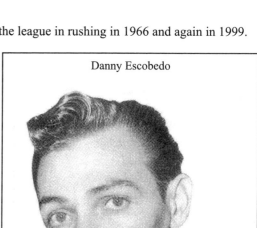
Ernest Hemingway

1965 – The first Chicago International Film Festival is held.

University of Chicago football coach Amos Alonzo Stagg dies at age 102. He ranks 5th in all time victories as a coach, having held that position at the university 41 seasons. He coached a total of 70 years at various colleges and was still coaching punters at age 98. He will be elected to both the Football and Basketball Halls of Fame, and the NCAA Division III championship game is named the Stagg Bowl in his honor.

Martin Luther King Jr. leads a civil rights march on Chicago's city hall.

Gayle Sayers of the Chicago Bears is the NFL rookie of the year. He will lead the league in rushing in 1966 and again in 1999.

Fairfield resident and Shelton gang nemesis Charlie "Blackie" Harris is convicted of killing two residents and setting fire to their farmhouse. Harris is age 69 at the time of his sentencing. Harris spent a total of 28 years of his life in prison.

Virginia Marmaduke, famous reporter for the *Chicago Sun*, serves as hostess for the Illinois Pavilion at the World's Fair held at Flushing Meadow in New York City. Marmaduke, who was born in **Carbondale**, worked for the *Herrin Daily Journal* and was a thorn in the side of Shelton gang mobster **Blackie Armes**. She left for Chicago after divorcing her husband and became famous for stories about her beat – blood, guts, and sex – not necessarily in that order. She once dated the actor **George Raft** who hung out with gangsters and portrayed them in film.

Danny Escobedo

1966 – Illinoisan Charles Percy, an executive at Bell and Howell, wins election to the U.S. Senate by unseating long-time Democrat, Paul Douglas. In September, the middle of the campaign, Percy's daughter Valerie was murdered (stabbed 10 times) in the Percy Chicago suburb home at **Kenilworth**. Her murder is never solved.

Martin Luther King Jr. leads a civil rights march in **Cicero**, a Chicago suburb, and is shocked by the violent and racist reception he receives from white residents there. People lined the streets hurling threats and insults at him. King later said that the hatred was so strong that he had expected to be shot during the march.

Senator Everett Dirksen, Chicago mayor Richard Daley, and Governor Otto Kerner convince President Lyndon Johnson to build a large atom-smashing complex known as Fermilab, in **Batavia**, 35 miles west of Chicago. This multi-million dollar project drew scientists from all over the globe, searching for the secrets of the universe.

ILLINOIS NAMES AND NICKNAMES

Illini: Algonquin word meaning "the men" and "accomplished"

Illinois: French added "ois" ending giving the meaning "land of superior men"

Garden of the West, Canaan of the West

Hub of the Nation

Crossroads of the Nation

Prairie State

Land of Lincoln

Sucker State

Little Egypt (southern Illinois)

Land of Second Chance

Inland Empire, The Delta of America

Prisoners stage a riot and kill three guards and wound several others at **Menard Prison** in Chester.

The **Marion Power Shovel**, with a bucket capacity of 180 cubic yards begins operations at the Percy "Captain" strip mine.

Bobby Hull of the Chicago Blackhawks wins the Hart trophy as Pro Hockey's MVP. He repeats in 1966 and is succeeded the next two years in a row by Chicago's **Stan Mikita**.

Fluorspar (fluorite) is chosen the state mineral. It is used in making fiberglass and welding rods, and a byproduct (fluorine) is added to toothpaste and drinking water to prevent tooth decay. Illinois is the **nation's leading producer**.

The National Guard is needed to quell a riot in Chicago when the police use Billy clubs on black youths, who illegally open a fire hydrant so they can play in the water.

Robert Coover publishes *The Origin of the Brunists*, a novel about coal mining life in Williamson County.

Martin Luther King Jr. leads a civil rights march in the Marquette Park section of Chicago. King and his followers were protesting segregated housing in that city's white ethnic enclave. During the march, angry whites hurled racial epithets and stones. One of them struck King in the head, causing him to fall to the ground on one knee. "I have seen many demonstrations in the South, but I have never seen anything so hostile and hateful as I've seen here today," King said about Chicago.

The Fab Four, also known as The Beatles, are in Chicago as part of a world tour. But controversy swirls around them because they had recently proclaimed that they were **more popular than Jesus**. Radio stations promised to quit playing their records and bonfire rallies were held in the Bible Belt to burn Beatle records. While in Chicago, the group held a press conference in the **Astor Towers Hotel** where John Lennon apologized for the remark. In 1970 the Beatles partnership was dissolved in a London Court. The Beatles greatly admired Buddy Holly and the Crickets, and took the name Beatles as a tribute to their rock and roll idol.

Illinois **leads the nation in exports**, ranked ahead of New York and California.

Tommy Agee of the Chicago White Sox is named Rookie of the Year.

The Chicago Bulls become a new franchise in the NBA.

Richard Speck, the loner with the "Born to Raise Hell" tattoo on his left arm, murders 8 nurses in a nursing school dormitory located on Chicago's south side. He is caught, not by Chicago's Finest, but by a doctor who recognized him when he was brought to a hospital after an attempted suicide. Speck's German father was from **Oquawka** and his Dutch-Irish mother was from **Kirkwood**. He had been staying with his sister in **Monmouth**. Speck was tried in Peoria and sentenced to die in the electric chair. He spent the rest of his life at Joliet Prison when a higher court rules that people opposed to the death penalty should not have been excluded from the jury.

Steve Sandler stars on the East St. Louis High football and basketball teams.

1967 – The John McAdams highway from **Alton to Grafton**, part of America's Great River Road, is completed. McAdams was with the *Alton Telegraph* and was the moving force behind the project.

Daisey Powell dies. She was a former court reporter with a flair for using colorful language and was a strong supporter of Paul Powell. She was routinely seen at **Big Boy's Tavern in Vienna** where she held court and kibitzed with Paul Powell supporters over several rounds of drinks. Her funeral service drew thousands of people and even included a visit from **Governor Otto Kerner**.

The **"Chicago Picasso"** is unveiled in a ceremony at Civic Center Plaza. It was modeled after Picasso's 42-inch original. The work stands 50 ft. high and weighs 162 tons. Picasso refused to accept a fee for his prototype and gave the design to the "people of Chicago."

Carl Sandburg, the guitar-playing troubadour poet with that famous face carved from granite, dies. His ashes are scattered near his boyhood home in **Galesburg** under Remembrance Rock, named for one of Sandburg's books.

Chicago is hit by a record blizzard – 23 inches over two days, January 26-27. Midway Airport reported drifts that were ten feet high.

Chicago's **Riverside Amusement Park** closes. Edward Grimm bought the property as an investment, then quickly closed the park and developed the land into a light-industrial site. DeVry Technical Institute is located on the site.

Chicago's McCormick Place is destroyed by fire.

The North Clark Street Garage is torn down in Chicago. It had been the site of the infamous St. Valentine's Day massacre back on February 14, 1928. Numerous people grabbed bricks and kept them as souvenirs.

Charlie Trippi, running back for the Chicago Cardinals, is elected to the football Hall of Fame at Canton.

The Chicago Crime Commission publishes a booklet that describes the major geographical areas of Mob control in Chicago: The Loop – Gus Alex; Near North Side - Joseph DiVarco, Joseph Arnold; Northwest Suburbs – Leonard Patrick, Ross Prio; Far West and West Suburbs – Sam Battaglia, William Dadano, Sam Giancana; South Side – Ralph Pierce; South and Southwest Suburbs – Frank LaPorte, Fiore Buccieri.

Chicago only manages to rank fourth as the nation's homicide capital, losing out to Atlanta, Washington D.C and Dallas.

1968 – In May, Governor Otto Kerner hands the reigns of government to Lieutenant Governor, Sam Shapiro, to accept an appointment as a federal Court of Appeals judge. After the riots and upheavals after the M.L. King assassination, Kerner heads a commission appointed by President Johnson to study the causes for the civil disorders. The Kerner Commission's main conclusion was that we as a nation were becoming increasingly divided and were "moving toward two societies, one black, one white – separate but unequal."

After the assassination of Dr. Martin Luther King, riots break out in Chicago, and after stores are looted and tenements burned to the ground, the National Guard is called in to restore order. About ten people were killed, 500 injured, 3,000, arrested and 162 buildings were burned. Mayor Daley gave police **"shoot to kill"** orders for anyone seen throwing a Molotov cocktail.

An earthquake from the New Madrid fault, registering 5.5 on the Richter scale, is felt as far north as **Alton**.

The State of Illinois celebrates its Sesquicentennial—150 years of statehood.

Radio announcer Paul Harvey

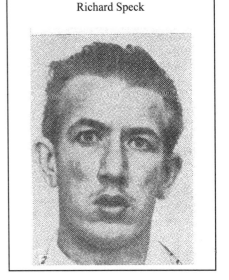

Richard Speck

Martin Luther King Jr. is assassinated in Memphis by **James Earl Ray**, a native of **Alton**.

Sam Shapiro and Paul Simon of **Troy** run for governor and lieutenant governor. Shapiro lost out to Republican Richard Ogilvie, but Simon pulled off an upset by winning the second spot. In a political oddity, the state now had a Republican governor and a Democrat for lieutenant governor.

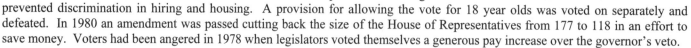

The new 1970 state constitution required that the governor and the lieutenant governor must be from the same party. Ogilvie even carried Madison County, a Democratic stronghold. Some say it was due, in part, to Illinois House **Speaker Ralph Smith** being an **Alton** resident. Ogilvie proposes legislative spending programs that steals the thunder from free-spending Democrats. This includes an expansive new highway program, moving mental patients to private nursing homes, and huge increases in aid to public education. He also names a special counsel to help land a new airport near **Columbia/Waterloo** to supplement Lambert Field in St. Louis. It is hoped that such a move will help revitalize poverty-stricken East St. Louis. In another move to help East St. Louis, a community college is established to focus on vocational and technical training. Most of the money is to come from the state since no East St. Louis taxes will be used to run the program. Some 30 years later the college will be closed by the state due to charges of inefficiency and mismanagement.

Another constitutional convention convenes, producing the state's fourth governing framework, adopted in 1970. The League of Women voters criticized the old document as being agrarian oriented and cited the need for a stronger governorship. The general feeling among voters was that the document was old and outdated. The new constitution included a section on ethical standards. An expanded Bill of Rights prevented discrimination in hiring and housing. A provision for allowing the vote for 18 year olds was voted on separately and defeated. In 1980 an amendment was passed cutting back the size of the House of Representatives from 177 to 118 in an effort to save money. Voters had been angered in 1978 when legislators voted themselves a generous pay increase over the governor's veto.

The Democratic national nominating convention is awarded to Chicago by Lyndon Johnson as a reward for Mayor Richard Daley's loyal support of the president's policies. Anti-war protestors flocked to the city and were allowed by authorities to sleep in Lincoln Park. There were 3 factions at the convention: Hubert Humphrey was the favorite of conservatives and moderates; Senator Eugene McCarthy, an early critic of the war, held a bloc of votes; a third bloc was committed to Robert Kennedy who had won most of the primaries but had been assassinated in June by Palestinian Sirhan, Sirhan.

Chicago police were on full alert due to prior threats to assassinate Mayor Daley and Hubert Humphrey. There were also threats to put **LSD in the city's water supply** and disrupt travel and communications. Daley wasn't about to allow "hippies" and "radicals" disrupt his town. He placed the city's 12,000 police on 12-hour shifts and called in 7,500 army troops and 6,000 national guardsmen. When the delegates voted down the anti-war plank of the party platform, **anarchy reigned in the streets**. What had earlier been a few isolated confrontations between police and protestors soon turned into total chaos. It all started when an American flag was taken down by protestors in Grant Park who then attempted to **raise a communist flag**. The police waded into the crowd and started using their nightsticks. Then they began lobbing tear gas. The crowd began chanting, "**The whole world is watching**." Radical leaflets promised seduction of delegate's wives and daughters. Demonstrators committed acts of public obscenity, public fornication, vandalism, and threw rocks and bottles at police and guardsmen. About 650 people were arrested.

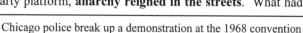

Chicago police break up a demonstration at the 1968 convention

At the convention, Senator Abraham Ribocoff denounced the "**Gestapo tactics**" of Chicago police. Daley was incensed when a government inquiry (The Walker (Dan) Report) termed it "**A POLICE RIOT**."

Liberals were outraged (conservatives ap-plauded) when Mayor Daley told police to "shoot to kill" arsonists and "shoot to maim" looters.

Bobby Seale and 7 others went on trial, charged with conspiracy. They became known as the "Chicago 8." Judge Julius Hoffman presided and Mayor Daley was subpoenaed as a defense witness. **Abbie Hoffman** proposed that he and Daley settle the matter with their fists but Daley merely laughed at him.

Bobby Seal of the **Black Panthers** acted up in court with behavior that was so obscene (Judge Hoffman was called a racist) and disrespectful, he was bound and gagged. Hoffman ended up sending him to prison for contempt of court and separated his trial from the rest. After that, the trial became known as the "Chicago 7." Defense called a long string of left-leaning celebrity witnesses, including Norman Mailer, "beat" poet Allen Ginsberg, Julian Bond, and Dick Gregory.

The seven on trial were **Jerry Rubin** and Abbie Hoffman of the YIPPIES (Youth International Party), Renie Davis and Tom Hayden of SDS (Students for a Democratic Society), David Dellinger, and two professors, John Froines and Lee Weiner. Hayden of course, later married actress **Jane Fonda**. The charge was conspiracy to riot.

Jerry Rubin (seated) L-R = A. Hoffman, John Froines, Lee Weiner, David Dellinger, Rennie Davis & Tom Hayden

William Kunstler argued in the lengthly and controversial 1969 trial that the defendants were merely exercising their right to free speech and that it was the unruly Chicago police who caused the riot. Displays of outrageous behavior included the draping of a North Vietnamese flag over the defense table. One day the defendants showed up for court **dressed in mock judicial robes**.

The trial of the "Chicago 8" began on September 24. **Abbie Hoffman**, Jerry Rubin, David Dellinger, **Tom Hayden** (he later married Jane Fonda), Rennie Davis, John Froines, Lee Weiner and Black Panther Bobby Seale were charged with violating the 1968 Anti-Riot Act – crossing state lines for the purpose of inciting a riot. The jury consisted of ten women and two men, with two female jurors being black.

The trial is full of high drama and high jinks as defendants were disruptive and disrespectful. Arlo Guthrie, Judy Collins, "Country Joe" McDonald, Pete Seeger, Alan Ginsberg and Timothy Leary were defense witnesses. On October 29 Judge Hoffman ordered Seale **bound and gagged**. On November 5 Seale was severed from the rest and sentenced to 4 years for contempt. Even defense attorney William Kunstler was given 4 years for contempt. But the Court of Appeals dismissed all contempt citations, saying contempt jail terms for more than 6 months required jury trials.

From October 8-11 a radical group known as the Weathermen went on a rampage in the Gold Coast section of Chicago, protesting the trial of the "Chicago 8" and yelling charges of racism. Before it was over, several Weathermen were shot and scores of police and citizens were injured. The damage was estimated to be over a million dollars.

The five-month trial ended with a not guilty verdict on the conspiracy charge but 5 were convicted of the lesser charge of crossing state lines to incite a riot. Their sentences were later overturned when an appeals court held that the judge had waited too long to impose sentences and erred in not allowing defense to question jurors about their values and beliefs.

To commemorate the Sesquicentennial of Illinois statehood, the original capitol building, now a museum and library, is restored.

The U.S. issues a postage stamp commemorating the statehood of Illinois; first day of issue is at **Shawneetown.**

This is the last year that gold pass cards are issued by the Illinois Central Railroad for 50-year veterans.

Ferguson Jenkins of the Chicago Cubs leads the league in strikeouts with 160.

East St. Louisan Barbara Teer founds the National Black Theater in Harlem, cited by President Reagan as one of 63 important cultural institutions in America.

Hamilton County experiences a powerful earthquake that registers 5.5 on the Richter scale.

The Illinois prison system is scandalized when a tabloid television program with Bill Curtiss shows a video of Richard Speck in Stateville Prison "living it up" with a fellow prisoner in a private room rather than a jail cell. Speck is shown using drugs and strips down to his skivvies, revealing a strange torso that has been injected with hormones to give him a more female appearance. Viewers are astounded when Speck brags about living the good life in prison.

George Patty, a Vancouver food company executive, submits the top bid to acquire a garage wall, complete with bullet scars. It was the backdrop for the St. Valentine's Day Massacre.

Dan Malkovich of **Benton** begins publishing a magazine, *Outdoor Illinois*. He is the father of actor John Malkovich.

Green County farmer Alec Helton leads archaeologist Stu Struever to a cornfield that for years had been yielding Indian arrowheads and pottery shards. A year later the Northwestern University professor returned with a group of students to excavate the site. They were astounded to discover that the Koster farm was one of the most important archaeological sites in the entire state, dating back about 5,000 years. Fourteen distinct layers or horizons were discovered. Digging at the Dickson Mound site ended years ago, and the gigantic hole was backfilled. A museum at **Kampsville** has become a favorite tourist attraction.

1969 – The state of Illinois, led by Governor Richard Ogilvie, enacts a law requiring citizens to pay a state income tax. The new **income tax** imposes a flat rate of 2.5% for individuals and 4% for corporations and was not graduated. Every single downstate congressman voted against senate bill 1150, but it still passed. This unpopular measure helps insure that Ogilvie will be a one-term governor.

A new state law declares marijuana to be a noxious weed.

Illinois leads the nation in the production of roses and gladioli.

An organization known as the **Cairo United Front** pressures Governor Ogilvie to appropriate funds to help the financially and racially troubled city. Ogilvie sends state troopers to the city and seeks to repeal an old state law allowing the formation of vigilante groups. It seems that one such organization, the White Hats, is formed in Cairo to counteract actions by various civil rights groups.

Writers Ed Pound and Ande Yakstis break a hot story for the *Alton Telegraph*. They say that Illinois Supreme Court justice **Ray Klingbiel of Moline** and Chief Justice **Roy Solfisburg** had each improperly accepted $2,000 worth of stock in a bank, in exchange for writing a favorable opinion for an officer of the bank. A board of inquiry called for the immediate resignation of the two justices, which was promptly forthcoming.

Taylor Pensoneau of **New Berlin** says that Southern Illinois newspapers are often derisively referred to as the **Pygmy Press**, but in this instance, the *Alton Telegraph* received accolades from all over the state.

Dickson Mound excavation at the Koster Dig

Senator **Everett Dirksen of Pekin** dies after surgery for lung cancer. He was known as the Republican senate minority leader and for the narration of a patriotic LP record called "Gallant Men." Governor Ogilvie appointed Ralph Smith to take his place but Smith was later defeated in the general election by Illinois Treasurer, Adlai Stevenson III.

Students protesting the Vietnam War **burn down Old Main** on the SIU campus at Carbondale. The National Guard was called out, but the rioting and tear gas got so bad that the school closed a month early for its summer hiatus.

Carbondale is involved in another controversy when SIUC officials authorize $900,000 for the construction of a new home for President **Delyte Morris**. The State Board of Higher Education begins cracking down on out-of-control university budgets. The controversy ends when W. Clement Stone donates $1 million in stock to cover the cost of construction.

Ground is broken for the construction of the National Accelerator Laboratory at **Batavia**, Illinois, to house the world's largest "atom smasher." With the completion of the project in 1972, Illinois became the **leading state in the field of nuclear power** and nuclear research facilities. The lab was financed by the AEC and is run by a consortium of 52 universities, including the U of I.

Leo Durocher's Chicago Cubs, led by future Hall of Famers Ernie Banks, Billy Williams and Ferguson Jenkins, blow a 9 and 1/2 game lead in August. The team inexplicably collapses, setting the stage for the Miracle Mets to win the pennant and pull off an upset victory over the Baltimore Orioles.

Chicago police make a surprise raid on the apartment of **Fred Hampton**, the leader of the city's Black Panthers. A gun-blazing 7 minute gun battle erupts and Hampton and Mark Clark are killed. Two Chicago policemen had been killed in an earlier shootout with the Black Panthers. Angry black leaders claimed the raid was simply a pretext for killing Hampton. This incident led to the emergence of a black voting block within the city that ultimately led to the election of Harold Washington as mayor.

The John Hancock Center is completed in Chicago.

At the urging of Governor Ogilvie, **Elza Brantly** of the State Police agrees to become Warden at Menard Prison in Chester.

SIUE's **Buckminster Fuller**, inventor of the geodesic dome, proposes to cover part of East St. Louis with a giant Plexiglas dome.

Judith Anne Ford of **Belvidere** becomes the first blonde in ten years to be named Miss America.

The convention to draw up a new Illinois state constitution convenes in December, containing 13 blacks and 15 women. It is the state's 6th convention and 4th constitution. This was the 6th of its kind in the state, the first dating back to the Kaskaskia convention of 1818. Meetings are held in the old Capitol Building. Voters go to the polls on December 15 to accept or reject it. Voters adopt a new state Constitution but decide to retain the old cumulative voting scheme that was first incorporated into the 1870 constitution. When voting for members of the House of Representatives, voters are given three votes to cast. He or she may use one for each of three candidates or cast all three votes for one candidate. This usually results in the minority party winning at least one of the three representative seats up for election. Illinois voters ratify the new state constitution in December of 1970.

Despite editorials from the **Belleville** *News-Democrat* calling for the rejection of the new state constitution, voters accept the document that now goes into effect. The newspaper did not like the new income tax provision, saying it gave carte blanche to unbridled taxation. Southern Illinois, as a whole, rejected the new constitution, but overwhelming approval by Cook County residents nullified their vote. Two other provisions that were voted on separately and defeated: abolition of the death penalty and lowering the voting age to 18.

The University of Chicago publishes the *Chicago Manual of Style*, to aid authors, editors and publishers.

Cub outfielder **Rick Monday becomes a national hero** and acquires the nickname "Mr. Red, White and Blue" when he prevents anti-Vietnam War protesters from setting fire to Old Glory at Dodger Stadium.

Paul Powell (*Bell. News-Democrat*)

1970 – **Merrill Ottwein**, who developed **Cottonwood Station** in west **Glen Carbon**, purchases the old **Three Mile House**, located 3 miles on the outskirts of Edwardsville. He planned to renovate it but got caught up with other projects. **Doug and Beverly Elliott** purchased the property, renovated it, and had it placed on the National Register of Historic Places. Then they turned it into a restaurant. There were reports of odd noises and strange occurrences, and rumor had it that the place was haunted. In 1980 radio personality **Jim White** secured permission to broadcast a Halloween program from the Three Mile House. The building was destroyed by fire in 1985.

On February 20, five members of the **Chicago 7** were sentenced. Froines and Weiner were found not guilty. The other 5 were found not guilty of conspiracy but guilty of crossing state lines with intent to incite a riot. Defendants were allowed to make statements before sentences were imposed. Rubin offered the Judge a copy of his book, *Do It*. Hoffman recommended that the judge lighten up and try some LSD. Davis promised to convert the prosecutor's children to the radical cause when he got out. The 5 were sentenced to 5 years in prison and fined $5,000 each.

Dignitaries from all over the state flock to **Vienna** to pay their respects to the late Paul Powell, who died October 10. The most important person at the funeral was Chicago mayor, **Richard Daley**. In his Springfield hotel room, associates found $800,000 in cash in shoeboxes. Powell's estate was estimated at $2.85 million, including racetrack stock. The state sued for recovery, arguing that the money came from bribes. An out-of-court settlement awarded the state $1.6 million.

The state of Illinois celebrates its first "Earth Day" in April.

Bellevillian Alan Dixon, Minority Whip in the Illinois Senate, is elected state treasurer, occupying the position vacated by Adlai Stevenson III (Democrat) who became the U.S. Senator.

The center of U.S. population is now located on the Lawrence Friederich farm, between **Mascoutah and New Menphis**. Every ten years it moves about 42 miles west and seven miles south. In 1980 it was near Desoto, Missouri (Jefferson County) and in 2000 it was located in Phelps County near **Rolla, Missouri**. Back in 1790 when the first census was taken, the center of population was near Baltimore, Maryland.

The population of Illinois reaches 11,113,976.

Rail passenger service declines so much all over the nation that President Nixon signs into law a bill creating Railpax, a federally subsidized passenger service. It would evolve into Amtrak.

The Illinois Environmental Protection Act sets new standards to prevent air and water pollution.

George Halas becomes president of the National Football Conference of the NFL. Brian Piccolo, Bears' running back, dies from cancer and is lionized in the film *Brian's Song*.

Ernie Banks hits his 500th home run, ensuring his enshrinement in the Hall of Fame.

1971 - **Monks Mound** on Route 40, in the State Park area of **Collinsville**, is the site of a strange gathering of about 1,000 people who came from all over the world to promote peace and harmony on Earth. Sort of a strange choice for a place where human sacrifice was once practiced. Apparently the people who promoted the event believed the area to be a sacred place.

Former governor **Otto Kerner** is indicted and sent to jail for tax evasion and on federal charges stemming from illicit transactions involving racing stock.

Seven men in an underground fluorspar mine near **Golconda** die from exposure to hydrogen sulfide gas. This leads to the formation of a state mine rescue station at **Elizabethtown.**

Mining fluorspar, circa 1925 (author's collection)

The new Religious Center opens at SIUE with its main feature consisting of a geodesic dome designed by Buckminster Fuller, the dome's inventor.

A strike by Illinois coal miners reduces the state's bituminous output by 13 percent.

Chicago's **Union Stockyards**, after 106 years of operation, ceases operation. Chicago lost out to places like Kansas City, Missouri, which was closer to the cattle-raising country.

Paul Simon of Troy/Makanda

1972 - Chicago lawyer **Dan Walker** accomplishes the impossible. He bucks Richard Daley's political machine and wins the governorship of Illinois. In doing so, he beat the favorite for the nomination, **Paul Simon of Troy**, who was already Lieutenant Governor of the state, but linked with the Daley machine in Chicago. Following on the heels of the Powell scandal, Walker, an iconoclast independent, promises to put an end to "racetrack politics" in Illinois.

Polls showed Simon had been the overwhelming favorite to defeat incumbent governor, Richard Ogilvie. Author Taylor Pensoneau says the contest was called the Bow Tie v. Red Bandanna Dan. Simon was given his nickname by Bill Ryan, a reporter with the *Alton Telegraph*. Walker's running mate was **Carbondale Mayor Neal Eckert**, a member of the Eckert Farms family in south **Belleville**.

Walker's populist candidacy, a grass roots four month walking trek of 1,197 miles, started in 1971 at **Brookport**. Walker also visited **Golconda, Elizabethtown, Old Shawneetown**, and moved north up to SIUE at **Edwardsville**. His campaign was managed by **Charles and Sue Kolker**, white liberals who lived in East St. Louis and helped **James Williams** become the city's first black mayor. After Williams' upset win, Charles became the city's lawyer.

But Walker would soon go from the Governor's mansion, the pinnacle of success, to the nadir of 17 months in a Minnesota prison. He was defeated for a second term and became involved in some business dealings that caused his ruin. After being noted for an austere lifestyle while governor, he divorced his wife of 30 years, married a younger woman, and began to live life in the fast lane. In the end, Walker pleaded guilty to perjury and fraudulent conduct (bilking a savings and loan) and was sentenced to **seven years in prison** in 1987.

Some blamed his failure to win a second term on his perceived lack of humor and his unwillingness to compromise. In later years Walker said that the other politicians never understood that he was a genius, IQ-wise.

Big Earl Shelton returns to **Fairfield** for a visit and tells the Wayne County *Press* that he has been living in Jacksonville, Florida.

Illinoisan Rock Hudson stars in TV series "McMillan and Wife," co-starring Susan St. James. He portrays a San Francisco police commissioner, and the popular program lasts 6 years.

Ferguson Jenkins of the Cubs wins the Cy Young award.

Collinsville High School's new Greenwood Campus opens. It is on a site that was originally purchased for the construction of a new JFK Hospital, but the idea folded in 1967 due to lack of financial support.

Governor Ogilvie signs a bill exempting pension plan payments for seniors from the state income tax.

Governor Ogilvie and Senator Charles Percy participate in a "**Superman Day**" ceremony in **Metropolis**.

The 7th Circuit Court of Appeals **reverses the convictions of the Chicago 7**. This was based on the discovery that the FBI had bugged the offices of the defense attorneys during the trial. The court was also critical of Judge Hoffman's refusal to allow defense question potential jurors about their cultural biases.

Illinois Central Industries continues its diversification and acquires Midas Mufflers and Pepsi Cola General Bottlers of Chicago. Diversification now accounts for 1/5 of all Illinois Central Railroad revenue.

Forty-five persons are killed in an Illinois Central train accident in Chicago.

After 79 years of service, the last "All aboard!" call is given for passenger service at Chicago's Central Station.

Illinois Central begins using continuous welded rail, and by this date more than 1,200 miles of it have replaced the old clickety-clack rails. It also undergoes a name change, Illinois Central Gulf, when it merges with the Gulf, Mobile and Ohio. The railroad also discards the diamond logo in favor of the Big I.

A United Airlines 737 crashes near Midway in Chicago on December 8. Dorothy Hunt, the wife of Watergate burglar E. Howard Hunt, was one of the 45 people killed. Authorities found $10,000 in her purse, giving rise to all sorts of conspiracy theories. Most likely, the money was simply a payoff for services performed by her husband.

An elephant by the name of Norma Jean is killed by lightning. She belonged to the Clark and Walters Circus and had been chained to a tall tree in **Oquawka** when a thunderstorm broke. Unable to move the 6,500-pound carcass, Norma Jean was buried on the spot. A memorial topped by an elephant statue marks her burial site near 5th and Mercer. In 1988 John Behnke of SIU made a 15- minute documentary film entitled *Norma Jean*.

The state of Illinois constructs a dam and forms Lake Kincaid for the purpose of supplying water to the Murphysboro region.

Chicago White Sox slugger Dick Allen blasts 37 homers, setting a club record, tied by Carlton Fiske in 1985.

The member of the McDaniel family of **White County** reports seeing a "bigfoot" type creature that he labels a "whangdoodle." He reportedly fired a shotgun at the creature, but it was unaffected and scampered away.

156

1973 - A movie about the life of **Charlie Birger** is made, *Bad Charleston Charlie*, glamorizing his life as a twenties gangster.

Ridgway High wins the state basketball championship in their division.

Harry A. Blackmun, born in **Nashville**, Illinois, is part of the Supreme Court majority opinion in Roe v. Wade, giving women legal access to abortions.

The Sears Tower, the **world's tallest building** is completed at 1,454 feet. By 2002 it was no longer the tallest building in the world. However, it is still the tallest building in North America. The Scars Tower is so big, it was given its own zip code of 60606. A skydeck is located on the 103rd floor. Like the stainless steel arch at St. Louis, the Tower sways back and forth in the wind about 7 inches.

Richard Crowe begins a Supernatural Tour business in Chicago. The two-hour adventure covers haunted sites and things like the curse of "Cap" Streeter, ghost ships on Lake Michigan, the ghost of the water tower, "cement shoes" during Prohibition, and the mysterious Lake Michigan Triangle.

The last commercial lead mine in **Jo Daviess County** closes down for good.

Illinois school children select the white oak as the state tree because it grows in every Illinois county and is a durable hardwood. The tree grows to a height of about 100 feet.

Hall of Famer Stan Mikita of the Blackhawks helps design a helmet that will eventually become standard equipment for all players.

Israel is attacked in October by the combined forces of Egypt, Syria, Jordan, and Iraq, and is nearly defeated in the Yom Kippur War due to a lack of ammunition, planes, and tanks. As **East St. Louisan** Walter Boyne points out in *The Two O'clock War*, the U.S. resupplied Israel with a tremendous airlift, code named Operation Nickel Grass. The coordination point for this massive airlift is Scott Air Base, located east-northeast of **Belleville** near **Mascoutah**. Named for Corporal Frank Scott, the first enlisted man killed in a flying accident, the base is the headquarters for MAC (Military Airlift Command). When the Soviets threatened to intervene with troops, the world teetered on the brink of nuclear war as the U.S. raised its military readiness status from DefCon 4 to DefCon 3. A furious counterattack resulted in an Israeli triumph that was ended by an uneasy truce.

A frightened couple report seeing a hairy monster in Riverside Park in **Murphysboro**. In the weeks that follow, several other residents phone in creature sightings. Reporters investigated the story and created the legend of the Big Muddy Monster.

1974 – Ground is broken for the construction of a new hospital in **Maryville**, on Route 162. It was named for Oliver Anderson, the man who donated the largest sum of money for its construction.

Marc Chagall is on hand when his "Four Seasons" mosaic was unveiled in a ceremony at the First National Plaza at Dearborn and Monroe Streets. It is 70 ft. long by 14 ft. high by 10 ft. wide and was nicknamed "the boxcar mosaic." Privately funded, it was Chagall's gift to the city.

The clubhouse and grandstand are destroyed in a fire at Fairmount Park in **Collinsville**. While the old facility is rebuilt, races are held for two years at Cahokia Downs on the edge of East St. Louis on Route 15.

Stan Hitchcock of **Nashville** writes "The Ballad of Dan Walker."

Paul Simon, now a resident of Little Egypt, is elected to the U.S. Congress.

David McIntosh publishes *Folk Songs* and *Singing Games of the Illinois Ozarks*.

Fort Massac Encampment Days, now an annual event in October, is held for the first time.

The four-lane Interstate 24 Bridge that crosses the Ohio River into Kentucky opens.

A Miners Memorial is erected and dedicated in **Zeigler**. It features a statue of a miner holding a pick.

Nate Thurmond of the Chicago Bulls sets an NBA record of a **quadruple double** in a game against Atlanta. He had 22 points, 14 rebounds, 13 assists, and 12 blocked shots.

The Eads Bridge at East St. Louis is no longer used for rail traffic.

Seventy-Sixer star, Doug Collins of Benton

1975 - **Otto Kerner**, former governor of Illinois, is released from a prison in Lexington, Kentucky, after serving seven months. He won parole due to poor health. Kerner had been indicted for conspiracy, bribery, mail fraud, tax evasion and perjury in connection with racetrack owners in Illinois.

Cicero deputy liquor commissioner **Robert Mengler** pleads guilty to taking payoffs in return for granting liquor licenses. Cicero has about 190 liquor serving establishments.

The Illinois IHSA initiates the practice of holding a state tournament for high school girl's basketball.

The Chicago Bears select running back Walter Payton in the college draft.

Kevin Luthi of **DuQuoin** reports seeing a 5-foot tall kangaroo jumping around in his cornfield.

LaRue Swamp, on the western edge of Pine Hills, is designated a National Heritage Landmark. The ecological miracle was formed thousands of years ago when it was the alluvial plain of the Mississippi and Big Muddy rivers. The last glacial period, called the Liman Advance, pushed the rivers away to their present beds. For several weeks on the spring and fall, the access road is closed to traffic to enable snakes and reptiles to migrate without loss of life. This unusual event has been reported in Ripley's "Believe It Or Not."

1976 – SIUC basketball team, at one point in the season, climbs to 18th in the national rankings in NCAA Division I.

East St. Louisan Julie Menendez makes history by becoming the first person to coach two Olympic sports. He is the coach of the U.S. soccer team, and back in 1960 he coached Cassius Clay (M. Ali) to a gold medal in boxing at Rome.

Republican Jim Thompson defeats Democrat Michael Howlett. Interestingly, Howlett promised not to raise taxes during his term if elected. Thompson only serves a two year term because a new law changed the gubernatorial election to an "off election year" (non-presidential) so voters could concentrate on state races. He is then elected to three more terms, the only person to do so. He was an exceptional campaigner and was seen as a doer and a builder. His negatives include a reversion to patronage politics (giving jobs to friends and supporters) and pork barrel spending which by 2002 had gotten out of hand. His pluses included support for county and state fairs, road building, prison expansion, more health care facilities and 14 scandal-free years of Illinois politics (quite an achievement).

During the campaign he married **Jayne Carr**, an attorney who had been a former student of his at Northwestern, and their daughter Samantha was the first in 72 years to be born to a governor occupying the governor's mansion.

Millions of Illinoisans get inoculated against the swine flu, but the dreaded infection never materializes.

Ronald Reagan challenges President Gerald Ford for the nomination of the Republican Party. He loses to Ford in the end, but there was a stunning rumor going around that Reagan would be the nominee, and Ford might be his running mate.

Milton Friedman of the University of Chicago wins the Nobel Prize for economics. His theories will be used during the Reagan years to develop supply-side or trickle down economics.

1977 - Due to rising crop prices and the increasing value of farmland, many farmers borrow large sums of money at high interest rates to increase the size of their farms to enable them to better compete with the large producers.

The state legislature is tied up 6 weeks as a record 186 roll calls are taken in an effort to choose an Illinois senate president.

During the winter of 1977-78 the state is hit by its worst blizzard ever, causing nearly a billion dollars in damages.

Route 66 in the state is completely replaced by Interstate 55, making it possible to drive from Chicago to St. Louis without any stops. Much of the road is now delegated to being a frontage road for the interstate. On Jan. 17th city employee Gus Schultz took down the "End of Route 66" sign in Chicago.

Governor Thompson rein-states a new and improved death penalty law for 16 categories of murder.

The skeleton of a woolly mammoth of the Pleistocene epoch (13,000 years ago) is

Annex Motel/Café in Litchfield, a Route 66 landmark

unearthed at the Blackwell Forest Preserve, east of **Batavia**. It is now housed in **Oak Brook's** Fullersburg Woods Environmental Education Center.

1978 – Kevin Stallings, a 6-6 all-star guard for the **Collinsville Kahoks**, leads the Midwest Junior College Athletic Association in scoring and assists. The former Kahok All-American averaged 20 points a game for Belleville Area College Dutchmen.

Galesburg celebrates the centennial of **Carl Sandburg's** birth. The U.S. government issues a 13-cent stamp to commemorate the event, and folk singer **Burl Ives** comes to town and leads a group rendition of the song, "Goober Peas" (peanuts). Sandburg once called Ives the greatest ballad singer of all time.

Part of the movie *Stingray*, starring Mark Hamill of *Star Wars* fame, is filmed in **Edwardsville**.

A man is killed when he successfully parachutes from a plane and successfully lands on top of the arch, then loses his balance and falls off.

The popular **Mississippi River Festival** comes to a close at SIUE. MRF was held at the outdoor grass "natural amphitheater," on the north end of the campus, starting in the late 1960s. It was the brainchild of President John Rendleman. MRF included per-formers such as Bob Hope, Bill Cosby, the King Family, Arlo Guthrie, Iron Butterfly, Joan Baez, Joni Mitchell, Bob Dylan, Bette Middler, Barry Manilow, and others. Its largest crowd was a 1971 performance by The Who that drew 30,000 people. Excessive amounts of trash, injuries from fights, and illegal substance abuse by patrons helped bring the era to an end.

Luke Grisholm writes an article for Official UFO Magazine titled, "The Night an American Town Died of Fright," the story of a **UFO attack on Chester**, Illinois.

Frank Collin, head of the National Socialist Party of America, holds a parade in Skokie, after more than a year of heated controversy by those who objected to his beliefs. His First Amendment free speech issue was supported by the ACLU and the U.S. Supreme Court. The parade is finally held, although the numbers were small. A TV movie called *Skokie*, starring Danny Kaye as a Holocaust survivor, was made shortly thereafter.

The Chicago *Daily News*, after 103 years of publication, ceases publication due to declining circulation.

Hannah Gray becomes president of the University of Chicago, the **first female president of a major university**.

Mayor Jane Byrne of Chicago

1979 - **Edwardsville's** LeClaire area was placed on the National Register of Historic Places in 1979. N.O. Nelson built a company town there that was inspected by **Nellie Bly**, the famous reporter for the New York World in 1894. She described it in glowing terms.

A snowstorm determines the next mayor of Chicago. Jane Byrne defeats incumbent Michael Bilandic (serving out the remaining term of Mayor Daley) to become Chicago's first woman mayor. Chicago was hit by a huge snowstorm that paralyzed the city. When investigations were made into the inefficiency of the snow removal it was discovered that favoritism, graft and nepotism had been involved in the awarding of snow removal contracts. Ironically, Byrne had been a Daley appointee until Bilandic fired her. The vitriolic Byrne was limited to one term due to constant controversy during her tenure.

Donald McHenry of **East St. Louis** is sworn in as the 14th and youngest person to head the U.S. delegation to the United Nations. He replaced the controversial Andrew Young who had resigned in the wake of a controversy engendered by his unauthorized contact with the Palestinian Liberation Organization.

The left engine falls off a DC-10 airplane **killing 275 people at O'Hare** Airport, the world's busiest. It is the nation's worst air disaster up to that time. Lindsay Wagner, better known as the Bionic Woman, was supposed to be on that flight but felt uneasy about it and switched plans at the last minute.

White Sox owner **Bill Veech** stages an anti-disco music promotion at a doubleheader. Radio personality Steve Dahl was hired to destroy disco records between games as part of the promotion. Fans who brought disco records were admitted for 98 cents. 59,000 fans crammed the ballpark to capacity, and another 15,000 milled around outside. After the first crate of records was destroyed, fans stormed onto the field and went berserk, tearing up sod and flinging records Frisbee fashion. The second game had to be cancelled and forfeited. Howard Cosell blamed announcer Harry Caray for the circus-like atmosphere that led to the riot.

Pope John Paul II visits Chicago and holds a mass in Grant Park, attended by 200,000.

Bruce Sutter of the Cubs wins the Cy Young pitching award.

The Chicago Bulls lose a flip of the coin and a chance to draft Magic Johnson. They are forced to settle for David Greenwood instead.

1980 - Alan Dixon, a **Belleville** attorney who is Secretary of State, wins the election and becomes a U.S. Senator. He will serve two terms and then be replaced by **Carol Mosley-Braun** of Chicago.

The Chicago City Ballet is established.

Illinois population levels off for the first time in its history, showing 11,427,414, a gain of little more than 300,000 from the last census. The census shows a huge loss of white population, fleeing the troubled cities and moving to the suburbs in what becomes known as white flight. Nowhere is this more dramatic than in the city of East St. Louis. Nearly half of the 70 largest cities in the state during this decade lost population.

The prices for farm products drop to record lows with corn bringing as little as two dollars a bushel. Due to these depressed prices, there are record numbers of farm foreclosures by banks.

Ronald Reagan

Evanston-born Elizabeth McGovern wins Best Supporting Actress Oscar for her role in *Ordinary People*.

Tampico-born, **Dixon**-reared Ronald Reagan is elected President of the U.S. He is the first to be born in the state of Illinois. Prior to his election he was a sports broadcaster in Iowa, successful actor, President of the Screen Actor's Guild and two-term governor of California.

Reagan wins two terms and is one of our most popular (and, like F.D.R – hated) presidents. His manner of speaking, his humor, his optimism, and his vision for America, endeared him to many. His hard line with the Soviet Union (he called them the Evil Empire) and his "Mr. Gorbachev, tear down this (Berlin) wall" speech which played no small role in the collapse of the Soviet Union in 1989.

Illinois school children vote to make the white-tailed deer the state animal. The bluegill will become the state fish.

Kellen Winslow of East St. Louis breaks Mike Ditka's record for career catches by a tight end.

The Chicago *Tribune* buys the Cubs and features them nationally on WGN, their television superstation.

John Wayne Gacy, a resident of **Des Plaines**, is convicted of murdering 30 boys and young men and then burying them in the crawl space of his home. Gacy was known for dressing up as a clown and entertaining the neighborhood children. He spent his next years at Menard Prison in **Chester** and was given a lethal injection at Joliet in 1994.

Killer Clown John Wayne Gacy

1981 - Coach Arthur Marshall's **East St. Louis** Lincoln Tigers win 4 consecutive state titles in track in 1981, '82 '83, '84.

Cicero is said to be part of the territory controlled by Joseph Ferriola, whose nephew is Harry Aleman.

East St. Louis jazz musician **Miles Davis marries actress Cicely Tyson** at Bill Cosby's house on Thanksgiving Day. Andrew Young performs the marriage ceremony.

A fifteen-cent postage stamp honoring Everett Dirksen is issued with a first day cover at **Pekin**.

On May 25, Daniel Goodwin, wearing a Spiderman costume fitted with suction cups, climbs the outside of the Sears Tower, a feat that takes over 7 hours. In November he climbs the Hancock Tower, despite attempts to knock him off with hose sprays from the fire department.

The Chicago Sting defeat the New York Cosmos in overtime to win the National American League Soccer Championship.

The Chain of Rocks Bridge, the old terminus of Route 66 in Illinois, no longer used for traffic, is the setting for the final scene in Kurt Russell's *Escape From New York*.

1982 – A tornado hits the north end of **Edwardsville** and does considerable property damage, but there is no loss of life. Another tornado hits **Marion**, killing ten people.

Bennie Lewis, coach of the **East St. Louis** Lincoln Tigers, wins the state championship in basketball. He will win an unprecedented three more in 1987, '88, and '89.

Cahokia Mounds becomes the tenth site in the U.S. to be listed by UNESCO as a place of "universal value to mankind."

Joseph Cardinal Bernardin is appointed Archbishop of Chicago.

Increased foreign competition and production problems cause the Caterpillar Tractor Company to lose $182 million, its first losses since the depression years of the 1930s.

In a devastating economic blow to the city, **Hiram Walker distillery leaves Peoria** and relocates in Fort Smith, Arkansas.

Adlai Stevenson III challenges Republican James Thompson in the governor's race and loses by about 5,000 votes, one of the smallest margins ever.

Thirty-four states ratify the Equal Rights Amendment to the Constitution passed by the U.S. Congress in 1972, but thirty-eight are required to meet the ¾ requirement of the U.S. Constitution. Illinois

Chain of Rocks Bridge near Granite City/Mitchell

was one of 16 states that failed to ratify, and only one of two northern states (Utah). The amendment dies. Constitutionally, proposed amendments have a 7-year life span, but congress gave ERA a three-year extension. Thanks largely to Phyllis Schlafly of **Alton** and her Eagle Forum, it doesn't get ratified. In the final days, 7 Illinois women went on a 37-day hunger strike, and numerous women chained themselves to railings in the state capitol. Ironically, the state constitution already guaranteed women equal rights.

Illinois plays Alabama in the Liberty Bowl and loses by a score of 21-15.

Jim McMahon, the quarterback at BYU who broke Danny White's (Dallas Cowboys) record for passing efficiency, is selected by the Bears in the draft.

Harry Caray, longtime broadcaster for the St. Louis Cardinals (he left in 1969), joins the Cub broadcast team after stints with the Oakland A's and the White Sox.

A Chicago madman laces several bottles of Extra-Strength Tylenol with cyanide. Seven victims die within a span of 48 hours. James Lewis was sentenced to 10 years in prison for trying to extort money from Johnson & Johnson, the makers of Tylenol. Johnson & Johnson had to recall $100 million worth of Tylenol. James admitted the extortion scheme but denied being responsible for the killings. The perpetrator is never caught and a $100,000 reward for the **Tylenol murders** is still offered.

1983 – **Harold Washington** wins 51 percent of the vote and becomes the first black mayor of Chicago. At the time, Chicago was about 50 percent black and 50 percent white. Councilman Edward Vrdolyak forms a coalition of 29 aldermen and stages a bitter fight to block Washington's appointments and agenda. Washington ran as an independent Democrat and did not have the backing of the political machine. He wanted to serve five successive terms, but he died of a heart attack before finishing out his first term. A controversy of sorts was created after his death when nine aldermen voted to remove an unflattering artistic depiction of Harold Washington from an art museum that was on display. It was in the Art Institute and titled "Mirth and Girth" and depicted Washington in women's underwear, stemming from the rumor that's how he was dressed when he suffered his fatal heart attack.

Harold Washington's inauguration

The FBI conducts a sting operation called **Operation Greylord** to nab corrupt judges, lawyers and officials in the Cook County judicial system. Ultimately, nearly 100 people were indicted, including 17 judges, 15 of whom were convicted, including Judges Wayne Olson and Harold LeFevour.

East St. Louisan Johnny Poe, of the New Orleans Saints, leads the NFL in interceptions.

A debt crisis grips Illinois farm country. Due to falling crop and land prices, farmers find themselves saddled with huge debts. Farm debt rose from $5.1 billion in 1977 to $11.3 billion. Banks foreclose on numerous farms that are sold by auction at bargain prices. Families are bitter about losing farms that had been in the family for over 100 years.

The **University of Chicago** has 7 Nobel Prize laureates on its faculty, and 53 others had either taught or studied there.

A 20-cent U.S.-Germany commemorative stamp is issued by the U.S. Post Office at **Germantown**.

The Illinois legislature passes a no-fault divorce law.

The University of Illinois' football team is undefeated in the Big Ten Conference with a 10-2 record.

Mike Singletary plays his rookie season for the Bears at middle linebacker, but he is not a starter.

Thomas Brimberry, who built a multi-million dollar house in a middle-class **Granite City** neighborhood, is convicted at Alton of embezzling $16 million from Stix and Company brokerage in St. Louis. Brimberry's wife is later sent to prison for 33 months. She was caught in a sting operation in **Collinsville** trying to sell expensive jewelry that was supposed to have been turned over to the IRS to settle their tax debt.

1984 – A scene in *American Flyer*, starring Kevin Kostner, a movie about bicycle racing, shows the St. Louis Arch and the Veterans/Martin Luther King Bridge in East St. Louis.

East St. Louisan Al Joyner, brother to Jackie Joyner, wins Olympic gold in the triple jump at Los Angeles.

Dr. John Dale Cavaness, a prominent southern Illinois physician and surgeon, is arrested in St. Louis. He is charged with the murder of his son (Sean) in St. Louis County. After failing a polygraph test authorities finally concluded that the doctor, a perfectionist who was heavily into bovine genetic engineering, killed his two sons because they just didn't measure up. It was a shocking case of filicide, a father killing his own offspring, like thinning a herd of cattle.

In his 1985 trial, he claimed to be innocent. The trial was held in Clayton at the St. Louis County Courthouse. **Steve Goldman** prosecuted the case but was not allowed to tell the jury that another son, Mark, had been shot to death in the woods of Little Egypt seven years earlier. The jury found Cavaness guilty as charged and recommended the death penalty. The Dr.'s southern Illinois supporters thought the trial was a travesty and figured the conviction would be overturned on appeal. On November 17, 1986, a prison guard found Cavaness hanging in his cell from an electrical cord. It was a case that had polarized **Eldorado** and **Harrisburg** between those who were sure he was innocent and those who thought he was guilty as sin.

His funeral was held in the First Presbyterian Church in Eldorado, officiated by Reverend Langham.

Paul Simon wins election to the United States Senate.

The first Bald Knob Passion Play at Alto Pass is given.

The Chicago Cubs win the divisional championship, giving rise to a fear that they might lose their label of Lovable Losers. The apprehension is short-lived when they are defeated in the National League championship series.

Illinois population stagnates, growing a miniscule 0.7 percent since 1980.

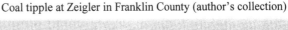

Coal tipple at Zeigler in Franklin County (author's collection)

Forty-four percent of Illinois coal production at this time is through strip mining. Eagle mines in **Gallatin County** are the only ones to ship coal by barges. The rest use railroads.

Fluorspar, the state mineral of which Illinois once produced 70 percent of the national total, is used as a flux in the steel industry. Illinois production begins to suffer because of cheaper material being shipped in from Mexico.

Fortune 500 publishes its annual list, and Illinois has 52 companies on it. Most of them are located in Chicago.

The Illinois-Michigan Canal, abandoned for more than 50 years, is converted into a 60-mile long park between **LaSalle** and **Joliet**, the first such park in the nation.

The Chicago Sting wins the North American Soccer League championship, defeating the Toronto Blizzard.

President Reagan visits his boyhood home in **Dixon** to celebrate his birthday on February 6.

Illinois loses to UCLA in the Rose Bowl by a score of 45-9.

Walter Peyton of the Bears breaks Jim Brown's career rushing mark of 12,312 yards. Rick Sutcliffe of the Cubs wins the Cy Young pitching award.

The Chicago White Sox play the longest game in American League history, defeating the Milwaukee Brewers 5-4 in 25 innings on a homer by Harold Baines.

Michael Jordan makes his debut at guard for the Chicago Bulls. His early nickname is Air-atola, a takeoff from the Ayatollah of Iran. It later becomes **Air Jordan**. Although not selected first in the draft, he wins the Rookie of the Year award in the NBA.

Steve Dahl and Gary Meyer of radio WLUP Chicago set the town on its ear with their discussion format antics. Larry Lujack of WLS was the highest paid personality during the 70s and 80s.

1985 –A tornado hits **Litchfield** on Palm Sunday and destroys several livestock belonging to Charlie Rodewald.

Architect Helmut Jahn unveils his colossal postmodern State of Illinois Center in the Chicago Loop. One critic calls it " a chunk wedge of little grace or elegance." Built with government funds, the structure cost twice the budgeted amount and was beset with air conditioning problems. In 1992 the General Assembly voted to rename it the James Thompson Center, for the governor who chose the radical design over a half dozen more conservative ones. It was quickly dubbed "Starship Chicago." The building has numerous restaurants and contains a complex of offices for government workers.

The Chicago Sanitary District builds **Deep Tunnel**, a tubular storm sewer 130 miles long. It is the third largest project of its kind in the world. Not only did the project protect homes and businesses from flooding, it lowered pollution in Lake Michigan.

The department of agriculture estimates that each acre of Illinois farmland loses one ton of soil each year due to erosion.

The average farm size at this time is about 250 acres. The definition of a farm is a parcel of land that produces at least $1,000 worth of agricultural products annually.

Large retailing firms headquartered in Chicago at this time include Jewel Tea (started in 1899 by Frank Skiff), Sears, Montgomery Ward, McDonalds, Walgreens, National Tea, and Marshall Field.

James Thompson Center in Chicago (author's collection)

East St. Louis High wins the state championship in football, defeating a Chicago team by the score of 46-0. Led by **Bryan Cox and Arthur Sargent**, they are also named **national champions**. Cox later played for the Chicago Bears and won a Super Bowl ring with the Patriots in 2002.

Mike Ditka's Chicago Bears, with Mike Singletary, Jim McMahon, Walter Payton, and William "the Refrigerator "Perry go 15-1 and win the Super Bowl against the New England Patriots.

Winnetka actor Rock Hudson, a closet homosexual, is the first big name actor to die from AIDS.

The most famous highway in America, Route 66, is decertified in a brief ceremony.

Governor Thompson signs a law requiring automobile drivers to wear seat belts.

McDonald's fast food franchise owner Ray Kroc dies. His estate is valued at $500 million. McDonalds passes Sears as the largest retail real estate owner in the country.

Oprah Winfrey begins her television career in Chicago. She quickly becomes one of the richest women in America and one of the most influential.

White Sox knuckleball pitcher Hoyt Wilhelm is inducted into the Hall of Fame.

1986 – Robert Hasting's *A Penny's Worth of Minced Ham*: *Another Look at the Great Depression*, and Charles Caraway's *Foothold on a Hillside*: *Memories of a Southern Illinoisan*, are published by SIU Press in Carbondale. Of the two books, critics generally agree that Caraway's book has more humor and gives a more realistic depiction of the struggles in the era of the Great Depression.

Frank Maltese, Cicero's assessor, goes to prison for gambling conspiracy charges. He admits to having links with the Ernest "Rocco" Infelice crime family.

Adlai Stevenson III, former U.S. Senator, challenges Republican Jim Thompson for the governorship and loses. Thompson announced an ambitious program called Build Illinois where $2.3 billion is earmarked for subsidized housing projects and road improvements.

Thanks to generous incentives, Mitsubishi and Chrysler announce a 50-50 deal to build an auto plant at **Bloomington/Normal**. Despite the fact that the Mitsubushi Eclipse and the Plymouth Laser are basically the same car and have the same engine, consumers in the state buy the Eclipse and neglect the Laser which eventually goes out of production. $40 million in state funds are earmarked **to train 2,500 workers how to read** for the plant.

Harold Washington tries to muster support for a 1992 World's Fair in Chicago, but there is little enthusiasm since political correctness has diminished the popularity of Columbus.

A live rock concert for Farm Aid is staged by **Willie Nelson** at Memorial Stadium in Champaign. An estimated $9 million was raised. The concert also helped publicize farmers' financial woes.

After 17,000 cases and 5 five deaths from salmonella poisoning, Governor Thompson fires the state public health director. The outbreak was traced to spoiled milk produced at the Jewel Food Stores' dairy in **Melrose Park**.

Cathleen Webb announces on national television that she had falsely accused Gary Dotson, her boyfriend, of rape in 1977. But state authorities did not believe her. Governor Thompson commutes his sentence to time served but does not issue a pardon.

The U.S. Post Office issues a $2 stamp honoring William Jennings Bryan in the Great Americans Series issued at **Salem**.

Studs Terkle

Chicagoan Studs Terkle's *The Good War* wins the Pulitzer Prize.

Tom Seaver of the Chicago White Sox records his last career win, number 311.

The East St. Louis Housing Authority is taken over by HUD due to criminal mismanagement.

1987 - Gary Gaetti of **Centralia** wins a World Championship ring when the Minnesota Twins defeat the St. Louis Cardinals in seven games. It is the first time in history that the home team won every game in a seven game series. Gaetti later played for the Cardinals and Cubs.

An earthquake of 5.0 magnitude on the Richter Scale hits southeastern Illinois.

Harold Washington wins a second term and dies suddenly of a heart attack at his desk on November 25, the day before Thanksgiving. More than 200,000 mourners passed by his casket to pay their respects.

A U.S. 22 cent postage stamp honoring Jean Baptiste duSable is issued at Chicago.

1988 – Illinois U.S. Senator Paul Simon launches a serious bid for the Democratic nomination for president but will lose out to Michael Dukakis.

Jackie Joyner-Kersee (courtesy *Belv. News-Democrat*)

Jackie Joyner wins the Heptathlon in Seoul, Korea, and is named Sports Illustrated's Woman of the Year.

A nuclear powered Trident sub is named the ***USS Melvin Price***, for the East St. Louis congressman who served in the House of Representatives for forty years. The **Granite City** Army Support Center and lock and dam #26 at Alton are also named for him.

Oscar Micheaux of **Metropolis** is given a star on the **Hollywood Walk of Fame**. He was the first African-American to produce and direct a film.

Lights are installed at **Wrigley Field** for the first time in its history and night baseball comes to the home of the Chicago Cubs. Rick Sutcliffe was given the honor of being the starter who threw the first pitch on August 8th.

Mike Ditka of the Chicago Bears becomes the first tight end inducted into the Hall of Fame at Canton, Ohio.

There are 10,000 McDonald's hamburger franchises in America. Ray Kroc's original dream was to have a thousand of them.

Christie Hefner closes the doors on Chicago's Playboy Club at 919 North Michigan on Chicago's Magnificent Mile.

A one block stretch of Wacker Drive is renamed Paul Harvey Drive to honor the radio star.

1989 - The 38th annual Christmas Parade is held in **Metropolis**.

Richard M. Daley, Cook County State's Attorney and son of former mayor Richard Daley, is elected mayor. There was a special election to fill the post for the remaining two years of Harold Washington's term. Daley served as Illinois State Senator from 1972-80. In 1991 he won a second term, defeating former mayor Jane Byrne in the Democratic primary. He won a third term in 1995 and a fourth term in 1999.

Carol Mosley-Braun, after serving 10 years in the legislature, runs on Washington's "Dream Ticket" for recorder of deeds. Her victory made her the first African-American woman to hold executive office in Cook County.

East St. Louis High, led by Dana Howard, is both the state and national champions in football. Howard goes on to attend the **University of Illinois** where he breaks Dick Butkus' Big Ten record for tackles in a game (25) and teams with Kevin Hardy, Simeon Rice, and John Holecek as the nation's best linebacking corps two years in a row. He was voted the best linebacker in the nation his senior year.

The big bluestem is designated as the state's official prairie grass. It is also called turkeyfoot grass.

1990 - St. Clair County celebrates its bicentennial as the oldest county in the state.

East St. Louisan Jimmy Connors, with more major tennis titles than anyone else in the world, is proclaimed **"Mr. Tennis."**

East St. Louisan **Eric Wright** wins his 4th Super Bowl ring, playing with Joe Montana and the San Francisco 49ers.

Drs. Richard and Jean Graber, retired ornithologists, donate War Bluff Valley as a sanctuary to the Illinois Audubon Society. It is three miles north of **Golconda**, off Highway 146. (618-446-5085)

The **Route 66 Hall of Fame** opens at Dixie Truckers Home in **McLean**. It is the most visited attraction on all of Route 66. Its purpose is to honor people and businesses whose careers or experiences along the road helped give it such special flavor in this state. By 2001 there were 48 members including truck drivers, waitresses, farmers, a newspaper editor, an inventor, gas stations, a drug store, a movie palace, a drive-in theater, the Chain of Rocks Bridge, and several roadhouses and diners. Induction ceremonies are held each June as part of the association's motor tour.

Jimmy Connors of East St. Louis/Belleville

Judge Roger Scrivner awards deeds to the **East St. Louis** City Hall and the Alcoa plant site at 3300 Missouri Avenue to Walter DeBow to settle a $3.5 million jury award to Debow for injuries he suffered while incarcerated in the city jail. A court settlement in 1993 allowed the city to regain title to the land and to City Hall because DeBow could not afford to pay the taxes on his new property.

A new **Comiskey Park** is built for the Chicago White Sox. Downstaters were visibly upset because the Illinois legislature voted to use state tax revenues for the project. The new park was built adjacent to the original and after demolition of the old structure, the space was used for parking. Relief pitcher Bobby Thigpin racks up an amazing 57 saves in one year.

African-Americans constitute about 15 percent of the state's total population and now outnumber whites in Chicago for the first time.

The state loses 2 representatives and 2 electoral votes as a result of the national 1990 census. Its electoral vote stands at 22. Los Angeles replaces Chicago as the second largest city in the nation by population.

Tina Turner of East St. Louis

Voters go to the polls and reject the possibility of calling for a new constitutional convention. By law, this prospect must be presented to voters every twenty years.

University of Illinois professor Jerome Friedman shares the Nobel Prize for proving protons, electrons and neutrons are made up of smaller particles called **quarks**.

Sue Hendrickson, a South Dakota paleontologist, unearths the remains of a Tyrannosaurus Rex (king of the tyrants). Named Sue, it's displayed at the Field Museum in Chicago.

The U. of Illinois ties for first in the Big Ten with an 8-4 football record.

Ryne Sandberg strokes 40 homers as a 2nd basemen for the Chicago Cubs. Only Davey Johnson of Atlanta and Rogers Hornsby of St. Louis hit more at that position. The Cubs traded Larry Bowa for Sandberg in a 1982 trade with the Phillies.

The Chicago White Sox have a no-hitter thrown at them, but they manage to defeat the Yankees 4-0.

Michael Jordan scores 69 points against the Cleveland Cavaliers.

Every year a section of Route 3 in **Union County** at Winter's Pond is closed to allow snakes and turtles to migrate to their seasonal quarters.

Alton resident Paula Sims is convicted of murdering her daughter in a sensation trial held at **Peoria**. St. Louis County Medical Examiner Mary Case was an important witness for the prosecution. The story was made into a television movie that starred Robbie Benson (Paula's husband Robert) and Richard Thomas (prosecutor Don Weber).

After a 28-year moratorium on the death penalty, Charles Walker is executed at Stateville Prison for the murder of a couple near **Mascoutah**.

1991 - Tina Turner, a former resident of **East St. Louis**, is elected into the Rock and Roll Hall of Fame.

The Chicago Bulls, led by Scotty Pipin and Michael Jordan win the NBA championship against the L.A. Lakers. They will make it a three-peat, winning again in 1992 and 1993.

The Chicago Public Library gets a new 10-story home on State Street that is dubbed the Harold Washington Library. It is a traditional classic looking structure with a Tiffany dome. A *Tribune* architecture critic called it a "heavy, lackluster statement." It is **the world's largest** with 757,000 square feet.

The first gambling boat on the Mississippi River is the 500-passenger Alton Belle.

Republican Governor Jim Edgar, a former Secretary of State, signs Kimberly Bergalis-type legislation requiring health care workers infected with aids to notify their patients. He also signs a bill giving the state its first state income tax hike since the law was first enacted.

In April, Richard M. Daley wins his first full 4-year term as Chicago mayor.

The University of Illinois defeats Virginia in the Citrus Bowl by the score of 31-21. Illinois finished the season ranked tenth in the nation. It is their first post-season victory in 26 years. QB Jeff George led the way with three touchdown passes and over 300 total yards passing.

The Chicago Blackhawks win the Norris Division of the Campbell Conference with a 41-33-6 record. Ed Belfour wins Rookie-of-the-Year and the Vezina trophy for outstanding goalie.

A vicious tornado hits Will County (near Chicago), killing 28 people and injuring 350.

Huge amounts of money are voted by the legislature for the bailouts of financially troubled inner-city schools in Chicago and **East St. Louis**.

Marjorie Judith Vincent of **Oak Park**, the daughter of Haitian immigrants, is named Miss America.

They started in Europe and spread to America – those crop circle hoaxes appear in the southern Illinois town of **Troy** and will reappear a year later.

It is estimated that only ten percent of the state remains forested. When pioneers first arrived it was about 40 percent.

The Chicago Bulls win their first NBA championship with Pippin and Jordan.

1992 – Carol Mosley-Braun, angered over incumbent Alan Dixon's vote to confirm Supreme Court nominee Clarence Thomas, challenges him for the U.S. Senate seat. In what was declared The Year of the Woman, she defeated Dixon in the primary and went on to defeat Republican Richard Williamson in the November general election. It was the first time Dixon, former Illinois Secretary of State, had ever lost an election. Mosely-Braun becomes the **first African-American woman elected to the U.S. Senate**.

Braun's numerous junkets and poor handling of several personal financial dealings caused her to have poor ratings, and she became a one-termer, losing the 1998 election to Republican Peter Fitzgerald. After her loss, President Bill Clinton appointed her to serve as ambassador to New Zealand.

Five nuns from the Ruma Province are murdered while serving in war-torn Liberia. A statue was erected in their honor two years later at the **Ruma Convent**. The five who lost their lives were **S. Agnes Mueller, S. Barbara Muttra, S. Kathleen McGuire, S. Mary Kolmer, and Shirley Kolmer**.

Coach Nino Fennoy's **East St. Louis Lincoln Tigerettes** win their **9th consecutive state track title**. **Jackie Joyner**, the World's Greatest Female Athlete, was a mainstay on his earlier teams.

East St. Louisan LaPhonso Ellis becomes the first rookie to start all eighty-two games for the Denver Nuggets and makes the NBA All-Rookie Team.

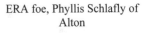

ERA foe, Phyllis Schlafly of Alton

Phyllis Schlafly of Alton, mother of 6, is named the Illinois Mother of the Year. Schlafly has been a national spokesperson for conservatives since the publication of *A Choice, Not an Echo* in 1964. It was a book supporting Barry Goldwater's campaign for the presidency. She has since written 13 other books. She is the head of the Eagle Forum which puts out "The Phyllis Schlafly Report," now in its 27th year. Schlafly, organizer of "Stop ERA," is generally given the lion's share of the credit for defeating the Equal Rights Amendment for women, which she said was far too radical, could result in women being drafted to fight wars and would be harmful to traditional families.

This is known as the year of the Great Chicago Flood. The Great Lakes Dredge and Dock Company punched a hole in the bed of the Chicago River with pilings. The posts caused a severe leak into some abandoned freight tunnels that ran beneath the downtown area, causing the basements in the Loop to flood. The estimated damage was about a billion dollars.

Madison and St. Clair Counties now supply the city of St. Louis with 20 percent of its labor force.

The state's tallest tree, standing 138 feet high with a circumference of 32 and ½ feet, is felled by strong winds at Morris in **Grundy County**. It was about 180 years old.

Outboard Marine of **Waukegan** spends $21 million for the cleanup of PCBs to clean up the toxins in the harbor. For six years residents are not allowed to fish in the harbor because of contaminants.

Mary Ann McMorrow becomes the first female justice on the Illinois Supreme Court.

Presidential candidate Ross Perot chooses **Abingdon** native **James B. Stockdale**, a former Vietnam POW and Medal of Honor winner as his running mate.

The city of **Zion's** official city seal, containing a Christian cross, is found by the U.S. Supreme Court to be offensive and in violation of the First Amendment. The ruling also affects the town of **Rolling Meadow**.

Chicago Cub star second baseman Rhyne Sandberg signs a $30 million contract. This is more money than the *Chicago Tribune* paid for the entire team in 1981.

The Cub's centerfield scoreboard, erected in 1937, has yet to be tagged by a home run ball.

The Chicago Bulls set the league's fourth best mark with a 67-15 won-lost record and win the NBA world title against Portland.

The scene where Bill Murray steps in a puddle at Punxsutawney, PA, is actually shot in **Woodstock**, giving rise to an annual Groundhog Day celebration every Feb. 2.

1993 – **Bellevillian** Taylor Pensoneau co-authors with Bob Ellis, *Dan Walker*: The Glory and the Tragedy, the story of Dan Walker who served as Democratic governor of Illinois from 1973-1977.

The East St. Louis/ St. Louis light rail MetroLink is completed, connecting the two cities by using the top deck of the Eads Bridge. The Casino Queen gambling boat (East St. Louis) opens.

The **Great Chicago Flood** sends thousand of office workers home for a week long vacation. An abandoned freight tunnel under the city developed a crack and in poured millions of gallons of water from the Chicago River, flooding the streets and basements of Chicago. Damage and business losses totaled an estimated billion dollars before the crack was repaired and water was pumped out of the tunnels. The chief tunnel inspector was fired, and the city had to pay out millions in damage claims.

The wife of Frank Maltese, Betty Loren-Maltese, is appointed interim president of Cicero's government. She wins three successive elections.

Chicago and its suburbs now account for 70 percent of the state's industrial output.

The Chicago Bulls make it a Three-peat by winning their third consecutive NBA title in a row.

Richard and Susan Armstrong buy a large, vacant Methodist Church two blocks from the square in **Hillsboro.** After two years of remodeling open it as the Church Street Pub with dining room seating for 100. One of the large stained glass windows of the old church features a portrait of John Wesley, founder of the Methodist movement.

Americans are shocked to hear an announcement from Sears that it will no longer produce its famed annual catalog.

Chanute Air Base at **Rantoul** is closed as part of a cost cutting program by the Defense Department.

1994 – The old **Clark Bridge at Alton** is replaced with an exciting new one of fan suspension design.

1995 – Troy Taylor of **Alton** publishes his first book, *Haunted Decatur*.

Chicago suffers through a devastating heat wave in the middle of July that is responsible for as many as 733 deaths, mostly among the elderly.

The **world's tallest fountain** is built on the riverfront in East St. Louis. Its main geyser sprouts 627 feet and is surrounded by a reflecting pool with four 100-foot fountains.

The Ozark-Mahoning Company at **Rosiclare**, the state's only surviving major producer of fluorspar (calcium fluoride) announces that it's prime source of the mineral near Cave-in-Rock has been mined out.

1996 **East St. Louisan** and Assumption High graduate Dick Durbin is elected to the U.S. Senate, filling the vacancy by a retiring Paul Simon. In the 2000 election he was seriously considered as a running mate for Al Gore.

Sonny Irvin, owner of A-1 Limos, and conductor of ghost tours of the city of **Alton**, is chosen by Fate Magazine to be the grand prize in their yearly "Haunted Weekend" contest. In doing research for his tours, Sonny worked with **Belleville psychic Shirley Blaine** who assured him that the **Blaske Building** was another haunted site. The building was constructed in 1916 by Sparks Milling and was used to house their offices. Several people reported paranormal experiences in the basement of the building including moans, groans and unexplained squeaking doors. (Good grief! It's hard to believe civilized Americans actually believe in apparitions and doppelgangers.) The building is currently owned by Con Agra.

Quincy High School (courtesy Neal Strebel)

The ACLU files suit against the old Montgomery Courthouse in **Hillsboro**, claiming that an old neon sign on top violates separation of church and state. The sign was put up by a Sunday school group in 1941 and proclaimed, "The World Needs God." District judge Richard Mills ruled in favor of the ACLU, and the sign was taken down.

The town of **Hillsboro** is noted for Hillsboro Glass, which makes the brown glass for Hiram Walker whiskey bottles.

Chicago-area U.S. Representative **Dan Rostenkowski**, chairman of the powerful Ways and Means finance committee, pleads to mail fraud and is given a jail sentence.

After a 28-year absence, the Democratic national nominating convention returns to Chicago, a city now governed by Richard Daley's son. In a quiet, carefully managed convention at the United Center, President Bill Clinton is nominated for a second term.

The unlikely **Northwestern Wildcats**, the Big Ten's most cerebral team, go 10-2 and win the Big Ten Championship in 1995 and a trip to the Rose Bowl on January 1. Coach Gary Barnett wins almost all of the Coach-of-the-Year honors. They had a slim lead in the 4th quarter but succumbed to the USC Trojans by a score of 41-32.

The Chicago Bulls, after finishing an incredible 72-10 regular season record, defeat the Seattle Supersonics in June to collect their 4th NBA title. Pippin, Jordan and Dennis Rodman (the league's leading rebounder) were the team stars. Tony Kukoc won the NBA Sixth Man award.

Illinois leads the nation in the production of corn, pumpkins, onions, horseradish, soybeans and Swiss cheese. O'Hare field in Chicago is the world's busiest airport. Our per-capita income ranks 7th among the 50 states.

The twin Petronas Towers in Malaysia replaces the Sears Tower as the World's Tallest Building. However, Chicagoans pointed out that the Sears Tower still had the highest occupied floor.

1997 – Taylor Pensoneau of **Belleville** writes his second book, *Governor Richard Ogilvie: In The Interest of the State*, published by Southern Illinois University Press.

Wayne Johnson, chief investigator for the Chicago Crime Commission, co-authors the book, *The New Faces of Organized Crime*.

The Chicago Bulls win their 5th NBA title.

1998 – John Hallwas, a professor of English and an archivist at Western Illinois University at **Macomb** writes *The Bootlegger*. It takes place in the small coalmining town of Colchester in **McDonough County**. The story chronicles the life of the town from its first settlers, through the Civil War, the Gilded Age, the Gay Nineties, World War I and the era of Prohibition. It also tells the story of Kelly Wagle, a petty criminal (bootlegger) folk hero who is murdered. The book is actually more of a documentary than a novel.

Sammy Sosa of the Chicago Cubs hits 66 home runs, surpassing the 61 hit by Roger Maris of the Yankees.

The Chicago Fire pro soccer team captures the MLS trophy.

The Chicago Bulls win their 6th NBA title and make it a second Three-peat by winning their third in a row.

1999 – The old Chain of Rocks Bridge along Route 66 is reopened and used by walkers, birdwatchers and bike pedalers.

2000 - East St. Louisan Darius Miles, a high school senior, is taken 3rd in the NBA draft by the L.A. Clippers. East St. Louisan Jackie Joyner-Kersee is named Female Athlete of the Century by Women's Sports Illustrated magazine.

Chicago population reaches 2,896,016 and the overall population of the state climbs to 12,419,293, placing it fourth among all the states.

2001 - Kaskaskia Island gets a $1.5 million new two-lane bridge. To get to Kaskaskia, one must go through St. Mary's, which is about eight miles south of St. Genevieve, MO. This bridge sits between Jefferson Barracks and the bridge at Chester. The 1990 U.S. Census set the population of Kaskaskia Island at nine people. The old bridge was blown up, falling into the old, dry channel. Then it was cut up for scrap.

Governors of Illinois (D=Democrat, R=GOP)
D - Shadrach Bond : 1818-1822
D - Edward Coles : 1822-1826
D -Ninian Edwards : 1826-1830
D -John Reynolds : 1830-1834
D - William Ewing : Nov-Dec 1834
D - Joseph Duncan : 1834-1838
D - Thomas Carlin : 1838-1842
D - Thomas Ford : 1842-1846
D - Augustus French : 1846-1853
D - Joel Matteson : 1853-1857
R - William Bissell : 1857-1860
R - John Wood : 1860-1861
R - Richard Yates : 1861-1865
R - Richard Oglesby : 1873
R - John Beveridge: 1873-1877
R - Shelby Cullom : 1877-1881
R - John Hamilton : 1883-1885
R - Richard J. Oglesby : 1885-1889
R - Joseph Fifer : 1889-1893
D - John Altgeld : 1893-1897
R – John Tanner : 1897-1901
R - Richard Yates : 1901-1905
R - Charles S. Deneen : 1905-1909
D - Edward Dunne : 1913-1917
R - Frank Lowden : 1917-1921
R - Len Small : 1921-1929
R - Louis Emmerson : 1929-1933
D - Henry Horner : 1933-1937
D - John Stelle : 1940-1941
R - Dwight Green : 1941-49
D - Adlai Stevenson : 1949-53
R - William Stratton : 1953-1961
D - Otto Kerner : 1961-1968
D - Sam Shapiro : 1968-1969
R - Richard Ogilvie : 1969-1973
D - Dan Walker: 1973-1977
R - Jim Thompson : 1977-1991
R - Jim Edgar: 1991- 1999
R - George Ryan : 1999-2003
D – Rod Blagojevich – 2003-

It is a little known fact that one of the early settlers of **Kaskaskia** set out to establish trade beyond the western border of Illinois and **was responsible for the creation of the famed Santa Fe Trail**.

An extension of the MetroLink light rail system opens in St. Clair County. Formerly it ran from Lambert Field in St. Louis, through downtown St. Louis, and ended in East St. Louis. The new extension goes to **Belleville** along Routes 50 and 161 to Belleville College, and from there to Mid-America Airport at Scott Air Base.

George Culley of **Pinckneyville** writes a "letter to the editor" in which he compares the plagues of Biblical Egypt with modern-day plagues of Egypt in southern Illinois. He cites: hunger, unemployment, alcoholism, drug addiction, homelessness, natural disasters (fires and floods), poverty, drought, occultism, and Dave Phelps' congressional district being redrawn. Mayor James

Wilson of **Cairo** confirmed that Burkart Foam planned to close its plant in Oct.

In mid-July, the head of the state board that oversees the finances of East St. Louis threatens to shut the city down unless they can start meeting deadlines and come up with a budget that is six months overdue. About half of the city's $33 million budget comes from the state.

John Hunter, a **Belleville** police officer, wins $32,000 on "Who Wants to be a Millionaire?" It could have been $64,000 had he or his lifeline known that an "X" through a triangle on a clothing label means Do Not Bleach. He wrongly guessed that it meant Do Not Iron.

Michael Jordan (courtesy Chicago Bulls/F. Medina)

Illinois remained the nation's second leading grain producing states with a record soybean crop and a corn harvest that almost equaled the previous year. Illinois farmers harvested a record 477.9 million bushels of soybeans, 3 percent above the previous record set in 1998. Yield was 45 bushels per acre. The Illinois corn harvest was 1.65 billion bushels, 1 percent less than in 2000. Corn yield was 152 bushels per acre. Only Iowa harvests more corn and soybeans than Illinois, but not by much.

The University of Illinois, led by Kurt Kitner, wins the Big Ten football title with a 10-2 record. Kitner led the fighting Illini to a stunning **five come-from-behind victories**.

Sandburg High of **Orland Park** defeats **Edwardsville** for the AA state soccer championship by a score of 1-0.

A ground-breaking ceremony is held for the Abraham Lincoln Library and Museum.

2002 – The city of **Collinsville** authorizes funds for the construction of an **inflatable dome** to be constructed near Interstate 255. Inside the dome will be seating for about 10,000-12,000 people. It is expected that the dome will be used for sporting events, concerts, etc. There are similar plans for a dome to be constructed on **Choteau Island**, in the Mississippi River, north of Granite City near Interstate 270. This site is a little trickier because it is an old landfill that has been covered with dirt. Construction will be monitored by the EPA to make sure the landfill is not disturbed. It is anticipated that an extra foot or two of fill dirt would be hauled in to the site before construction would begin.

Harry Statham, coach of the **McKendree College** basketball Bearcats at **Lebanon** for 36 years, becomes one of only 4 college coaches to achieve 800 victories in mid-January. This is more victories than Lou Henson of Illinois or Bob Knight of Indiana or Norm Stewart of Missouri. At the time, his purple and white clad warriors were ranked 16th in the nation in NAIA Division I.

Brandee Hewlett, a **Belleville East Lancer**, wins the state bowling championship with a couple of three game series of 642 and 610 to win the title.

SIU Carbondale basketball team defeats Texas Tech (coached by Bobby Knight) and Georgia (77-75) at the United Center in Chicago to make it into the NCAA Sweet Sixteen for the first time since 1977.

A deadly F-3 tornado hits Wayne County in April and does severe damage in **Sims, Keenes, Fairfield, and Wayne City**. It was clocked at a top speed of 206 mph and caused destruction for a 20-mile stretch. One person was killed and about 50 were injured.

A week later another tornado hits **Shiloh** in St. Clair County. People are upset when they hear the tornado warning siren go off ½ hour later. Officials blamed this on a computer malfunction the night before and the fact that the storm cell had low level circulation which is difficult to pick up on radar.

Officials arrest a man in a Chicago suburb April 30th. He was accused of aiding terrorism by using his Benevolence International Association as a front organization and funneling money to Osama Ben Laden's Al Quaida network.

Magician David Copperfield's tour bus visits **Greenville's Demoulin Brothers**. The world famous magician collects novelty items such as collapsible chairs, once manufactured at the factory in Greenville. Back in the 1970s Demoulin Brothers rented graduation gowns for high school exercises. Currently, their staple is band uniforms.

On May 1 **Greenville** suffered an unusual disaster – 6 different tornadoes ripped through the southern part of town causing extensive damage along Route 140. Fortunately, the tornadoes were only rated as F-1s on the Fujita scale so there was no loss of life. The storms later struck **Kinmundy** where 16 homes sustained damage. Over 35 structures were damaged by the series of tornadoes.

The biggest casualty was the 300-400 year-old white oak tree that was blown over and destroyed by the wind. This was the tree that was the model for Greenville's logo.

Danny Jackson cracked a 2 run homer to break a 1-1 tie and lead the Edwardsville Tigers to a regional title against Belleville West. Nathan Culp fired a 6 hitter to hold the opposition in check. The tigers were scheduled to play Alton for the sectional title. At the IHSA state track meet in **Charleston**, Stephen Pifer took first in the 1,600 meter run for Class AA schools. Edwardsville would go on to take 2nd place in the state tournament.

According to Pat Gauen of the *St. Louis Post-Dispatch*, forty-two people were convicted of selling or buying drivers licenses for bribes when Governor George Ryan was Secretary of State. Ryan's political campaign and its manager were also charged with racketeering. Polls indicated that nearly 2/3 of voters favored the resignation of Ryan which he refused to do. He did, however, choose not to run for reelection. Democrat Rod Blagojevich easily won the race to become the new governor.

The Eli Bridge Company in **Jacksonville** remains the only maker of Ferris Wheels in the USA.

A study ranks Illinois as the fourth largest high tech employer in the USA.

Coal mining remains the third most dangerous profession in the USA.

One of the main characters in the Bruce Willis film about a World War II POW camp in Germany, **Hart's War**, is a racist cop who hails from **East St. Louis**.

Cicero Town President, Republican Betty Loren-Maltese is convicted for having helped loot Cicero's treasury of $12 million. Five others are also convicted, including **Michael Spano** and one town official reputed to be the mob boss of Cicero.

One hundred and sixty prison inmates on death row petition lame-duck Governor George Ryan for clemency. Earlier in his tenure, Ryan had suspended all forthcoming executions based on what he felt to be a large number of prisoners being declared innocent on the basis of DNA evidence.

The nation is shocked when two men driving a moving truck are dragged from their vehicle and beaten to death by an angry mob. The driver, who had been drinking, lost control of his vehicle, and his van crashed into 3 young girls who were sitting on the steps of a house at 3900 South Lake Park Avenue. A crowd of about 100 stood around and did nothing while as many as 20 men participated in the attack. Police later charged 7 men with the crime. Everyone involved in the incident was African-American.

Due to extensive remodeling of Soldier's Field, the Chicago Bears play their home games at the University of Illinois' football stadium.

Erika Harold, of **Urbana**, a graduate of the University of Illinois and an African-American of mixed parents, is selected as Miss America.

Illinois leads the nation with about 30 deaths resulting from the West Nile Virus transmitted by mosquito bites.

Chicago city council unanimously passes an ordinance requiring all corporations doing business with the city to research their records to determine if they benefited from slavery. They are the first large city in the nation to pass such an ordinance. The idea is that these companies (railroads, insurance companies, etc.) will at some future date be required to issue a formal apology and put forth some plan of **reparations**. The plan is very controversial because polls suggest that 45 percent of African-Americans are against the idea, and 70 percent of whites oppose reparations. Proponents claim it will have a healing effect, but opponents say it will be divisive and produce white backlash.

The student union building at **Wheaton College** is renamed the Todd Beemer Building. Beemer was the passenger on the 9-11-01 Flight 93 and led the attack on the Arab hijackers by saying, "Let's roll." The plane then crashed in a Pennsylvania field instead of the White House, believed to be the intended target. Beemer was a 1991 graduate of Wheaton College.

In a poll of college history professors, Abe Lincoln, for the first time in decades loses his top spot as America's greatest president, falling to second place behind Franklin D. Roosevelt. This is not too surprising since 85 percent of all college history professors are Democrats (by their own admission) who support spending outlays for social programs similar to those of FDR's New Deal.

Edwardsville High School takes second place in prep football playoffs for the second straight year.

An official from Mayor Daley's office travels to Switzerland and comes back with the idea for **Cows On Display**. Local artists encouraged to execute cow sculptures of various shapes and sizes to be displayed all over the city. The idea is wildly successful and grabs national spotlight.

Edwardsville, led by coach Tim Funkhouser, wins second place in the state baseball tournament, losing out to Sandburg High of Orland Park. Sandburg was 23-9 while Edwardsville finished 32-8. Dan Atkinson of the Sandburg Eagles, who pitched a one-hitter, was tourney MVP.

Atlanta's Hartsfield Airport claims to be the world's busiest airport, replacing O'Hare, which still tops the list in terms of number of flights.

Paul Newman and Tom Hanks star in the film *Road to Perdition*. It is a fictionalized story about the Looney gang that terrorized the quad city area of northwestern Illinois back in the 1920s and 1930s. In the Max Collins story, the Hanks character works for Looney (changed to Rooney in the film) and his son witnesses a mob murder. After his wife and other son are killed by the mob, Hanks flees with his other son to Chicago, seeking **Frank Nitti's** protection and permission to retaliate. The Quad Cities include **Rock Island, Moline, Davenport** and **Bettendorf**, Iowa.

Evan Jones of Glen Carbon tossing horseradish at Collinsville's annual Horseradish Festival in 2003

Al Capone's signed police booking card with his fingerprints, when he was arrested in 1929 at Philadelphia, PA on a concealed weapons charge, sells for $42,576 at auction.

Illinoisan Dennis Hastert, the wrestling coach from **Aurora**, is Speaker of the U.S. House of Representatives.

2003 – The University of Illinois has approximately 31,000 students.

The state of Illinois ranks third in the nation with respect to total interstate highway miles.

Lake County in north suburban Chicago is the nation's second ranked county in the nation in terms of average household income.

Cicero President/Mayor **Loren Maltese** is sentenced to 8 years and a day in prison for looting the city of Cicero's treasury. Maltese apparently spent millions of the dollars on gambling at casinos and in Las Vegas.

Governor George Ryan angers law enforcement officials all over the state by using his constitutional power of pardon. A few days before the end of his term of office ends, Ryan pardons 167 convicts in the state on Death Row and commutes their punishment to a life sentence. He says that his justification for taking such drastic action is that the criminal justice system is broke. Four men were pardoned outright as Ryan maintained that confessions were tortured out of them by Chicago police. Incoming governor Rod Blagojevich, a liberal Democrat, was quick to condemn the action, saying that blanket actions of this sort are seldom a good idea.

Former Chicago Bears coach and restaurant owner Mike Ditka goes on Fox television news program "The O'Reilly Factor" and criticizes the city's proposal to ban smoking in all restaurants due to employees and patrons being subjected to secondary smoke. Ditka is also highly critical of Governor Ryan's blanket pardon of Death Row inmates, commuting their sentences to life in prison.

Old gravesites are discovered atop a hill covered with ask and oak trees on Harlan Booten's farm in Gallatin County. The bodies were discovered after Booten leased his property's mineral rights to a coal company. It is believed that the plot site may be the first cemetery for African-Americans in the state of Illinois. The slaves probably worked at the nearby saltworks at **Equality**, the only place in the state where slavery was legal.

Chicago ranks second only to New York City as a financial market.

At the trial of Scott Fawell, a former George Ryan aide, prosecutors introduce a 555 page list that showed how the former Secretary of State and Governor doled out hundreds of political patronage jobs, state contracts and favors for people with clout. One of the names on the list was former Chicago Outfit boss, **Tony Accardo**.

1968 Masters Golf Champ Bob Goalby of Belleville (*B. N. Dem.*)

Twenty-one people are crushed or smothered to death at the Epitome nightclub in Chicago. Witnesses said it all started when guards used pepper spray or mace to break up a fight between two women. Some of the exit doors had been locked. It was estimated that approximately 1,500 people were inside the two-story building at the time of the incident.

The Chicago Bears and Chicago/Phoenix Cardinals are the only two original pro football franchises still in existence.

The U.S. Mint issues the Illinois quarter in its tribute to all the states series.

Chicago wins the best cast/picture award from the Screen Actors Guild; it garners a total of 6 Oscars at the Academy Awards.

The University of Illinois defeats Ohio State to win the Big Ten basketball tournament. Fans are outraged when the NCAA only gives them a 4th seed in the tournament, despite their 24-6 record. They finished second to Wisconsin in the Big Ten conference, thrashing all the teams soundly at home, but losing a number of close ones on the road. Brian Cook is the Big Ten scoring champion. They lose to Notre Dame in the second round of the tournament.

For the 43rd year in a row, the Chicago River is dyed green for St. Patrick's Day in March.

SIU at **Carbondale**, led by Kent Williams, nearly upsets Mizzou in the first round of the NCAA Tournament, losing 72-71.

Cub manager Dusty Baker draws heavy criticism for claiming African-American players take the heat better than Caucasians.

The Bearcats of McKendree College in **Lebanon** are ranked number two in the nation with over thirty basketball victories. They make it to the Final Four but are defeated in the first round.

Sammy Sosa of the Cubs clouts his 500th homer in April, making him the 18th player in the major leagues to reach that coveted mark. Later in the season he is tossed from a game for using an illegal corked bat.

U.S. Senator Peter Fitzgerald announces that he does not intend to seek re-election for another term in 2004.

Catherine Drexel, founder of the Adorers of the Precious Blood Convent at **Ruma**, is canonized in a ceremony at the Vatican.

President Bush becomes the first Commander-in-Chief to land on a moving aircraft carrier when he arrives on the deck of the *USS Abraham Lincoln* to tell the nation that the war for Iraqui Freedom has been a success.

The nation is shocked by a home video that is shown on national TV of a hazing incident involving about a hundred students (counting boys who watched) on a girls' powderpuff football team in suburban **Northbrook**. Several juniors were injured by seniors when the ritual grew vicious, and initiates were beaten and smeared with animal feces.

Adrianne Curry of **Joliet** is selected by TV Guide Magazine as one of three models destined for stardom in the near future. The bandana-wearing brunette was chosen for her homegirl edgy looks (whatever that means), attitude and streetwise allure.

2004 – Former NBA all-star and Chicago Bull's coach Doug Collins, of **Benton**, is selected by NBC as a color analyst for the upcoming Olympic games in Athens, Greece. Chicago becomes controversial for its policy sanctioned by city officials making it a **sanctuary city**. This means that local law enforcement is uncooperative in reporting Chicago illegal aliens to the federal INS.

INTERESTING TOWN FACTS

Note: In describing important historical landmarks, railroads, churches, factories and the like, it is important for readers to understand that these things or places, once integral to a specific area or town, might no longer exist. If the population is not listed, that means it is probably less than 225. Some of this material was given to me by town residents and librarians and I had no way to verify it. If you see erroneous info, please contact me at bnunesbook@aol.com so it can be corrected in next edition. I'm sorry if your town is missing; send relevant items and I'll try to include them in a revision or new edition.

Abington: In Knox County, south of Galesburg; home of the inventor of the first mousetrap; birthplace of Medal of Honor winner James Stockdale, Ross Perot's running mate for president; **83-foot tall totem pole** in town; Abington pottery is now very collectable; pop. 3,612

Addison: Chicago suburb; German-Lutheran town named for Joseph Addison, an English essayist; radio station WMBI on Mill Road; voice of the Moody Bible Institute; Dave and Buster's Million Dollar Midway recreational center (630/543-5151); Marcus Imax Theater (630/88-1901); Dave & Buster's Games; pop. 35,014

Great Northern Migration statue in Bronzeville

Albany: Whiteside County on the Great River Road in northwestern Illinois; Indian Mounds State Historic Site; Albany to Thompson bike trail; devastating 1860 tornado; pop. 895

Albion: Seat of Edwards County near the Wabash River and Indiana border on Route 15; on famous Illinois Prairie; founded by George Flower and Morris Birbeck; back in olden times (1066) England was called Albion; huge shale pits famous for making and shipping brick in early years; this English settlement had the state's first municipal public library in 1819; currently housed in the oldest building being used as a library in the state; Jeff Keener pitched (underhanded-sidearmed) for St. Louis Cardinals and manager Whitey Herzog and his World Championship ring; home of Champion Labs and Luber-Finer, makers of air and oil filters; pop. 1,933

Aledo – Seat of Mercer County; town fathers couldn't reach a decision so they drew letters out of a hat to determine the town's name; northern Illinois town home to a Rhubarb Festival every June; has 3-story restaurant called The Slammer that was once an old jail; meals are served in jail cells; Roosevelt Military Academy; *American Shetland Pony Journal*; pop. 3,613

Algonquin – In Henry County on Rock River; named for a ship that, in turn, was named for an Algonquin Indian tribe; northwest Chicago suburb; Algonquin Princess paddle wheeler on Fox River (847/658-3660) Raging Buffalo Snowboard Park (847/836-7243); pop. 23,276

Alma: Town in Marion County named for Crimean War battle; pop. 386

Alsip: Southeast Chicago suburb; named for the Alsip family; incorporated in 1927 to prevent encroaching cemeteries from elbowing out truck farms; Swap-O-Rama – Chicagoland's largest flea market (708/344-7300); Calumet Sag Channel; pop. 19,725

Altamont: Effingham County on U.S. 40; organized in 1872 and named for a rise of ground; home to B&O and Pennsylvania railroads; was a wheat-shipping center, clothing manufacturer and maker of egg crates; Ben Winter Museum (618/483-6665) features old steam engines and threshing machines; annual Schuetzenfest (shootfest) ; prep Indians; the *Independent*; pop. 2,283

Alto Pass: Union County: its 111 ft. tall Christian cross on Bald Knob is the **largest in the United States**; pop. 388

Alton High, home of the Redbirds (Neal Strebel collection)

Alton: In Madison County, named for a son of Rufus Easton, the town's founder; called Bluff City, the City of Seven Hills; its Owens Glass Works were the largest in the world; Piasa monster rock/cliff painting; monument dedicated to Elijah Lovejoy who was murdered; legend holds that **Jean Lafitte**, the pirate who helped Andrew Jackson win the battle of New Orleans, is buried in the Mississippi near Alton; local Negroes lived on low-lying ground called **Dogtown**; Look Magazine's All-America City in 1959; prominent steamboats *Golden Eagle, Gossamer* and *Kate Kearney*; Alton Giant Robert Wadlow – nearly nine feet tall, 490 pounds, size 36 shoe – World's Tallest Man – life size statue of him near old Shurtleff College (oldest college building in the state); Smallpox Needle monument to over 1,300 Confederate soldiers who died at Alton prison camp; beautiful new Clark Bridge; birthplace of Rocky Mountains explorer, Stephen H. Long; home to Alton Belle gambling casino; old Western Military Academy; Fast Eddie's (Eddie Sholar) popular eaterie/tavern at 4th , Pearl and Broadway (618/462-5532), said to be the largest (by volume) in the state; Melvin Price Lock 26 and Dam; site of last Lincoln-Douglas debate; National Great Rivers Museum traces history of locks and river transportation; Alton Square shopping mall; has popular Underground Railroad Tour; birthplace of Miles Davis; Fate magazine calls Alton the **most haunted small town in America**; churning waters from dam prevents freezing, making waters a favorite feeding spot for wintering bald eagles; home to prep Redbirds; Great River Road; radio WOKZ; pop. 30,496

Amboy: In Lee County east of Tampico; Charles Dickens' brother (Noel) started a newspaper here in 1854; home to the mercantile firm of Carson Pirie Scott & Company, owned by three Scotch Irish immigrants; *Amboy News*, Illinois Central and Burlington Railroads; Amboy Depot Museum; Amboy Old-Time Pharmacy; pop. 2,561

Andalusia: Rock Island County; located just south at a point where the Rock River flows into the Mississippi; named for a province in southern Spain; B.W. Clark started a famous ferry business here in 1863 located at the western end of the Great Sauk Trail that ran across northern Illinois from Chicago; pop. 1,050

Andover: Henry County off Interstate 80 near Bishop Hill; Swedish singer Jenny Lind, the Swedish Nightingale, endowed a chapel that is open to the public; pop. 594

Bunny Bread logo ®

Anna: Union County; hometown to Frank Willard, creator of famed comic strip, Moon Mullins; hometown to R. Jack Lewis who started the **Bunny Bread** business; known in pioneer times for its deposits of potter's clay; home to Neptune, the War Bond selling pig during World War II; Anna State Hospital for mental patients was the site of a big fire in 1895; pop. 5,136

Annawan: On Route 6 near Interstate 80; Henry County; old Hennepin Canal just north of town; pop. 868

Antioch: Lake County on Route 54, this northeastern Illinois resort town presumably named for New Testament Biblical town; is principal community in the Chain – O' – Lakes area created by Wisconsin Glacier; near Spring Grove Fish Hatchery; Soo Line Railroad; pop. 8,788

Aptakisik: Named for a local Indian; town of Half Day also named for his translated English name

Arcola: In Douglas County, platted in 1855; Broomcorn Capital of Illinois; Louis Klein Broom Museum; Broom Corn Festival in September; named for a town in Italy by Illinois Central officials; large Amish community nearby (the Plain People); birthplace of Johnny Gruelle, creator of **Raggedy Ann and Andy** (annual festival in May (800/336-5456); home to Raggedy Ann and Andy Museum on Main Street; has America's only **Hippie Memorial**, created by Bob Moomaw, an eccentric artist who claims he was never a hippie; Illinois Amish Interpretive Center; Rockome Gardens and Restaurant (217/268-4216), home of America's only **Amish theme park** complete with home-made candy and buggy rides; employees and attendants are either bearded or bonneted; for a quarter you can challenge a chicken named **Bird Brain** to a game of tic-tac-toe (the fowl usually wins); a skeleton pounds the white and ebony keys of an eighty-eight in the **Haunted Cave**; beautiful garden and pond area has placards with pithy Amish sayings like "The best garden club is a hoe handle;" Arcola *Record-Herald*; prep teams called Purple Riders; pop. 2,652

Moon Mullins

Argo: Home to Ted "Killer" Kluszewski, homerun hitter for the Cincinnati Reds in 1950s; Argo brand corn starch

Argonne: Central-east Chicago suburb on Interstate 55 home to Argonne National Research Laboratory (708/252-5562)

Argyle: On the Winnebago County line; a Scottish settlement originally called Scottish Grove

Arlington Heights: Chicago suburb served by Chicago & North Western; home to Arlington Park Race Track, largest in Chicago area; had English turf track when it opened in 1929; **Equipoise** set world record here in 1932 (847/255-4300); Metropolis Performing Arts Center; Reinberg Forest Preserve; Arlington Heights is 106 feet higher than Chicago; pop. 76,031

Aroma Park: Kankakee County at confluence of Kankakee and Iroquois rivers; 821

Arthur: "Where You're a Stranger Only Once;" platted in 1873 by officials of Paris & Decatur Railroad; incorporated 1877; home to the Amish people mostly clustered in Moultrie, Coles and Douglas counties; frugal Amish became very prosperous farmers; Penn Central Railroad; its *Graphic-Clarion* was the first to feature the comic strip "**Mannequins**" by Don Chambers; pop. 2,203

Ashburn – Known as Redwood City

Ashland: In Cass County, **birthplace of Henry Clay**, the Great Compromiser; his home in Kentucky was named Ashland; pop. 1,361

Assumption: Christian County; named for a parish in Louisiana; pop. 1,261

Astoria: Fulton County; named for John Jacob Astor; town is an amalgam of two previous settlements, Washington and Vienna; was on the old stagecoach line from Peoria to Quincy; pop. 1,193

Athens: In Menard County near Springfield; pronounced with a long A; on Route 29 (J.D. Jones Highway); Abe Lincoln met with the Long Nine here in a room above the post office, now a museum (200 South Main); home to the prep Warriors; pop. 1,726

Raggedy Ann

Atkinson: Henry County on Route 6, once a coal mining region settled mostly by Belgians; pop. 1,001

Atlanta: In Logan County; established in 1853 and originally called Xenia; 1865 fire burned most of town to the ground; unusual 8-sided library; on old Route 66; GM & O Railroad; pop. 1,649

Atlas: At the intersection of IL 96 and U.S. 54; once the seat of Pike County; Brigham Young once lived here for 7 weeks

Atwood: Home of the prep Rajahs (girls are called Rajenes); old timers said, "See you at the wood," hence Atwood; pop. 1,290

Auburn: "Redbud City of Illinois" in Sangamon County; pop. 4,317

Aurora: Kane County; named for the goddess of dawn; billed as "The City of Lights," on the Fox River just east of DeKalb; founded by Joseph McCarty who looked first at Chicago and disdained it as a good place for raising bullfrogs; CB&Q railroad shops; two rival towns – East and West Aurora merged in 1857; Stolp's Island a famed dueling site; 1881 streets illuminated by electric lights, the first in the state, reflecting the name Aurora; home to Unstad Collection of Antique Weapons, Jennings Seminary, Aurora College, Phillips Park; its municipal buildings located on island in the middle of the river; Paramount Arts Center is a

Marmion Military Academy in Aurora

restored 1931 art deco theater palace (630/896-6666) Blackberry Historical Farm Village; home to Hollywood Casino; Grand Army of the Republic Museum has Civil War memorabilia (630/897-7221) Mooseheart Orphanage for about 275 boys and girls (630/859-2000); Harambee African-American Cultural and Sports Heritage Center; Ageless Classics Transportation Museum ((630/896-0888); Fox River Paintball (630/585-5651); SciTech hands-on science center (630/859-3434); home to U.S. House Speaker **Dennis Hastert**; pop. 142,150 (3rd in state)

Ava: In Jackson County on Highway 4 and 151; originally called Headquarters; named for Ava Johnson who was the daughter of the postmaster; incorporated in 1894; not far from Carbondale; **Calahan Gang** rustled horses and robbed travelers; Trico High prep teams called the Pioneers; Kent Keller, a local congressman, responsible for building of Route 151 which connected the bottomland along Routes 3 and 4 with Ava; had an old stave factory; home to St. Elizabeth Church; pop. 662

Bannockburn: Lake County; named for town in Scotland; incorporated 1929; pop. 1,429

Barrington: Northwest Chicago suburb on the dividing line between Cook and Lake counties; named for a town in Massachusetts; Chicago millionaires built palatial homes here after World War I; home to Jewel Tea; Carl von Malmborg had a secret formula for making a strong gold-colored metal; home to Health World, an interactive museum for kids (847/842-9100); Robert Marketing makes Vegiform, plastic molds to place over growing plants to make them into unusual shapes; **"Babyface" Nelson** was killed at Langendorf Park by G-men in a shootout that killed 2 G-men but not before they blasted Nelson with 17 rounds; his body dumped near St. Paul's Cemetery; one of 5 Illinois towns with the word Barrington in its name; Fernwood Shetland Stable; pop. 10,168

Barry: Pike County on U.S. 36 west of Pittsfield; terrorized by Missouri "bushwackers" during the Civil War; town name is a misspelling of Barre, Vermont; pop 1,368

Bartlett: Named for early settler Luther Bartlett; Chicago suburb near Elgin; home to Villa Olivia Ski Resort; pop. 36,706

Bartonville: A suburb of Peoria once inhabited largely by coal miners; Keystone Wire; pop. 6,310

Batavia: Kane County; west-central Chicago suburb; called Rock City (for its stone quarries); Windmill Capital of America (3 windmill makers after Civil War); founded by Christopher Payne; named by New York settlers for their town in New York; municipal service buildings were located on an island in the Fox River; its Bellevue Rest Home is where Mary Todd Lincoln was committed; her room has been preserved with décor of the time; birthplace of Denver Nugget pro basketball star, **Dan Issel**; features scenic Batavia River Walk on Fox River; home of the Fermi Acceleration Lab (home to those interesting cosmic creatures known as quarks and quirks); Fermilab boasts world's largest energy particle accelerator with a circular tunnel 4 miles in circumference for studying the nucleus of an atom (630/840-3000); center also features a large herd of buffalo; paper making center; pop. 23,866

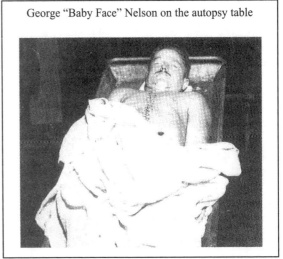

George "Baby Face" Nelson on the autopsy table

Bates: On Route 36, home to a 2-mile long experimental highway built by the state in 1921, with 63 different stretches of pavement

Beardstown: In western Illinois on Route 67 in Cass County and on the Illinois River; named for Thomas Beard, founder and ferryboat operator; the Burlington Railroad crosses the river at Beardstown; town seriously flooded in 1922; Abe Lincoln dramatically defended a young boy accused of murder here in 1858; young lad was son of Hanna Armstrong, a woman who had befriended Abe at New Salem; Lincoln won by **using an almanac** to show that the moon was not full on the night of the murder, casting doubt on the testimony of the accuser; Baehr and Hemplull archaeological Indian sites 13 miles below Beardstown on Illinois River; Rudie Black Gun Museum; Sanganois Conservation Area; pop. 5,766

Beaverville: In Iroquois County, eastern Illinois; home to St. Mary's Catholic Church; KBS Railroad, pop. 391

Beecher: In Will County and named for preacher **Henry Ward Beecher**; Southeast Chicago suburb; home to Plum Creek Nature Center (708/946-2216); pop. 2,033

Beckemeyer: Clinton County near Carlyle Lake; named for Beckemeyer family; pop. 1,043

Belgium: On Route 1 in Vermilion County; named for European town; pop. 486

Belknap: South of Vienna; located on the floodplain of the original path of the Ohio River; near the Cache River State Natural Area famous for its bald cypress trees and more reminiscent of snake-infested Louisiana bayou terrain than Illinois

West Haven Pool at Belleville

West Haven Swimming Pool, Smithton Road, Belleville, Illinois

Belleville: Hometown to 3 governors; formerly known as Compton Hill; chartered in 1819, county seat of St. Clair County, the oldest in the entire state; producer of bleached asparagus; incredibly, Belleville did not get a railroad until the arrival of the Louisville & Nashville in 1870; name translates to Beautiful City; known as the Stove Capital of America because it manufactured so many of them; called Dutch Town because of its large German population; site of Our Lady of the Snows, **world's largest outdoor Catholic shrine** (200 acres 800/533-6279); featured drive-by exhibits include The Journey (story of the Bible), The Mary Chapel (beautifully painted ceiling) Lourdes Grotto (reproduction of famous French cave) The Way of the Cross (statues illustrate the Gospels), The Agony Garden (beautiful scenery), The Way of the Lights (incredibly magnificent lighted nativity scene); home of Southwestern Illinois College; home to Belleville East Lancers and Belleville West Maroons; Belleville Maroons and East St. Louis Flyers big football rivals; 1950's annual Turkey Day game brought out 11,000 spectators; Bellevillians taunted Flyers by calling them "pig killers" (due to nearby stockyards), and Flyer fans returned the insult by calling opposition "morons" instead of Maroons; home to golfers **Jay Haas** and **Bob Goalby**, birthplace of actor **Buddy Ebsen**; St. Louis TV personality **John Pertzborn** is a resident; St. Louis *Globe-Democrat* political cartoonist Don Hesse lived here; annual Art Fair in May; Marsh Stencil Co.; population 41,410

Bellevue: A suburb of Peoria; French for "beautiful view;" noted for building television and radio towers

Bellwood: Chicago suburb home to Borg Warner Company and Chicago Screw Co.

Belvidere: Boone County; City of Murals; northern Illinois town in the valley of the Kishawaukee River founded in 1836; important stop on Chicago-Galena stage route; home to National Sewing Machine; home to popular Potawatomie chief, Big Thunder; after his death, his body sat in state near the courthouse; souvenir hunters filched most of his personal items, even his clothes; Big Thunder gravesite now marked by a memorial boulder; Jennie Hodgers, **a female, volunteered to fight in the Civil War** under the pseudonym of Albert D. Cashier(e); set the record for longevity before being caught; Balliet Antiques; Beaver Creek Pottery; Judith Ford named Miss America in 1968; pop. 20,820

Bement: Piatt County; 7 miles south of Monticello; incorporated in 1874; Lincoln and Douglas met here to set up the schedule for their debates; named for an official of the Great Western Railway; pop. 1,784

Benld: In Macoupin County, named for Ben L. Dorsey, an early settler; according to lore, the man painting the railroad depot sign got drunk and didn't finish it; alternate theory: a storm blew half sign off and they kept the name; home to Coliseum dance hall/casino owned by the Tarro brothers; Sammy Kaye, Tommy Dorsey, Guy Lombardo, Count Basie, Chuck Berry and Ike and Tina Turner all played the Coliseum; Illinois Terminal Railroad; pop. 1,541

Hard Day's Night Bed and Breakfast (courtesy Lori and Bruce Eisenhauer)

Benton: Named for Missouri Senator Thomas Hart Benton; it was here that gangster Charlie Birger was the last man publicly hanged in the state in 1928; **Hard Day's Night Bed and Breakfast** – former home of Louise Caldwell, George Harrison's (the famous Beetle) sister (618/438-2328); Jail Museum has rope used to hang Charlie Birger, a couple of his machine guns, Birger jail cell, a replica of the gallows, and a wicker basket similar to the one his body was placed in after the hanging; John A. Logan home site at 204 South Main; **Doug Collins**, pro basketball star, coach and announcer hails from Benton; prep teams are called the *Rangers*; pop. 6,880

Berkeley: Chicago suburb on Chicago & Northwestern Railway; optimistically named itself after Berkeley, California; pop. 5,245

Bernadotte: Small town in Fulton County; home to old army base, Camp Ellis (roughly 17,500 acres) built in 1942-43 used for training purposes; became inactive around 1945 and most structures moved or torn down; facility processed about 125,000 men; it was a self-sufficient city with its own water supply, railroad, landing strip and 2200 buildings; later used to house 5,000 German prisoners; named for a Swedish King

Berwyn: Chicago residential suburb located next to Cicero full of old Route 66 signs; named for a town in Pennsylvania; has large Bohemian population, Charles Piper and Wilbur Andrews early important real estate developers; many of its residents worked at Western Electric in Cicero and were killed in *Eastland* incident; Morton West High School; pop. 54,016

Wesley Methodist at Bloomington

Bethalto: Madison County on Route 111; name is a contraction of Bethel, a religious name and "alto" from the town of Alton' Bethalto Airport; Dugger Pool Company; prep teams called the Eagles; pop. 9,454

Bethany: Moultrie County near Decatur; founded in 1877; originally called Marrowbone; two starving trappers camping on Marrowbone Creek survived by sucking the marrow out of animal bone to survive; town renamed Bethany for Bethany church in Tennessee; Bethany Timberwolves; *Bethany Echo*; pop. 1,287

Bishop Hill: Near Galva, a Swedish communal colony in Henry County, settled by followers of Eric Jansson (Janson) and Jonas Olson to escape religious persecution by the Lutheran Church. In Sweden, only Lutherans were allowed freedom to worship. Bishop Hill is in Henry County, the **leading hog producing region in the state**, followed by Pike County; named for Biskopskulla, Sweden, Jansson's birthplace, the town's founder; the communal venture ended around 1862; Bishop Hill Cemetery contains graves of 96 settlers who died during the winter of 1846-47; Henry County Historical Museum; Steeple Building 1854 church has clock missing minute hand; legend says settlers so busy only hours were important, not minutes; Jordbruksdagarna (I hope I spelled this right) Harvest Fest in September; Swedish artist Olof Krans; pop. 100

Bloomingdale: Central-east Chicago suburb; home to Stratford Square Mall; Indian Lakes Resort; Medina Country Club; pop. 21,675

Bloomington: "Hub of the Corn Belt;" named for a profusion of flowers in the area; nickname is Prairie City; situated on Bloomington Plain, a long drift left by Wisconsin glacier; early name was Keg Grove (Indians discovered a cache of pioneer Whisky and had a wing-ding party); changed to Blooming Grove; state Republican party organized here in 1856; Normal its twin city; birthplace of **Elbert Hubbart** who wrote "A Message to Garcia," about the Spanish-American War; Illinois Wesleyan University; Illinois Normal University; home of State Farm Insurance; stage actress Margaret Illington (a combination of Illinois and Bloomington) site of Lincoln's "Lost Speech" (so good no one thought to write it down); home to Adlai Stevenson, great-grandfather to Governor Stevenson (1948-52), elected to U.S. Congress by the Greenback Party in 1874, one of the party's few victories; home of **Gene Funk**, seed research scientist; Hollywood of the Aerialists; home to dozens of circus performers such as Antoinette Concello, Eddie Ward, Howard, Fred Green and Mickey King; birth-place of McLean Stephenson, star of television series "M.A.S.H.;" its Franklin Avenue is only street in America with a University at both ends (Illinois State and Illinois Wesleyan); newspaper

is the *Pantagraph;* tourism sites: McLean County Museum of History; David Davis Mansion (he was appointed to U.S. Supreme Court by Lincoln), Prairie Aviation Museum; Shirk Products claims to be only factory in U.S. that makes **Beer Nuts** (originally

called Virginia Redskins); home to Dorothy Gale, niece of Frank Baum who died less than a year after she was born – Dorothy character in *The Wizard of Oz* is named for her; Clover Lawn Mansion (309/828-1084); birthplace of George Pullman's first "sleeper" railroad car; ostentatious Ewing Castle belonged to Hazel Ewing whose father was associated with William Wrigley Jr., the chewing gum magnate; area north of Bloomington called the Grand Prairie; **home to Capt. Ryan Anthony Beaupre, killed in Operation Iraqi Freedom, 2003**; stockyards area called Butcher's Alley; Capital of "Flying Trapeze Acts" (Green brothers); pop. 64,808

Steeple Building at Bishop Hill (Neal Strebel collection)

Blue Island: Located about eighteen miles south from Chicago's Loop; Calumet Sag Channel; Little Calumet River; has a population consisting largely of German and Italian extraction. It is the only hill on the Chicago plain, being a prehistoric glacial ridge. Early settlers perceived a blue haze cloaking its dense woods; home to Libby Foods plant; pop. 23,463

Blue Mound: Macon County on Route 48; early settlers saw mound covered with blue flowers; Meridian Hawks; Whistle Stop Restaurant famous for ragtime weekend dinner/ show/ piano entertainment; town is near Weldon Springs State Park; Decatur & East St. Louis Railroad; pop. 1,129

Bolingbrook – Southwest Chicago suburb; in Will County close to Naperville; located on Interstate 55 and old Route 66; Montana Charlie's on outskirts is one of few surviving authentic Route 66 sites; home to indoor amusement park/shopping mall complex called Old Chicago; Rocket Ice Arena; the roller coaster scene in *The Fury* was filmed in Old Chicago; not incorporated until 1965 and first mayor was John Leonard who spearheaded the drive to incorporate; newspaper is *The Beacon*; prep teams called The Raiders; Midwest Street Rods; pop. 56,321

Bourbonnais: Just north of Kankakee; founded by Francois Bourbonnais as a French trading post that attracted French-Canadians to the area; Noel LeVasseur first settler; Perry Farm; Strickler Planetarium (815/939-5395) at Olivet Nazarene University; Northfield Square Mall; pop. 15,256

Bowen: At the intersection of IL Routes 61 and 94; hometown of Josephine Williams, mother of Senator Barry Goldwater who ran for President in 1964; pop. 535

Bradley: Kankakee County; on Route 45, named to honor David Bradley who built a farm implement factory here; pop. 12,784

Braidwood: Will County; huge coal mining area; Chicago mayor Anton Cermak, a Bohemian, worked in mine here until he was 17; Fossil Ridge; Scotsman James Braidwood sunk one of town's first mine shafts; Mazon Creek fossils; pop. 5,203

Breese: Largest town in Clinton County; on the Cahokia Vincennes Trace which became Route 50, named to honor Judge Sydney Breese; famed early jurist and resident of the town; the **Vander Pluyms**, from Holland, one of the oldest family names in town; home to Excel Bottling Co. producing Ski

Louie Vander Pluym of Breese (courtesy Marillyn Watts of Belleville)

Soda; **King Edward VII** of England went on a hunting trip near Breese in 1860 and became lost in the Santa Fe Bottoms; Cholera Cross built by man whose family was spared from the dread disease; Cougars and Mater Dei Knights prep teams; pop. 4,048

Bremen: On Route 50, near Chester, in southwestern Illinois; home to 98-foot single span covered bridge (first erected 1854) a few miles west on Route 150; bridge is on Mary's River

Bridgeport: Lawrence County; also known as Hardscrabble; oil producing region; Red Hills State Park; near Wabash River; pop. 2,168

Bridgeview: Cook County town with more factories than most Chicago suburbs; pop. 15,335

Brighton: North of Alton near Jerseyville; home to Cardinal ace relief pitcher, Jason Isringhausen; pop. 2,196

Brookfield: Home to Chicago suburb famed Brookfield Zoo where harried parents take children to see carnivorous mammals, poisonous reptiles and screaming primates; founded by real estate speculator Sam Gross; pop. 19,085

Brooklyn: Next to East St. Louis stockyards, town founded by 11 ex-slave families from Missouri, platted and named by white abolitionists; **largest all-Negro community in the state**; named Lovejoy when it incorporated in 1874; nine railroads converged here; pop. 676

Brookport: Massac County; on Route 45 in southeastern Illinois across the river from Paducah, KY; home to the Irvin S. Cobb Bridge connecting the state to Kentucky; near the juncture of the Tennessee and Ohio Rivers; the original Ohio River cut across southern Illinois just south of Golconda and flowed westward past Karnak before heading southwest to present-day Olive Branch and joining the Mississippi River considerably west of the present site of Cairo; pop. 1,054

Buffalo Grove: Northeast Chicago suburb; originally called Nanusha, the Indian word for buffalo; originally laid out as St. Marion; declined after railroad went through nearby Polo: Raupp Memorial Museum; Soo Line Railroad; pop. 42,909

Buncombe: In southern Illinois near Vienna; Vertical Heartland Rock Climbing School (618/995-1427)

Bunker Hill: In Macoupin County; named for Revolutionary War Battle; has bronze memorial statue of Abe Lincoln on large granite base with a kneeling "Lady Liberty" (unveiled in 1904); Larkin Stark, a cooper smith and important early settler in 1837; Wolf Ridge early name for the area due to a den of wolves; pop. 1,801

Burbank: East-central Chicago suburb; Haunted Trails Family Entertainment Center; pop. 27,902

Burksville: Near Route 3, just south of Waterloo; home to Illinois Caverns State Natural Area featuring sinkholes and spooky bat-filled caves; spelunkers required to sign a liability release before exploring is allowed

Bushnell: McDonough County; famous for its large terminal packing house market home to Peter Newell who illustrated Lewis Carroll's *Alice in Wonderland*; Bushnell Water Tank Co.; named for I.N. Bushnell, president of Northern Cross RR; pop. 3,221

Byron: Ogle County on Route 2 south of Rockford, known as the Black Hawk Trail; named for English poet Lord Byron who lost his life in the Greek War of Independence against Turkey; settled by New Englanders; near Rock River Farm, Medill McCormick's estate; Leaf River south of town; farther south is Stronghold, a medieval-type castle built by Walter Strong of the Chicago *Daily News;* site of the Dresden nuclear power plant; underground railroad stopover; pop. 2,917

Cahokia: St. Clair County; built on Cahokia Creek in American Bottom; oldest settlement in Illinois, its courthouse (built 1737 as a residence) near Route 3 is the oldest in the state; home to two-story Jarrot Mansion (1810), first brick building in the state (has a crack caused by the 1811 earthquake); Church of the Holy Family (1699, oldest west of Appalachians); site of old Curtiss-Steinberg Airport in 1930s and Park Air College; home to prep Comanche teams; pop. 16,391

Cairo: Seat of Alexander County; Goose Capital of the World; Illinois' southernmost town; The Confluence of America; the Walled Town (because of its levees); home of ginkgo trees, mimosa, canebrakes and cotton fields; surrounded on three sides by gray Ohio and brown Mississippi waters; in 1886 its river and rail shipments gave it the highest per-capita commercial valuation in the U.S.; immortalized by Mark Twain when Cairo was the destination of Huck and Jim in *Huckleberry Finn;* Cairo is farther south than Richmond, Virginia; points of interest: **the Hewer statue**, a nude by George Barnard, was exhibited at St. Louis World's Fair, old post office, U.S. Custom House Museum;

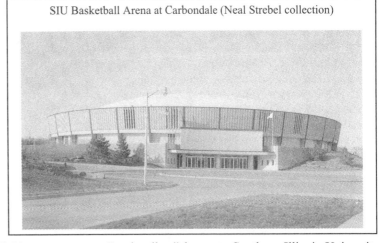
Morse Motel at Cairo on U.S. Highway 51

Halliday House, Magnolia Manor (618/734-0201), Birds Point (lowest spot in the entire state); George Rogers Clark statue at Fort Defiance; Cairo Library has rare Tiffany grandfather clock and a bronze fountain titled "Fishing Boys" by famous sculptor Janet Scudder; annual Magnolia Festival; Riverboat Memorial picnic area (618/776-5281); near Horseshoe Lake Conservation area where 200,000 Canadian geese take refuge; Charles Dickens scathingly called Cairo a "detestable morass . . . a place of fever, ague and death;" (he was angry because he lost money in land investment there); conversely, Mark Twain said Cairo was a good place to "get out of the river;" during Civil War, Cairo was U.S. Grant's headquarters; home to TV personality **Peter Lind Hayes**; flagpole of Grant's river packet *Tigress*, sunk by shore batteries at Vicksburg, is in Lansden Park; home to George "Pop" Hart, a noted watercolor painter; pronounced "Kerro;" prep Pilots; *Cairo Citizen*; pop. 3,632

Old Post Office in Canton (Neal Strebel collection)

Calumet City: Sin Town; owes its existence due to growth of Hammond, Indiana; had reputation of being a wide-open town, similar to East St. Louis; named for the peace pipe of local Indians; originally called Village of West Hammond; home to River Oaks Mall; 1901 fire destroyed G. H. Hammond Meat Packing, town's only major industry; Schrum family among the first settlers; pop. 39,071

Calumet Park: Chicago suburb originally called DeYoung; Calumet Sag Channel; pop. 8,516

Cambridge: Seat of Henry County; in northwestern Illinois; home to Benjamin Walsh an entomologist (bug scientist) who had a collection of 30,000 insects; co-founder and editor of the American Entomologist; killed in 1869 near Rock Island in a railroad accident; near the Quad Cities; Rock Island & Peoria Railroad; pop. 2,180

Campbell: Home of the Moore House, lived in by Rueben and Matilda Moore. Matilda was Abe Lincoln's stepsister

Camp Point: Adams County; home to noted historian **Alan Nevins** who won Pulitzers for biographies of Grover Cleveland and Hamilton Fish; between Beardstown and Quincy; pop. 1,244

Canton: Founded by Isaac Swan; largest town in Fulton County, home to the world's largest coal strip-mining area (Central States Collieries); called Canton because founder believed it was antipodal (opposite side of the Earth) to Canton, China; hit by tornado in 1835; home to P & O Plow Works, very large until incorporated by International Harvester, also at Canton; disc harrow and corn stalk cutter invented here; huge coal deposits here; **triple C economy** – corn, cattle, coal; pop. 15,288

SIU Basketball Arena at Carbondale (Neal Strebel collection)

Capron: On Route 173, settled by Norwegian pioneers; pop. 961

Carbondale: Largest city in Jackson County; Big Muddy River just west of town; Daniel Brush, a Vermonteer considered town's founder; a division point on Illinois Central Railroad and in center of southern Illinois coal fields; name means "coal valley;" home to Southern Illinois University

(24,000 students); near Shawnee National Forest; Giant City State Park; General John Logan and family live in Carbondale several years; SIU attended by **Dennis Franz** of NYPD Blue, comedian/activist Dick Gregory, St. Louis Cardinal quarterback **Jim Hart**; NBA star **Walt Frazier**; SIU Salukis (royal hunting dog of the ancient Egyptians); Egyptian Drive-in on Highway 148 dates back to 1948 (618-988-8116); Woodlawn Cemetery site of **first observance of Memorial Day**; Crab Orchard Lake and National Wildlife Area covering 43,000 acres (618-997-3344); prep Terriers; *Carbondale Times*; *Southern Illinoisan*; pop. 20,681

Carlinville – Home to **Blackburn College**, named for founder Rev. Gideon Blackburn; its county courthouse called the "White Elephant" because it was one of the most costly rural courthouses ever built ($1 million in 1870); judge's chair alone cost $1,500; it was a thing of architectural magnificence; Lincoln spoke in Carlinville but "black Republicanism" was not well received there; town big on tree planting on Arbor Day thanks to Will Otwell; home to author Mary H. Austin, member of the literary glitterati of her era - died in 1934; GM&O Railroad; largest collection of **Sears pre-cut homes** in the nation; Ortic Farm a **Capone hideout**; pop. 5,685

Carlock: Home to Woodford County Cemetery where town's founder, Robert Carlock is buried; Carlock a staunch Democrat and foe of Abe Lincoln; traditionally, Democrats were buried in Woodford Cemetery and Republicans buried in McLean County Cemetery, just across the road; pop. 456

Carlyle: Clinton County seat; named for Englishman, Thomas Carlyle; home to Lake Carlyle, the largest man-made lake in the state (site of annual sailboat regatta); Carlyle Dam Visitor's Center (618/594-5253); rustic General William Dean (Korean War) swinging bridge over Kaskaskia River (only one in the state); John Hill's Fort located here during War of 1812; old Eagle Salt Works; native son **Jack Slade** a legendary outlaw; old Goshen Road from southern Illinois went through Carlyle on its way to Edwardsville; **Ned Buntline** (inventor of the Dime Novel and Colt gun, Buntline Special) once owned a newspaper in Carlyle; prep Indians; *Union Banner*; pop. 3,406

Dean Suspension Bridge on Goshen Road at Carlyle (Illinois Dept. Tourism)

Carmi: White County; on Route 1 and the Little Wabash River; named for the Biblical son of Reuben, grandson of Jacob; marks transition between open prairie and the hill country of southern Illinois; in center of tri-state oil producing region; home to the **Human Hangman**, Phil Hannah, the man who tied the knot for Charlie Birger and dozens of others; L. Haas Museum; town once celebrated annual Rooster Day; had an underwear factory back in 1939; Main Street Café (618/382-4838); prep Bulldogs; *Carmi Times*; pop. 5,422

Carpentersville: Kane County; northern Illinois town settled by Angelo Carpenter of Massachusetts; he established Illinois Iron and Bolt Company, early economic mainstay; pop. 30,586

Carrier Mills: Saline County; town faces the Illinois Ozarks; named for William H. Carrier who built a sawmill in 1870; known locally as "Cat Skin;" pop. 1,886

Carrollton: Seat of Greene County; home of **Major Marcus Reno** who fought alongside Custer at the battle of the Little Big Horn; named for Charles Carroll, a signer of the Declaration of Independence; pop. 2,605

Carol Stream: Chicago suburb; named for developer Jay Stream's daughter; Container Corporation of America; pop. 40,438

Carterville: Site of the first coal mine in Williamson County; Laban Carter was one of town's co-founders; home to John A. Logan College; known as a coal mining town located on mainline of Illinois Central; miner David Wallace introduced practice of taking **canaries into mines** to check for poisonous gas; prep Cubs; *Carterville Courier*; pop. 4,616

Carthage: Seat of Hancock County in western Illinois; a mob from this city attacked the jail and killed Mormon leaders Joseph & Hyrum Smith in 1844; old Carthage Jail acquired by Mormons and bullet holes and bloodstains on walls preserved; Lincoln spoke in Carthage in 1858; home to Carthage College, first Lutheran college in Midwest, and radio station WCAZ; CB&Q RR; pop. 2,725

East side of town square at Carrollton (Neal Strebel collection)

Cary: McHenry County; named for early settler, William Carey; home to Norge ski meets

Casey: On Route 40 in Clark County; 1910 oil boom; home to Richard's Farm Restaurant located in a converted barn (217/826-2034); Saturday Night Auction held every week at the Auction House in downtown area (217/932-6186); named for Zadoc Casey, an early politician; annual Bocce Ball Tournament; pop. 2,942

Caseyville: St. Clair County; named for Irishman/politician Zadoc Casey who platted the town; B&O and Pennsylvania railroads came through north end of town; early coal mining town; situated on Route 157; Zadoc Casey considered founding father of Marion County; population 4,310

Catlin: Vermilion County; a suburb of Danville; named for J.M. Catlin, president of the Great Western Rail Company

Cave-In-Rock: Ohio River town in Hardin County at site of large cave in bluff on the river, once used by counterfeiters and river pirates; pop. 346

Cedarville: Stephenson County; northern Illinois town that is the burial site of Jane Addams; pop. 719

Centralia: Billed itself as Queen City of Egypt; along with nearby Central City (German settled), named for Illinois Central

Railroad; Population Center of USA, Oil Center of Illinois, Gateway to Egypt (houses and businesses use Egyptian motif); in early years known as Crooked Creek; for decades its Orphan basketball team has had more wins than any high school team in the nation; girl teams known as Orphan Annies; originally the Cardinals, the boys' basketball team dressed shabbily in 1942; someone remarked that they looked like a bunch of orphans – like the Lillian Gish movie, *Orphans of the Storm*; once home to Hollywood Candy Company, maker of **Payday**, **Smooth Sailing** and **Zero** candy bars; home of *Thunderbolt Express*, first temperature controlled refrigerated (packed with ice) cars for shipping fruit to Chicago in 1868; IC switched from burning wood to coal around 1866 in its huge repair facilities at Centralia; birthplace of opera singing star Jean Maderia who grew up in East St. Louis; the baseline from which the townships in the state are numbered north and south, passes a few miles south of town; Louisville & Nashville Railroad passed through southern part of town; Southern Railroad also went through Centralia; the

Little person and midget car advertising Zero candy bars from Centralia

CB&Q was city's 2nd largest employer in 1889; Lincoln and Douglas visited state fair held here in 1858; coal mining town that experienced an oil boom in 1938; home to *Morning Sentinel* newspaper; famous residents include Bobby Joe Mason (Harlem Globetrotters), **Gary Gaetti** (baseball) and **Roland Burris** (first African-American elected to statewide office); Carillon Bell Tower with 65 bells and an eight foot long keyboard; Fairview Park has Engine #2500 old railroad steam engine; Warren Murray Hospital for children; pop. 14,136

Cerro Gordo – Piatt County near Decatur; named for a battle in Mexican War; translation means Fat Hill; Hope Welty Library named for resident who started town's first library in her home; originally on Sangamon River until it moved to be next to stagecoach and railroad line; on Routes 105 and 32; prep teams called Broncos; highest point on Norfolk & Western RR between Detroit and St. Louis; pop. 1,436

Champaign-Urbana: Twin Cities; home to the University of Illinois; Urbana founded 1822 by Willard Tompkins; Illinois Central bypassed the city by a mere two miles to its dismay, giving rise to West Urbana; 1855 Urbana tried to annex West Urbana but citizens revolted and incorporated as Champaign, after Champaign County in Ohio; columnist and baseball fanatic **George Will** born in Champaign in 1941; University of Illinois Library is third largest in U.S. behind Harvard and Yale; *Champaign News-Gazette; Urbana Courier*; Illinois Central Railroad; Krannert Art Museum; Lorado Taft statue in front of Altgeld Hall welcomes U of I students; Lorado Taft statue of Lincoln as a lawyer in Urbana's Carle Park; Champaign population 67,518; Urbana pop. 36,395

Alma Mater statue at Altgeld Hall by Lorado Taft at the University of Illinois

Chandler: On Route 78 near its intersection with highway 64; founded by Dr. Charles Chandler; while hurrying to Springfield to buy land adjacent to his farm ahead of a rival, he was lent a horse by a sympathetic stranger. When he later hired a man named Lincoln to survey his land, he was surprised to learn it was the stranger who had loaned him the horse. Back then, it was the custom not to buy land within 80 acres of a neighbor, giving him the option of buying more land at $1.25 an acre when he could afford it.

Channahon: Will County; settled in 1832 at the confluence of Des Plaines and Du Page rivers; from an Indian word meaning meeting of the waters; Briscoe Indian Mound; pop. 7,344

Charleston: Named for postmaster Charles Moron; home to Mildred Lawrence, novelist for young adults; seat of Coles County; on the route of the famed Lincoln Trail Highway, a road built from Vincennes, Indiana, through

Eastern Illinois University at Charleston (Neal Strebel collection)
Teachers College, Charleston, Ill.

Marshall, Charleston, Decatur, Springfield and ending at New Salem (later extended to Petersburg) to mark the route traveled by the

179

Lincoln family as they came from Indiana to Illinois in 1930; site of fourth Lincoln-Douglas debate; site of Eastern Illinois University; site of Second Lincoln Family Home in Illinois as well as a third one; Lincoln Log Cabin Historic Site; graves of Sarah and Thomas Lincoln in Shiloh Cemetery (Abe's step-mother and father); home to tallest statue of Abe Lincoln in world – six stories tall, clutching a copy of the Emancipation Proclamation; population Morton Park has a replica of the Liberty Bell; site of Charleston Riot – armed conflict between 300 men during the Civil War; Penn Central RR; pop. 21,039

Chatsworth: Livingston County; laid out in 1858, its growth spurred by arrival of Toledo, Peoria & Western Railroad; Chatsworth train wreck in 1887 one of worst in history with 85 people killed and scores injured; pop. 1,265

Chebanse: Iroquois-Kankakee County line; from Indian word meaning "little duck;" German farm community

Chenoa: McLean County; established in 1854 at juncture of Chicago & Alton and Oquawka Railroads; Steve's Café (now owned by Ken and Peg Sipe) on old Route 66; name from Indian word *chenowa* meaning "white dove;" pop. 1, 845

Cherry: On highway 89 in north central Illinois, 8 miles northwest of Peru; scene of state's worst mine disaster in 1909; named for coal developer James Cherry; the mine had to be sealed with concrete to extinguish the fire; pop. 509

Cherry Valley: Northern Illinois town near Interstate 90; home to Kegel Motorcycle Company and Diner, world's oldest Harley-Davidson dealership; pop. 2,191

Chester: On Route 3, seat of Randolph County, named for Chester, England; on Bluffs overlooking the Mississippi River; flour, castor beans and coal

Chenoa Motel at Route 24 and U.S. Route 66 (author's collection)

dominated items shipped from its early docks; hometown for the famed cartoon character **Popeye** and his creator, Elzie Seegar (Popeye statue near Chester Bridge); Popeye Parade first weekend in September; Spinach Cal Collectibles sells Popeye memorabilia; home of Menard Prison (built on land owned by Menard; 1889 home to Asylum For Criminally Insane (changed to politically correct version - Mental Health Center) Greenwood/Evergreen Cemetery has grave and marker for Shadrach Bond, state's first governor; nearby is covered bridge that spans Marys River, scene of several stage robberies and murders; Chester Riverfront Mural; prep teams called Yellowjackets; home to Harry Hamilton, author; his book became a movie, *Banjo On My Knee* (Barbara Stanwick); *Herald-Tribune*; pop. 5,185

Chicago: Mud Hole of the Prairie, Blues Capital of the World; Pork City, The City That Works, Second City, The City of Big Shoulders, The Windy City, Chi-town; its Home Insurance Company was the first skyscraper in the world in 1884; home to Brookfield Zoo, Lincoln Park Zoo; Stephen Douglas Tomb & Memorial; Standard Oil Building and its copper wall displaying music-related items; Federal Reserve Bank; Time-Life Building, Chicago Harbor lighthouse; fourth largest city in America; Chicago itself is dominated by the Black and Hispanic populations; whites dominate the city's 175 suburbs; DuSable Museum of African-American Art (773/947-0600); Oriental Institute Museum (773/702-9521); Polish Museum (773/384-3731); Terra Museum of Art (312/664-3939); Museum of Contemporary Art (312/289-2660); Museum of Science & Industry (773/684-1414); Art Institute of Chicago (312/443-3600); Peggy Notebaert Nature Museum (773/755-5100); Broadcast Museum (312/629-6000); Chicago Historical Society (312/642-4600) Museum of Surgical Science (312/642-6502) Nike Town – display of athletic shoes and sports memorabilia (312/642-6363; Untouchables Tours (773/881-1195); Supernatural Tours (708/499-0300) Hotel Monaco's interactive rock n' roll shrine (312/960-8500); Centennial Fountain and Arc – a 90-foot jet stream creates an arc across the Chicago River for 10 minutes on the hour (312/922-3432); Disneyquest – Indoor interactive theme park (312/222-1300); Hancock Center Observatory – elevator to 94th floor for panoramic view of Chicago (888/875-8439) Sears Tower Observatory – elevator to 103rd floor for scenic view (312/875-9696); Chicago Board of Trade is world's largest and oldest; Shedd Aquarium; Roosevelt University; Saint Xavier College; shop the Magnificent Mile on State Street – That Great Street; Here's Chicago: multimedia show on Chicago history (312/467-7114) pop. 2,896,016

Chicago Heights: Home to Svoboda Nickelodeon Museum, displaying a large collection of music boxes; Prairie State College; Drama Group community theater; built on Valpariso Plain, one of the largest terminal moraines in the world; it was here that the Hubbard Trail crossed the east-west Sauk Trail;

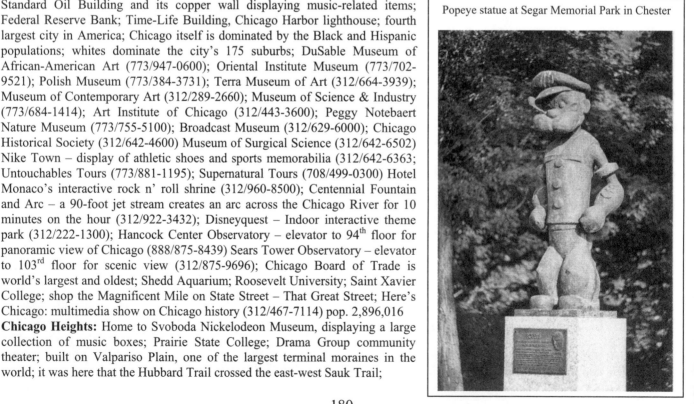

Popeye statue at Segar Memorial Park in Chester

Chicago Fire Monument
(photo: Charles and Kirsten Viola)

Charles on Lake Michigan
(photo: Charles and Kirsten Viola)

Chicago Tribune Tower (Charles and Kirsten Viola)

The Wrigley Building (Charles and Kirsten Viola)

Chicago Board of Trade
(photo: Charles and Kirsten Viola)

The Monadnock Building
(photo: Charles and Kirsten Viola)

The Rookery Building
(Charles and Kirsten Viola)

NOOD Regatta
(photo: Charles and Kirsten Viola)

182

**University Hall at Northwestern University
(photo: Charles and Kirsten Viola)**

**Rockefeller Chapel at Univ. of Chicago
(photo: Charles and Kirsten Viola)**

**Nuclear Energy Memorial at U. of Chicago
(photo: Charles and Kirsten Viola)**

**Main Northwestern University buildings in Chicago
(photo: Charles and Kirsten Viola)**

**Lake view of Shedd Aquarium
(photo: Charles and Kirsten Viola)**

**Chicago's Merchandise Mart
(photo: Charles and Kirsten Viola)**

**Museum of Science and Industry
(photo: Charles and Kirsten Viola)**

**John Hancock Tower and Bloomingdale's
(photo: Charles and Kirsten Viola)**

184

Lion statue at Chicago Art Institute
(photo: Charles and Kirsten Viola)

Frank Lloyd Wright home and studio
(photo: Charles and Kirsten Viola)

Cows on Parade in Chicago
(photo: Charles and Kirsten Viola)

Navy Pier on Lake Michigan
(photo: Charles and Kirsten Viola)

Chicago Adler Planetarium
(photo: Charles and Kirsten Viola)

Buckingham Fountain
(photo: Charles and Kirsten Viola)

Harry Caray's Restaurant
(photo: Charles and Kirsten Viola)

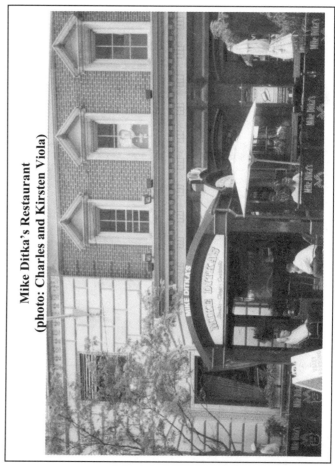

Mike Ditka's Restaurant
(photo: Charles and Kirsten Viola)

**Nathan Moore House by Frank Lloyd Wright
(photo: Charles and Kirsten Viola)**

**Chicago's Lyric Opera House
(photo: Charles and Kirsten Viola)**

**Chicago's Marshall Field's Store
(photo: Charles and Kirsten Viola)**

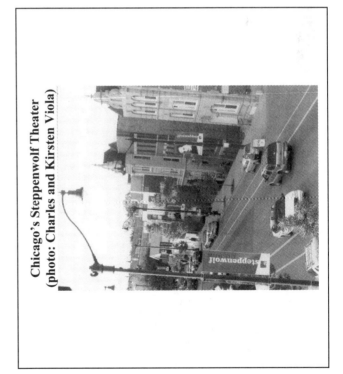

**Chicago's Steppenwolf Theater
(photo: Charles and Kirsten Viola)**

Chicago's Oriental Theater
(photo: Charles and Kirsten Viola)

Unnamed sculpture by Pablo Picasso
(photo: Charles and Kirsten Viola)

Chicago Water Tower
(photo: Charles and Kirsten Viola)

Sculpture at Michigan Ave. Bridge
(photo: Charles and Kirsten Viola)

Absalom Wells the first settler; birthplace of **Bret Saberhagen**, star pitcher for the Kansas City Royals; pop. 32,776

Chicago Ridge: Southeast Chicago suburb; Chicago Ridge Mall; home to one of the largest truck terminals in America; pop. 14,127

Chillicothe: Peoria County; settled by pioneers from Chillicothe, Ohio; Santa Fe RR; pop. 5,996

Chrisman: Edgar County; platted in 1872 by Matthias Chrisman; pop. 1,318

Christopher: Coal mining town in Franklin County

Cicero: Large west Chicago suburb; home base for Al Capone, his brothers and associates, situated in a hotel near the Western Electric plant which employed 40,000 people; its employees were the ones killed (812) in *Eastland* tragedy. Al was called the King of the Gangsters; early settlers Hetty Green and Portus Weare; town once noted for its 100 industrial plants; WHFC radio station; home to Sportsman's Park and Hawthorne racetracks; Ceco Steel Co.; pop. 85,616

Cissna Park: Iroquois County; center of an Apostolic Church community known in Illinois as the New Amish; known for their simple and plain manner of dress and worship services (church building is without ornamentation); Cissna Park Tile; pop. 811

Union Stock Yards Gate desig. by Burnham & Root (courtesy Gary Barber)

Clarendon Hills: Chicago suburb named by Burlington Railroad for a town in England; pop. 7,610

Clinton: De Witt County: site of Lincoln's famous aphorism – "You can fool some of the people all of the time . . ."; seat of DeWitt County; it was here Lincoln first met George McClellan, an engineer for Illinois Central who later became his ambivalent Civil War commander (Lincoln said he had a case of the "slows"); Barnett Hotel is where all the old notables stayed: life-sized statue of Lincoln by Van den Bergen; Clinton Lake – a 5,000 acre cooling facility for Illinois Power Company's nuclear plant; Clement H. Moore Homestead (Twas the night before Christmas . . .); Weldon Springs Recreational Area was once site of Chautauqua meetings featuring William Jennings Bryan, Billy Sunday and Carry Nation; its Days Inn has a series of fantasy suites with décor themes such as Cupid (romance), Jungle, Roman, Space Odyssey and Sahara; Vespasian Warner Library; pop. 7,485

Coal Valley: Rock Island County; home to Niabi Zoo with lions and tigers; pop. 3,606

Cobden: Union County; named for English director of Illinois Central Railroad; hometown to **Agnes Ayers**, silent screen actress who starred in *The Sheik* with Rudolph Valentino; prep teams called "Appleknockers;" Parker Earl of this town is said to have invented refrigerated railroad car; Cobden Museum with Indian artifacts, open on weekends by 3 amateur archaeologists (618/893-2067); Thomas Museum; pop. 1,116

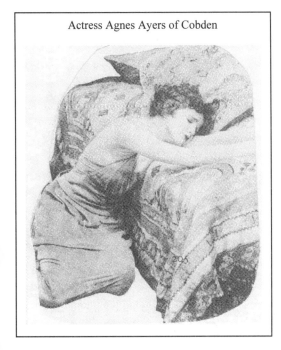
Actress Agnes Ayers of Cobden

Coffeen: Small coal mining town about 7 miles southeast of Hillsboro. It was the site of a big coal strike in 1897. Union organizer **Alexander Bradley** traveled all over southern Illinois that year to persuade laborers to join the United Mine Workers. Their membership rose from a paltry 226 to more than 30,000. He rallied strikers at places like Collinsville, Belleville, DuQuoin, Virden and Murphysboro. He was referred to as The General, and his is one of the great success stories in the history of labor. He was buried at Mt. Olive's Miners' Cemetery in 1918; pop. 709

Alexander Bradley painting on Mt. Olive's Union Hall

Colchester: McDonough County; named for a coal town in England; pop. 1,493

Collinsville: St. Clair/Madison Counties; first settled in 1810 and known as Downing Station; named for several members of the Collins family that came here from Litchfield, Connecticut; Cow Bell Capital of America - because Blum Company made so many of them; its Kahoks (named for a fictitious Indian tribe) are third winningest high school basketball team in the nation (legendary coach Virgil Fletcher); Brooks Catsup water tower is the **largest in the world** (the Heinz people were shocked to learn this); home to annual Model Train Show, spring and fall postcard conventions, Italianfest and Horseradish Festival; home of Fairmont Park racetrack and Cahokia Mounds State Park; home to Tom Tippett, author of *Horse Shoe Bottoms*, the first novel in the state about coal mining (1935) Miners Theater built by five Collinsville locals of the United

Mine Workers of America; high school band won national recognition under Franklin C. Kreider; home to George Musso (Chicago Bears), Hootie Evers (Detroit Tigers); Tom Jaeger (Olympic gold medal swimmer) and Kenny Oberkfell of Maryville attended Collinsville High and starred for baseball Cardinals; state soccer champs in 1991, 1992 and 3rd in 1993; baseball champs 1941 and 1980; Cahokia Mounds Historic Site and Interpretive Center (618/346-5160) a United Nations World Heritage Site (along with Egyptian pyramids and Great Wall of China); 4 prep soccer state championships; pop. 24,707

Colp – Named for mine owner John Colp; a wild Southern Illinois coal mining town known by the moniker Pistol City in 1905

Columbia: Monroe County; on Route 3, freshly scrubbed appearance of this town reflects its German ancestry; site of Fort Piggott (Grand Ruisseau or Great Run), named for the man who later founded East St. Louis; one of the major stops on the old Kaskaskia-Cahokia Trail; Keokuk limestone quarry a major industry for decades; named by George Rogers Clark for Columbia/lady liberty; known for its karst topography, sunken spots due to collapsed Keokuk limestone caves; prep Eagles; *Clarion-Journal*; pop. 7,922

Coulterville: Randolph County; on Highway 13, named for James Coulter, town's first settler; his Stone House, as it is called, still stands; home to **George Khoury** founder of Khoury League baseball for youths; old Ziegler Mine #11 still operating; the old Adami Hotel with its mineral springs and bath was once a big tourist attraction; p. 1,230

Countryside: Chicago suburb on the Joliet Road section of old Route 66; pop. 5,991

Cowden: On Highway 128, named for Marcus Cowden an early landowner and mechanic; in Dry Point Township known for currently being dry with reference to alcohol; Cowden-Herrick prep teams called the Hornets; home to Thompson Mill covered bridge, built in 1843; pop. 612

Crest Hill: Will County near Joliet; has a monument to Lidice, the Czech town obliterated by Hitler in retaliation for Hangman Heydrich being killed by the resistance in Czechoslovakia during World War II; memorial service each year; pop. 13,329

Old Chester Knitting Mills in Collinsville (courtesy Neal Strebel)

Creston: Home to the B.R. Pierce family that brought a herd of Angus cattle from Scotland in 1871 and is said to be the oldest herd in America, reproducing itself generation after generation; pop. 543

Crete: Will County; southeast Chicago suburb; Adventure Trails Family Entertainment; Balmoral Park Racetrack; town name picked from the Bible at random; pop. 7,346

Creve Coeur: Tazewell County; built from plans made by LaSalle to enable Louis XIV to broaden his empire; name means "broken heart;" pop. 5,448

Crystal Lake: McHenry County; named for a nearby crystal clear lake; Chicago & Northwestern Railway; pop. 38,000

Cuba: Fulton County: so named because the numerous ponds around the town reminded founders of the island of Cuba; pop. 1,418

Cullom: Livingston County; home of Hahn Industries, maker of concrete figurines; pop. 563

Cypress: Home to a rare natural sandstone formation in southern Illinois called Rainbow Arch; about a mile west of town off Route 37; it is about 66 feet long and 7 feet high; pop. 271

Dahinda: Home to an unusual Barn Bed and Breakfast (309/639-4408) on scenic Spoon River; barn (it's air conditioned) built old-fashioned way with wooden pegs and square nails

Dallas City: On main line of Santa Fe RR near Nauvoo; named for George Dallas, vice-president of the U.S. 1845-49; pop. 1,055

Danforth: Iroquois County; named for A.H. Danforth who brought 30 families from Holland to settle; p. 587

Danville: Seat of Vermilion County; formerly the site of a Piankeshaw village at the junction of two forks of the Vermilion River; site of important saltlick in pioneer days; named for early settler Dan Beckwith; home to Ward Lamon, lawyer, friend and bodyguard of Lincoln; home to a GM plant, Hyster Fork Lift Company, Quaker Oats plant, **Chuckles Candy** Company; prep athletes called Vikings; birthplace of comic actor **Jerry Van Dyke** ("Coach" and "My Mother the Car"), born in 1931; brother Dick Van Dyke graduated from Danville High in 1944; birthplace of **Robin Yount**, American League MVP in 1982 and

Vermilion Street in Danville (courtesy Neal Strebel)

Vermilion Street, Danville, Ill.

1989; Vermilion County Museum; has a sidewalk called **Celebrity Way**, paying tribute to famous Danvillians like singer Bobby Short; turtle races held at fairgrounds every June; radio station WDAN; Danville Correctional Facility; prep teams called the Vikings; William Fithian Home; state's top coal producer in 1850; Vincennes Trace; pop. 33,904

Darien: Southeast Chicago suburb; Carmelite National Shrine; Darien Sportsplex; pop. 22,860

Decatur: Seat of Macon County on Sangamon River, named for Stephen Decatur, hero of Tripolitan War around 1800; town located on a bend in Sangamon River; site damned in 1923 to form 13-mile long Lake Decatur; home to Millikin University (named for a generous local bank owner); Milliken Big Blue; home of A.E. Staley who built a soybean empire, proposing that soybean not only be used as cattle forage but industrial raw material as well (A.E. Staley now Tate & Lyle); home of Illinois Power; the state's first radio station, WDZ, located here; Fairview Park, radio station WJBL; Decatur was final 1830 destination of Abe Lincoln's family in its trek from Indiana to Illinois ; Lincoln and family lived just west of town, abandoned homestead after only one year; statue of a

Lincoln Square in Decatur (Skip Gatermann of St. Louis collection)

young, barefoot Abe Lincoln at the square; Lake Decatur; Scoville Petting Zoo and Museum (217/421-7435); Mari-Mann Herb Farm (217/422-8800); ADM corporate headquarters located here; the Transfer House is town's most famous landmark; famous for 5 **Kreckel's Kustard** fast food restaurants with promotional advertising by Chicken Cadillacs, sedans fitted with a rooster head on the top and a large tail on the trunk; said to be one of the **most haunted towns in America**; haunted Greenwood Cemetery due to Sangamon River flood that unearthed Confederate and Union Civil War dead; cemetery also haunted by Greenwood Bride, a woman who committed suicide after her fiancé was murdered; resident Hieronymus Mueller patented several inventions for a new "motorwagon;" prep teams MacArthur Generals, Eisenhower Panthers; word Decatur means "dweller at the sign of the cat;" Ralston Purina plant; Spitler Woods State Park; pop. 81,860

Deerfield: Home of Orphans of the Storm, an animal shelter founded by dancer **Irene Castle**; home of **Sarah Lee** (whom nobody doesn't like) Bakery Company; Milwaukee Railroad; pop. 18,420

DeKalb: Barb City; **Barbed Wire Capital of America**; home to Northern Illinois University (25,000 students) and Joseph Glidden, the inventor of barbed wire (the Devil's Rope); named for Baron DeKalb, a German military leader who volunteered his services in the Revolution and was killed in 1780 at the Battle of Camden, S.C.; home to C.L. Gunn, pioneer in seed research; restored Egyptian Theater, a Middle East-style movie palace with statues of Ramses II flanking the stage (815-758-1215); Ellwood House Museum; Sweet Corn Festival every August; Pumpkin Festival in October; home of the first county farm bureau (1912); pop. 39,018

Delavan: Tazewell County; founded in 1863 by Edward Delavan who auctioned off parcels of land; pop. 1,825

DePue: Bureau County riverport community on Lake Depue; glacial moraine forced Illinois River to make a 90 degree turn here; zinc smelting an important early industry; **William Cullen Bryant** received his inspiration for "To A Waterfowl" from Lake Depue while visiting his brother; pop. 1,842

Des Plaines: Originally called Rand to honor Socrates Rand, town's founder; name changed because located near Des Plaines River; Methodist camp meetings held here annually; home of Illinois' first McDonalds; home to Des Plaines Historical Museum, **McDonalds Museum**; home of the **Choo-Choo Restaurant** where meals are delivered by a toy train (847/298-5949); Chicagoland Sports Hall of Fame; once home to 127 different companies; pop. 58,720

Cypress Inn and Sugar Bowl in DesPlaines (Skip Gatermann collection)

Desoto: Named for Spanish explorer who discovered the Mississippi (yes, the Indians already knew of its existence); hit by devastating tornado in 1925 killing about 80 persons, including 38 children trapped in collapsed school; pop. 1,653

Divernon: Off Interstate 55/ old Route 66 in Sangamon County near Dixon Mounds; *Divernon News;* home to Divernon Dragons prep teams; old coal mining town; pop. 1,201

Dixon: The Petunia Capital of the World; on Route 30 and Rock River, seat of Lee County; named for John Dixon, early resident who operated a trading post and ferry; cement industry important to its early economy; Fort Dixon has a large bronze statue (by Leonard Grunelle) of Abe Lincoln as a captain in the Black Hawk War; At Fort Dixon, Lincoln met with two future presidents during Black Hawk War – Jefferson Davis and Zachary Taylor; Winfield Scott, Albert S. Johnston, Joe Johnston, and John Reynolds also were stationed here; **Charles Walgreen,** of drug store fame, lived here; **Ronald Reagan** grew up in Dixon; Reagan's Boyhood Home ((815/288-3404); The Reagan Trail (11 Illinois communities important in his life); Nachusa Hotel hosted presidents Lincoln, Grant, Theodore Roosevelt,

William Howard Taft (our heaviest president) and Reagan (our first divorced president); built in 1837, it is oldest hotel in state; claims to have had the **state's first bathtub**; Reagan was a lifeguard at Lowell Park and is credited with saving dozens of lives; Dixon-Marquette cement plant; Illinois Central RR; pop. 15,941

Dixon Springs: In southeastern Illinois, home to the **Chocolate Factory** (618/949-3829) and Lake Glendale recreation area

Dolton: South of Lake Calumet Harbor founded by the 4 Dolton brothers; served by about 5 railroads; pop. 25,614

Donovan: On Route 52; settled by Swedish immigrants; ironically, a mostly dry community named for a keeper of the wet Buckhorn Tavern; pop. 351

Dowell: Sprouted in 1916 around Kathleen Mine; named for George Dowell, legal advisor for Progressive Miners of America; **Minnesota Fats**, considered the greatest pool player who ever lived, resided here; pop. 441

Downers Grove: Chicago suburb incorporated in 1873 and named for Pierce Downer who settled here from Vermont at the confluence of two Potawatomie trails; known as a commuting suburb; Eastern Art Arcade; Laser Quest tag complex; Downers Grove Cemetery, located in the heart of the business district, was a bone of contention for decades; home to Joy Morton Arboretum (630/719-2400), has The Ginko Restaurant and gift shop (630/968-0074); home to **Peter Pan** peanut butter company, home to **Pepperidge Farm** baked goods company; Ogden Avenue a main thoroughfare; pop. 48,724

Alan Pinkerton of Dundee

Dundee: Northern Illinois town home to **Alan Pinkerton**, head of Union Army's spy service; Haeger Pottery Factory (847/426-3033); Santa's Village in East Dundee features shows, rides and Polar Dome Ice Rink (847/426-6751); prep team are the Cardinals

Dupo: St. Clair County; from the French prairie du pont, "prairie across the bridge" (bridge constructed by Cahokians across a creek); site of large railroad yards, oil boom in 1928 with 300 wells that petered out quickly; just north is scenic Falling Spring Drive, lined by a majestic wall of limestone bluff; oil field existed due to the Waterloo-Dupo anticline in the region, an arched section of terrain; claims to be the oldest "white settlement of continuous occupation" in Illinois; prep Tigers; *Dupo Herald*; pop. 3,933

DuQuoin: Perry County on the old Shawneetown-Kaskaskia Trail; named for Chief Du Quoigne, a Kaskaskia Indian of French extraction; for decades the site of a state fair with the world-famed harness horse race, The Hambletonian; fairground track called The Magic Mile; current fair starts 10 days before Labor Day and runs through the holiday (618/542-9373); one of nation's largest strip mines located there in mid-1930s; Harvey Pitt's Waterfowl Museum; Illinois Cent. RR; prep Indians; *Evening Call*; pop. 6,488

Dwight: Livingston County: established in 1854 by the Chicago & Alton Railroad; named for Henry Dwight, the survey engineer; home to famous Keeley Institute for treatment of drug and alcohol addiction; Keeley was one of first to believe that drunkenness was a disease not a moral weakness (still hotly debated); Dwight Correctional Center for Women; Prince of Wales came here to hunt in 1860; Becker's Route 66 Marathon Station; Feddersen's Pizza Garage; GM&O and Penn Central railroads; pop. 4,363

Gingerbread House at Santa's Village in East Dundee

East Alton: Madison County; home to Olin Corporation Brass Mill and Winchester Western Cartridge, small arms ammunition; pop. 6,830

East Dubuke: Jo Daviess County; the northwesternmost town in the state; named for Julien Dubuque; pop 1,995

East Dundee: In DuPage County on Fox River across from West Dundee; Chicago suburb home to Santa's Village theme park; theme park divided into Old MacDonalds Farm, Coney Island and Santa's World; Racing Rapids Park; settled by German immigrants after failed 1848 revolutions in Europe; home to Haeger Potteries exhibited at Chicago's Century of Progress fair 1933-34; pop. 2,955

East Moline: Rock Island County; Farm Implement Capital of America; International Harvester; near Campbell's Island State Park (Major John Campbell defeated a band of Indians during Black Hawk War); Quad City Race Track; Buddy L Toys; pop. 20,333

East Peoria: Tazewell County; across the river from Peoria; heavy industrial site; pop. 22,638

East St. Louis: St. Clair County; named for Louis IX of France who was killed while on one of the Crusades; Porkopolis (because of its stockyards), City of Champions (because it has so many IHSA high school sports titles); fountain on Mississippi riverfront is the **tallest in the world**, shooting 627 feet high; had first paved road in the state (St. Clair County Turnpike); fastest growing city in America from 1890-1920; second only to Chicago as the U.S. leading rail center; its stock yards led the nation in horse, mule and hog market; called the **Hellhole of the Nation** by W.C. Fields; its Cahokia power plant largest in Mississippi Valley (smokestacks were 21 feet in diameter; plant devoured a ton of pulverized coal every 30 seconds); 15 barge lines preempted the waterfront; **Jackie**

Joyner-Kersee Youth Center; Casino Queen and Crown Hotel; home to **Jimmy Connors**, Jerry Costello, **Miles Davis, Tina Turner, Bob Turley, Johnny Wyrostek,** and **Hank Bauer**; town was 13 percent Negro in 1939, now the blackest town of its size in America; population once 82,000, down to 31,542

Eddyville: On Route 145 in the Shawnee National Forest near Bell Smith Springs (a hiker's paradise) and Burden Falls; named for Henry Eddy, town founder

Edwardsville: Coal mining town on old **Route 66** with annual 66 Festival at Library Park; seat of Madison county, which dastardly Altonites tried to grab; Home of Governors (5); its high school Tigers baseball team was undefeated and ranked #1 in the nation in 1998; basketball standout Manny Jackson is current owner of Harlem Globetrotters; LeClaire Historic District; Southern Illinois University is located here; Madison County Historical Museum and Archive Center; Mark Hamill film, *Stingray* was filmed in Edwardsville; Jackson Browne recorded the songs "Cocaine" and "Shaky Town" for his *Running on Empty* album at the Edwardsville **Holiday Inn** on Route 157/Route 66;

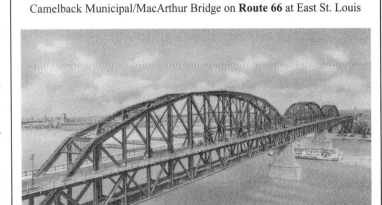

Camelback Municipal/MacArthur Bridge on **Route 66** at East St. Louis

Laurie Metcalf (Jackie on "Roseanne" television show) is a graduate of Edwardsville High; annual Halloween parade draws 11,000 spectators; streetcar tracks that headed out of town and down the bluffs went down Randle Street; Thomas Kirkpatrick first settler;

Propellex factory north of town makes explosives for pilot ejection seats and for capping burning oil wells; home to German artist Max Autenrieb; pop. 21,491

Effingham: At the junction of Routes 40 and 45; The "Heart of the USA" has the John Boos Co., the country's oldest maker of butcher blocks; Heart Theater 1930's movie house; My Garage Corvette Museum; K Square Mall; September Corvette Funfest; home to Lake Kanaga; has a Dixie Truckers Home, named for Lord Effingham of England who supported the colonists in the War for Independence; Flaming Hearts (they sound more like lovers than fighters) prep teams; WCRA radio; Illinois Glove Co.; pop. 12,384

Eldorado: Saline County; home of judge Samuel Elder, cofounder of Elder-Redo, town's original name; The City of Murals; in the Illinois Ozarks; known for its large migration of young men to East St. Louis and Alton for jobs; mothers would frighten children into behaving, not with the bogeyman but a threat: "If you don't stop doing

Edwardsville Holiday Inn, on old **Route 66**, now a Days Inn

that, I won't let you go to East St. Louis when you get older;" hometown to Dr. Dale Cavaness, who killed one son and possibly another, because they didn't "measure up;" pop. 4,534

Elgin: Chicago suburb first settled by James Gifford on the gentle bluffs of the Fox River; home to Elgin Watch Company; Emerson Hough who wrote *The Covered Wagon*; rear admiral Emmet O'Beirne a war hero; home to Gail Borden's milk condensing plant;

Elgin's Board of Trade largely set national dairy prices; Elgin Watchmakers College; Laura Davidson Sears Academy of Fine Arts; Elgin Observatory; David C. Cook Publishing Co. (Protestant Sunday School materials); home to **Frederick Maytag**, washing machine manufacturer known for its repairmen who have so little to do they get bored; Elgin Historical Museum; Grand Victoria Casino; Hemmens Cultural Center; South Elgin has Fox River Trolley Museum featuring 30 minute rides (847/697-4676); prep Maroons; artist Trygve Rovelstad; pop. 94,487

Elizabeth: E-town; Jo Daviess County in northwestern Illinois; named for Mrs. Elizabeth Armstrong who inspired and rallied defenders of Apple River Fort and helped fight off Indian attack until relief arrived; Apple River Fort; Arnold's Pumpkin Patch; Chicago Great Western Railroad Museum; The Wedding Chapel; pop. 682

Elizabethtown: On Route 146; Hardin County seat: Old Rose Hotel (named for Sarah Rose, 618/287-2872), since

Elgin Watch Company in Elgin (Skip Gatermann collection)

193

late 70s a bed and breakfast, until 1978 was the oldest continuously operated hotel in the state, dating back to 1812; only county seat in southern Illinois not to have a railroad; home to historic stone furnace used to smelt iron in early pioneer days; named for Elizabethtown, KY; pop. 348

Cattleman John Gillette

Elk Grove: Chicago suburb home to McDonald's "Hamburger College" (or is it now a university?) where degrees in hamburgerology are awarded; Peony Festival; pop. 34,727

Elkhart: Founded by John Shockey; on Elkhart Hill, a prominent wooded area surrounded by flat prairie; home and burial site of Governor Richard Oglesby, three-time governor of Illinois; on old Route 66; on Old Edwards Trace pioneer trail; Captain Bogardus (national shooting champion) traveled with Buffalo Bill's Wild West Show; prep teams called Mt. Pulaski Toppers; Elkhart Hill juts up from rest of the prairie; resident **John Gillett** was **"Cattle King of the World"** with 16,500 acres of land for his Shorthorn cattle; a crack shot, Adam Bogardus toured with William F. Cody's Wild West Show; pop. 443

Elkville: Southern Illinois town; narrowly averted disaster when hit by huge fire in business district in 1936; pop. 1,001

Ellis Grove: Fort Kaskaskia Historic Site; Pierre Menard House (Illinois' first lieutenant governor) has lower level museum; pop. 381

Ellisville: Small town in Fulton County; on Spoon River Scenic Drive; claims to have the smallest library (in terms of space) in the state

Elmhurst: Chicago suburb named for majestic elm trees; first known as Cottage Hill; public library on old home site of Seth Wadham; home to the Lizzardo Museum of Lapidary (rock polishing) Art (630-833-1616); home of Elmhurst College in Thomas Wilder Park; Carl Sandburg lived in old Torode House; novelist Rosamond du Sardin resided in Elmhurst; home to **Keebler Bakery** where funny little elves make all those yummy cookies; Elmhurst Art Museum; Illinois Prairie Park, a 55-mile long path for equestrians, joggers and cyclists begins here; home to American Movie Palace Museum, houses scale models and artifacts from old nickelodeons and movie palaces (630-782-1800); sports announcer Harry Caray's tombstone in All Saints Cemetery reads "Holy Cow;" population 42,762

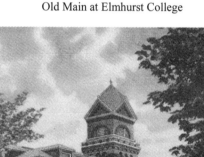
Old Main at Elmhurst College

Elmira: Known as the Scotch settlement; was an important stop on Underground Railroad

Elmwood: Peoria County on Route 78; home to noted sculptor **Lorado Taft**, first noticed for his works at the Columbian Exposition; his "Eagles Nest" artist colony is now part of Northern Illinois University; his bronze, "Pioneers of the Prairies" in Central Park, bears the inscription: "To the pioneers who bridged the streams, subdued the soil and founded a state;" Palace movie theater is longest continuously operating theater in the state, dating back to 1914; home to Lorado Taft Museum (309/742-7791 p.m. only); pop 1,945

El Paso: Woodford County; home of **Lester Pfister**, pioneer in the development of new and improved seed products; experiments took ten years before successful, and he was subject to much ridicule for placing paper bags over ear-shoots and tassels; on crossroads of Routes 51 and 24; pop. 2,695

Elsah: Jersey County; important early steamboat stop on Mississippi River, north of Alton; popular tourist spot with quaint shops and restaurants; home to Principia College (Christian Scientist), home to the Sample House, built in 1931; now known as the Mistake House, it features a variety of building materials and structures used for test purposes (618/374-2131); Elsah was the first instance where the entire New England-like town placed on the National Register of Historic places; 22-mile-long Sam Vadalabene Bike Trail; pop. 635

Elwood: Chicago suburb home to Abraham Lincoln National Cemetery; pop. 1,620

Enfield: White County; home of the **Enfield Horror**, a three-legged, big-headed monster that terrorized a local farmer named Henry McDaniel back in 1972 (Some towns will claim anything to get noticed.); Ann Rutledge once lived here; pop. 625

Equality: In Gallatin county on Louisville & Nashville RR; site of Old Crenshaw Slave House and Nigger Spring, only place in state where slavery was allowed for processing salt at the United States Salines; name comes from French slogan: Liberty, Equality, Fraternity; pop. 721

Eureka: Seat of Woodford County; **Pumpkin Capital** of the World; home to Eureka College, built by the Disciples of Christ, founded by Alexander Campbell; Ronald Reagan played football for Eureka College; Mennonite home for the aged; pop. 4,871

Evanston: Northeast Chicago suburb; Frances Willard and others founded the Women's Christian Temperance Union (WCTU) here; home to Dave's Down-to-Earth Rock Shop, which has a remarkable collection of prehistoric creatures, including the **Tully Monster** (discovered by F. Tully), declared to be the genuine Illinois' state fossil (found only in the Mazon Creek area south of Evanston. The *Tullimonstrum Gregarium* was a foot-long tube-shaped invertebrate that lived millions of years ago in the Illinois Sea (847/866-7374); Father Marquette landed at natural harbor here in 1674; An aristocratic and self-sufficient community on Lake Michigan, town named for John Evans a Methodist Episcopalian who helped found the university; sobriquets: "the finest New England village in the Midwest" and "the safest city in America" (traffic-wise); "the City of Conspicuous Consumption;" long known as a "dry" city; separated from Chicago by Calvary Cemetery; home of Kevin Cronin, founder of REO Speedwagon, which had a #1 hit in 1981, "Keep on Loving You;" points of interest: Dyche Stadium, Dearborn Observatory; Levere Memorial Temple (national headquarters of Sigma Alpha Epsilon fraternity); Grosse Pointe Lighthouse (Marquette landed here 1674), Northwestern University; headquarters of Rotary International; **Charles Gates Dawes House**; its high school was the first to use closed-circuit television (they're either very rich or very innovative); birthplace of political columnist Drew Pearson; pop. 74,239

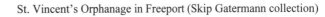

Charles Dawes house in Evanston

Evergreen Park: Chicago suburb known for its evergreens and as the "Village of Churches;" pop. 20,821

Fairbury: Has several Apostolic Churches (Illinois Amish) in the community; pop. 3,968

Fairfield: Wayne County on Route 45; General Lew Wallace (**Ben Hur**) spent a few days here defending his interests in a land suit; worked on manuscript while staying at the Jackson Hotel; stomping grounds of the Shelton brothers gang; William E. Borah, the U.S. senator from Idaho in the post-World War I era was born near Fairfield; pioneers proclaimed there was "no fairer field;" prep Mules; pop 5,421

Fairmont City: First known as Willow Town; an industrial suburb of East St. Louis; birthed by a roundhouse of the Pennsylvania Railroad; home to American Zinc, the world's second leading producer of zinc, used in galvanizing; also home to General Chemical, VC Fertilizer and B&O Railroad; Horseshoe Lake State Park (2,600 acres) is due north on Route 111 (618/931-0270); large Mexican population; name is misnomer since terrain is flat; pop. 2,436

Fairview: Home to the state's largest landfill covering over 80 acres, built on strip-mined land and lined environmentally; pop. 493

Fairview Heights: Home to a large shopping mall on Route 159 called St. Clair Square, one of the most profitable malls in the entire state; town did not incorporate until 1969; pop. 15, 034

Findlay: Near Lake Shelbyville; has Festival of Lights with over two-and-a-half million lights, making it America's second largest Yuletide light festival; draws more than 200,000 visitors annually; pop. 723

Fish Hook: Birthplace of Robert Hughes in 1926. He weighed 11.5 pounds at birth; by age 32 he weighed 1,069 pounds, earning the title, **World's Heaviest Man**; died in 1958 when he contracted a disease and was too large to fit through hospital doors; buried at Benville Cemetery in Mt. Sterling

Flora: Clay County: on Route 45, named for the daughter of one of its founders; home of Egyptian Seed Exchange and Redtop Growers' Warehouse Association; pop. 5,086

Flossmoor: Chicago suburb; residential German town; Scotch name means "gently rolling countryside;" pop. 9.301

Forest Park: Chicago suburb located on the Des Plains River; known for its many cemeteries; Waldheim Cemetery has monument to men hanged in Haymarket Riot; Showmen's Rest in Woodlawn Cemetery is for deceased circus performers, the first plots given to 65 performers killed in a train wreck at Gary, Indiana, in 1918; Forest Park baseball museum is dedicated to early stars of baseball; **Michael Todd**, Elizabeth Taylor's husband, who died in a plane crash, is buried here in Forest Home Cemetery (yes, it's another one of those darned haunted cemeteries); Hemingway's parents also buried here; said to be "more dead than alive because of its plethora of cemeteries; pop. 15,688

Forreston: Cabbage growing community home to an annual Sauerkraut Festival; pop. 1,469

Fort Sheridan: In Lake County, named for Civil War general; motto: Essential to Freedom Since 1887

Fox Lake: In northeastern Illinois near Route 12; popular resort and tourist area; near Chain - O'- Lakes State Park; named for the Fox Indians; pop. 9,178

Fox River Grove: Home to the Norge (Norway) Ski Club, one of the oldest ski organizations in America, founded in 1905. The club was featured on the very first episode of "Wide World of Sports;" 4,362

Frankfort: Will County; "The Town With 1890's Charm" on U.S. Highways 30 & 45; Highway 30 part of the Lincoln Highway, part of an early New York to San Francisco route; paved with concrete in 1914, one of the first in the state; restored Trolley Barn; named for Frankfurt, Germany; pop. 10,391

St. Vincent's Orphanage in Freeport (Skip Gatermann collection)

Franklin Grove: In north-central Illinois, east of Dixon; home of the Lincoln Highway Association's National Headquarters; pop. 1,052

Franklin Park: Chicago suburb; south of O'Hare Airport; served by four railroads; pop. 19,434

Freeburg: In St. Clair County; home to sports teams called the Midgets; home to the Star Mine; IC Railroad; pop. 3,872

Freeport: Stephenson County; site of 2nd Lincoln-Douglas debate; prep teams are called the Pretzels (they'll tie the opposition in knots); in the driftless area of the Pecatonica River Valley; first settled by William "Tutty" Baker; wife complained of his sharing meals with strangers, saying: "This place is getting to be a regular free port for anybody who comes down the trail." – hence the maritime name of Freeport, unusual for a landlocked town; settled early by unsuccessful miners in Galena; it was at Freeport where Douglas said "I am not for the dissolution of the Union under any circumstance." Freeport Arts Center; Stephenson County Historical Museum; Rawleigh Arts Museum; Jane Addams Trail; Krape Park; Pumpkin Junction; site of the unusual James Bruce round barn; Structo Company toy cars; Arcade Manufacturing (hardware); pop. 26,443

Fullersburg/Hinsdale – Home of Loie Fuller, international dance star; performer at the Follies-Bergère; known for her voluminous skirts and layered petticoats

Fulton: Whiteside County; on juncture of Routes 30 (the nation's first trans-continental highway) and 84 (Great River Road) on the Mississippi River in northwest Illinois, named for the inventor of the steamboat; John Baker was town's first settler, building a 3-room log cabin; Daniel and Lucinda Reed were town's first doctors; tomatoes and cucumbers early cash crops; celebrates annual Dutch Days Festival; 9-story windmill proclaims town's Dutch heritage; old Dement House Hotel was an imposing 6-story structure; Dr. Henry M. Kennedy House was head office of Modern Woodmen of America, a fraternal life insurance society; Heritage Canyon is built into a rock quarry and features numerous old-time buildings; Lock and Dam 13; pop. 3,881

Pre-Civil War (steamboat architecture) homes in scenic Galena (Neal Strebel)

Funks Grove: Named for early settler Isaac Funk who was famous for raising cattle; pioneered the use of corn as feed for cattle and hogs; Funk Brothers Seed Company; also noted for making maple syrup (learned from the Indians); syrup still available at gift shop 309/874-3220

Galena: Named for a silvery substance called lead sulfide, also known as galena; third behind Chicago and Springfield as a tourist site; Located on the banks of the Galena River; home to Lewistown Trail that ran from Galena to Springfield; monikers: Crescent City, The Cultural and Commercial Capital of the old Northwest, The City That Time Forgot; northern terminus of Illinois Central Railroad, when first completed, the longest line in the world; its mines placed under government aegis in 1807 to prevent plundering; Grant's home (150,000 visitors a year) was given to him by citizens after he returned from the Civil War; home tours in June and September with interesting examples of a variety of period architecture; Belvedere Mansion (has artifacts from movie, *Gone With the Wind*); Dowling House; U.S. Grant Home; Galena Wax Museum with over 50 figures; Vinegar Hill Lead Mine with guided tour; snowboarding at Chestnut Mountain Resort; in 1840s led the nation in production of lead; Galena/Jo Daviess County History Museum (815/777-9129); Grant Hills Antique Auto Museum; most crooked Main Street in Illinois (direction, not honesty); Galena Road with Stone Arch Bridge Memorial was most important trail in northern Illinois; Chamber of Commerce (815/777-0203); Desoto House Hotel; Farrar's Cabin; pop. 3,460

Cottage Hospital in Galesburg (Neal Strebel collection)

Galesburg: Seat of Knox County; **World's Greatest Mule Market**; home of "Mother" Mary Bickerdyke, known as the **Cyclone in Calico**, an angel of the battlefield, who went to the front to nurse injured Civil War soldiers; home of Knox College and poet Carl Sandburg; Hiram Revels of Mississippi, the first Negro to be elected a U.S. Senator (during Reconstruction) was a Knox College graduate; city conceived by George Washington Gale of Oneida, NY, and planned before settlement around 1835; at this time, Illinois and Indiana was often referred to as the Middle Border; resident Olmstead Ferris introduced popcorn to England by making a presentation to Prince Albert and Queen Victoria; childhood prank in 1950s was to call a store and ask them if they had Prince Albert (tobacco) in a can. If answer was yes, response was: "Well, you'd better let him out before he suffocates;" important stop on Underground Railroad; Galesburg Railroad Museum; Carl Sandburg Historic Site (309/342-2361); Remembrance Rock, a glacial remnant, marks grave of Sandburg and his wife; Galesburg Antique Mall; Orpheum Theater where Jack Benny and Marx Brothers performed; annual national Stearman Airplane Fly-In (309/343-1194); Lincoln-Douglas debate site at Knox College Old Main; prep teams called Silver Streaks for Burlington Northern shops are there; *Galesburg Register-Mail*; Ronald Reagan's family moved here when he was 4 years old; incredibly, **Nancy Davis (Reagan)** also lived for a while in Galesburg, being adopted by Loyal Davis, a Chicago neurosurgeon and Galesburg native; pop. 33,706

Galva: Henry County; a Swedish settlement named for the Swedish seaport of Gefle; Galva is an Anglicized version of this name; home of Jacobsen's Home Bakery famous for making ruska, a delicious sweet bread; not far from Bishop Hill; Best Displays (carpet displays) located here; Dixline – maker of funeral casket hardware; home to **Rollin Kirby**, a famous political cartoonist of the Wilson-Harding-Coolidge/Hoover/FDR era; home to western fiction writer **Luke Short**; pop. 2,758

Gays: Only town in the world that features a **double-decker outhouse** (in 1869 it serviced a two story building); pop. 259

Genesco: Henry County on Route 6, settled by New York residents from Bergen and Genesco; near Lock 24 of Illinois and Mississippi Canal; Ropp Farm; pop. 6,480

Geneva: Seat of Kane County; on both sides of the Fox River; soldiers returning from Black Hawk War extolled town's virtues; it became a supply center for families moving farther west; Swedish Days Festival; home to Gower Champion who won Tony awards for choreographing *Bye, Bye, Birdie, Hello Dolly* and *42ⁿᵈ Street*; died in 1980 of a rare blood disease; pop. 19,515

Genoa: Seventeen miles north of DeKalb; home to Lt. General Glenn Barcus who commanded the 5th Air Force in Korea; settled by pioneers from Genoa, New York; when pronounced, the emphasis is on the "o" as in Gen-O-ah; pop. 4,169

Georgetown: In Vermilion County; on Route 1 near the Indiana Border; named for George Haworth, an early settler; *Georgetown Independent News*; prep teams called Buffaloes; WITY nearby radio station; pop. 3,628

Marchand's Steak House in Germantown (Neal Strebel collection)

Germantown: Birthplace of **Red Schoendienst**, St. Louis Cardinals' baseball player elected to Hall of Fame; on old Germantown Road is a "Cholera Cross" first erected in 1832 to give thanks to God for sparing the family of Joseph Altepeter from cholera; named for its numerous German settlers; pop. 1,118

Gillespie: On Route 16 off Interstate 55 in Macoupin County; the ITS streetcar line that went to Springfield ran down main street; incorporated in 1853; named for Joseph Gillespie, a circuit judge who was a friend of Abe Lincoln's, whom he met in the Black Hawk War; Gillespie was responsible for bringing the Indianapolis & St. Louis Railroad, later called The Big Four; the Chicago & Northwestern Railroad sunk the Superior Mine shaft, and the Gillespie area had 3 of the largest mines in the world; prep teams called the Miners; birthplace of actor/singer **Howard Keel**; pop. 3,412

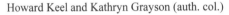

Howard Keel and Kathryn Grayson (auth. col.)

Girard: Macoupin County; named for Frenchman who operated a sawmill; *Girard Gazette*; pop. 2,245

Glen Carbon: Madison County; next to Edwardsville; between routes 157 and 159; name translates to "coal valley;" its coal mines shut down around 1930; founded 1892 by the Madison Coal Co.; home to covered bridge on Glen Carbon Road; reconstructed Yanda log cabin; gangster Charlie Birger's brother lived here and was respected member of the community; new fire house, library, city hall and post office; currently one of the fastest growing communities in the state; gangster Charlie Birger's brother ran a store here and was a respected citizen; pop. 10, 425

Glencoe: Name is a combination of "glen" – a valley site, and "Coe"- the maiden name of the wife of Walter Gurnee, one of the ten founders; home of Chicago Botanic Garden; home to poet Archibald MacLeish; pop. 8,762

Glen Ellyn: Thomas Hill, an early resident, named the community for his wife, Ellyn and a picturesque glen at the base of Cooper Hill; home to Willowbrook Wildlife Haven, featuring a Touch and Feel Museum (630/942-6200); Stacy's Tavern Museum, restored 1846 stagecoach inn; pop. 26,999

Glenview: Chicago suburb; home to Signode Corp. and publisher Scott Foresman; pop. 41,847

Glenwood: Chicago suburb home to Annie Lee Art Gallery (708/757-7100); Country Club Paintball; pop. 9,000

Godfrey: Madison County; on Route 67 near Alton; home to Monticello College for women established by Ben Godfrey; site now Lewis and Clark College; pop. 16,286

Golconda: Lusk's Ferry; smallest county seat (Pope) in Illinois; site of Buel House & Davidson Cabin, state's only remaining structures from the Trail of Tears; town named for a faraway precious gem market in old India and means "land of great wealth;" called the Deer Capital of Illinois because of the good hunting there; The Mansion bed and breakfast (618/683-4400); Smithland Pool/lake; Whispering Angel Gifts; home to One Horse Gap, petroglyphs at Millstone Knob and Clarida Hollow; population 726

Golden: On IL 94 in Adams County; has operating wooden, wind-powered grist mill built in 1872; pop. 629

Golden Gate: In Washington County; was birthplace of **Bat Masterson**, lawman/friend of Teddy Roosevelt; pop. 629

Goreville: Southern Illinois town in Johnson County, named for early settler and merchant, John Gore; home to Ferne Clyffe State Park; 1,000 acres of bluffs, shallow caves, dells, brooks, domes, cascades and rills (618/995-2411); pop. 938

Grafton: Jersey County's oldest town; on the Great River Road; named for the Grafton Mass. and the Duke of Grafton; site where Illinois River flows into the Mississippi; limestone quarries; James Mason, an early leader, predicted Grafton would become Illinois' chief river port; near Pere Marquette State Park with beautiful stone lodge (618/785-2331) and tourism cabins; lodge has 700-ton stone fireplace and has world's largest chess set with a board 12 feet square; Raging Rivers Water Park; near Pere Marquette Lodge and park, built by the CCC in 1930's; restored 1884 Ruebel Hotel now a restaurant; new $6.00 ferry service to St. Charles, Missouri; pop. 609

Grand Chain: In Pulaski County, named for a 6 mile chain of rocks that were a navigational hazard in the Ohio River

Main lodge and gift shop at Pere Marquette State Park (Neal Strebel col.)

Grand Detour: Ogle County; early French name: Grand De Tour for an oxbow bend in the Rock River; major Leonard Andrus of Vermont an early settler who built road to Dixon; near Castle Rock State Park; home to blacksmith John Deere (also from Vermont), inventor of the steel plow in 1837, perfect for Illinois prairie soil; Deere's first plow was an abandoned Sheffield steel saw blade from the Andrus mill; Deere and Andrus later became partners; Deer historic site (815/652-4551)

Grand Tower: In southwest Jackson County on Route 3 west of Big Muddy River; site of Tower Rock, a famous 62-foot high landmark in the Mississippi River, **smallest U.S. National monument;** also home to Fountain Bluff outcrop which eons ago was once located in Missouri, and Devil's Backbone Park; Devil's Tea Table; just south is Grand Tower Island – a near island due to an old meander of the Mississippi nearly forms an island of the area; Devil's Backbone is a geological feature consisting of a narrow ridge of inclined strata; pop. 624

Oil pipe suspension bridge at Grand Tower

Granite City: Madison County; Soccer Capital of Illinois; Six Mile Prairie (six miles from St. Louis) on American Bottom, founded by Neidringhaus brothers of St. Louis to circumvent toll monopoly charged by Wiggins Ferry and Terminal Railroad in East St. Louis; named for durable pots and pans it produced called Graniteware; six different streets converge on unique round "town square;" known as the Pittsburgh of the West because of its steel mills; Look Magazine's All-America City; home of **Karo Syrup**; Granite City Steel; American Steel; Commonwealth Steel; known as one of the Tri-Cities, along with Madison and Venice; Six Mile Museum; home to cowboy star Whip Wilson; lock and dam #27; home to Union Starch, National Lead, Granite City Steel, and Royal Crown Cola; Lock and Dam #27, built in 1953, is the last one on the river; native Danny Jones has fourteen 300 games sanctioned by bowling authorities; 10 IHSA Soccer Championships; prep Warriors; pop. 31,301

Granville: Putnam County; home to Red Ruffing, star pitcher for New York Yankees; Samuel Parr, a noted chemist; mine accident cost him four toes on his left foot, forcing him to become a pitcher instead of an outfielder; 3 World Series wins; inducted into Hall of Fame in 1967; farmer convention here in 1846 lobbied for creation of U.S. Dept. of Commerce; Hopkins Township Museum – art and statuary museum has reproductions of world famous artwork; pop. 1,414

Grayslake: Chicago suburb; home to Lake County Fairgrounds, Glunz Raspberry Farms, Glunz Winery; Meister Brau (master brew) Westphalian draft horses; pop. 18,506

Greenup: Cumberland County on Route 40, named for William Greenup, first clerk of the territorial legislature; 1832 replica covered bridge over the Embarras River, the longest of its type in the state; population 1,532

Greenville: Off Interstate 70, seat of Bond County; Richard Bock Sculpture Museum; (618/664-6724) its DeMoulin Brothers made practically all of the circus costumes used by U.S. performers; home to Greenville College, founded by Free Methodists (old saying from the days when people thought enough about their religion to argue about it: "A Methodist is a Baptist who learned how to read," or vice versa); boyhood home of Robert Ingersoll who became famed agnostic lecturer (he was one of those troublesome PKs – a preacher's kid); home of Greenville Correctional facility; Nevco Scoreboard (electronic sports scoreboards); Rinco Instruments; South Central Motorplex for race car fans; pop. 6,955

Griggsville: Pike County; on IL 107; Purple Martin Capital of the World (brought in to solve mosquito problem – each consumes 2,000 insects daily); site of the Abolition Riot of 1838 between pro-slave and abolitionist forces; pop. 1,258

Gurnee: Named for Chicago mayor Walter Gurnee; site of a 300-acre Six Flags Great America theme park (featuring the American Eagle roller coaster with a 147-foot drop) located here, north of Chicago next to Lake Michigan; Sweet Basil Hill Farm bed and breakfast with a 7 acre sheep farm/ranch; Gurnee Mills Outlet Mall across from Six Flags with 200 stores; Bass Pro Shop (847/856-1229); pop. 28,834

Half Day: Lake County; name is an English translation of Potawatomie Chief (Aptakisic) who lived there

Hamilton: Hancock County; south of Nauvoo on Route 96, part of the Great River Road, across the Mississippi from Keokuk, Iowa; site of Keokuk Dam and Lock # 19; town named for founder Artois Hamilton; pop. 3.029

Hamletsburg: Small bucolic town in southeastern Illinois (Pope County) at the juncture of the Cumberland and Ohio Rivers

Hampshire: Kane County; dairy country; home to Eberly's Honey Hill Apiaries with 1,600 hives (847/464-5165); town originally called Henpeck; pop. 2,900

Hancock: Home to Cpl. Evan T. James, 20, killed in Operation Iraqi Freedom 2003

Hanover: Jo Daviess County; Mallard Capital of the World; On Route 80 and the Apple River; flour and woolen mill important early industries; named for Hanover, Germany; not far from Mississippi Palisades State Park; home to Whistling Wing Duck Hatchery that ships thousands of ducks to game preserves all over the world. Hanover is located on the Mississippi Flyway and many of the ducks are released into the wild; pop. 836

Hardin: Seat of Calhoun County, last town on Illinois River; large apple-growing town and county; John Shaw, known as the Black Prince, controlled early politics in area, said to often rig elections; Hardin has a bridge lift on the Illinois River with a complete section that rises straight up to allow large boats to pass underneath; named for John Hardin, a hero killed in the Mexican War; pop. 959

Harrisburg: Seat of Saline county; in Illinois Ozarks near Garden of the Gods sandstone formations; 230 ft. radio tower of WEBQ a landmark; 13 coal mines opened here in 1905; coal refuse known as gob piles occasionally caught fire producing eerie flickers of light; home to famed Whiskey Chute district of bawdy saloons and joints for miners; platted by sawmill proprietor James Harris; *Daily Register*; pop. 9,860

Hartford: Madison County; established in 1915 on Route 3 on the American Bottom; birthplace of actor Clint Walker; home to International Shoe in its glory days; over 27,000 hides processed in a single week. It took 110 separate processes to prepare hide for shoe leather taking a full 37 days to convert from rawhide to pliable leather; brand new **Lewis and Clark Interpretive Center** (618/251-5811; pop. 1,545

Harvard: McHenry County; in northeastern Illinois near Wisconsin border; served by junction point of two branches of Chicago & North Western RR; **Milk Capital of the World**; Starline Model Dairy Farm; home to Harmilda, a life-sized Fiberglas cow in the middle of Main Street to pay tribute to town's dairy industry; annual Milk Days Festival; pop. 7,996

Harvey: Chicago suburb on the Little Calumet River; birthplace of **Lou Boudreau**; a baseball Hall of Famer; he was an exceptional outfielder and batting champ in 1944 and MVP of the 1948 World Series for the Cleveland Indians; also an all-star basketball player; home to Allis-Chalmers, Harris Hub Company; pop. 30,000

Harwood Heights: Chicago suburb; incorporated 1947; name IS an amalgam of *Har* from Harlem and *wood* from Norwood Park Township; pop. 8,297

Havana: Mason County; "Catfish Riviera of Illinois;" founded by Ossian Ross who instituted a ferry service where the Spoon River empties into the Illinois River; became a shipping point for grain produced in the area; seine fishing an important early industry; Lincoln and Douglas spoke here during 1858 senatorial race; Chautauqua National Wildlife Refuge; near Dixon Mounds historic site; part of a large, flat bottomland area called the Havana Lowland; pop. 3,577

Hebron: Named for a Scottish hymn and pronounced HEE-brin; on Route 47 near Wisconsin border; dairy farming community; has a water tower shaped and painted like a basketball to honor its 1952 state championship team; prep Green Giants probably prep basketball's greatest achievement defeating Quincy in the championship game without ever substituting; Paul and Phil Judson twins on that team; school enrollment was a miniscule 98 students; called Green Giants for the school's proclivity for producing tall hoopsters; pop. 1,038

Hennepin: Putnam County; named for Father Hennepin, early Recollet Franciscan missionary and explorer; site of Benjamin Lundy's abolitionist newspaper, *The Genius of Universal Emancipation*, later printed at Lowell; Jones & Laughlin Steel; pop. 707

Henry: Marshall County; on the Illinois River; old sign: "Best Town in Illinois by a Dam Site;" dam was later blown up; home of Steamboat Elsie, for whom boat captains blew their whistles as they traveled past her house, out of respect for her love of the river; home to B.F. Goodrich chemical plant and Hormel Co.; named for Gen. James Henry of Blackhawk War; pop. 2,540

Herod: On Route 34; southern Illinois town home to Gary DeNeal, author of *A Knight of Another Sort* (Charlie Birger) and publisher of the bi-monthly *Springhouse Magazine*; site of an old volcano, **the only one in the entire Midwest**; slightly northeast is the Garden of the Gods featuring interestingly shaped sandstone formations; named for early settler Thomas Herod

Herrin: In Williamson County on Route 148; became nationally infamous when its citizens killed 19 coal mine guards and scab workers in 1922; prep teams are called *Tigers*; won state basketball championship in 1957; town named for Isaac Herring, one of the first settlers; called Herrin Prairie; noted for White City Amusement Park with giant dance hall played by all the big bands; famous for KKK shootouts on the city streets in 1920s; Borg-Warner plant; annual Herrinfest Italiana in May on Memorial Day Weekend; pop 11,298

Heyworth: McLean County; near Bloomington; founded on old campsite of Kickapoo Indians; home to Simkins War Museum; named for Lawrence Heyworth, a member of Parliament and railroad stockholder; pop. 2,431

Highland: On Route 40; Little Helvetia in Madison County; it had more Swiss immigrants than any town in America; birthplace of female jockey, Barbara Jo Rubin; once home to Pet Milk Company; home to Korte Construction, one of the largest industrial firms in St. Louis metropolitan area; the Midwest edition of the *Wall Street Journal* is printed in Highland; site of weekly stock car races on a track at Lindendale Park; site of yearly Madison County Fair where big attraction is combine demolition derby; home to Wicks Pipe Organ Company that has branched into making experimental plane kits, rolltop desks and grandfather clocks; Heinrich Bosshard wrote *Sempacher Lied* which became part of the Swiss national anthem; pop. 8,438

St. Mary's Catholic Church in Herrin

Highland Park: Chicago suburb; on site of two old Potawatomie villages; home to Deerfield High; Ravinia Park long a great summer music center with large pavilion, summer home to the famed Chicago Symphony (847/266-5100); pop. 31,365

Hillsboro: Seat of Montgomery County; Eagle Picher metal company, American Zinc; pop. 4,359

Hinckley: DeKalb County; platted by F.E. Hinckley, a railroad officer; pop. 1,994

Hinsdale: Chicago suburb; on Route 34, named for W.H. Hinsdale, an early director of the Chicago, Burlington & Quincy Railroad; another community named Fullersburg was annexed in 1923; nearby is Mayslake, the country estate of coal magnate, Francis Peabody; birthplace of tennis star, **Marty Riessen**; Robert Crown Center for Health Education; pop. 17,349

Homer: Champaign County; town either named for Homer, the Greek poet, or by a group of town planners when one said, "That'd be more homer (homelike) to me; pop. 1,200

Homewood: South of Chicago; German/ Dutch town; originally platted in 1852 by James Hart and called Hartford; American Can Company; pop. 19,543

Hoopeston: Located on Route 1 near Danville in Vermilion County; once known as America's "sweet corn capital;" the high school sports teams go by the unusual name "**Cornjerkers**;" was once a big canning center; named for Thomas Hoopes, an early settler; *Hoopeston Chronicle*; radio station WHPO; pop. 5,965

Hooppole: Henry County; located on highway 78 near swampy Green River; derives name from local coopers who cut hickory hoops (bands) for their barrels; resident A. Haff began practice of dehorning Texas longhorns to keep them from injury; originally arrested and fined in 1880, it became common practice when he demonstrated no pain involved; Green River was haven for thousands of passenger pigeons but hunters made them extinct

Hope: Birthplace of Mark and **Carl Van Doren**, both

Louis Latzer Homestead in Highland (founder of Pet Milk)

Pultizer prize winners – Mark for poetry and Carl for a biography of Ben Franklin

Hudson: McLean County; near Lake Bloomington; birthplace of Melville Stone, founder of *Chicago Daily News* and general manager of the Associated Press; name source from original settlers of Hudson Valley in New York who secured town lots by luck of the draw; known as the Hudson Colony; site of last village of Potawatomie in the area; pop. 1,510

Huntley: McHenry County; founded by Thomas Huntley as a station at the Chicago & Northwestern Railway

Hutsonville – Named to honor the Hutson family that was massacred by Indians in 1813; pop. 568
Irvington: Strawberry Capital of Egypt (southern Illinois) in 1890s; pop 736
Itaska: DuPage County; Weidenmiller Company; Nordic Hills Resort; life here is mostly about golf; pop 8,032
Jacksonville: Morgan County; the Schoolhouse of Illinois; named for Andrew Jackson; home to Ben Grierson who led his cavalry forces on a brilliant 600-mile raid (Grierson's Ride) into enemy territory, disrupting communications and supply lines. Rail lines and telegraph facilities were destroyed. It was the basis for the John Wayne film, *The Horse Soldiers*; visited by William Cullen Bryant in 1832 who was duly impressed; home to Illinois College, founded largely through the efforts of the Yale Band led by Edward Beecher, brother to the famous Henry Ward Beecher (daughter, Harriet Beecher Stowe); also home to MacMurray College; has

Soldiers Monument, Central Park, Jacksonville (Neal Strebel collection)

area of town called Portuguese Hill; strongly New England in its early character; a speech at Jacksonville earned Stephen Douglas the title "Little Giant;" William Jennings Bryan, a graduate of Illinois College, practiced law here; Beecher Hall; pop. 18,940
Jamaica: Vermilion County; named for island in West Indies
Johnston City: Williamson County; caught up in Klan wars, Herrin Massacre and Birger/Shelton gang wars; World Billiard Tournament; pop 3,557
Jerseyville: Seat of Jersey County; originally named Hickory Grove; Little Red House part of Underground Railroad; Jersey County Fair; Apple Festival; Ainad Shrine Circus in June; numerous settlers came from New Jersey; 1866 Colonel Fulkerson Mansion; South Victorian Restaurant (618/498-4011); first free schoolhouse in Illinois; pop 7,984
Joliet: Seat of Will County on the Des Plaines River; The Land of Make Believe; Gaming Center of the Midwest (4 casinos); called "City of Spires" for its many church steeples; originally named for Shakespeare's Juliet to match a nearby town named Romeo, it was mistakenly called Joliet (to honor the explorer) at the time of incorporation; native son Edwin Teale a notable author; home of Stateville Correctional Center; Route 66 Raceway; WCLS radio; Joliet Stateville Penitentiary; Wallpaper Capital of America; limestone quarries; horseshoe producer; points of interest: Bird Haven, Pilcher Arboretum, baroque Rialto Square Theater, performed in by Fanny Brice and Al Jolson; has largest hand-cut chandelier in U.S. (815/726-6600) College of St. Francis; high school won so many band competitions it was barred from competition: Empress Casino (800 - HARRAHS); had the nation's first junior college; on northern end of I&M Canal; noted for making wallpaper; population 106,221

Jonesboro: Seat of Union County; site of third debate between Abe Lincoln and Stephen Douglas in 1858; Lincoln sat on porch of old Union House Hotel (burned 1937) and watched Donati's Comet; pop 1,853
Justice: Cook County; its Resurrection Cemetery (708-458-4770) the home of "Resurrection Mary," an active poltergeist first spotted by residents with overactive imaginations in 1939; ghost belongs to either Mary Bregovy or Mary Duranski, both of whom were killed in separate car crashes coming home from a dance; German/Irish community; pop. 12,193
Kampsville: Area called The Nile of North America; home to Koster farm site in Greene County, one of most important archaeological digs in America; free ferry boat service across Illinois River to Brussels; pop. 302
Kankakee: Indian for "beautiful land;" scene of the Kankakee Torrent, a huge glacial meltwater flood that occurred about 15,000 years ago; named for Kankakee

Stinson Memorial Library Jonesboro/Anna (Skip Gatermann collection)

River which flows through it; home to Illinois Central and Penn Central Railroads; home to George Gray Barnard, noted sculptor who did *The Hewer* (in Cairo), *Prodigal Son* and *Crouching Venus*; large producer of TNT during World War II; birthplace of NBA basketball star **Jack Sikma**; Strickler Planetarium (815/939-5395); two of Frank Lloyd Wright's houses are in area; the Bradley House was his first done in the "prairie style;" prep teams called Kays; home to baseball manager Casey Stengel and Frank Waterman, fountain pen manufacturer; pop. 27,491
Kansas: Edgar County; named for Kansas (Sioux) Indians; pop 842
Karnak: Was the last town in southern Illinois (known as Little Egypt) to be named after a place in Egypt; pop. 619
Kaskaskia: First state capital; thanks to 1881 flood, this Illinois town is the only one located west of the Mississippi River in Missouri; home to **Liberty Bell of the West** (on the island); liberated from British rule by George Rogers Clark; Kaskaskia Island

and the bell are on the west side of the Mississippi, Kaskaskia Historic Site and Pierre Menard Home are on the east side of the river (618/859-3741)

Keensburg: On Route 1 between Mt. Carmel and Grayville; near Beall Woods State Park; home to AMAX Wabash Coal Mine; the Harrisburg seam here is about 6 feet thick; pop. 252

Writer Eugene Field

Kenilworth: Cook County; named for one of Sir Walter Scott's novels; writer Eugene Field buried here; native Daniel Terra was named Ambassador at Large for Cultural Affairs by President Reagan; pop. 2,494

Kewanee: Henry County: Winnebago Indian for "prairie chicken;" Hog Raising Capital of the World; native son John Hyatt; **invented celluloid**; home to Kewanee Boiler Factory; Boss work glove factory, Francis Park and Woodland Palace (the estate of Fred Francis, a brilliant engineer/mathematician); Francis, a practicing nudist, patented a watch-making tool for Elgin Watch and retired in his mid-thirties and lived off royalties; older part of town known as Wethersfield, founded by religious leaders from Connecticut who deemed it necessary to counter Catholic influence in Illinois; home to Chicago, Burlington & Quincy Railroad (known in its early years as the Military Tract Railroad); Boss work gloves; Walworth Valve Manufacturing (known for making monkey wrenches); pop. 12,944

Kincaid: Christian County; large Peabody Mine; Commonwealth Edison plant with two 500 foot stacks provides electricity to Chicago; In the heyday of coal mining in the 1920s, Peabody employed 2,300 workers at their two mines; named for James Kincaid, Peabody official who planned the town; pop. 1,441

Kinmundy: Northeast of Salem; has Ingram's Log Cabin Village with 13 authentic log buildings dating as far back as 1818 (618/547-7123); pop. 892

Aerial view of Kankakee business district (Neal Strebel collection)

Knoxville: Knox County; home of the Wolf Covered Bridge over the Spoon River, built in 1848; population 3,183

Lacon: Seat of Marshall County; old major Illinois River port; weekly newspaper *Lacon Home Journal* dates back to 1837; pop. 1,979

Ladd: Bureau County; Italian community named for George Ladd of Peru who built a local railroad; pop. 1,313

LaFox: Chicago suburb; Garfield Farm Museum

La Grange: Named for Lafayette's homestead in France; also a town of that name in Tennessee; first suburb developed along Chicago, Burlington & Quincy Railroad; site of Masonic Children's Home; The Corral Youth Club; pop. 15,608

La Harpe: Hancock County; named for the French explorer Benard de la Harpe; pop. 1,385

Lake Forest – Described by one state publication as a "rich man's dormitory for Chicago;" its Deerpath Avenue was on old buffalo/deer route to Lake Michigan; home to Lake Forest College and Barat College; the setting for the academy award-winning film directed by Robert Redford, *Ordinary People*; pop. 20,059

Kewanee: New Central Grade and Junior High School (Skip Gatermann col.)

Lake Villa – On highway 59 in northeastern Illinois; resort community; near Allendale Farm School modeled after Father Flannigan's Boys Town in Nebraska; pop. 5,864

Lake Zurich: Northeastern Illinois summer resort center founded in 1836 by Chicagoan Seth Paine; changed name from Cedar Lake to Lake Zurich; pop. 18,104

Lanark: Home of the Illinois poet Glenn Ward Dresbach; Standish House bed and breakfast (815/493-2307); pop. 1,584

Lansing: Chicago suburb; home to Lansing Historical Society and Museum that has replicas of the Inaugural Ball gowns of all the First Ladies (708-474-6160) Hollywood Park family entertainment center; named for early pioneer John Lansing; pop. 28,332

LaSalle: LaSalle County: Terminus of the Illinois-Michigan Canal on Illinois River; home to Hegeler Zinc Company (ore came from Galena); LaSalle-Peru-Ogelsby College; at Fort Wilbourn, Lincoln enlisted for the Blackhawk War; Starved Rock State Park; Matthiessen State Park; native Zez Confrey wrote the popular 1920s song, "Kitten On The Keys;" pop. 9,796

Lawrenceville: On Route 50, originally known as the Old Trace Road, an Indian and Buffalo trail connecting Louisville and Cahokia. The B&O Railroad tracks roughly parallel Route 50, and this line generally marks the northern boundary of what is referred to as southern Illinois; town lies on west bank of Embarras River (pronounced Am-braw - so tricky to navigate it embarrassed skilled pilots); seat of Lawrence County; known as spindletop country for its oil, starting with first gusher in 1906; home of Indian Oil Refinery; Elizabeth Reed hanged here – **only woman in Illinois so executed**; Lincoln Trail State Memorial Monument on Route 50; pop. 4,745

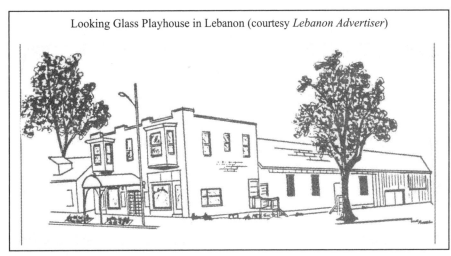

Looking Glass Playhouse in Lebanon (courtesy *Lebanon Advertiser*)

Lebanon: Its McKendree College houses the oldest existing cast metal bell in the United States; home to Mermaid Inn, owned by a retired Sea Captain who **claimed to have seen mermaids**; town visited by both Lincoln and Charles Dickens in 1840s; located on old St. Louis to Vincennes stagecoach route; Looking Glass Prairie; Looking Glass Theater; home to Emerald Mound, 2nd largest earthen Indian mound in the state; prep teams called Greyhounds; pop. 3,523

Leland: In northern Illinois, south of Shabbona; Hang Glide Chicago on routes 23 and 34; pop. 970

Lemont: Chicago suburb; French for "the mountain;" the only known cookie jar museum in the world with over 2,000 containers collected by Lucille Bromberek; home to St. James of the Sag, Cook County's oldest church; erected on site of old Indian burial ground and said to be Illinois' most haunted church (yes, and everyone has an exact duplicate somewhere out there known as a doppelganger); ghost monks have been sighted at the cemetery near the church, performing Gregorian chants in Latin (630/257-7000); Camp Sagawau forest preserve; pop. 13,098

Lena: Stephenson County; near Wisconsin border; near Lake Le-Aqua-Na State Park which is derived from the name Lena and aqua (Latin for water); home to the Chris Jensen Round Barn; pop. 2,887

Lerna: Has the log cabin home that belonged to Abe Lincoln's stepmother and father, Sarah and Thomas; pop. 322

LeRoy: McClean County; features another one of those famous Dixie Truckers Home café and gas stations; pop. 3,332

Lewistown: Seat of Fulton County, named for the son of Ossian Ross, a veteran of the War of 1812; home to Edgar Lee Masters, a Chicago lawyer turned poet, famous for *Spoon River Anthology*; located in central Illinois, nearby is the Dickson Mound State Museum on a 63 acre park where Native American burial mounds have been excavated and are on display; the first town laid out in the Military Tract; Stephen Douglas once spoke at nearby Proctor's Grove in 1858 to a crowd of 5,000 people; Ross later founded the town of Havana where he lived in retirement; Lincoln gave "Return to the Fountain" speech here; Dickson Mound Indian burial site; pop. 2,522

Edgar Lee Masters' Home in Lewistown

Lexington: McClean County; named for Revolutionary War battle of Lexington; home to some original pavement on the famed road known as Route 66; town founded near settlement of Kickapoo and Delaware tribes; not a single scalp was lost during the Black Hawk War, Chicago & Mississippi Railroad arrived in 1857; pop. 1,912

Libertyville: Lake County; originally known as Independence Grove; on Route 45; Daniel Webster and Samuel Insull owned land here; home of Foulds Spaghetti Plant; Mundelein College is nearby, named for Catholic Archbishop of Chicago; Architect David Adler's summer home is here – now a cultural center; Lambs Farm has17 foot tall Fiberglas statue of a cow, a 15 foot woodsman and a 10 foot tall milk bottle; The Lambs is a 63 acre residence and work site dedicated to helping the handicapped with 250,000 visitors annually; has David Adler Cultural Center (847/367-0707) Marlon Brando once lived here and worked as an usher in a local theater; Adlai Stevenson farm is now part of Lake County Forest Preserve; Samuel Insull estate; The Holiday Shop – year-round Christmas store; Mickey Finn's Brewery; Gene Harris Shetland Pony Ranch; pop. 20,742

Lincoln – Seat of Logan County; town named to honor Abe Lincoln because he had drawn up the legal papers for the three men who platted the town; Lincoln tried to discourage use of the name by telling them: "I never knew of anything named Lincoln that amounted to much;" Brainerd Park was old, large Chautauqua meeting site; its Chautauqua buildings and park grounds were among the largest in the state; original settlement called Postville; town has a large watermelon statue (217/732-8687) to commemorate an event in 1853 when Abe Lincoln dedicated the town with a watermelon; Logan Correctional Center; Logan County claims the geographic center of the state; Kickapoo Town, southwest of Lincoln, was site where Ann Gilham and 3 of her children were captured by Indians; it took her husband several months to find her and bargain with the Indians for her release in 1790; has rare brick-paved section of Route 66; pop. 15,369

Lincolnshire: Chicago suburb; Marriott's Resort and Theater; Flatlander's Restaurant and Brewery; home of Adlai E. Stevenson; pop. 6,108

Lincolnwood: Cook County town noted for elm trees planted in 1830s; pop. 12,359

Lisle: Chicago suburb; known as Arboretum Village; current home of the Morton Arboretum where 4,800 species of plants are featured on a 1,700 acre site; Lisle Station Park; Jurica Nature Museum; pop. 21,182

Litchfield: Montgomery County; named for an early town Terre Haute & Alton Railroad official, on old Route 66 and in the center of an important coal field that spread over 6 counties; in 1859 was scene of first commercial oil production in the state; home to large Brown Shoe Factory, Roll-A-Way Skate Company; International Stove, Planet Mill; prep teams called Panthers; Niehaus Cycle Sales; Sky View Drive-in Theater on old Route 66 – continuous since 1950; pop. 6,815

Odd Fellows' Children's Home in Lincoln (author's collection)

Lockport: Will County; home of inventor John Lane who made steel plows in 1835; founded and platted in 1836 by I&M Canal commissioners to serve as headquarters for the I&M Canal; site where Chicago Sanitary Ship Canal linked with Des Plaines River in 1900 making the **Chicago River flow backward**, featured in Ripley's "Believe It Or Not;" site of first locks on upper Illinois River uniting Great Lakes and Mississippi waterways for barge traffic; this lock determines the volume of water withdrawn from Lake Michigan; Illinois and Michigan Canal Museum (815/838-5080); home to Dellwood Park; Pioneer Settlement (14 structures); Rialto 1926 Theater (815/726-6600); pop. 15,191

Lombard: Chicago suburb; called **Lilac Town** as a result of William Plum estate; Plum collected species of lilacs from all over the world; Lombard Lilac League annually holds Lilac Pageant (630/629-3799); Yorktown Cinema Complex has 18 screens; Boogie Nights dinner and dancing; Sheldon Peck Homestead; Whirly Ball family entertainment (630/932-4800) platted by Chicagoan Josiah Lombard in 1868; Sheldon Peck House functioned as a station on Underground Railroad; town depicted in two novels by Katherine Reynolds, *Green Valley* and *Willow Creek*, birthplace of actress Mary Elizabeth Mastrantonio who starred in Kevin Kostner's *Robin Hood* ; pop. 42,322

Long Grove: Located at Routes 83 and 53; historic village originally called Mutterscholz by German settlers; currently known as an antique haven with 90 shops; Long Grove Apple Haus (847/634-0730) features cider and apple butter; Long Grove Confectionery (847/634-0080) is noted for its sugary delights; pop. 6,735

Louisville: Seat of Clay County; pronounced Lewis-ville not Looieville; pop. 1,242

Lyle: Home to Benedictine College

Lyons: Cook County; located on the old portage between Chicago and Des Plaines rivers; largely a Chicago suburb residential town; twenty-foot statue of Marquette and Joliet; calls itself the Gateway to the West; Hoffman Tower; Houdek's Steak House; pop. 10,255

Litchfield Elks Lodge 654 B.P.O.E. built in 1922 (courtesy Neal Strebel)

Mackinaw: Tazewell County; sometimes spelled Mackinac; name means "turtle" in Ojibway; pop. 1,452

Macomb: Seat of McDonough County, settled by New Englanders; Home to Western Illinois University which has a geology museum; name honors Alexander Macomb, Commander-in-Chief of the U.S. Army (1828-1841) who fought the British at Lake Champlain in War of 1812; home of Argyle (Scottish town that gave us Argyle socks) Lake State Park; manufacturing center; Forest of Arden, a professor's private estate where his students gave performances of *As You Like It* and *Midsummer Night's Dream*; summer training camp for the **St. Louis Rams**; pop. 20,000

Macon: Home to Pvt. Jonathan L. Gifford, 20, killed in Operation Iraqi Freedom 2003

Madison: Madison County; Eagle Park; platted in 1889 by St. Louis industrialists for the purpose of building the McKinley Bridge; home to a newly built NASCAR racetrack located just off Interstate 70 near East St. Louis; American Car Foundry; pop. 4,545

Maeystown: Southeast of Waterloo; entire town has been designated a National Historic District, only 2 Illinois towns so designated; founded by Jacob Maeys in 1852; German settlers came from Bavaria Reinpfalz

Mahomet: Champaign County; probably named for a local Indian tribe; eastern Illinois; home of Early American Museum in Lake of the Woods Park on State Route 47 (217/586-3360); thousands of artifacts reflecting early pioneer life; has the Mahomet Aquifer, a bountiful groundwater reservoir; pop. 3,100

Makanda: Named for Kaskaskia Chief Kanda; gravesite of a three-legged dog named Boomer who was killed in 1859 while trying to warn his engineer master of a hotbox fire on a train. The grave marker is located south of the train depot; in his honor, a dormitory at SIU Carbondale was named Boomer Hall; early railroad conductors shouted "My-candy" to announce arrival at the town; residence of Senator Paul Simon; "about as exciting as a day in Makanda" an age old put-down; home to Giant City State Park (its sandstone formations looked like a city built by giants) and lodge with 34 rustic cabins (3,700 acres – 618/457-4921); Fern Rocks Nature Preserve; Little Grassy Lake (161 campsites (618/457-4836); once the largest fruit shipping point on the I.C.R.R; pop. 419

Picturesque Makanda, gateway to Giant City State Park (courtesy Mike Coles)

Manito: Mason County; variation on Algonquin word Manitou, which means "Great Spirit;" p. 1,733

Manteno; Kankakee County; named for the half-Indian daughter of Francois Bourbonnais, a French scout; pop. 6,414

Marengo: Small northern Illinois town home to McGill Metal Products, one of world's largest makers of mousetraps; home to Egbert Van Alstyne, composer of the song, "In The Shade of the Old Apple Tree;" pop. 6,355

Marine: Madison County town that was named by sailors who settled there; pop 910

Marion: Seat of Williamson County; public square is where politician John Logan, a Democrat, gave a pro-Union speech that was largely responsible in winning southern Illinois to the Northern cause during the Civil War; agnostic Robert Ingersoll and politician/general John Logan lived here; both organized Civil War regiments and became colonels; first aerial bombing attack on U.S. soil (**Ripley's Believe it or Not**) happened here when Shelton gang dropped bombs from a Curtiss "Jenny" on Charlie Birger gang's hangout known as Shady Rest; near Crab Orchard Wildlife Refuge at Crab Orchard Lake, one of the state's largest man-made lakes; Illinois Center shopping mall; actress Judith Ivey was a Marion High Wildcat; p. 16,035

Township High School at Marion (courtesy Neal Strebel)

Marissa: St. Clair County town; from the Hebrew town Mareshah; Matthew Hamilton House a link on Underground Railroad; Marissa Coal Museum; Schneidewind Barn Museum (618/295-2726); pop. 2,141

Maroa: Macon County; town council pulled letters from a hat for the name; pop.1,654

Marseilles: LaSalle County; pronounced mar-sales; located on a stretch of rapids in the Illinois River; named for a town in France; home to Marseilles Canal to get around the rapids; 4,655

Marshall: Seat of Clark County on Route 40; founded by William Archer and named by him to honor his idol, Chief Justice John Marshall; home to author James Jones; Indiana writer Booth Tarkington visited the town in boyhood years and made it the setting in his novel, *Penrod*; 1841 Archer House is Illinois' oldest hotel; annual frog jumping contest; pop. 3,600

Broadway Street Scene, Mattoon (author's collection)

Mascoutah: St. Clair County town with the Mascouten Indian tribe name (it means prairie), originally called Mechanicsburgh; located near Scott Air Base and Mid-America Airport; served by L&N Railroad; pop. 5,659

Matteson: Cook County Chicago suburb; home to Lincoln Mall on Route 30; named for Governor Joel Matteson; pop. 12,928

Mattoon: In Coles County off Interstate 57; named for William Mattoon, an official on the Illinois Central; Highway 45 and the Lincoln Memorial Highway intersect here; U.S. Grant mustered the 21st Illinois Infantry into service at Mattoon; home of Thomas Chamberlin who founded the *Journal of Geology* in 1893; south of Mattoon is the Shelbyville Moraine, marking the maximum advance of recent glaciation; Paradise Lake was stocked annually with 750,000 fish from Mattoon Hatchery; Mad Gasser of 1944 is an urban legend based on stories about a man with a gas mask who surreptitiously went around spraying some kind of unknown gas on a few town folk; psychologists attribute incidents to a bad case of "war jitters" and mass hysteria; prep teams called the Green Wave; radio stations WLBH, WMCI; *Mattoon Journal Gazette*; home of Arland D. Williams who was one of the people in the 1982 Air Florida plane crash at Washington D.C.; he helped rescue several others before he drowned; U.S. Grant flagpole; pop. 18,291

Maywood: Large northwest Chicago suburb; Chicago industrial expansion created need for home sites; pop. 26,987

Maeystown: A 150-year-old German community, north of Prairie du Rocher west of the Great River Road; Maeystown General Store sells Shaker furniture; Corner George Inn a bed and breakfast; Eschys Bar & Restaurant; pop. 100

Cobblestone Bandstand in a Park at Metamora

McHenry: Located on the Fox River on Route 120, called Gateway to Chain -O'- Lakes; settled by Dr. Christy Wheeler; on route of Chicago and Northwestern Railroad; popular vacation and resort area; Moraine Hills State Park just 3 miles south of town; park's Lake Defiance was created by a leftover chunk of melted glacier; Volo Bog State Natural Area just east of town; named for an army officer in the War of 1812 and Blackhawk War; pop. 21,501

McLean: Home of the Route 66 Hall of Fame at the Dixie Truckers Home; museum and gift shop opened in 1990; full of memorabilia dedicated to the Mother Road (309/874-2323); pop. 808

McLeansboro: Hamilton County seat; racehorse country; site of County Fair; on Routes 14 and 242; named for Dr. William McLean who built the first house in the area; home of high school sports teams known as the Foxes (and Foxettes?) – no, uh, Lady Foxes; People's Bank, next to the McCoy Library is classic example of American Baroque architecture; Chicago Bulls star and Utah Jazz coach **Jerry Sloan** hails from here; served by L&N Railroad; radio station WMCL, home of Cuzin Eddie Show; pop. 2,945

Melrose Park – Chicago suburb near O'Hare with large Italian population; birthplace of singer/dancer Carol Lawrence, wife of Robert Goulet; Stern Corporation is the **only U.S. maker of pinball machines**; Jewel Foods; pop. 23,171

Mendota: World's Greatest Little City; from the Dakota word *mdote* meaning "mouth of the river;" Sweet Corn Festival every August; on highways 51 and 34; important Asparagus Co. canning center; Del Monte Company; 1837 hometown to the famous pro-Confederate ex-schoolteacher, William Quantrill, who led the Civil War border ruffian raid on Lawrence, Kansas, killing 180 innocent civilian men and boys. This massacre has no equal in America. Also home to Helen Hockison, one of the nation's first female cartoonists whose works often appeared in The New Yorker; to its north is the Bloomington Moraine, one of the longest known to geologists; to the south is the LaSalle coal district; hosts a Tri-county Fair; Time Was Museum; pop. 7,272

Meredosia: Morgan County; Button Capital of America (Boyd Button Co. made pearl buttons from mussel shells); at mouth of Meredosia Lake; home to a section of the Northern Cross, the state's first railroad (which ended in failure); name comes from a corruption of the French for Marais (swamp) and d'osier (of basket reeds); native son Frank Skinner did the music score for dozens of films, including *Shenandoah* and *Bedtime for Bonzo*; pop. 1,041

Mermet: Small, southeastern Illinois town by Mermet Lake; named for French Vicar, Jean Mermet

Metamora: In Woodford County; Metamora Courthouse is one of two remaining in Lincoln's 8th Circuit; Adlai E. Stevenson house, erected 1858, home to Grover Cleveland's vice-president; named for the play "Metamora," about Chief Massasoit, last of the Wampanoags back east; pop. 2,700

Metropolis: Seat of Massac County; only town in the U.S. with this name; in 1970s had a **Superman statue** built and billed itself as his hometown; newspaper is *The Planet;* has street named Lois Lane; Superman Celebration (800/949-5740) every June; original Fiberglas statue replaced with one of bronze in 1992; Super Museum and gift shop (618/524-5518) home to Fort Massac Park off Interstate 24; a reconstructed fort and statue of G.R. Clark mark the site; an annual "encampment" is held there the third week in October with musket demonstrations and costumes and crafts of the Colonial Era; Fort Massac Museum (618/524-9321); Robert Stroud, better known as the "Birdman of Alcatraz" is buried in a local cemetery; Superman Museum on Market Street has outfits worn by **Christopher Reeve**; visitors greeted by a colorful 15-foot statue of the "Man of Steel;" home to Merv Griffin Theater and Players Casino on the riverfront (800/929-5905); Major Elijah P. Curtis Home and Museum; prep Patriots; pop. 6,700

Robert Stroud, the "Birdman of Alcatraz"

Midlothian: Cook County; its Bachelor's Grove Cemetery is said to be most haunted spot in area; some say ghost stories concocted to scare off youths who vandalized the place; Madonna of Bachelor's Grove is a female ghost who walks the grounds holding a dead baby in her arms; golfing community named for a shire in Scotland where golf originated; pop. 14,315

Milan: Rock Island County; named for Italian town but locals pronounce it with a long "I;" pop. 5,348

Milford: On Route 1 in Iroquois County; the mill by the ford – town name origin; established 1830; pop. 1,369

Milledgeville: Carroll County; home to Kraft Foods plant; name comes from "mill" at the "edge" of "ville"

Miller's Grove: In Johnson County near Carbondale/Vienna; founded in mid-1800s by escaped slaves (Miller Family) from Nashville, Tenn.; sheriff of the county protected them; it became a haven for other free Negroes; Nigger Knob was highest point in the area; fires were built on the hill as a signal for slaves arriving at Golconda from the south; slaves also hid in nearby caves and inside the cisterns where they used straps to hold on while they hid during the day; B.G. Roots, the Illinois Central Railroad surveyor at **Tamaroa**, used his home and railroad boxcars to help the slaves flee to **Centralia**, then to **Illinoistown**, then to **Alton** and points north in a zigzag pattern; the town is now defunct (from Eugene Baldwin of **Skokie**)

Millstadt: Town in southern Illinois southwest of Belleville; German name means Milltown; originally Mittelstadt; pop. 2,794

Minooka: NE part of state; name from Algonquin words *mino* and *oki* meaning good land; pop. 3,971

Mokena: Will County; town name from the Algonquin word for "turtle;" pop. 14,583

Moline – One of the Quad Cities on the Mississippi on the Iowa border; name comes from a French word Moulin, meaning "mill;" town plotted by a mill company in 1838 and incorporated 5 years later; early settlers German, Belgian and Swedish; calls itself the Farm Implement Capital of the World; home to Playcrafters Barn Theater with performances in a remodeled dairy barn; Southpark Mall features 150 stores; Celebration River Cruises; Deere and Company Center features Deer implements; John Deere Pavilion; another building on Deer Commons remodeled to look like a 1950's Deere dealership and features antique tractors; Center for Belgian Culture (309/762-0167); 10 miles southeast at Coal Valley is the Niabi Zoo; Niabi is an Indian term that means "spared from the hunter's arrow;" *Moline Dispatch*; prep team called Maroons; home to The Mark – a regional sports/concert arena; Vincent Bendix invented self-starters for automobiles; Moline Maroons were home to an early semi-pro team owned by Ben Kerner called the Tri-City Hawks; home to artist Paul Norton; pop. 43,100

Momence: Kankakee County; platted in 1844, incorporated 1874; called Border Town (civilization on the edge of wilderness); named for Isadora Momence, half-breed daughter of a Potawatomie chief; Momence Gladiolus Festival; pop. 3,171

Monmouth: In western Illinois, named for the Revolutionary War battle in New Jersey where Molly Pitcher carried water and manned the canon; called Prime Beef Capital of the World; known in pioneer days for its deposits of potter's clay; sports teams: Zippers and **Zipperettes** (no kiddimg); home to American Bankers Life Insurance; Monmouth College's Holt House gave birth to Pi Beta Phi and Kappa Kappa Gamma Sororities; cattle raising country; birthplace of Ralph Greenleaf who became the world champ at billiards at age 19; not far from Bogus Hollow, a ravine near the Mississippi bottom lands home to a band of notorious counterfeiters; birthplace of **Wyatt Earp**, famed frontier lawman; Earp Home (309/734-6419) Earp monument in City Park; OK Corral Show Shootout May-August (309/734-6419); Ronald Reagan's family briefly lived here at 218 South Seventh Street; Western Stoneware Company and Pottery Barn (309/734-2161; Monmouth Airport is oldest continuously operating facility in the state; pop. 9,841

Wyatt Earp: lawman, gunfighter, saloon keeper

Monticello: Seat of Piatt County; named for Jefferson's home in Virginia; located on site of old Kickapoo and Potawatomie hunting ground; James Piatt and Major James McReynolds were important early settlers; home to Monticello Rail Museum inside a restored Illinois Central train depot; home to Robert Allerton Park; the park features a statue of Apollo that is 12 feet tall; called the Sun Singer, it shows Apollo with outstretched hands, welcoming the morning sun; Allerton commissioned Swedish sculptor Carl Milles to execute the work for his beautiful estate; Allerton the son of wealthy Chicago stockyards baron, Samuel Allerton; Millionaire's Row named for historic houses; around turn of century, Monticello had one of highest per-capita incomes in the country; pop. 4,500

Mooseheart: On the Fox River, known as the Child City, founded by James Davis and named for his membership in the Loyal Order of the Moose; provides home, education, vocational training for children of deceased members of the lodge; by 1938, more than 3,000 children had been admitted to Mooseheart

Morris: Seat of Grundy County; on Route 47 along the north bank of the Illinois River close to where it is joined by the Des Plaines; named for Isaac Morris, one of the commissioners of the Illinois and Michigan Canal; near Gebhard Woods State Park; an important early grain shipping center; Dresden Nuclear Power Plant is nearby; east of town in Evergreen Cemetery is gravesite of Shabbona, Potawatomie who sided with settlers in Blackhawk War; Gebhard Woods State Park; skydiving at Morris Municipal Airport; nearby Goose Lake Prairie Park has no lake, having been drained long ago for farming purposes; nearby Jug Town, now defunct, was once a prosperous tile and pottery center; pop. 11,928

Morrison: East of Fulton; county seat of Whiteside on Route 30; on the route of Chicago & North Western Railway; James Sargent, inventor of the time lock for bank vaults, placed his invention in the door of Morrison's First National Bank, the first in the U.S.; about 6 miles from Morrison is the Abbot Farm where a notorious band of counterfeiters; Ben Boyd was the gang's master engraver who was caught and sent to Joliet; members of his gang plotted to steal Lincoln's body to get him released from prison; home to Robert A. Millikan, physicist, educator, and recipient of the 1923 Nobel Prize for measuring the charge on an electron; population 4,400

Morton: Tazewell County; on Interstate 55 near Peoria; Pumpkin Capital of the World due to Libby Food Company processing plant; pop. 15,198

Morton Grove: Cook County; home to Par King, one of the best miniature golf courses in the state (847/965-3333); named for Levi Morton an official for the Chicago, Milwaukee & St. Paul Railroad; Revelle plastic model kits; pop. 22,451

Mound City: Seat of Pulaski County; in southern Illinois on Highway 51 and named for nearby Indian mounds; its Marine Ways, an incline with a steam wench, site of Civil War construction and repair of ironclads, tinclads, turtles, rams for use on the inland waterways; site of U.S. National Military Cemetery with 27 identified Confederate soldiers and 2,441 unknown ones; headquarters for the Western River Fleet during Civil War; keels for 3 Union gunboats laid here; town completely flooded by the Mississippi in 1937; pop. 692

Mount Carmel: On Route 1; seat of Wabash County; named for place mentioned in the Bible; located at juncture of Wabash and White River; first town in the state to be prospected for oil; home to Robert Ridgway, famed naturalist who wrote 8-volume *Birds of North America*; home to **Brace Beemer**, who played the **Lone Ranger** on radio; annual Lone Ranger Day; **Don Liddle**, who pitched for the NY Giants in the 1954 World Series; Penn Central and Southern Railways; pop. 7,982

Brace Beemer: voice of Lone Ranger 1940-55

Mount Carroll: Seat of Carroll County; named for Charles Carroll, a signer of the Declaration of Independence; home of Raven's Grin Inn (815/244-4746), a giant funhouse designed by Jim Warfield; The War Memorial is listed in Ripley's Believe It Or Not as the only memorial with an annex (to accommodate extra names); monument sculpted by Lorado Taft; town hosts annual Mayfest; Timber Lake Playhouse is a summer stock theater (815/244-2035); pop. 1,832

Mount Morris: On highway 64 in Ogle County near Oregon; settled by pioneers from Maryland; home of Mount Morris College, most of whose buildings burned in a 1931 fire; home to Kable Brothers Printing; in 1855 the Illinois Central came through nearby town of Polo instead of Oregon; rock formations known as Devil's Backbone, Castle Rock and Big Cut are due south; has Freedom Bell, a replica of our Liberty Bell that was dedicated by Ronald Reagan in 1963 and was at the Illinois pavilion at the World's Fair in New York in 1964; pop. 3,013

Mount Olive: Coal mining town in Macoupin County on old Route 66; home to Alexander Bradley, known as "the General" because of his ability to form miners into a formidably army of unionists; also home to "Mother" Mary Jones, the black-bonneted woman who fearlessly worked for the cause of labor after the death of her husband and four children in 1867; Clarence Darrow called her a formidable force for workingmen; monument erected to her, miners and General Bradley in 1936; 15,000 people attended her funeral; named for the site in the Bible; pop. 2,150

Mount Prospect: Cook County; home to George Stevens, a metal worker who made a grille that he named George's Bar-B-Q Kettle. The name eventually evolved into **Weber Grill** Company; Friedrich Busse of Hanover, Germany an important early settler; Randhurst Shopping Center; pop. 56,285

Casmir Pulaski, martyr of the U.S. cause

Mount Pulaski: Succeeded Postville as seat of Logan County; Logan County was home to William Scully, a rich Irishman who settled here; as he made his way west, he made huge land purchases, becoming one of the greatest landowners in the United States; Abe Lincoln argued cases in the local courthouse; Illinois Central Railroad; Illinois has a school holiday in March to honor the patriot Casmir Pulaski; pop. 1,600

Mount Sterling: Seat of Brown County; located on a slight elevation and named by founder Robert Curry for the "sterling quality" of its soil; in central-west part of state; Cornelius Vandeventer the area's first settler; located on a major route of westward migration during the 1849 California gold rush; pop. 2,070

Mount Vernon: Called King City because it "crowns" southern Illinois; county seat of Jefferson County; named for Washington's home; near juncture of Interstates 64 and 57; home to Appellate Court of Greek Revival design graced by fluted Ionic columns and a twin flight of cast iron stairs; home of the

Rams prep teams; Abe Lincoln argued a tax case in the appellate courthouse; **Clara Barton** used same courthouse as a hospital following 1888 tornado; gateway to expansive Rend Lake wildlife area; home to Mitchell Art Museum (618/242-1236) includes works of George Bellows, Mary Cassat, Thomas Eakins plus unique outdoor sculptures in surrounding park; Times Square Shopping Mall; Dale's Motorcycle and Classic Car Museum; large General Tire factory gives group tours; Vern Wood Press prints Midwest editions of *Time*, *Newsweek* and 17 other publications; home to Ken Trout, an SIUC grad who founded Excel Corporation in Dallas in 1988 and became a millionaire; Orient #3 was largest coal mine in the state; home to 5 railroads; pop. 16,269

Marillyn E. Watts & Lois M. Bowman at Muddy post office

Moweaqua: Shelby County near Decatur, site of 1932 Christmas Eve coal mine accident killing 54, including 7 sets of brothers; home to Moweaqua Coal Mine Museum; Indian name means "muddy water" from nearby Flat Branch Creek; another version says it is Potawatomie for "weeping woman;" pop. 1,800

Muddy: Located on floodplain of Big Muddy River; town of about 100 in Saline County has the **nation's smallest active post office with a lobby**; once home of Little Ridge Coal Mine; a wet town in a dry county; home to New York Central Railroad; did not incorporate until 1956; entrepreneur John Molinarolo bought most of town during Depression and urged miners to "hang on," offering them low rent; located near Harrisburg which was a dry town, and its locals came here to drink at a large, popular nightclub

Mulberry Grove: On Route 40, noted for its shipments of molding sand from Hurricane Creek for metal castings; pop. 671

Mundelein: Northern Illinois Chicago suburb; town originally named Area; changed name to Mundelein in 1929 to honor George Mundelein, a popular Chicago Archbishop; Quig's Country Store; Chicago utilities magnate Samuel Insull owned extensive property here; pop. 30,935

Murphysboro: On Route 3, seat of Jackson County; birthplace of **General John Logan**, considered America's greatest Civil War political general; devastated by 1925 tornado; not far from **Fountain Bluff** in Illinois Ozarks, a unique rocky bump on the landscape which has a 60 foot fire watchtower; so named for numerous springs sprouting from its rock formations; General Logan Memorial; nearly 3 dozen commercial orchards near town; annual Apple Festival; Murphysboro Charcoal Company had brick kilns for production; four old, domed brick structures located off Highway 149; The Molly O is a restaurant and bar that was once the depot for the Mobile & Ohio RR; pop. 13,295

Naperville: DuPage County; early settlers were forced to flee to Chicago's Fort Dearborn due to the Black Hawk War; Fort Payne built here in 1832 to protect settlers; early pioneer was Joseph Naper who built a saw mill and platted the town; lost county seat to Wheaton through skullduggery; historic building is Premption House Tavern North Central College; Bailey Hobson House; a linear Riverwalk follows the DuPage River for several miles; recreated Naper Pioneer Settlement; Centennial Beach – world's third largest chlorinated body of water (who looks up these things?); DuPage Children's Museum (hands on activities); Downtown Riverwalk; Taylor Brewing Company; Kroehler Furniture; Bell Laboratory; pop. 128,358 (4th in the state)

Nashville: Seat of Washington County; on Route 127 off Interstate 64; named by early settlers for their hometown of Nashville, Tennessee; Nashville Memorial Park; **Harry Blackmun** born here – gave majority Supreme Court decision in Roe v. Wade in 1973; its Presbyterian Church was first organized in 1832 and is one of state's oldest; Fall Festival Days 3rd week in September; Kirk **Rueter**, star pitcher for San Francisco Giants, attended Nashville High; pop. 3,147

Nauvoo: The City Beautiful; City of Checkerboard Streets; Mormon Town; once the largest city in the state (11,000); this place was established by Joseph Smith, founder of the Mormon religion, and his followers; has remains of temple and 15 restored buildings; after Mormons left for Utah, the site was occupied by French Icarians, a socialist utopian sect; Women Statuary Garden dedicated to honoring women of the past; Joseph Smith Historic Center; Mansion House (home of the prophet Joseph Smith) Red Brick Store (operated by Joseph Smith); Brigham Young Home; Nauvoo State Park; pop. 1,200

Nebo: Small town in Pike County; Cal Rodgers stopped here in 1911 during the nation's first transcontinental flight from New York to California; his aeroplane, which he bought from the Wright brothers, was named the Vin Fiz Flyer, for a grape-flavored soft drink marketed by Chicago's Armour Company which helped sponsor the flight; Rodgers also made stops in Chicago, Lockport, Streator, Springfield, Peoria, and Middletown (to fix a leak); a marker to memorialize the event was placed along the Von Fiz Highway in Nebo; pop. 408

Neoga: Cumberland County; Illinois Central Railroad; name is an Iroquoian Indian word that means "place of the gods;" pop. 1,854

New Athens: Laid out by Narcisse Pensoneau in 1836; home to Whitey Herzog, manager of the World Champion St. Louis baseball Cardinals; home to New Athens Drag Boat Races; the A in Athens is long as in "able;" pop. 1,981

New Baden: Clinton and St. Clair counties; named for region in Germany; pop. 3,001

New Berlin: West of Springfield on Interstate 72; home to Taylor Pensoneau, head of the Illinois Coal Association; pop. 1,030

New Hanover: In Monroe County, home to Rehmer's Chicken Hatchery

New Haven: In Gallatin County; Seymore Hughes, a resident of our state's 3rd oldest town, made prized walking canes from tree planted by daughter of Jonathan Boone, brother to pathfinder Daniel Boone; according to legend, the catalpa tree grew from a riding whip one of Boone's daughters carelessly stuck in the ground after an outing; American Discovery Trail enters Illinois from Indiana here; pop. 477

Residence of Dr. J.C. McMillan, New Berlin

Newman: Founded in 1857 and named for the son-in-law of Methodist circuit rider Peter Cartwright; town had a canning factory and a dairy products plant making casein (Elmer's glue); pop. 956

New Salem: Twenty minutes northwest of Springfield; site of reconstructed frontier village where Abe Lincoln served as surveyor storekeeper and postmaster; Anne Rutledge's father was one of the founders of New Salem; founded in 1829 because it was in the center of the state, it prospered for about 5 years then experienced a rapid decline; a ghost town by 1840; Lincoln left in 1837

Newton: Seat of Jasper County; home to folk singer and actor **Burl Ives** who recorded the song "Holly, Jolly Christmas;" nearby is Jordan Hill, formed by sidecutting action of Embarras River; Burl Ives Bridge; Illinois Central Railroad; pop. 3,069

Niles: Cook County; home to the Bradford Museum of Collector Plates, the largest such collection in the world; home to a full-scale replica of the **Leaning Tower of Pisa**, which actually disguises a water tower (847/647-8222); pop. 30,068

Nokomis: Montgomery County; named for the grandmother storyteller in Longfellow's *Hiawatha*; Penn Central and Chicago & Eastern; pop. 2,389

Normal – Takes its name from the Normal University located there, now called Illinois State; founded by Jesse Fell who planted 12,000 trees there; Fell, a resident of **Bloomington**, also responsible for the founding of **Pontiac, Lexington, Towanda, Clinton, Le Roy and El Paso**; horse Louis Napoleon helped make Normal the **Norman Horse Capital of the U.S.**; home of the **original Steak and Shake** (1934) fast food restaurant with the slogan, "Food in sight, it must be right;" pop. 45,386

Northbrook: Chicago suburb; **Speed Skating Capital of the World** (1972 Olympic skaters Diane Holum and Anne Henning); home to the company that produces **Cracker Jack** snack popcorn and peanuts; Northbrook Court Shopping Center; pop. 33,435

North Chicago; Originally called South Waukegan; Abbott Laboratories; Baxter Laboratories; G.D. Searle Co., American Hospital Supply; Chicago & Northwestern Railroad; pop. 35,918

Northfield: Home to Kraft Foods, started by James Kraft and Thomas McInnerney;   5,389

Norway: On the Fox River near Ottawa, home to the first permanent settlement of Norwegians in America (they came to escape persecution by those dastardly Swedes), founded by Cleng Peerson (the Norwegian Daniel Boone); site of a crashed plane, nose down, placed there as a tribute to farmers who lived through the agricultural "crash" of the 1980's; erected by Melvin and Phyllis Eastwold and Norwegian Implement Company

Oakbrook – Chicago suburb that started out as a polo club; home to the headquarters of McDonalds hamburger franchise; Ray Croc Museum; home to the largest archery center in the world; home to 14 very large polo fields (did you know left-handed polo players were not allowed to compete?); home of E. Hemingway and Edgar Rice Burroughs; Oakbrook Center – an upscale/ patrician shopping plaza; Czech Heritage Museum; Operational Graue Mill; Oak Brook Polo Club (Sunday matches in summer and fall 630/990-2394) population 9,200

Oakbrook Terrace: Chicago suburb, home to Drury Lane Theater; pop. 2,300

Oakland: On IL 133 in the northeast corner of Coles County; Hiram Rutherford House belonged to a man who harbored a family of slaves; Abe Lincoln represented Robert Matson, the owner, but the court freed the slaves after a hearing; Centennial Park has captured WW I German cannon; pop. 996

Oak Lawn: Chicago suburb; during World War II, the only place in the nation besides Tusgegee Institute where Negroes could earn aviator wings; served by the Wabash Railroad; pop. 55,245

Oak Park: Chicago suburb settled in 1833 by Joseph Kettlestrings; has numerous homes featuring Frank Lloyd Wright's Prairie School of Architecture (In case you're wondering, he lived there.); was the largest community in U.S. with a village form of government; known in early years as a "bone dry" town; property deeds had anti-dram shop clauses; in 1890s referred to as Saints' Rest because of its many churches; famous Lloyd Wright houses (Walking Tour 708/848-1500) include: Moore House, Heurtley House, Gale House, Beachy House, Hills House, Thomas House; home to Oak Park Conservatory, First Congregational Church; William Barton Bible Museum, Saint Edmunds Catholic Church, Hephzibah Home (Question: How rich do you have to be before you can slap a name on your house?); Frank Lloyd Wright Home and Studio; Historic Pleasant Home; Unity Temple demonstrates Wright's use of poured concrete; Hemingway Home and Museum; Oak Park Conservatory; long known for being a dry province; pop. 53,600

Oblong: Crawford County; on Route 33 between Newton and Robinson, home to the Oblong oil pool area and the Oil Field Museum; old newspaper headline joke: **OBLONG BOY MARRIES NORMAL GIRL**; town name ostensibly comes from the shape of its corporate limits; pop. 1,580

O'Dell: Established in 1854 and named for William O'Dell; on Chicago & Alton Railroad; situated on old Route 66; pop. 1,014

Odin: - Marion County; named for the chief Norse god by Illinois Central officials to attract Scandinavian immigrants; called the "**Hellhole of the Illinois Central**" due to young scalawags who frequently stole passenger's luggage; also served by the B&O RR pop. 1,122

O'Fallon: St. Clair County; platted in 1854 and named for railroad developer, John O'Fallon; located on Route 50; its high school marching band program is considered one of the ten best in the entire nation; birthplace of actor William Holden; large numbers of its residents work at nearby Scott Air Force Base; prep teams called Panthers; pop. 21,910

Olney: Home of the White Squirrels (Neal Strebel collection)

Oglesby: Important early cement center, named for Governor Oglesby; important limestone outcrop in Vermilion Valley nearby; near LaSalle Peru; Bailey Falls where creek empties into the Vermilion River; pop. 3,647

Okawville: Site of famed mineral springs bath and hotel complex off Interstate 64 (618/243-5458); home to Poos Museum; pop. 1,355

Olney: Seat of Richland County; considered an oil town; named for John Olney, lieutenant in Civil War; home of the famous white/albino squirrels; home of Larchmond, residence of Robert Ridgway, naturalist who some say originally brought the squirrels; other maintain **albino squirrels** brought to town by a hunter who put them on display in a saloon; because squirrels are protected, cat pets must be on a leash when outdoors; believe it or not, these squirrels (some call them rats with bushy tails) have right of way on all Olney streets; Red Hills State Park; pop. 8,631

Olympia Fields: Cook County; strictly a residential area; coach Amos Alonzo Stagg was one of the community's organizers; pop. 4,732

Omaha: In Gallatin County; named by a railroad official for Omaha, Nebraska; pop. 263

Onarga: Nursery capital of the Midwest (trees and shrubs, not children); at juncture of Routes 45 and 54 in Iroquois County; pop. 1,438

Ontarioville: Northern Illinois town located near the Illinois Pet Cemetery; 6 acre tract is for birds, cats, dogs, rabbits, etc. with some gravesites having granite or marble tombstones

Oquawka: In Henderson County on the Great River Road in northwest Illinois; from an Indian word meaning yellow banks; a Mississippi River crossing site for Indians on hunting expeditions; founded by the Phelps brothers in 1827; known for manufacturing pearl buttons from mussels; home to Henderson covered bridge, built in 1866; has statue of Norma Jean, a 6,500 pound circus elephant killed there by a bolt of lightning; pop. 1,539

Pleasure Boat Junction in Ottawa, Illinois

Oregon: Seat of Ogle County on Routes 2 and 64; On Rock River near Lowden State Park (named for Governor Lowden); praised in 1843 by Transcendentalist Margaret Fuller who visited the Eagle's Nest Colony nearby, calling it the "Capital of Nature's Art;" island in Rock River named for her; some works housed in Oregon Library and Art Gallery; Soldier's Monument on courthouse lawn by Lorado Taft; Lincoln Boulder has a plaque honoring September 9 speech; - has wrong inscription of August 16, 1856; north of town is **Black Hawk Monument**, 48 feet tall, the tallest reinforced concrete statue in the world (815/732-6828); critics maintain that the chief's countenance should be angry looking; Oregon Courthouse burned in controversy between thieving Banditti leader John Driscoll and his men and an opposing vigilante group known as regulators; pop. 4,060

Orion: Henry County; named for Orion the Hunter of mythology fame; pop. 1,713

Orland Park: Chicago suburb; home to Antique Row; Orland Square Shopping Center; pop. 51,077

Ottawa: LaSalle County glass-making town; from the Indian term "adawe" meaning to trade; one of the state's most scenic cities; at the junction of the Fox River with the Illinois River; Town of Two Rivers; platted by the Illinois and Michigan Canal commissioners; birthplace of Johnston McCulley, creator of that Hispanic do-gooder of the old West, Zorro; site of first Lincoln-Douglas debate; Lincoln Sun Dial marks spot where Lincoln mustered out of the service at end of Black Hawk War; Buffalo Rock

State Park just west of town; near Starved Rock State Park (home to Effigy Tumuli, five earthen sculptures shaped in the form of a catfish, snake, turtle, frog and a water strider (815/433-2220); they are the **largest outdoor sculptures in the world**; Michael Heizer Starved Rock Lodge and Cabins (815/667-4211) Libby-Owens-Ford glass plant in nearby Lof-town once produced wide assortment of glass products (GM windshields); Peltier Company made glass marbles of the "mibs," "cats eye," "shooter" and "boulder" variety; Ottawa Scouting Museum (memorabilia associated with scouting (815/431-9353); W.D. Boyce statue, **founder of American Boy Scouts**; Reddick Mansion on town square was part Underground Railroad, rumored to have underground tunnel to river; later served as town library; Keen Kleener Cleanser Co.; pop. 18,307

Otterville: In Jersey County; site of first free schoolhouse in the state

Ozark: Southern Illinois town that has annual Pumpkin Land in October (618/777-2802)

Palatine: Cook County; named for a region in Germany; L.B. Anderson Terry-Jean Shetland Pony Stables; pop. 65,479

Palermo: In Edgar County near Indiana; site where Chief Pontiac met with George Groghan, British deputy superintendent of Indian Affairs in 1765; parley ended Pontiac's Conspiracy of the French and Indian War era

Palestine: The original seat of Crawford County; named for the Biblical land of milk and honey; its early pioneer Eaton family were known for their big feet. When a nearby fort was constructed it was called Fort Foot; home to one of the six land offices in the state; birthplace of Augustus French who later became governor; Auntie Gogin, a local milliner (hat maker) is considered Illinois' first businesswoman; Fort LaMotte and Labor Day Rodeo; pop. 1,366

Palos Heights: Chicago suburb; Lake Katherine Nature Preserve including Calumet-Sag Canal; named for a seaport in Spain; pop. 11,260

Pana: Christian County; established 1856; City of Roses; on Route 51; in old days, 5 firms shipped 15 million cut roses annually; local coal supply provided heat for glass hothouses; home to Kitchel Park; near the Illinois State Penal Farm, called Peanut Farm by locals; town name is of Indian origin; pop. 5,614

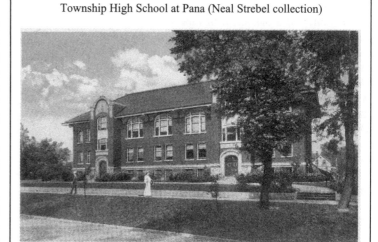

Township High School at Pana (Neal Strebel collection)

Panama: In Bond County; John L. Lewis of the United Mine Workers began his career here; pop. 323

Paris: Kickapoo hunting grounds until 1819; Seat of Edgar County named for Paris, Kentucky, where early settlers were from; Lincoln spoke here on behalf of John Fremont in the presidential election of 1856; Lincoln's kinsman Dennis Hanks killed here by a runaway team of horses; during Civil War a center of pro-Confederate activity, "Copperheads" planned to attack the city but Union troops foiled plan; old **sport of goosepulling** originated here – hanging a goose from a tree with a greased neck, and riders on horseback tried to tear off goose's head; winner awarded a bloody goose; annual Honeybee Festival; calls itself the Honeybee Capital of the Nation; the *Beacon News*; Penn Central RR; pop. 9,077

Park Forest – Chicago suburb; Freedom Hall; Illinois Philharmonic Orchestra; Illinois Theater Center; America's Original GI Town; pop. 23,462

Park Ridge: On northwestern city limits of Chicago; founded by George Penny who operated a brickyard from the local red clay; first called Pennyville, then Brickton; rail point for Chicago & Northwestern Railroad; named for the ridge that separates the Mississippi and St. Lawrence river watersheds; pop. 37,775

Patoka: Named for an Indian chief, this small town experienced an oil boom in 1937; pop. 633

Paxton: Off Interstate 57 on Route 9; county seat of Ford County; settled by Swedes in the 1850s and incorporated in 1865; pop. 4,525

Pecatonica: Winnebago County; from an Indian word that means "river of many bends;" pop. 1,997

Pekin: Seat of Tazewell County; home of prep teams called the Dragons, **formerly called Chinks**; birthplace of actress **Susan Dey** of television's "L.A. Law;" site of Lincoln's Black Nance where he defended an escaped slave; birthplace and gravesite of Senator Everett M. Dirksen; annual Marigold Festival; Union League of America, a patriotic organization, founded here in 1862; noted for its distilleries; major grain terminal; Quaker Oats plant; pop. 33,857

THE AMISH IN ILLINOIS

The Amish are loosely defined as people belonging to sects known as Mennonites, German-Amish or Swiss Apostolic Church. They tended to wear dark simple clothing and eschewed the use of frivolous buttons. Sometimes they were referred to as "hook and eye people" for the fasteners they used. Men usually wore beards but not mustaches. They tended to cluster together in Woodford, Tazewell, and Bureau Counties near the Illinois River. In 1939, it was estimated that their numbers in the state were about 10,000. Fairbury, Meadows, Arthur, and Gridley were Amish towns.

Modernism and mechanization were scrupulously avoided. The horse and buggy was long used for transportation instead of the corrupting and worldly automobile.

Peoria: Called Au Pé in its early history; named for one of the 5 Illinois Tribes; some claim it to be the oldest settlement in the state; founded by LaSalle in 1680 when he built Fort Crevecoeur: first permanent European settlement on mid-American continent; Progressive City, Whiskey Town; surveyed by Alexander Hamilton's son William in 1826; pork packing an important early industry; home to the Caterpillar Company, maker of bulldozers; Illinois' 3rd largest town; called the "Capital of Central Illinois;" whiskey and earthmoving capital of the world; home to Bradley University (sports teams called Braves), home to Glen Oak Park; disparaged by comedians who say its very name suggests all that is parochial in America; home to agnostic, Democratic lawyer, Bob Ingersoll; Lakeview Museum of Arts and Sciences; Lakeview Planetarium; Wheels O' Time Museum; Jack Daniels distillery; Peoria Mineral Springs and mineral water; home to the part of the state known as the military tract; site of gangster Bernie Shelton murder; radio station WMBD (Teddy Roosevelt called it the World's Most Beautiful Drive); Par-A-Dice Hotel and Casino in East Peoria; How will it play in Peoria? a nationally famous saying originating in melodrama days of old vaudeville; named an All-America City by

Bradley Polytechnic Institute at Peoria

Look Magazine; Peoria Historical Society (309/674-1921); African-American Museum Hall of Fame; Constitution Gardens; Lorado Taft Museum (309/742-7791; part of the **Ruhr Valley of America** stretching from Chicago to East St. Louis; *Peoria Journal-Star*; pop. 112,936 (5th in the state)

Peotone: In Will County off Interstate 57, some say name comes from an Indian name; others say a clerk for Illinois Central Railroad threw a bunch of letters together and came up with town name; locals jokingly say it's an Indian word that means "a good place to live;" has 1871 mill, a restored old Dutch windmill, only about 4 originals left in the state; when Dillinger escaped from Crown Point Jail (Indiana's Alcatraz) his car broke down about two miles outside of town; *Peotone Vedette* newspaper; prep teams called Blue Devils; home for many years to Bennett Industries that developed the first 5-gallon plastic pails for commercial shipping; about a mile south on Route 50 is Miami Gardens (now Edwin's) a two story brick building that was allegedly one of Capone's speakeasies and brothels with underground parking; was said to have underground tunnels to escape police raids; Junction City Restaurant with cabbage stack locomotive at the front door; pop. 3,385

Percy: Small town on the eastern edge of Randolph County; originally called Short's Prairie, for early settlers Eli and Betsy Short; it may have been Short, not Richard M. Johnson, who killed the Indian leader Tecumseh at the battle of Thames in Ontario, Canada

First National Bank in Pinckneyville (courtesy Neal Strebel)

during the War of 1812; home to General Madison Miller Mine and Willis No 6; Syndicate Shaft Mine; the Streamline Tipple; Lickiss General Store; Percy Flour Mill; W.N. Griffin Hotel; Myers Cycle Sales; pop. 942

Peru: Incorporated in 1838; at Routes 6 and 51, adjoins city of LaSalle; on the northern bank of the Illinois River; its name is an Indian word meaning land of plenty; LaSalle outstripped Peru because Peru is on a steeper site; old Peru Wheel Company and Star Union Brewery important early businesses; Illinois River Bridge; western end of Illinois-Michigan Canal; Wesclox Big Ben clocks; pop. 9,835

Petersburg: Burial site of **Edgar Lee Masters**, **Ann Rutledge** and Vachel Lindsay; Laid out in 1833 by George Warburton and Peter Lukins; John Taylor and Hezekiah King bought the town on the Sangamon River and hired Lincoln to do a new survey; many New Salem residents moved here when it was made the seat of Menard County in 1839; pop. 2,299

Phoenix: Chicago suburb home to Washington Park racetrack with Mount Vernon replica clubhouse; pop. 2,157

Pinckneyville: Seat of Perry County; named for C.C. Pinckney of South Carolina who gave us the slogan: "Millions for defense, but not one cent for tribute;" home of a new minimum-security prison; prep Panthers won state basketball titles in 1948, 1994 and 2001; Illinois fish farmers co-op; pop. 5,464

Pittsfield: Seat of Pike County; founded by New England settlers from Pittsfield, Massachusetts; important pork packing center; John Hay, later U.S. Secretary of State, spent two years here as a student; boulder in Central Park commemorates place where Lincoln gave a speech in 1858; calls itself Pork Capital of the World with 450,000 hogs marketed annually; special Pig Days Festival (217/285-2971); pop. 4,211

Plainfield: Will County, founded by a Frenchman named Du Pazhe around 1790; named for its prairie topography; fur trading post operated by American Fur Trading Co.; a stop on the rounds of Jesse Walker who was known as the "Daniel Boone of Methodism;" the town was an early rival of Joliet but Joliet's population exploded after completion of Illinois-Michigan Canal; near the Du Page River named for Du Pazhe; pop. 13,038

213

Plano: Kendall County; from the Spanish word for plain; In 1835 a Norwegian Quaker led a group of settlers here; further migration was stimulated by Ansten Nattestad who returned to Norway and circulated a promotional pamphlet; in 1866, church headquarters of the Reorganized Church of the Latter Day Saints, established by Joseph Smith III who was Joseph Smith Jr's. son; it was Joseph Smith Jr. who founded the Church of Christ of Latter Day Saints (Independence, MO) lived here and was president of the church in 1860; they eventually moved to Lamoni, Iowa; the first grain reaper was made in Plano by John Hollister and W.W. Marsh; they sold 600 harvesters in 1867; called itself the "biggest little industrial city in the world;" pop. 5,633

Pocahontas: Bond County; on old Route 40; was a stagecoach stop on the Cumberland Road; named for Indian girl who saved the life of Captain John Smith of the Jamestown colony in Virginia (her father Powhatan was about to club him to death); she married John Rolfe, who introduced tobacco to England; home to the Powhatan, a 24-7 restaurant; pop. 727

Powhatan Restaurant/Motel off Interstate 70 at Pocahontas

Polo: Ogle County; Zenas Aplington the founder; Lincoln once stayed at his home; named for Italian explorer-adventurer, Marco Polo; U.S. Grant bought hides from here to be used in his Galena leather shop; near White Pines Forest State Park; pop. 2,477

Pomona: Jackson County; nearby Saltpeter Cave was important in early manufacture of gunpowder; Pomona Natural Bridge

Pontiac: Seat of Livingston County; named for the Ottawa chief who opposed the British in the French and Indian War; founded in 1837 and named by Jesse Fell, a friend of Abe Lincoln; Winston Churchill College; on Chicago & Alton Railroad; Soldiers and Sailors Monument at courthouse dedicated by Theodore Roosevelt; home to Riverview Park, bounded on three sides by the Vermilion River; the expression "out at Pontiac" means someone is serving time at the State Penitentiary; Log Cabin Inn on Route 66; old State Police headquarters; Central States Threshermen's Reunion Labor Day weekend; pop. 11,864

Posen: Near Chicago on the Dixie Highway; the **most Polish town in Illinois**, owing its existence to Polish real estate salesmen who sold lots to their countrymen; incorporated when unneighborly Harvey tried to annex; pop. 4,730

Prairie du Rocher: More than 200-years-old; located on the American Bottom; name means "prairie by the bluffs;" founded in 1722 as a result of Scotsman John Law's outlandish investment scheme known as the Mississippi Bubble promotion; settled mostly by French immigrants; some claim it to be the oldest town in the state; near Fort Chartres Historic Site with annual October encampment (618-284-7230); near Modoc Rock Shelter, important Indian archaeological site; Fort Chartres Rendezvous early November (618/284-7230); pop. 613

Preston: Near Chester, home to James Thompson, the man who surveyed and platted parts of Chicago; Randolph Street in that town is named for his native Randolph County; Chicago mayor Big Bill Thompson was one of his descendants

Princeton: On Route 6; seat of Bureau County; laid out in 1833 by settlers from Massachusetts; home of abolitionist preacher, Owen Lovejoy, younger brother to Elijah Lovejoy who helped form Republican party in Illinois; home to John Bryant House, a brother of William Cullen Bryant; home to 1863 red covered bridge (only one in state open to traffic); annual Pork Barbeque; Dover moraine just north of town; Burlington Railroad; pop. 7,501

Princeville: Peoria County; settled by Daniel Prince; platted by William Stevens in 1837; pop. 1,621

Prophetstown: On the Rock River at the site of a village led by White Cloud, the prophet who railed against encroaching whites; his village destroyed in May of 1832 at start of Black Hawk War; remark in 1908 said soil so rich around Prophetstown that it was probably the only rural area in the state "where tillers of the soil have automobiles;" annual Booster Rooster Day was a big event; home to Riverside Park; pop. 2,023

Old Orpheum Theater in Quincy

Quincy: Founded in 1822 and named for John Quincy Adams; Model City, Gem City; westernmost city in the state; unofficial capital of western Illinois; part of the military tract; founded by Willard Keyes and John Wood who later became governor; hotbed of abolitionist activity; major industrial city of the state; seat of Adams County; located on the bluffs of the Mississippi, the site of an old Sauk Indian settlement; suffered cholera epidemic in 1832; old Mission Institute the contentious scene between pro and antislavery groups, burned to ground by Missouri bushwackers; known as hog producing region in early years; for about 20 years, second largest city in the state; scene of 6th Lincoln-Douglas debate in Washington Park; Edgar Goodspeed's translation of the New Testament was published in 1923; Augustine Tolton, the first Negro Roman Catholic priest in America, was educated in Quincy; radio station WTAD, Q106, WGEM-TV, KHQA-TV; home to prep teams called Blue Devils; important sites include: Browning House, Wood House, White House, Riverview Park; Indian Mounds Park (has statue of George Rogers Clark), Baldwin Park,

Moormon Manufacturing Co. in Quincy (author's collection)

Quincy National Cemetery; Soldiers and Sailors Home; once hosted World Free-Fall Convention at Baldwin Field; Quinsippi Island Antique Auto Museum (217/223-4846); All Wars Museum (217/222-8641); Thunder on the Bay (217/426-4191); annual Dogwood Festival 1st week in May; Quincy Memorial Mississippi Bridge on Route 24; home of Quincy University; a tree in a cemetery at northeast end of town has a large unusual burl that looks like the historic Jesus carrying a lamb in his arms; sometimes called the Apparition Tree; home to Villa Katherine, an Arabesque castle built by George Metz around 1900 and named for his mother (217/224-3688); Moorish architecture and decorations collected by Metz on a two-year trip to North Africa; home to Alan Nevins, prominent American history historian; Gardner Museum of Architecture; Natural History and Art Museum; All-America City 1968, 1984; prep teams are called the Blue Devils; *Quincy Herald-Whig*; John Wood statue (from Sherry Sparks of **Fowler**) pop. 40,366

Raleigh: In Saline County; home to Robert Ingersoll Law office; Webber brothers were large tobacco buying and processing partnership; pop. 330

Rantoul: On Interstate 57 and IL 136 in Champaign County; named for Robert Rantoul, member of Illinois Central Board of Directors; home of Chanute Field; home to Octave Chanute Aerospace Museum and gift shop; Military Aviation Hall of Fame including 34 aircraft; (217-893-1613); Aviation Camp for grades 7-12; National August Hot Air Balloon Championships; 2002 World Freefall Convention with 3500 skydivers; tandem skydive $179.00; hot air balloon rides $150.00; Paintball Tactics (217/893-0595); prep teams are called the Eagles; 3rd oldest active base for 76 years; processed 2 million military personnel in that time; Tuskegee Airmen unit first formed here in 1941; later moved to Alabama; pop. 12,857

Red Bud: Randolph County; on Route 3, named for red bud trees in area; tableland south of the village is known as Horse Prairie for horses that escaped from the early French settlers and roamed the area; pop. 3,422

Renault: McHenry County; named for Frenchman Philip Renault - brought first slaves to Illinois country to work in mines

Richmond: On Route 173 near Wisconsin border; home to a remarkable village full of antique shops; pop. 1,091

Ridgway: Gallatin County; named for naturalist Robert Ridgway; popcorn capital of the world because so much of it is grown here; annual Popcorn Day Festival, the second Saturday in September to honor John Schmitt, the man who introduced growing popcorn to Gallatin County; pop. 928

Riverdale: Cook County: named for its site along the Little Calumet River; Acme Steel Co.; pop. 15,055

River Forest: First settled by Ashbel Steele on the east bank of Des Plaines River; a Chicago suburb next to Oak Park; named for a forest preserve; was used as a workshop for Frank Lloyd Wright and has many homes of his design; Frink and Walker Stagecoach Line connected town to Chicago; Daniel Thatcher persuaded Chicago & North Western to build through line; Thatcher House Historic site; Trailside Museum of Natural History; Rosary Catholic College; Concordia Teacher's College, Dominican House of Studies; Frank L. Wright buildings include: Winslow House, Edgewood Place, Roberts House, Richard Bock Studio, Harlem House, River Forest Women's Clubhouse – first women's clubhouse in state; pop. 11,635

River Grove: Chicago suburb; home of Triton College; Cernan Earth and Space Center (708/583-3100), named for astronaut Eugene Cernan, born in Chicago and raised in Maywood; named for the DesPlains River on its western border; pop. 10,688

River Park – Home to Richard Rhodes who **patented the first hearing aid** in 1879

Riverside: One of Illinois few "planned" communities; laid out in 1866 by Frederick Olmstead and Vaux, New York architects who laid out Central Park and

First National Bank in Red Bud (author's collection)

Columbian Exposition grounds; community resembles a park on the Des Plaines River; called the "womb of the metro area" because it sits on the portage between the St. Lawrence and Mississippi watersheds; pop. 8,895

Roanoke: Woodford County; founded by settlers from Roanoke, VA; Santa Fe Railroad

Robbins: Near Chicago; nearly an all-black town, founded by Eugene Robbins and settled by workers who helped build Columbian Exposition buildings; pop. 6,635

Robbs: In southern Illinois, home to Milestone Bluff, north off Route 147; ancient Indian dwelling and burial site

Robinson: On Route 33, seat of Crawford County; home to Marathon oil refinery; home to Heath Candy Co. maker of Heath, Payday and Zero candy bars; located in the Illinois Basin, site of large oil deposits; oil formed from breakdown of marine organisms; petroleum first found in the area in 1906; local author James Jones wrote "**From Here to Eternity**;" Illinois Central and Penn Central; pop. 6,822

Burpee Museum of Natural History at Rockford

Rochelle: Northern Illinois town on Route 51 in Ogle County; site of Del Monte cannery; resident Charles Butterfield wrote song "When You and I Were Young, Maggie;" town called "Asparagus Capital of Illinois;" restored Standard Oil Filling Station now a visitor's center; Railroad Park is where main lines of Burlington Northern, Santa Fe and Union Pacific cross; Blackhawk Chocolate Trail; new meat packing plant built here in 1962; pop. 8.800

Rochester: Sangamon County, near Springfield, just off old Route 66; Cardinal Hill Candles & Crafts (217/498-9375); pop. 2,893

Rock Falls: Platted in 1837, connected to Sterling by a dam and road across Rock River in 1857 a feeder canal connects it to the Illinois and Mississippi Canal about 30 miles south; Lawrence Park is on an island between the two cities; pop. 9,580

Rockford: Bisected by the Rock River, located 18 miles south of Wisconsin; Forest City (122 trees per block), City of Beautiful Homes; has large population of Swedish descent; stages from Chicago to Galena crossed the Rock River at a shallow, rock-lined area, - hence Rockford; the state's second largest city; world's largest, most valuable watch and clock collection; famous for its sock production; its Warner Lambert Corp. produces biodegradable golf tees and packaging "peanuts" made from potato starch; contains a Time Museum displaying an amazing variety of timepieces from prehistoric times to modern; radio station WROK; its Forest City Nine amateur baseball team in 1870 (with A.G. Spaulding and "Pop" Anson) considered the champions of America, trouncing the Cincinnati professional team 12-5; John Manny invented a reaper/mower in the 1850's that revolutionized agriculture; points of interest: Burpee Art Gallery, of Natural History; Erlander Home Museum, Tinker Swiss Cottage, native Leland Howard was Chief of the U.S. Bureau of entomology (insects) from 1894-1927; Beattie Park, Sinnissippi Park; newspaper is the *Register Star*; prep team the West Rockford Warriors; "the sun never sets on Rockford labels;" pop. 150,115 (2nd in the state)

Rock Island: Seat of Rock Island County; originally called Stephenson; founded by Germanicus Kent and his slave, Lewis Lemon, along with Thatcher Blake in 1834; called The Forest City and City of Gardens; part of the Quad Cities area on the Mississippi; about 2,000 vessels docked here annually in days of old steamboating; laid out by George Davenport an early settler (Davenport, Iowa); **Dred Scott** lived here with his master at Fort Armstrong; 1855 railroad bridge first to span the Mississippi; Confederate prisoners housed here on the two-mile-long island; radio station WHBF; Lock and Dam #10; home to International Harvester; home to Rockford Speedway (stock car racing); Mississippi River Visitor Center with slide show; Magic Waters Waterpark; Discovery Center Museum (hands on); Midway Village with 24 restored historic buildings; Rockford Art Museum; Tinker Swiss Cottage Museum (5,000 objects); Sinnissippi Gardens; Rock Island Arsenal (prison for captured Confederates during Civil War); Moline is its twin city; points of interest: Augustana College, features Channel Cat Water Taxi offering river tours; January and February prime time for viewing bald eagles who winter here; Modern Woodmen of America Building; Black Hawk State Park; Jumer's Casino on the riverfront; Lock and Dam #15 and Visitor's Center; Black Hawk State Park (309/788-0177); prep Rocks; annual August Indian Powwow; pop. 39,684

Old Fort Theater at Rock Island

Rockton: Winnebago County; started as two settlements on each side of Rock River; pop. 5,296

Rockwood: On Route 3 south of Chester; from the two nouns rock and wood; early source of wood for steamboat boilers; its rock quarries provided the stone to build famed Eads Bridge at East St. Louis, the first major bridge to span the Mississippi; Indian Mound, about 20 feet high, is nearby

Rolling Meadows: Chicago suburb; incorporated in 1955; near Arlington Race Track; pop. 24,604

Romeoville: Chicago suburb; Isle A La Cache Museum; Philip Lynch Theater; fastest growing community in Illinois in 1967; UNO-VEN Refining Co.; pop. 21,151

Roodhouse: Greene County; named for railroad official John Roodhouse; about 20 miles south of Jacksonville, home to William Sullivan, owner of the Eli Bridge Company that has made Ferris Wheels for a hundred years in Jacksonville. Sullivan got the idea of making smaller, portable Ferris wheels after riding in the original at the Columbian Exposition in Chicago; pop. 2,214

Roscoe: Home to Spc. Brandon J. Rowe, age 20, killed in Operation Iraqi Freedom 2003; pop. 6,244

Roselle: Northwest Chicago suburb named for Roselle Hough who set up a flax mill (for linen) on Meacham Creek; pop. 23,115

Rosemont: Chicago suburb; Allstate Arena; Donald Stephens Museum of Hummels; Rosemont Theater' pop. 4,224

Roseville: City of roses and prime beef in Warren County; Truman Eldridge first settler; pop. 1,083

Rosiclare: On the Ohio River southwest of Elizabethtown; named for Rosi and Clare, two daughters of an early French settler; known for its high grade deposit of **fluorspar, the state mineral**; home of the Hardin County Fluorspar Museum; fluorspar first discovered by James Anderson while digging a well; pop. 1,213

Rossville: Vermilion County; bills itself as The Village of Unusual Shops; Rossville Packing Co. and BAW Industries; named for Jacob Ross, early settler; pop. 1,217

Roxana: Madison County; hometown to Shell Oil Company employing 3,000 people; former home (for 6 years) of Robert Wadlow, the world's tallest man, until family moved to Alton; named for Roxanne, the wife of the owner of Royal Dutch Shell; pop. 1,547

Rushville: Seat of Schuyler County; named for Dr. Benjamin Rush, patriot of the Revolution; Abe Lincoln participated in a friendly

Author Marguerite Henry

wrestling match while stationed here during Black Hawk War; Lincoln wrestled Dow Thompson who "threw" him twice, winning the match; Lincoln said that Thompson "was as strong as a grizzly bear;" home to Scripps Park, land once owned by Edward Scripps, the newspaper mogul who was born here; County Jail Museum; when Stephen Douglas came to speak here in 1858 the town decided to mark the occasion with a salute from a cannon; the heavily charged cannon, loaded with scraps of wet leather, exploded but miraculously no one suffered serious injury; home to Francis Drake who became governor of Iowa and has Drake University named for him; pop. 3,212

Sadorus: First settlement in Champaign County; along the path of the Potawatomie Trail of Death; in 1838 officials in Indiana ordered the removal of the Potawatomie to Kansas, resulting in 39 tragic deaths; pop. 426

St. Anne: Kankakee County; founded by a priest rejected by his Bourbonnais parish; founded on St. Anne's Day; annual pilgrimages made each year on St. Anne's day because church has a bone fragment believed to have belonged to St. Anne, mother of Mary and Jesus' grandmother; annual "Sainte Ann Day;" pop. 1,212

St. Charles: West of Chicago on Fox River; has Giant Antique Market and a large flea market first weekend of each month; paddlewheel riverboat excursions; was home to School For Boys who were under court sentence – had a school plus 22 buildings that housed about 45 boys each; Fox River Trail for bikes and walking; Living History Month in August; (630/584-6967); Moorish-style Hotel Baker features the Rainbow Room, a backlit dance hall with a glass-block floor (630/584-2100); Pheasant Run Dinner Theater Complex featuring name stars (630/584-6300); Dunham Hunt Museum; Ruth Garfield Farm Museum features a Fall Festival; *St. Charles Chronicle* (630/584-8485); home to Marguerite Henry who wrote the novel *Misty*, about a Justin Morgan breed of horse; pop. 27,896

St. Elmo: Fayette County; named for the patron saint of mariners; on Route 40, founded in 1830 by a group of Catholics from Kentucky; home to Chicago & Eastern Illinois railroad shops; oil became the touchstone of prosperous times when the town experienced an oil boom in 1930; pop. 1,456

St. Jacob: On Route 40, part of Triad school district (Marine, St, Jacob and Troy) Nearby Fort Chilton was built during War of 1812. Abraham Howard, fort's commander once chased after a troublesome Indian for 90 miles before he returned and proudly displayed a scalp of straight coal-black hair; pop. 801

St. Joseph: Champaign County; Joseph Kelly was a tavern keeper and the town's first postmaster; pop. 2,912

Salem: Marion County; on Route 50; founded by Capt. Samuel Young who left the river area as a result of the

Park Hotel in Salem: birthplace of William Jennings Bryan

1811 New Madrid earthquake and looked for a more stable place; The Iuka Half-way House, a stagecoach stop on the Vincennes-St. Louis Trail; **Miracle Whip** salad dressing was invented here by Max Crosset at his café on North Washington (sold to Kraft Foods in 1931 for $300); W.J. Bryan 3-time presidential candidate for Democratic party; redtop seed capital of the world; 1944 G.I. Bill of

Rights idea originated at its American Legion Post; home to an oil boom in 1939; home to William Jennings Bryan statue executed by Gutzon Borglum of Mount Rushmore fame; William Jennings Bryan Home; Bryan prosecuted John Scopes for teaching evolution in Tennessee; Scopes grew up in Salem and attended the University of Illinois; in 1939 boasted the nation's second largest oil field; pop. 7,909

Salisbury: In central Illinois, home to Colin Folk Art, a museum dedicated to the works of artist George Colin (217-626-1204)

Sandoval: Marion County; at juncture of Routes 50 and 51, mining and farming community on B&O Railroad; freight transfer site between IC and B&O; hurt by overnight conversion of B&O to standard gauge, making transfers unnecessary; named for lieutenant Sandoval who served under Cortes, the famous Spanish conquistador (spoiler of paradise if you prefer political correctness); pop. 1,434

Palace Modern Cabins on Route 50 at Sandoval

Sandwich: Originally called Newark; named for Sandwich, New Hampshire, which was probably named for the Earl of Sandwich who discovered the Hawaiian Islands and the sandwich (he was too busy at gaming tables to eat regular meals); Sandwich Antiques Market with over 500 dealers; home of the DeKalb County Fair; pop. 6,509

Savanna: Carroll County; on the Mississippi River; named for a grassy plain; on state Route 80 on the southern edge of Mississippi Palisades State Park with its famed Silurian dolomite rock formations; terminal for the Chicago, Milwaukee, St. Paul and Pacific Railroad; also terminal for CB&Q Railroad; home of Plum River Falls; near a point close to Rock Island Military and Prophetstown Trails to Galena; area scouted for hostile Indians during Blackhawk War; pop. 3,542

Savoy: Located adjacent to Champaign and incorporated as a village; does not have its own high school; pop. 4,476

Schaumburg: In Cook County; unusual in that Schaumburg Township never had a railroad for many years; early settlers came from Schaumburg-Lippe area in Germany; prep sports teams called Saxons and Conant Cougars; German town famous for the Jennings Slot Machine; home to Woodfield Mall, world's largest indoor shopping mall when built around 1971; home to Motorola Corporation; Athenaeum Museum; Habana Cigar House; Rainforest Café; The Waterworks indoor water park; Medieval Times Dinner and Tournament Show; Spring Valley Nature Sanctuary with 3.5 miles of nature trails; Schaumburg Flyers – minor league baseball team; home to silent film star Dorothy Dalton and bandleader Wayne King; **home to Lance Cpl. Jakub Henryk Kowalik, 21, killed in Operation Iraqi Freedom 2003**; pop. 75,386

Shawneetown Territorial Bank, 1816 (Mike Coles photo)

Seneca: LaSalle County; named for a tribe of New York Indians; home to Clark Stafford who has a 10-foot-tall concrete statue of Elvis he uses in parades; called the "Prairie Shipyard" during World War II for the landing craft LST boats (made by Winnie the Welder and Rosie the Riveter) and floated to New Orleans; pop. 2,053

Sesser: In Franklin County next to Rend Lake (3,300 acres); formed by damming the Big Muddy and Casey Fork Rivers; has Wayne Fitzgerrell State Park with 250 campsites (618/629-2320); Rend Lake Resort has first class lodge and guest cabins; boat-el; PGA 27 hole golf course (618/629-2211); pop. 2,128

Schiller Park: Chicago German suburb incorporated in 1914; Julia Kolze was Illinois' first woman mayor in 1934; pop. 11,850

Shabbona: DeKalb County northern Illinois town named for Indian loyal to the whites; pop 929

Shawneetown: Seat of Gallatin County; named for local Indian tribe; its bank (with 5 massive sandstone columns) purportedly turned down Chicago officials who requested a $2,000 loan for development (historian Robert Howard calls this story a myth but a rejection letter dated July 5, 1838 exists); financial center of Illinois from 1818-1831; visited by General LaFayette in 1825; only other town besides Washington D.C. platted by the federal government; **Insect War** between local tribes started when two boys from different tribes were playing together and quarreled over which should own a very large grasshopper they had captured; home to the Marshall House, the only brick building in early Shawneetown built by John Marshall; B&O and L&N Railroads; bridge over Ohio River on Illinois Route 13; pop. 1,410

Sheffield: Bureau County; on U.S. 6 and 34, home to the first Danish Evangelical Lutheran Congregation in the U.S.; dumping ground for low-level radioactive wastes; pop. 946

Shelbyville: Home to Lake Shelbyville (217/774-2020) with 172 miles of shoreline, has a visitor's center; lake holds back the Kaskaskia and Okaw rivers; project started in 1963, completed 1970; home of Horace Tallman who invented first successful pickup hay baler; Shelby County Courthouse; Oliver Tractor Company; pop. 4,971

Sheldon: Iroquois County; Penn Central & Toledo, Peoria & Western cross here; named for a railroad official; pop. 1,232

Shiloh: St. Clair County; first known as New Germany; has a white frame church that is the oldest Methodist church structure in the state of Illinois; Glen Addie Mansion on Shiloh Road; 640 acres taken from Shiloh Valley to create Scott Air Base; pop. 7,643

Silvis: Located in northwestern Illinois near the Mississippi River; named for early settler R.S. Silvis; has a roadway named Hero Street. Around the turn of the century large numbers of Mexicans settled here to work in the freight yards. Many of them lived on Second Street, only a block and a half long. During World War II and the Korean War, that tiny neighborhood sent 57 young men to the battlefields. According to Defense Department statistics, no area of comparable size contributed more soldiers. In 1971 Second Street was renamed **Hero Street**. A monument now stands to commemorate those who served and those who died; pop. 7,269

Simpson: In Southern Illinois, home to **Buffalo Rock**, 3 miles northeast of town off Route 147; outline of a buffalo, thought to be drawn by Indians, is on the side of a sandstone cliff

Lincoln's Monument and Tomb at Springfield (Illinois Department of Conservation)

Skokie: Chicago suburb settled by immigrants from Luxembourg; billed itself as the "world's largest village;" Skokie Northshore Sculpture Park (70 sculptures on two acres); led Illinois in West Nile Virus deaths; lost most of their songbirds due to virus; built on a drained swamp; Potawatomie Indian settlement; then became large orchard area; Hebrew Theological College; Old Orchard Shopping Center; *Skokie Review*; pop. 63,348

Sleepy Hollow: Kane County in northeastern Illinois; home to Helen "Ma" Sunday who was married to evangelist Billy Sunday and shared in his work; the couple spent their summers here; home to D. Ray Wilson, author of the **Illinois Historical Tour Guide**; pop. 3,553

Somonauk: In DeKalb County, from a Potawatomie word meaning, "paw paw;" CB&Q Railroad; pop. 1,295

South Holland: cook County; Dutch community established around 1840 on Little Calumet River; truck farming important; once known as the Onion Set Capital of America; Midwest Carvers Museum; pop. 22,147

South Stickney: Cook County; in 1968 the largest unincorporated community in Illinois

Sparta: Randolph County; Comic Book Capital of America; home to Spartan Printing, the company that once printed most of our nation's comic books in the 1950s, employing 1,000 people; home to Roscoe Misselhorn museum; film *In The Heat of the Night* shot here; home to historic octagonal Charter Oak School; Hunter Field named for Hunter brothers who were daredevil pilots and friends of Charles A. Lindbergh; pop. 4,486

Springfield: Founded by Elisha Kelly; Flower City, City of Churches; named for spring creek; state's 4th largest city; home of the state's first race riot in 1908 where 6 people killed (2 whites, four blacks) and 70 injured, leading to the formation of the national NAACP; birthplace of singer June Christy (sang for Stan Kenton orchestra) has Lincoln's two-story home, Oliver Parks Telephone Museum; GAR Museum; Camp Butler National Cemetery (Confederate POW Camp); Lincoln tomb at Oakridge Cemetery; radio stations WTAX and WCVS; annual Illinois State Fair; points of interest Lincoln Home, Globe Tavern (Abe and Mary lived here in a

rented room from 1842-1844, Dana-Thomas House, **classic Frank Lloyd Wright house**; Illinois State Museum (217/782-7387); Old State Capitol; Thomas Rees Memorial Carillon with 67 imported bells; Lincoln-Herndon law office, Concordia Theological Seminary, **Lincoln Tomb**; birthplace of 1950's star Philadelphia Phillies pitcher, **Robin Roberts**; Illinois State Museum Store (217-782-7387); Illinois Natural Resources Gift Shop; the famed Mason-Dixon line runs just a few miles south of Springfield; Cozy Dog Drive-in (217/525-1992); radio personality Spizz Singer; pop. 111,454 (6th in the state)

Frank L. Wright's Dana-Thomas House in Springfield (IL Dept. of Tourism)

Spring Valley: On Route 6, north-central Illinois; once the site of extensive mining operations, succeeded by manufacturing; union leader John Mitchell a resident here; pop. 5,398

Staunton: A coal mining community on old Route 66; John Wood of Virginia was its first settler in 1817; has annual Tour de Donut bicycle race where points are earned for donuts consumed at rest stops; pop. 5,030

Steelville: In Randolph County; Kloth's Antiques Store just west of town at Routes 4 and 150; named for early settler John Steele of Tennessee; pop. 2,077

Steger: Chicago suburb; Piano Capital of America; named for John Steger who started piano factory; pop. 9,682

Sterling: On Route 30, directly across the Rock River from Rock Falls; small towns of Chatham and Harrisburg united to form Sterling; each town had its own preference and the name Sterling was chosen by a flip of a coin; Daniel Harris of Galena important early settler; home of several prize winners – Jesse Williams for *Why Marry?;* the first play (1917) ever to receive a Pulitzer Prize; Odell Shepard for *The Life of Bronson Alcott* (biography Pulitzer) and Don Fehrenbacher a history

Archibald Hefer/R.P. Lumber Store in Staunton (R.P. since 1977)

Pulitzer for *The Dred Scott Case*; Lincoln Boulder commemorates speech Lincoln gave here in 1856 in support of John Fremont; home to P.W. Dillon Home Museum (owner of Northwestern Steel and Wire Company); home to Sterling Municipal Coliseum and Grandon Civic Center; Chief Shikshak Bison Ranch; Gierhart's Scouting Museum (815/626-0609); bills itself as the "Heart of American Hardware;" pop. 15,451

Stickney: Chicago suburb; Hawthorne Downs Racetrack; large Czech population; Commonwealth Edison plant; pop. 6,148

Stillman Valley: Site of the first battle of the Blackhawk War where Major Isaiah Stillman and his militiamen were defeated by Chief Black Hawk; the war lasted 15 weeks; pop. 1,048

Stockton: Illinois' Highest Town; on Route 78 near Wisconsin border and Apple River Canyon State Park; Mount Carroll; pop. 1,926

Stonington; Christian County; named by settlers who came from Stonington, Connecticut; pop. 960

Streamwood: Chicago suburb near Elgin; "the City With a Smile;" pop. 36,407

Streator: Livingston and LaSalle counties; first called Hardscrabble; long known for its famed glass bottling works and coal and clay producing mines; changed to Unionville to honor men who went to war; name changed to Streator to honor the coal company president; home to George "Honey Boy" Evans, a member of Chicago's Mastodon Minstrels (black face) in 1890s, wrote song, "In The Good Old Summertime;" home to Clarence Mulford, creator of the western, "Hopalong Cassidy;" industrial town served by 7 railroads; pop. 14,190

Prime Steak House in Stickney (courtesy Neal Strebel)

Sullivan: Moultrie County; calls itself the "Northern Gateway to Lake Shelbyville;" situated on the Lincoln Heritage Trail; originally known as Asa's Point; home to the Little Theater for summer stock plays; pop. 4,326

Summit: Cook County; for many years this town had the name Argo on its post office because the bulk of the mail it received was for the Argo cornstarch plant there; so named because it is located on the continental divide in the state of Illinois; situated on an almost imperceptible crest of the watershed; rain falling on east side of town drains into Great Lakes; rain falling on other side drains into Mississippi River and Gulf of Mexico; Corn Products Company largest corn processing refinery in world; pop. 10, 637

Sumner: Lawrence County; southeastern Illinois oil town named for first settler, Ben Sumner; home to Red Hill Raceway on Route 1; pop. 1,022

Swansea; St. Clair County sandwiched between Belleville and Fairview Heights; named for seacoast town in Wales; resident Philip Gunlach patented seed drill planter; Mike and Christine Gillespie House; pop. 10,579

Sycamore: Seat of DeKalb County; this is the English name for the Potawatomie word "Kishwaukee;" its earliest name was Orange; north of DeKalb on Route 23; founded by Carlos Lattin; *Sycamore True Republican*; pop. 12,020

Tamaroa: Perry County; French name for local Kiawkashaw Indian tribe; nearby are the Maple Lawn Gardens, a cornucopia of narcissuses, daffodils, peonies and other flowers; town named by Illinois Central officials who built a train depot there; pop. 740

Tamms: Alexander County; home to a correctional center and the prep Pharaohs; pop. 724

Tampico: Birthplace of **President Ronald Reagan,** who also lived in Monmouth and Dixon and attended Eureka College; Reagan was a play-by-play sports announcer for Cub games by delayed broadcast (the announcer reads about the course of the game over the wire service and then makes up the details as he goes along); pop. 772

Ronald Reagan as an announcer

Taylorville: Southeast of Springfield; seat of Christian County; prominent coal mining area; KKK very active here during 1920s; resident Ed Purcells helped develop radar in WW II; prep teams called the Tornadoes; pop. 11,427

Teutopolis: Effingham County; T-Town, City of Teutons; home of the Wooden Shoes high school sports teams, so-called because a shoemaker, enjoying the schools sports teams, gave the coach a pair of wooden shoes in 1935; on Route 40, a German Catholic community settled in 1839 by a group from Cincinnati, Ohio; St. Francis of Assisi Church; northern Germany tended to be Lutheran while southern Germany remained Catholic after the Reformation; home to Teutopolis Monastery Museum (217/857-3586); pop. 1,559

Thebes: Once the seat of Alexander County, has old Greek Revival courthouse, situated on a bluff, where Dred Scott was once detained in the dungeon/jail on the lower level; originally named Sparhawk's Landing; mentioned in Edna Ferber's novel, *Show Boat* (song "Old Man River" comes from the play); not far from Thebes is Horseshoe Lake, a 2,000 acre lake and a 1,400 acre island in the middle that is a game preserve and feeding ground for fowl; site is a point of convergence for 2 of the 3 major flyways for Canadian geese; in 1935 more than 5 tons of turtles were taken in traps to protect the game fish there; island planted annually with cereal crops for fowl food; this area resembles a Louisiana bayou and is considered a hunter's paradise; pop. 478

Thomson: Home to yearly Melon Days on Labor Day; Burlington Railroad Depot Museum; pop. 559

Thornton: Cook County; large stone quarry; old German town; pop. 2,582

Tilton: Vermilion County; named for L. Tilton, president of the Northern Cross Railroad; pop. 2,976

Tinley Park: Chicago suburb; Centennial Lanes computerized bowling; New World Music Theater; Odyssey Fun World; Fungus Town - mushroom canning center; Rock Island Railroad; pop. 48,401

Tolono: Champaign County: located at crossroads of Illinois Central and Great Western Railroads; south of Champaign; Abe Lincoln gave his "farewell address" to the people of Illinois in February of 1861, before leaving for the White House; pop. 2,700

Tonti: Town in Marion County named for Henri Tonti, LaSalle's faithful lieutenant

Toluca: Marshall County; coal mining town named by Mexican workers for a city in Mexico; pop. 1,339

Towanda: McLean County; Indian name meaning, "where we bury the dead; " pop. 493

Tremont: Tazewell County: named for three hills in the area; Lincoln challenged to a duel here by James Shields; pop. 2,029

Trenton: Clinton County on Route 50; named by early settler William Lewis for his hometown of Trenton, New Jersey; pop. 2,610

St. Mary's Catholic Church in Trenton

Troy: Hometown to Paul Simon, Lieutenant Governor, U.S. Senator and presidential candidate; noted for its large truck stop plaza at Route 162 and Interstate 70; its Triad school district consists of Troy, St. Jacob and Marine; pop. 8,524

Troy Grove: LaSalle County; home to **Wild Bill Hickok,** lawman with 72 notches on his gun when murdered by Jack McCall in Deadwood, South Dakota; Hickok shot in back while holding what came to be known as "dead man's hand" – aces and eights; pop. 305

Tunnel Hill: Southern Illinois town near railroad tunnel owned by Big 4 Railroad (St. Louis, Cleveland, Chicago, Cincinnati); located a mile west off Highway 45 near Vienna; built in 1871 by Pennsylvania Railroad; tunnel is about 540 feet long

Tuscola: Seat of Douglas County; an Indian word meaning level plain; Uncle Joe Canon practiced law here; on route of Illinois Central Railroad; platted in 1857 and incorporated in 1861; two major gas lines meet here; one of the states' four Dixie Truckers Home; pop. 4,448

Union: Home to an Illinois Railway Museum (56 acres with working steam engine train ride 815/923-2488); McHenry County Historical Museum; Donley's Wild West Town Museum (staged gunfights between lawmen and desperadoes, western memorabilia, death masks of notorious gunmen 815/923-9000 or 2214); pop. 576

Urbana: Named for Urbana, Ohio; home of the Frasca Air Museum (217/367-8441), housing aircraft used in the movies *1941* and *Midway.*; home of the University of Illinois; John Philip Sousa Library and Museum; Krannert Art Museum; population 36,395

Utica: Called the Burgoo Capital for a soup of the same name made from vegetables and assorted critters

Valmeyer: In Monroe County; home to one of the largest mushroom farms in America, located in nearby caves; in early history, Steven Miles purchased huge segment of land and started a **feudal empire;** his mausoleum on bluffs at Eagle Cliff; pop. 608

Vandalia: Seat of Fayette County; at juncture of Routes 40 and 51; Wilderness Capital; Illinois' second capital city and home to the 18 ft. high **Madonna of the Trail** statue; home to artist James Berry; old 1836 State Capitol; pop. 6,975

Venice: Madison County; one of the tri-cities on the American Bottom; named for town in Italy because it flooded so often; ferry service to St. Louis established in 1804; large rail switch yard built here around 1901; McKinley Bridge connected Venice with St. Louis; Kerr Island, inhabited by Negro squatters, became attached to mainland; "Bad-eye" Bill Smith's Hyde Park Club; pop. 2,528

Vernon Hills: Cuneo Museum and Gardens; pop. 20,120

Vienna: Named for a pioneer woman named Vienna who lived in the area; home to Trail of Tears Memorial Park (618/833-4910), commemorating the tragic removal of southeastern Native Americans to Oklahoma; home to Paul Powell, Secretary of State who died and left a fortune in shoeboxes; *Vienna Times* Building; Tunnel Hill State Trail; pop. 1,234

Villa Grove: Douglas County; was once known as the Pancake Capital of the World due to annual pancake festival; tradition discontinued because it became too expensive; one year enough pancakes were consumed to form a Bunyanesque stack of flapjacks a mile and a half high; pop. 2,553

Trinity Lutheran Church at Pekin (courtesy Neal Strebel)

Virden: Situated near Springfield; site of famous 1898 riot at coal mine during strike dispute; **10 miners and 6 guards killed;** Freeman-Crown II mine currently operating – nearby Farmersville has Freeman # 3 mine; prep teams called Bulldogs; served by 3 railroads; pop. 3,488

Virginia: Seat of Cass County; platted in 1836 by Henry Hall and named for his native state; pop. 1,728

Volo: Hamlet in N.E Illinois on Route 20; dominated by St. Peter's Church, modeled after the one in England on the Salisbury Plain near Stronehenge; Antique Auto Museum (815/385-3644); Volo Bog State Natural Area; pop. 200

Vladimirovo: Near Freeport; Illinois' "Little Russia"

Wadsworth: Chicago suburb; resident James Onan, a contractor, lives in a gold-plated 1/100 replica of the Great Pyramid of Egypt (six-stories tall); outside the home is a 40-foot statue of Ramses II, built by Disney Studios for a movie; inside the house is a recreation of **King Tut's Tomb** (847/662-6666); home of Tempel Farms, a 6,000 acre site with **Lipizzan stallions** giving performances from June through August (847/623-7272); home of Des Plaines River Wetlands Demonstration Project with 450 acres of marshes, a botanical and birdwatcher's delight, located on Highway 41 at Wadsworth Road; pop. 3,083

Walnut: North-central Illinois town home to Don Marquis, humorist, dramatist and poet who wrote with Joel Chandler Harris for Uncle Remus Magazine; named for a grove of Walnut trees; pop. 1,461

Wamac: Illinois Central Railroad town whose name comes from first letter of the counties in which the town lies – Washington, Marion and Clinton; long-time favorite watering hole for residents of surrounding "dry" towns; the state's Third Principal Meridian intersects with the east-west Base Line near here; pop. 1,378

Warren: On highway 78 about a mile from Wisconsin border, settled by Alexander Burnett along the old Sucker Trail which ran from St. Louis to Wisconsin; named for the founder's son; also located on the old Galena/Chicago Railroad line; home to painter William Lathrop, who moved east after winning New York awards; home to Abner Dalrymple, Chicago White Stockings star and Paul Minebarger, adviser to Chiang Kai Shek; two stagecoach lines crossed here, the old Sucker Trail which went south to St. Louis and the Chicago-Galena Trail; pop. 1,496

Warrenville: DuPage County; named for settler Colonel Julius Warren who arrived in 1833; pop. 13,363

Warsaw: Hancock County; named for the city in Mrs. Porter's novel, "*Thaddeus of Warsaw*; located between Quincy and Nauvoo; its Geode Park is one of the few places in the state where rock specimen collecting is allowed; home to Forts Johnson (1814) and Edwards (1817), the latter built under the direction of Zachary Taylor; Thomas Sharp print shop and museum (he opposed the Mormons); Resident John Hay thought the town should have been named Spunky Point; pop. 1,793

Waterloo Country Club (courtesy Skip Gatermann)

Wartburg: In Monroe County: named for castle in Germany where Martin Luther translated the Bible into German

Washington Park: Suburb of East St. Louis on Route 111, its Emerson Electric plant built the Honest John army rocket & B-52 fire control systems in late 1950s; pop. 5,345

Waterloo: Seat of Monroe County; adjacent to original settlement of Bellefontaine (beautiful spring); Emory Peter Rogers an important early settler; before passage of stricter marriage laws in 1937, had reputation of being the Gretna Green of metropolitan St. Louis (In colonial days, young couples from London who wanted to marry eloped to Gretna Green near

Scotland due to its lax marriage restrictions.); signs advertising "quickie" marriages by a justice of the peace with reasonable fees lined the roads for several miles around the city limits; the Marquis de Lafayette stayed at the old Ditch Tavern when visiting the area in 1825; its St. Paul's Church **has a rooster on top** instead of the traditional Christian cross; some Protestant churches felt the

cross to be a Catholic symbol; named for site of Napoleon's defeat in Belgium; Moredock Lake; pop. 7,614

C&NW Railroad Station at Waukegan

Watseka: Iroquois County seat; named for Watch-e-kee (pretty woman) Potawatomi wife of Gurdon Hubbard of John Jacob Astor's American Fur Company; it was a business marriage to cement relations with local Indians; Hubbard grew tired of her in two years and gave her to his partner, La Vasseur when he quit the business; Hubbard's Trace went from Vincennes to Chicago; home of Max Nordeen's Wheels Museum featuring rare and unique automobiles; native Henry Bacon **designed the Lincoln Memorial** in D.C.; pop. 5,670

Wauconda: Lake County; Justus Bangs and Elihu Hubbard early settlers; name comes from an Indian word meaning "great spirit;" Northeast Illinois on Route 12; Lake County Museum with fabulous collection of postcards by **Curt Teich**; prep Bulldogs; pop. 9,448

Waukegan: Indian name means Little Fort for a small French stockade; a Lincoln speech here in 1860 was not finished due to an outbreak of fire; later became heavily industrial; its Lake County Chamber of Commerce building, erected in 1847 is on National Register of Historic Places; Winthrop Harbor has charter fishing boats for catching salmon (847/BIG-FISH); south of Waukegan is Great Lakes Naval Training Center; has a Walk of Fame that includes **Jerry Orbach** of "Law and Order" fame; football Hall of Famer **Otto Graham**, science fiction writer **Ray Bradbury** (*Fahrenheit 451* and *Martian Chronicles*); won an Oscar for his screenplay of *Moby Dick* (I have always thought Moody Dick would have been a better name for that temperamental whale); Orion Howe, a 14-year-old drummer boy during the Civil War, received Congressional Medal of Honor; Pfanstiehl Chemical; pop. 87,901

Waverly: Morgan County; named for the Waverley novels of Sir Walter Scott; huge underground storage site for natural gas; pop. 1,346

Wenona: 815/853-4665; From an old Indian name; off Interstate 39, old Burgess Farms raised draft horses that were bought all over the world; on border of Marshall and LaSalle counties; home to Dennis Frings, a noted painter; prep teams called the Fieldcrest Knights; its "Welcome to Wenona" sign features a prominent spoil or gob pile; such piles were leftovers as a result of longwall mining (as opposed to room-and-pillar) and were simply waste material separated from coal; unsuspecting tourists are told that these are merely old cones from inactive volcanoes; pop. 1,065

Coal Miners Memorial at West Frankfort (Eisenhauer)

Westchester: Chicago suburb; organized by utilities mogul, Samuel Insull; pop 16,824

West Dundee: Small northern Illinois town settled mainly by Scots and Brits and named for Dundee, Scotland; Alan Pinkerton migrated here from Dundee, Scotland, and opened a cooperage shop and came to know Lincoln through abolitionist activities; in 1850 he became Chicago's first detective; pop 5,428

Western Springs: Cook County on Route 34, incorporated by a Quaker group in 1866; named for local mineral springs believed to have medicinal benefits (people back then also bought concoctions from flim-flam snake oil drummers (salesmen); John Dillinger drove a taxicab here for a while; police ran him out of town after customers complained that he was surly; pop. 12,493

West Frankfort: Coal mining community in Franklin County; Name comes from Frank Jordan's Fort; the 2nd worst coalmine disaster in the state occurred here in 1951 killing 119; home to WFRX radio station; home to annual Church of God state camp meeting; most important city north of Cairo in 1830; pyramid-shaped monument pays tribute to all coal miners; Ken Gray's Political Memorabilia and Antique Car Museum (618/937-6100); has large Lithuanian settlement; once had two post offices; Orient 2 Mine largest in world; pop. 8,196

Westmount: Near Route 34; small community home to Illinois Pet Memorial Cemetery, platted in 1926 by a grateful man whose dog once saved his life; pop. 24,554

West Salem: Actually located east of Salem; settled by Moravians; Ripley's Believe It Or Not says tombstone of Emma Pfeil is world's smallest tombstone 5 and7/8 x 10 and 1/2x2 inches; pop. 1,001

Westville: Vermilion County on Route 1; home of the first night prep football game in Illinois, 1928; pop. 3,175

Wetaug: In southern Illinois' Pulaski County; named for tribe of Cherokee who passed through on way from Georgia to Oklahoma (Trail of Tears); its large spring stopped flowing after 1896 earthquake

Wheaton: Chicago suburb, seat of Du Page County; "The Button of the Bible Belt;" home to 24 different religious organizations; home of **Elbert Gary** who became Chairman of the Board of U.S. Steel and helped build Gary on the sand dunes of Indiana; name honors Warren and Jesse Wheaton, town godfathers; home of Wheaton College (Rev. Billy Graham's alma mater), built by Wesleyans; **Billy Graham** Center Museum (630/752-5909); residents stole county seat from Naperville by absconding with all the records in the dead of night; home of Red Grange, the Wheaton Iceman; arrival of Galena & Chicago Union Railroad helped the town grow; home of Theosophical Society Temple; birthplace of Grote Reber, inventor of the radio telescope; **home of the first 18 hole golf course in America** (Chicago Golf Club), back in 1893 (Oh, those rich Chicago suburbs!); home to about 25 religious organizations and publishers; First Infantry Division Museum (630/668-5161) at Cantigny – 500 acres, formerly property of publisher Robert McCormick; Cosley Zoo; pop. 55,416

White City: In Macoupin County, just east of I-55; obtained its name from the 52 white residences that coal officials brought over from the St Louis World's Fair of 1904 to start a company town

Whitehall: In Greene County; has Annie Louise Keller memorial, a statue crafted by Lorado Taft to pay tribute to a schoolteacher who lost her life rescuing her students during a 1927 tornado; also, grave of the Little Drummer Boy of Shiloh; pop. 2,629

Whittington: Southern Illinois town off interstate 57, south of Mount Vernon; home to Rend Lake Resort and Rend Lake Shooting Complex (all shotguns) and Archery Facility (618/629-2368)

Willisville: In Perry County; on Route 4 in southern Illinois, named for Dickey Willis; settled by Sicilians who came over to work in the Dickey Willis coal mine; incorporated in 1900; its old time privy cleaners (scavengers) were required to have a license and had to do their work between the hours of 10:00 p.m. and 5:00 a.m.; Wilco Dairy Barn said to be one of largest in the world; when the Willisville Bank lost its charter to the town of **Ava**, it was said that the whole operation was moved to Ava in the back of a car; pop. 1,439

Wilmette: Cook County; named for Chicago's first settler, Antoine Ouilmette; has beautiful Baháí Temple – North American headquarters of the Baháí religion named for a Persian religious leader; believe in the unity of all religions and a universal language; home to No Man's Land, an area that sold illegal fireworks (problem solved by annexation); Kohl Children's Museum; home of Mallinckrodt College; pop. 27, 651

Wilmington: Will County on the Kankakee River; called "Island City" because the river splits the downtown area; Peter Stewart House an important stop on Underground Railway; Schutten-Aldrich House is an unusual 3-story octagonal house; home to the Launching Pad Café that features **The Gemini Giant**, another one of those outrageous Fiberglas statues, 30-foot tall; originally a lumberjack, the statue was modified to look like a spaceman by being fitted with a space helmet while his hands hold a toy space rocket (815/476-6535); pop. 5,134

Winchester: On Route 36, seat of Scott County; when

Beautiful Baháí Temple in Wilmette, the religion's North American headquarters

platted in 1836, surveyors allowed a Kentucky local to name the town in exchange for a jug of whiskey; public square has bronze statue of Stephen Douglas who began his career as a teacher here in 1833; Birthplace of G.V. Black, **Father of Modern Dentistry**; wrote numerous books and articles on dentistry; invented many dental instruments; on Route 36; pop. 1,650

Winfield: DuPage County; Kline Creek Farm tourist site; Erastus Gary the first settler; pop. 8,718

Winnebago: In Winnebago County, named for the Indian tribe; pop. 1,840

Winnetka: Cook County; Potawatomie word for "beautiful land;" suggested by Mrs. Charles Peck, wife of the founder; Incorporated in 1869; prides itself in its excellent schools; New Trier Township named for a town in Germany that was once an outpost of the old Roman Empire; Harold Ickes, a member of FDR's cabinet hailed from Winnetka; pop. 12,419

Winthrop Harbor: In Lake County near the Wisconsin border on Lake Michigan; named for the Winthrop Harbor and Dock Company that planned the town; most northeastern town in Illinois; pop. 6,670

Wonder Lake: McHenry County; lake formed by damming Nippersink Creek; pop. 7,463

Wood Dale: Du Page County: Edward Lester of Vermont was town's first settler; named for a wooded valley; pop. 13,535

Wood River: Madison County: located on the American Bottom, early town in area called Benbowe City was wild and turbulent, brawls and shootings frequent; in 1917, Shell Oil built a huge refinery complex; home to Standard Oil refinery which razed Benbowe City; in 1925 it had the largest concrete swimming pool in America, built by Standard Oil refinery; Lewis and Clark expedition started here; Union Tank Car Co.; WRTH radio; pop. 11,296

Woodridge: DuPage County; Seven Bridges Ice Arena; nearby Boy Scout camp; pop. 30,934

Woodstock: Named for a town in Vermont; seat of McHenry County; home to cartoonist Chester Gould, creator of **Dick Tracy** as a crime-fighter counter to the antics of Al Capone; Chester Gould Museum; home to Woodstock Typewriter; Todd School for Boys has a

Fire Department at Wonder Lake (author's collection)

famous alumnus – Orson Welles; Woodstock Opera House (815/338-5300) has live theater where Orson Welles and Paul Newman once performed; seat DD 113 is always reserved for Elvira, a female ghost who haunts the scene; she hung herself in a bell tower after being jilted back in 1903 (815/338-5300); dairy farm and resort area; Chicago & Northwestern Railroad; newspaper is the *Sentinel*; pop. 20,151

Worden: Madison County: John Worden, an English land developer, donated land for a right of way for the Wabash Railroad; pop. 905

Worth: Cook County: Calumet Sag Channel runs just south of town; pop. 11,047

Wyanet: On Route 6, situated at the Illinois and Mississippi (Hennepin) Canal; has some interesting land formations nearby due to the Bloomington Moraine; pop. 1,028

Wyoming: Stark County; named for the Wyoming Valley in Pennsylvania; pop. 1,424

Zeigler: Franklin County town named for Zeigler Coal Company; laid out like the city of Paris with a hub in the center and spokes radiating out; Napoleon favored this design because a cannon at the hub could command several streets; heavy mine violence here after the turn of the century; pop. 1,669

Zion: Chicago suburb in Lake County in the extreme northeast corner of the state founded in 1900; a religious colony founded by Scottish zealot John Dowie who imposed blue laws and forbade alcohol, tobacco, oysters, humming, cosmetics, tan-colored shoes and believed that the earth was flat. "Where God rules, man prospers," was his motto.

Dowie started attracting large crowds after Buffalo Bill's cousin, Sadie Codie, went to him because of an illness and was cured. The Cody's were in town for the Columbian Exposition. No trains were allowed to stop in Zion on Sundays. A lace factory imported from England provided jobs for residents. A successor, Wilbur Voliva, began the nation's first Christian radio broadcast, WCBD, in 1922. Things eventually fell apart and outsiders finally began moving into the town; has annual Passion play at the Christian Arts Auditorium (847/746-2221) (Zion Historical Society 847/746-2427); Illinois Beach State Park; The Power House – interactive display; pop. 22,866

Massive Shell Oil Complex at Wood River (courtesy Gary Barber and Shell Oil)

ILLINOIS COUNTIES, DATE CREATED, COUNTY SEAT

Adams: 1825 - named for President J.Q. Adams; Quincy, **Alexander**: 1819 - named for William Alexander an early settler, Cairo, **Bond**: 1817 - named for Shadrach Bond, first governor of the state; Greenville, **Boone**: 1837 - named for Daniel Boone; Belvidere, **Brown**: 1839 - named for General Jacob Brown of the War of 1812; Mount Sterling, **Bureau**: 1837 - named for Pierre de Bureo, early Indian trader; Princeton, **Calhoun**: 1825 - named for Vice-president John C. Calhoun; Hardin, **Carroll**: 1839 - named for John Carroll, a signer of the Declaration of Independence; Mount Carroll, **Cass**: 1937 - named for Lewis Cass, secretary of war; Virginia, **Champaign**: 1833 - named for Champaign County in Ohio; Urbana, **Christian**: 1839 - named for a Kentucky county; Taylorville, **Clark**: 1819 - named for George Rogers Clark; Marshall, **Clay**: 1824 - named for Henry Clay; Louisville, **Clinton**: 1824 - named for De Witt Clinton, governor of New York; Carlyle, **Coles**: 1830 - named for governor Edward Coles; Charleston, **Cook**: (largest county by population) 1831 - named for Daniel Pope Cook territorial delegate to Congress; Chicago, **Crawford**: 1816 - named for presidential candidate from Georgia, William Crawford; Robinson, **Cumberland**: 1843 - named for the Cumberland Road; Toledo, **De Kalb**: 1837 - named for Baron de Kalb, a German officer killed at the battle

The White Barn in Casey, Illinois

of Camden in the Revolution; Sycamore, **De Witt**: 1839 - named for De Witt Clinton of New York; Clinton, **Douglas**: 1859 - named for Stephen A. Douglas; Tuscola, **Du Page**: 1839 - named for the Du Page River; Wheaton, **Edgar**: 1823 - named for John Edgar, Kaskaskia merchant; Paris, **Edwards**: 1814 - named for Ninian Edwards, governor of Illinois Territory; Albion, **Effingham**: 1831 - named for Lord Effingham, who supported the colonists in Parliament; Effingham, **Fayette**: 1821 - named for the Frenchman, the Marquis de Lafayette; Vandalia, **Ford**: 1859 (the last county created in the state) - named for Governor Thomas Ford; Paxton, **Franklin**: 1818 - named for Ben Franklin; Benton, **Fulton**: 1823 - named for Robert Fulton, inventor of the steam boat, **Gallatin**: 1812 - named for Albert Gallatin, Secretary of the treasury; Shawneetown, **Greene**: 1821 - named for General Nathaniel Greene of the Revolutionary War; Carrollton, **Grundy**: 1841 - named for Felix Grundy of Tennessee, a War Hawk in the War of 1812; Morris, **Hamilton**: 1821 - named for Alexander Hamilton; McLeansboro, **Hancock**: 1825 - named for John Hancock, signer of the Dec. of Independence; Carthage, **Hardin**: 1839 – (smallest county by population) named for a county in Kentucky; Elizabethtown; **Henderson**: 1841 - named for a Kentucky County; Oquawka, **Henry**: 1833 - named for Patrick Henry; Cambridge, **Iroquois**: 1833 - named for the Iroquois tribe; Watseka, **Jackson**: 1816 - named for Andrew Jackson; Murphysboro, **Jasper**: 1831 - named for Sergeant William Jasper, who replaced the American flag shot away by the British at Fort Moultrie; Newton, **Jefferson**: 1819 - named for Thomas Jefferson; Mount Vernon, **Jersey**: 1839 - named for the state of New Jersey; Jerseyville, **JoDaviess**: 1827 - named for Joseph Daviess, a Kentuckian killed at the battle of Tippecanoe; Galena, **Johnson**: 1812 - named for Richard Johnson, hero of the battle of Tippecanoe; Vienna, **Kane**: 1836 - named for Elias Kane, Illinois senator; Geneva, **Kankakee**: 1853 - an Indian name; Kankakee, **Kendall**: 1841 - named for Amos Kendall, member of Andrew Jackson's Kitchen Cabinet; Yorkville, **Knox**: 1825 - named for Washington's secretary of war, Henry Knox; Galesburg, **Lake**: 1839 - named for Lake Michigan; Waukegan,

LaSalle: 1831 - named for the explorer, La Salle; Ottawa, **Lawrence**: 1821 - named for commander James Lawrence, captain of the *Chesapeake* who said: "Don't give up the ship;" Lawrenceville, **Lee**: 1839 - named for Richard Henry Lee, signer of Dec. of Independence; Dixon, **Livingston**: 1837 - named for Edward Livingston, secretary of state; Pontiac, **Logan**: 1839 - named for Dr. John Logan pioneer physician; Lincoln, **McDonough**: 1826 - named for Thomas McDonough, hero of the battle of Lake Champlain in the War of 1812; Macomb, **McHenry**: 1836 - named for William McHenry, soldier in the Black Hawk War; Woodstock, **McLean**: (largest county in area) 1830 - named for John McLean, Illinois senator; Bloomington, **Macon**: 1829 - named for Nathaniel Macon, Revolutionary War hero; Decatur, **Macoupin**: 1812 - the name is of Indian origin, meaning "white potato;" Carlinville, **Madison**: 1812 - named for President James Madison, Edwardsville, **Marshall**: 1839 - named

Zion Home at Zion, Illinois

for chief justice John Marshall; Lacon, **Mason**: 1841 - named for a county in Kentucky; Havana, **Massac**: 1843 - named for Fort Massac; Metropolis, **Menard**: 1839 - named for Pierre Menard, lieutenant governor of Illinois; Petersburg, **Mercer**: 1825 - named for General Hugh Mercer, killed at the battle of Princeton; Aledo, **Monroe**: 1816 - named for President James Monroe; Waterloo, **Montgomery**: 1821 - named for Richard Montgomery who was killed at Quebec in the Revolution; Hillsboro, **Morgan**: 1823 - named for General Daniel Morgan, hero of the battle of Cowpens; Jacksonville, **Moultrie**: 1843 - named for General William Moultrie, Revolutionary War soldier; Sullivan, **Ogle**: 1836 - named for an early pioneer and militia officer; Oregon, **Peoria**: 1825 - named for an Indian tribe; Peoria, **Perry**: 1827 - named for Oliver Hazard Perry, hero of the battle of Lake Erie; Pinckneyville, **Platt**: 1841 - named for the Platt family; Monticello, **Pike**: 1821 - named for the explorer, Zebulon Pike, Pitsfield, **Pope**: 1816 - named for Nathaniel Pope, secretary of Illinois Territory; Golconda, **Pulaski**: 1843 - named for Polish patriot Casmir Pulaski, killed at Savannah during the Revolution; Mound City, **Putnam**: (smallest county in area) 1825 - named for Israel Putnam of the battle of Bunker Hill; Hennepin,

1863 red covered bridge at Princeton, Illinois

Randolph: 1795 - named for Edmund Randolph, Washington's attorney general; Chester, **Richland**: 1841 - named for an Ohio county, Olney, **Rock Island**: 1831 - named for Rock Island in the Mississippi at the mouth of Rock River, Rock Island, **St. Clair**: 1790 (the state's first county) - named for Arthur St. Clair, governor of the Northwest Territory, Belleville, **Saline**: 1847 - named for the salt springs which abound in the area; Harrisburg, **Sangamon**: 1821 - an Indian name meaning "good hunting ground;" Springfield, **Schuyler**: 1825 - named for General Philip Schuyler of the Revolutionary War; Rushville, **Scott**: 1827 - named for a county in Kentucky; Winchester, **Shelby**: 1827 - named for General Isaac Shelby, first governor of Kentucky; Shelbyville, **Stark**: 1838 - named for John Stark, Revolutionary War hero, Toulon, **Stephenson**: 1837 - named for Benjamin Stephenson, Illinois colonel In the War of 1812, **Tazewell**: 1827 - named for Littleton Tazewell, governor of Virginia; Pekin, **Union**: 1818 - named to commemorate a union revival meeting; Jonesboro, **Vermilion**: 1826 - named for the Vermilion River; Danville, **Wabash**: 1824 - named for the Wabash River on Indiana border; Mount Carmel,

The Little Theater on the Square at Sullivan, Illinois

Virginia: Seat of Cass County; founded in 1836 by Dr. H.H. Hall; 13 miles east of Beardstown on Route 125
Warren: 1825 - named for Dr./General Joseph Warren, killed at Bunker Hill, Monmouth, **Washington**: 1818 - named for George Washington; Nashville, **Wayne**: 1819 - named for General Anthony Wayne; Fairfield, **White**: 1815 - named for Leonard White, state senator; Carmi, **Whiteside**: 1836 - named for General Samuel Whiteside of the War of 1812 and the Black Hawk War; Morrison, **Will**: 1836 - named for Conrad Will, pioneer settler; Joliet, **Williamson**: 1839 - named for a county in Tennessee, Marion, **Winnebago**: 1836 - named for the Winnebago Indians; Rockford, **Woodford**: 1841- named for a county in Kentucky; Eureka.

FORMER U.S. SENATOR PAUL SIMON'S TOP TEN LIST

The ten most influential Illinois politicians in my years of public service? It's not an easy call, but I'm going to cheat a little – which some of them did – and give you a slightly larger list alphabetically:

Russell Arrington: State Senate leader, and a real leader. He had a great mind and would have been a Republican Governor or Senator but for a somewhat prickly personality. Diplomacy was not his strength.

The two Adlais: **Governor Adlai Stevenson** cleaned up the then-corrupt Illinois State Police, and through state police raids reduced blatant bribery by county and local officials, and helped Illinois in many other ways. Senator Adlai, his son, had a more low-key style. His father could not be described as flamboyant, but compared to his son he earned that adjective. The son's contributions in the Senate did not receive great attention, but were solid, including a restructuring of Senate committees and procedures.

An unknown except to politicians: **Gene Callahan**. He worked for several of us, including serving as chief of staff for Senator

Alan Dixon of Belleville. Rigidly honest, he knew how to get things done, including being tough when he had to be.

Richard J. Daley: For many years the most powerful office-holder in the state. His keys to success: hard work, and following issues and office-holders down to amazingly small details. His son has many of his father's qualities, but serves in a different era, and cannot manipulate things through patronage like his father did.

Everett Dirksen: A man of flexible principles, he played key roles on many issues through his adroit 180-degree shifts. A landmark bill that probably would not have passed without his assistance was the Civil Rights Act of 1964. Earlier he had opposed the legislation.

Paul Douglas: A giant physically and in every other way. In a period when corruption tainted Illinois everywhere, he headed efforts for higher ethical standards, protection of consumers, and anything that would help the impoverished, including championing civil rights. No one outside of Martin Luther King and Lyndon Johnson (amazingly!) played a greater role in the ultimate passage of basic civil rights. No state in the union had higher ranked senators than Illinois when the double Ds of Dirksen and Douglas were in office.

Dick Durbin of East St. Louis. It may be premature to evaluate our senior Senator, but he is highly respected by his colleagues and as a result plays an important role in the Senate. In 2000 when Al Gore had the Democratic nomination for president locked up, the *New York Times Magazine* story on the vice-presidential spot – then wide open – said that Democratic Senators collectively favored Dick Durbin.

Jim Edgar: Played a key role in getting the Illinois financial picture improved, not something everyone understands or appreciates. But his performance as our state's chief executive made him the most popular GOP figure in the state.

Dennis Hastert of Aurora and **Bob Michael**: Both leaders of the GOP in the House, both are disposed to win through working with others rather than the Gingrich-style hardball confrontation that leads to bitterness. Both have been a credit to our state and to the nation.

Mike Madigan: A man of few words. If you want to visit with him, make it a meal, otherwise plan to get your business over quickly. His dominance of the House in Springfield is legend. Part of that is because he is cautious about making commitments, but when he does, count on it. The most powerful Democrat in the state, outside of the Governor. Whoever eventually succeeds him is not likely to be as strong. He combines being a good politician with a strong sense of public service.

Gov. Richard Ogilvie with Rep. Les Arends of Melvin, Senator Everett Dirksen, Senator Charles Percy (author's collection)

Richard Ogilvie: Not a dynamic per-sonality, but a courageous governor who asked for an income tax. It has been of huge help to the causes of education and health care and other issues important to the state. But it **probably cost him his re-election**.

Paul Powell: He served in an era that tolerated corruption that would land him in prison today. My confrontations with him were frequent. But he clearly played the role of leader effectively – often for the public good, often for his own good.

Dan Rostenkowski: Legal difficulties plagued the end of his career in the U.S. House, following practices tolerated when he grew up in Illinois politics. But time brought changes. A strong leader before his legal difficulties, to his credit he has emerged from those troubles to continue to play an influential role on the Illinois and national scene.

William G. Stratton: Governor during part of senior Mayor Richard Daley's reign, in many ways he had similar traits: great attention to detail, more than any governor I have known, and he was adept at "wheeling and dealing."

George Ryan: This will surprise many. His problem: playing the old-style politics. But no Illinois governor of the past century – except one – has received as much national attention and influence as George Ryan. Adlai Stevenson exceeded the Ryan national attention and influence once nominated for President, but prior to that he had achieved a respected role, but not as much national attention as George Ryan did with two courageous actions: on the death penalty and by becoming the first governor of any state to **visit Castro's Cuba** and call for a change in U.S. policy.

James Thompson: He loved politics and because of a very outgoing personality – much different than George Ryan or Jim Edgar or Adlai Stevenson – he played an extremely influential role. He knew how to get his melody played by the discordant group called the Illinois General Assembly.

Harold Washington: He brought excitement and greater influence for Chicago's minorities, but his articulate voice and reconciling manner helped make more of a sense of community out of Chicago. That skill did not prevail in the City Council, but outside City Hall it did. He brought enthusiastic cheers with his presence at a Bud Billiken Day parade or any other African-American group – but he did the same with a Lithuanian or Polish crowd where he would mangle a foreign phrase he had tried to memorize. He loved to read, and the city library is appropriately named for him.

ILLINOIS RAILROADS - THE GREATEST IN THE WORLD BY Mark Godwin of Lebanon

This first survey will cover the railroads of the central region of Illinois as defined by the Baltimore & Ohio Railroad on the south and the Toledo, Peoria & Western on the north. Running at a diagonal across the region are lines linking St. Louis with Chicago as well as rail lines running across the middle of the state bypassing both cities. Mixed in are short lines, regional carriers, Street Car and interurbans, and even a former narrow gauge. (**See map on page 136 for the Chicago lines.**) The railroads of Egypt (Southern Illinois) are covered next and include the Baltimore & Ohio and everything south of Route 50 on down to Cairo, Illinois.

The railroads of the 19th century and interurbans of the late 19th and early 20th centuries helped connect a continent and served as important links to the future. They were the "blue chips," the "dot coms" of their era. Promoted as a safe way to make a fortune, they often experienced boom and bust, going through reorganization, mergers, receiverships and numerous alphabet soup name changes. They spawned some of the early Captains of Industry (Robber Barons, if you prefer) - names like Jay Gould and Cornelius Vanderbilt. (**Chicago railroad map p. 136**)

The first railroad in Illinois and, in fact, the first west of the Pennsylvania Alleghenies, was a seven-mile long road constructed in 1837. It did not carry any passengers. Instead, it was a private road built for the expressed purpose of hauling coal from the bluffs of a coal mining community called Pittsburg(h) (near Belleville), and traveled a mere six miles to the Wiggins Ferry site on the Mississippi River at Illinoistown, which later became East St. Louis. The trains ran on strap iron rails nailed on wooden boards and spiked to ties laid directly on the ground without rock ballast. At first they were pulled by mules and horses, and later wood-burning steam engines were brought in. The owners overestimated the demand for coal in St. Louis, and the early years were not prosperous ones. But by 1860, as railroads switched from wood to coal as a fuel, it became the richest dollar-per-mile railroad in the country.

THE ILLINOIS CENTRAL, chartered in 1851, set out to build a main line between Cairo and Galena, aided by the first federal land grant to a railroad. This was during the administration of President Millard Fillmore. The U.S. lacked the capacity to make rails, so they were ordered from England. They arrived in U-shape form so they could be placed in the hold of a ship. They were re-heated and straightened out on arrival. The first IC passenger train reached Cairo on August 7, 1855.

A branch line running diagonally to Chicago began at Centralia. An independent company built a connecting line between Belleville and East St. Louis that opened in the mid-1850s. The line was extended to DuQuoin in 1873 and became an IC property in 1895. The IC Railroad Bridge from Cairo to Kentucky was finished in 1889. At that time it was the **longest metallic structure across a river anywhere in the world**.

Chicago and New Orleans were first linked to service by rail to Cairo and then by a steamboat line to New Orleans, owned by the I.C. To connect Chicago and New Orleans by rail, the IC began to buy rail lines between Cairo and New Orleans. IC purchased or established traffic agreements with the New Orleans, Jackson and Great Northern and the Mississippi Central. The Ohio River was crossed between Cairo and Columbia, Kentucky, with a car ferry. The Ohio River Bridge was not completed until 1889. Lines south of Cairo were converted to standard gauge (4 ft. 8 & 1/2 inches) from the South's 5 ft. "broad gauge" in July of 1881.

Illinois Central Railroad

The IC purchased the East St. Louis Peabody Short Line in 1960 and merged it with the IC a year later.

In 1972 the IC merged with the Gulf, Mobile & Ohio, creating the Illinois Central Gulf. Last year the IC was purchased by the Canadian National Railroad.

A luxury train of the old IC was the *Panama Limited* on the eighteen-hour trip from Chicago to New Orleans. Between Chicago and St. Louis, the chief passenger trains were the *Green Diamond* and the *City of Miami*.

THE RAILROADS OF ALTON: Long an important river port, Alton was backed by the Illinois Legislature as the western terminus for any railroad crossing the southern portion of the state. **In a plot to diminish St. Louis' role as a rail center**, the state had directed railroads in Illinois not to terminate on the east bank of the Mississippi River opposite St. Louis. This, of course, hurt the growth of East St. Louis, known back then as Illinoistown.

229

Alton's first railroad was the Alton & Sangamon, with construction beginning in 1850. It was planned by Captain Benjamin Godfrey to link Alton with **Springfield**, and it would be the first railroad in Madison County. The line was extended to **Normal** in 1853 and **Joliet** in 1854. The railroad was reorganized and then renamed the Chicago & Mississippi. This line merged with the Chicago, Alton & St. Louis in 1856, later taking the name Chicago & Alton. The line was acquired by the B&O in 1930. In 1947 it became part of the extensive GM&O.

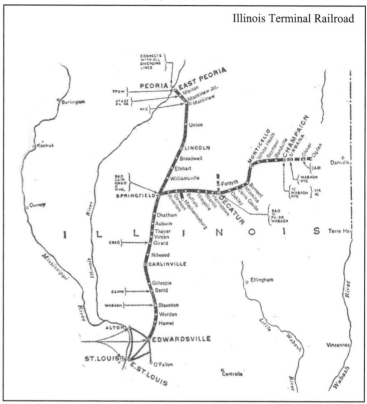

Illinois Terminal Railroad

With the building of the Eads Bridge in 1874 at East St. Louis, the die was cast, and Alton never achieved the prominent rail status envisioned. Nevertheless, the number of railroads in Alton continued to grow.

The Alton & Terre Haute (predecessor of the Big Four) incorporated in 1851, chose Alton as its western terminus. Local trackage was constructed in 1853 and Terre Haute was reached in 1856. It became part of the CCC & St. Louis/Big 4 in 1899.

The Rockford, Rock Island & St. Louis was chartered in 1870, and construction was completed in 1870. In 1875 the company was reorganized as the St. Louis, Rock Island & Chicago and became part of the Burlington in 1876.

In 1881-82 the St. Louis, Jerseyville & Springfield built a line between **Springfield** and **Grafton** on the Illinois River. The river was reached by a grade down the bluffs at **Elsah**. The original plan was to ease the grade by using a tunnel. However, the contractor struck water and was never able to get the flooding under control. This required the building of a steeper grade than what had been desired. Work on the tunnel closed, never to be taken up again.

The Wabash Company had its eye on the St.LJ&S and offered to lease with the option to purchase the line. Both lines went into receivership, and the merger never took place.

Instead, the St.LJ&S was purchased in late December of 1887 by the St. Louis, Alton & Springfield. Work began on a new route to the river to avoid the steep grade at Elsah. That new grade reached the Mississippi at **Loch Haven**, and the push was on to reach Alton to the south. By December 1888, **Hop Hollow** (on the edge of Alton) was reached and after the Chicago & Alton attempts to block entry to the city were removed, rails finally reached Alton in January of 1889. That same year, 4.3 miles of rail were laid providing a direct link between Loch Haven and Elsah.

In 1892, the line was purchased at foreclosure sale by the St. Louis, Chicago & St. Paul Railroad. It was under the ownership of the St.LC&St.Paul that work was begun to reach **Granite City**. Wood River was reached by spring of 1893 before reentering receivership. Work to reach Granite City did not begin again until the following spring, with operations to Granite City starting in July 1894. The St.LC&St.Paul again entered receivership and found itself part of the Chicago, Peoria & St. Louis in 1900, but a change in ownership and name did nothing to clear away the red ink.

Having no longer a need for the route, the CP&STL sold off its Litchfield branch to the Litchfield & Madison in 1905.

Sale of the Litchfield branch helped the CP&STL to finance its extension to the East St. Louis river port. Started in 1903 but delayed by costly repairs following the massive flooding that same year, once completed in 1906, the CP&STL had access to all St. Louis area railroads either by direct connection or via the Terminal Railroad of St. Louis.

Profitable for a while, inflation deferred maintenance during World War I and a down turn in the economy pushed the line toward receivership again. In late 1924 the line was parceled out and sold off. The northern portion of the line went to the Chicago & Illinois Railroad while the southern part went to the Chicago, Springfield and St. Louis (Springfield to Loch Haven).

In 1924 James Duncan, president of the Litchfield & Madison (a CP&St.L cast off) purchased the Grafton to East St. Louis portion but did not merge the two lines. This recently rescued Alton & Eastern took a turn for the worse when Duncan died the following year. Service began to deteriorate as the Duncan family showed no interest in the railroad.

Desperate customers on line approached the Illinois Terminal RR to help. The IT leased the line in 1931, and later purchased it.

THE ORIGINAL ILLINOIS TERMINAL: The Illinois Terminal started as a steamrail connection built by Illinois Glass Co. on **Alton's** east side to Henry Street to allow rail connections to their plant. The IT was incorporated July 8, 1895. One third of a mile of rail was laid in 1886 allowing access to the Chicago & St. Louis, the CB&Q, the NYC, the M&IB&B and the MKT. In 1889 work began to extend the line to **Hartford**. Access from Hartford to **Edwardsville** was gained by leasing a Wabash branch line already in place. For a short time there existed a paper railroad called the Illinois and Mississippi Valley, created by the IT in order to be able to satisfy a legal requirement for the IT to operate this far from Alton. The line was soon to disappear when merged with the IT in 1899.

Operations began on November 5th. Regular freight operations began Nov. 14th followed by the first regular passenger train on Nov. 26th with connections being made with the CP& St. Louis and NKP in Edwardsville in Jan. 1900.

The Wabash branch proved to be an operational headache being too steep and having tight curves. Work was done to correct these problems through realignment of the right of way in the fall of 1904. That same year work began on Federal yard located just outside Alton's eastern city limits for tax purposes. The new yard had a capacity of 50 cars and featured a roundhouse and car shop. In 1907 it was separated from Illinois Glass, and its headquarters were moved from Illinois Glass property to Second and Alby Streets in Alton.

THE ST. LOUIS, TROY & EASTERN: Donk Brothers Coal began construction on a railroad from East St. Louis to Donkville, and its coal mines were reached in December of that year. Work had begun in October on the Collinsville & Troy Railroad. The 7-mile line was completed in February 1900 and operated independently from the T&E until sold in Oct. 1902.

On October 5th 1905 the St. Louis & Illinois Belt Ry was incorporated for the purpose of linking the Edwardsville area railroad with the St Louis, Troy & Eastern. The 5-mile gap between **LeClaire** (in Edwardsville) and Troy Junction on the T&E was bridged in Aug. 1909. By late 1909 this line was extended south to reach the Pennsy at Formosa Junction. Operationally, these all became the same line when the T&E became the St.L&IB.

These lines became part of the Illinois Traction System (streetcars) by lease in 1928 and were purchased in 1930.

THE LITCHFIELD & MADISON: "The St. Louis Gateway" – The Chicago, Peoria & St. Louis had originally leased the St. Louis & Chicago Ry line between Springfield and Litchfield and then built its own line between Litchfield and East St. Louis in 1889-1890. When the CP&St.L lost its lease of the StL&C Ry, it went shopping for another route between St. Louis and the Illinois State Capital, and the line to Litchfield became a branch line.

In 1900 the CP&StL purchased the St. Louis, Chicago & St. Paul and the former St. Louis, Jerseyville & Springfield line through **Alton** to again have access to **Springfield**. The CP&StL no longer had a use for the Litchfield branch and leased it to the newly formed Litchfield & Madison in 1900. The new L&M purchased the line in 1904.

The former branch line became more of a terminal line, servicing a few on line customers, however the principal commodity carried was coal. In 1912 the L&M carried nearly one million tons of freight, 90% being coal. South bound trains from coal mines in the **DeCamp**, **Staunton**, **Worden** and Edwardsville and Litchfield areas, a few on-line grain elevators and customers in **Edwardsville** terminated in the **Madison** yard where cars were handed off to the Alton & Southern, the CP&StL, the clover Leaf, the TRRA of St. Louis and the Wiggins Ferry Company.

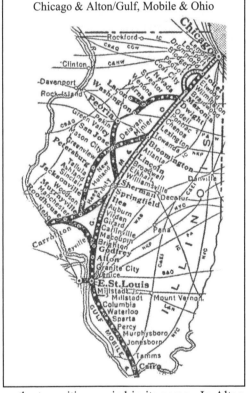

Chicago & Alton/Gulf, Mobile & Ohio

Interchange was made with the CB&Q in 1922 when the L&M began to use ½ miles of Q track to reach the Q's yard in Litchfield. In 1925 interchange was made with the Chicago & North Western by using 8 miles of C&NW track to run from DeCamp to **Benld** and giving C&NW access to the St. Louis market.

Litchfield & Madison headquarters, general offices and car shops were located in **Edwardsville** where the L&M interchanged with the Illinois Traction System, the Wabash, the St. Louis, Troy & Eastern and the Clover Leaf (Nickelplate). The Illinois Central had trackage rights on the L&M from **Glen Carbon** to Madison and L&M rails saw 6 passenger and 10 IC freight trains a day.

From the 1950s, the C&NW connection handed off two time freights a day. Iron ore of the C&NW generated an average of 5,900 car loads annually, destined for the steel mills of Granite City. By 1957, C&NW owned 95 % of L&M stock and merged with the L&M in 1958.

CHICAGO & ALTON/GM&O: Alton's own Alton & Sangamon was chartered in 1847 and reached **Springfield** in 1851. **Bloomington** was reached in 1854 and Joliet in 1855 under the name Chicago & Mississippi, and was renamed the St. Louis, Alton & Chicago.

Reorganized in 1861 as the Chicago & Alton, it first entered Chicago using Rock Island track and now was able to provide freight and passenger service between the two cities carried in its name. In Alton, steamboat connections were made to reach St. Louis. This railroad was sometimes known as the "Carry All."

Between 1861 and 1864, the C&A used trackage rights on NYC predecessor TH&A to reach St. Louis. In 1864 the C&A gained entrance to Chicago by leasing the Joliet & Chicago. By 1871 only the lake steamers hauled more coal into Chicago.

In 1870 the C&A leased the Louisiana & Missouri River (Louisiana to Mexico, Missouri) and in 1878 leased the Kansas City St. Louis & Chicago (Mexico to Kansas City) creating a K.C/Chicago route.

In Alton, the main line left the riverfront and ran up the middle of Piasa Street. A stone passenger depot, built by the Alton & Sangamon in 1850, was located at 5th and Piasa Streets. In 1886 the C&A and the Big 4 (NYC) built Alton Union Depot on the riverfront at Market and Front Streets, and the original depot became a C&A freight house. Built of brick and stone, the Union depot featured a hotel and restaurant and was built to resemble a steam locomotive.

The original Alton & Sangamon ran up Piasa Street to reach **Godfrey**. The hill was an operational headache due to numerous grade crossings and the steep climb away from the riverfront. Helper engines were often required to assist northbound trains. In 1894, an easier route was built by passing downtown, the cut off started at Wann Tower in **Wood River** and rejoined the original main at Godfrey. The original line was kept primarily to have access to the freight house and local industries but all main line freight and passenger trains used this cut off, and only local passenger trains stopped at the down town depot.

In the 1920s, the C&A had planned to abandon the Union depot and move passenger operations to Godfrey. Alton citizens and the mayor opposed the move. The College Avenue depot site on the cut off was previously only a platform for mail service. After the College Avenue depot was built in 1928, most passenger operations shifted from Godfrey and the riverfront to the new depot. In 1904 the C&A was briefly under the control of the Union Pacific/Rock Island and in 1907 the Clover Leaf. By 1912 the C&A was in financial trouble in part to loss of coal business and in part to loss of traffic on the KC/Chicago line. The Baltimore & Ohio purchased the C&A in 1929 creating the Alton Railroad. When the Alton entered receivership in 1942, the B&O desired to cast off the Alton line. In 1945 the Gulf, Mobile & Ohio purchased the Alton for $1.2 million. Merger occurred in 1947.

In 1924 the Alton Limited passenger train made the trip from St. Louis to Chicago in 6 and ½ hours. After the GM&O merger, the "Alton Limited," the "Abe Lincoln" and the "Ann Rutledge" made the same trip in 5 hours and 10 minutes.

Stops along the route included: **Bloomington, Braceville, Braidwood, Carlinville, Chenoa, Chicago, Dwight, Gardner, Granite City, Jacksonville, Joliet, Lemont, Lincoln, Lockport, Mason City, Normal, Odell, Pontiac, Springfield, Washburn, Washington, and Wilmington.**

CHICAGO BURLINGTON & QUINCY/M&IB&B: The idea of a bridge over the Mississippi River at Alton was first put forth in 1839. South of Alton the Eads Bridge spanned the river at East St. Louis in 1874, drawing away rail traffic from Alton. By 1885 the idea of a bridge at Alton was renewed when the Central Missouri announced plans for an Alton Bridge. Financial trouble brought the project to a halt. Work began again in 1889 with some grading being done before the contractor also stopped.

The Chicago Burlington & Quincy had two lines that passed near Alton. Originally an independent line, the Rockford, Rock Island & St. Louis was completed in 1867 and ran from Rock Island (**made famous in a 1950s song by Lonnie Donnigan**) through east Alton to East St. Louis. It was acquired by the Q in 1877. In the 1870s the St. Louis, Keokuk & North Western approached St. Louis from the Missouri side of the river. In the 1880s, the Q had used the Wabash route into St. Louis via the Wabash bridge at St. Charles, but owners were not happy with the cost imposed by the Wabash and planned to span the Missouri River with their own bridge and maybe a bridge at Alton to link up with their Illinois line.

Chicago, Milwaukee & St. Paul

The Q Missouri River bridge and route to St. Louis was completed in 1874, spanning the Missouri at Bellefontaine. While the Q and the Big Four considered an Alton bridge in 1891, it fell to the St. Clair, Madison & St. Louis Belt to build the Alton bridge. Construction began in 1892 and was completed in 1894.

Built too late to get a large share of rail revenue, the Alton bridge never attained the success of the Eads Bridge. Most main lines had already been built to East St. Louis while a majority of rail lines reaching Alton were branch lines or secondary lines. While the bridge proved successful, the financial backing to build it proved weak. Without the expected revenue to service the debt, the bridge company entered receivership in 1897 and was seized by the Madison County sheriff for back taxes.

In July 1904 the Missouri & Illinois Bridge and Belt was created and gained control of the bridge and neighboring track in Feb. 1905. The M&IB&B was owned by most of the same partners that owned the Terminal Railroad in East St. Louis.

The Q, which had previously complained of the cost of using the Wabash bridge in St. Charles now complained of excessive costs of the Alton bridge. Having run 9 passenger trains a day over the bridge in 1895, the Q began routing trains via East St. Louis in 1902. The M&IB&B took over the passenger operation between Alton and West Alton (in Missouri).

The Q again began talking of building a new bridge of its own somewhere between Alton and East St. Louis. That bridge never saw the light of day and by 1920 the Q was the largest user of the Alton bridge. By 1947 most stock was held by the Q except for that held by Mopac.

The Corps of Engineers decision to replace the aging Alton Lock and Dam #26 spelled the end of the Alton bridge. The last train crossed over in 1990, and the bridge was razed in 1991.

NEW YORK CENTRAL: Fanning out from Indianapolis, 4 New York Central lines entered Illinois. A secondary main to **Cairo** has been covered in *Southern Illinois: An Illustrated History*. A subsidiary company line to Peoria will be covered later in this chapter while the NYC line to Chicago will be covered by a later book in this series.

The Alton & Terre Haute was incorporated in 1851. It chose **Alton** as its western terminus reaching **Wood River** in 1853 and Terre Haute via **East Alton** in 1856. The A&TH used shared trackage with the Chicago & Alton to reach East St. Louis, and merged with the Belleville & Illinoistown in 1855. The A&TH was renamed the Terre Haute, Alton & St. Louis. In 1861 it was renamed the St. Louis, Alton & Terre Haute.

In Indiana, the Indianapolis & St. Louis built a line between Indianapolis and Terre Haute. The I&StL was chartered in 1867 and opened in 1870. The St. Louis, Alton & Terre Haute entered receivership in 1868 and was leased by the I&StL creating a line from

Indianapolis thru **Pana, Mattoon, Litchfield** and Alton. The Cleveland, Columbus, Cincinnati & Indianapolis acquired the I&StL in 1882, known as the 'B Line" because their operations were centered around Bellefontaine, Ohio. In 1889 the Cleveland, Cincinnati, Chicago & St. Louis was formed with the merger of the B Line and the Cincinnati, Indianapolis, St. Louis & Chicago. Known as the "Big 4," the New York Central gained control of their stock in 1930 and leased the Big 4.

The original line entered the St. Louis metro east via **Litchfield, Bethalto** and East Alton. With St. Louis gaining prominence over Alton, there was a shift in the main line. In 1904, starting at **Hillsboro**, the new main headed for St. Louis via **Mitchell** and the East Alton/Alton track became secondary. The Bethalto-Litchfield branch was abandoned in the late 1960's.

The New York Central was itself first incorporated in 1853 and was known as the "Water Level Route" due to its preferences for the comparatively flat routes created by river valleys. Their New York to St. Louis passenger train was the "Southwest Limited."

In 1968 the NYC merged with the Pennsylvania Railroad to create the Penn Central which, in turn, became Conrail in 1976.

THE ALTON, JACKSONVILLE & PEORIA:

One of the most successful interurbans in the Metro East was the Illinois Terminal's St. Louis and Alton commuter line and its predecessor, the Alton, Granite & St. Louis.

Sharing a station stop on Alton's riverfront was one of the less successful, the short-lived Alton, Jacksonville & Peoria. The name reflects the unleashed enthusiasm common in many interurban companies during the Golden Age of the interurban era. As the name implies, the founders had great ambitions, planning to reach distant Peoria, 65 miles to the north.

Starting at the foot of Piasa Street at the CP&StL depot near Alton's city hall, the AJ&P used Alton city street car trackage running up Piasa paralleling the C&A to 3rd Street and turning off 3rd street onto its own trackage on Bell and headed north.

The Alton to Godfrey line (5 ½ miles) was built in 1907. Profitable for only a short time, the AJ&P entered receivership in 1911 and only with great difficulty was able to muster the resources to reach Jerseyville in 1912. In 1914 it was reorganized as the Alton & Jacksonville.

The Interstate Commerce Commission ruled that the AJ&P should probably have never been built. It served a sparsely populated area, already served by the CB&Q. Alton and Peoria were already linked by steam railroads and one more was unnecessary. The line closed in 1918.

The AJ&P owned 6 passenger cars and 14 freight cars. It had ordered 3 cars from St. Louis Car Co., but they never took delivery. These were sold to the **Waterloo** Line.

THE NICKEL PLATE ROAD AND THE NARROW GAUGE:

To tell the story of the Nickel Plate RR in Illinois, we must first tell the story of the Toledo, Cincinnati & St. Louis and the narrow gauge trunk.

In 1877 the Toledo, Delphos & Indianapolis had laid narrow 3-foot gauge

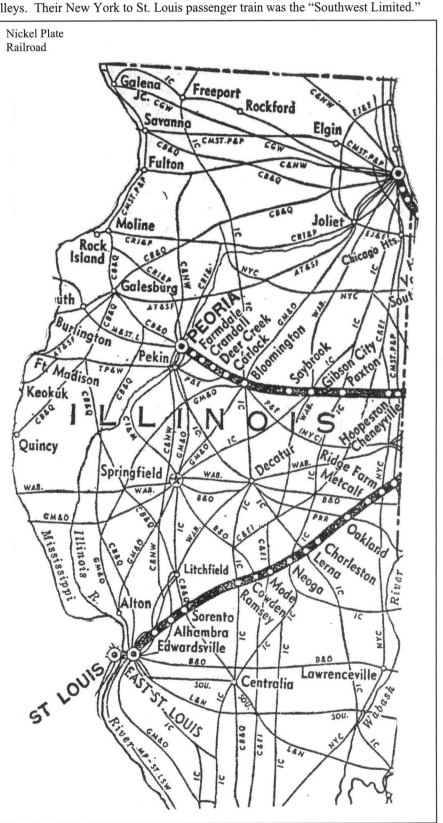

Nickel Plate Railroad

233

track just north of Delphos. Within two years the TD&I had become part of the Toledo Delphos and Burlington, whose goal was to link northern Ohio to Burlington, Iowa.

The line had been extended to Kokomo, Indiana, by 1880 but a Burlington terminus never became a reality. Instead, the company set its sights on Mexico City as the TD&B became the northern portion of the Grand Narrow Gauge Trunk, a network of regional lines intended to link the Midwest and Mexico. The 780-mile Toledo, Cincinnati & St. Louis reached East St. Louis in 1882.

Mexico City was as illusive as Burlington, Iowa, as the southern members of the Grand Narrow Gauge trunk built no farther south than Houston, and the middle segment between East St. Louis and Cairo showed little interest in the interchange of freight cars. The grand dream began to collapse, and Ohio trackage was sold off and converted to standard gauge.

The Toledo to E. St. Louis line would have died if not for the discovery of oil and gas along the tracks. The Frankfort, Indiana, to East St. Louis segment was converted to standard gauge in 1889 after a name change.

The reorganized Toledo, St. Louis & Kansas City adopted the trefoil as its symbol. The clover leaf as it was known for a time went bankrupt in 1893 and was sold to the bond holders who renamed it the Toledo, St. Louis & Western. In 1907 the Clover Leaf purchased controlling stock in the Alton. The financial burden pushed it into receivership again in 1914.

THE LAKE ERIE & WESTERN: This railroad was a consolidation of several small roads that stretched from Fremont, Ohio, to **Bloomington**, Illinois. New York banker George Seney began assembling these lines in 1879 and in 1881 turned east to reach Cleveland when he became dissatisfied with the way the NYC routed his freight, creating the New York, Chicago & St. Louis. Described by an Ohio paper as a "nickel plated railroad," the name stuck. By 1887 the LE&W extended to Peoria.

Rail tycoon Jay Gould expressed an interest in the NKP so to keep it out of his reach, NYC's Vanderbilt bought it. However, anti-trust legislation required he sell it. Rather than have it end up as a Gould property, Vanderbilt opted to sell it to the Von Sweringen brothers who were instrumental in upgrading the line after suffering from benign neglect as a NYC property.

In 1923 the NKP, LW&W and Clover Leaf were consolidated as the New York, Chicago & St. Louis. In 1933 the NKP came under the control for a time of the C&O which rehabilitated the line from Peoria and East St. Louis to Alton for the use of heavier freight engines. By 1942 the NKP was back in the control of the of the bond holders and merged with the N&W in 1964.

The NKP passenger train to St. Louis was the "Westerner."

Norfolk Southern, which inherited the NKP from N&W, abandoned most of the Clover Leaf division around 1989, keeping a section between **Madison** and **Coffeen** for power plant access. That was abandoned a few years ago, and now the only part in operation is between **Metcalf** and **Neoga**, operated by the Eastern Illinois Railroad.

To follow the line even today, the narrow gauge characteristics are still very much in evidence, as the right-of-way follows the profile of the land, with steep grade and sharp curves.

THE CHICAGO & ILLINOIS MIDLAND AND THE CP&St.L – Before we can tell the story of the Chicago & Illinois Midland, we must first visit the history of an earlier regional carrier and its even earlier component, the Peoria, Pekin & Jacksonville, the Jacksonville Southwestern, and the Springfield & Northwestern.

The Peoria, Pekin & Jacksonville had been envisioned to link the **Havana/Pekin** area to the then new Rock Island Railroad near **LaSalle**. Chartered in the name Illinois River Railroad, the chief engineer who laid out the original line was fired when it was discovered he was buying land along the proposed right of way. With his departure, the line was re-oriented by a mile, bypassing town sites he had envisioned.

Construction began in Havana in Sept. 1857. The first rails were spiked down in Pekin on July 4, 1859. Work was impeded by flood and fire at the Pekin engine house and by financial trouble.

Operations began in the summer of 1860, but until rails were extended to **Peoria** and **Jacksonville**, the first and last part of any journey each way was via boat and stagecoach. It was said that the PP&J was nicknamed the "Push, Pull and Jerk."

In July 1859, the PP&J contracted with the Peoria & Hannibal to build from Peoria to the south and build a bridge over the Illinois River, but work was stopped by the onset of the Civil War. By the fall of 1863 due to debt the PP&J was sold, and the new company leased the P&H.

The Illinois River was finally crossed at Pekin in 1864. The CB&Q tried to prevent the PP&J from entering Peoria. The roadblock was removed after the PP&J went to court, but this did not prevent a couple of knock down/drag out fights between crews of the CB&Q and the PP&J.

Passenger service on the new section began Nov. 1864. The P&H was purchased in 1868 with the first train to Jacksonville July 4, 1869.

Profitable for a while, the PP&J entered receivership in 1878 and was sold. In 1881 ten miles of track from Peoria to Pekin were sold to the Peoria & Pekin Union. In 1882 the PPU closed the Illinois River Bridge. In 1881 the line was leased to the Wabash, St. Louis & Pacific.

Chicago Burlington & Quincy Depot and Riverside water tower

THE SPRINGFIELD & NORTHWESTERN: Work began on the Havana to Springfield line in 1879. The **Havana/Petersburg** section was opened in 1872 with Springfield being reached Nov. 1874. Soon after the line went into receivership since there was little business generated by the line.

The Wabash leased the S&N to link it with the PP&J with the intent to purchase both, but by 1884 the over extended Wabash went into receivership, and the courts ordered that they release both.

The Wabash wanted these lines back and created a company to purchase both and then went looking for some one to lease them until they could be merged with the Wabash.

The Hook family already managed the Jacksonville Southeastern that ran from **Jacksonville** to **Centralia** via **Litchfield** and a line from Litchfield to **Columbriana** on the Illinois River. They then created the Chicago, Peoria & St. Louis to lease the PP&J and the SNE as well as the JSE (to get around stock holders objections to the JSE leasing these other lines).

Desiring a direct route between Springfield and St. Louis, they built the Peoria, Springfield & St. Louis between Litchfield and Springfield. Northbound traffic out of St. Louis could then reach Springfield via Litchfield on the leased North & South Railroad between Litchfield and Springfield or a round about route via Litchfield, **Jacksonville**, **Peoria**, and back to Springfield on the CP&StL route crossed at Litchfield. In 1890 the CP&StL used TRRA to gain access to East St. Louis and St. Louis.

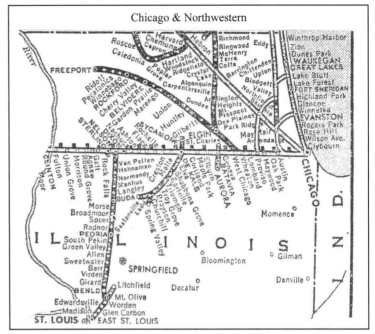
Chicago & Northwestern

In 1890 the CP&StL reached Chicago via **Peoria** to **Eureka** on the Toledo, Peoria & Western and then the Santa Fe to Chicago. Called the "Red Express," the Pullman passenger service did not last as the JSE got caught in a rate war and lost the use of the ATSF to Chicago. CP&StL passenger trains terminated in Peoria after 1893. In a possible attempt to regain access to Chicago, work began on a connection with the Rock Island but this was never completed.

The Hook family and the CP&StL stockholders had long been in conflict over how to spend profits from the line. When the CP&StL entered receivership in 1893, the system was divided between factions and began to be sold off. Parts of the line to **Columbriana** went to the Alton Railroad in 1903. The **Walnut Hill** to Centralia line went to the Southern Railroad in 1898. The Jacksonville to Centralia line went to the CB&Q.

A further blow to the CP&StL came when the North and South Railroad that formed part of the Springfield to St. Louis route received a better offer and cancelled the CP&StL line in 1895. For a time the CP&StL used trackage rights on the Bluff Line between **Springfield** and **Waverly** and former J&SE (now the Jacksonville, Louisville & St. Louis) to reach CP&StL rails at Litchfield, then discontinued the Bluff Line track in favor of the J&SE rails again.

However, the Bluff Line closing the CP&StL/Springfield/ Peoria traffic for itself and by July 1897 had control of the CP&StL and under the trackage use of the J&SE rails. By fall of 1897 the CP&StL used the Bluff Line between Springfield and St. Louis providing through service using CP&StL (Peoria to Springfield) and Bluff Line (Springfield to St. Louis).

And what became of the North and South? It entered receivership and became part of the Illinois Central between Chicago and St. Louis.

With CP&StL traffic diverted to the Bluff Line and the loss of the North and South line, the **Litchfield** trackage (no longer accessed Springfield) was downgraded to a branch line of the CP&StL and was sold to the Litchfield & Madison.

The CP&StL entered receivership in 1909. Received under the director William Charles Hurst, the CP&StL entered receivership in 1914. Hurst returned in 1917, as did profitability. World War I freight traffic boosted income, but the burden of war related loadings and deferred maintenance while under the administration of the Federal Government the CP&StL defaulted as debt rose again. Hurst was brought back and profits returned in 1920.

However, by 1922 the CP&StL had filed to abandon or sell off the line to service the debt. In 1923 the receivers put it on the auction block, but there were no takers. With no buyer for the whole lot, the line was sold off in pieces starting in 1924. James Duncan, President of another CP&StL cast off the L&M bought the **Grafton** to East St. Louis section that became known as the Alton & Eastern. In 1925 the **Springfield** to **Pekin** section was being considered by the Chicago & Illinois Midland. The Jacksonville & Havana RR bought the line between those two towns.

Broken pieces of the CP&StL were attempting to reassemble elsewhere. The Chicago, Springfield & St. Louis had purchased the **Springfield** to **Lock Haven** (on the Mississippi near Alton now served by the Alton & Eastern).

Desiring to reconnect two isolated portions of the J&H and the CS&StL a trackage rights agreement was negotiated with the CB&Q between **Jacksonville** and **Waverly** and between the two companies purchased three Brill Co. motor cars for passenger service (one went to the J&H and two to the CS&StL.

235

The grand plan called for building a connection between Jacksonville and Waverly and to connect with the Minneapolis & St. Louis in Peoria creating a St. Paul to St. Louis system. However both entered receivership in 1930 without ever putting the trackage rights agreement into effect. The J&H was abandoned in 1937. The CB&Q bought the Jacksonville trackage. The Chicago, Springfield & St. Louis carried on alone until abandoned in 1941.

Four miles of track in the **Jerseyville** area became the Jerseyville & Eastern to serve 11 local businesses. This line survived from 1940 to 1965. In our state capital, the Springfield Southwestern bought 8 miles of track, Springfield to **Currai**, for access. This track was abandoned in 1949 with the closing of Citizens Coal Mines A&B.

The CP&StL had several lightly populated areas with a sometime meandering route through an area already served by other railroads with more direct routes. Much of the line has faded back into the landscape but one part survives even today.

THE CHICAGO & ILLINOIS MIDLAND: The Chicago & Illinois Midland had its humble beginnings as the Paunee Railroad in 1888. Owned by local farmers to have an outlet for their produce, four miles of track were laid from Paunee west to the P&J. In 1892 five more miles were added to **Auburn** to connect with the Chicago and **Alton**.

In 1905 the Illinois Midland Coal Company was created by partnership of Commonwealth Edison of Chicago and the Peabody Coal Company to develop coal deposits south of Springfield for Chicago area power plants, and were able to gain control of the Pau--nee.

In 1905 the Paunee was extended east to tap newer coal deposits at **Sicily** and **Tovey**. The next year the name was changed to Chicago & Illinois Midland. In 1907 the new C&IM reached **Taylorville** where it connected with the Baltimore & Ohio and the Wabash. Finally in 1917 a con-nection was made at **Compro** with the Chicago & Northwestern.

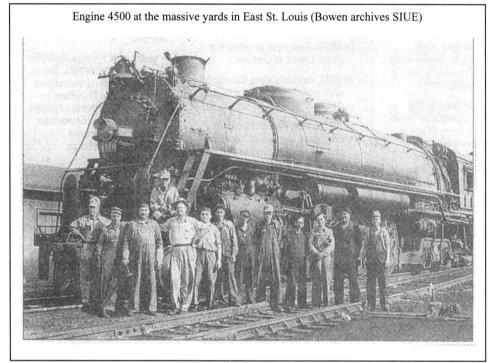
Engine 4500 at the massive yards in East St. Louis (Bowen archives SIUE)

Most of these rail connections were for the purpose of shipping coal north to Con Ed power plants in Chicago. Always looking for a way to reduce transportation costs, the Con Ed considered the idea of shipping coal north via barges on the Illinois River. This was desirable as all Con Ed plants were located on the river for a source of cooling water. The original plan was to extend the C&IM west to the Illinois River but as an alternative, in 1926 they bought the CP&StL line between Peoria, Havana and Springfield. To reach the coal deposits south of Springfield, the C&IM gained trackage rights on the Illinois Central between Springfield and the C&IM at a junction called CIMIC (C&IM and IC).

The upper portion of the Illinois River had not yet been developed to allow barge traffic, and for a time most coal traffic on the C&IM went to the new Con Ed power house at **Powerton** on the Illinois River south of **Pekin**, which opened in 1928.

Coal traffic on the Illinois River began in 1933 when coal dock A was opened at Havana. An improved facility called Dock B was opened in 1937.

For a while, 6 million tons of coal was shipped out on the C&IM with ½ going to the Powerton plant and ½ to the Havana dock.

The C&IM considered electrifying the main line, a natural as their best customer either mined coal or generated electricity by burning that same coal. Plus parent company Con Ed was a property of Sam Insull the great Chicago area interurban tycoon. It seemed a natural choice, but in the end the closest the C&IM came to being an interurban was the purchase of a few light weight passenger coaches of the same design as one of the Insull interurbans, due to the fact the C&IM went shopping for passenger cars at the same time Insull had ordered cars. These "interurban" coaches were delivered without trolley mechanisms but were otherwise fully equipped. They were pulled by C&IM steam engines.

C&IM also considered acquiring the CP&StL spin off, the Chicago, Springfield & St. Louis that ran from Springfield to Lock Haven on the Mississippi near Alton to be able to carry general freight between St. Louis and **Peoria**. The C&IM in the end opted not to repeat the error of predecessor companies and passed on the idea of becoming a bridge route carrier.

Coal continued to be the principal commodity carried by the C&IM though they were always active in soliciting other on line traffic. In 1953 Peabody #10 mine opened east of **Paunee**. But the character of the C&IM and the coal traffic were in the process of change.

Long a holdout to dieselizing its locomotive fleet, the C&IM had become a Midwestern haven for steam long after other area carriers had converted to internal combustion. However, due to the age of their steam fleet and the difficulty in getting replacement parts, the C&IM began to dieselize in 1955.

236

In 1964 a mine mouth power plant was built at the Peabody #10 mine. In 1967 a mine month power plant was built at **Kincaid** and coal traffic dropped. With high sulfur Illinois coal on the EPA hit list and more strict clean air standards in effect, the C&IM saw a drastic shift again in coal traffic. Where once coal had been sent off line, now C&IM was receiving low sulfur western coal from Wyoming bound for Powerton as well as the coal dock at Havana, bound for Chicago via the Illinois River. Sam Insull had been opposed to purchasing the Peoria/Havana track, now it proved to be important in bringing in western coal traffic.

In 1966 the C&IM was sold to the Genesee & Wyoming, a Greenwich, Connecticut, based company which owns a number of short lines and renamed the C&IM, the Illinois Midland.

In 1999 the Havana coal dock was purchased by SCH after being closed for 4 years to again receive western coal.

NEW YORK CENTRAL/PEORIA & EASTERN – Fanning out from Indianapolis, 4 New York Central lines entered Illinois. A secondary main to Cairo has been covered in the first book, (Southern Illinois), also the secondary/subsidiary (the P&E) to Peoria will be covered in the next book in this series.

In the Midwest, the NYC main to St. Louis was a consolidated series of regional lines strung across Ohio, Indiana and Illinois.

Choosing **Alton** as its western terminus, the Alton & Terre Haute was incorporated in January 1851. It reached **Wood River** via **East Alton** in 1853 and Terre Haute, Indiana in 1856 using trackage shared with the Chicago & Alton. When it reached St. Louis/East St. Louis, the line was renamed the St. Louis, Alton & Terre Haute in 1861.

In Indiana, the Indianapolis & St. Louis built between Indianapolis and Terre Haute. The St.LA&TH entered receivership in 1868 and was leased by Indianapolis and St. Louis creating a line from Indianapolis through **Pana** and **Mattoon** to Litchfield to East Alton.

The line came under the control of the CCC&I in 1882 and became part of the Big 4 in 1899. The Big 4 became part of the NYC and was merged with the NYC in the 1930s.

The original line entered the metro east via Litchfield and East Alton. With St. Louis gaining prominence over Alton, there was a shift in the main, and the new St. Louis bound line started at **Hillsboro** heading to St. Louis via **Mitchell** in 1904.

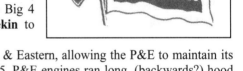

THE PEORIA AND EASTERN – The Peoria and Eastern was a consolidation of several railroads. An early component was the Mad River & Lake Erie built in 1835. The Indiana, Bloomington & Western (Pekin, Illinois, to Springfield, Ohio) purchased the Wood River & Lake Erie to gain a port on the Great Lakes.

Broken up during the panic of 1887, it was reorganized as the Ohio, Indiana & Western, becoming the Peoria & Eastern in 1890 prior to being merged with the Big 4. The Big 4 purchased the line between Indianapolis and Springfield, Ohio, and leased the **Pekin** to Indianapolis segment as a separate corporation.

In 1930 the Big 4 was leased by the New York Central which subleased the Peoria & Eastern, allowing the P&E to maintain its own identity within the NYC until the creation of Conrail in 1976. Dieselized in 1955, P&E engines ran long, (backwards?) hood first, just the same as NYC.

Entering Illinois at **Danville** on the east, it entered the **Peoria** area at **Pekin** and used Peoria & Pekin Union track to reach Peoria's Union Station. The P&E "Peoria" was the last passenger train to call at Peoria's Union Station and once that structure was closed in 1955, P&E passenger service was cut back to Pekin, necessitating a name change to the "Corn Belt Express." P&E train #11 departed Indianapolis at 7 a.m. and arrived in Pekin at 12:45 p.m.

P&E's counterpart train #12 departed Pekin at 2:35 p.m. and arrived in Indianapolis at 7:46 p.m.

When a bridge collapsed between **Bloomington** and **Pekin**, NYC successor Conrail decided not to rebuild and instead chose to use trackage rights on Norfolk Western (NKP) between Bloomington and Peoria and then use Peoria & Pekin's union rails to regain access to the P&E from the western end to serve in line customers. Later, P&PU took over their job until the line was abandoned.

Abandoned east of Danville, portions of the line between **Urbana** and Bloomington are still in service. Running out of **Decatur**, Norfolk Southern crews access the former P&E off the former Wabash line at **Mansfield** to service Anderson Grain at Reising (west of **Champaign**) and services two other customers in **Urbana**, the track east of Urbana was abandoned around 1996. In the Bloomington area, the P&E is used for car storage.

THE WABASH: The oldest component of the Wabash was the Northern Cross. The Northern Cross was completed in 1840, and it stretched from **Meredosia** to **Jacksonville**. Two years later it reached Springfield. The railroad's name comes from the fact that it was part of a vast internal improvements scheme by the state

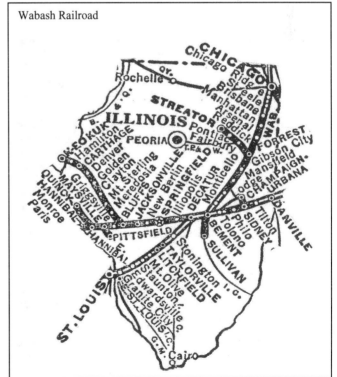

Wabash Railroad

legislature in the northern part of the state. There was also to be a Southern Cross in the lower part of the state but the railroad, canal, and plank road scheme, coupled with the Panic of 1837, bankrupted the state by 1841. The Northern Cross had strap iron rails that had a tendency to curl up and stab the cars – and sometimes the passengers. Called "iron horses" by the Indians, the railroads two engines (*Rogers* and *Illinois*) had to stop often for more wood and water. The two engines soon broke down for lack of spare parts. After that, what little traffic remained was pulled by mules. Chartered in 1837 to run from **Quincy** to the Indiana border, the Wabash line became the Great Western of Illinois.

Other parts of the future Wabash were built in Missouri to link St. Louis to Iowa and Kansas. Kansas City was reached in 1868 and Council Bluffs, Iowa (across the Missouri River from Omaha, Neb.) was reached in 1879. These lines were known at the St. Louis, Kansas City & Northern after 1872.

By 1858 the Great Western merged with the Toledo & Wabash which itself was the result of the 1856 merger of the Toledo & Illinois and the Lake Erie, Wabash & St. Louis, thus creating a system reaching from Toledo to **Quincy** and Keokuk.

In 1879 the Wabash merged with the St. Louis, Kansas City & Northern creating the Wabash, St. Louis & Pacific, the name reflected owner Jay Gould's vision to create the first transcontinental railroad out of his vast holdings. The Wabash being only one part.

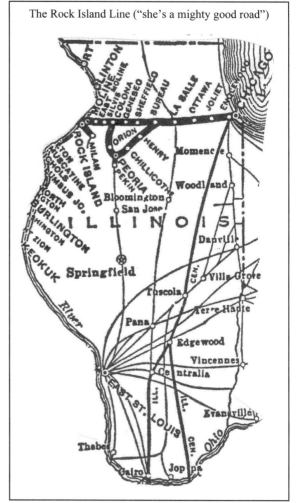

The Rock Island Line ("she's a mighty good road")

Ever expanding, the Wabash acquired the Chicago & Paducah, which ran from **Streator** to **Effingham**. Under Wabash control, the C&P was expanded to Chicago in 1880. Wabash also leased the Cairo & Vincennes at that time and leased the TP&U.

Around 1880 Wabash built a line to Detroit, and its Toledo trackage became a secondary line.

By 1884 the Wabash was over extended (at more than 3,000 miles) and could not finance the debt of expansion and lost much leased lines as the Cairo & Vincennes while the rest of the Wabash was divided up into several railroads.

By 1887 the new Wabash was back with an eye to expand farther east. In 1898 it accessed a route to New York and the east via Detroit and trackage rights on the Grand Trunk through Canada to Buffalo.

As America entered the motorcar age, the Wabash put its main line through the middle of Illinois to good use as it provided a direct route from the Motor City to Kansas City bypassing both Chicago and St. Louis. **Decatur** was the hub of the Wabash, and its main shops were there.

By 1963 the Pennsylvania RR had control of the majority of Wabash stock. However with the merger of the New York Central and the Pennsy, there was no place for the Wabash, and it went instead to the Norfolk Western in 1964. N&W merged with the Southern in 1982 to create the Norfolk Southern.

Well known passenger trains on the Wabash were the "Blue Bird" on the Chicago/St. Louis route in competition with the GM&O. Another train was the "Banner Blue Limited." There also was the "City of St. Louis" and the "City of Kansas City," the latter being a streamline train beginning in 1946 with through coaches and Pullman service to the West Coast on the Union Pacific.

Certainly the most famous Wabash passenger train was the "**Wabash Cannon Ball**" immortalized by a song of that name. Interestingly, the song predated the train by many years, and the lyrics refer to stations never served by the real Cannon Ball.

DANVILLE STREETCARS: Birthplace of William McKinley, Father of the Illinois Traction System, Danville's own streetcar system was envisioned as early as 1867. A proposed Danville Horse-pulled Railway was never built. However the Citizens' Street Ry did open in 1883. By 1887 the CS Ry was hauling rail workers on a branch to Danville Junction and had 5 miles of track, 8 cars and 41 mules.

In 1891 the Cannon brothers created the Danville Gas, Electric Light & Street Ry. By Aug. 1891 the railway was electrified and became the Danville Street Ry and Light Co.

In 1901 William B. McKinley (not to be confused with President McKinley) bought the line, and by 1904 it had 14 miles of rail and 28 cars. McKinley added 3 Illinois Traction subsidiaries, the Danville & Northern, Danville & Eastern (2&1/2 miles) and the Danville & Southeastern (3 miles).

The D&E served the Chicago & Eastern Illinois shops, but the envisioned goal of Terre Haute (high ground), Indiana, was never reached.

Around 1922 sixteen Birney one-tram cars were introduced to reduce operating costs. In 1926 Danville purchased its first buses.

By 1935 the Danville had 16 miles of streetcar track and operated 12 cars, but in 1936 the Danville City Lines had taken over with streetcar operations ending in 1936.

THE KEOKUK JUNCTION RAILWAY: The Keokuk Junction was incorporated in Sept. 1980 to use former Rock Island track in Keokuk, Iowa, and it acquired the former RI track in 1981. In Dec. 1986 the KJ purchased 28 miles of former Toledo, Peoria & Western from **LaHarpe** to Keokuk, giving the KJ interchange with the TP&W in La Harpe, Illinois.

The line was purchased by Pioneer Rail Corp. in March of 1996. A big customer in LaHarpe is the big Roquette American Grain elevator which also owns the former Huberger Corn processing plant. Until recently the KJ had two Philadelphia & Western electric cars for public excursions.

"Tip Up" – THE TOLEDO, PEORIA & WESTERN: Predecessor Peoria & **Oquawka** was chartered in 1852. Construction began in 1855 in East Peoria. The Illinois River was bridged in 1857 allowing access to Peoria and construction progressed west to **East Burlington**, Illinois.

Two years later the P&O went bankrupt and came under the control of the Chicago, Burlington & Quincy. The P&O Eastern Extension RR reached **Effner** on the Indiana border in 1860. The line was completed when it reached Logansport, Indiana, the same year. It was renamed the Logansport, Peoria & Burlington in 1861 and in 1864 was reorganized as the Toledo, Peoria & Warsaw.

The "Pioneer" - Chicago's first locomotive 1848

The Mississippi & Wabash was building east linking **Warsaw** and **Carthage** and became part of the TP&W at this time, to which along with other construction enabled it to reach the Mississippi in 1868 and cross the river to Keokuk in 1871. That same year a branch was built to **Lomax** to give the TP&W a connection with the CB&Q and by trackage rights on the Q from Lomax to Burlington, IA.

Due to financial troubles the road was reorganized and renamed the Toledo, Peoria & Western in 1880 and for a short time was leased by the Wabash. The 50-year lease in fact lasted only until 1884 when the TP&W took back the line. In 1893 the Pennsylvania and the Burlington took control of the TP&W by purchasing large blocks of stock.

In 1926 Greg McNear purchased the TP&W at foreclosure for $1.3 million and turned the TP&W into a bridge carrier between connections with the PRR on the east end and the Santa Fe in the west, bypassing Chicago and St. Louis congestion.

In 1941 McNear proposed radical new work rules he felt were needed to modernize operations. Union men were opposed to these changes and went on strike for higher wages instead of McNear's plan for hourly wages. Soon after work stoppage began two strikers were shot and killed at **Gridley**, Illinois, by railroad guards. McNear himself was killed when walking home from a baseball game. The murder was never solved.

Reorganized again in 1952, the ATSF bought the line in 1960 and sold half to the Pennsy.

Conrail, the merger of the NYC and PRR, was created in 1976. The traffic pattern created by the new company no longer required the PRR connection to the TP&W. To prevent losing its eastern connections, the TP&W bought the former Pennsy line between Effner and Logansport. The PRR sold its half interest to the TP&W to the ATSF in 1979, and the TP&W disappeared into the ATSF in 1983. Under the Santa Fe banner, the former TP&W saw a greater emphasis placed on containerized freight traffic. (standardized freight containers hauled on flat cars). Serving auto assembly plants in Lafayette, Indiana, and **Normal**, Illinois.

In February of 1989 the Santa Fe sold the line to a company headquartered in Cooperstown, NY. A reborn Toledo, Peoria & Western reappeared sporting a new look. Replacing solid red diesels of the old TP&W and the blue and yellow of the Santa Fe, the new TP&W engines carried a sharp gray and white "Lightning Stripe" paint scheme reminiscent of the New York Central.

THE "PEE POOH" - PEORIA & PEKIN UNION: Today's P&PU forms an upside down U on both sides of the Illinois River, linking Pekin, East Peoria, Peoria and **Bartonville**. Incorporated in Sept. 1880 to own and operate the Peoria area rails of the 4 founding railroads after conflict between the 12 rail companies entering the Peoria Gateway resulted in violence and sabotage over rights of way and access to area customers.

The original founding members were a Wabash subsidiary (later spun off as the TP&U), Indiana, Bloomington & Western (later the Peoria & Eastern) the Peoria, Decatur & Evansville (Illinois Central and the Peoria, Pekin & Jacksonville (Chicago & Illinois Midland). By World War I membership expanded with the addition of the Lake Erie & Western (later the Nickel Plate/Norfolk Western), the Iowa Central (later the Minneapolis & St. Louis/Chicago & North Western) the Chicago & Alton (later GM&O/IC), the Vandalia (Pennsylvania), the Chicago, Burlington & Quincy (Burlington Northern), and the Illinois Terminal. Members Rock Island and the Rock Island & Peoria were later consolidated under the RI banner.

Crossing the Illinois River on its own bridge, the P&PU linked all these railroads together, providing switching services and engine servicing. Most railroads had their own yards and used the P&PU to transfer cars between one railroad and another. Those without yards used the P&PU main yard.

All railroads used the P&PU Union Station except the IT and the RI, which had their own depots. Union Station, built in 1883, saw 28 passenger trains daily from the owner roads as well as P&PU's, own commuter runs. In 1898, Union Depot saw 90 passenger trains a day, and 102 trains were scheduled for Peoria by 1900.

With the downturn in passenger business after World War II, Peoria's Union Station was closed in 1955 and torn down a few years later. The Rock Island depot survives as a restaurant on the Peoria Riverfront while the IT depot for a time after the end of electric passenger service to Peoria in 1950, It was used as the Peoria Police Department and now houses the Peoria Electric Department.

When the IT arrived in Peoria in 1907, the P&PU originally refused to interchange freight with electric interurbans, claiming they did not have to because the IT

Chicago & Eastern Depot and War Memorial at West Frankfort

did not use their steam engine service facilities. Legal action was required before the P&PU opened a connection to IT rail.

While the traction did have their own depot in Peoria, on one occasion IT passenger cars traveled on P&PU rails. Around 1954 a barge struck the IT bridge, isolating several passenger cars in Peoria. As the bridge would be out of service for some time and the cars were needed elsewhere on the system, a plan was devised to move the cars. The Illinois Terminal interchanged with the P&PU cars on the river in East Peoria but had no rail connection in Peoria where these cars were stranded.

However, Peoria streetcar tracks passed very close to P&PU Union Depot. The station was to remove a portion of the passenger platform at the depot and build a temporary extension from the end of the Peoria street car track to reach P&PU rails in front of the depot. IT cars then ran down to the end of the city street car tracks, lowered their poles and were pushed on to the steam road track. Once all cars were on P&PU tracks, a steam engine pulled the train across the river and delivered them to the IT interchange in E. Peoria.

The Peoria & Pekin Union's original bridge was built in 1872. The current bridge was installed in 1910 and was rebuilt in 1984. With the closing of the PP&U bridge after being struck by a barge, the P&PU bridge played an even more vital role in Peoria area rail transit.

A competing terminal railroad was created by the Rock Island. Called the Peoria Terminal, it even had its own bridge over the Illinois River until the 1970s. With the end of the Rock Island, some trackage was operated by the P&PU. Today part of the Rock Island/Lower Rock Island and Peoria trackage is owned by the city of Peoria and north side Suburban Peoria Heights. Called the "Peoria & Peoria Heights," the P&PU was contracted to operate the line to access on line customers.

At this writing, the P&PU no longer operates the P&PH,

Illinois Central Station at Champaign

but rather the contract has gone to Pioneer Rail Corp. However, the city of Peoria has announced plans to convert the southern portion of the P&PU to a bike trail that would cut off several industries still on the line. The plan is to extend the Union Pacific spur serving the Pioneer Industrial Park to reach their trackage.

Following the mega mergers of the late 20th Century, the P&PU still serves the Illinois Central, Norfolk Southern, Union Pacific, Burlington Northern/Santa Fe, the Chicago & Illinois Midland, the New Toledo, Peoria & Western, and the Iowa Interstate which uses former RI line from **Bureau**.

MATTOON CITY RAILROAD AND THE CENTRAL ILLINOIS TRACTION: Incorporated in 1902, over the next two years the Mattoon City Ry built local street railways in Mattoon and **Charleston**. Starting with 2 cars and 1 and ¼ miles of track, by 1904 the 10 mile gap had been filled between the two communities.

A disastrous wreck in 1907 with multiple fatalities (including the dispatcher who committed suicide) pushed the line into receivership. In 1910 the Central Illinois Public Service took over and renamed the line the Central Illinois traction.

In 1912 CIPS purchased the **Paris Street Ry** with the idea to link Mattoon with the Indiana, Terre Haute & Western Railway, but the gap was never closed.

Charleston operations ended in 1925. Mattoon and interurban operations lasted until 1927 when the company switched to buses.

THE LINCOLN STREET RAILWAY: As early as 1867 there were plans for a horse-drawn railway for the city of Lincoln which never materialized. However, Lincoln received a gift too large to put under their tree when on Christmas Day, 1871, Lincoln received its own trolley line. It operated 4 or 5 cars on a 4 and ½ mile stretch of track. Cars ran on ½ hour headways, 15 minutes on the Illinois Central depot line.

240

In 1907 an extension was made to the Chautauqua grounds. During the Chautauqua discussion session extra cars were leased from Springfield. The Lincoln Street car line had no physical connection to any other railroad so Springfield cars were brought in on the Illinois Traction and transferred to Lincoln rails where the street car line crossed the ITS at the Broadway Street crossing. Cars were manhandled 90 degrees from the ITS to Lincoln rails. The process was repeated when the cars were sent home.

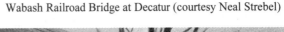

Wabash Railroad Bridge at Decatur (courtesy Neal Strebel)

The city was probably too small to justify a streetcar line, and earnings were always low. Going through a series of defaults and receiverships and name changes before being purchased by the city, it was leased to Central Illinois Car & Electric for a dollar a year. In doing so, it became only the second streetcar company in Illinois owned by a city.

Operated by two different utility companies in 1925, the line could not compete with the autos or paved roads and ended service around 1929, to be replaced by a city run bus company.

THE SPRINGFIELD, CLEAR LAKE & ROCHESTER RAILWAY: Organized in 1906, by June of 1909 the 15 mile line was completed with 11 miles linking Springfield to **Rochester** with a branch to **Clear Lake**. The line had some affiliation with early Illinois Traction System companies and was later allied with the Sangamon Valley Ry and the Hillsboro Street Ry.

In 1910 it was called the Springfield Suburban, and after 1910 it was known as the Mississippi Valley Interurban Railway. Operating 4 cars, the line was primarily intended for resort traffic, which proved too seasonal in nature to be a year-round success. Built "on the cheap" and receiving little maintenance, the Illinois Railroad Commission in 1912 ordered services halted until it was made safe. No money was available and services were ended.

THE KANKAKEE & URBANA TRACTION – "THE UNIVERSITY ROUTE;" Work began on the Kankakee and Urbana Traction in 1912. Rantoul was reached in 1913 but it took until 1916 to reach Paxton. The 25-mile line had another 25 miles to reach the Chicago area via Kankakee, but the gap was never closed.

Passenger service consisted of 8 round trips daily including Chanute Field and served two on line grain elevators. Freight was interchanged with the Illinois Central at **Rantoul** and the Wabash and Illinois Traction in **Urbana**.

Feeling the pressure of competition with the paved road and automobiles, two light weight one man cars were purchased (earlier cars had come from the Alton, Jacksonville & Peoria), and in 1924 passenger service was cut to 3 trips to **Paxton** with express runs only to Rantoul.

This line entered receivership in 1926 and ended services in March of the same year.

THE SPRINGFIELD: The state's capital, Springfield Consolidated Railway was created in 1893 as a merger of several street railways, the earliest dating from the horse-drawn Springfield City Railway of 1866. Competition and violent confrontation between the various horse-drawn and steam "dummy" lines prompted the call for a merger.

Electrification began around 1893, and expansion of the new company was completed by 1900. However the violence continued during the labor unrest and strike in 1917 prompting the city to call out troops to restore order.

Illinois Central train at Springfield's Union Station (Neal Strebel)

In 1922 Illinois Power Company took over the Street Railway and power company, by which time the system had 41 miles of track and 35 cars. (17 Birney cars had arrived in 1920.) The first 9 buses arrived in 1924.

After the Depression, the Springfield Transportation Company was created in 1933 to take over the streetcar and bus service while Central Illinois Light took over the power company. The last streetcar ran Dec. 21, 1937 and the track was removed by 1939.

THE RAILROADS OF SOUTHERN ILL. BY MARK GODWIN

The great state of Illinois is second only to Texas in total rail miles. Most railroads that operate in the state either have main lines that pass through the southern portion of the state on their way to major markets (Chicago, St. Louis), or have branch lines that reach into this region. There are more railroad bridges above East St. Louis than below that point because both the Mississippi River and floodplain are narrower in the north.

Our survey will cover the steam railroads as well as their interurban and streetcar brethren. Rail companies will be referred to by the names they carried for most of their corporate existence before the era of mega-mergers that saw so many lines meld into new titles or cease to exist all together.

The **BALTIMORE & OHIO**, which crosses the top portion of southern Illinois, is the oldest common carrier in America. To some historians, the B&O marks the northern limits of Egypt, the nickname for Southern Illinois. In 1828 the B&O's first stone was laid by Charles Carroll, the last surviving signer of the Declaration of Independence.

The first rail link between East St. Louis and the east coast, via Cincinnati, was the Ohio & Mississippi. Chartered in 1848 in Indiana, the Illinois legislature opposed building the line unless it terminated at Alton as a means to divert traffic there at the expense of St. Louis. The Illinois charter was granted in 1851 after great pressure was put on the legislators. Work began in 1852 and was completed in 1857 with the western terminus at East St. Louis rather than Alton. Thus began the rise to prominence of that great city.

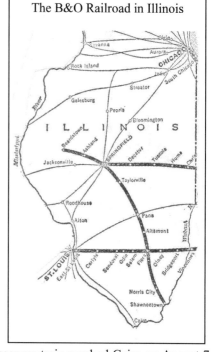

The B&O Railroad in Illinois

In November of 1893 it was consolidated with the B&O as the B&O Southwestern. In addition to its main line through southern Illinois, the B&O had a branch line that originated in **Springfield** and ran south through Flora where it crossed the B&O main line and terminated on the north shore of the Ohio River at Shawneetown. The branch line was originally a two-part disconnected line called the Springfield & Illinois Southeastern, which dates from 1870. The O&M purchased the line in 1875, and these isolated segments were later connected to form a 222-mile line from Shawneetown to Beardstown.

In 1977 the former Illinois & Southeastern was purchased by Trans Action Lines Limited and named the Prairie Trunk Railway, with the last five miles into Shawneetown shared with the Seaboard (L&N). The PTRY had in 1983 four locomotives and twenty-nine cars, but it is no longer operating. Operations were suspended in 1984, and the line was abandoned in 1985.

In 1973 the B&O, the Chesapeake & Ohio and the Western Maryland were merged to become the Chessie System, named for the C&O mascot, Chessie the cat. In 1979 the Chessie System was combined with the Family Lines (a merger of L&N and Seaboard). Speculation about the name of the new railroad was that it would be called the Family Cat. However, the new company took the name Chessie Seaboard or CSX.

The B&O's most famous passenger trains were the *Pullman Car Capital Limited* and the *National Limited*.

The **ILLINOIS CENTRAL**, chartered in 1851, set out to build a main line between Cairo and Galena, aided by the first federal land grant to a railroad. This was during the administration of President Millard Fillmore. The U.S. lacked the capacity to make rails, so they were ordered from England. They arrived in U-shape form so they could be placed in the hold of a ship. They were reheated and straightened out on arrival. The first IC passenger train reached Cairo on August 7, 1855.

A branch line running diagonally to Chicago began at **Centralia**. An independent company built a connecting line between Belleville and East St. Louis that opened in the mid-1850s. The line was extended to **DuQuoin** in 1873 and became an IC property in 1895. The IC Railroad Bridge from **Cairo** to Kentucky was finished in 1889. At that time it was the **longest metallic structure across a river anywhere in the world**.

Chicago and New Orleans were first linked to service by rail to Cairo and then by a steamboat line to New Orleans, owned by the I.C. To connect Chicago and New Orleans by rail, the IC began to buy rail lines between Cairo and New Orleans. IC purchased or established traffic agreements with the New Orleans, Jackson and Great Northern and the Mississippi Central. The Ohio River was crossed between **Cairo** and Columbia, Kentucky, with a car ferry. The Ohio River bridge was not completed until 1889. Lines south of Cairo were converted to standard gauge (4 ft. 8 & 1/2 inches) from the South's 5 ft. "broad gauge" in July of 1881.

The IC purchased the **East St. Louis** Peabody Short Line in 1960 and merged it with the IC a year later.

In 1972 the IC merged with the Gulf, Mobile & Ohio, creating the Illinois Central Gulf. A few years ago the IC was purchased by the Canadian National Railroad.

A luxury train of the old IC was the *Panama Limited* on the eighteen-hour trip from Chicago to New Orleans. Between Chicago and St. Louis, the chief passenger trains were the *Green Diamond* and the *City of Miami*.

The **MOBILE & OHIO** was organized in 1848, and it reached the Ohio River in 1883. The southern Illinois segment between St. Louis and Cairo started out as a narrow gauge (3 ft.) railroad. Construction of the Cairo and St. Louis began in 1871 with Cairo being reached in 1875. Known as the Cairo Short Line, the C&St.L was renamed the St. Louis & Cairo in 1882. In 1886 the Mobile

& Ohio leased the Cairo Short Line and began to convert it to standard gauge.

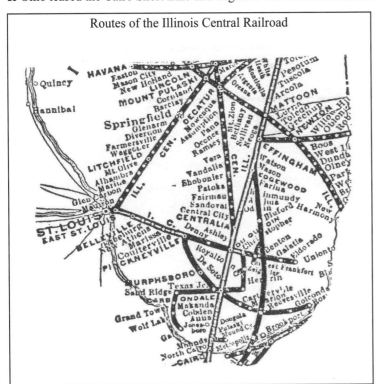

Routes of the Illinois Central Railroad

By 1920 the M&O was operating six passenger trains into St. Louis. In 1940 the M&O was merged with the Gulf, Mobile & Northern, creating the Gulf, Mobile & Ohio. The GM&O acquired the Chicago and Alton in 1947.

The first streamlined passenger trains to run in the South were the GM&O Rebel trains. The train to St. Louis was the *Gulf Coast Rebel*. North of St. Louis to Chicago was the *Abe Lincoln*.

In 1972 the GM&0 merged with the Illinois Central to create the Illinois Central Gulf. The new railroad had redundant lines both north and south of St. Louis. The IC line between St. Louis and Springfield was abandoned in favor of the GM&O route. South of St. Louis the GM&O route is now largely abandoned with rail still in use around the Sparta area for power plant access at Baldwin, and the extreme south end now used by the Cairo Terminal.

The **LOUISVILLE & NASHVILLE**, known as the Dixie Route, started out as the St. Louis & Southeastern, chartered in Illinois in 1869. Once consolidated with two other lines, including the Evansville, Henderson & Nashville, purchased in 1872, a line was created from St. Louis to Evansville, Indiana, across southern Illinois. The L&N (chartered in 1850) purchased the EH & St. Louis from the St.L & Southeastern in 1879. L&N's competitor, the Nashville, Chattanooga & St. Louis (chartered in 1851),

purchased the St. Louis & SE around the same time the NC&St.L had announced plans to build a bridge over the Ohio at Evansville. This prompted the L&N to begin purchasing stock in that road. Once the L&N had controlling interest in the NC&St.L, it took control of the **East St. Louis** to Evansville route for itself.

In 1882 the L&N established a trackage agreement with the Louisville, Evansville & St. Louis, known as the Louisville Air Line for its smooth straight rail between Mt. Vernon and Louisville.

Formal merger between the L&N and the NC&St.L took place in 1957. In 1971 the L&N absorbed the Monon and the Memphis branch of the Chicago and Eastern Illinois. The L&N merged with the Seaboard in 1975, creating the Family Line, which merged with the Chessie system in '79, creating the CSX. Most of the line between **Nashville**, Ill., and East St. Louis is abandoned, as is the branch from McLeansboro to **Shawneetown**. The abandoned line between East St. Louis and Belleville (along Routes 50) and 161), is now the St. Clair County extension of the MetroLink electric rapid transit system that goes from the airport in St. Louis to Southwestern Illinois College at Belleville.

The **SOUTHERN RAILROAD** was built by the Louisville, Evansville & St. Louis

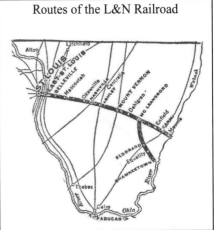

Routes of the L&N Railroad

Consolidation Railroad in the early 1880s. It was known as the Louisville Air Line because of its straight route. The Southern Railroad was chartered in the state of Virginia in 1894 and is a consolidation of twenty smaller railroads throughout the South. The Air Line was purchased by Southern in 1898.

In **Belleville** the yard and depot complex were built by the Air Line north of "A" Street and west of 2nd Street. The depot was built in 1884 near the ten-stall roundhouse and turntable. A freight house was located in the yard. The spur line connected with Southern's main line at North 20th Street.

Having to back trains in or out of the depot was an operational headache, so the depot was moved to North Illinois Street in 1911. The wood trestle over Richland Creek was kept to access the freight house and was not removed until 1970. A portion of the freight dock and freight house survive now on old Southern Railroad tracks behind

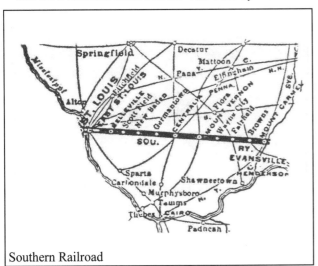

Southern Railroad

the Belleville car dealership property of Oliver C. Joseph, complete with a dining car painted for O.C.'s favorite railway, the Great Northern.

The engine service facilities in East St. Louis were at **Fireworks Station** (site of a fireworks factory that later blew up). Nearby was the freight yard. The large Copeman Yard, south of **Alta Sita**, was easily reached by the Terminal Railroad's belt line, the Alton & Southern and Southern's Venice & Carondelet belt line.

Southern merged with Norfolk Western in 1982 creating the Norfolk Southern.

MISSOURI PACIFIC and the **MISSOURI & ILLINOIS**: As the name implies, the Missouri Pacific was envisioned as a St. Louis link to the West Coast. The line from St. Louis was chartered in 1849, and work began the next year. Kansas City was reached in 1865 after the Civil War.

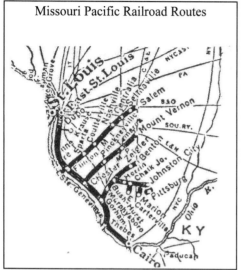

Missouri Pacific Railroad Routes

In 1852 the state of Missouri granted a charter for the Pacific Railroad to build a branch out of St. Louis to reach southeastern Missouri. This became the St. Louis Iron Mountain & Southern which merged with the MP in 1917.

In Illinois, the Illinois Southern was created in 1900 as successor to the Centralia & Chester with the grand plan to cross the Mississippi and bypass St. Louis on the way to Kansas City. Bismarck, Missouri, and connection with the Iron Mountain was made in 1903. The Mississippi River was crossed via rail car ferry between Kellogg, Illinois, and St. Genevieve, Missouri. The Illinois Southern was reorganized in 1911 and placed in receivership in 1915.

Owned by a number of lead companies, the Missouri & Illinois was created in 1921 to acquire the Illinois Southern. In 1929 MoPac gained control by purchasing controlling interest. At that point the M&I leased the Mississippi River & Bonne Terre Railway (chartered in 1890). After reorganization in 1933, and emerging from bankruptcy in 1944, the M&I and the MR&BT were merged in 1945.

Car ferry operations at Kellogg ended in 1961. In 1964 MoPac acquired the rest of M&I stock and merged the Mo & Illinois with the parent company in 1978.

Traces of the car ferry operations are still visible on both sides of the Mississippi. On the Illinois side, the car ferry dock is now part of a coal/barge loading facility.

The **CHICAGO & EASTERN ILLINOIS** had its beginnings as the Evansville & Illinois in 1849. Known as the Chicago, Danville & Vincennes in the 1870s, it went through a name change again in the 1880s. In 1890 the line had branches to Evansville and via **Shelbyville** through **Salem** to **Joppa** on the Ohio River and Thebes on the Mississippi by 1900.

In 1902 the C&EI fell under control of the St. Louis & San Francisco. To link these two together, the C&EI used trackage rights of the N. Y. Central Big 4 route from Pana to St. Louis via Hillsboro by 1904.

Around 1911 the C&EI purchased coal properties in southern Illinois. In a 1920 reorganization, the coal properties were sold off along with several branches. A coal strike in 1922 cut deeply into coal traffic.

In 1930 the C&EI offered passenger trains with air conditioning. Its Chicago/St. Louis trains were the *City of Progress* and the *Spirit of Progress*, but

Chicago & Eastern Illinois Routes

passenger business lost out to the competition - the IC, the Wabash and GM&O after World War II.

Southern Illinois passenger service in the 1930s was provided by American Car & Foundry self-powered "doodle bug" passenger cars and in the 1950s by Bud Company Rail diesel cars.

In 1952 the CE&I bought the twelve-mile **Mount Vernon** area short line, the Jefferson Southwestern. In 1954 it bought the abandoned St. Louis & O'Fallon in order to gain access to East St. Louis. In 1969 the Evansville, Indiana, branch was sold to the L&N and the CE&I was merged with MoPac in 1976.

The **NEW YORK CENTRAL** is one of the nation's oldest railroads, having its origins in 1831 as the Mohawk and Hudson. Its southern terminus in Illinois was at **Cairo**.

In 1852 the Terre Haute & Alton was created as competition to the city of St. Louis. In 1882 it came under the control of the Cleveland, Columbus, Cincinnati & Indianapolis (known as the Big 4).

In the 1880s the Big 4 consolidated a number of smaller companies to link **Danville** and Cairo. The Danville to Cairo line was merged first with the St. Louis, Alton & Terre Haute and later with the Big 4, a NYC subsidiary.

New York Central Routes

The NYC merged with the Pennsylvania in 1968 to form Penn Central which went bankrupt in 1973. Congress created from its ruins the Conrail Company which actually showed a profit and was sold to CSX and Norfolk Southern.

The **PENNSYLVANIA RAILROAD**: In 1847 the Mississippi & Illinois was created to build from East St. Louis to Terre Haute via Vandalia. In 1865 the St. Louis, Vandalia & Terre Haute was chartered. From East St. Louis, Highland was reached in 1868, Effingham in 1869 and Indianapolis in 1870. In 1880 the Vandalia Road became part of the Pennsylvania. The Pennsy, known as the Standard Railroad of the World, was incorporated in 1846.

A financially troubled PRR was merged with the NYC to create an equally troubled Penn Central in 1968, and it became profitable as the Conrail component. There were no branch lines in southern Illinois.

The **CRAB ORCHARD & EGYPTIAN**: Known as the "Pig Hauler," the CO&E is a railroad fantasy come true, that of being able to run one's own railroad.

Passenger operation began in 1973 on a leased Illinois Central branch line between Marion and the ICG main at Carbondale. Using the IC depot in Marion, the "weekends only" passenger excursions ran from downtown Marion to a "Y" track a few miles west of town where the train was turned and run back to Marion. Using former IC electric trailer coaches, the first trains were pulled by a former CIPS 2-4-2 Saddle Tank steam engine. The water tank that had sat astride the boiler was removed, and a larger capacity, more traditional looking tender converted from a former steam engine canteen car was attached behind.

The excursion group purchased the line in 1977 and took over what little freight business remained on the line. Passenger operations ceased after the loss of the depot in a fire in 1978. Freight traffic increased and the CO&P went shopping for a larger engine to handle the extra tonnage.

A 2-8-0 steam engine arrived in 1979 to shuffle freight cars between Marion industries and the former Missouri Pacific (now Union Pacific) interchange, the only rail connection to the outside world as the rest of the tracks to Carbondale had been pulled up.

The freight business, which includes serving off-line customers who truck their products to Marion to be loaded on flat cars for shipment, increased to the point where the steam engine has been retired and replaced by four diesel electric locomotives.

The CO&E now also serves local industries in nearby Herrin on another abandoned IC branch line. The **Herrin** branch has no direct connection to **Marion** and instead interchanges with the Burlington Northern/Santa Fe.

The engines carry the company logo of a white pyramid under the cab window but are painted in the local school colors for Marion and Herrin, depending on which community they are operating in.

Logos on the side of company highway trailers for loading on flat cars to be shipped across the country carry a pig wearing an engineer's cap setting atop the cab of a steam engine, symbolic of the "piggy back" trailer on flat car service offered by the CO&E.

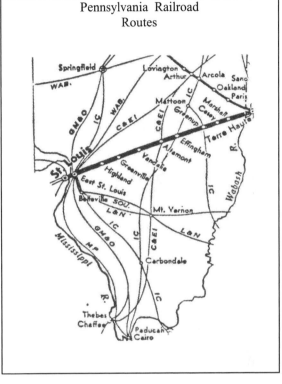

Pennsylvania Railroad Routes

From a modest beginning in 1977 when the CO&E carried only four cars per month, it improved in 1994 to 166 cars per month. The small steam engine went to a tourist attraction in Jackson, Missouri, and the bigger engine went to a tourist line in Boone, Iowa.

The Chicago, Burlington & Quincy trackage in southern Illinois was part of a 413-mile system designed to link Springfield and St. Louis, originally called the Chicago, Peoria & St. Louis.

The Jacksonville North Western and South Western Railroad had purchased the Illinois Farmers Railroad in 1872. The Jacksonville Southeastern had purchased the JNW & NE at foreclosure and pressed on with an extension to **Centralia** in 1883. In 1886 the Louisville & St. Louis Railroad (created by the JSE) built a line from Centralia to Denver and had a connecting line with the L&N. This was completed in 1887. A short section between Walnut Hill and Centralia became part of the Southern line to St. Louis.

In 1889 the JSE created the Peoria, Springfield & St. Louis and built a line between the JSE main in **Litchfield** to St. Louis that was reached in 1890.

That same year a long simmering conflict between the stock holders and the Hook family that managed the company erupted. The various components of the line went into receivership, and the system began to be divided up and sold off. The Chicago, Peoria & St. Louis was severed from the JSE. The **Jacksonville** to Centralia line was purchased by the CB&Q in 1905. Between 1914 and 1916 the CB&Q extended the line from Centralia into

Missouri and Illinois Railroad Routes

Southern Illinois to reach the coal fields and gain access to Paducah, Kentucky.

The Q merged with the Great Northern, the Spokane, Portland and Seattle and the Northern Pacific to become the Burlington Northern in 1970. The Burlington recently merged with the Santa Fe to create the Burlington Northern/Santa Fe.

EAST ST. LOUIS JUNCTION: An enduring image of American western movies is the cattle drive. After the end of the Civil War, the vast herds of cattle raised on the plains of the American West began their journey to the hungry markets back East by being driven to railroads to be loaded on cattle cars destined for major rail cities, such as St. Louis. From there, dressed beef completed the journey in refrigerated cars cooled by ice.

The East St. Louis Junction Railroad, which was organized in 1873, was located in National City, adjacent to the northwest part of **East St. Louis**. The Junction was owned by the St. Louis National Stock Yards Company.

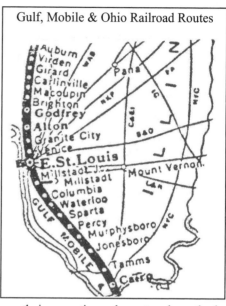

Gulf, Mobile & Ohio Railroad Routes

The railroad's biggest customer was the National City Stockyards itself, but it also served the meat packing houses of Morris, Armour, Hunter and Swift, along with feed suppliers, cold storage warehouses and a few light industries. The East St. Louis Junction connected with every railroad in the East St. Louis area either by direct connection or by interchange with the Terminal Railroad Association of St. Louis. Loaded stock cars would be delivered to the Junction where a fleet of steam locomotives would distribute them to the various sidings in National City. The TRRA would also deliver iced refrigerator cars for the Junction Railroad, which when loaded with dressed beef, would be delivered to the connecting railroads. In October of 1920, the Junction handled 14,000 loaded cars.

Empty stock cars would be blasted clean by high-pressure hoses before being returned to their original railroad.

After World War II, the line began to dieselize its locomotive fleet, and the last of the steam engines were retired. And about this time the fleet of ice reefers were replaced by diesel-powered mechanized refrigerator cars, making the neighboring TRR's ice loading facilities obsolete.

In the 1950s more beef was being shipped by trucks as meat packers began to move their operations closer to where the herds were being raised, reducing the need for stock trains. Thus began the decline of stock related traffic and the Junction Railroad.

The Junction's last major customer, Hunter Packing, closed its National City operations in 1982. Portions of the line were leased by the Chicago & North Western for switching purposes in 1975. In 1986 a devastating fire destroyed the stock yards office building with the loss of all company records and history.

ALTON & SOUTHERN constructed a twenty-one mile belt line around the St. Louis metro east area. It had its origins when the parent Aluminum Ore Company of East St. Louis became dissatisfied with its rail services from the Southern Railroad. In 1910 the Denverside Connecting Railroad (named for an East St. Louis neighborhood) had been chartered to construct a connection with the East St. Louis and Suburban's freight line, the St. Louis & Belleville Electric. Successor, Alton & Southern Railway, constructed a rail line from the aluminum plant at 3300 Missouri Ave. south in a connection with the Illinois Central Railroad at Valley Junction and on south through Monsanto/Sauget to the Fox loading terminal on the east bank of the Mississippi.

In 1913, a renamed Alton & Southern Railroad built north to connect with every railroad that ran east and west through the metro-east, including the St. Louis & O'Fallon, the L&N, B&O, and the Pennsy. Once reaching the Madison/Granite City area after World War I, it crossed the Illinois Terminal's steam railroad (the St. Louis, Troy & Eastern) and the Chicago & Northwestern (Litchfield & Madison).

The original "Rogers" engine, built in 1838, purchased by Northern Cross Railroad

The Alton & Southern never reached Alton but instead terminated its line at Lenox Tower just north of **Granite City** in 1925 where it connected with the Wabash, the CE&I, the Big 4 (NYC) and the Chicago & Alton. The A&S leased the St. Louis & Ohio River facilities and in doing so was able to use the St. Louis & OR engine facilities. This also gave the A&S access to the Belleville area. Illinois Central, which served the same area, was concerned about the competition in **Belleville** and secured an agreement from the A&S that they would not compete with the IC for coal traffic. Traffic from Belleville was light, and that line has been abandoned for some time. The old St. Louis & Ohio River railroad property was retained in the East St. Louis area, and in the early 1960s a modern double hump yard was constructed. Hump yards are the most efficient way to sort and handle large numbers of cars. Cars are pushed up an incline or hump and at the top are released and roll by their own weight down the other side through a series of complicated switches to a pre-selected destination track.

Due to the limited space available, the A&S's inclines approaching the dual humps are on a curve. Switch engines must push freight cars around a curve as they climb for the summit. The yard is busy enough that often two strings of cars are running up the humps simultaneously.

In 1968 the Alcoa Company sold the Alton & Southern 50/50 to MoPac and C&NW. In 1972 the C&NW sold its half to the St. Louis & Southwestern (Cotton Belt). In 1982 the MoPac was merged with the Union Pacific and in 1996 UP gained control of the Cotton Belt when it bought the parent company, Southern Pacific.

The A&S continues to operate one of the major terminals and switching rail lines in the metro east.

The **TERMINAL RAILROAD ASSOCIATION**: The building of the Eads Bridge in 1874 across the Mississippi at St. Louis made it possible for trains from Illinois to gain quick access to St. Louis. Before that, cars had to be taken across by the Wiggins Ferry Company (of East St. Louis) on special boats. However, once opened, there was no legal provision for trains to cross, as railroads chartered in Illinois had no such charter in Missouri and vice versa. Nor could the bridge or tunnel company run trains. It took another year to sort out the problem. The solution was the creation of auxiliary railroad carriers created in both states to haul freight across the river.

Railroads in St. Louis became concerned in 1881 when Jay Gould acquired the tunnel under downtown St. Louis, the bridge and switching railroads serving the bridge. They feared this would lead to just one railroad controlling the only bridge across the river.

In 1889 the Terminal Railroad Association of St. Louis was created. Original members were the Ohio & Mississippi (B&O), the Big 4 (NYC), L&N, MoPac, Iron Mountain, and the Wabash. Soon after the turn of the century most other St. Louis area railroads had joined. The TRRA leased the Eads and the Merchants Railroad Bridge (near **Madison**) and operated over 100 miles of rail on each side of the river.

The TRRA switches and classifies cars for the landlord railroads, transfer blocks of cars between the numerous rail connections several local industries, and also allows landlord roads trackage rights to run their own trains across TRRA rails.

The TRRA forms one of three belt lines on the metro east side. On the north end the TRRA has industrial trackage in the Granite City Area. Heading south, the line passes through Madison where the TRRA's large hump yard is located, crosses the PRR and B&O tracks in north East St. Louis where it then turns south and runs parallel to Southern's belt line (the Venice & Carondelet) and

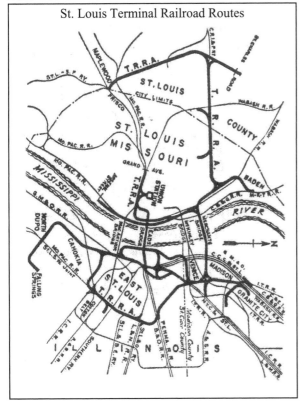

St. Louis Terminal Railroad Routes

then heads southwest to **Dupo** where it interchanges with MoPac. Between these two points, the TRRA crossed and connected with all railroads in the metro east.

There are also tracks serving the riverfront and the eastern approaches to the MacArthur, Eads and Merchants Bridges. The **East St. Louis** Relay Depot was in the tangle of rails near the approach to the Eads Bridge. The depot is now gone and the line to Dupo unused.

TRRA's main engine servicing facility on the east side was in **Brooklyn**. It is now closed.

In its heyday, East St. Louis, with an area of twelve square miles, had 27 rail lines with 550 miles of track.

PRAIRIE CENTRAL RAILWAY: The Wabash Valley had been created in 1978 to run on former Pennsy tracks, linking Decatur and Paris. Its line later passed into the hands of Trans Action Lines. In 1982 Trans Action leased the Penn Central (old NYC) line between **Paris** and **Lawrenceville** and purchased the Lawrenceville to **Mt. Carmel** line and was renamed Prairie Central. This line is now abandoned after operations were suspended in 1984.

CAIRO TERMINAL: The 20 mile switching line began in Jan. 1983, using 2 and 1/2 miles of abandoned Conrail track in Cairo. By mid 1983, 17 and 1/2 miles of former IC track between **Cairo** and **Elco** were acquired. In 1986 the line had 2 locos and 112 freight cars. However, the Cairo Terminal subsidiary Jackson & Southern R.R. engine #103 has been seen on the property. (The J&S is a former MP branch between Delta and Jackson MO, operated by CT.)

PEABODY COAL: Of all the coal operations in southern Illinois, Peabody Coal stands out due to their unusual paint scheme applied to buildings and operating equipment. For a business associated with the dirt and grime of mining and hauling coal, Peabody has chosen an unexpected combination of colors - yellow and green, often with a red border. Rolling stock frequently would feature a large lump of coal with a red flame.

Of all Peabody Coal operations in southern Illinois, perhaps the most interesting was the mine/rail operations around Lenzburg, **Marissa** and Baldwin.

Built originally to ship out coal from the Baldwin #1 underground mine and the River King #6 strip mine near Marissa, the traffic pattern has shifted a couple of times. While once all loads of coal were outbound on the IC via their connection at **Lenzberg**, in the 1970s coal from these two sources were either going to Illinois Power's Baldwin power plant or to the Kaskaskia River Port Dock #1 for loading on barges.

With the construction of Peabody's Randolph coal preparation plant, at least 50% of the output went to the IP plant in Baldwin with the balance going to the river dock.

The Randolph preparation plant, whose most prominent structure was a pair of tall concrete silos and their conveyors, cleaned and sized the coal from the mines and stored it in the silos until time to ship it out.

When the mines and the coal dock were active, two different types of coal trains could be seen. Peabody Coal diesels would haul twelve car trains the five miles to the power plant, dump their load and then push those same cars back to the coal prep plant for reloading. During the back-up move, the brakeman would ride in a special cab in the end of the last car to sound the horn and ensure the way was clear. Generally, two trains were operated in this fashion with one out bound from the coal loader while the empty train was returning for a refill. This would go on all day.

In addition, there was the Kaskaskia River Port Dock, opened around 1977. The red KRPD engines would pull their coal hoppers from the coal prep plant and run the ten miles to the river where they would go through a balloon track over the car dump and return to the Randolph plant engine first. Once back at the coal prep plant, they would swap empties for another string of load and repeat the process.

Today, economics and politics have brought changes to the operation. The mines which produced high sulfur coal are closed, and the land has been reclaimed. The coal prep plant sits idle. While the coal dock for now is not shipping out any coal, the Baldwin power plant's demand for coal has not stopped. Now, to meet more stringent clean air standards, the Baldwin plant burns a combination of high sulfur and low sulfur coal. The low sulfur coal comes from out west in Wyoming and arrives by Union Pacific unit coal train over the old IC connection at **Lenzburg**.

While currently idled, the KRPD is reported to be ready to begin operations once the local mine is reopened.

PEABODY COAL AT SHAWNEETOWN: In the 1980s Peabody was running twelve car coal trains from the Eagle Mine through **New Shawneetown** to their coal dock at Old Shawneetown on the Ohio River. The operation is now closed, and no railroads run to Shawneetown anymore, though at one time L&N and B&O (in later years Prairie Central) ran to this Ohio River town.

Peabody Coal has long been known for hosting a wide variety of exotic and rare first generation diesels at its coal operation across Missouri, Illinois and Indiana, as well as across the Ohio River in Kentucky, all in a variation of the company's paint scheme. Visiting these sites once proved as interesting as sampling a Forrest Gump box of chocolates as you never knew what you would find.

Even after selling off the Peabody Short Line (between East St. Louis and **Freeburg** for the old Cahokia power plant), Peabody's River King Mine at Freeburg continued to host a number of exotic diesels. Another location in southern Illinois sporting Peabody diesels at one time was the mine at **New Athens**. Not to ignore other local operations in southern Illinois, Consolidated Coal had a engine at its # 2 mine at **Pinckneyville** and engines at the rail-to-barge transfer dump at Kellogg, located on the site of the former M&I car ferry. First generation diesels can still be found there though coal is delivered to the dump by modern Union Pacific diesels.

Old Ben coal mine #21 at Sesser once sported its own diesel as did Old Ben #24 at **Benton**.

Zeigler Coal had an engine stationed at its mines in **Sparta** and **Coulterville**.

Sahara Coal Company had an engine at its **Harrisburg** mine as did Freeman United Coal at **Waltonville**.

Amax Coal once had two diesels at **Mt. Carmel** that delivered coal to a power plant in Indiana.

Power plants, as well as coal mines, can have switch engines to shuffle cars about. The Baldwin plant had one, so did the Central Illinois Public Service plant to Grand Tower, and so did the Southern Illinois Power Company plant at **Joppa** as did the power plant on Lake Egypt near **Marion**.

INTERURBAN AND STREET CAR LINES IN SOUTHERN ILLINOIS

The Coal Belt Electric Railway of Marion was the only interurban in the state operated for most of its life as a steam road subsidiary.

Mount Olive Wabash train wreck: 5-23-07

Built by a group of investors in association with the Illi-nois Midland Coal Co., operations began in 1902. The 13- mile line connected Marion and Herrin. There was a 3- mile branch to **Carterville** coming off the main at Energy. In the early years there were several other small branches, such as the one to **Spillertown** (which lasted until 1907).

The line was acquired by steam road Missouri Pacific in 1906 after which time it appeared in MoPac time tables. Passenger service was hourly with schedules covered by seven street car-type passenger cars.

The line dropped freight service in 1914 that was taken over by parent company MoPac, the principal commodity being coal. Paved roads cut into ridership. A down turn in coal traffic and a loss of passenger traffic occurred in 1922, and by 1926 the line had been discontinued, though some trackage was retained by MoPac for freight access.

CAIRO ELECTRIC & TRACTION COMPANY: ALSO CAIRO & ST. LOUIS. Utility tycoon and U.S. Senator from Illinois, William McKinley, in the late 19th and early 20th centuries, bought utility companies and street railway companies throughout Illinois, Iowa and Missouri. His grand plan was to link many of these together to create an electric interurban stretching from Chicago to Kansas City.

While Chicago and Kansas City were never linked by an interurban, he was successful in connecting all major central Illinois cities with St. Louis. Another part of his grand plan was to build an interurban linking St. Louis and Cairo.

THE EAST ST. LOUIS & SUBURBAN RAILWAY CO.

REACHES THE FOLLOWING PLACES OF INTEREST ALONG ITS WIDELY EXTENDED SYSTEM

BELLEVILLE
CASEYVILLE
O'FALLON
LEBANON
COLLINSVILLE
MARYVILLE
EDWARDSVILLE

TRI-CITIES
HORSE SHOE LAKE
NAMEOKI
LONG LAKE
HARTFORD
LAKE VIEW
ALTON

Toward that goal he built the Cairo Electric & Traction Co. and the Cairo & St. Louis. Construction began in 1909 and was completed in 1910.

Using CE&T street trackage, the Cairo & St. Louis used trackage rights on the Illinois Central to reach Mound City 8 miles to the north where it returned to its own tracks to reach its northern terminal. The line had seven passenger cars and three freight motors. It never reached St. Louis and was abandoned in August, 1931.

SOUTHERN ILLINOIS RAILWAY & POWER CO. Southern Illinois Railway & Power, owned by CIP, opened in 1913 and was built to steam road standards as the road did a substantial freight business (mostly coal) as well as hauling passengers on the fifteen-mile line.

Passenger service was provided by seven passenger cars that ran on an hourly schedule. Cars ran from Eldorado, through Harrisburg to Carrier Mills, though most passengers traveled only to and from Harrisburg from either end of the line. The power house and car shops were located in Muddy.

The SIR&P company had its own fleet of gondola cars pulled by an electric freight motor. Business was so good that there were plans to extend the line west to Carbondale and south to **Rosiclare** on the Ohio River. However, a depressed coal market put an end to expansion plans.

Competition with paved roads and bus companies put an end to passenger service, followed shortly by freight service in 1933.

MURPHYSBORO & SOUTHERN ILLINOIS RAILWAY: Built in 1909, the Murphysboro Electric Railway & Light Co. was a three mile street railway that was linked with the seven mile interurban M&SIR to reach **Carbondale** using private right of way. Paved roads and auto traffic cut into profits, and the line closed in 1927.

FRUIT GROWERS REFRIGERATOR & POWER CO.: Operational by 1907, the three-mile street car line connected Anna and Jonesboro. By 1925 the Central Illinois Power Company system had taken over the line and replaced the street cars with buses though trackage in Anna was kept for a time to deliver coal to the state mental health hospital.

CENTRALIA AND CENTRAL CITY TRACTION CO. The line once linked Central City on the north with **Wamac** on the south through Centralia. Cars ran mostly on street trackage with some private right of way near Wamac.

CITY RAILWAY OF MOUNT VERNON: This street car line ran from Columbia and Olive on the north to Logan & 24th on the south. These lines connected at 9th & Broadway and then ran east to the Chicago and Eastern Illinois depot.

ELIZABETHTOWN, on the Ohio River, also had a street car system, but little is known of the line.

EAST ST. LOUIS & SUBURBAN/ COLUMBIA & WATERLOO: From East St. Louis, the 110 mile railway system ran west across the Eads Bridge to St. Louis, and fanned out east into Illinois to reach Belleville, O'Fallon, Lebanon, Collinsville, Glen Carbon, Edwards-ville and Alton. The first line, com-pleted in 1894, ran from East St. Louis to Belleville along the St. Clair County Turnpike (State Street). Collinsville and Edwardsville were connected in 1898. A line starting at French Village and extending to O'Fallon and Lebanon was finished in 1904. The twenty-two mile line from East St. Louis to Dupo, Columbia and Waterloo opened for business in 1912. The suburban's Blue Goose bus service was started in 1925. After highways in the area were paved around 1925, passenger business fell off consider-ably. All streetcar services ended in 1935.

Electric Interurban between Murphysboro (Walnut & 13th Streets) and Carbondale

LEWIS AND CLARK IN ILLINOIS

Every young school student knows that Meriwether Lewis and William Clark were sent on a grand adventure by President Thomas Jefferson to explore the newly acquired Louisiana Territory. However, what is usually left out is the story about all the places they visited in Illinois, and how much time they spent here before embarking on their challenging journey.

William Clark had been living with his older brother, George Rogers Clark, at the foot of the rapids along the banks of the Ohio River. George Rogers Clark, of course, was the man who played the key role during the Revolution to wrest Illinois country from British control. Jefferson had earlier approached George about leading such an expedition, but he declined, recommending his younger brother instead. William Clark had previously visited Illinois Country, staying at the residence of Shadrach Bond Sr. in Kaskaskia, whose nephew became the state's first governor. This visit gave Clark important social contacts in the area.

Meriwether Lewis, Jefferson's secretary, lacked combat experience, but he had served with Anthony Wayne's army following the great victory over the natives at Fallen Timbers. It was in this capacity that he first met young William Clark. Their starting point was at Clarksville, across the Ohio River from Louisville, Kentucky. The pair first crossed into Illinois from Kentucky on November 11, 1803. At the time, Illinois had not yet achieved statehood and was still part of Indiana Territory. Illinois was sparsely populated with only about 2,500 whites living here at the time.

Edwardsville's Kirkpatrick home: built 1805 after Lewis and Clark were in area

Jefferson instructed the pair to collect information on Indians, fur trade possibilities, climate, minerals, soils, and waterways. Interestingly, one of the things they would be searching for was the Northwest Passage - that fabled all-water route to the Pacific that explorer after explorer searched for in vain. Although they did not find that all-water route, (it doesn't exist) they carefully recorded every detail of their two-and-a-half year journey and paved the way for the settlement of the Great Plains, Far West, and the growth of our great nation. They carefully mapped every inch of the way and brought back hundreds of scientific specimens.

Most of their extensive preparations for the trip were made in Illinois where they stayed a total of 181 days. It was in Illinois that they secured provisions and supplies and recruited about 3-dozen men who became part of their Corps of Discovery team. Lewis was fastidious, keeping detailed records and maps of everything. He noted in his journal that the launching point for their incredible journey was Camp River DuBois, at the mouth of the Wood River near present-day Hartford.

Their first stopping point in Illinois was Fort Massac, which is now a state park. They conferred briefly with Captain Daniel Bissell and then continued on their journey. George Rogers Clark, the "George Washington of the West," and his Long Knives spent one day here back in 1778, on their way to pluck Kaskaskia from British control. Massac was a frequent stopover point for settlers heading farther west. This made the place a prime recruiting area for our intrepid explorers. George Droulliard was one such man. His mother was a Shawnee Indian, and his father was French-Canadian. He was fluent in English, French and Native-American. He became the group's premier interpreter and hunter.

Fort Massac (Illinois Dept. of Tourism)

One of the people with them at this point was an African-American. His name was York, and he was Clark's slave. During the exploration part of the trip, most Indians who met him were in awe, for they had never before seen a black man.

Next they moved farther south down the Ohio River to **Cairo** at the confluence of the Ohio and Mississippi Rivers. Today this is the site of Fort Defiance State Park. Fort Defiance was used as a staging area by U.S. Grant and the Union troops during the Civil War. While at Cairo, Lewis said he caught a 128-pound blue catfish (we have only his word for it). At Cairo they also practiced using the latest navigational instruments for determining latitude and longitude.

They encountered difficulty going against the current of the Mississippi as they headed north for Kaskaskia. With the men rowing against the current, they progressed only ten or twelve miles a day. As they passed the mouth of the Big Muddy River, Lewis observed the existence of coal in the area, a mineral that would later play an important role in Southern Illinois economy. They reached **Kaskaskia** on November 28th. Kaskaskia was one of the old French settlements on the American Bottom, a small strip of alluvial plain that was the most historic in the entire state. The settlements there constituted the cradle of Illinois civilization.

Lewis and Clark's difficulty in progressing upstream made them realize it was going to take more men to make the arduous journey, so they continued the recruiting process. One of the new recruits was sergeant John Ordway, who became the third man in the chain of command. One person they visited with at Kaskaskia was Pierre Menard, who played such a key role in early Illinois politics. The beautiful French colonial home that he subsequently built at Kaskaskia was called the "Mount Vernon of the West."

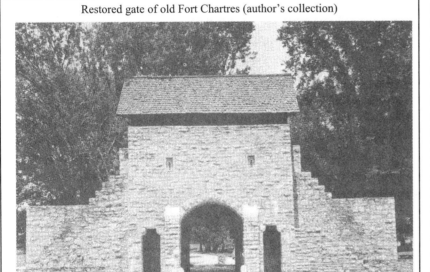

Kaskaskian Pierre Menard

After stocking up for winter supplies and enlarging their crew, on December 3rd Clark resumed the northward journey up the river without Lewis, next stopping at **Cahokia**. He passed the ruins of old **Fort Chartres** along the way. Lewis took the quicker overland route on horseback so that he could meet with officials in St. Louis. This historic place called Cahokia, founded back in 1699, was the first European settlement on the Mississippi. This was genesis - where it all began. The Bottom was extremely fertile, but it was subject to mosquitoes, ague, malaria and frequent flooding. Cahokia became the post office site from which the group communicated with President Jefferson back in Washington D.C. The Church of the Holy Family and the old courthouse were at the Cahokia site. They are two of the oldest buildings in the state of Illinois. It was here that Lewis and Clark conferred with Nicholas Jarrot, one of the prominent citizens of that town - a landholder and slave owner. Jarrot lived in a two-story mansion, built in 1799, the first brick structure in the state of Illinois. Jarrot, a shrewd land speculator (9,000 acres), also owned the ground near present-day **Collinsville** that featured the Cahokia Mounds ancient Indian site at the juncture of Canteen Creek and Cahokia Creek.

Restored gate of old Fort Chartres (author's collection)

When Lewis met with officials in St. Louis, Jarrot went with him as an interpreter and advisor. St. Louis had about 1,000 inhabitants at the time. They met with Spanish authorities and asked for permission to explore Upper Louisiana. The officials replied that permission would be granted in the spring, after the transfer of Louisiana Territory into American hands was completed. Spanish officials suggested that they winter in St. Louis, but the two men chose to set up Camp Dubois (Camp Wood) on land that was owned by Nicholas Jarrot, across from the mouth of the Missouri River.

On December 10 the group moved a short distance upstream from Cahokia to Illinoistown, the present site of **East St. Louis**. Lewis then went back to St. Louis, most likely crossing the river at Piggott's Ferry. Piggott, who died in 1799, is considered the founder of East St. Louis. His ferry was located almost in the exact same spot where the Casino Queen is presently located. While across the river, Lewis

Lewis and Clark Keelboat inside the Hartford Interpretive Center (IL Tour.)

began to gather data and information about the Missouri River. Much of his information was gleaned from Antoine Soulard, the surveyor general of Upper Louisiana. Lewis questioned Soulard about the population of Louisiana Territory. Thomas Jefferson wanted this information because he was thinking about sending all Indians in the East to live west of the Mississippi River, while all whites on the other side would move back East.

While camping at Illinoistown, Lewis and Clark were close to the great Cahokia Mound at this point, but they make no mention of seeing it in their diary or notes. By 1803, the native-Americans who had built the mound had completely disappeared from the area. The natives living there at the time had no knowledge of how or why the mound was built.

On December 11 Clark and the group moved north again toward their winter campsite at Camp River Dubois. Most scholars believe it was on the south side of the Wood River. Due to the vagaries of Mother Nature and numerous floods that subsequently changed the landscape, the exact location of the campsite is not known. Along the way, they passed a few scattered settlers at Six Mile Prairie (future **Granite City**), so named because it was six miles from St. Louis. On reaching their destination, they built several cabins and surrounded them with a wooden stockade. The U.S. flag they flew at the campsite had 15 stars on it, but it did not reflect several new states that had recently been added to the union. Lewis again went back to St. Louis to take care of business matters and purchase supplies (salt, pork, candles, turnips, corn, flour, biscuits, gunpowder, etc.). Captain Clark imparted discipline to the men, built *esprit de corps*, and started packing provisions.

St Louis, though part of the Louisiana Purchase, had not yet formally been transferred to the United States. When Napoleon conquered much of Europe, he placed his brother on the throne of Spain and took possession of Louisiana territory by fiat. When Jefferson sent ministers to France to inquire about buying the port of New Orleans, the cash-strapped Napoleon astounded them by selling the whole territory for a few cents an acre.

On December 20 there was a ceremony in New Orleans to transfer Louisiana to American possession. The transfer of Upper Louisiana did not take place in St. Louis until March 9, 1904. The French citizens at St. Louis were unhappy about the transfer but it was a settled matter.

As months passed at Camp Dubois, a determined team spirit was established by the men in what psychologists refer to as a "bonding" process. Final preparations and team selection of 33 men were made. The expedition, consisting of a heavily loaded keelboat (with swivel cannon) and two canoes, began on the rainy afternoon of May 14th, 1804. Thus began their long trek into a dangerous and inhospitable territory. After they embarked, they did not return to their point of departure for 28 months, but it was a joyous, triumphant end to a long and difficult trip. They traveled through 11 future states before they reached the Pacific Ocean. The 11 pillars at the state memorial represent each of those 11 states.

The new Lewis and Clark Interpretive Center on the west side of Route 3 at **Hartford**, Illinois, opened in the fall of 2002. It is an impressive 14,000 square foot building that features an exact-scale, 55-foot replica of the wooden keel boat used on the journey. The display features full mast and sail and has a unique cutaway section to demonstrate how the interior space was used. By the summer of 2003, the center included a replica of the five cabins and palisaded (vertical log) fortress at Camp Dubois.

Meriwether Louis (L) and William Clark
(Michael Haynes art)

When the Corps of Discovery team officially pushed off on May 14, 1804, they were cheered by a number of Illinois settlers who had gathered, including some from the Goshen settlement south of **Edwardsville**. They did not arrive back in St. Louis until September 23, 1806.

Meriwether Lewis fell on hard times in later years, meeting with several professional and personal failures. He became an alcoholic and died in 1809 at Grinder's Inn, on the Natchez Trace near Nashville, Tennessee. There were reports that he had been mur-dered, but it was probably a suicide. William Clark settled down in St. Louis and married Julia Hancock and reared a large family. He married Harriet Radford in 1821, about a year after Julia's death in 1820. Clark died in 1838 and is buried in Belle-fontaine Cemetery in North St. Louis on Riverview Drive, not far from Broadway.

The famed **John Colter** was one of the men on the expedition. He went on to become a "mountain man," engaging in the fur trade, and was the first white man to see Yellowstone Park. This author still remembers reading in high school the story of his "race for life," after being captured by Indians.

One hundred years later, a World's Fair was held in St. Louis, in part, to commemorate the expedition. The journey of Lewis and Clark paved the way for a great migration of settlers and an influx of immigrants to the trans-Mississippi region. Citizens of Illinois can take great pride in the role their forefathers played in this historic vision quest. The fascinating story of that saga is part of history's great tapestry that tells us who we are as a people and where we came from. One can only wonder what it must have been like to endure the hardships they encountered. They suffered through sunstroke, hailstorms, dysentery, sore muscles and snakebites. But their courage and spirit was rewarded with the sight of great herds of thousands of buffalo, and the thrill of straddling the continental divide and being among the first Americans to see the Pacific Ocean.

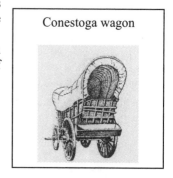
Conestoga wagon

Ken Burns recently did a PBS documentary on Lewis and Clark. In it, he points out that when we examine the life, times and exploits of past heroes, we learn much about the "inner workings of our remarkable Republic." And, in doing so, we discover much about ourselves.

www.lewisandclark.org is the Lewis and Clark Heritage Trail Website
www.lewisandclarkillinois.org is the Illinois Lewis and Clark Bicentennial Commission
Lewis and Clark Center at Hartford: 618/251-5811
www.enjoyillinois.com   1-800-2CONNECT

INTERESTING STATE FACTS

1. Illinois celebrated its Sesquicentennial (150 years) in 1968. Illinois ranks 7th in overall population.
2. The law-making body, the General Assembly, consists of 59 Senators and 118 Representatives.
3. The Governor, the law-enforcing arm of the government, is elected to a 4-year term.
4. The Supreme Court, consisting of 7 members, elected to 10-year terms, interprets the laws
5. Illinois has 74 major universities and colleges.
6. Hogs are the number one farm animals raised, followed by beef cattle and sheep.
7. Farms cover approximately 75 percent of the state.
8. Illinois is spread out over more than 56,400 square miles; it is 24th in size among the 50 states. It ranks first in the production of a rock called Tripoli.
9. Illinois is 218 miles at its widest point; 385 miles is its greatest distance north to south. It ranks fourth in the country in miles of road.
10. Glaciers once covered 90 percent of what is now Illinois.
11. Tornadoes have caused more deaths in Illinois than any other state.
12. Illinois is known as The Prairie State and Land of Lincoln.
13. The highest point of the state is Charles Mound (1,235 ft.) in the Driftless Area of Jo Daviess County. Chicago is the third largest publishing town in the country.
14. The lowest point of the state is in Alexander County on the Mississippi River at 279 feet above sea level.
15. Although the Ohio River forms the southeastern border of the state, the river is wholly owned by the greedy state of Kentucky, whose border ends on the north shore of the river.
16. Illinois has 22 U.S. Representatives and 2 U.S. Senators (Dick Durbin and Peter Fitzgerald), giving it 24 electoral votes.
17. Coal exists beneath 2/3 of the state; Illinois has the greatest reserves of any state in the union.
18. The state mineral is fluorspar, not coal; state bird – cardinal (chosen because it does not leave the state during winter), state tree – native white oak; state motto – "State Sovereignty – National Union;" state animal – white tailed deer; state flower – native violet; state insect – monarch butterfly; state wiggle – the Square Dance; state fossil - Tully Monster (a harmless invertebrate)
19. The state is part of a geographical region called the Great Central Lowlands.
20. Four of the 10 tallest buildings in the world are in Chicago; Chicago is/was home to Boeing, Kraft Foods, American Flyer, Motorola, United Airlines, Quaker Oats, Wurlitzer, Rockola, and Seeburg jukebox; Bally, Gottlieb and Williams pinball
21. Illinois has 500 rivers and streams with 2,000 miles of navigable canoe routes.
22. Carlyle, Rend and Crab Orchard are all man-made lakes in a state not noted for its large number of lakes.
23. The circuit court of Cook County has over 140 judges, making it the largest court in America.
24. Illinois has 102 counties and 72 state parks.
25. Southerly winds from the Gulf of Mexico have a moderating effect on southern Illinois climate, giving the area 240 frost-free days, enabling it to grow cotton and tobacco.
26. Illinois, with 900 streams, generally has good drainage except in the central eastern part of the state, which hampered early settlement.
27. At the juncture of the two rivers, the Ohio is a distinctly bluish-gray, while the Mississippi is a muddy brown (see pic on back cover).

28. Maple syrup farming is carried on near **Lacon, Oakland, Shirley**, and several other communities in central Illinois. One tree, on average, may give as much as thirty gallons of sap during the 30-day sap-running season.
29. Article 6 of the Northwest Ordinance proclaimed Illinois Country to be free of slavery, but it was permitted at the Saline Salt Works near Equality where a man named Crenshaw built The Old Slave House. When the 3-story frame house was built, a beech tree seedling from George Washington's gravesite was brought from Mount Vernon and planted next to the Crenshaw House. The slaves were housed on the third floor and slept in small cells with wooden bunks. The room contained two whipping posts used when punishment was needed. The house still stands as a reminder that slavery once existed in Illinois.
30. The town of **Elgin** once had a large and thriving dairy industry. Gail Borden built a milk condensing plant there in 1865, the second of its kind in the entire nation. Condensed milk was in great demand during the Civil War because it was less bulky and less perishable than fresh milk. Borden's factory saved the town of Elgin from becoming a ghost town only a quarter of a century after it was founded.

31. There is a place in England called Stonehenge, famous for its "hanging" stones placed in a circle. Did you know that the state of Illinois had its own Woodhenge? During a 1960 excavation about 3,000 feet from Monks Mound at Cahokia Mounds near Collinsville, a number of oval pits were discovered. Their purpose was a mystery until the base of an old cypress log was found in one of the pits. According to carbon 14 dating tests, these circles with upright logs were constructed around A.D. 1,000. The diameter of American Woodhenge is 410 feet. It is a precise circle probably made with a rope and peg compass. The posts were about two feet in diameter. No one quite knows their actual height, but they were probably at least 20 feet tall.

Young Abraham Lincoln with his stepmother by Charles Bracker

Because the earth is tilted on its axis and rotates around the sun in an elliptical path, the point of sunrise and sunset move along the horizon from north to south and then back from south to north. The speculation is that this structure, like Stonehenge, was a sun calendar, making it the only one on the continent, north of Mexico.

32. There are no living descendants of our sixteenth president with the name Lincoln. Robert Todd was the only surviving Lincoln at the time of his father's assassination. Robert Todd died in 1930. He had one son named Abraham Lincoln II, but he died from blood poisoning in 1890 following an operation on a carbuncle under his left arm. Robert was not buried next to his father in Springfield because the crypt only had six places. There would have been room for Robert but not his wife, and she wanted to be buried next to her husband. All three of them are buried at Arlington Cemetery in Virginia.

33. The Chieftan Pontiac made war on the British and Americans during the French and Indian War in an effort to stop their encroachments on their land. In June of 1769 he tried to seize the fort at Detroit but failed. Realizing he had failed in his efforts, he made peace with his enemies. In 1969 he went to the Spanish fort in St. Louis, commanded by Sieur de Bellerive, the Frenchman now in the employ of the Spanish. Pontiac heard about a party being given at Cahokia by the British. Bellerive warned him not to go because he was not liked by the British. Pontiac went to the party dressed in a French army uniform given to him by the Marquis de Montcalm. Some Englishmen hired an Illini to kill Pontiac for a barrel of whiskey.

Abraham Lincoln II by Charles Bracker

During Pontiac's walk back to St. Louis he was killed, his skull crushed by a tomahawk. His body was taken to St. Louis and buried there, although there is no marker to indicate his final resting place. Pontiac's tribesmen, seeking revenge, made war on the Illini. The Illinois Indians tried to escape their enemies by seeking refuge on the flat-topped surface of a place the Indians called The Rock, on the Illinois River at old Fort St. Louis, built by LaSalle in 1682. According to legend, they were encircled and starved into submission, giving the place a new name, Starved Rock. They were almost totally annihilated.

LEGENDS AND LORE of ILLINOIS

1. According to historian John Allen, people of southern Illinois have long been referred to as "suckers." The term may have been used as a derogatory comparison of the poor, common folk of southern Illinois to that useless growth on tobacco plants. It could also have come from southern Illinois residents who traveled up the Mississippi to work at the lead mines in **Galena** each spring, at about the same time the sucker fish, an ugly bottom-feeding species, traveled north to spawn. "Here come the suckers from southern Illinois," was a common refrain up north. Another version holds that small crawfish holes held water that could be sucked dry and early travelers, searching for fresh water, spotting one, yelled "Here's a sucker."

Starved Rock near Peoria

If you think "sucker" is bad, those native to Indiana were called "hoosiers" and Missourians were called "pukes." Wisconsinites became known as "badgers" because early miners in that state holed up like badgers during the long winter.

2. Historian **Grover Brinkman** told about the **world's smallest tombstone**, located in West Salem. The grave marker for **Emma Pfeil** in a Moravian cemetery is five and 7/8 inches by two inches.

3. On the outskirts of Centralia, incorporated as a city in 1913, it had a population in 1939 of 1,232. It did a flourishing business as an oasis for nearby towns that were "dry." A historic plaque south of Wamac on the east side of Route 51 designates the site where the third Principal Meridian intersects with an east-west baseline. At least sixty percent of the land in Illinois, including Chicago, was measured from these important coordinates.

Grover Brinkman

4. **Peter Cartwright** was a famous Methodist circuit rider whose territory was from Shawneetown to Galena. He left Kentucky and came to Illinois because it was a slave state. He was an eloquent speaker and converted an estimated 10,000 people. He ran for a seat in the legislature but was defeated by Abe Lincoln. Peter, a man of broad chest and powerful arms, became the subject of stories and legends due to his rivalries with that scalawag, **Mike Fink**, "King of the Keelboats" whose exploits were showcased in the 1950s Disney TV movie, ***Davy Crockett and the River Pirates***. Following is a typical Mike Fink swagger song:

I'm a ring-tailed roarer and a ring-tailed screamer too!
I was raised on grizzly bear milk and cradled with a wildcat.
I'm half horse and half alligator and people call me the Mississippi Snag.
I can eat a dozen rattlesnakes for breakfast and drink a barrel a' whiskey besides.
I can out-run, out-hop, out-jump and out-fight any man in this whole country!
Ya-hoooooooo! Yip-eeeeeeee!
Stand back and gimme room!

5. There were approximately thirty-two railroads that operated in southern Illinois below Route 50. Most of these were standard gauge, 4 ft., 8 and 1/2 inches. A commonly given explanation for this rail width is that this was the spacing of Roman chariot wheels. British Parliament established this width as law in 1845. The Ohio and Mississippi, which ended at East St. Louis, was built at a width of 6 ft. and converted to standard gauge in 1871. The 340-mile conversion was done in one day by huge numbers of track gangs.

Circuit Rider Peter Cartwright by Larry Sanders of Rockford

6. **Henry Dillinger** and **George McKinney** of Murphysboro were great pioneer storytellers. In one of their tall tales they claimed to have scooped out the channel of the Big Muddy River with their own hands. When they were asked why it was so crooked, they replied that they worked on it day and night. The straight part was dug during the day, and the crooked parts happened at night, they explained.

7. Over a thirty-year period from the 1920s to the 50s, it has been estimated that about fifty members of the Shelton Gang were either murdered or died under mysterious circumstances.

8. The founder of Rock Island and Davenport, Iowa, was an interesting man named George Davenport. After 10 years of military duty and several narrow escapes with death at the hands of Indians, he went to work as a food contractor to provide provisions for American troops. He arrived at Rock Island in 1816 with two regiments of soldiers. They erected the first buildings on Rock Island. The fort they constructed was named for Secretary of War, John Armstrong.

George Davenport's home

One day Davenport was attacked by drunken Indians. One Indian musket ball came within inches of his head. As they prepared to kill him one Indian called out, "Saganosh! Saganosh!" (He is an Englishman.) To the pro-English Indians of this area these words were magic, saving his life. Davenport later became a successful fur trader, packing his furs, tallow, and beeswax in barrels and selling everything in St. Louis. Davenport became a prominent citizen of the area and piloted steamboats and was appointed postmaster. He was a colonel in the Black Hawk War and urged President Jackson to pay the Indians for their land east of the Mississippi. Davenport, who amassed a fortune, gave up the business of Indian trading and became a land baron around what is now called the Quad Cities..

9. The first use for Illinois oil was medicinal. The Indians skimmed it off pools of water and used it on insect bites and stings. The white men bottled it and sold the balm as Seneca Oil.

10. An old tradition in Illinois that was started by the French was the **shivaree**, whose loose translation means "headache." Sometime during the newlywed's first week of marriage, friends would gather outside their house, just after they went to bed, and wake them with revelry by serenading with songs and racket made from blowing horns and beating on pots and pans. If the young couple refused to come out of the house, a rug was placed over the chimney to force them out.

The husband would be taken away in a wheelbarrow or on a log, and the wife was kidnapped and hidden. The husband then had to go looking for her. Various mischief was then committed in the home while the newlyweds were gone. Typically, salt would be mixed with sugar, and beds would be short-sheeted. When it was over, the couple was expected to serve drinks, and then they would be toasted by the group.

11. **Pioneer Medicine**: The pioneer doctor was a far cry from today's modern practitioners. A foot gashed by the slip of an axe . . . a man stricken with ague, an outbreak of smallpox, a soldier dying of a gangrenous wound – these and other hazards in pioneer life created a desperate need for doctors in early Illinois.

Early pioneer circuit-riding physician

The simple equipment of a country doctor included a mortar and pestle for mixing herbs and medicines, a set of balances for weighing amounts of powders, homemade splints, bandages, a few simple drugs, syringes, hot water bottles, and an assortment of crude instruments. Among these were a saw (for amputations) pliers (tooth extraction) and a "pulsometer." This dumbbell-shaped device was six inches long and filled with a red liquid. It was used to impress dubious patients that they were getting a thorough and accurate diagnosis. The patient grasped one end of the contraption and bubbles rose to the other. This, of course, had nothing to do with the patient's condition, but it was usually quite impressive. The early doctor had to make his own pills and tinctures, in fact, he mixed up all his medicines.

Most often the doctor rode a circuit over his territory as he made house calls. Their fees were usually small and even then were often paid in promises, seldom money. Farm products called "truck" (hence the origin of the phrase truck farming) were the general medium of payment.

There were no anesthetics and for amputations, patients were held down and given a bullet to clamp down on to suppress screams. This is the origin of the phrase, "bite the bullet." Cautery was another method of treating wounds. To stop the flow of blood and kill infection, a hot poker was pressed to an injury for several seconds.

Most doctors went along with home remedies, superstitions and the use of charms. The right front paw of a mole was tied around a child's neck to ward off attacks of "croup." A ball of asafetida tied in a white cloth and worn around the neck supposedly prevented milk sickness. Gum camphor worn around the neck supposedly warded off malaria. For colds, a child wore a spider in a pouch around his neck until it died. Tea made of white ants, a lick of a lump of alum, and eating some Indian turnip ground in molasses, were other folk remedies. In case of colds the throat and chest were rubbed with goose grease. In case of fever, pioneers consumed a mixture of the juice of garlic and onions, crawled toward the east under a double-rooted raspberry briar, or ate a mixture of ground flax seed and licorice, vinegar, raisin, and sugar-candy. If children, sick with fever, didn't respond to these treatments, the child would be put to bed, covered well, and given tea made from snakeroot, dogwood, willow, or sassafras. It was said to be best if the child ate from a blue bowl, wore a bit of blue ribbon (better if stolen), or drank from a blue bottle.

Household samp mortar (Robert Fair of Rockford)

12. Pierre Radisson. A French explorer told about how the first lead was mined near the present town of **Galena** in the 1730s. First, the ore was pounded into smaller pieces with a "samp mortar." Then two or three large trees were cut down, and the trees were trimmed into logs about five feet long. Next a small basin was dug into the ground. The logs were made into a boxlike structure with a metal grate that was placed over the pit. The unsmelted ore was dumped into the box that was then burned from below. The ore was smelted by the fire, and the lead fell into the pit for recovery.

The federal government passed a lease ordinance in 1785 that gave the U.S. government right to the land around the Fever River. Those who worked the mines kept 2/3 of the profit while 1/3 went to the government. In the end the lease system proved difficult to enforce and was eventually abandoned.

13. The first historical society in the state was at **Vandalia**.

14. Historian **John Allen** once told a story about the beautiful dogwood and redbud trees that flower so prominently each spring in southern Illinois. The back country legend holds that Christ was crucified on a cross made from the dogwood. He took pity on the tree and said that never again would it grow large or straight enough to be used as a cross. From that point in time, the blossoms of the dogwood took the shape of a cross, with two long petals and two short ones. And the markings at the end of each petal are said to represent Christ's nail prints.

15. Hill folk claim that redbud trees are usually found growing near the dogwood. They call it the "Judas tree" because it is said that after Judas betrayed Christ, he went out and hanged himself from the branch of a redbud.

16. The Kaskaskia River, known as the "river of big cat fish," was originally called the Okaw River by the French. The French spelled it Cascasquia which was abbreviated into Cas, which they pronounced Kah. The word was corrupted into Okaw by English settlers.

17. Early settlers believed that the Great Mound, on Route 40 between Collinsville and East St. Louis, was built by one of the lost tribes of Israel.

Early fur trapper

18. Illinois pioneers used goose grease to treat chest colds and made a cough syrup from sorghum, ginger, pepper and vinegar.

Illegal liquor was called "moonshine" because it was an activity mostly carried on at night, under the convenience of moonlight.

19. Trade and barter were common in colonial America. It was animal skins and fur that brought the first white men to Illinois Country – not gold. The furs quickly became the **coin of the realm** and were a substitute for money. While Lewis and Clark were in Southern Illinois the local Indians offered Clark several furs in exchange for his dog, but he turned them down. For one beaver skin a trapper could buy a half-pound of beads, a kettle, one pound of shot, five pounds of sugar, one pound of tobacco, two awls, twelve buttons, two fishhooks, and twenty flints for his musket. English royalty used ermine for their robes. Rich men desired lynx for their bedcovering and beaver for their hats. The Native-Americans stopped producing goods for themselves and hunted and trapped for furs that they exchanged for goods, guns and whiskey. Major Morrill Marston, commandant at Fort Armstrong (**Rock Island**) in 1820 reported that furs brought in by the Sauk and Fox Indians consisted of the following: 2,760 beaver skins, 922 otter, 500 mink, 200 wildcat, 13,440 raccoon, 12,900 muskrat, 680 bear, and 28,680 deer.

20. Then there is the story of **Lakey's ghost** based on the murder of an early settler near McLeansboro. The quite personable man was cutting logs one day for the purpose of building a cabin. His neighbor came to see him and discovered that someone had dispatched the man with his own ax and severed his head from his shoulders. Lakey had no known enemies, and the murder was never solved.

Shortly after Lakey was buried, two men were traveling along a road that bordered Lakey's Creek, and they suddenly were joined by a headless horseman on a black steed. The gruesome companion silently rode with them until they crossed the stream. Near the center of the stream, the ghostly apparition turned away and disappeared into the mist. It was then that the men remembered that ghosts are unable to cross moving water. This incident was repeated often with other travelers, and it was said that the headless horseman was looking for his killer.

21. Some of the earliest settlers in Centralia were the **Crosby brothers** who left East St. Louis for good after the 1844 flood and resettled in the center of the state. Centralia was named for the Illinois Central Railroad and was long self-advertised as "The Gateway to Egypt." It was platted by the railroad in 1853 and has a dominant German population. German influence was seen in the fact that English and German was taught in its schools as well as the dominant architecture in many homes, and in numerous *Saengerfestes* (songfests). (From George Ross of **Sandoval**)

22. There is an ancient Indian buffalo painting, actually an outline on the side of a sandstone cliff, on a low bluff in **Gum Spring Hollow** in Johnson County, about three miles south of the town of **Ozark**. Ozark also has Pumpkin Land during the month of October (618-777-2802).

Alton's famed Piasa Monster

23. At **Turkey Track Rock**, in Jackson County, near Routes 151 and 3, there are rocks with Indian carvings (petroglyphs: petro = rock, glyph = picture) of turkey tracks, human eyes and human hands, and people sitting.

24. Scattered throughout southern Illinois are the remains of nine Indian forts, built on a projected finger of a high bluff. The sites could only be scaled with great difficulty, and moving the stones from below the cliff required great effort. These places are known variously as Indian Kitchen, Millstone Bluff, War Bluff near **Raum**, and Cornish Bluff and Trigg Stone Fort, both in Johnson County.

25. Along the bluffs of the Mississippi, north of **Alton**, is the painting (a reproduction of an Indian pictograph) of the legendary **Piasa Bird**, known by the Indians as the Bird of Evil Spirit. The fiendish looking creature, first seen by Marquette and Joliet in 1673, and first sketched in 1826, had the body of an alligator and feet with talons, pointed teeth, enormous wings, and the face of a man with antlers on its head. It is generally regarded as the **greatest Indian painting in North America**.

Named for a local creek, the bird was presumably the thunderbird or storm spirit of the Illiniwek. Historian Wayne Temple maintains that the bird as presently depicted, was not the same figure seen by Marquette.

The creature was said to have lived in a cave and feasted on Indians, swooping down and carrying them away to be devoured in its lair. Finally, the brave young chief of the Illini, Ouatoga, took twenty armed warriors with him and stood brazenly on a rock to defy the monster. The evil one swooped down to kill its intended victim, and at the last second, the hidden warriors emerged and killed the beast with their poisoned arrows.

The original painting, in red, green and black, was quarried away for railroad ballast in 1847. Local Boy Scout groups erected a metal picture on the bluff face in the 1980s.

26. In the 1880s there was a central Illinois man named James Strang who bought huge sections of land and raised cattle. His holdings became so extensive that an 1882 issue of Harper's Magazine did a story on him. The article referred to him as a man with eccentric ideas and called him "**An American King**."

27. John Allen says the most notable "witch" of southern Illinois was **Eva Locker** who lived on David Prairie in Williamson County. Witches are said to be human beings who have made a pact with the devil in return for super-natural powers. A woman was said to become a witch by drawing her own blood and then making a pact with the devil by dedicating it to him. Eva cast spells on those she disliked, causing them to suffer a variety of maladies that ranged from warts, boils, uncontrollable twitching, and fits. She could milk the cows of her neighbors by merely hanging a towel on a rack in her kitchen. Five minutes later she would twist it and wring the milk into a bucket.

Charlie Lee of Hamilton County became a noted witch-master, called upon to nullify witches' spells.

28. The Native-Americans of southern Illinois, dating back 10,000 years, have left their mark. The "great mound" on old Route 40, on the outskirts of East St. Louis, was the largest man-made structure in America when the Pilgrims landed at Plymouth Rock. Its base is larger than that of the great pyramid of Egypt, and it is the largest earthen structure in the world. It contains 21,690,000 cubic feet of dirt that was carried in buckets by the Indians who built it. When early settlers on the American Bottom (please, the correct term is bottom, not bottoms) asked Indians they encountered about it, they knew nothing of their ancestors who once lived there. They left no written records for us to decipher their history.

1882 sketch of James Jesse Strang, the American King

Due to lack of written records and Native American oral history, archaeologists have long quibbled over certain conclusions drawn about the culture that once existed here.

29. There is a small island in the Mississippi River near **Grand Tower** in Jackson County called Tower Rock. According to an Indian legend, there was a Wyandotte brave who was loved by a Fox Indian maiden. But she told him that she had already been promised by her father to a warrior of the Fox. She climbed Tower Rock and leaped to her death, 100 feet below. Saddened and despondent, her true love followed her in death, making this place known as Lovers Leap.

The Indians in Wisconsin had warned Marquette and Jolliet about the rock, and local natives believed that manitous and demons inhabited the swirling waters. In later years, river pirates pillaged boats in the area and then retreated to their hideout at Sinner's Harbor up the Big Muddy River.

Crime and Punishment in Southern Illinois

Malingering slaves were made to pick and eat the worms feeding on tobacco plants.

Horse thievery - death by hanging

Larceny - tied to a whipping post and given 39 lashes

Disobedient child - jailed until humbled

Negro or mulatto found 10 miles from home without written consent - 10 lashes

Malicious gossip - 3 hours in the stocks

Sheriff guilty of letting a prisoner escape - he serves out the sentence

Selling liquor to Indians - $5.00 fine for each quart sold

Militia service was required of all men between 16 and 60

Negro caught trying to run away - his heel tendons are cut

---

30. At La Belle Fountain, John Milton Moore, the son of James Moore, was born. He was the first English child born in the area. There was a Virginian named Briggs who fought the British with George Rogers Clark and in 1784 settled in Bellefontaine (beautiful spring or fountain) 1/2 mile south of Waterloo (named for the site of Napoleon's defeat). While traveling to Cahokia in 1788, Briggs was captured by Indians. He was taken to a Kickapoo village about 250 miles away. By traditional ceremony and custom, he was adopted into the tribe. He was urged to take an Indian maiden but remained faithful to his wife. Through a French trader, he was able to ransom himself for 107 bucks (deerskins, hence the possible origin of the word buck for a dollar). Ten weeks after his capture, Briggs, given up for dead, returned home. He later became **the first sheriff of St. Clair County**.

31. There was a young man named **Willie Potts** who grew up near Ford's Ferry, not far from Cave-In-Rock. His father owned a tavern near there, and following in his father's footsteps, he began to engage in a career of robbery. He fled the area and plied his trade elsewhere for fear of capture. After a number of

years, older and with a different appearance, he decided to return home. He revealed his true identity to his friends, but when he visited his parents, he decided not to tell them who he was until the next day. The father, long known for his criminal activity, decided to rob the stranger. When they both went outside for a drink of water, he plunged his knife into the man's back.

When Willie's associates came looking for him the next day, the father was horrified to learn that he might have murdered his own son. They dug up the body and looked for a "lucky" birthmark on the shoulder, in the shape of a 4-leaf clover. The parents found the mark **just above the spot where the knife went in his back**.

Baptist church at New Design, built in 1832

32. A historic marker exists in **Vandalia**, Illinois, marking that city as the western terminus of the great **National Road** that started from Cumberland, Maryland, and was to end at either Alton or Illinois Town (East St. Louis). The government ran out of funds, so the road ended at Vandalia, which was then the state capital. It was also known as the Cumberland Road and the Great Western Mail Route. The road was authorized in 1806 by President Jefferson. A large statue was placed at the end of the road in 1928. It was called the **Madonna of the Trail**, and it shows a woman walking forward with a babe in arms and a child clinging to her skirts. The 18 ft. high statue was erected by the D.A.R. and is on the old statehouse lawn.

The powerful Wiggins Ferry in East St. Louis convinced the state legislature to appropriate funds to extend the road from **Vandalia** to **East St. Louis**.

33. There was a tavern built along Highway 50 in Marion County called the **Halfway House**, because it marked the midpoint between Vincennes and St. Louis. It was built in 1818, and meals were about 25 cents, and lodging was 12 and 1/2 cents.

34. The settlement of **New Design** was founded on the bluffs in **Monroe County** in 1782 by a Virginian. In 1783 John Seeley settled in New Design and started the **first school in Illinois**. Reverend James Smith came from Kentucky to preach at New Design in 1787. Four people were baptized in nearby Fountaine Creek. In 1796 the Rev. David Badgley started the **first Baptist church in Illinois** at New Design.

35. One of only eight remaining **covered bridges** in the state has been restored in Randolph County. It was opened in 1854 and was built by the Randolph County Plank Road Company. The bridge itself was built by Wilhelm Misselhorn, a professional builder from Germany. He was the grandfather of Roscoe Misselhorn, the famous artist. It rests on stone piers and crosses Mary's River on a road that connected **Chester** and **Sparta**. Although it is the only covered bridge in southern Illinois, most observers agree that it is the most photogenic, often being used on Christmas cards.

Covered bridges protected the floor timbers from rot and kept horses calm because they could not see the water below. At one time, Illinois had 132 covered structures.

Plank roads were constructed of 8 ft. long boards that were four inches thick and ten inches wide. They should not be confused with earlier corduroyed roads that were merely logs laid side by side.

36. Tobacco is no longer a significant crop in Illinois, but at one time the state ranked third among all states in production behind Virginia and Kentucky. The Illinois Indians raised tobacco, but used it only for religious and ceremonial use. They never smoked for pleasure until the white man came. Tobacco in early times was thought to have special value for curing rheumatism and removing warts. Tobacco was part of Indian mythology for they believed that when one of their members died, his spirit was helped on its journey to the "Happy Hunting Grounds" by a sufficient amount of smoking. It turned out that the variety of tobacco native to Illinois was not the type that the settlers enjoyed. They preferred leaves from Kentucky and Virginia plants.

Shop interior at the Rock Island Arsenal showing 75mm. cannon

37. During World War I the Rock Island Arsenal, between Moline, Illinois and Davenport, Iowa, was reactivated. The armory shops were opened again in the autumn of 1916 to produce rifles for the allies. In 1917, when the U.S. entered the war, the arsenal's orders multiplied. The French 75 mm. cannon recuperator was produced at the arsenal with the help of French advisors. By the end of the war, 20,000 different war items were produced. These included artillery cartridges, artillery vehicles, and .30 caliber rifles. Approximately $90 million was spent at the arsenal for war production. In July of 1916 there had been 2,263 employees there but that expanded to 13,263 by war's end.

The war was particularly hard on the large Illinois German-American population whose loyalty was questioned. Anything that smacked of German heritage was looked down on. Streets with German names were changed. Enrollment in German languages classes fell off dramatically in high schools. Shakespeare was taught in literature rather than Schiller. Conductors avoided playing pieces by Bach and Beethoven at concerts. Sauerkraut was referred to as "Liberty Cabbage" and dachshunds (badger dogs) were called "liberty pups." In **Belleville**, the Deutsch-Amerikanischer Bund put out a loyalty to the U.S. statement. The Belleville Turnverein (athletic club) Americanized the name of their organization and began calling themselves Turners.

38. **Alton** was the home of the **tallest man who ever lived (8' 11.1," 490 lbs., 44 1/2 AA shoe)**. **Robert Wadlow** was about a foot and a half taller than Kareem Abdul Jabbar, and he was nicknamed the "Gentle Giant." His height was a quirk of nature because everyone else in his family was "normal" size. He made many special public appearances, and these events helped pay for his medical and clothing expenses which were huge because everything had to be tailor made. He had to be fitted with special braces on his legs so that he could walk. A graduate of Alton High School, he died at the age of twenty-two in 1940 from blood poisoning in an infected blister that was made by his braces. He weighed 491 pounds when he died and was buried in a ten-foot coffin that took 12 pallbearers to carry. A life-size statue of him is in Alton on College Ave. across from the old Shurtleff College.

39. **Billy Bryan** was a railroad man in the tradition of Casey Jones. Like Jones, he also worked for the Illinois Central. He was a conductor on the Mudline Branch that ran diagonally from Johnston City to the Mississippi River Bridge at Cape Girardeau. He supposedly started off each day with fifteen shots of Egyptian corn whiskey. A gregarious man, he became a legend with passengers and was known for regularly bending the rules to accommodate those he served. The company wanted to fire him but knew they couldn't because of his popularity. He retired in 1909 on the eve of his 70th birthday.

The Liberty Bell of the West

40. In 1845 one of Vital Jarrot's slaves sued for his freedom. **Lyman Trumbull** represented the slave in the case of **Jarrot v. Jarrot**. Trumbull successfully argued that the slave should be free because slavery had been forbidden in Illinois by the Northwest Ordinance of 1787. This case ended slavery in Illinois. Trumbull, the senator from Illinois after the Civil War (he lived in Alton from 1855-73), was the author of the **13th Amendment** to the U.S. Constitution, outlawing slavery.

Vital Jarrot, who briefly served as mayor of Illinoistown/East St. Louis, was ruined by the Panic of 1873. Destitute, he traveled to South Dakota, lured there by General Custer's tales of gold. He found no gold, fell ill of fever, and died at the age of seventy-one.

41. No person living in southern Illinois has likely ever seen a **passenger pigeon** in the wild. Ornithologists estimate that their numbers once reached five billion in America. They thrived in this region on insects, seeds, berries, acorns and beech nuts. Smooth and graceful in flight, writers often referred to them as "blue meteors." James Audubon, the French naturalist, reported seeing millions of them in one flight in southern Illinois.

42. **Chatsworth** had a large beet factory for producing sugar back in 1863. It was on a plot of 104 acres purchased by Jacob Bunn of **Springfield**. Its 225-foot high chimney was the tallest in the state and the factory drew many visitors. There were about 550 employees who worked in the field and in the factory. The beets were washed and then crushed. The pulp became fodder for cattle, and the liquid contained the sugar. Fifty tons of sugar was produced the first season. In 1872 the factory moved to **Freeport** because of poor soil and water shortages in Chatsworth. Chatsworth subsoil was blue, flat clay and contained large amounts of potassium nitrate (saltpeter). The venture closed in 1876.

43. The most famous bell in southern Illinois is the **"Liberty Bell of the West."** It was sent in 1743 by Louis 15th to the Church of the Immaculate Conception in **Kaskaskia**. It was pulled by raft up the Mississippi River from the port of New Orleans. It was the first church bell west of the Appalachians. When George Rogers Clark captured Kaskaskia in 1778, the bell proclaimed the news and thus acquired its name. The bell is 11 years older than the Liberty Bell in Philadelphia, and it is inscribed with the French word for 'liberty.'

Jacob Bunn (German) of Springfield

44, The oldest *Protestant* bell came into use in 1830 at **Vandalia** in a Presbyterian church.

45. There is a Spanish bell, presumably cast in the 8th century, in the chapel at **McKendree College in Lebanon**. It came from an old mission in Santa Fe, New Mexico, and was brought to the Illinois State Fair in 1858. **President Cobleigh** was taken with the heirloom and purchased it for the college after the fair was ended. Mounted in a relatively new tower, the bell has been deemed the **oldest in the nation**.

46. Two notable **Belleville** buildings include Saint Peter's Cathedral, built in 1837 (the largest in Illinois), and the national Shrine of Our Lady of the Snows on Route 15. This is the **world's largest outdoor Catholic shrine**.

47. Carlyle Lake is the largest man-made lake in the state of Illinois.

Carterville's David Wallace was the man who introduced the idea of taking canaries into mines to check for deadly pockets of gas.

48. The **G.S. Suppiger Company**, tomato canning factory and maker of Brooks (tangy) Catsup, had facilities at 800 South Morrison. The company went out of business in the early 1960s but left a 77-foot high water tower on a 100 foot base (built in 1950) that began rusting away. A few years ago, a preservation committee was formed and $75,000 was raised to pay for repainting. It is now a landmark and is recognized by Guinness as the **world's largest catsup bottle**.

49. After the turn of the century, a St. Louis newspaper reported the death of the last carrier pigeon in captivity in a zoological garden in Cincinnati. The last killing of one in the wild occurred at Wisconsin in 1899.

Millions of the birds were trapped or killed and sent to large cities for consumption. They frequently were slaughtered at live trap shoots. They were trapped or destroyed in large numbers at roosting places or nesting grounds. Sulfur fumes were used to kill them at roosting places. They were captured at their nesting places through the use of a **stool pigeon** whose eyes had been sewn shut.

50. The world's tallest fountain is located on the riverfront in East St. Louis. Across from the St. Louis Arch, the Gateway Geyser was completed in the 1990s and shoots an incredible 627' high. There is a reflecting poll surrounding it that has four other jets that shoot streams of water 100' high.

51. In 1990-91 coach Tom Pile's **Edwardsville** High baseball team won an incredible 64 games in a row, the second longest winning streak in the nation.

52. In 1907 Granite City's Corn Refining Products Company began making world-famous **Karo Syrup**.

53. Old Stone Face, on Eagle Mountain in the Garden of the Gods near Harrisburg is said to resemble 1930s/40s actor Wallace Beery.

54. **Sand Cave** in southern Illinois is the largest sandstone cave in North America.

55. Once there was a great Pawnee chief named Oronoo. The only Indian who was taller or more accurate with a bow than he was a beautiful Indian maiden named **Kishwaukee**. She wanted to marry Oronoo, but his heart yearned for a maiden of a different tribe, although Kishwaukee did not know this.

Eventually Kishwaukee discovered that Oronoo's true love was the daughter of an elderly chief whom she had married. Jealous Kishwaukee then told her husband that his daughter was aiding his enemies (the Pawnee) and was hatching a plot to kill Kishwaukee. The chief believed his wife and made his daughter drink poison. But she was so pure in heart the poison had no effect on her. Soon afterward, the chief's daughter married Oronoo of the Pawnees. One night, when the chief and Kishwaukee were alone, she stabbed and scalped him.

In the morning she fled to the Pawnee village and told Oronoo what she had done. Instead of killing her for her deed, the Pawnee medicine man placed a curse on her. "She shall still live till the Pawnee leave their hunting grounds . . . the cursed of the Great Spirit and the terror and warning of all who look upon her. The fire that sweeps the prairie shall surround, but not consume her; the hurricane that uproots the forest shall lightly pass her by; and the lightning shall leave her unscathed. But before this unending life begins, she must suffer an agonizing death!"

When Kishwaukee heard this curse she went screaming to a nearby stream, threw herself in and drowned. She sank to the bottom of the stream that today bears her name.

On the exact spot where she stood when her doom was pronounced, there soon appeared an ash tree that in many ways resembled her strong figure and form. The Indians believed it was Kishwaukee reincarnated. Their belief was strengthened by the fact that during subsequent prairie fires the flames always seemed to miss the tree. Tornadoes that roared through the area did likewise.

56. If maps of Illinois in 1787 already showed a grid of parallels of latitude and meridians of longitude, why was it necessary to establish principal meridians and base lines to sell property at land offices? Jeff Pauk of **Edwardsville** says it was to give cardinal reference points so surveyors could be exact. Although parallels and meridians existed back then, the technology simply didn't allow for surveyors to determine their exact locations. They faced the same problem when it came to determining elevation. That is why most cities posted an elevation datum mark at a prominent place in town. It became a reference point used by all surveyors for determining local elevations.

Gateway geyser at East St. Louis

57. Weaving and clothmaking were forbidden by law in French Illinois. Colonies were not supposed to compete with cloth-makers back in France. All cloth had to be purchased from the king's storehouse or from merchants who brought it up the river from New Orleans.

58. What was the disease known as *ague*? The American Bottom, the flat alluvium stretching from Alton to Chester was considered by many to be an unhealthy place. Ague was the name doctors gave to a strange fever that often beset settlers. It was thought that the swampy area with rotting vegetation and a noxious gas that created a miasma. It wasn't until many years later that the cause of the malaria-like problem was caused by mosquitoes.

Natural Bridge at Pomona (courtesy Illinois Dept. Tourism)

59. McKinley Kantor, acclaimed author of *Andersonville*, used the **Herrin** shootout between S. Glenn Young and Ora Thomas as the basis for a short story. However, its local was in the far west.

60. A lady from **Carterville** was asked by the Bush White House to make a Christmas ornament based on some historic structure in the state. One artisan from each of the 50 states was asked to do a similar task to help decorate the 2001 Christmas tree. The ornament she chose was the **Pierre Menard Home at Kaskaskia**. It is a good example of architecture brought up from New Orleans by the French with its dormered attic and columned porch sweeping the length of the house.

61. Brian **Shipp**, a student at SIUE remembers competing against **Jason Isringhausen** when they were both in high school. Jason is considered one of the premier relief pitchers in the game with 73 "saves" over the last two seasons. Ship attended Southwestern High. It is about 40-45 minutes south of Springfield. Jason hails from **Brighton,** and he was signed by the St. Louis Cardinals last year when he became a free agent. In 2001 Jason had 34 saves in 43 chances and a 2.65 earned run average.

62. **Granite City** was home to a man who became a famous criminologist with the FBI. His name is **Clinton Van Vanzant** who currently lives near Fredericksburg, Virginia, and he is one of America's foremost criminal profilers. He has been on Larry King's CNN prime time talk show numerous times. His house has heavy security and is surrounded by an electric fence and surveillance cameras.

63. Some people think that the **House of Plenty Restaurant** in Highland is haunted. Located in an 1890s Victorian mansion on 9th Street in Highland, the place was once owned by a certain Tim Gruaz who ran a business selling steamship tickets to places in Europe. Many of the people in Highland were of Swiss descent, and it was common for those who had money to visit their native land on summer voyages. There was a bon-voyage dinner celebration at the house for one couple planning to take such a tour. Unfortunately the ship sank and everyone on board perished.

Judy and Ken Ernst, who formerly were in the bakery business, have turned the place into a popular restaurant. They and their children have reported strange goings-on at the place. Some think the place is inhabited by a friendly ghost.

Giant City State Park at Makanda (courtesy Ill. Dept. Tourism)

64. In **Edwardsville there** is the area known as Hexabuchel. Hexabuchel translates to **"witches back,"** and it is at the north end of town by Old Alton Road and 2nd Street. It is believed the name came from a woman who once lived there who was thought to have the power to cast spells on people.

The **Riverbend region** of southern Illinois is that part of the state from Grafton to East St. Louis, from Calhoun to St. Clair County, where the Mississippi River bends or bulges in an eastward direction. It is considered to be one of the most haunted sections of Illinois. Alton is bedeviled by spirits for numerous reasons. Elijah Lovejoy, the abolitionist newspaper editor was murdered there in 1837. Over 1,000 Confederate prisoners died there during the Civil War. Pirate Jean LaFitte, the man who helped Andrew Jackson win the Battle of New Orleans, is said to be buried along the Mississippi near there. And the spirits of Native Americans who were devoured by the Piasa monster remain along the bluffs where they met their untimely demise.

The ghost of **Robert Prager**, who was lynched for repeatedly making unpatriotic remarks during World War I, walks the streets of Collinsville. Belleville is beset with a similar problem due to **angry citizens lynching David Wyatt**, a black man who had shot and killed the County Superintendent of Schools for refusing to renew his teaching certificate.

It is said that late-night screaming can occasionally be heard just west of the Casino Queen and near the downtown section of East St. Louis. It was here that a bloody riot took place in 1917, killing 9 whites and 39 Negroes.

Cahokia residents have reported the ghostly apparition of a slave who was executed in colonial times for casting spells on white French settlers.

It has been said that Elijah Lovejoy's murder placed a curse on the city of **Alton**. Before his death, Alton was the most important town in this part of the state. City fathers had high hopes it would someday rival St. Louis. It was a center of culture and learning. Intellectuals left the city. Plans to have railroads go through Alton collapsed. A financial panic ensued, and land and property values plummeted. The city was widely condemned in newspapers around the country. Lovejoy's murderers were never brought to justice. The National Road, which was planned to end at Alton, went farther south and stopped at the water's edge in East St. Louis.

65. The **Blue Pool** is an area similar to the **Bermuda Triangle,** but it is on the Mississippi just north of Alton. It is legendary for its depth and in earlier, more superstitious times was said to be bottomless. There have been so many fatal swimming and boating accidents at the Pool that locals claim it to be haunted.

Troy Taylor is president of the American Ghost Society and has written numerous books including *Haunted Alton* and *Haunted Illinois* and *Haunted Decatur*. His Illinois book covers ghost stories from Cairo to Chicago. He and his wife Amy run the Riverboat Molly's Bookstore on 515 Third Street in Alton (618-465-1086). Their Internet web page is www.prairieghosts.com.

66. How did Rudolph Wanderone acquire the nickname **Minnesota Fats**? Wanderone was born in New York and was sometimes called New York Fats. When Hollywood made the movie *The Hustler*, the Jackie Gleason character was given the sobriquet **Minnesota Fats** because it had a good sound to it. Fats lived with his wife Evelyn in Dowell for over 40 years. The George Jansco family were promoters who owned Jansco Showbar – now Hurley's Show Bar Tavern (near Interstate 57), where Fats played. The film *Baltimore Bullet,* starring James Coburn, was about professional pool tournaments held in Johnston City.

67. How did the river affect architecture in Alton? Many of the homes on the bluffs overlooking the Mississippi had Belvederes which were similar to the **Widow's Walk** found on homes in Massachusetts and Rhode Island. River towns up north such as **Quincy** and **Savanna** have similar architecture.

DuQuoin Fair (courtesy Ill. Dept. of Tourism)

68. Where is the **mysterious "vortex"** alleged to exist by numerous people in southern Illinois? According to **Brian DeNeal** it is at Max Creek between **Tunnel Hill** and **Vienna**. Hikers on the River-to-River Trail claim to have experienced strange phenomena when trekking by the meandering creek. Those affected by the vortex claim to have suffered fainting spells, headaches, and pressure in their heads causing earaches. Some believe that there is an unusual magnetic force in the area that has mystical healing powers, curing maladies such as backache and rheumatism.

69. Where is the 35-foot cast bronze statue of the Good Shepherd? The statue shows Christ holding a lamb, and it is at San Damiano (St. Damien) retreat center on the Ohio River in Pope County. This 200-acre retreat is about 10 miles east of **Golconda**, 2 miles south of the intersection of Illinois Routes 146 and 34. The 26 cottages and Tuscan style conference center are in the beautiful Shawnee National Forest. It opened in 1992. Phone: (618) 285-3507.

70. Johnny Bob Harrell was a self-styled militia leader/anti-Communist in **Louisville** (pronounced Lewisville) Illinios, not far from **Flora** and **Olney**. His home (a 24 room estate) was modeled after George Washington's Mount Vernon. In 1961 130 FBI agents raided his property. He was arrested and charged with harboring a Marine deserter. Harrell jumped bail and failed to appear for his 1963 trial. Harrell also got into trouble for withdrawing his children from public school. Survivalist training sessions were held on his property every June. The basement of the home was said to be connected to a series of hidden passages. His conservative followers numbered around 25,000, and they eagerly awaited his monthly newsletter.

71. What led to Boy Scout camp Warren Levis, near **Godfrey**, Illinois, being recognized by the National Park Service? The 287-acre camp used to be part of the Underground Railroad for escaped slaves. Charlotte Johnson did much of the research that led to the recognition. The land back then was owned by the Hawley and Spaulding families. Escaped slaves would swim across the Mississippi River from slave state Missouri or cross the river when it was frozen. The families gave assistance to the slaves helping them to move on to freedom. A.T. Hawley deeded the land to the scouts in 1924.

72. Why did the early American Indians call some creatures Thunderbirds? According to ancient lore and legend of Native Americans there were large birds with curved beaks, sharp talons and very large wingspans. These enormous birds were powerful enough to carry off cats, dogs, goats and even children. They likened the sound of their flapping wings to thunder rolling across the plains hence the name Thunderbird.

73. The southernmost part of Illinois, that region south of Route 50, answers to the name of Egypt. Three of its towns, Thebes, **Cairo** and **Karnak**, were ascribed names that were borrowed from that ancient land along the Nile. But years before these towns were platted, there was another Egyptian name that was prominent in this part of the state. It was the name of Goshen, known to be the Egyptian land of Biblical times where the Israelites lived in captivity before the Exodus.

Old Rose Hotel at Elizabethtown

The name of Goshen was first used to describe a settlement just south of **Edwardsville**. The name was given to the area by the Reverend David Badgley who came there in 1799 looking for a suitable place to settle. He found the place, like that land of old in Egypt, to be fertile and accordingly selected it as a site for a settlement. Badgley is credited with being the first Protestant minister in Illinois.

Badgley was acting as a scout for a group back east and when they read his favorable report they began moving there around 1800. By 1802 it became known as the Goshen settlement. It remained an unusual place for it never incorporated as a village. A church organization of the Methodist persuasion was established there and was accepted into the Western Kentucky Conference, along with others from Shiloh, Wood River, New Design, and Kaskaskia, in 1803.

Bald Cypress in the Cache River Wetlands (courtesy Illinois Department of Tourism)

It is thought that the Goshen group erected the first Methodist building in the state in 1806. A camp meeting was held on "Mr. Good's" property in 1807. These services were presided over by Reverend William McKendree, of later McKendree College fame.

John Reynolds, who later became governor, lived at the settlement from about 1807 until the close of the War of 1812. During the war a company of Rangers were recruited from Goshen and other nearby settlements, and a blockhouse, protected by a wooden stockade, was constructed and named **Fort Russell**. Munitions were stored there, and several expeditions against the Peoria tribes to the north were launched from the fort. Captain William Whiteside, a prominent leader in the Indian campaigns, was stationed there.

In 1818 an effort was made to raise money by a lottery. Notices were posted in Kaskaskia and St. Louis newspapers that the offered prize was 100 Merino sheep at Goshen.

Another indication that this was an important early settlement is the fact that the Goshen Road was named for it. This road started at the United States Salines (saltworks), near **Shawneetown**, and traversed in a northwesterly direction to Edwardsville. It is one of the very few roads indicated on early government maps. Later maps used by the Post Office Department also show the road.

The reason for the road's early importance was due to the nature of early river travel. People trying to reach the area flatboated down the Ohio River and landed at Shawneetown. If they wanted to go to Kaskaskia, Goshen, or St. Louis, they cut across the state by land because no steamboats yet plied the Ohio or Mississippi Rivers. Keelboats could be shoved upstream with long poles, but the progress was a discouraging one-mile per hour. Flatboats were usually dismantled for lumber at the end of a voyage. The road went through or near such places as **Eldorado, Galatia, Frankfort** (now West Frankfort), Mt. Vernon, Carlyle, Silver Creek, and then Edwardsville. The road was later extended to Alton. The road passed through numerous other villages, but most of these have been gone for more than a century. Little is left to mark the old Goshen Road except a historical marker between the towns of **Edwardsville** and **Glen Carbon**. There is a sandstone marker near the old road in Hamilton County that marks the grave of Peter Cartwright's daughter, killed by a falling tree as the family moved into southern Illinois. Peter Cartwright is remembered as a renown Methodist circuit rider.

JOHNSON COUNTY – A profile of one of Illinois' 102 counties

Tunnel Hill in Johnson County (Ill. Dept. Tour.)

Johnson County's first government, is that theoretically, was of England under King James I. When he granted the London Company title to Virginia with a charter that extended from the Atlantic to the Pacific Ocean. In 1682 LaSalle claimed the Mississippi valley and called it Louisiana for King Louis XIV. What came to be called Illinois country was part of what was known as Upper Louisiana. The French tried to maintain their hold on Illinois country by settlement but lost out to the British in the French and Indian War, ended by the Treaty of Paris, 1763. After we declared our independence in 1776, we reverted to being part of Virginia. But Virginia ceded the territory to the new federal government in 1779, and in 1784 we became part of the Great Northwest Territory. Johnson County was organized from Randolph County in 1812. It is watered by the Cache and Big Bay Creeks. It is on about the same latitude as Richmond, Virginia. Other counties were created out of Johnson County. Union County was created from its land in 1818. In 1843 Johnson County was reduced to its present size by the creation of Massac and Pulaski Counties, making it one of the smallest counties in the state. It is also one of the most hilly sections of the state. The Ozark Ridge is really part of the foothills of the Ozark Mountains. These cliffs, made of sandstone, limestone and shale, offer spectacular scenic vistas and great spots for hiking and picnicking.

Memphis silt loam, Yazoo clay (found near the Cache River) and Waverly silt loam are the most common soils of the county. The average rainfall is a little over 40 inches.

The county was named in honor of Richard M. Johnson, a native of Kentucky and a friend of Governor Edwards, who was also from that state. During the War of 1812, at the battle of Thames, Colonel Johnson was credited with killing Tecumseh, the great Indian chief. He was a Jacksonian Democrat and became vice-president under Martin Van Buren in 1836.

Farming and cattle raising were the main pursuits in the county's early years. Hereford, Angus and Shorthorn were raised for beef. Truck farming became popular in areas along the Chicago and Eastern Illinois after its arrival. As late as 1923, the county had no significant factories or mines as was common in other counties. For a while, charcoal was produced in clay ovens at Belknap.

Goreville had a cannery. Some surface coal was mined at Burnside. White Hill had a stone quarry that produced 7,000 tons a day in 1913. Charles Marshall, of Belknap Township, owned the largest farm in 1923, consisting of 2,810 acres. The Belknap Drainage System was organized in 1903. This levee system protected about 6,000 acres of land and extended from Old Foreman to Rago. The Cache River Drainage System was organized in 1911 and includes 4 other counties. The bald cypress trees of the Cache River wetlands are the **oldest living things east of the Mississippi**. Forty percent of the state's endangered species live in these swamps, depicted in the Tommy Lee Jones movie, *U.S. Marshals*.

The Cairo & Vincennes Railroad, whose president was A.E. Burnside of Civil War fame, arrived in 1872. It ran diagonally from the northeast corner of the county to the southwest corner. It later merged with the Big Four or New York Central. The St. Louis, Alton and Terre Haute entered the county in 1888 and went all the way to Paducah. It later became part of the Illinois Central. The Burlington railroad entered the county in 1910.

Pounds Hollow in the Shawnee National Forest (courtesy Mike Coles)

The county's first courthouse was in the home of John Bradshaw, at or near Elvira. Territorial law called for courthouses to be located near the center of each county. In 1818 the county seat was moved to Vienna. The current courthouse was built in 1868. A brick jail was erected in 1887. Most places stopped placing debtors in jail around 1800, but as late as 1816 Johnson County impounded Peter Prow and Catherine Price for debt.

Tavern rates were regulated by law in 1828. Lodging was 13 cents, and meals were twenty-five cents.

The ox was the first animal to be used for draft purposes. The horse came later. George Elkins, born in the county in 1825, says he did not see a wagon and a team of horses until he was 21.

One of the reasons corn was converted to whiskey by so many people is that it brought a better price and was cheaper to transport. Equality was the only place to obtain salt and usually a farmer made a trip to buy enough to last all year and quite often brought back enough to sell to a few neighbors.

Early settlers made their own light by using grease lamps. These consisted of cotton wicks immersed in a vessel full of grease leaving one end of the wick high enough out of the grease to burn. These were eventually replaced by tin molds for making tallow candles and these, in turn, were replaced by oil lamps with protective hurricane glass.

Vienna was the site of a number of agricultural fairs, but in the 1880s the Fair Associations lost money and they had to be abandoned, only to be revived a few years later by a new group. The first aeroplane to visit the county landed at the Vienna Fair in 1912. Back then it was called a flying machine.

Fox hunting was long a favorite sport but, unlike England, the fox was not killed.

Vienna did not get a township high school until 1919. The library was built in 1911 with the assist of a $5,000 donation from the Andrew Carnegie Founda-tion.

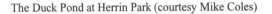
The Duck Pond at Herrin Park (courtesy Mike Coles)

The town of **Wartrace** used to be known as Grantsburg. It is said to have taken its name from the hanging of a horse thief by a mob. It happened shortly after the Civil War, and it was hoped that this would be the last trace of war in the area.

Long one of the most isolated sections of Egypt, it includes: **Vienna*** (Trail of Tears Memorial Park), West Vienna, Belknap, Grantsburg (named for President Grant), Ganntown, **New Burnside** (named for General A.E. Burnside), Ozark, Tunnel Hill, **Goreville** (named for settler John Gore), **Bloomfield, Reevesville, Cypress, Castle Rock**, the Devil's Stairway at Ferne Clyffe, Big

Bay Creek, Dutchman Lake at Vienna and the Vienna Correctional Center and Lake Egypt. The Triple T Cedar Lake Ranch near Vienna has 180 campsites (695-2600).

Tunnel Hill is a village at the head of a short tunnel owned by the Big 4 Railroad. Cypress took its name from the tall cypress trees on the Cache bottomland. Ozark was a main shipping point for fruit grown in the county, and a large warehouse was located there. **Vienna**, like Chicago, started out as an Indian trading post. The town was either named for the capital of Austria or the wife of Frank Hayward, who married Vienna Reynolds in 1841. In 1939 Vienna's population was only 874 people.

Illinois State Hospital at Anna (Bruce and Lori Eisenhauer)

Apple orchards became prevalent in the county and Heaton Brothers apples from **New Burnside** won a gold medal at the St. Louis Worlds Fair of 1904.

It has been said that John C. Freemont, the Republican candidate for president in 1856, only received two votes from Johnson County - Merida Spencer and H.M. Ridenhower. It was considered to be a terrible disgrace in those days to be a Republican. There were 3,583 men from Illinois drafted during the Civil War, but none of them were from southern Illinois. Johnson County had 1,426 volunteers.

The Cairo & Vincennes Railroad constructed a line in the county in 1871-72. The St. Louis, Alton & Terre Haute came through the county in 1888-89. By 1910 the Chicago & Eastern Illinois and the Burlington had arrived.

A neighborhood known as **Hell's Neck** was home to an 1898 feud between two clannish families, the Arnetts and Stanleys. This heated conflict cost several people their lives.

Ralph Chapman, a Johnson County product, was named captain of the University of Illinois football squad in 1913.

There were few "coloreds" living in Johnson County until 1923. Many of them came up from the South to assist in the new industry of raising cotton.

The small town of **Ozark** was on the Illinois Central branch of the railroad line from **Carbondale** to Paducah and is on the very top of the main ridge of the Illinois Ozarks.

Near **Cypress** there is a place called **Bun's Cave** where hoboes used to hang out during the Depression.

Goreville is the site of **Ferne Clyffe** State Park that contains the area's largest shelter bluff.

Nearby is Indian Bluff, the place where George Rogers Clark camped overnight on his march from Massac to Kaskaskia.

Heron Pond is a nature preserve owned by the state of Illinois. It is located off Belknap Road, south from Vienna on Route 45. There is a walking path about a mile long into a cypress swamp that was formed at the end of the Pleistocene Period. It was the southernmost point to which the great sheet of ice advanced in southern Illinois. It looks like an exact replica of the Florida Everglades except there are no alligators.

The Cache River State Natural Area, near **Belknap**, boasts a 1,000 plus year-old bald cypress tree, the **state champion** at +40 feet in circumference.

The home of **Paul Powell**, the state politician who died in 1970, is on display on Vine Street in **Vienna**. It is not far from Courthouse Square. His first wife was killed in the devastating tornado that hit **West Frankfort** in 1925. The office in his home is filled with political memorabilia.

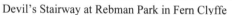

Devil's Stairway at Rebman Park in Fern Clyffe

OIL IN ILLINOIS

Marion Hubbert, of the University of Chicago, once explained that oil and natural gas in Illinois are found in pools or it is trapped in porous sedimentary rocks, originating from layer after layer of decomposed marine life dating back many millions of years. This conversion process is believed to have taken as long as 300 million years.

Interestingly, there is one scientist of note (Immanuel Velikovsky) who theorizes that our petrochemicals are a result of some ancient cosmic storm eons ago, and the earth soaked up the gooey matter, acting much like a giant sponge.

Gas production first began in the state in 1853 when marsh gas was taken from wells drilled near **Champaign**. This gas was produced from rotting vegetation buried under the glacial deposits. In the 1860s, several wells were drilled in Clark County, but commercial production in that area did not begin until some forty years later. In the 1880s natural gas was discovered in the Litchfield area and was being sold for domestic use.

In the early years of searching for oil, water seeped into the wells and caused problems. It was not until the turn of the century that well casing technology solved the problem so that excess water could be drained off. By this time, geologists also discovered that oil and gas collected at anticlines, beneath the crests of uplifted layers of rock. The LaSalle anticline in eastern Illinois became a rich oil producing region around 1904. These discoveries pushed Illinois to third place among states in annual petroleum production. By 1913 the boom years of oil production in Clark, Cumberland, Edgar, Crawford, and Lawrence counties was essentially over. The state's production fell off from 33 million barrels in 1910 to a paltry 5 million in 1936.

The oil economy quickly revived when the new technology of seismic exploration allowed geologists to find hidden anticlines. By 1940 the state's production had risen to 147.6 million barrels a year. Clay, Richmond, Jasper, and Marion counties prospered during this period. Production fell off again after 1940 as finding new sites to replace old ones lagged.

Most people don't usually think of Illinois as a significant oil-producing region, but it has been pumping out crude oil since shortly after the turn of the twentieth century. A map of our oil producing areas looks pretty much like a bunch of scattered dots – some strange kind of psychological Rorschack test. However, most oil well sites are found in the southeastern part of the state in what is known to geologists as the Illinois Basin, centering in Crawford and Jasper Counties. Most prominent are sites along Interstate 64 between **Mount Vernon** and the Indiana border, and just north of the interstate in places like **Fairfield, Oblong** and **Robinson**.

In Illinois the depth of the deposits, or pay zones, varies from 500 feet to about 3,950 feet. From the highway one can see numerous grasshopper pumps rhythmically bobbing up and down, with their upright cylindrical storage tanks somewhere nearby. Sometimes one can also spot what are called "heater treater" structures that are used to separate warmed oil from its accompanying salt water by a simple gravitational process

Old oil well near Mt. Carmel, Wabash County

where the oil, being less dense, rises to the top. The water is pumped down another well, and the oil goes to a storage tank.

Another method of oil extraction is known as water flooding or secondary recovery. In this technique, water is pumped under pressure into the pay zone, where it displaces the oil and pushes it to the pump site. Sometimes it takes as little as 1,000 barrels of water to accomplish this. Detergents can be added to the water to make it easier for the oil to seep through the porous rock. In the most common technique, the five-spot pattern, water is pumped into the reservoir rocks from different spots around the well, making a pattern much like the five spots on a domino. Unfortunately, this method leaves behind over half of the oil reserve.

A terciary method of assisting the extraction process is called hydraulic fracturing. A fluid with the consistency of a milkshake is injected into the reservoir and the pressure is great enough to fracture the rocks around the well. The newly opened fractures make the reservoir rocks more porous, allowing oil to flow more easily into the well area.

Through hydraulic fracturing and water flooding, Illinois oil production rose to about 82 million barrels in 1956. Unfortunately, production in the state has been declining ever since, amounting to only about 12 million barrels annually in recent years.

A more recent extraction technique is the injection of carbon dioxide into areas around the well to push the oil closer to the well.

When a site is prospected for oil, the first thing done is the construction of a drilling rig with a spindletop. The old rigs were wooden structures, and they were left in place after the drilling was completed. Today they are made of metal and are dismantled and reused elsewhere. As the drilling process begins and progress is made through various layers of earth and rock strata, core samples are taken and analyzed. As the well progresses, a 4-6 inch casing is inserted into the drilled area. When it is believed that oil has been found, a smaller pipe is inserted inside the casing, and an explosive charge called a Go-Devil is lowered to the bottom. This explosion blows a hole in the side of the casing, allowing crude oil to seep into it.

Whether or not you get what is known as a "gusher" depends on how much pressure is in the strata. If the oil is under strong pressure, they place a choke on the top of the well, and this regulates the flow of gas. Water and gas often come up with the oil as a by-product. In older times, the gas was burned or "flared" off. Nowadays the gas is sent to a compressor where it is converted into a liquid composed of propane, butane, methane and ethane.

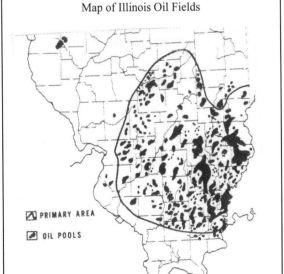

Map of Illinois Oil Fields

PRIMARY AREA

OIL POOLS

The water is often collected and injected back into the ground to help force the oil up the well.

The oil that is pumped out of the ground is sent to a collection tank. The pipe leading from the well to the tank often sits on top of the ground.

When a well penetrates an oil reservoir, it is much like a balloon that gradually begins to deflate. In some large oil fields there is a certain amount of subsidence (sinkage) because of this deflation. A similar phenomenon occurs when extensive coal deposits are removed. Most homeowners who live in an area that is honeycombed with mines take out mine subsidence insurance to protect their investment.

Gary Barber, a Houston, Texas, engineer (formerly of **Edwardsville**) explains that crude oil contains other contaminants such as sulfur, and these are removed during the refining process. Particulate matter in suspension is separated and is converted into asphalt for applying to roads. The term asphalt actually has two meanings. First, it is merely the sludge that exists at the bottom in a normal barrel of crude oil that is pumped from the ground. At room temperature this mixture is nearly a solid. The second definition is the mixture of this sludge with sand and gravel to form a material that is used to build or resurface roads.

Road asphalt is combined with crushed rock and sand for road construction purposes. Refineries also make pitch that is used for roofing tar. The asphalt at the bottom of a barrel can be mixed with diesel fuel to form "bunker fuel" that is used to power ocean going vessels. Ships generally are powered by a special internal com-bustion engine that runs on this heavy fuel.

Let's use a typical well that you might see in a farmer's field off Interstate 64 in Wayne County as an example. Over a 24-hour period the well might produce a minimum of 5 barrels (42 gallons per barrel) a day. That is roughly the break-even point due to electrical costs for the pump motor, and other expenses incurred in the collection and shipping process. The average well produces about 20 barrels a day or 800 gallons. If the going price of crude on the world market is $20 a barrel, that's over $400 a day. Electrical costs per day run about $100.00. The farmer who owns the land receives about one eighth or $50 a day, and the company that installs and maintains the well gets the other $250. Wells around **Mattoon, Taylorville** and **Nashville** generally pump more than 20 barrels a day.

After the **Carlyle** dam was built and the lake created, you saw a lot of oil wells drilled around the perimeter of the lake. That's because all the weight of that water sitting on the lakebed created pressure and placed the oil in the rock strata under greater pressure, making it more economically feasible to drill for oil.

In the old days geologists specifically looked for dome-shaped rock formations because they knew this often meant that oil was trapped in the strata of such a formation. The oil sometimes collects in pools, but it is often trapped in porous rock such as shale or sandstone.

By 1962, oil had replaced coal as the state's most valuable mineral, and it employed some 60,000 people.

Over the years some 150,000 wells have been sunk in Illinois to explore for gas and oil deposits. Oil has been found in 47 counties by 1,200 companies. Oil production in Illinois currently stands at about 11 million barrels of oil a year.

"Down Among the Oilfields" – old poem, author unknown

We're down among the oil fields
Where you never have the blues
Where the bandits steal the jitneys
And the marshals steal the booze
Where the buildings horn the skyline
Where the populace is boost
Where they shoot a man for pastime
Where the chickens never roost.

Where the stickup men are wary
And the bullets fall like hail;
Where each pocket has a pistol
And each pistol's good for jail;
Where they always hang the jury
Where they never hang a man.
If you call a man a liar, you
Get home the best you can.
Where you get up in the morning
In a world of snow and sleet

And you come home in the evening
Suffocating in the heat.
Where the jitneys whiz about you
And the street cars barely creep
Where the burglars pick your pockets
While you "lay me down to sleep"
Where the bulldogs all have rabies
And the rabbits they have fleas,

Where the big girls like the wee ones
Wear their dresses to the knees.
Where you whist out in the morning
Just to give your health a chance
Say "Howdy" to some fellow who
Shoots big holes in your pants.
Where the owls are afraid to hoot
And birds don't dare to sing
For its hell down here in Oil Land
Where they all shoot on the wing.

Karst landforms (Illinois Geological Survey)

THE ROMANCE OF ILLINOIS COAL

Between 1833 and 1925 over one and a half billion tons of coal were removed in Illinois, yet the total amount was estimated only one percent of our coal. With 15 distinct bituminous coal seams, only the state of Pennsylvania has produced more.

Back in the old days when we threw a shovel of coal into the furnace, few of us realized that we were handling a product that had its origins billions of years ago. This was when the surface of the planet was mainly covered with water and swamp land. The climate and conditions were perfect for the growth of carboniferous plants – giant ferns, trees and shrubs. The air buzzed with mammoth insects of infinite variety, while gargantuan beasts (dinosaurs) and reptiles inhabited the waters and land.

Old photo of mule hauling coal in Illinois mine

In the mines of France there have been found in the strata of coal and rock the fossils of many of these species in a splendid state of preservation. These fossils included flies, grasshoppers, roaches, spiders, locusts, and dragonflies – some of which measured nearly two feet from wing tip to wing tip.

It has been estimated that the original amount of coal deposits in the United States exceeded three trillion tons. Of this amount, the original coal deposits in Illinois alone were placed at 18 billion tons. Illinois ranks second only to Pennsylvania in that respect. The first discovery of coal in the U.S. was made in the latter part of the 17th century by explorer Father Hennepin at **Ottawa**, Illinois. In our state, the coal beds were formed when our inland sea receded and Illinois became a great marsh or swamp with luxuriant plant growth. Peat beds were formed after year after year as these plants and formed layer after layer. (Peat is an early stage of coal formation.) There was relatively little earth disturbance, so most of our coal is found in beds that are relatively level.

Coal was discovered in an unusual manner on the American Bottom around 1811 by a group of Monks living on Cahokia Mound. They noticed that in some way a tree near the bluffs took fire, and even its roots burned. The roots kept burning until it was found that the roots reached into a seam of coal, and the coal was on fire. From about 1850 to 1950 about a third of all coal produced by the state was used by the railroads. And for years about half the coal produced has been consumed by the Chicago district.

What many people don't realize is that most seams of coal are only about two and a half to fourteen feet thick. In the early days of mining, for every ton of coal mined, there was about one and a half ton of coal wasted or left in the mines as supporting pillars. Modern methods of mining and improved equipment have greatly reduced this percentage.

There are 3 methods to mining coal in Illinois: the drift, the strip and the shaft.

Where the coal bed outcrops on a hillside or a ravine the drift or slope method is used. A drift mine differs slightly from a slope mine in that the former follows the seam in on a level, while the slope mine is driven downward at an angle from the surface to reach a vein of coal that does not outcrop.

One of the greatest obstacles to mining deep shaft coal is the great amount of water that collects in a mine that has to be continually pumped out. In Illinois alone, more than a billion gallons of water are pumped out of the bituminous mines annually. A general average figures about fifteen tons of water pumped out for every ton of coal mined.

Majestic Coal Company at DuQuoin

Majestic Coal Co., Du Quoin, Ill.—2

Another problem faced by miners was the danger of the roof of a mine collapsing. Timbers were used to shore things up, but many mines chose to spray the underside of a roof with a cement mortar called "gunite." It was sprayed on one to three inches thick with a "gun." Mines that were about 300 or 400 ft. deep had temperatures that hovered around 60 degrees. It was necessary to create numerous air passages in mines to provide adequate ventilation to insure the dilution of poisonous and explosive gases generated by the coal, mine water and explosives. It was common in area mines to use the room and pillar method of mining. The greater the depth of the mine, the closer the natural pillars were spaced. It was not uncommon for the tremendous weight on the pillars to push down on the clay floor causing the floor to heave, a condition known as a "squeeze." If the floor was hard, the pressure on the pillars sometimes caused them to collapse, closing the mine.

Every year the shafts of the mines must be sunk deeper and deeper, as the more accessible veins of coal are worked and exhausted. Pumps for the work cost thousands of dollars each, so there is an enormous investment in this equipment alone. A large force of men, besides those actually employed in mining coal, must always be available to keep mine machinery in repair, as mining operations cannot be interfered with, except in cases of great emergency. Since the mining is done during the day, repairs and maintenance are usually carried out at nights and on Sunday. The water from the mines has such high mineral content that it cannot be used in the boilers at the collieries.

Strip mining, also called open-pit mining, is possible when the seam of coal is an exposed outcrop or close to the surface. The loosened cover or "spoil" can be thrown aside, and large power shovels can be used to load the coal on trucks or railroad cars. When there is no outcrop, the digging must be started by digging a 70 ft. wide ditch next to the seam. This ditch is called a box cut. Surface coal usually has lower sulfur content because of oxidation. In the early years strip mining left ugly scars on the land with a series of furrows with topsoil mixed with subsoil. The state legislature enacted laws requiring mine companies to restore and reforest the land after the coal has been extracted.

Consumption of coal in America reached a peak around 1918 with over 700,000 men employed.

Back in 1915 a large ocean liner, in making a record trip across the Atlantic, used 4,725 tons of coal, enough to keep 945 families in fuel for an entire year. In a single year, one great steamship company paid seven million dollars for the coal necessary to operate its fleet of steamships, or fifty percent more than it paid for provisions for crews and passengers.

Coal was first brought to the East St. Louis area from a mine in the bluffs near a small village named Pittsburg (near present-day Routes 157 and 15. The coal was first hauled by mules and horses along tracks with wooden rails. Pilings had to be driven in Pittsburg Lake (Grand Marais) so that a bridge could be constructed across the body of water. East St. Louis was in a rudimentary stage of development at that time (around 1832), and the coal was delivered to the riverfront. From there it was loaded on Samuel Wiggins' ferryboats and transported across the Mississippi to the city of St. Louis. The railroad fared poorly in its early years because the company overestimated the demand for coal by St. Louis. Wood was still the preferred fuel, even in steam locomotives that came along. But demand for coal slowly increased, and by the 1860s the ten-mile long railroad was the richest dollar-per-mile railroad in the nation. By 1875 coal could be delivered to any part of East St. Louis on a railroad track for six cents a bushel. Manufacturers could buy in bulk at $1.50 a ton.

Coal is not only useful as a household fuel, and in manufacturing, but it also has a number of useful by-products. Here is what one-ton of bituminous (soft) southern Illinois coal will yield: 1500 pounds of coke; 20 gallons of ammonia water; 140 pounds of coal tar. Coal tar, by distillation, will yield 70 pounds of pitch, 17 pounds of creosote; 14 pounds of heavy oils, 9.5 pounds of naphtha yellow, 6.3 pounds of naphthalene, 4.75 pounds naphthol, 2.25 pounds alizarin, 2.4 pounds solvent naphtha, 1.5 pounds phenol, 1.2 pounds aurine, 1.1 pounds anthracite and 0.9 pounds toluene. Coal is also used in the production of perfume, plastics and dyes.

From toluene is obtained the substance known as saccharine, produced by the Monsanto plant near Cahokia and another in St. Louis. Saccharine is 230 times sweeter than sugar. Saccharine was long used for medicinal purposes and in the manufacture of confections.

Southern Illinois coal has a high sulfur content which is a pollutant. Around 1951 St. Louis passed an ordinance banning the use of soft coal and required the use of anthracite coal from places such as Pennsylvania. Other cities followed suit, delivering a crushing blow to the local coal industry.

Back then, there was a general formula used in estimating the amount of coal a family would need to get through a typical southern Illinois winter. Experts generally figured one ton per room per season, plus an extra half-ton. So, on this basis, a typical five-room house would ordinarily require almost six tons of coal. Coal was delivered by truck and emptied into the coal bin of the house, located in the basement. Access was gained by a metal door, usually located in the block foundation. By the early-to-mid 1950s, many homes converted to a stoker. This was a machine with a hopper that was attached to the furnace. Instead of using lump coal, stoker coal was pellet sized and was automatically fed to the furnace by a motor-operated worm screw at the bottom of its hopper. Instead of an ash residue, stoker coal produced "clinkers" which were very abrasive on the hands. By the late 1950s, many homes converted again, this time to natural gas. Old coal furnaces were often retrofitted with gas burners.

William Rend (Rend Lake) who operated coal mines along the Big Muddy River

Most of the towns along the bluffs near East St. Louis, Granite City and Alton, owed their prosperity to their coal mines which served industries in those towns along the riverfront. The Glen Carbon area was heavily mined, and the subterranean landscape is honeycombed with mine shafts and connecting tunnels. Many homeowners carry mine subsidence insurance as an addendum to their homeowner's policy for protection. There was an elementary school in Collinsville and a state police station in Maryville that had to be abandoned due to subsidence problems.

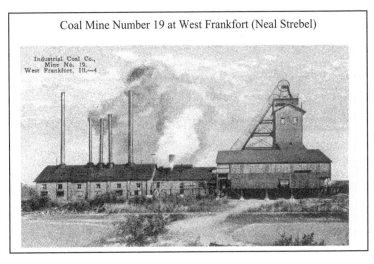

Coal Mine Number 19 at West Frankfort (Neal Strebel)

Most people cannot imagine the huge quantities of coal that are used to produce electricity. Commonwealth Edison had a plant in Kincaid in 1969 that used a conveyor belt to take coal to generators for Chicago electricity. The consumption at this plant back then was 4 million tons a year. That is the equivalent of more than two train loads a day with each train pulling 100 cars containing 50 tons of coal each. The plant has two 500-foot high stacks that are equipped with air-pollution abaters, including electrostatic precipitators that cost $6 million to install. Lake Kincaid, covering 4 square miles and averaging about 13 feet deep, built by damming a creek, supplies water to the steam condensers.

The huge Cahokia Power Plant at East St. Louis, with its set of six huge smokestacks, consumed an almost equal amount of coal for the industrial suburbs across the river from St. Louis in their 1950s heyday.

The artificial gas industry in East St. Louis dates back to 1865 when the East St. Louis Gas and Coke Company was chartered by the state. In 1907 the company was consolidated with Belleville Gas and Electric to form the St. Clair County Gas and Electric Company. By 1950 Illinois Power and Light Company had their gas plant at 2060 Lynch, across from Mepham/C.K. Williams Paint Company. They had a regulating station at 627 North 89th Street. Their offices were at 417 East Missouri Avenue. Union Electric, which generated electricity from burning coal at the Cahokia Power Plant, had their offices in East St. Louis at #7 Collinsville Avenue, next to the Southern Illinois Bank. They built a new office at 5th and Broadway in 1957. For the most part, Illinois Power supplied the city with gas, and Union Electric took care it its electric needs. In both cases, southern Illinois coal was the source of the fuel that was used.

C.H. Quackenbush says that the most common gas used in southern Illinois was coal gas. This was manufactured by placing coal in a superheated clay retort, which was then closed to exclude air. The heated retort freed the volatile or gaseous matter from the coal. These gases were then carried through a series of pipes and appliances which condensed, washed and scrubbed the crude gas, and by mechanical and chemical means removed the impurities from the product and made it ready for the 400 uses which gas is applicable.

A second method of making gas from coal was known as the carbureted method. The gas is manufactured by passing steam through a bed of coal or coke in an incandescent state. The action of the hot fire on the steam passing through it decomposed the steam into hydrogen and oxygen. These gases were united with carbon gases from the fuel bed to create water gas. The mixture in that state had little illuminating value, so it was then passed to another machine where it was mixed with an oil vapor. This whole mixture was then fixed into a permanent gas by contact with superheated fire brick. It was then scrubbed and cleaned in a similar manner as the coal gas. Water gas was often used to enrich coal gas, thereby giving it greater illuminating value.

Gas ball at Ingleside, Illinois (courtesy Neal Strebel)

The distribution of gas from the storage holder was carried on through a system of about sixty miles of cast iron pipe of diameter varying from four to sixteen inches. The flow of gas through mains is similar to water flowing through pipes, but the pressure is much less, being about 1/9 of a pound per square inch. Wrought iron pipes were laid from the main to the consumer's basement at no charge. Contrary to public opinion, gas meters, which measure the amount of use, are very accurate. They cannot register unless gas at that time is passing through it.

"SIXTEEN TONS" – Popular song in the mid-1950s sung by Tennessee Ernie Ford

You load sixteen tons and what do you get?   Another day older and deeper in debt,
Saint Peter don't call me 'cause I can't go,   I owe my soul to the company store.

271

EASTERN EUROPEANS and minorities IN EGYPT

Dr. Stanley Kimball of SIUE has written extensively about Eastern Europeans in southern Illinois. He maintains that Eastern Europeans have played an important role in this part of the state. Theirs is a rich tradition that has largely gone unrecognized. Part of the reason is due to discrimination. The settlers who were already here when they first arrived tended to be Protestant and from Western Europe. They often looked down on the new arrivals who were clannish, spoke a foreign tongue, and were usually Catholic or Eastern Orthodox.

It can be said in general that Eastern Europeans came to this area looking for jobs and a better life for their families. But political freedom and religious and ethnic persecution also played a significant role. When there were pogroms (riots) against Russian Jews, many of them migrated here. The same can be said for persecution by the Ottoman Empire of Armenians and other Christian groups in the Balkans.

There were only a few Slavic, Hungarian, or Lithuanian immigrants in this area before 1875. But as coal mining became a major activity and **Granite City, Madison and East St. Louis** expanded industrially, Eastern Europeans came seeking labor-intensive jobs in factories, steel mills, and packing houses that required little education. They established ethnic enclaves like **Hungary Hollow** in Granite and Goose Hill in East St. Louis near Indian Lake. **Alton** was a magnet in the north, and **Chester** drew them in Southern Illinois.

St. Mary's Greek Orthodox Church at Benld

The decennial census has established that there are over fifty different ethnic groups in Southern Illinois. It would be fair to say that these early immigrants were discriminated against and verbally insulted, especially in the urbanized areas. These groups found themselves the target of epithets such as **Bohunks, Hunkies, Polacks, and Huns**. Some tried to lessen the taunts by Americanizing their names. The letters vich, ski (Polish), or sky (Czech) were occasionally left off the end of a name. Or a Polish name like Zely might become Green.

At coalmines in places such as **Herrin, Benton, West Frankfort, Harrisburg, DuQuoin, Marion**, and **Carterville**, the social economic status could easily be discerned. The owners tended to be old family WASP Americans. The skilled workers came from northwestern Europe, and the lowest paid, unskilled workers were usually from southeastern Europe. Additional tension was created when this new tier of immigrants became drawn to the radical doctrines of bolshevism, socialism and anarchism - especially Bulgarians and Slovenes. To make matters worse, Presidents Lincoln, Garfield and McKinley were assassinated by Catholics.

The **Italians** and Slavs were separated from other townsfolk by language, manners and custom; they had difficulty adjusting to new folkways and mores. Out of sheer necessity, these groups banded together and formed religious and social institutions that helped them survive. They kept their language and traditions alive in parochial schools. They built churches, lodges and music or sports societies. A **Croatian, Czech**, or **Ukrainian** Hall performed a variety of functions and served as a place for weddings, showers, funerals, dances, and benevolent assistance.

Due to the influence of public schools, their children, with each passing generation, became more and more "Americanized." Unfortunately, this caused them to lose contact with their ancient folk heritage. They became less provincial in outlook than their parents, but at the cost of their old world roots.

The **Bulgarians** came to the area late, arriving after 1900 and settling mostly in the three cities of Madison, Granite City and East St. Louis. The first Bulgarian Orthodox Church in America was built in **Granite City**. The unusual quality of the Bulgarians was that they originally were predominantly single males. The *Naroden Glas,* in Granite, was America's first Bulgarian newspaper. Economic improvement came slowly through bootstrap operations. By 1950 Bulgarians owned forty-three businesses in Madison.

A group of southern Slavs, known as the **Croats**, started coming to southern Illinois around 1890, working mostly in the mining and smelting industries. In 1906 they organized the Croatian League of Illinois, which ultimately had over 100 lodges. They also organized several Tamburitzan Orchestras.

The **Czechs**, from Bohemia and Moravia in the old Austro-Hungarian Empire, first arrived in the area in 1851 at Collinsville, and then fanned out. The early Czechs came to rural southern Illinois because they heard about free homesteads to people who settled their families on farms. Immigrants from the later period settled in cities and found jobs on the railroads, packinghouses, steel mills and factories. Many spoke little or no English when they first arrived, so Czech Schools were established to teach adults English and to instruct children in old ways and traditions. Sokol (Czech for falcon) gymnastics classes were organized.

Citizenship classes were taught in the Czech Halls. Czechs built an impressive National Hall in **Edwardsville** in 1906. They formed benevolent societies, Taborite unions and Bohemian societies. In 1933 these societies merged into the Czech Society of America. Their largest settlement was in East St. Louis near the **Stock Yards.** They built SS. Cyril and Methodius Church on 11th Street. When the Nazis took over Czechoslovakia in 1938, the organization formed a Czech Mafia to fight Hitlerism.

Second generation Czechs became merchants, shopkeepers and tradesmen, often building two-story businesses with their homes on the upper level. By the third generation, the Czech young people were fully "Americanized" and often married outside their ethnic enclave. Most knew only a few words and phrases from their original native tongue.

The **Hungarians**, known as the Magyars, came to southern Illinois around 1850, following Louis Kossuth's failed revolution. As previously noted, a large number of them settled in Hungary Hollow in **Granite City**. They were never strong enough to build their own lodge or church in East St. Louis, but about sixty of their families worshipped at St. Elizabeth's, and they were in generous numbers in Washington Park and Fairmont City. Hungarians were tarred with a large brush by established Western European groups as being related to gypsies, who were said to steal little children from their families.

The Baltic **Lithuanians** began arriving in the U.S. around 1860. They were from western Russia and Eastern Germany. Their largest concentration was in East St. Louis near 1509 Baugh where they built their Immaculate Conception Church, first a frame structure, and later a brick one in the old world architectural style. Masses were usually in Latin, except for Sunday morning sermons, which were Lithuanian.

People of **Jewish** extraction have long migrated to southern Illinois from all over the world. Despite a rich heritage chronicled in the Old Testament, they had no country of their own in modern times. Punished for continued rebellion against Roman rule, they were driven out of their homeland after 70 A.D. in what came to be known as the Diaspora (scattering of the Jews).

Known for their resourcefulness and tenacity, they managed to prosper despite universal persecution from Catholics and Protestants. Knights on their way to the Crusades to free the Holy Land from the "infidel" Moslems killed hundreds of Jews in Europe. Ferdinand and Isabella persecuted Jews in Spain. Riots against Jews in Russia were called **Pogroms**. Hitler used the Jews as scapegoats for German defeat in World War I. When he came to power he methodically killed six million of them in the Holocaust.

Southern Illinois, especially East St. Louis, offered avenues of entrepreneurship for Jews, and they quickly mastered the rigors. A uniquely industrious people, they entered professions such as banking, doctoring, lawyering, pharmacology and dentistry. They became very knowledgeable about gold, silver and precious stones and put this adeptness to use in the lucrative jewelry business. They were also very good small company entrepreneurs.

The Jewish people settled first in St. Louis, but large numbers of them were attracted by business opportunities across the river when East St. Louis began to experience its remarkable growth. They built their synagogue in an affluent part of town at 9th and Pennsylvania.

When the Pilgrims landed at Plymouth Rock in 1620, a Greek Eastern Orthodox Church was already established at St. Augustine, Florida. The Orthodox Church took hold in New Orleans during the Civil War. But Greeks first came to this country in large numbers at the turn of the century. Like most Eastern European immigrants, they were attracted to southern Illinois by the existence of labor-intensive jobs. In 1925, under the leadership of William Boudoures, they established a congregation and built a church at 1133 Gaty Avenue in East St. Louis. Around 1951 they moved to a new location at 6900 State Street. The new church had an interesting touch of **Byzantine architecture** with two round domes and arched entryways.

Illinois coal fields that gave minorities opportunities for jobs

Coal Area

Granite City's A.O. Smith Co. that employed many Eastern Europeans

A. O. Smith Corporation Plant, Granite City, Illinois

The **Greek Orthodox** group does not celebrate Easter on the same day as Roman Catholics and Protestants. This is due to their adherence to the old Julian calendar, rather than the Gregorian, for religious purposes. There is a difference of about thirteen days between the two calendars. The Greeks owned many businesses in East St. Louis including: Kimon Tsichlis (Crystal Candy Kitchen), Louis Hages (Toddle Inn), William Boudoures (Majestic Cleaners), John Terris (Thissier's Grill), Bill Lampros (Apollo Restaurant), Charles Terris (Publix Cafeteria), Gus Boukas (G/B Sandwich Shop), Christ Demetrulias (Hermes Candy Company), Harry Kotsiras (Liberty Lunch Room), Bill Millas (Millas Key Club Restaurant), Andy Bisbecos (Candy Andy's Tavern), Nick Anastis (Deluxe Restaurant). This author lives in a subdivision at Glen Carbon developed by Nick Demetrulias, formerly of Cahokia/East St. Louis.

The **Poles** started arriving here in large numbers around 1850 from Polish areas in Germany, Austria and Russia. Illinois has more Poles than any other state except New York, and Chicago has the second biggest concentration of Poles in the world. The largest group that seemed to favor the rural areas was the Poles. In southern Illinois, they settled mainly in **Glen Carbon, DuBoise,**

Belleville, Collinsville, East St. Louis, Nashville, O'Fallon, Madison, Fairmont City and **Posen**. There was a Polacktown section in East St. Louis, and they built St. Adalbert's Church and School on 7th and Summit. In Granite City, they built SS. Cyril and Methodius. The reason there are so many Slavic churches with this name is that they were the two Orthodox priests from Greece who Christianized the Slavs back in the 9th Century. They also invented the Cyrillic alphabet. Washington and Perry Counties have large numbers of Poles who were brought to the area by the Illinois Central Railroad which wanted communities established at various points along the line. The city of **Posen** took its name from the town of Poznan, in western Poland.

There are significant Polish numbers in **DuQuoin, Pinckneyville, Rice, Todd's Mill**, and Ashley (named for John Ashley, an early settler). The Poles have built more churches, lodges and schools than any other Slavic group because they have traditionally been the most loyal Catholics.

In 1874 ten Polish families came to what was first called **Coloma**, Illinois, later changed to **DuBois**. They left Poland to escape persecution imposed by Otto Von Bismarck in what was called the Prussian Kulturkamp. As more families arrived, they decided to build an impressive Catholic cathedral known as St. Charles. Work on the Roman/Byzantine structure was started in 1908. This huge edifice, with magnificent stained glass windows, dominates the rural area with its twin spires that rise 116 feet. The "Cathedral on the Prairie," as it is usually called, is on U.S. highway 51.

Fluorspar mines in Southeastern Illinois employed minorities

The **Russians** came here as early as 1893, emigrating from areas near the Carpathian Mountains. They formed musical groups in **Madison, Benld, Mt. Olive, Livingston (St. Michael's)**, and **Witt**. They built two churches in Benld and two in Madison, and established cemeteries in Edwardsville and **Livingston**.

The Slovaks, from an old part of Hungary, settled here in the 1860s. They were mainly in Madison, East St. Louis, Benld, **Hillsboro, Livingston, Marissa, Mt. Olive, Pana** (Pana was once known as the rose capital of Illinois), **Virden, Granite City,** and **Staunton**. Slovaks are mostly Catholics, but a few are of the Lutheran persuasion.

The **Slovenes** are from western Yugoslavia and didn't migrate here until about 1880. They settled mainly in the coal mining areas of southern Illinois.

The **Ukrainians**, also known as Ruthenians, come from southern Russia and first arrived here around 1880. In Madison they built St. Mary's Catholic Church. They are of the Uniate faith, which means that while they recognize the leadership of Rome, they follow Eastern Orthodox rituals. In 1921 they built a Ukrainian Hall on 9th Street in East St. Louis.

There was a significant **Armenian** population in East St. Louis, and they were noted for running many of the dry cleaning establishments. Armenians came to

The American Steel foundries at Granite City

this country to escape persecution by the Turks. Turks are Moslem while Armenians are Christians who lived in southern Turkey. Armenians are said to be the first people to adopt the Christian faith. The "ian" at the end of many of their names means "son of" and refers to one's father. The Ottoman Turks instituted a purge against the Armenians during World War I, driving them into the Syrian Desert. A number of the Armenians who moved to East St. Louis had been rug merchants in St. Louis. They originally clustered in the area around 15th and Broadway and attended Irving School at 15th and Walnut. Armenian businesses included: Loris Tourijigian (Archie's Tavern), Arnold Maksudian (Eagle Cleaners), Aram Norsegian (Boismenue Cleaners), Harvey Noubarian (East Side Cleaners), Haig Apoian Law Office, Amie Mirzi (Varsity Cleaners) Joe Gashgarian (Lincoln Cleaners) and Caspar Vartanian (Lily Cleaners).

Back in 1957 African-Americans numbered roughly 67,000 out of a population of about a million people in southern Illinois. East St. Louis had about 80,000 people and blacks constituted about forty percent of that number. Segregation confined them to the south end of town. **Brooklyn, Dewmaine, Future City** and **Colp** were southern Illinois towns that were mainly colored towns. African-Americans in the 1940s and '50s often had to endure a harsh poverty that was made easier by a family life with rich and colorful traditions that reached back into the era of slavery.

Shirley Motley Portwood, in her autobiographical *Tell Me a Story*, relates what it was like back then as a child living in Pulaski, Massac, and Alexander counties in extreme southern Illinois. Negroes migrated to this mostly rural tri-county area after the Civil War, and by the turn of the century it had one of the highest concentrations of black population outside the south. They moved here because there were more freedoms in a northern state, but the land and climate similar to the place they had left. Better opportunity was reflected in the fact that quite a large number of blacks owned farmland in Pulaski County.

Blacks in Illinois could vote, while most in southern states had lost that right through intimidation and Jim Crow laws. De facto

The Old Slave House near Equality where slaves were kept

segregation still existed, of course. Portwood states that blacks in **Mound City** went to Lovejoy Grade School and Frederick Douglass High, both segregated. They ate only in black-owned restaurants and sat in the back of the bus and in the balcony of the Roxy Theater in **Mounds**. It wasn't until the mid-50s that they were allowed to live in the dormitories at SIU Carbondale. If they took sick, they were placed in segregated wards at the hospitals. And when they died, they were buried in all-black cemeteries.

She describes a life of hardship and self-doubt for most blacks back then. It was a time of outdoor toilets, wood burning stoves trying to heat four rooms, cardboard in the bottom of one's shoes, and clothes that were patched and mended. Whites had most of the political and economic power and were determined to keep it.

An exceptional black was **Hugo Chambliss** of Mounds who grew prosperous with his Front Street real estate business. Even most of the whites in Little Egypt had little money because southern Illinois, although rich in scenic beauty, was poor compared to the rest of the state. Many of the blacks who worked the farms did so under the status of sharecroppers. Some blacks worked as laborers at places like Bruce's Mill or the Illinois Central Railroad.

Portwood says it was scary to hear about occasional stories of lynchings across the river in Kentucky or Missouri.

Klansmen terrorized Negroes and Catholic immigrants

Children grew up in the fear that something terrible would happen to them if they sassed a white or merely looked them in the eye. And if a black person sold produce or jelly from house to house, they had to knock on the back door of a white person, never the front.

Children pitched in at harvest time with picking and chopping cotton. Adults usually dragged nine-foot long cotton bags behind them while those of children were considerably shorter. It was also possible to earn 50 cents a bushel picking string beans. A few earned money to supplement the family income by sewing and doing house cleaning for white women whose husbands were professionals such as doctors or dentists. But most black women helped with the work and chores on the farms.

African-Americans came to southern Illinois in three great migrations. The first was immediately after the Civil War; the second was at the end of the 1800s when they were brought in as strikebreakers by coal mine owners, and the third was the World War I era to work in the new industries. It is a shame that when the centennial histories of counties and towns are written, the contributions of African-Americans are often overlooked. Their struggles and triumphs, their culture and traditions, deserve to be told and become a part of the American past.

DID YOU KNOW?

1. The **smallest national monument in America** is Tower Rock in the Mississippi River near **Grand Tower**.
2. Illinois is the only state in the union that elects its representatives by cumulative voting to ensure minority representation.
3. Thanks to chicanery, Illinois is the **smallest state ever added to the union** – census takers were bribed to inflate population figure.
4. Chicago is the **second largest Polish city in the world** – hence Casmir Pulaski Day as a statewide school holiday.
5. A bomb raid by the Shelton brothers on gangster rival Charlie Birger is considered the first aerial attack on American soil.
6. The Illini Indians had a calumet for peace and a calumet for war. A calumet adorned with a red feather was a sign of war.
7. Illinois is in the heart of **Tornado Alley**. Texas has more twisters overall than Illinois, but ours are the deadliest in the nation.
8. Monks Mound near **Collinsville**, larger than Egypt's Great Pyramid, is the most significant archaeological site in the USA.
9. The **Piasa Monster** petroglyph on the bluffs at **Alton** was considered the most significant Indian painting in America.
10. The **Liberty Bell of the West**, in the Memorial Building at **Kaskaskia**, is older than the famed Liberty Bell in Philadelphia.
11. The State Historical Museum has the wooden leg of Santa Anna, captured by John Gill of Pekin who fought in the Mexican War.

12. The national **ERA** for women was never ratified, thanks to Phyllis Schlafly of **Alton**, the nation's most potent conservative female.

13. **Dixon's** Nachusa Hotel hosted presidents Lincoln, Grant, Taft, T. Roosevelt and Reagan, and was the first in Illinois with a tub.

14. The *Chicago Tribune's* headline, "Dewey Defeats Truman" in 1948, is the **biggest gaffe ever in newspaper publishing history**.

15. The **Adler Planetarium**, built in Chicago in 1930 for the Century of Progress fair, was the first in the western world.

16. Chicago-born Walt Disney won 39 Oscars for his work as a filmmaker, the most ever.

17. The Kaskaskia were the most numerous of the Illinois tribes and also the most favorably inclined to accept the teachings of Christianity.

18. Abraham Lincoln of Illinois remains the only President of the U.S. to have secured a patent for an invention.

19. Eli Bridge Company in **Jacksonville** is the only company in the United States that makes Ferris Wheels.

20. The expression "your name is mud" comes from Dr. Samuel Mudd, the man who treated Booth's leg after Lincoln's assassination.

21. Lincoln grew a beard late in 1860 after an 11-year-old girl, Grace Bedell, wrote him, suggesting he would look better with one.

22. Architect **Frank Lloyd Wright** once proposed to build a mile high skyscraper with atomic powered elevators.

23. More than half of the people in the entire state live in metropolitan Chicago.

24. Lake Michigan is the fourth largest freshwater lake in the world.

25. It is a geographical oddity that at the juncture of the Wabash and Ohio rivers, there is not a single town of significant size.

26. **Buckminster Fuller**, inventor of the geodesic dome, once proposed to cover a significant portion of downtown East St. Louis.

27. The largest cottonmouth ever killed in Illinois came from Mermet Lake in Massac County and measured a whopping 49.5 inches

28. Illinois has the nation's #1 martyr for freedom of the press (Elijah Lovejoy) and the #1 martyr for religious freedom, Joseph Smith.

29. When George Rogers Clark captured **Cahokia** and **Kaskaskia** from the British in 1778, Illinois became a Virginia county.

30. Members of the **Mormon Battalion** in the Mexican War discovered gold at Sutter's Fort that led to the '49 California gold rush.

31. The Chicago Historical Society claims to have the skin from the snake that tempted Eve in the Garden of Eden, donated by eccentric Charles Gunther; it also has a rare **Tucker automobile** and one of the few original copies of the Declaration of Independence.

Sesquicentennial medallion

32. **Angel Fluff** is a drink that mixes Mississippi River water with Mogen David wine, Early Times whiskey and Pepsi Cola.

33. A Mississippi highball is a glass of water from the Mississippi River.

34. The deepest spot of the Mississippi in southern Illinois is at **Grand Tower**, with a depth of 100 feet.

35. **Cairo**, Illinois, is the reference point for the beginning of what is referred to as the Upper Mississippi River. (mile 0.0)

36. Theodore Kazynski, better known as the *Unibomber*, attended **Evergreen Park High School** in South Chicago.

37. No dinosaur bones have ever been found in the state of Illinois.

38. In the Pennsylvanian geologic era, when most of Illinois coal was formed, the state was located near the equator.

39. The Horseshoe Lake area in southern Illinois is called the "**Canada goose capital of the world**."

40. The Capone gang wars in Illinois led to the creation of the first forensic science lab in Illinois at Northwestern University.

41. Abe Lincoln attended school only when he was not needed for chores at home. His total schooling amounted to only 1 year.

42. Only about 11 percent of the state's population lives in rural areas.

43. Only about 10 percent of Illinois' original forests remain, and a quarter of that figure exists in the Shawnee Forest in southern Illinois.

44. Chicago is the **national hub for Amtrak**, the national passenger service railroad.

45. Illinois has 59 Senators elected to 4-year terms, 118 Representatives elected to two-year terms.

46. More than 70 recipients of the Nobel Prize either graduated from or were employed by the **University of Chicago**.

47. The official state Website is www.state.il.u.s, state capital Website is www.springfield.il.us, Chicago Website is www.ci.chi.il.us

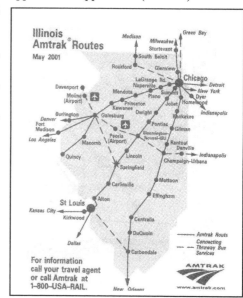

48. Corn dogs were invented by the Waldmire family at **Springfield's Cozy Dog Drive-in** on Route 66.

49. Chicago is as far north as Boston, Massachusetts, and **Cairo** is as far south as Richmond, Virginia.

50. Illinois ranks first in the nation as an exporter of agricultural products.

51. Chicago is considered the **world's leading convention center**.

52. The town of Pullman, planned by railroad magnate George Pullman, was the nation's first planned industrial town.

53. The Mississippi is the general dividing line between radio and television stations, with those to the west starting with "K" and east starting with "W."

54. The call letters of station WGN in Chicago stand for World's Greatest Newspaper because it's owned by the *Tribune*.

Tower Rock (Rock of the Cross) in the Mississippi at Grand Tower

55. Abe Lincoln **suffered from bouts of melancholy** and avoided carrying a pocketknife if he knew he was going to be alone.

56. The demand for **badger hair shaving brushes** nearly caused the animal's extinction in northern Illinois.

57. Abe Lincoln tried more cases before the Illinois Supreme Court than any other lawyer in the state.

58. Fourteen northern counties, seeking lower taxes, **voted to secede** from the rest of the state in 1842 and join Wisconsin.

59. The first mining boom in America occurred at the lead mines in **Galena**. The Indians used white lead for making warpaint.

60. The tri-state twister that hit southern Illinois in 1925 is the 2nd longest continual path ever recorded for a tornado (219 miles).

61. Lusk Creek Canyon, in the rugged hills of the Shawnee Forest in **Pope County**, is considered the most beautiful spot in Illinois.

62. **LaRue Swamp** in southwestern Illinois contains more plant species than the entire Great Smoky Mountains National Forest.

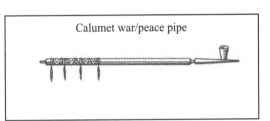
Calumet war/peace pipe

63. The highest point in Illinois is Charles Mound in the driftless (unglaciated) area near Wisconsin. It is 1,241 feet above sea level, but it is less than 300 feet higher than the level area surrounding it. The lowest part of the state of Illinois is at Bird's Point near **Cairo,** 268 feet above the sea. Over this 400-mile distance between the two points the gradient (slope) is about 2 and ½ feet per mile.

64. Founded in 1848, the **Chicago Board of Trade** is the world's largest and oldest futures and options exchange.

65. The 1871 fire that destroyed much of Chicago, started by Mrs. O'leary's cow, burned her barn but did not destroy her house.

66. The Chicago suburb of **Downers Grove** has about 100 homes that were "kit built" and were sold through a specialty Sears catalog.

67. Graue Mill in **Oak Brook** was a station on the Underground Railroad in Illinois.

68. Ernest Hemingway spent the first 6 years of his life in **Oak Park**, Illinois.

69. Tempel Farms in **Wadsworth** is the largest of its kind in the U.S. and features the famous Lipizzan stallions of Austria who perform to ballet music.

Lippizan stallion at Wadsworth

70. **Belvidere** is known as the City of Murals because 250 artists painted 12 murals on downtown walls in 48 hours back in 1997.

71. The Lincoln statue in **Dixon** is the only one in existence that shows him in military dress from the Blackhawk War.

72. The Upper Limits Rock Gym in **Bloomington** features one of the tallest climbing gyms in all of Illinois.

73. **Danville Stadium**, built in 1946 for the Brooklyn Dodgers' farm team, was the location for the 1992 movie, *The Babe* (John Goodman), and *A League of Their Own* (1991), starring Tom Hanks.

74. Sixty-five percent of the pumpkins grown in the U.S. are grown in the Havana-Manito-Beardstown area near Mason County.

75. **Carl Sandburg's** "The War Years," consists of 4 volumes and has more words than all of Shakespeare's plays.

76. Avanti Foods at **Walnut** is housed in a Swiss Chalet and has been turning out cheese products since 1932 (815/379-2155).

77. The caves at Devil's Backbone Park, near **Grand Tower**, were used in 1798 as hideouts by river pirates.

78. **Metropolis** is the obvious choice as **Superman's hometown** because it is the only U.S. city by that name. (Picture of statue at right)

79. There is a state law that bans the taking of any white squirrel from the town of Olney, Illinois.

80. The **Gateway Geyser** in **East St. Louis** is the world's tallest, spewing forth a stream of water 630 feet high, as tall as the St. Louis Arch.

81. The middle fork of the **Vermilion River** is the only river in Illinois, Iowa, or Indiana designated as a national scenic river.

82. **Moses Austin**, on his way to found the great state of Texas, traveled through Illinois in 1797 and described Illinois Country as being beautiful and fertile.

83. December of 1917 was the coldest in history for Illinois. For the first time in history it was possible to walk across the Mississippi River at **Cairo** on ice.

84. Tornadoes are more common in the Illinois Mississippi River basin than anywhere in the world.

85. If you are out in the open and you spot a tornado, run to the north of its path because the winds are less violent on the north than on the south side of a tornado.

86. There are 133 trees native to Illinois, including: tamarac larch, butternut walnut, pignut hickory, quaking aspen, cow oak, slippery elm, hackberry, red haw, sassafras, witchhazel, pawpaw, cucumber, prickly ash, poison sumach, wahoo, shittimwood (I hope I spelled it right.), buckthorn, nannyberry, and the catalpa (Indian cigar tree).

St. Paul's Church
Highland, Illinois

87. Incredibly, the rich fertile Grand Prairie was once thought by early pioneers to be unfit for cultivation. The absence of trees was one of the reasons settlers came to this wrongheaded conclusion.

88. Despite being hunted extensively for food, the deer population increased as more pioneers arrived in Illinois. The reason for this seems to be that they found protection in the neighborhood of man from beasts of prey that assailed them in the wilderness.

89. **Illinois was originally free of rats**. It seems they first arrived at our shores from other towns with the coming of steamboats, and they came ashore from the boats.

90. The Indian population in Illinois at the time of statehood is estimated to have been a mere 12,000, or one for every 5 square miles.

91. The early Illinois Indians loved to eat venison, buffalo and bear meat, but cared little for fish.

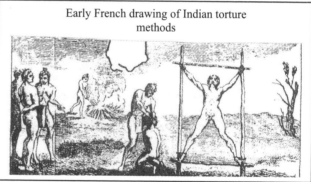

Early French drawing of Indian torture methods

92. "The wealth of Illinois is in her soil, and her strength lies in its intelligent development." – Carved on the walls of the College of Agriculture at Urbana.

93. Illinois plants need ten different elements or they will not develop. They are: carbon, hydrogen, oxygen, sulfur, iron, magnesium, calcium, nitrogen, phosphorus, and potassium. (Yes, Texas plants probably need the same 10 elements.)

94. Illinoisans will kill for a delicious ear of bi-color sweet corn in mid-July. Corn is grown on ¾ of all the farms in the state. But Europeans view this crop with disdain and grow very little of, preferring to feed it to their farm animals.

95. **Sorghum molasses** were once consumed by Illinoisans in large quantities. Sorghum is a grain/grass that came from Syria. Sugar and syrup were extracted from its stem, and the rest of the plant was used for fodder and silage. First the cane was passed between two stone rollers and the juice was pressed out. The juice was then placed in large iron kettles over a hot wood fire. Impurities were skimmed off as the juice boiled.

Sorghum plant

96. Mules were more common in the southern part of the state because they can take the heat of the sun better than horses. In general, a draft mule cost more than a draft horse.

97. Every kind of clay product known to man can be found in Illinois soils except for china.

98. **Collinsville**, an old coal town, has no zinc deposits, but in 1920 it had a large zinc smelting factory. The reason for this is that zinc required large amounts of coal for the heat required to separate the metal from the ore. It was cheaper to ship the ore to the coal fields than to ship the coal to the zinc mines.

99. Mineral water, produced from 23 commercial springs in the state, sold for 5 cents a gallon in 1920.

100. The largest railroad repair shops during railroad's heyday were located at **Centralia, Mattoon, Decatur, Danville, Bloomington** and **Galesburg**.

101. Illinois had so many miles of railroad that by 1920 almost no place in the state was more than 15 miles from a railroad and 95 percent of the state was within 5 miles of a rail line.

102. The railroads of Illinois once owned enough right-of-way sufficient to reach across the United States from ocean to ocean five times.

103. **Hardin** and **Calhoun** counties were the only two counties in the state without railroads.

104. Early Illinois federal-aid roads by 1920 were as follows: The *Lincoln Highway* from Chicago to Clinton, Iowa; the Chicago-*Waukegan Road* from Chicago to **Waukegan**; the *Chicago-East St. Louis Road* that went through, **Ottawa, LaSalle, Peoria, Springfield**, and **Carlinville**; the *Dixie Highway* from Chicago to **Danville**, and the *National Road* from Terre Haute to **East St Louis**.

105. By 1920 Illinois had a system of public highways sufficient in combined length to reach a third of the way to the moon.

106. The town of **Peoria** owes its existence to the fact that it was the best place for travelers to ford the Illinois River.

Diamond stack, coal burner, and Burlington Zephyr

107. The town of **Oquawka**, a busy steamboat port, was seriously considered as a railroad crossing point on the Mississippi. The decision, however, went to Burlington, Iowa. By 1910 Oquawka's population fell drastically while Burlington stood at a robust 24,324.

108. The city of Chicago is built on a low flat plain that was once the bed of a great lake – Lake Chicago. The city is about 26 miles long and 15 miles wide.

109. The only access to **Calumet Harbor** is by water on Lake Michigan that actually belongs to the state of Indiana.

110. **Yorkville**, in the Fox River basin, is the smallest county seat in Illinois.

111. One of the early Illinois trails was called Meridian Road because it extends across the state from north to south and closely parallels the 89th meridian from Rockford to Cairo.

112. Most Illinoisans don't know where their soil came from. It's very simple. Soil takes millions of years to form, and it comes from decayed rock. It often contains sand and decayed plant matter (humus).

113. All land in Illinois was surveyed using the Third Principal Meridian (longitude) as a reference point. This square township system, divided into 36 square miles, is different from the "metes and bounds" English system used in the East. (In case you're wondering, the first meridian is the boundary between Ohio and Indiana.) Thus the location of a 40-acre tract of land in Illinois may be described as the SE quarter of the NW quarter of Section 16, Township 35 North, Range 10 East of the Third Principal Meridian. This land is found in Will County near Joliet.

Kroc's original McDonald's in DesPlaines

114. Most towns near rivers have official datum points that are posted stating that a certain point in the city is so many feet above sea level. The datum of East St. Louis is posted on the Eads Bridge. Edwardsville's is imprinted on a brass plate near some steps at the old courthouse.

115. Illinois has what is known as a continental climate that gives us 4 distinct seasons and abundant rainfall. Geographically we are part of the central lowlands in the Great Central Plain. Seventeen countries of Europe are smaller in size than Illinois.

116. Potsdam sandstone underlies the entire state. It was formed during the Cambrian Period when a sea covered Illinois, and great quantities of sand were washed from surrounding land into the sea.

117. When you see ridges of land in Illinois that exist on otherwise flat prairie, chances are good that it is a terminal moraine. This was rock, sand, pebbles and soil deposited at the end of a glacier. These moraines are named for towns where they exist. Shelbyville, Bloomington and Valparaiso are the most prominent ridges in Illinois.

118. Illinois is ranked 23rd in area among the states, but first in the value of its farm land.

119. **Summit**, the highest point in Chicago, is only about 12 feet higher than Lake Michigan. This gives you a good idea about the flatness of Chicago.

120. Twenty-three of the forty-eight states furnish water that flows across Illinois or along its borders.

121. Neither the Pacific Ocean nor the Atlantic Ocean have any significant impact on Illinois weather. The prevailing westerlies and Appalachian Mountains shut out most of the ocean influence from the east, and the western ocean is simply too far away. However, the moisture bearing winds from the Gulf of Mexico do bring frequent rain to the state.

122. The greatest change in recorded Illinois weather occurred on May 10, 1911, when the temperature fell 61 degrees in a 24-hour period.

Chicago White Sox new ballpark

123. The most incredible weather occurred on December 20, 1836. The temperature was about 40 degrees Fahrenheit and it was raining. All of a sudden the rain turned to a freezing slush. Chickens were caught in the freeze and froze in their tracks, their feet held fast to the ground. A man riding to Springfield on a horse was frozen to his saddle. The man and saddle were removed from the horse and thawed apart in a warm room.

124. January is the coldest month, and July is the warmest month, on average, in the state of Illinois.

125. Mammals native to Illinois include: opossum, woodchuck, muskrat, beaver, bison, hoary bat, pocket gopher, wolf, black bear, shrew, mink, badger, mole, otter, deer, squirrel, prairie mouse, panther, bobcat, lynx, coyote, and weasel.

126. Illinois birds include: cardinal, grouse, turkey, pigeon, turkey vulture, screech owl, kingfisher, yellow-bellied sapsucker woodpecker, chimney swift, hummingbird, flycatcher, lark, blue jay, crow, bobolink, cowbird, blackbird, grackle, sparrow, waxwing, shrike, wren, warbler, creeper, chickadee, titmouse, kinglet, robin, bluebird, thrush, purple martin scarlet tanager whippoorwill, cuckoo, hawk, and bald eagle.

127. Illinois soil types include: peat (at least 35 percent organic material), muck (25 percent of decomposed organic material mixed with clay), clay (25 percent or more of clay), loam (containing 30-50 percent sand), sands (75 percent or more sand), gravels (75 percent or more gravel and sand).

128. Illinois is in the path of the Mississippi Flyway, the migration route used by waterfowl through 14 Midwestern states. More than 1.1 million ducks and geese winter in Illinois every year. Goose Lake Prairie, 60 miles southwest of Chicago, contains the **largest native prairie in Illinois**.

129. The early French colonials were not very good at farming, but they were very sociable and found every excuse for merrymaking and social gatherings where there was much music and dancing. They were exemplary in their domestic relations and showed great affection for their children. They were generally kind to their slaves. They were not a quarrelsome lot as seemed to be the case with American colonists of British descent.

130. The British took control of French Acadia by terms of the Treaty of Utrecht, 1713. They renamed the place Nova Scotia (New Scotland) and expelled the French. This became the basis for Longfellow's story about *Evangeline*.

131. When George Rogers Clark left Kaskaskia and headed for Vincennes, he passed through **Sparta, Oakdale, Salem, Olney** and **Lawrenceville**.

132. Chicago's U.S. Cellular Field (formerly Comiskey Park) hosted the 74th annual All-Star Game. The American League won by a score of 7-6, giving the American League home field advantage in the World Series. The first All-Star game was played at Wrigley Field in 1933.

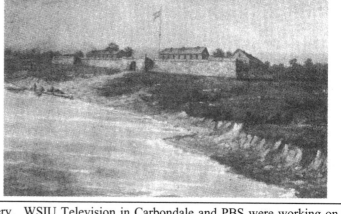
Mural of old Fort Chartres in the state capitol

133. Charlie Birger's gang, consisting of five men robbed the Bond County State Bank at **Pocahontas** on November 30, 1926. Birger and his gang operated mainly in Williamson County, but they had interests in East St. Louis as well. They were lured to Pocahontas by a huge miners' payroll. Their take was $9,577.53. Area resident Nick Gregory owns the safe that was robbed that day. It has a bullet hole in the side from the ensuing shootout after the robbery. WSIU Television in Carbondale and PBS were working on a documentary on the life of Birger in the summer of 2003.

134. The Big Four Railroad consisted of the Cleveland, Cincinnati, Chicago and St. Louis. It was so named because it linked the four biggest cities in the Midwest. It was absorbed by the New York Central.

135. The large balloon and diamond smokestacks on the early steam engines were enlarged at the top because they had baffles and screens in them that were supposed to catch wood embers and prevent prairie fires. Unfortunately this was not very effective, and it is one reason why railroads switched from burning wood to coal.

136. The first product Chicago's Motorola tried to develop was a record player for automobiles. At the time, the most known player on the market was Victrola, so they called themselves Motorola.

137. French Massacre of the Fox Indians: Every high school history textbook tells how the French got along with the Indians while the American pioneers engaged them in warfare. In Illinois, there is a glaring exception to this generalization. Friction between the French and Fox Indians began when the French, angered because the Fox charged tolls at portages near the Illinois-Wisconsin border, determined to exterminate them. This warfare started in 1712 and lasted variously until 1730. In that year the French encouraged the Iroquois tribes in the Indiana region to make war on the Fox tribes in northern Illinois. War parties of the Mascouten and Kickapoo tribes put the Fox warriors and their families in flight. The Fox warriors held their enemies off until they finally reached the banks of the river that now bears their name. This place, on the Fox River in present-day Kendall County, is where the Little Rock and Big Rock creeks unite with the Fox River. It is also the site of the ancient Indian village of Maramech. Here the fleeing Fox were surrounded by their adversaries, and they prepared for a siege.

Columnist Hedda Hopper with one of her famous hats

The enemies of the Fox, finding that they could not break through Fox fortifications, sent for their French allies. The French governor of Illinois and commander at Fort Chartres, Louis de Bellerive responded. He moved north with a huge force of 500 men. The Fox, seeing that their situation was hopeless, began to consider surrendering. But ten more Frenchman and 200 Indians arrived from Detroit with word that no quarter was to be given to the Fox. The Fox discovered an unguarded section of the forest and fled their fortifications. But their pursuers caught up with them, overwhelmed them with their superior numbers, and most were tortured and killed.

There is a monument at Maramech for those who died in this heroic last stand against impossible odds.

FAMOUS QUOTES ABOUT CHICAGO

Cyrus McCormick

Sarah Bernhart: "Chicago is the pulse of America."
D.H. Lawrence: "It rained and fogged in Chicago and muddy-flowing people oozed thick in the canyon-beds of the streets. Yet it seemed to me more alive and more real than New York."
Ashley Montague: "Hell has been described as a pocket edition of Chicago."
Carl Sandburg: "Here is the difference between Dante, Milton, and me. They wrote about Hell and never saw the place. I wrote about Chicago after looking over the place for years and years."
Rudyard Kipling: "Having seen Chicago, I urgently desire never to see it again. It is inhabited by savages. Its water is the water of the Hughli, and its air is dirt."
Louella Parsons: "There are two types of people in this country. There are the ones who love Chicago and the ones who think it is unmitigated Hell."
Stuart Rosenburg: "Chicago is the ultimate American city – rich, deep, insane."
George Steevens: "Chicago, queen and guttersnipe of cities, cynosure and cesspool of the world."
Studs Terkel: "Chicago is not the most corrupt American city – it is the most theatrically corrupt."

The famous Chicago Theater

Oscar Wilde: "Your city looks positively dreary."
Shane Leslie: "Chicago has all the possibilities of becoming the earth's final city, the Babylon of the Plains."
John Peyton: "The city is situated on both sides of the Chicago River, a sluggish, slimy stream, too lazy to clean itself. . . "
Old Saying - "Chicago has the best cops money can buy."
"Chicagoans seem to experience a perverse vicarious thrill of pride in such flamboyant outrages as the St. Valentine's Day Massacre." **1968 article in "The Economist"**
Al Smith: "Chicago is the most loved and most hated city in the United States and perhaps in the world."
Nelsen Algren – "Chicago is a joint where the bulls and the foxes live well and the lambs wind up head-down from the hook."
"Chicago – a city where they are always rubbing a lamp and fetching a genii, and contriving and achieving new possibilities." – **Mark Twain**
British author Arnold Bennett: "Chicago: it's ugly but immense."
"Chicago is more suited for raising bullfrogs than humans." – **Joseph McCarty** who decided to settle in Aurora instead

POISONOUS, TREASONOUS, TRAITORS IN CIVIL WAR ILLINOIS

Venerable historian John Allen wrote *It Happened In Southern Illinois* in 1968. In this wonderful book, he described some of the ante bellum and Civil War events in Illinois.

A good majority of early settlers who moved into this part of Illinois arrived from Southern states such as Tennessee, Kentucky, Virginia and North Carolina. Most came simply for economic betterment while a minority left their state to escape the slave environment. No matter what their motive, they almost always maintained ties to friends and family left behind.

In the 1824 election there was a strong effort to legalize slavery in Illinois by adopting a new constitution that sanctioned it. The southernmost part of the state overwhelmingly wanted to adopt slavery, but the proposal was narrowly defeated. Further indication of the pro-slave sentiment in the state is demonstrated by the murder of Elijah P. Lovejoy, the abolitionist Alton newspaper editor in 1837. There is strong reason to believe the mob actions in this incident reflected a majority of people in that town in the River Bend area of the Mississippi. Even more interesting is the fact that Alton is on the northernmost fringe of southern Illinois where proslave sentiment was not thought to be that strong.

The 1858 senatorial race between Abe Lincoln and Stephen Douglas further illuminates the point. In the famed series of debates, Lincoln argued a strong freesoil position of the newly formed Republican Party, while Douglas adopted a morally neutral stance on the subject of slavery with his popular sovereignty theme. Most forget that it was Douglas who won this election – not Honest Abe. It must also be remembered that there was no such thing as direct election of Senators by popular vote back then. It was the state legislature, not the people, which elected Douglas. However, it is safe to assume that representatives generally reflected the will of their constituents.

Thus on the eve of the Great Conflict, southern Illinois, a region that came to be perceived as an area of great strategic importance, came to the war with a marked proslavery inclination. This bias resulted in some leading political figures (mostly Democrats) failing to support the national cause for the Union when war came. It also helps explain the intrastate dissention and strife that lasted for most of the duration of the conflict. It was this tense atmosphere that spawned the likes of William Quantrill, a schoolteacher (he lived for a spell at Mendota) who committed the most vile act of the entire Civil War, the sack of Lawrence, Kansas. That atrocity was followed up with the massacre of 90 Union soldiers at Baxter Springs, Kansas, near Joplin, Missouri. Bleeding Kansas had been a battleground for quite some time before the Civil War between Jayhawkers (anti-slavery, pro Union guerrillas) and their proslave counterparts, known as **Bushwhackers or Border Ruffians**. **Cole Younger, Frank James, Jesse James, Jim Younger and Bob Younger** were some other prominent Bushwhackers. The current intense sports rivalry between the universities of Kansas and Missouri can trace its origin to these past bloody events. And it was this atmosphere that led to the creation of numerous dissent groups who came to be known as **Knights of the Golden Circle, Sons of Liberty and Copperheads**.

Clingman

When open conflict did come in 1861, it was natural for those in Illinois with southern roots and sentiments to openly express their beliefs and feelings. Many became staunch advocates for the Confederacy and numerous young men joined the rebel army and proudly wore the gray uniform. About 30 men from **Marion** joined up with a group of Tennessee Volunteers. It was common in many parts of the state for southern sympathizers to hold mass meetings. One such gathering took place at **Carbondale** early in 1861. As federal forces slowly took control of the state, these people were forced to meet secretly or go underground. A mob in **DuQuoin** rescued a knot of deserters from a deputy marshal. There was talk of making a raid on **Jacksonville,** a known abolitionist town, by a group camped at Apple Creek. Jacksonville had incurred Copperhead wrath for its *Journal* having dared to print the Knights' constitution and secret oath. The *Journal* also mocked Southerners by daring to print some of their resolutions passed at Winchester:

Resolved: That coloreds is contagious, and, if permitted to come here, we, having a strong predisposition, might catch 'em.

Resolved: That God made us, but we don't exactly know whether he made coloreds or not . . . .

Resolved: That coloreds stink considerable, especially free coloreds

Resolved: That coloreds have no business to be coloreds nohow.

There were minor riots in **Peoria, Joliet** and **Mount Sterling** on draft registration day.

It was also necessary for a contingent of federal troops to guard the Illinois Central Bridge over the Big Muddy River during most of the war's duration. By the end of the war, the Knights of the Golden Circle probably had about 100,000 members scattered throughout the state.

Yet this large number of southern sympathizers did not prevent southern Illinois counties from meeting their full quota of men for the Union cause. Hamilton County, a reputed hotbed of discontent, led the state in the percentage of registered men who enlisted. Franklin and Williamson counties also had reputations for treasonous activity, but ranked high in percentage of eligible men enlisting.

The most notorious group in the state was the Clingman (Klingman) Gang that operated mostly in Bond, Fayette and Montgomery counties. The group was led by Josiah Woods, a native of Missouri, who often used the alias Clingman. They made various claims about being members of the Confederate Army, but they mainly were a bunch of renegades who terrorized the surrounding countryside. They sometimes wore the butternut colored pin or badge that marked them as Copperheads. They camped out in the woods by day and committed most of their foul acts under the cover of darkness. There are numerous newspaper accounts of their activities and lawlessness, and Clingman's deeds have been chronicled in a number of articles in historical journals and periodicals. The Centennial History of Illinois in Volume 3 gives a good account of the Clingman group:

"Toward the end of the war there were many desertions from the army and a great dissatisfaction with the progress of the war among certain areas.

"Armed resistance on the part of anti-war forces was a constant fear in the minds of union men. A heavy demand for Colts' revolvers, guns, and ammunition was noticed by storekeepers whose supplies were drained by buyers from copperhead districts, guerrilla bands, formed in the rural regions of southern Illinois, conducted demonstrations in places as large as **Charleston**, **Jacksonville**, and **Vandalia**; a band operating in Union county destroyed property of loyal men and assaulted unionists who fell in its hands. Armed rebel sympathizers often met in numbers for military organization and drill. Union men were seized and whipped and sometimes driven from their homes; in numerous instances they were shot down, even in their own homes, by rebel sympathizers.

"Many of these acts, it must be remembered, were done in a spirit of retaliation for the lynch law visited upon more or less harmless peace advocates. The latter, indeed, had at the start the more grounds for complaint against the outrages perpetrated on them by the super-patriots of the day. The Democrats complained that Governor Yates had repeatedly condoned such acts of violence. They invoked the law of reprisal in their defense, having in vain counseled obedience to law and an appeal to it for redress in all cases of lawlessness. They felt that responsibility for having to organize for their own protection and to make reprisals in kind, rested upon their opponents.

"In the closing years of the war this organized retaliation became extremely serious. Gangs of bushwhackers, horse thieves and deserters from both armies swelled the ranks of the copperhead desperadoes in the river counties and for a long time threw all central and southern Illinois into a panic. Under the daring leader named Clingman, one band of armed guerrillas did especial damage in the vicinity of Montgomery County until it was broken up on the summer of 1864."

In **Greenville**, a company of men was formed for the purpose of combating Clingman's gang. **Greenville, Donnellson, Pocahontas, Carlinville, Litchfield, Jerseyville, Walshville** and **Dudleyville** were staunchly patriotic. **Mulberry Grove** was said to be a hotbed of secessionist activity. In rebel places like Hurricane and Shoal Creek, old Secesh (secessionist) songs were sung at gatherings. The outlaws were derisively called Copperheads because they struck without warning like the deadly snake.

James Langdon, a **Quincy** surveyor, wrote a letter to General Jacob Ammen saying ". . . There is no place in the state . . . where treason is spoken so boldly as in this city . . ."

The *Alton Telegraph* reported in a March 8th 1864 issue: "Another disgraceful affray between the Copperheads and soldiers occurred at **Hardin**, Calhoun County, on Friday last. A copperhead cheered 'hurrah for Jeff Davis' and was promptly shot down by a soldier. The Copperheads then gathered and hung three soldiers and shot three others dead."

Some said that Clingman intended to set up a confederacy with **Havana** as the capital. Clingman was reportedly a crack shot and was said to be able to ride his horse at full speed and manage to put a bullet in a fence post. A heavily wooded area north of **Van Burensburg** was a favorite campsite of the Clingman ruffians who sometimes numbered over 100 men. There were many who thought his sympathy with the Southern Cause was merely a ruse to cover up his lawless inclinations. He and his men invaded numerous homesteads and under threat of pain or death, demanded food, money, weapons and sometimes horses.

Clingman met an untimely death after he was finally run out of the state. An angry mob of about a dozen men dragged Joe Woods from a jail in March of 1867 at Sedalia, Missouri, and lynched him. This was in retaliation for Woods' (Clingman's) having shot a man in the back, killing him in cold blood.

For a fascinating and in-depth account of copperhead activity in Illinois during the Civil War, one can purchase a hardbound copy of Carl L. Stanton's well-researched book, *They Called It Treason*. Send a check for $26.00 to his address: Box 429, Bunker Hill, IL 62014. Much of this article was based on his interesting and scholarly work.

JOHN A. LOGAN - SOUTHERN ILLINOIS' GREATEST HERO

John A. Logan, southern Illinois' most powerful and important political leader of the Civil War era, was a fascinating person. His life personified the human drama of this time because he reflected the social and political thoughts of the region he lived in. He was born and raised at **Brownsville,** in Jackson County, on an aristocratic 160-acre farm along the **Big Muddy River**. In 1839, when a new county was created out of Sangamon County, Abe Lincoln suggested that it be **named for John Logan's father** (also named John), who was a physician and a member of the state legislature. They were good friends despite the fact that Lincoln was a Whig and Logan was a Democrat.

The Civil War was about divided loyalties—brother against brother, and Logan's story is exemplary. His state remained loyal, but Logan's native Egypt triangle was completely surrounded by southern states. Logan's metamorphosis from a Democrat to

Republican and from a Negrophobe to Negrophile is extraordinary. He was the prototype of the mid-nineteenth century American whose attitudes toward Negroes went through a dramatic change. Egypt was technically in the north, but it was below the Mason-Dixon line and a hotbed of southern sentiment. But, it also went through a dramatic change, its citizens hesitant at first to fight in "Mr. Lincoln's War." Then slowly it began mustering support for preserving the Union by sending an ever-increasing number of volunteers to fight for the cause.

GOLCONDA HERALD, April 17, 1861

Should you of the North attempt to pass over the border of our state, to subjugate a Southern state, you will be met this side of the Ohio River. . . . You shall not shed the blood of our brothers until you have passed over the dead bodies of the gallant sons of Egypt.

John and his brother Tom were educated at Shiloh Hill Academy in Randolph County, not far from Kaskaskia. In 1847, following the sentiments of Mississippi Valley Democrats who supported President Polk, he enlisted to fight in the Mexican War. But an outbreak of measles struck his company, killing nine and confining him to the infirmary. By the time he recovered, the war was over.

He secured a law degree at Louisville, Kentucky, and began his practice at **Benton**, Illinois. In 1852 he was elected to the Illinois legislature at Springfield. The first major piece of legislation that he sponsored was an 1853 bill that forbade the introduction of any more Negroes into the state.

In 1855 he fell in love with, and married, a girl named Mary Cunningham of **Shawneetown**. For a while she had resided in the Wilcox House, a hotel on Front Street in Metropolis. He was elected to the 20th Illinois General Assembly in 1856. In 1858, and again in 1860, he was elected as a member to the U.S. Congress where he became a staunch supporter of Stephen Douglas. Logan campaigned for Douglas in the 1860 presidential campaign, but it was Lincoln "the Abolitionist" who won the election. Like most Illinois Democrats, Logan supported loyalty to the Union but opposed using force against the secessionists. Deep down in his soul, he was half-Yankee and half-Southerner. After the Confederates fired on **Fort Sumter**, Logan still sought compromise, supported by constituents who held meetings all over southern Illinois protesting Lincoln's call to arms.

Hearing that a battle was to be fought near Washington D.C., he secured permission to go with the troops by promising to watch at a safe distance as a spectator. Though dressed in civilian clothes, he picked up the musket of a fallen soldier and participated in the battle of **Bull Run** by firing a few shots at the enemy.

When it became apparent that all compromise efforts were doomed to failure, Logan came back to Marion and gave a pro-Union speech from the bed of a wagon. He passionately and successfully asked for volunteers to help him form a company. But many of his friends now became bitter enemies. Even his mother and one of his brothers criticized him for abandoning southern principles. His wife's brother opted to fight for the Confederacy. But the effect of Logan's switch in positions was dramatic. By forming a company, anti-war tide ebbed in Egypt and turned in favor of the government. Logan was made a colonel in the 31st infantry regiment, and they trained at **Fort Defiance** in Cairo.

General John A. Logan (left) with other members of Gen. Sherman's staff

Logan's first action was under the command of U.S. Grant, and it was a small skirmish at Belmont that ended in a draw. Logan suffered the ignominy of having his horse shot out from under him. Shortly after this engagement, he resigned as a member of Congress.

Logan next participated in Grant's capture of the strategic forts Henry and Donnelson on the Tennessee and Cumberland Rivers, not far from Paducah, Kentucky. Logan was wounded in the shoulder and taken back to **Murphysboro**. For his courage and bravery in battle, he was promoted to general and given charge of a brigade.

It was after the capture of Fort Donnelson that Grant earned the nickname, "Unconditional Surrender" Grant.

When Logan went back to his command, Grant, due to his actions in the loss at Shiloh, Tennessee, was replaced by General Halleck from **St. Louis**. Grant, discouraged, was going to quit the army and go back to his family in St. Louis, but Logan and others convinced him to stay. After fighting alongside William T. Sherman against P.T. Beauregard, in western Tennessee, Logan was given a twenty day leave and went back to Carbondale where his family was now living. He discovered that his brother-in-law had been arrested for anti-Union activities. When he returned to the war, he learned that he had been given command of twenty-three regiments.

Logan and Grant now moved against the Confederate citadel at Vicksburg. A few men under Logan, angered upon hearing that Lincoln had issued the Emancipation Proclamation in January of 1863, resigned and went home. Logan urged his men to stand by the flag and fight for an open and free Mississippi River. The *Jonesboro Gazette* took him to task for supporting abolition.

Logan was recommended for promotion but the U.S. Senate rejected his nomination. Governor Yates appealed to Lincoln, citing Logan's record and the effect his promotion would have on Democrats in Illinois. Lincoln pressed again for Logan's promotion to major general and was successful. Lincoln and Grant liked Logan because of his ability to inspire his men and press the attack. He was very popular with his men and with his dark eyes and dark mustache, he acquired the nickname "Black Jack." His persona soon took on an aura of myth and romance.

Vicksburg fell on July 3, 1863, and it was a crushing loss for the Confederacy. The war in the West was now essentially lost. Logan rode side by side with Grant as federal forces entered Vicksburg, and Logan was made temporary commander of the city.

Following this, Logan returned briefly to **Carbondale** and went on a whirlwind speaking tour to drum up support for the Union. His **DuQuoin speech** was hailed enthusiastically. Though still a Democrat, he was slowly moving toward Republican positions on the issues. He even won over his rebel brother-in-law who joined the Union forces.

Grant sent Logan and Sherman to Chattanooga to break the bottleneck created by Braxton Bragg, but Logan arrived too late and Union forces had already won the day. Logan was now in charge of the 15th Corps. By December, reports were filtering back from home that there was a "Logan for Governor" campaign being launched.

In the spring of 1864, Sherman, Logan, and George Thomas moved on Atlanta in a campaign that would bring the enemy to its knees. Logan's courage under fire was remarkable. He had an uncanny ability to charge back and forth along the line, ignoring the frequent hail of bullets, rallying his men. Logan soon was given command of the Army of Tennessee, consisting of three corps.

Abe Lincoln: Springfield photo in 1846

Despite his able performance, command of the Army of Tennessee was taken from Logan and given to General O.O. Howard. Logan returned to his command of the 15th Corps. It was a bad decision by Sherman, but it was made, in part, due to his dislike of political generals (like Logan) who frequently went back to their native states to keep in touch with their political base. General Joe Hooker was so disgusted by the move that he resigned his position in protest. Sherman took Atlanta in September, and Logan, though disheartened by his demotion, once again increased his fame and distinguished himself in action.

The presidential election now dominated the scene. Lincoln was renominated in Baltimore after much talk of replacing him with John C. Fremont. The Democrats met in **Chicago** and nominated General George McClellan, a peace candidate, declaring that the war had been a failure. There was some talk of placing John Logan on the ticket with him. Logan went back home, not to accept such a nomination, but to campaign for Lincoln. Logan spoke in **Carbondale, Springfield, Chicago, Belleville, Alton, Centralia, Harrisburg, Vienna, Metropolis, and DuQuoin**. A "Logan for Senator" movement soon gained momentum.

After the election, he went to Washington D.C. and had a conference with Abe Lincoln where he confidentially assured him of a positive outcome of the war. He then rejoined his command with Sherman, who was preparing to attack South Carolina after having captured Savannah. They swept through Columbia, South Carolina, and moved north towards Virginia to link up with Grant, who was now commander of the Army of the Potomac. Logan was grieved by the news of Lincoln's assassination but much relieved on hearing the news of Lee's surrender to Grant.

With the war over, General Howard was made head of the Freedman's Bureau, and Logan regained command of the Army of Tennessee. The Logans were expecting a baby in the late summer of 1865, and he made preparations to resign from the army. Everything was complicated by President Andrew Johnson's offering him the position of Ambassador to Mexico. He refused and was offered the Japan ministry, but that too was turned down. While in Washington, he talked to Republican leaders who said they would back him for the Senate. Logan then worked with Governor Richard Oglesby and Ben Stephenson to **help found the national Grand Army of the Republic**. Logan hoped to use GAR support to help unseat Senator Lyman Trumbull. By now Logan was a full-fledged Republican. But Logan had to be content with winning a seat to the U.S. House of Representatives.

In 1870 Logan won election to the U.S. Senate (1871-86) defeating **Bellevillian, Gustave Koerner.** In 1877 he won a second term when the legislature selected him over Richard Oglesby. Logan, now known as the "Black Eagle," supported Grant's unsuccessful bid for a 3rd term. In 1884 he ran unsuccessfully as a Republican candidate for the U.S. vice-presidency. John A. Logan died in 1886 and is buried in Washington, D.C.

Logan participated in all the Western campaigns with Grant and served with General Sherman on his march through Georgia. He fought in 8 major campaigns, and received several wounds. He was given a special medal of valor in 1863, one of only six that were awarded.

GALLATIN COUNTY (Gleaned from *Old Handbook of Gallatin County* by Jon Musgrave, 2002, $32.00 from Ill History.com, Box 1142, Marion, IL 62959)

Michael Sprinkle is thought to have been the first white settler of the county. He settled near Shawneetown around 1800.

The largest Indian mound in southern Illinois is known as Boyd's Mound (with a base of 4 acres), and it is situated nearly 5 miles north of Shawneetown. The burial site is also known as Sugar Loaf mound. One day some Indians called on the house of an Early settler, Dr. John Reid. Mrs. Reid was home with her infant son Alexander Reid who was in his cradle. One of the squaws with the group looked at the infant and exclaimed "me swap," leaving her own papoose in the baby's place. When Dr. Reid came home and found his wife crazed with grief, he came up with an idea. They cleaned and washed the redskin baby, put clean clothes on him, and took the child back to the Indian camp. The surprised mother was more than happy to make the exchange.

Ninian Edwards, governor of Illinois Territory, created Gallatin County as the 4th one in the state in 1812, following St. Clair, Randolph and Madison counties. The first county seat was Shawneetown, but it was later moved to Equality.

The widow Peggy Logsdon was a midwife who lived on the southern extremity of Shawneetown next to the Ohio River. One night she heard someone calling for her services from across the river on the Kentucky shore. When she went down to the river bank where she kept a skiff she discovered it to be missing. She found a log with a stout limb thrusting perpendicularly up in the air. She stripped off all her clothes, placed them on the limb, and swam safely across, pushing the log before her.

A noted landmark in the county is the **Devil's Anvil**, a large rock near the road between **Equality** and **Golconda**.

A group of citizens from Gallatin, Pope, Saline, and Hamilton Counties presented General Grant with a horse named "Egypt."

On Oct. 24th, 1861, the U.S.S. *Conestoga* and 300 infantry steamed up the Ohio River from Paducah to below Shawneetown, to intercept 70 Knights of the Golden Circle reported to be leaving Illinois to join the Confederate army.

On August 13, 1864, Col. Adam "Stove-Pipe" Johnson, commanding Confederate Guerrillas, crossed the Ohio River below Shawneetown at Saline Bar (just above the mouth of the Saline River), attacked 3 stranded steamers, and captured their cargoes. The Shawneetown Artillery arrived, and the band of 100 marauders fled back to Kentucky.

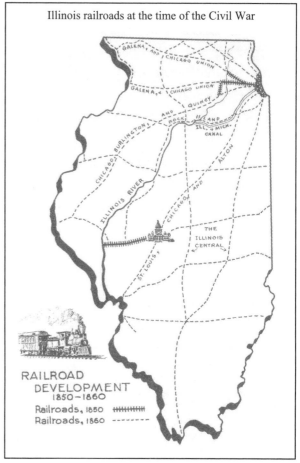

Anvil Rock in the Shawnee Hills

Illinois railroads at the time of the Civil War

A MACOUPIN COUNTY MAN IN THE CIVIL WAR (from edited Memoirs of W.R. Eddington)

I was born April 2, 1842, at **Woodburn**, Illinois in . . . Macoupin County. There were no free school houses here until I was 14 years old. I was 6 years old when I first attended a tuition school with the term lasting 3 months. I completed 6 of the school terms. In 1856 I attended 3 terms at a public school with each term lasting 6 months. In the winter of '61 and '62 I taught a couple of 6-month terms at the school.

My father died in 1855 at the age of 43. He drank himself to death. But I had a good mother, and she raised 9 children, 6 boys and 3 girls.

I once made a trip to **Springfield** when I was 13 to help my cousin drive a team of horses and several cows. For long distances on the way there was not a single house. The wild prairie grass was higher than a man's head and full of wild prairie chickens, with millions of wild pigeons, geese, ducks, cranes and pelicans flying overhead. And as we went into the city of Springfield there were but a few stores and places of business. The State House had not been built at the time.

When the Civil War broke out I wanted to enlist in the army but my mother was not willing and as I was not of age, I could not get in without her consent, so I waited until the second year.

Early on the morning of August 7, 1862, I with four of the neighbor boys left our home and went to **Bunker Hill** and took a train to **Gillespie** where they were making up a Company for the war. There we signed the roll for a 3-year enlistment in the U.S. Army. We slept that night in a boxcar loaded with wheat. The next morning we were put on a train and headed for **Springfield**. We got Sibley tents the same day. There was a hole in the top to let the smoke out. They were big tents, about 8 feet high and were supposed to hold about 15 men each. We had to get a man from another regiment to show us how to put them up.

The next day we drew blankets and uniforms. Then we were sent out to clear off a place to drill and parade. Then we were sent out to drill 5 hours each day and dress parade in the evening.

On September 8 we were drawn up in ranks and inspected by one of the officers to see if we were fit for the service. He said, "How are your eyes?" I told him I could not see anything but the light with my right eye. He looked me over and said, "You'll do, you pass."

My first duty while at Camp Butler was guarding a large covered wooden railroad bridge that spans the Sangamon River to prevent anyone from trying to set it on fire.

I was elected 5th sergeant of Company A. We were sent to Cincinnati, Ohio, to protect the town from rebel troops that were only 20-miles away. There was a pontoon bridge across the Ohio. It was built by stretching a long rope across the river and fastening each end securely to the banks. A lot of skiffs or small boats were tied to the front end of them to this rope and a joist of timber is laid from one boat to the next until it reaches all the way across the river. Then boards are laid across these joists which makes a floor for the bridge, and the whole structure is anchored down to the bottom of the river with heavy iron anchors. . . .

On December 20th we took steamboats down the Ohio to **Cairo**. We were joined there by other boats and proceeded to Chickasaw Bayou, one of the defenses of Vicksburg on the north. The Rebels had their big guns, rifle pits, and breastworks planted on hills, some as high as 100 feet. Down where we were, all was water and swamps. The weather was terrible cold, and we were not allowed to have a bit of fire. I thought I would freeze to death. We had a good spring for drinking water, but the Rebels poisoned it and killed some of our men. In our first battle we got licked. Our bullets went right over their heads as they stood in the rifle pits.

We evacuated our position and were transferred to a place on the Arkansas River where the Rebels had built a big fort. We surrounded the enemy and then were ordered to advance. Our forward movements were met by a hurricane of bombs, grapeshot, canister, shrapnel shot and thousands of musket balls. We got the order to lie down. We fell flat on our faces and began to crawl forward, lying on our breast and shooting and then rolling over on our backs and passing the but (sic) of our guns down between our feet and loading our guns as we lay on our backs. We then shoved the gun forward, rolled back on our breast to shoot and always creeping a little closer toward them.

While lying on our breasts the man next to me on my left was struck by a bullet which took the top out of the second button on his coat, cut the third one off and went through all his clothing and lodged against his breast bone without breaking the skin. I heard the ball hit him and reached over and tore his clothes open. The ball fell to the ground. He picked it up and put it in his pocket with the remark, "I am going to take that ball home."

We had got within about 40 yards of the Fort when the order was given to fix bayonets and charge. We jumped up, put on our bayonets and away we went on the run, over the ditch, over their breastworks and right in amongst them. In the charge the man next to me had the first finger of his hand shot off, and the ball passed so close to my ear it stung me so bad that I thought my ear was shot off. I slapped my hand over it but found no blood, and I still have my ear. They threw down their guns and put up their hands. The battle was fought, the victory won, and for the present, the shooting was done. We captured about 5,000 prisoners and all their cannons and guns and munitions. Some of them had Enfield rifles that had been smuggled to them from England.

We gathered the prisoners and put them on boats and sent them to **Alton** where they were put in the old State Penitentiary. Next we gathered up the wounded for both sides and sent them on boats to hospitals to be cared for by doctors and surgeons. Many of them had to have their arms or legs cut off, or their bodies probed to find lodged bullets. Such is the horrors of war. (from *Macoupin Goes to War* by Carl Stanton, Box 429, Bunker Hill, Illinois, 62014)

Robert Ingersoll, the man who would become known as the **Great Agnostic**, lived in southern Illinois. He taught school in **Metropolis**. Ingersoll also taught in **Greenville, Marion** and **Mount Vernon**. He lived in **Raleigh** when it was the county seat of Saline County. For a while he was a deputy clerk in **Shawneetown**. He became a lawyer and resided in Marion. Ingersoll left Marion in 1856 and settled in **Peoria**. When the Civil War broke out, he became a colonel and organized the 11th Illinois Cavalry. In the 1880s he went on the lecture circuit and attacked the orthodox beliefs of most Christian churches. He was a prominent orator and had significant influence on Mark Twain and Clarence Darrow.

Ingersoll's irresponsible behavior nearly got him killed back in early pioneer days. The incident occurred at Shawneetown, which became the site of the state's **first successful insanity plea** in a murder trial. A man named Sloo was told that a county clerk had wolf-whistled at his daughters when they were in there. He promptly came back into town and shot the offending clerk. But he killed the wrong man. It was Bob Ingersoll, the *deputy clerk,* who he unknowingly meant to kill. District Attorney **John A. Logan** unsuccessfully prosecuted the case.

Ingersoll, noted for being a "free thinker" and having a sharp wit, once described the Gallatin County Courthouse as a "cigar box with a pimple on top."

MAKING MAPLE SYRUP IN ILLINOIS

One legend has it that one day, a long time ago, a squaw in part of central Illinois was gathering wood for a fire. As she passed by a maple tree she noticed some sap leaking out. She tasted it and liked it. After collecting some of it, she cooked it with that night's venison. So began maple syrup.

"Sugaring off" time, as it was called, occurred in the early spring when the vernal warmth of the sun began to push buds open on dogwood trees and caused the sap to flow. The sap-running season usually begins around the first of February and lasts about a month. There are usually only about 10 "good" days out of a one-month season. V-shaped cuts were made in the tree bark, and small wooden buckets were attached to trees with "schculder" yokes to collect the dripping sap. Wooden buckets were replaced by metal buckets and, in turn, by plastic bags. Plastic bags came into use because it was discovered that the bags let sunlight through which kills bacteria harmful to the product's taste. The most recent improvement is plastic tubing which allows the sap from many trees to be collected in one 200-gallon vat. To tap 400 trees requires 20,000 feet of tubing. To get a good sap flow you need cold, freezing nights and warm days. The cold nights are needed to make the starch turn to sugar and the warm days to make the sap run. In 1957 the syrup sold for $1.75 per quart. The syrup was used by pioneers mainly at breakfast time and poured liberally over home made buckwheat cakes.

Hardly anyone in Illinois makes maple "sirip" anymore, 'cept the folks at Funk's Grove where its been a family tradition for over 150 years. The maple syrup industry is mostly a vast commercial enterprise produce in New York and New England. Yet for those who like the sound of "homemade" and "handcrafted" because it means something made by someone who takes pride in their craftsmanship, Funk's "sirip" is a treat to behold.

ILLINOIS STATE PARKS AND NATIONAL FOREST (Dep. Illinois Conservation)

**World's largest comic book mural at Metropolis
("Doc" and Kate Brasel of Watson, IL)**

**Grave vault of Klansman S. Glenn Young at the Herrin Cemetery
("Doc" and Kate Brasel photo)**

**Coal Miner's Memorial at Herrin
(Mike and Kate Brasel photo)**

**Superman memorabilia and Museum at Metropolis
(Mike and Kate Brasel)**

Illinois Colleges and Universities
2002–2003

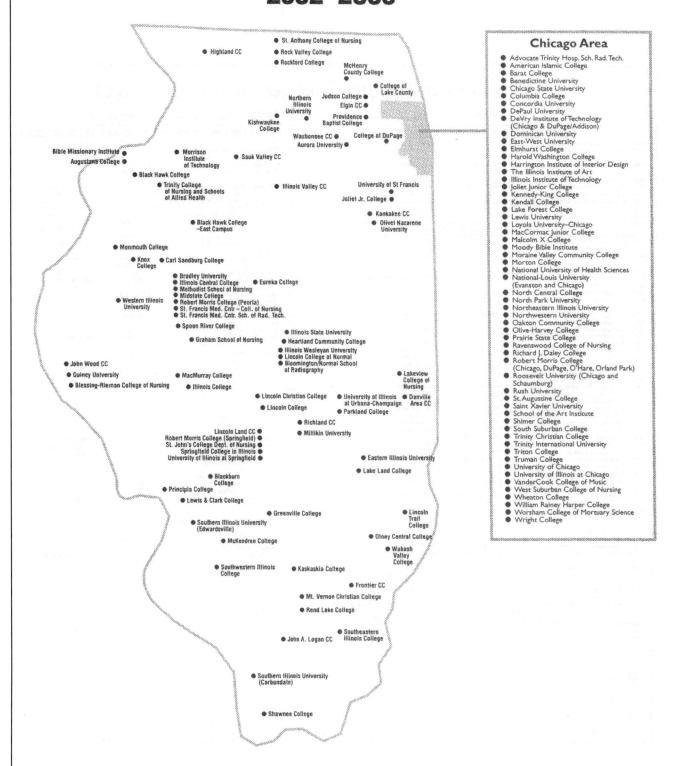

St. Anthony College of Nursing
Highland CC
Rock Valley College
Rockford College
McHenry County College
College of Lake County
Northern Illinois University
Judson College
Elgin CC
Providence Baptist College
Kishwaukee College
Waubonsee CC
College of DuPage
Aurora University
Bible Missionary Institute
Morrison Institute of Technology
Augustana College
Sauk Valley CC
Black Hawk College
Trinity College of Nursing and Schools of Allied Health
Illinois Valley CC
University of St Francis
Joliet Jr. College
Black Hawk College –East Campus
Kankakee CC
Olivet Nazarene University
Monmouth College
Knox College
Carl Sandburg College
Bradley University
Illinois Central College
Eureka College
Methodist School of Nursing
Midstate College
Western Illinois University
Robert Morris College (Peoria)
St. Francis Med. Cntr – Coll. of Nursing
St. Francis Med. Cntr. Sch. of Rad. Tech.
Spoon River College
Illinois State University
Graham School of Nursing
Heartland Community College
Illinois Wesleyan University
Lincoln College at Normal
Bloomington/Normal School of Radiography
John Wood CC
Lakeview College of Nursing
Quincy University
MacMurray College
Blessing-Rieman College of Nursing
Illinois College
Lincoln Christian College
University of Illinois at Urbana-Champaign
Danville Area CC
Lincoln College
Parkland College
Richland CC
Lincoln Land CC
Millikin University
Robert Morris College (Springfield)
St. John's College Dept. of Nursing
Springfield College in Illinois
University of Illinois at Springfield
Eastern Illinois University
Lake Land College
Blackburn College
Principia College
Lewis & Clark College
Greenville College
Lincoln Trail College
Southern Illinois University (Edwardsville)
Olney Central College
McKendree College
Wabash Valley College
Southwestern Illinois College
Kaskaskia College
Frontier CC
Mt. Vernon Christian College
Rend Lake College
Southeastern Illinois College
John A. Logan CC
Southern Illinois University (Carbondale)
Shawnee College

Chicago Area

- Advocate Trinity Hosp. Sch. Rad. Tech.
- American Islamic College
- Barat College
- Benedictine University
- Chicago State University
- Columbia College
- Concordia University
- DePaul University
- DeVry Institute of Technology (Chicago & DuPage/Addison)
- Dominican University
- East-West University
- Elmhurst College
- Harold Washington College
- Harrington Institute of Interior Design
- The Illinois Institute of Art
- Illinois Institute of Technology
- Joliet Junior College
- Kennedy-King College
- Kendall College
- Lake Forest College
- Lewis University
- Loyola University–Chicago
- MacCormac Junior College
- Malcolm X College
- Moody Bible Institute
- Moraine Valley Community College
- Morton College
- National University of Health Sciences
- National-Louis University (Evanston and Chicago)
- North Central College
- North Park University
- Northeastern Illinois University
- Northwestern University
- Oakton Community College
- Olive-Harvey College
- Prairie State College
- Ravenswood College of Nursing
- Richard J. Daley College
- Robert Morris College (Chicago, DuPage, O'Hare, Orland Park)
- Roosevelt University (Chicago and Schaumburg)
- Rush University
- St. Augustine College
- Saint Xavier University
- School of the Art Institute
- Shimer College
- South Suburban College
- Trinity Christian College
- Trinity International University
- Triton College
- Truman College
- University of Chicago
- University of Illinois at Chicago
- VanderCook College of Music
- West Suburban College of Nursing
- Wheaton College
- William Rainey Harper College
- Worsham College of Mortuary Science
- Wright College

Compliments of ACT™ and the Illinois ACT Council

ILLINOIS COUNTIES

Achilles, Rolfe. *Made in Illinois*. Illinois Manufacturer's Association, 1992.

Adair, Anna. *Indian Trails to Tollways*. Homewood: IL, 1968.

Adams, J.N. *Illinois Place Names*, Edited by W.E. Keller. Springfield: Illinois State Historical Society, 1989.

Allen, John. *Legends and Lore of Southern Illinois*, Carbondale: IL, Southern Illinois University, 1963.

Altman, Jack and Ziporyn, Marvin, *Born to Raise Hell*, New York: Grove Press, 1967.

Altman, Linda Jacob. *The Decade That Roared*, New York, Henry Holt, 1997.

Alvord, Clatrence. *The Illinois Country 1673-1818*. 1920. Urbana: University of Illinois Press reprint, 1987.

Andrews, Wayne. *Battle for Chicago*, Harcourt, Brace, 1946.

Angle, Paul. *Bloody Williamson*. New York: Alfred A. Knopf, 1952.

Angle, Paul, ed. *Prairie State: Impressions of Illinois*: 1673-1967. Chicago, 1968.

Asbury, Herbert. *History of the Chicago Underworld*, 1942.

Ayars, James. *The Illinois River*. New York, 1968.

Bachelder, Louise. *Abraham Lincoln: Wisdom and Wit*. Mount Vernon, N.Y.: The Peter Pauper Press, 1965.

Bardsley, Marilyn. *Eliot Ness: The Man Behind the Myth*.

Bateman, Newton and Selby, Paul, ed. *Encyclopedia of Illinois,* Chicago: Munsell Publishing, 1909.

Baughman, Judith, ed. *American Decades – 1920-1929*. Detroit: Manly Inc. Books, 1996.

Behr, Edward. *Prohibition: Thirteen Years that Changed America*.

Bergreen, Laurence. *Capone: The Man and the Era*. New York, Simon and Schuster, 1994.

Bielski, Ursula. *Chicago Haunts*, 1998.

Black Hawk: An Autobiography. Urbana: University of Illinois Press, 1990.

Blashfield, Jean. *Awesome Almanac: Illinois*, Wisconsin: B & B Publishing, 1993.

Boardman, Fon Jr. *America And The Jazz Age*. New York: Henry Walck, 1968.

Boardman, Barrington. *Isaac Asimov Presents: From Harding to Hiroshima*. New York: Dembner Books, 1988.

Bogart, Ernest, et al. *The Centennial History of Illinois*, 5 Volumes, Springfield: Illinois Bicentennial Commission, 1922.*Botkin, B.A.* A Treasury of Railroad Folklore. *1943.*

_____ *A Treasury of Mississippi River Folklore.* 1950.

Bridges and Davis. *Illinois: It's History and Legacy*, Scholarly Press.

Brinkman, Grover. *Southern Illinois*. Weekends Inc. Salen, IL, 1973.

Broverman, Helen and Dorothy Drennon, ed. *History of Christian County*, Jacksonville: Prod. Press, 1968.

Brownell, Baker. *The Other Illinois*. Duell, Sloan and Pierce, 1958.

Cahill, Tim and Ewing, Russ. *Buried Dreams* (John Gacy). New York: Bantam Books, 1986.

Caraway, Charles. *Foothold on a Hillside*, Carbondale: SIU Press 1986.

Carrier, Lois. *Illinois: Crossroads of a Continent*, U of I Press, 1999.

Carpenter. John. *Illinois, From its Glorious Past to Present*. Chicago, 1963.

Carter, William. *Middle West Country*, Boston: Houghton Mifflin Company, 1975.

Centennial History of Madison County, edited by W.T. Norton, 1912.

Centennial Committee. *Centennial History of Illinois*. (multivolume). Springfield, 1920.

Chambers, Don. *Mannequins: At Home in Illinois and Western Indiana*, Soybean Farm Press, Savoy, IL, 2001.

Chapman, Mrs. P.T. *A History of Johnson County*. Herrin News Press, 1925.

Chicago Days: 100 Defining moments in Chicago History, (by the *Chicago Tribune* staff).

Church, H.V. *Illinois: History, Geography, People, Government*. Chicago: D.C. Heath, 1925.

Cicconne, Richard. *Chicago and the American Century*, Chicago: Contemporary Books, 1999.

Clayton, John, compiler. *The Illinois Fact Book and Historical Almanac*, 1673-1968, Carbondale: SIU Press, 1970.

Counties of Illinois: Their Origin and Evolution, Springfield, Illinois Secretary of State.

Corliss, Carlton. *Main Line of Mid-America: the Illinois Central*. New York: Creative Age Press, 1950.

Cowdery, Ray. *Capone's Chicago*, Minnesota, Northstar Commemoratives, 1987.

Cromie, Robert and Joseph Pinkston. *Dillinger: A Short and Violent Life*, Evanston, IL., Chicago Historical Bookworks, 1990.

Cronon, William. *Nature's Metropolis: Chicago and The Great West*, New York: W.W. Norton, 1992.

Danilov, Victor. *Chicago's Museums*, Chicago Review Press, 1991.

Davis, James Edward. *Frontier Illinois*. University of Indiana Press (teaches at Illinois College, Jacksonville), 1998.

Dedman, Emmett. *Fabulous Chicago*, New York: Random House, 1953.

Delorme's *Illinois Atlas and Gazetteer*. 2000.

Demaris, Ovid. *Captive City*, Lyle Stuart, 1969.

Deneal, Gary. *A Knight of Another Sort*. (Charlie Birger) Carbondale: IL, Southern Illinois University Press, 1998.

Deutsch, Sarah. *From Ballots to Breadlines: American Women From 1920-1940*. Oxford: Oxford University Press, 1994.

Elazar, Daniel. *Cities of the Prairie*, New York: Basic Books, 1969.

Donald, David. *Lincoln*, New York: Simon and Schuster, 2002.

Dunne, Edward F. *Illinois: The Heart of the Nation*. Chicago: Lewis Publishing, 1933.

Fadner, Dr. Frederick. *The Gentleman Giant,* (Robert Wadlow – the Alton Giant)1941.

Fensom, Rod and Foreman, Julie. *Illinois: Off the Beaten Path*. Chester: CT. Globe Pequot, 1987.

Flanders, Robert B. Nauvoo: Kingdom on the Mississippi. *Urbana: University of Illinois Press, 1965.*

Fliege, Stu. Tales And Trails of Illinois. *University of Illinois Press, 2003.*

Ford, Thomas. *History of Illinois From 1818-1847*, ed. by Milo Quaife. Chicago: Lakeside Press, 1945.

Foster, Olive. A Student's Guide to Localized History. *New York: 1968.*

Fox, Stephen. *Blood and Power*. William Morrow, 1989.

Frank, Gerold. An American Death *(M.L. King). New York: Doubleday Books, 1972.*

Galligan, George, and Jack Wilkinson. *In Bloody Williamson*, 1927. 1985 reprint by Williamson County Hist. Society, 1985.

Gray, James. The Illinois, *Prairie State Books, 1989.*

Graf, John and Skorfad, Steve. Chicago: Monuments, Markers and Memorials, *Images of America, 2002.*

Hansen, Harry. Illinois: A Descriptive and Historical Guide, *New York: Hastings House, 1974.*

Hanson, Erica. The 1920s. *San Diego: Lucent Books, 1999.*

Harris, Stanley, Harrell, William and Irwin, Daniel. Exploring the Land and Rocks of Southern Illinois Carbondale, IL Southern *IL U Press, 1977.*

Hartley, Robert. *Louis and Clark in the Illinois Country*, 2002.

Heimel, Paul. *Eliot Ness: The Real Story*, 1997.

Henderson, Lyndee J. *Illinois Firsts: The Famous, Infamous and Quirky*. July 2003.

_____ *More Than Petticoats: Remarkable Illinois Women*, 2003.

Herald, Jacqueline. *Fashions of a Decade*: The 1920s. New York: Facts on File, 1991.

Hicken, Victor. *Illinois in the Civil War*. University of Illinois Press, 1991.

Hoffman, Dennis. *Scarface Al And The Crime Crusaders*.

Hoffman, John, ed. *A Guide to the History of Illinois*. 1991.

Horrell, William, Henry Piper and John Voigt. *Land Between the Rivers*. Carbondale: Southern Illinois University Press, 1973.

Horsley, Doyne. *Illinois: A Geography*. Bolder, Colorado: Westview Press, 1986 (well illustrated).

Howard, Robert P. *Illinois: A History of the Prairie State*, Grand Rapids: Ferdmans, 1972.

Hubbard, Freeman. *Railroad Avenue: Stories and Legends*. San Marino, Calif.: Golden West Books, 1964.

Illinois History. (written for and by Jr. High and High School students - various volumes, numbers and years).

Illinois: Land and Life in the Prairie State. Illinois Geographical Society, 1978.

Illinois State Historical Society. *Chronology of Illinois History*, 1972.

Jackson, Donald, ed. *Black Hawk: An Autobiography*, University of Illinois Press.

Jefferies, Richard W. *The Archaeology of Carrier Mills*, Carbondale: SIU Press, 1987.

Jensen, Richard. *Illinois: A Bicentennial History*. New York: W.W. Norton, 1978.

Johnson, James. *The Lincoln Land Traction*. Wheaton: IL, Traction Orange Company, 1965.

Johnson, Scott and Kistler, Julie. *Once There Were Giants*, (Hebron basketball) Bloomington: IHSA, 2002.

Journal of the Illinois State Historical Society (various volumes, numbers and years).

Kefauver, Estes. *Crime in America*. New York, Doubleday and Co, 1951.

Keiser, John A. *Building for the Centuries: Illinois: 1865-1898*, Urbana: U of I Press, 1977.

Kimball, Stanley, ed. *The Mormons in Early Illinois*. Southern Illinois University at Edwardsville.

Klein, Jerry. *Peoria Industry: A Pictorial History*, St. Louis, G. Bradley Publishing, 1997.

Krohe, James Jr. *Midnight at Noon* (coal mining in Sangamon County) Springfield: Sangamon Cnty. Hist. Soc., 1975.

Kummer, Patricia. *Illinois Geography*, Capstone Press, 1996.

Lantz, Herman R. *People of Coal Town*, New York: Columbia University Press, 1958.

Lathrop, Ann. *Illinois, its People and Culture*. Minneapolis: 1975.

Lathrop, H.O. *Geography of Illinois*. Boston: Ginn and Co., 1935.

Lewis, Lloyd and Smith, Henry. *Chicago: The History of its Reputation*, New York: Harcourt Brace and Company, 1929.

Lindberg, Richard. *Return (Again) To The Scene Of The Crime*, Cumberland House Publishing, 1999.

Lindop, Edmund. *Dazzling Twenties*, New York: Franklin Watts, 1970.

Mahoney, Olivia. *Go West: Chicago and American Expansion*, Chicago: Chicago Historical Society, 1999.

Marsh, Carol. *The Hard to Believe – But It's True, Book of Illinois History*, 1990. (elementary level)

Mason, John. *A Gazetteer of Illinois*, 1993.

McAuliffe, Emily. *Illinois Facts and Symbols*, 1998.

McPhaul, Jack and McGuire, James. *Deadlines and Monkeyshines: The Fabled World of Chicago Journalism*.

McPherson, Alan. *Fifty Nature Walks in Southern Illinois*, Vienna, Il., Cache River Press, 1993.

Meyer, Douglas. *Making the Heartland – A Geographical History*, 2000. (good section on early Illinois roads)

Miller, Donald L. *City of the Century* (Chicago).

Moore, William. *Dateline Chicago*. New York: Taplinger, 1973.

Mowry, George. *The Twenties: Fords, Flappers and Fanatics*. Englewood Cliffs: Prentice Hall, 1963.

Murphy, Jim. *The Great Chicago Fire*, New York: Scholastic Books, 1995.

Murray, David. *Charles Percy of Illinois*, New York: Harper and Row, 1968.

Neeley, Mark E. *The Abraham Lincoln Encyclopedia*. New York: McGraw-Hill, 1982.

Nelson, Ron. *Illinois: A Geographical Survey*, Bloomington: Illinois Geographic Society, 1996.

Nevins, Alan. "The Frontier in Illinois History," *Journal of the Illinois State Historical Society*, (Spring 1950): 28-45.

Nunes, Bill. *Southern Illinois: An Illustrated History*, Thomson-Shore Printers (self-published), 2001.

Nunes, Bill. *East St. Louis: An Illustrated History*, (self-published, 288 pages, 500 pictures), 1998. (out of print)

Oblinger, Carl. *Divided Kingdom* (mining in central Illinois), Springfield: Illinois State Historical Society, 1991.

Pease, Theodore. *The Story of Illinois*. Chicago: University of Chicago Press, 1969.

Pensoneau, Taylor. *Brothers Notorious*: (the Shelton Gang), New Berlin: Downstate Publications, 2001.

Peterson, Virgil W. *Barbarians in Our Midst, A History of Chicago Crime and Politics*, Boston: Liottle, Brown Co., 1952.

Phillips, Rudy. *Rudy's Life in Shawneetown*, 1928-80, Shawneetown: 1980.

Peithmann, Irvin. *Echoes of the Red Man*. New York: Exposition Press, 1955.

Pietrusza, David. *The Roaring Twenties*. California: Lucent Books, 1998.

Pohlen, Jerome. *Oddball Illinois*, Chicago Review Press, 2000.

Puhala, Bob. *Illinois: Off the Beaten Path*, Connecticut: Globe Pequot Press, 2003.

Quaife, Milo. *Chicago and the Old Northwest: 1673-1835*, Chicago University Press, 1913.

Rhodes, Eric. *Radio's First Seventy-Five Years*, Streamline Publishing, 1996.

Ridgley, Douglas C. *The Geography of Illinois*. Chicago, 1927.

Roehrick, L. ed. *Illinois Historical Markers and Sites*. South Dakota: Enterprise Publishing Co. 1976.

Rothert, Otto. *Outlaws of Cave-In-Rock*, 1924.

Royko, Mike. *Boss: Richard J. Daley of Chicago*, New York, 1971.

Russo, Edward J., *Prairie of Promise, Springfield and Sangamon County*, 1983.

Russo, Gus. The Outfit: The Role of Chicago's Underworld in the Shaping of Modern America, 2002.

Santella, Andrew, Andre. *Uniquely Illinois*, 2002.

Sawyers, June. *Chicago Sketches*, Chicago: Wild Onion Books, 1995.

Schlarman, J.H. *From Quebec to New Orleans – The French in North America*. Belleville: Buechler Publishing, 1929.

Schoenberg, Robert. *Mr. Capone*, New York: William Morrow, 1992.

Scott, Quinta and Kelly, Susan. *Route 66*. Oklahoma: University of Oklahoma Press, 1988.

Sears, Stephen W. *The American Heritage History of the Automobile in America*, New York: Am. Heritage Pub., 1977.

Simon, Paul. *Freedom's Champion: Elijah Lovejoy*, 1994.

Smith, George Washington. *A History of Southern Illinois*, Chicago: Lewis Publishing, 1912.

Smith, George Washington. *History of Illinois and Her People*, 1927.

Snyder, John. *Selected Writings*, Springfield, State Historical Library, 1962.

Steil, Tim. *Route 66*. MBI Publishing, Osceola, WI, 2000.

Stein, Conrad. *Illinois*, Chicago: Children's Press, 1987.

Stover, John F. *History of the Illinois Central Railroad*, New York: McMillan Publishing, 1975.

Sutton, Robert, et al. *The Heartland*, Lake Forest: Deerpath Publishing, 1995.

Taylor, Troy. *Haunted Alton*. Alton, Whitechapel Press, 1999. (For autographed copy call 618/465-1080)
_____. *Haunted Illinois*, Alton, Whitechapel Press, 1999.

Teague, Tom. *Searching For Route 66*. Springfield: Samizdat House, 1991.

Terkle, Studs. *Chicago*. New York: Pantheon Books, 1986.

Theising, Andrew. *Made in USA: East St. Louis – The Rise and Fall of an Industrial River Town*. Virginia Publishing, 2003.

Thilenius, Jesse and Snider, Felix. *Tower Rock*, Cape Girardeau: Ramfre Press, 1968.

Thiem, George. *The Hodge Scandal*, New York, St Martin's Press, 1963.

Tingley, Donald E. *Illinois: The Structuring of a State, 1899-1928*, Urbana: U of I Press, 1980.

"Twenty Scenic Motor Tours to Take in Illinois." State of IL Division of Tourism, 1977.

Turner, Glenette. *The Underground Railroad in Illinois,* Glen Ellyn: Newman Educational Publishing 2001.

Tuttle, William. *Race Riot: Chicago in 1919*, New York: Atheneum Press, 1980.

Vogel, Virgil J. *Indian Place Names in Illinois*. Springfield, Illinois State Historical Society, 1963.

James Waddell. *Capone's Vault*, 1991.

Walton, Clyde. *An Illinois Reader*. DeKalb: IL, 1970.

Weis, John. *New, Historic Route 66 of Illinois*. Wilmington: AO Motivation, 1997.

Wallis, Michael. *Oilman: Frank Phillips*. Garden City, NY: Doubleday, 1988. (Sheltons in ESTL.)
_____. *Route 66: The Mother Road*. New York: St. Martin's Press, 2001.

Watters, Mary. *Illinois in the Second World War*. Springfield: Illinois State Historical Library, 1952.

Wendt, Lloyd and Kogan, Herman. *Big Bill of Chicago*. New York, Bobbs-Merrill Co., 1953.

Wendt, Lloyd and Kogan, Herman. *Chicago: A Pictorial History,* Bonanza Books, 1958.

Wendt, Lloyd and Kogan, Herman. *Lords of the Levee*, Bobbs-Merrill, 1943.

Wheeler, Adade. *The Roads They Made: Women in Illinois History*. Chicago: Charles Kerr Publisher, 1977.

Wilson, Colin. *A Criminal History of America*, Putnam's, 1984.

Wilson, D. Ray. *Illinois Historical Tour Guide*. (thumbnail sketches of Illinois towns), 1991.

WPA Guide to Illinois. Federal Writer's Project, New York: Pantheon Books, 1939/1983.

Johnson, Curt. *Wicked City: Chicago: from Kenna to Capone*, by December Press, Highland Park, IL 1994.

Wiggers, Raymond. *Geology Underfoot: In Illinois*, Missoula, Montana: Mountain Press Publishing, 1997.

Wills, Charles A. *A Historical Album of Illinois*, Connecticut: Millbrook Press, 1998.

Wolfe, Anya. *It Happened in Illinois*, Decatur: House of Illinois, 1974.

Zeuch, Lucius. *History of Medical Practices in Illinois*. Chicago: The Book Press, 1927.